The McGraw-Hill Reader

The McGraw-Hill Reader

GILBERT H. MULLER
The City University of New York
LaGuardia

McGRAW-HILL BOOK COMPANY

New York | St. Louis | San Francisco | Auckland
Bogotá | Hamburg | Johannesburg | London | Madrid
Mexico | Montreal | New Delhi | Panama | Paris
São Paulo | Singapore | Sydney | Tokyo | Toronto

THE
McGRAW-HILL
READER

1 2 3 4 5 6 7 8 9 0 D O D O 8 9 8 7 6 5 4 3 2 1

See Acknowledgments on pages 665-670.
Copyrights included on this page by reference.

This book was set in Palatino by Black Dot, Inc.
The editors were Phillip A. Butcher and David Dunham;
the designer was Nicholas Krenitsky;
the production supervisor was John Mancia.
R. R. Donnelley & Sons Company was printer and binder.

Library of Congress Cataloging in Publication Data

Muller, Gilbert H., date
    The McGraw-Hill reader.

    Includes index.
    1. College readers.   I. Title.
PE1417.M77   808'.0427   81-8126
ISBN 0-07-043978-8   AACR2

To
Parisa and Darius
My favorite readers

Preface   xvii

1
Personal Narrative   1

LANGSTON HUGHES Salvation   1
MARK TWAIN The Mesmerizer   4
CARSON McCULLERS Home for Christmas   9
BUDD SCHULBERG The Wonderful Lousy Poem   14
JOHN A. WILLIAMS The Figure Eight   18
SANTHA RAMA RAU By Any Other Name   22
JAMES THURBER The Night the Bed Fell   28
DYLAN THOMAS A Visit to Grandpa's   32
MAXINE HONG KINGSTON The American Father   38
MAYA ANGELOU The Deterioration of My Marriage   44
GEORGE ORWELL Shooting an Elephant   51
JAMES BOSWELL Wednesday, 12 January 1763:
A Man of Pleasure   58

2
The Sense of Place   63

HARRY CREWS Why I Live Where I Live   63
WASHINGTON IRVING A Sunday in London   67
MARGARET MEAD A Day in Samoa   69
N. SCOTT MOMADAY The Way to Rainy Mountain   73
HENRY DAVID THOREAU Economy   79
ELIZABETH BOWEN The Big House   84
JOSEPH ADDISON The Royal Exchange   89
E. B. WHITE Once More to the Lake   93
GEORGE ORWELL Marrakech   99
PHYLLIS McGINLEY Suburbia: Of Thee I Sing   105
JEAN-PAUL SARTRE American Cities   113
ANAÏS NIN Morocco   123

Contents

3
Manners and Morals 132

MARYA MANNES Wasteland 132
S. I. HAYAKAWA Sex Is Not a Spectator Sport 134
A. G. MOJTABAI Polygamy 137
ST. AUGUSTINE Adult Cruelty and Folly 141
AMIRI BARAKA Soul Food 143
BENJAMIN FRANKLIN The Art of Procuring
Pleasant Dreams 145
ELLEN GOODMAN Bamama Goes to College 150
D. H. LAWRENCE Do Women Change? 152
CHARLES LAMB A Bachelor's Complaint 157
JOSEPH ADDISON A Superstitious Household 163
JONATHAN SWIFT A Treatise on Good Manners and
Good Breeding 167
FRANCIS BACON Of Envy 172

4
Human Development and Behavior 177

VIRGINIA WOOLF The Death of the Moth 177
ROLLO MAY Powerlessness Corrupts 180
RUTH BENEDICT The Uses of Cannibalism 184
BENJAMIN FRANKLIN Remarks Concerning the
Savages of North America 189
FRANZ BOAS The Diffusion of Cultural Traits 194
JOAN DIDION In Bed 202
ANAÏS NIN Notes on Feminism 206
MARYA MANNES The New Therapy 211
CARL GUSTAV JUNG The Mother Archetype 216
SIGMUND FREUD Libidinal Types 220
RICHARD WRIGHT The Psychological Reactions of
Oppressed People 224
KAREN HORNEY The Oedipus Complex 229

5
Social Processes and Institutions 235

E. M. FORSTER My Wood 235
JANE JACOBS Conserving Old Work by Adding New 239
OLIVER GOLDSMITH An Election 242
J. B. PRIESTLEY Wrong Ism 245

ALEXIS DE TOCQUEVILLE Some Reflections on
American Manners 249
FRANCES FITZGERALD America Revised 253
LEWIS MUMFORD The Social Concept of the City 259
W. E. B. DU BOIS Of the Meaning of Progress 265
NICCOLO MACHIAVELLI The Circle of Governments 274
JONATHAN SWIFT A Modest Proposal 277
RUTH BENEDICT Are Families Passé? 285
BARBARA TUCHMAN An Inquiry into the Persistence of
Unwisdom in Government 295

6

Language, Writing, and Communication

309

HENRY DAVID THOREAU On Keeping a Private Journal 309
JOAN DIDION On Keeping a Notebook 311
S. I. HAYAKAWA Words and Children 318
RUSSELL BAKER Little Red Riding Hood Revisited 323
E. B. WHITE Calculating Machine 326
MORTIMER J. ADLER How to Mark a Book 328
AMIRI BARAKA Expressive Language 334
MARSHALL McLUHAN Sight, Sound, and the Fury 339
GEORGE ORWELL Politics and the English Language 348
JONATHAN SWIFT The Art of Political Lying 360
JOHN SIMON The Corruption of English 364
GENEVA SMITHERMAN White English in Blackface, or
Who Do I Be? 372

7

Literature, Media, and the Arts

383

JUDITH VIORST How Books Helped Shape My Life 383
SYLVIA PLATH A Comparison 388
D. H. LAWRENCE Why the Novel Matters 391
URSULA K. LeGUIN American SF and the Other 397
THOMAS DE QUINCEY On the Knocking at the Gate in
Macbeth 401
WILLIAM HAZLITT On Gusto 406
KATHARINE KUH Break-up: The Core of Modern Art 410
MARYA MANNES How Do You Know It's Good? 415
ROBERT WARSHOW The Gangster as Tragic Hero 422

PAULINE KAEL Movies on Television 427
JAMES BALDWIN The Uses of the Blues 438
VIRGIL THOMSON Taste in Music 448

8
Philosophy, Ethics, and Religious Thought

453

ROBERT COLES I Listen to My Parents and I Wonder
  What They Believe 453
EPICURUS We Should Seek Our Own Pleasure 459
EDITH HAMILTON Roots of Freedom 464
PLATO The Allegory of the Cave 467
IMMANUEL KANT The Ethical Systems of the Ancients 471
JOSEPH WOOD KRUTCH The New Immorality 477
MICHAEL NOVAK Sports: A Sense of Evil 480
ALBERT CAMUS The Myth of Sisyphus 484
HANNAH ARENDT The Human Condition 488
JOHN DONNE No Man Is an Island 493
BERTRAND RUSSELL Can Religion Cure Our Troubles? 495
ROBERT LOUIS STEVENSON Aes Triplex 504

9
Mathematics, Science, and Technology

512

T. H. HUXLEY We Are All Scientists 512
ALBERT EINSTEIN The Common Language of Science 519
LEWIS THOMAS On Societies as Organisms 522
BENJAMIN FRANKLIN Lead Poisoning 526
LOREN EISELEY How Natural Is Natural? 529
RACHEL CARSON The Changing Year 532
BERTRAND RUSSELL The Study of Mathematics 540
J. B. S. HALDANE On Being the Right Size 542
ART BUCHWALD To Clone or Not to Clone 548
ALDOUS HUXLEY Time and the Machine 550
ARTHUR C. CLARKE The Planets Are Not Enough 553
KENNETH B. CLARK The Science of Human Morality 561

10
Civilization

568

OLIVER GOLDSMITH National Prejudices 568

JOHN STEINBECK Americans and the Land   572

WILLIAM FAULKNER Address upon Receiving the Nobel
  Prize for Literature   578

JAMES BALDWIN Stranger in the Village   580

WOODY ALLEN My Speech to the Graduates   592

ARNOLD TOYNBEE Why I Dislike Western Civilization   595

EDITH HAMILTON The Lessons of the Past   602

F. M. ESFANDIARY The Mystical West Puzzles the
  Practical East   611

MARGARET MEAD One Vote for This Age of Anxiety   617

MARY BEARD Women and Civilization   622

HENRY ADAMS The Dynamo and the Virgin   629

KENNETH E. BOULDING After Civilization, What?   639

Glossary of Terms   650

Acknowledgments   665

Index   671

Narration

LANGSTON HUGHES Salvation   1
MARK TWAIN The Mesmerizer   4
JOHN A. WILLIAMS The Figure Eight   18
SANTHA RAMA RAU By Any Other Name   22
MAXINE HONG KINGSTON The American Father   38
GEORGE ORWELL Shooting an Elephant   51
W. E. B. DU BOIS Of the Meaning of Progress   265

Description

MARGARET MEAD A Day in Samoa   69
N. SCOTT MOMADAY The Way to Rainy Mountain   73
E. B. WHITE Once More to the Lake   93
GEORGE ORWELL Marrakech   99
ANAÏS NIN Morocco   123
MARYA MANNES Wasteland   132
LOREN EISELEY How Natural Is Natural?   529

Illustration

JOSEPH ADDISON The Royal Exchange   89
A. G. MOJTABAI Polygamy   137
ST. AUGUSTINE Adult Cruelty and Folly   141
BARBARA TUCHMAN An Inquiry into the Persistence of
   Unwisdom in Government   295
S. I. HAYAKAWA Words and Children   318

Contents
of Selected Essays
by Rhetorical Mode

J. B. S. HALDANE On Being the Right Size   542
JOHN STEINBECK Americans and the Land   572

Comparison and Contrast

PHYLLIS McGINLEY Suburbia: Of Thee I Sing   105
ALEXIS DE TOCQUEVILLE Some Reflections on
  American Manners   249
SYLVIA PLATH A Comparison   388
D. H. LAWRENCE Why the Novel Matters   391
EDITH HAMILTON Roots of Freedom   464
JAMES BALDWIN Stranger in the Village   580
F. M. ESFANDIARY The Mystical West Puzzles the
  Practical East   611

Analogy

D. H. LAWRENCE Do Women Change?   152
VIRGINIA WOOLF The Death of the Moth   177
HENRY DAVID THOREAU On Keeping a Private Journal   309
JAMES BALDWIN The Uses of the Blues   438
PLATO The Allegory of the Cave   467
JOHN DONNE No Man Is an Island   493
LEWIS THOMAS On Societies as Organisms   522

Definition

JONATHAN SWIFT A Treatise on Good Manners and
  Good Breeding   167
JOAN DIDION In Bed   202
LEWIS MUMFORD The Social Concept of the City   259
AMIRI BARAKA Expressive Language   334
GEORGE ORWELL Politics and the English Language   348
WILLIAM HAZLITT On Gusto   406
ROBERT WARSHOW The Gangster as Tragic Hero   422

Classification

SIGMUND FREUD Libidinal Types   220
J. B. PRIESTLEY Wrong Ism   245
NICCOLO MACHIAVELLI The Circle of Governments   274
URSULA K. LeGUIN American SF and the Other   397
IMMANUEL KANT The Ethical Systems of the Ancients   471

OLIVER GOLDSMITH   National Prejudices   568
KENNETH E. BOULDING   After-Civilization, What?   639

Process Analysis

HENRY DAVID THOREAU   Economy   79
FRANZ BOAS   The Diffusion of Cultural Traits   194
FRANCES FITZGERALD   America Revised   253
MORTIMER J. ADLER   How to Mark a Book   328
KATHARINE KUH   Break-up: The Core of Modern Art   410
RACHEL CARSON   The Changing Year   532
MARY BEARD   Women and Civilization   622

Causal Analysis

ROLLO MAY   Powerlessness Corrupts   180
E. M. FORSTER   My Wood   235
JANE JACOBS   Conserving Old Work by Adding New   239
GENEVA SMITHERMAN   White English in Blackface, or
Who Do I Be?   372
THOMAS DE QUINCEY   On the Knocking at the Gate in
Macbeth   401
BENJAMIN FRANKLIN   Lead Poisoning   526
ALDOUS HUXLEY   Time and the Machine   550

Argument and Persuasion

ELIZABETH BOWEN   The Big House   84
S. I. HAYAKAWA   Sex Is Not a Spectator Sport   134
ELLEN GOODMAN   Bamama Goes to College   150
RICHARD WRIGHT   The Psychological Reactions of
Oppressed People   224
JOHN SIMON   The Corruption of English   364
ROBERT COLES   I Listen to My Parents and I Wonder
What They Believe   453
ARNOLD TOYNBEE   Why I Dislike Western Civilization   595

Logic

JONATHAN SWIFT   The Art of Political Lying   360
VIRGIL THOMSON   Taste in Music   448
EPICURUS   We Should Seek Our Own Pleasure   459
JOSEPH WOOD KRUTCH   The New Immorality   477

MICHAEL NOVAK   Sports: A Sense of Evil   480
BERTRAND RUSSELL   Can Religion Cure Our Troubles?   495
T. H. HUXLEY   We Are All Scientists   512

Humor, Irony, and Satire

JAMES THURBER   The Night the Bed Fell   28
RUTH BENEDICT   The Uses of Cannibalism   184
OLIVER GOLDSMITH   An Election   242
JONATHAN SWIFT   A Modest Proposal   277
RUSSELL BAKER   Little Red Riding Hood Revisited   323
ART BUCHWALD   To Clone or Not to Clone   548
WOODY ALLEN   My Speech to the Graduates   592

Glossary of Terms   650

Acknowledgments   665

Index   671

The McGraw-Hill Reader presents classic and contemporary essays for today's college students. Addressing the growing national interest in core liberal arts programs, this text offers students and teachers a full range of prose models important to writing courses, reading sequences, and key undergraduate disciplines. All the selections, consisting of complete essays, chapters, and self-contained sections of chapters, have been selected for their significance, vitality, and technical precision. With its high caliber of material, its consistent humanistic emphases, and its clear organization, this text is lively, sophisticated, and eminently usable for college composition and reading programs.

The organization of *The McGraw-Hill Reader* is one of its most significant features. Composed of ten chapters, each containing twelve essays, the text moves from the personal to the global, embracing most modes of writing and most disciplines that college students encounter as undergraduates. Chapters 1 to 3 provide students with prose models largely of a personal, experiential, narrative, descriptive, or reflective nature—essays which enhance the acquisition of basic language skills. Following chapters cover core liberal arts disciplines, including the social sciences, the humanities, and the sciences, and culminate in a final interdisciplinary chapter on civilization that is integral to the scope and method of *The McGraw-Hill Reader*. While reinforcing earlier modes of writing presented in the text, these disciplinary chapters offer prose models that provide practice in techniques of analysis, criticism, argumentation, and persuasion. As an integrated text, *The McGraw-Hill Reader* seeks to reconcile expressive and abstract varieties of thought in order to treat the total reading and writing process. An alternate table of contents, listing seven carefully selected essays in each of twelve rhetorical categories, adds to the flexibility of the text.

A second distinct advantage of *The McGraw-Hill Reader*, perhaps the primary one for teachers who prefer to create their own approaches to composition and reading courses, is the wide range of material and the varied constituencies represented in the text. The 120 essays in this book have been selected carefully to embrace a rich international assortment of authors, to achieve balance among constituencies, to cover major historical periods, and to provide prose models and styles for class analysis, discussion, and imitation. The

Preface

authors in this text—whether Plato or Maya Angelou, Swift or Ruth Benedict—have high visibility as writers and thinkers of value. Some of these authors are represented by two or three essays. All the authors, writing from such vantage points as literature, journalism, anthropology, sociology, art history, biology, and philosophy, presuppose that ideas exist in the world, that we should be alert to them, and that we should be able to deal with them in our own discourse. Because the selections extend from very simple essays to the most abstract and complex modes of prose, teachers and students will be able to use *The McGraw-Hill Reader* at virtually all levels of a program. Above all, teachers can develop their own sequence of essays that will contribute not only to their students' reading and writing proficiency, but also to growing intellectual power.

The third major strength of *The McGraw-Hill Reader* is the uniform apparatus that has been designed for every essay. While there is a temptation not to include apparatus for some essays, particularly shorter, less complex ones—a temptation some leading anthologies have given in to—the premise here is that much can be learned from any well-written essay, especially if the apparatus is systematic in design. For each selection in this text there is a brief introduction. After each essay, there are ten questions organized in a common format created to reinforce essential reading, writing, and oral communication skills. These questions are organized in the following manner: questions 1 and 2, comprehension; questions 3 and 4, language and style; questions 5 to 8, compositional techniques and rhetorical strategies; question 9, discussion and prewriting; question 10, applications to writing. All specialized terms used in the questions are defined for students in the complete Glossary of Terms at the end of the text. The integrated design of these questions makes each essay—simple or complex, short or long, old or new—accessible to college students who possess mixed reading and writing abilities.

Supplementing *The McGraw-Hill Reader* is a comprehensive instructor's manual. Unlike many manuals, this one is a complete teacher's guide. *A Guide to the McGraw-Hill Reader* offers sample syllabi, well-considered strategies for teaching individual essays, sample rhetorical analyses, answers to questions, additional thought-provoking questions, comparative essay discussion formats, and tips for prewriting and guided writing activities. There is also a bibliography of criticism and research on the teaching of composition.

As teachers and students today, we might very well be inclined to agree with Dr. Johnson's definition of the essay as a "loose sally of the mind; an irregular, undigested piece; not a regular and orderly performance." There is, of course, an ideal essay lurking behind Johnson's whimsical definition. In this better sense of the essay, *The McGraw-Hill Reader* offers orderly performances. Here, there are regular prose models commensurate with our need and desire to read, write, and think well.

ACKNOWLEDGMENTS

It is a pleasure to acknowledge the support, assistance, and guidance of numerous individuals who helped to create *The McGraw-Hill Reader*. Foremost among these people are the many McGraw-Hill sales representatives who obtained teacher responses to question-naires when the text was in its formative stages. I also want to thank the excellent McGraw-Hill family of assistants, editors, and execu-tives who participated enthusiastically in the project from the outset and who encouraged me at every step.

The final design and content of *The McGraw-Hill Reader* reflects the expertise and advice offered by college teachers across the country who gave generously of their time when asked to respond to questionnaires submitted to them by McGraw-Hill sales representa-tives. These include: Howard Eitland, Boston College; Jack Williams, California State College, Stanislaus; John Gordon, Connecticut Col-lege; A. Harris Fairbanks, University of Connecticut; Scott Elledge, Cornell University; Bernard Beranek, G. F. Provost, Duquesne Uni-versity; J. A. LaBashak, Edinboro State College; Robert Hogenson, Ferris State College; John McGrail, Fitchburg State College; James Fetler, Foothill College; Lynn Garrett, Louisiana State University; Gloria Conforti, Loyola University of Chicago; Florence Frank, Uni-versity of Massachusetts; Robert L. Brown, University of Minnesota; Lee Nicholson, Modesto Junior College; Mary McHenry, Mount Holyoke College; Mary Wagoner, Univeristy of New Orleans; Linda Barlow, Walter Beale, Erika Lindemann, University of North Carolina; June Verbillion, Northeastern Illinois University; Penny Hirsch, Northwestern University; David Fite, University of Santa Clara; Tony Tyler, State University College, Potsdam; and Peter DeBlois, Syracuse University.

Warm appreciation is also extended to those college and university English professors who carefully read the manuscript in part or in its entirety, and who made many constructive suggestions for improvement. I am most grateful to Lillian Gottesman, Bronx Community College; Dennis R. Gabriel, Cuyahoga Community Col-lege; John Hanes, Duquesne University; James Mauch, Foothill Col-lege; Margaret A. Strom, George Washington University; Robert J. Pelinski, University of Illinois; Eugene Hammond, University of Maryland; Robert L. Brown, University of Minnesota; Jack Wilson, Old Dominion University; David Fite, University of Santa Clara;

Grayce F. Salerno, Seton Hall University; Carl Wooton, University of Southwestern Louisiana; and Susan Miller, University of Wisconsin.

Special recognition must also be given to those specialists in various liberal arts fields who provided advice: Jane S. Zembaty, Department of Philosophy, University of Dayton; Linda Davidoff, Department of Psychology, Essex Community College; Curtis Williams, Department of Biology, The State University of New York; and Diane Papalia-Finlay, Department of Psychology, University of Wisconsin.

Above all, I wish to thank Dr. Richard McAdams of Manhattan College for his help in designing biographical sketches and exercise materials and for his superlative work on *A Guide to the McGraw-Hill Reader*.

Finally, I am pleased to acknowledge support from the Mellon Foundation, the Graduate Center of The City University of New York, and the United States Office of Education (Title III) that enabled me to concentrate on the development of this text.

Gilbert H. Muller

The
McGraw-Hill
Reader

Personal Narrative

LANGSTON HUGHES

Salvation

James Langston Hughes (1902–1967), poet, playwright, fiction writer, biographer, and essayist, was for more than fifty years one of the most productive and significant modern American authors. In *The Weary Blues* (1926), *Simple Speaks His Mind* (1950), *The Ways of White Folks* (1940), *Selected Poems* (1959), and dozens of other books, he strove, in his own words, "to explain the Negro condition in America." This essay, from his 1940 autobiography *The Big Sea*, reflects the sharp, humorous, often bittersweet insights contained in Hughes's examination of human behavior.

was saved from sin when I was going on thirteen. But not really saved. It happened like this. There was a big revival at my Auntie Reed's church. Every night for weeks there had been much preaching, singing, praying, and shouting, and some very hardened sinners had been brought to Christ, and the membership of the church had grown by leaps and bounds. Then just before the revival ended, they held a special meeting for children, "to bring the young lambs to the fold." My aunt spoke of it for days ahead. That night I was escorted to the front row and placed on the mourners' bench with all the other young sinners, who had not yet been brought to Jesus.

My aunt told me that when you were saved you saw a light, 2 and something happened to you inside! And Jesus came into your life! And God was with you from then on! She said you could see and hear and feel Jesus in your soul. I believed her. I had heard a great many old people say the same thing and it seemed to me they ought to know. So I sat there calmly in the hot, crowded church, waiting for Jesus to come to me.

The preacher preached a wonderful rhythmical sermon, all 3 moans and shouts and lonely cries and dire pictures of hell, and then he sang a song about the ninety and nine safe in the fold, but one little lamb was left out in the cold. Then he said: "Won't you come? Won't you come to Jesus? Young lambs, won't you come?" And he held out his arms to all us young sinners there on the mourners' bench. And the little girls cried. And some of them jumped up and went to Jesus right away. But most of us just sat there.

A great many old people came and knelt around us and 4 prayed, old women with jet-black faces and braided hair, old men with work-gnarled hands. And the church sang a song about the lower lights are burning, some poor sinners to be saved. And the whole building rocked with prayer and song.

Still I kept waiting to *see* Jesus. 5

Finally all the young people had gone to the altar and were 6 saved, but one boy and me. He was a rounder's son named Westley. Westley and I were surrounded by sisters and deacons praying. It was very hot in the church, and getting late now. Finally Westley said to me in a whisper: "God damn! I'm tired o' sitting here. Let's get up and be saved." So he got up and was saved.

Then I was left all alone on the mourners' bench. My aunt 7 came and knelt at my knees and cried, while prayers and song swirled all around me in the little church. The whole congregation prayed for me alone, in a mighty wail of moans and voices. And I kept waiting serenely for Jesus, waiting, waiting—but he didn't come. I wanted to see him, but nothing happened to me. Nothing! I wanted something to happen to me, but nothing happened.

I heard the songs and the minister saying: "Why don't you 8 come? My dear child, why don't you come to Jesus? Jesus is waiting for you. He wants you. Why don't you come? Sister Reed, what is this child's name?"

"Langston," my aunt sobbed. 9

"Langston, why don't you come? Why don't you come and 10 be saved? Oh, Lamb of God! Why don't you come?"

Now it was really getting late. I began to be ashamed of 11 myself, holding everything up so long. I began to wonder what God

LANGSTON HUGHES

thought about Westley, who certainly hadn't seen Jesus either, but who was now sitting proudly on the platform, swinging his knicker-bockered legs and grinning down at me, surrounded by deacons and old women on their knees praying. God had not struck Westley dead for taking his name in vain or for lying in the temple. So I decided that maybe to save further trouble, I'd better lie, too, and say that Jesus had come, and get up and be saved.

So I got up. 12

Suddenly the whole room broke into a sea of shouting, as 13 they saw me rise. Waves of rejoicing swept the place. Women leaped in the air. My aunt threw her arms around me. The minister took me by the hand and led me to the platform.

When things quieted down, in a hushed silence, punctuated 14 by a few ecstatic "Amens," all the new young lambs were blessed in the name of God. Then joyous singing filled the room.

That night, for the last time in my life but one—for I was a big 15 boy twelve years old—I cried. I cried, in bed alone, and couldn't stop. I buried my head under the quilts, but my aunt heard me. She woke up and told my uncle I was crying because the Holy Ghost had come into my life, and because I had seen Jesus. But I was really crying because I couldn't bear to tell her that I had lied, that I had deceived everybody in the church, that I hadn't seen Jesus, and that now I didn't believe there was a Jesus any more, since he didn't come to help me.

QUESTIONS

1.   How does Hughes describe the revival meeting he attended? What is the dominant impression?

2.   Describe Hughes's shifting attitude toward salvation in this essay. What does he say about salvation in the last paragraph?

3.   Key words and phrases in this essay relate to the religious experience. Locate five of these words and expressions and explain their connotations.

4.   What is the level of language in the essay? How does Hughes employ language effectively?

5.   Where is the thesis statement in the essay? How does it prepare the reader for the ironic situation that develops?

6.   How much time elapses and why is this important to the effect? How does the author achieve narrative coherence?

7.   Locate details and examples in the essay that are especially vivid and

interesting. Compare your list with what others have listed. What are the similarities? The differences?

8. What is the tone of the essay? What is the relationship between tone and point of view?

9. Can giving in to group pressures have lasting effects on a person? Why or why not?

10. a. Recount an event in your life during which you surrendered to group pressures.
b. Write a narrative account of the most intense religious experience in your life.
c. Narrate an episode in which you played a trick on people simply to win their approval or satisfy their expectations.

MARK TWAIN

The Mesmerizer

Mark Twain (1835–1910) was the pseudonym of Samuel Lang-horne Clemens. In *The Adventures of Tom Sawyer* (1876), *Life on the Mississippi* (1883), and *The Adventures of Huckleberry Finn* (1885), Twain celebrated the challenge of the frontier experience and the promise of a new world. Adventurous, democratic, individualistic, hardheaded, and sentimental, he projected the image of the essential American, a role that did not always correspond to the bitter and tragic aspects of his later life. This selection, from Twain's autobiography, captures the young Clemens as a humorous crowd pleaser and perpetrator of hoaxes—characteristics that became central to his adult life and career.

An exciting event in our village was the arrival of the   1
mesmerizer. I think the year was 1850. As to that I am
not sure but I know the month—it was May; that detail
has survived the wear of fifty years. A pair of connected
little incidents of that month have served to keep the memory of it
green for me all this time; incidents of no consequence and not worth
embalming, yet my memory has preserved them carefully and flung
away things of real value to give them space and make them
comfortable. The truth is, a person's memory has no more sense than

his conscience and no appreciation whatever of values and proportions. However, never mind those trifling incidents; my subject is the mesmerizer now.

He advertised his show and promised marvels. Admission as usual: 25 cents, children and negroes half price. The village had heard of mesmerism in a general way but had not encountered it yet. Not many people attended the first night but next day they had so many wonders to tell that everybody's curiosity was fired and after that for a fortnight the magician had prosperous times. I was fourteen or fifteen years old, the age at which a boy is willing to endure all things, suffer all things short of death by fire, if thereby he may be conspicuous and show off before the public; and so, when I saw the "subjects" perform their foolish antics on the platform and make the people laugh and shout and admire I had a burning desire to be a subject myself. **2**

Every night for three nights I sat in the row of candidates on the platform and held the magic disk in the palm of my hand and gazed at it and tried to get sleepy, but it was a failure; I remained wide awake and had to retire defeated, like the majority. Also, I had to sit there and be gnawed with envy of Hicks, our journeyman; I had to sit there and see him scamper and jump when Simmons the enchanter exclaimed, "See the snake! See the snake!" and hear him say, "My, how beautiful!" in response to the suggestion that he was observing a splendid sunset; and so on—the whole insane business. I couldn't laugh, I couldn't applaud; it filled me with bitterness to have others do it and to have people make a hero of Hicks and crowd around him when the show was over and ask him for more and more particulars of the wonders he had seen in his visions and manifest in many ways that they were proud to be acquainted with him. Hicks—the idea! I couldn't stand it; I was getting boiled to death in my own bile. **3**

On the fourth night temptation came and I was not strong enough to resist. When I had gazed at the disk a while I pretended to be sleepy and began to nod. Straightway came the professor and made passes over my head and down my body and legs and arms, finishing each pass with a snap of his fingers in the air to discharge the surplus electricity; then he began to "draw" me with the disk, holding it in his fingers and telling me I could not take my eyes off it, try as I might; so I rose slowly, bent and gazing, and following that disk all over the place, just as I had seen the others do. Then I was put through the other paces. Upon suggestion I fled from snakes, passed buckets at a fire, became excited over hot steamboat-races, made love to imaginary girls and kissed them, fished from the platform and landed mud cats that outweighed me—and so on, all the customary marvels. But not in the customary way. I was cautious at first and watchful, being afraid the professor would discover that I was an **4** imposter and drive me from the platform in disgrace; but as soon as I realized that I was not in danger, I set myself the task of terminating Hick's usefulness as a subject and of usurping his place.

It was a sufficiently easy task. Hicks was born honest, I 5 without that incumbrance—so some people said. Hicks saw what he saw and reported accordingly, I saw more than was visible and added to it such details as could help. Hicks had no imagination; I had a double supply. He was born calm, I was born excited. No vision could start a rapture in him and he was constipated as to language, anyway; but if I saw a vision I emptied the dictionary onto it and lost the remnant of my mind into the bargain.

At the end of my first half-hour Hicks was a thing of the past, 6 a fallen hero, a broken idol, and I knew it and was glad and said in my heart, "Success to crime!" Hicks could never have been mesmerized to the point where he could kiss an imaginary girl in public or a real one either, but I was competent. Whatever Hicks had failed in, I made it a point to succeed in, let the cost be what it might, physically or morally. He had shown several bad defects and I had made a note of them. For instance, if the magician asked, "What do you see?" and left him to invent a vision for himself, Hicks was dumb and blind, he couldn't see a thing nor say a word, whereas the magician soon found out that when it came to seeing visions of a stunning and marketable sort I could get along better without his help than with it.

Then there was another thing: Hicks wasn't worth a tallow 7 dip on mute mental suggestion. Whenever Simmons stood behind him and gazed at the back of his skull and tried to drive a mental suggestion into it, Hicks sat with vacant face and never suspected. If he had been noticing he could have seen by the rapt faces of the audience that something was going on behind his back that required a response. Inasmuch as I was an imposter I dreaded to have this test put upon me, for I knew the professor would be "willing" me to do something, and as I couldn't know what it was, I should be exposed and denounced. However, when my time came, I took my chance. I perceived by the tense and expectant faces of the people that Simmons was behind me willing me with all his might. I tried my best to imagine what he wanted but nothing suggested itself. I felt ashamed and miserable then. I believed that the hour of my disgrace was come and that in another moment I should go out of that place disgraced. I ought to be ashamed to confess it but my next thought was not how I could win the compassion of kindly hearts by going out humbly and in sorrow for my misdoings, but how I could go out most sensationally and spectacularly.

There was a rusty and empty old revolver lying on the table 8 among the "properties" employed in the performances. On May Day two or three weeks before there had been a celebration by the schools and I had had a quarrel with a big boy who was the school bully and I had not come out of it with credit. That boy was now seated in the middle of the house, halfway down the main aisle. I crept stealthily and impressively toward the table, with a dark and murderous scowl on my face, copied from a popular romance, seized the revolver suddenly, flourished it, shouted the bully's name, jumped off the platform and made a rush for him and chased him out of the house before the paralyzed people could interfere to save him. There was a storm of applause, and the magician, addressing the house, said, most impressively—

"That you may know how really remarkable this is and how wonderfully developed a subject we have in this boy, I assure you that without a single spoken word to guide him he has carried out what I mentally commanded him to do, to the minutest detail. I could have stopped him at a moment in his vengeful career by a mere exertion of my will, therefore the poor fellow who has escaped was at no time in danger." 9

So I was not in disgrace. I returned to the platform a hero and happier than I have ever been in this world since. As regards mental suggestion, my fears of it were gone. I judged that in case I failed to guess what the professor might be willing me to do, I could count on putting up something that would answer just as well. I was right, and exhibitions of unspoken suggestion became a favorite with the public. Whenever I perceived that I was being willed to do something I got up and did something—anything that occurred to me—and the magician, not being a fool, always ratified it. When people asked me, "How *can* you tell what he is willing you to do?" I said, "It's just as easy," and they always said admiringly, "Well, it beats *me* how you can do it." 10

Hicks was weak in another detail. When the professor made passes over him and said "his whole body is without sensation now—come forward and test him, ladies and gentlemen," the ladies and gentlemen always complied eagerly and stuck pins into Hicks, and if they went deep Hicks was sure to wince, then that poor professor would have to explain that Hicks "wasn't sufficiently under the influence." But I didn't wince; I only suffered and shed tears on the inside. The miseries that a conceited boy will endure to keep up his "reputation"! And so will a conceited man; I know it in my own person and have seen it in a hundred thousand others. That professor ought to have protected me and I often hoped he would, when the tests were unusually severe, but he didn't. It may be that he was deceived as well as the others, though I did not believe it nor think it possible. Those were dear good people but they must have carried simplicity and credulity to the limit. They would stick a pin in my arm and bear on it until they drove it a third of its length in, and then be 11 lost in wonder that by a mere exercise of will power the professor could turn my arm to iron and make it insensible to pain. Whereas it was not insensible at all; I was suffering agonies of pain.

After that fourth night, that proud night, that triumphant 12 night, I was the only subject. Simmons invited no more candidates to the platform. I performed alone every night the rest of the fortnight. Up to that time a dozen wise old heads, the intellectual aristocracy of the town, had held out as implacable unbelievers. I was as hurt by this as if I were engaged in some honest occupation. There is nothing surprising about this. Human beings feel dishonor the most, sometimes, when they most deserve it. That handful of overwise old gentlemen kept on shaking their heads all the first week and saying they had seen no marvels there that could not have been produced by collusion; and they were pretty vain of their unbelief too and liked to show it and air it and be superior to the ignorant and the gullible. Particularly old Dr. Peake, who was the ringleader of the irreconcilables and very formidable; for he was an F.F.V., he was learned, white-haired and venerable, nobly and richly clad in the fashions of an earlier and a courtlier day, he was large and stately, and he not only seemed wise but was what he seemed in that regard. He had great influence and his opinion upon any matter was worth much more than that of any other person in the community. When I conquered him at last, I knew I was undisputed master of the field; and now after more than fifty years I acknowledge with a few dry old tears that I rejoiced without shame.

QUESTIONS

1. What reasons does Twain give for his triumph over Hicks?

2. Describe the persona that Twain creates for himself in the course of the narrative.

3. Twain uses abstract language in the first paragraph. Does Twain rely more on abstract or concrete language in the course of the narrative? Why?

4. Use these words in sentences: *embalming* (paragraph 1); *bile* (paragraph 3); *terminating* (paragraph 4); *incumbrance* (paragraph 5); *stealthily* (paragraph 8).

5. Why is Twain's introductory paragraph effective? In what way does the paragraph establish the tone of the essay?

6. What is the point of view in the essay? What advantage does Twain gain from his selection of point of view?

MARK TWAIN

7. Cite three instances of comic techniques and effects in the essay and explain their significance.

8. What is the function of Twain's editorializing in the account?

9. Speaking of memory, Twain declares that "a person's memory has no more sense than his conscience and no appreciation whatever of values and proportions." Do you agree or disagree with this opinion? Why do you hold this view?

10. Recall a memorable event that occurred in your neighborhood when you were a child. Write a narrative essay about your role in it.

CARSON McCULLERS

Home for Christmas

Carson McCullers (1917–1967) was the author of a small but impressive body of fiction, including *The Heart Is a Lonely Hunter* (1940), *Reflections in a Golden Eye* (1941), *A Member of the Wedding* (1946), and *The Ballad of the Sad Cafe* (1951). Although she was preoccupied in her fiction with the theme of loneliness, this selection from her autobiography reveals instead the love, joy, and sense of community permeating one episode from her Georgia childhood.

ometimes in August, weary of the vacant, broiling   1
afternoon, my younger brother and sister and I would
gather in the dense shade under the oak tree in the back
yard and talk of Christmas and sing carols. Once after
such a conclave, when the tunes of the carols still lingered in the
heat-shimmered air, I remember climbing up into the tree-house and
sitting there alone for a long time.

Brother called up: "What are you doing?"   2
"Thinking," I answered.   3
"What are you thinking about?"   4
"I don't know."   5
"Well, how can you be thinking when you don't know what   6
you are thinking about?"

I did not want to talk with my brother. I was experiencing the   7
first wonder about the mystery of Time. Here I was, on this August
afternoon, in the tree-house, in the burnt, jaded yard, sick and tired
of all our summer ways. (I had read *Little Women* for the second time,

Hans Brinker and the Silver Skates, Little Men, and *Twenty Thousand Leagues under the Sea.* I had read movie magazines and even tried to read love stories in the *Woman's Home Companion*—I was so sick of everything.) How could it be that I was I and now was now when in four months it would be Christmas, wintertime, cold weather, twilight and the glory of the Christmas tree? I puzzled about the *now* and *later* and rubbed the inside of my elbow until there was a little roll of dirt between my forefinger and thumb. Would the *now* I of the tree-house and the August afternoon be the same *I* of winter, firelight and the Christmas tree? I wondered.

My brother repeated: "You say you are thinking but you don't 8 know what you are thinking about. What are you really doing up there? Have you got some secret candy?"

September came, and my mother opened the cedar chest and 9 we tried on winter coats and last year's sweaters to see if they would do again. She took the three of us downtown and bought us new shoes and school clothes.

Christmas was nearer on the September Sunday that Daddy 10 rounded us up in the car and drove us out on dusty country roads to pick elderberry blooms. Daddy made wine from elderberry blossoms—it was a yellow-white wine, the color of weak winter sun. The wine was dry to the wry side—indeed, some years it turned to vinegar. The wine was served at Christmastime with slices of fruitcake when company came. On November Sundays we went to the woods with a big basket of fried chicken dinner, thermos jug and coffee-pot. We hunted partridge berries in the pine woods near our town. These scarlet berries grew hidden underneath the glossy brown pine needles that lay in a slick carpet beneath the tall wind-singing trees. The bright berries were a Christmas decoration, lasting in water through the whole season.

In December the windows downtown were filled with toys, 11 and my brother and sister and I were given two dollars apiece to buy our Christmas presents. We patronized the ten-cent stores, choosing between jackstones, pencil boxes, water colors and satin handkerchief holders. We would each buy a nickel's worth of lump milk chocolate at the candy counter to mouth as we trudged from counter to counter, choice to choice. It was exacting and final—taking several afternoons—for the dime stores would not take back or exchange.

Mother made fruitcakes, and for weeks ahead the family 12 picked out the nut meats of pecans and walnuts, careful of the bitter layer of the pecans that lined your mouth with nasty fur. At the last I was allowed to blanch the almonds, pinching the scalded nuts so that they sometimes hit the ceiling or bounced across the room. Mother cut slices of citron and crystallized pineapple, figs and dates, and candied cherries were added whole. We cut rounds of brown paper to

CARSON McCULLERS

line the pans. Usually the cakes were mixed and put into the oven when we were in school. Late in the afternoon the cakes would be finished, wrapped in white napkins on the breakfast-room table. Later they would be soaked in brandy. These fruitcakes were famous in our town, and Mother gave them often as Christmas gifts. When company came thin slices of fruitcake, wine and coffee were always served. When you held a slice of fruitcake to the window or the firelight the slice was translucent, pale citron green and yellow and red, with the glow and richness of our church windows.

Daddy was a jeweler, and his store was kept open until midnight all Christmas week. I, as the eldest child, was allowed to stay up late with Mother until Daddy came home. Mother was always nervous without a "man in the house." (On those rare occasions when Daddy had to stay overnight on business in Atlanta, the children were armed with a hammer, saw and a monkey wrench. When pressed about her anxieties Mother claimed she was afraid of "escaped convicts or crazy people." I never saw an escaped convict, but once a "crazy" person did come to see us. She was an old, old lady dressed in elegant black taffeta, my mother's second cousin once removed, and came on a tranquil Sunday morning and announced that she had always liked our house and she intended to stay with us until she died. Her sons and daughters and grandchildren gathered around to plead with her as she sat rocking in our front porch rocking chair and she left not unwillingly when they promised a car ride and ice cream.) Nothing ever happened on those evenings in Christmas week, but I felt grown, aged suddenly by trust and dignity. Mother confided in secrecy what the younger children were getting from Santa Claus. I knew where the Santa Claus things were hidden, and was appointed to see that my brother and sister did not go into the back-room closet or the wardrobe in our parents' room. 13

Christmas Eve was the longest day, but it was lined with the glory of tomorrow. The sitting-room smelled of floor wax and the clean, cold odor of the spruce tree. The Christmas tree stood in a corner of the front room, tall as the ceiling, majestic, undecorated. It was our family custom that the tree was not decorated until after we children were in bed on Christmas Eve night. We went to bed very early, as soon as it was winter dark. I lay in bed beside my sister and tried to keep her awake. 14

"You want to guess again about your Santa Claus?" 15

"We've already done that so much," she said. 16

My sister slept. And there again was another puzzle. How could it be that when she opened her eyes it would be Christmas while I lay awake in the dark for hours and hours? The time was the same for both of us, and yet not at all the same. What was it? How? I thought of Bethlehem and cherry candy, Jesus and skyrockets. It was 17

 HOME FOR CHRISTMAS

dark when I awoke. We were allowed to get up on Christmas at five o'clock. Later I found out that Daddy juggled the clock Christmas Eve so that five o'clock was actually six. Anyway it was always still dark when we rushed in to dress by the kitchen stove. The rule was that we dress and eat breakfast before we could go in to the Christmas tree. On Christmas morning we always had fish roe, bacon and grits for breakfast. I grudged every mouthful—for who wanted to fill up on breakfast when there in the sitting-room was candy, at least three whole boxes? After breakfast we lined up, and carols were started. Our voices rose naked and mysterious as we filed through the door to the sitting-room. The carol, unfinished, ended in raw yells of joy.

The Christmas tree glittered in the glorious, candlelit room.   18
There were bicycles and bundles wrapped in tissue paper. Our stockings hanging from the mantlepiece bulged with oranges, nuts and smaller presents. The next hours were paradise. The blue dawn at the window brightened, and the candles were blown out. By nine o'clock we had ridden the wheel presents and dressed in the clothes gifts. We visited the neighborhood children and were visited in turn. Our cousins came and grown relatives from distant neighborhoods. All through the morning we ate chocolates. At two or three o'clock the Christmas dinner was served. The dining-room table had been let out with extra leaves and the very best linen was laid—satin damask with a rose design. Daddy asked the blessing, then stood up to carve the turkey. Dressing, rice and giblet gravy were served. There were cut-glass dishes of sparkling jellies and stateliness of festal wine. For dessert there was always sillabub or charlotte and fruitcake. The afternoon was almost over when dinner was done.

At twilight I sat on the front steps, jaded by too much   19
pleasure, sick at the stomach and worn out. The boy next door skated down the street in his new Indian suit. A girl spun around on a crackling son-of-a-gun. My brother waved sparklers. Christmas was over. I thought of the monotony of Time ahead, unsolaced by the distant glow of paler festivals, the year that stretched before another Christmas—eternity.

QUESTIONS

1. Trace chronologically the preparations for Christmas by the McCullers family.

2. What is the author's attitude toward time? Paraphrase the last sentence of the essay.

3. This essay is rich in sensory language. Cite five words or phrases that

are especially vivid and analyze their effect. To which senses does the writing appeal?

4. Define these words: *conclave* (paragraph 1); *patronized* (paragraph 11); *blanch* (paragraph 12); *tranquil* (paragraph 13); *festal* (paragraph 19). Use them in sentences of your own.

5. McCullers writes in paragraph 7 that she "was experiencing the first wonder about the mystery of Time." How does this theme serve as the organizing principle for the essay? How does the author convey the mystery of time? What is her dual attitude toward time, and how does this serve as a structuring device in the essay?

6. What principles of emphasis do you find in McCullers's treatment of chronology?

7. How and why does the author connect the many and varied details in the essay? How effective are her details in conveying a sense of the author's childhood and of her evolving personality? How is this reflected in point of view?

8. How does the conclusion relate to the rest of the essay? Do you find the conclusion effective? Why or why not?

9. Do you still look forward to special holidays or celebrations, or does the type of anticipation of which McCullers speaks exist only for children? Why do children have different perceptions of time than adults?

10. Write a narrative account of a vivid holiday event in your childhood.

The Wonderful Lousy Poem

Budd Schulberg (1914–   ), American novelist, short story writer, screen writer, and contributor to major national magazines, is the author of *What Makes Sammy Run* (1941), *The Disenchanted* (1950), and *On the Waterfront* (1954). The son of "a Hollywood tycoon," Schulberg invests the following autobiographical account with the drama of film community life in the 1920s, even as he finds in a childhood crisis the sources of the creative process.

hen I was eight or nine years old, I wrote my first poem. 1
At that time my father was a Hollywood tycoon, 2 head of Paramount Studios. My mother was a founder and prime mover in various intellectual projects, helping to bring "culture" to the exuberant Hollywood community of the 1920s.

My mother read the little poem and began to cry. "Buddy, 3 you didn't really write this beautiful, beautiful poem!" Shyly, proud-bursting, I stammered that I had. My mother poured out her welcome praise. Why, this poem was nothing short of genius. She had no idea that I had such talent for writing. I must write more poems, keep on writing, perhaps someday even publish them.

I glowed. "What time will Father be home?" I asked. I could 4 hardly wait to show him what I had accomplished. My mother said she hoped he would be home around 7. I spent the best part of that afternoon preparing for his arrival.

First, I wrote the poem out in my finest flourish. Then I used 5 colored crayons to draw an elaborate border around it that would do justice to its brilliant content. Then I waited. As 7 o'clock drew near, I confidently placed it right on my father's plate on the dining-room table.

But my father did not return at 7. I rearranged the poem so it 6 would appear at a slightly more advantageous angle on his plate. Seven-fifteen. Seven-thirty. The suspense was exquisite. I admired my father. I liked to go to the studio and watch the rough cut of his new pictures in his big projection room. And sometimes he would let me sit in when his important writers came to the house for story conferences. He had begun his motion-picture career as a writer. He would be able to appreciate this wonderful poem of mine even more than my mother.

Sometimes our household was like a Hollywood version of 7

"Life with Father." It seemed as if the studio personnel were engaged in a great conspiracy to exhaust my father's patience. For instance, I never thought of movie stars simply as movie stars. I was accustomed to hearing them described as "those blank blank sons of blank stars!" Gloria Swanson, Marlene Dietrich, the formidable director Von Sternberg; the bigger they were, the more violent my father's denunciation.

This evening it was almost 8 o'clock when my father burst in,   8
and his mood seemed even more thunderous than usual. He was an hour late for dinner, but he could not sit down. He circled the long dining-room table with a Scotch highball in his hand, calling down terrible oaths on his glamorous employees. I can see him now, a big Havana cigar in one hand, the rapidly disappearing highball in the other, crying out against the sad fates that had sentenced him to the cruel job of running a teeming Hollywood studio.

"Imagine, we would have finished the picture tonight" my   9
father was shouting. "Instead that blank blank MORON, that blank blank BLANK suddenly gets it into her beautiful but empty little head that she can't play the last scene. So the whole company has to stand there at $1,000 a minute while this silly little BLANK, who's lucky she isn't behind the counter of a five-and-ten, walks off the set! Now I have to go down to her beach house tonight and beg her to come back on Monday. I may just strangle her instead and finish the picture with her stand-in doing her scenes with her back to the blank blank camera!"

My father always paced determinedly as he ranted against   10
the studio greats, and now as he wheeled he paused and glared at his plate. There was a suspenseful silence. He was reaching for my poem. I lowered my head and stared down into my plate. I was full of anxious daydreams. How wonderful it would be if this very first work of mine drove away the angry clouds that now darkened my important father's face!

"What is *this*?" I heard him say.   11

"Ben, Buddy has been waiting for you for hours," my mother   12
began. "A wonderful thing has happened. Buddy has written his first poem! And it's beautiful, absolutely amaz—"

"If you don't mind, I'd like to decide that for myself," Father   13
said.

Now was the moment of decision. I kept my face lowered to   14
my plate. It could not have taken very long to read that poem. It was only 10 lines long. But it seemed to take hours. I remember wondering why it was taking so long. I could hear him dropping the poem back on the table again. I could not bear to look up for the verdict. But in a moment I was to hear it:

"I think it's lousy," my father said.   15

I couldn't look up. I was ashamed of my eyes getting wet.   16

"Ben, sometimes I don't understand you," my mother was   17
saying. "This is just a little boy. You're not in your studio now. These
are the first lines of poetry he's ever written. He needs encouragement."

"I don't know why," my father held his ground. "Isn't there   18
enough lousy poetry in the world already? I don't know any law that
says Buddy has to become a poet."

I forget what my mother said. I wasn't hearing so well   19
because it is hard to hear clearly when your head is making its own
sounds of crying. On my left, she was saying soothing things to me
and critical things of my father. But I clearly remember his self-
defense: "Look, I pay my best writers $2,000 a week. All afternoon
I've been tearing apart their stuff. I only pay Buddy 50 cents a week.
And you're trying to tell me I don't have a right to tear apart his stuff
if I think it's lousy!"

That expressive vernacular adjective hit me over the heart like   20
a hard fist. I couldn't stand it another second. Leaving untouched the
chocolate soufflé, my favorite dessert, I ran from the dining room
bawling. I staggered up to my room and threw myself on the bed and
sobbed. When I had cried the worst of the disappointment out of me,
I could hear my parents still quarreling over my first poem at the
dinner table.

That may have been the end of the anecdote—but not of its   21
significance for me. Inevitably the family wounds began to knit. My
mother began talking to my father again. My father asked me
whether I would like to go to a prize fight. This was his favorite
recreation, and I learned at a tender age to value the prowess of our
California champions. I even began committing poetry again, though
of course I dared not expose it to my father.

A few years later I took a second look at that first poem, and   22
reluctantly I had to agree with my father's harsh judgment. It was a
pretty lousy poem. After a while, I worked up the courage to show
him something new, a primitive short story written in what I fancied
to be the dark Russian manner. My father thought it was overwritten
but not hopeless. I was learning to rewrite. And my mother was
learning that she could criticize me without crushing me. You might
say we were all learning. I was going on 12.

But it wasn't until I was at work on my first novel, a dozen   23
years later, that the true meaning of that painful "first poem"
experience dawned on me. I had written a first chapter, but I didn't
think it was good enough. I wanted to do it over. My editor, a wise
hand who had counseled O'Neill and Sinclair Lewis and William
Faulkner, told me not to worry, to keep on going, the first chapter
was fine. Keep writing, just let it flow, it's wonderful, he encouraged

me. Only when it was all finished and I was in a triumphant glow of achievement did he take me down a peg. "That chapter may be a little weak at that. If I were you, I'd look at it again." Now, on the crest of having written a novel, I could absorb a sharp critical blow.

As I worked my way into other books and plays and films, it became clearer and clearer to me how fortunate I had been to have had a mother who said, "Buddy, did you really write this —I think it's wonderful!" and a father who shook his head no and drove me to tears with his, "I think it's lousy." A writer, in fact all of us in life, needs that mother force, the loving force from which all creation flows; and yet the mother force alone is incomplete, even misleading, finally destructive, without the father force to caution, "Watch. Listen. Review. *Improve.*"   24

Sometimes you find these opposing forces personified in your editors, your associates, your friends, your loved ones. But finally you must counterpoise these opposites within yourself: first, the confidence to go forward, to do, to become; second, to temper rampant self-approval with hardheaded, realistic self-appraisal, the father discipline that barges into your ivory tower and with a painful truth jars your reverie of creative self-glorification.   25

Those conflicting but complementary voices of my childhood echo down through the years —*wonderful, lousy, wonderful, lousy*—like two powerful, opposing winds buffeting me. I try to navigate my little craft so as not to capsize before either. Between the two poles of affirmation and doubt, both in the name of love, I try to follow my true course.   26

QUESTIONS

1. Describe the response of Schulberg's mother and father to the boy's first poem. How do the mother and father contrast? What does Schulberg learn from the experience?

2. What was the relationship of Hollywood to home life in the Schulberg family?

3. Locate five colloquial phrases in the essay. What is the effect of this colloquial style on the tone of the essay?

4. Discuss the metaphorical language in the last paragraph of the essay. Locate metaphors and similes in other parts of the essay. Identify various allusions in the selection.

5. Trace Schulberg's development of conflict and suspense in the story he narrates. How does he handle these elements successfully?

6. How does Schulberg develop the time frame in the essay? What paragraphs treat the key event? Examine the paragraph that serves as a transition to later episodes. Compare and contrast Schulberg's presentation of the later episodes with that of the key episode.

7. Why is characterization important to the development of Schulberg's thesis?

8. Which paragraphs comprise the conclusion? What distinguishes these paragraphs from most of the other paragraphs in the essay?

9. Do you think that Schulberg explains the conflicts in the creative process in a convincing way? Why or why not? Do you accept his premise that fathers tend to be more critical and mothers more supportive of children's work and creative projects?

10. Relate an experience involving a project you created that resulted in conflicting responses from parents, relatives, or friends.

JOHN A. WILLIAMS

The Figure Eight

John A. Williams (1925–   ) has had a notable career as novelist, journalist, editor, and university professor. As a literary artist, Williams is one of the most significant interpreters of the contemporary American experience. Two of his eight novels, *The Man Who Cried I Am* (1967) and *Captain Blackman* (1972), are among the best political fiction of recent times. The essay that follows recreates with humor and horror a memorable grade school experience.

iss Wooley scared the hell out of all of us. She was a big, statuesque woman with quivering mustaches and thick-lensed glasses. She walked about the halls of the school with a heavy ruler; she seemed not to know what to do with it and when she walked the empty halls she beat it against the palm of her hand, "Pap! Pap!" And those of us who were in the corridors, perhaps around the corner she was approaching with clumping, menacing steps, scattered as pellets blasted from a gun. But sometimes, oblivious to all sounds, so intent were we in our trading of cowboy or baseball player pictures which came with gum,

1

JOHN A. WILLIAMS

we were surprised. Such leaping and whooping you never saw. And ducking—really, if I were to ever comment on my dexterity in dodgeball I would have to credit the arithmetic teacher, Miss Wooley.

No one fails in the second grade; I know, I tried hard enough 2 to because when you got to the third grade you had to study arithmetic from Miss Wooley, she of the fat, pasty face and the still eyes. It was inevitable, of course. I had to learn my numbers, as they called them at home. How could you survive in the world if you didn't learn numbers? "You'll be cheated to death," they said.

I've never known my friends to be so still, so attentive, so 3 mannerly. It was as if they passed through an invisible ray entering Miss Wooley's room, and it forced their faces into somber expressions which did not quite conceal the childish willingness to please.

The winter dragged into spring; we were learning the num- 4 bers. They became increasingly easy for me and I told myself that I had them beat. Oh, this is not to say that there were not some catastrophes. Miss Wooley teed off on James Dunbar one day. James was a lunk of a boy; insensitive from head to foot to practically everything. I always got on his side when we played tin can soccer in the schoolyard. James was dawdling at the board this day—I remember it well because I had had a tremendous crush on Marjorie Dey and she had told me my sneaks stank—when Miss Wooley dashed up behind him, in a rather unsporting manner, and clapped him across the buttocks with the ruler. James, startled out of his reverie, moved away from the board where he had drawn a tic-tac-toe affair. Miss Wooley seized his hands, as was her habit, and began belaboring them furiously. The class moved from one buttock to the other in a mass demonstration of empathy. James, however, was unmoved. Frenzied at his utter lack of cooperation, Miss Wooley began slamming the top of his head with the ruler. James, in a halfhearted way, raised his hands to cover his skull. But Miss Wooley would not have it. She moved into short range and the ruler became a dull-yellow blur and the sound of its meeting James' scalp in so rapid a succession was not unlike the reports from a light machine gun. Then the ruler broke. James backed out of the room. Miss Wooley turned back to the class which had degenerated into a trembling heap of popped eyes and chattering teeth. I didn't even have time to think of Marjorie Dey or of my sneakers.

You could say of Miss Wooley that she was not a discriminat- 5 ing woman; she beat just as furiously at girls as she did at boys. She always had a supply of those thick, yellow rulers some bank in town was forever passing out to the schools in a perverted public relations gesture. The day she thrashed Marjorie made me realize how close to home the teacher was getting. Poor Marjorie. I sought to comfort her when she came to sit down. I tucked my sneakered feet (Jesus, didn't they ever buy me anything but sneakers?) around the base of the chair and offered her some of my cowboy gum. She took it, but I had the feeling that she still disliked my sneaks.

Then we came to the figure eight. As soon as Miss Wooley 6 snapped from the board, her long, heavy fingers clutching the chalk with which she'd drawn that terribly intricate figure, I began to shake. God! I couldn't do *that* one! She must have known it would be difficult for some of us, because she smiled the way a cop smiles when he approaches you with a ticket and pencil. Not only that, but she tightened her grip on the ruler. Was it longer and thicker than usual? One by one my classmates took their places at the board and drew the figure. The room was a jiggling blur before me, but I heard the ruler. "Pap!" Then there would be the dutiful cry, "Oww!"

The row began to empty before me. I had forgotten about my 7 sneaks and Marjorie. I leaned forward, concealing my panic as best I could, and tried to get the movement of drawing the figure set in my pea-brain. I could not. Then, of course, it was my time to meet fate in the huge, threatening form of Miss Wooley. I think when I passed her and took my place at the board, she said to herself, "Hey, here's one I've missed all term."

I grasped the chalk and raised my hand to the board. There 8 was a sound at my feet. Looking first at Miss Wooley—to make certain she was not too close to me—I glanced down at the floor. There was the chalk. I looked at my fingers; there was nothing there. I turned my backside to the board, placed one arm over my head and dipped quickly for the chalk. I was back up before Miss Wooley could move. I placed the tip of the chalk against the board and for a second closed my eyes. I wanted God to take my arm and draw a figure eight for me, like I had prayed for since the class had begun that day. But God, goddammit, must have been out for lunch or something, because that chalk didn't move an inch! Yes, I was surprised when I opened my eyes and saw the chalk still in the same place. No eight on the board. "Pap!" from the other side of the room. I shot a terrified glance in that direction and prayed, not without some anger, because I had dutifully gone to Sunday school on Sunday, had said my prayers at night and had done my cussing in private. I felt I had something coming for all that devotion. I heard Miss Wooley again approaching my board. I pressed against the slate in a panic and a wriggly line squirted from the chalk onto the board. I looked at it in amazement; it was no eight. Clump! Clump! She moved closer. I grabbed an eraser and with vigorous motions which were supposed to convey to Miss Wooley the idea that in my next motion there would be an eight, slapped it against the board. Puffs of chalk exploded from beneath the eraser. I even knitted my brows to further impress Miss Wooley with my seriousness.

JOHN A. WILLIAMS

No luck. Pap! Pap, pap, pap! Boy, could that woman swing a ruler! I figured, as I heard her step back, that *now* I would do it. I scrambled for the board, all pretense gone, panic rampant in my eyeballs, tears jetting out, my wrists feeling not my own from the blows of that blasted ruler. An Indian teepee came out of my scribblings; I jigged away from the ruler, then jigged back to the spot where the teepee was. Swish! Swish! went the ruler. Everyone else was seated now. I jabbed the chalk into the board, and praying with all the sincerity in my heart, I placed upon it something that resembled an eight. I looked at Miss Wooley like a cornered dog. She surveyed the figure, surveyed me. With an almost imperceptible nod of her head, she signaled me to my seat. I was so filled with relief I forgot my usual caution and did not sidle by her with a wary look. Needless to say, she helped me by two feet on the way to my chair. I sat down thinking it was wrong for someone to have as much dislike for a person as I had for Miss Wooley. I looked at the eight on the board. It leaned to one side. Something else was wrong with it. I compared it to the other eights on the board. I had made mine from the wrong side.

I still do.

QUESTIONS

1. How does Miss Wooley run a classroom? What are Williams's impressions of her? How does the author use Miss Wooley's personal characteristics to convey his impressions?

2. Why was the author terrified by "the figure eight"?

3. Locate five examples of idiomatic language in the essay. Why is such language appropriate to the selection?

4. Describe the nature of the imagery used to depict Miss Wooley.

5. Why and how is Williams's introductory paragraph particularly effective?

6. How does Williams handle chronology in the essay? Why does he delay the episode about the figure eight until the end?

7. What is the tone of the essay? How does Williams achieve it?

8. The author's conclusion consists of a single short sentence. How effective is this strategy and why?

9. Williams as an adult and an author obviously has placed Miss Wooley in perspective. But can teachers like Miss Wooley have more lasting and perhaps detrimental impact on students? Why or why not?

 THE FIGURE EIGHT

10. Write a narrative essay recounting the worst or most terrifying teacher you had as a child. Focus on a critical episode that is most memorable to you.

SANTHA RAMA RAU

By Any Other Name

Santha Rama Rau (1923–   ) is an Indian novelist and essayist who throughout her career has interpreted the Eastern experience for Western audiences. She is a gifted travel writer and memorist. Her principal works include *Home to India* (1944), *Remember the House* (1955), and *Gifts of Passage* (1961). This narrative essay sensitively portrays the conflict in cultures perceived by the author in her early childhood.

At the Anglo-Indian day school in Zorinabad to which my sister and I were sent when she was eight and I was five and a half, they changed our names. On the first day of school, a hot, windless morning of a north Indian September, we stood in the headmistress's study and she said, "Now you're the *new* girls. What are your names?" 1

My sister answered for us. "I am Premila, and she"— nodding in my direction—"is Santha." 2

The headmistress had been in India, I suppose, fifteen years or so, but she still smiled her helpless inability to cope with Indian names. Her rimless half-glasses glittered, and the precarious bun on top of her head trembled as she shook her head. "Oh, my dears, those are much too hard for me. Suppose we give you pretty English names. Wouldn't that be more jolly? Let's see, now—Pamela for you, I think." She shrugged in a baffled way at my sister. "That's as close as I can get. And for *you*," she said to me, "how about Cynthia? Isn't that nice?" 3

My sister was always less easily intimidated than I was, and while she kept a stubborn silence, I said, "Thank you," in a very tiny voice. 4

We had been sent to that school because my father, among his responsibilities as an officer of the civil service, had a tour of duty to perform in the villages around that steamy little provincial town, where he had his headquarters at that time. He used to make his 5 shorter inspection tours on horseback, and a week before, in the stale heat of a typically postmonsoon day, we had waved good-by to him and a little procession—an assistant, a secretary, two bearers, and the man to look after the bedding rolls and luggage. They rode away through our large garden, still bright green from the rains, and we turned back into the twilight of the house and the sound of fans whispering in every room.

Up to then, my mother had refused to send Premila to school 6 in the British-run establishments of that time, because, she used to say, "you can bury a dog's tail for seven years and it still comes out curly, and you can take a Britisher away from his home for a lifetime, and he still remains insular." The examinations and degrees from entirely Indian schools were not, in those days, considered valid. In my case, the question had never come up, and probably never would have come up if Mother's extraordinary good health had not broken down. For the first time in my life, she was not able to continue the lessons she had been giving us every morning. So our Hindi books were put away, the stories of the Lord Krishna as a little boy were left in mid-air, and we were sent to the Anglo-Indian school.

That first day at school is still, when I think of it, a remarkable 7 one. At that age, if one's name is changed, one develops a curious form of dual personality. I remember having a certain detached and disbelieving concern in the actions of "Cynthia," but certainly no responsibility. Accordingly, I followed the thin, erect back of the headmistress down the veranda to my classroom feeling, at most, a passing interest in what was going to happen to me in this strange, new atmosphere of School.

The building was Indian in design, with wide verandas 8 opening onto a central courtyard, but Indian verandas are usually whitewashed, with stone floors. These, in the tradition of British schools, were painted dark brown and had matting on the floors. It gave a feeling of extra intensity to the heat.

I suppose there were about a dozen Indian children in the 9 school—which contained perhaps forty children in all—and four of them were in my class. They were all sitting at the back of the room, and I went to join them. I sat next to a small, solemn girl who didn't smile at me. She had long, glossy-black braids and wore a cotton dress, but she still kept on her Indian jewelry—a gold chain around her neck, thin gold bracelets, and tiny ruby studs in her ears. Like most Indian children, she had a rim of black kohl around her eyes. The cotton dress should have looked strange, but all I could think of was that I should ask my mother if I couldn't wear a dress to school, too, instead of my Indian clothes.

I can't remember too much about the proceedings in class 10

that day, except for the beginning. The teacher pointed to me and asked me to stand up. "Now, dear, tell the class your name."

I said nothing. 11

"Come along," she said frowning slightly. "What's your 12 name, dear?"

"I don't know," I said, finally. 13

The English children in the front of the class—there were 14 about eight or ten of them—giggled and twisted around in their chairs to look at me. I sat down quickly and opened my eyes very wide, hoping in that way to dry them off. The little girl with the braids put out her hand and very lightly touched my arm. She still didn't smile.

Most of that morning I was rather bored. I looked briefly at 15 the children's drawings pinned to the wall, and then concentrated on a lizard clinging to the ledge of the high, barred window behind the teacher's head. Occasionally it would shoot out its long yellow tongue for a fly, and then it would rest, with its eyes closed and its belly palpitating, as though it were swallowing several times quickly. The lessons were mostly concerned with reading and writing and simple numbers—things that my mother had already taught me—and I paid very little attention. The teacher wrote on the easel blackboard words like "bat" and "cat," which seemed babyish to me; only "apple" was new and incomprehensible.

When it was time for the lunch recess, I followed the girl with 16 braids out onto the veranda. There the children from the other classes were assembled. I saw Premila at once and ran over to her, as she had charge of our lunchbox. The children were all opening packages and sitting down to eat sandwiches. Premila and I were the only ones who had Indian food—thin wheat chapatties, some vegetable curry, and a bottle of buttermilk. Premila thrust half of it into my hand and whispered fiercely that I should go and sit with my class, because that was what the others seemed to be doing.

The enormous black eyes of the little Indian girl from my class 17 looked at my food longingly, so I offered her some. But she only shook her head and plowed her way solemnly through her sandwiches.

I was very sleepy after lunch, because at home we always 18 took a siesta. It was usually a pleasant time of day, with the bedroom darkened against the harsh afternoon sun, the drifting off into sleep with the sound of Mother's voice reading a story in one's mind, and, finally, the shrill, fussy voice of the ayah waking one for tea.

At school, we rested for a short time on low, folding cots on 19 the veranda, and then we were expected to play games. During the hot part of the afternoon we played indoors, and after the shadows

SANTHA RAMA RAU

had begun to lengthen and the slight breeze of the evening had come up we moved outside to the wide courtyard.

I had never really grasped the system of competitive games. 20 At home, whenever we played tag or guessing games, I was always allowed to "win"—"because," Mother used to tell Premila, "she is the youngest, and we have to allow for that." I had often heard her say it, and it seemed quite reasonable to me, but the result was that I had no clear idea of what "winning" meant.

When we played twos-and-threes that afternoon at school, in 21 accordance with my training, I let one of the small English boys catch me, but was naturally rather puzzled when the other children did not return the courtesy. I ran about for what seemed like hours without ever catching anyone, until it was time for school to close. Much later I learned that my attitude was called "not being a good sport," and I stopped allowing myself to be caught, but it was not for years that I really learned the spirit of the thing.

When I saw our car come up to the school gate, I broke away 22 from my classmates and rushed toward it yelling, "Ayah! Ayah!" It seemed like an eternity since I had seen her that morning—a wizened, affectionate figure in her white cotton sari, giving me dozens of urgent and useless instructions on how to be a good girl at school. Premila followed more sedately, and she told me on the way home never to do that again in front of the other children.

When we got home we went straight to Mother's high, white 23 room to have tea with her, and I immediately climbed onto the bed and bounced gently up and down on the springs. Mother asked how we had liked our first day in school. I was so pleased to be home and to have left that peculiar Cynthia behind that I had nothing whatever to say about school, except to ask what "apple" meant. But Premila told Mother about the classes, and added that in her class they had weekly tests to see if they learned their lessons well.

I asked, "What's a test?" 24

Premila said, "You're too small to have them. You won't have 25 them in your class for donkey's years." She had learned the expression that day and was using it for the first time. We all laughed enormously at her wit. She also told Mother, in an aside, that we should take sandwiches to school the next day. Not, she said, that *she* minded. But they would be simpler for me to handle.

That whole lovely evening I didn't think about school at all. I 26 sprinted barefoot across the lawns with my favorite playmate, the cook's son, to the stream at the end of the garden. We quarreled in our usual way, waded in the tepid water under the lime trees, and waited for the night to bring out the smell of the jasmine. I listened with fascination to his stories of ghosts and demons, until I was too frightened to cross the garden alone in the semidarkness. The ayah found me, shouted at the cook's son, scolded me, hurried me into supper—it was an entirely usual, wonderful evening.

It was a week later, the day of Premila's first test, that our   27
lives changed rather abruptly. I was sitting at the back of my class, in my usual inattentive way, only half listening to the teacher. I had started a rather guarded friendship with the girl with the braids, whose name turned out to be Nalini (Nancy, in school). The three other Indian children were already fast friends. Even at that age it was apparent to all of us that friendship with the English or Anglo-Indian children was out of the question. Occasionally, during the class, my new friend and I would draw pictures and show them to each other secretly.

The door opened sharply and Premila marched in. At first,   28
the teacher smiled at her in a kindly and encouraging way and said, "Now, you're little Cynthia's sister?"

Premila didn't even look at her. She stood with her feet   29
planted firmly apart and her shoulders rigid, and addressed herself directly to me. "Get up," she said. "We're going home."

I didn't know what had happened, but I was aware that it   30
was a crisis of some sort. I rose obediently and started to walk toward my sister.

"Bring your pencils and your notebook," she said.   31

I went back for them, and together we left the room. The   32
teacher started to say something just as Premila closed the door, but we didn't wait to hear what it was.

In complete silence we left the school grounds and started to   33
walk home. Then I asked Premila what the matter was. All she would say was "We're going home for good."

It was a very tiring walk for a child of five and a half, and I   34
dragged along behind Premila with my pencils growing sticky in my hand. I can still remember looking at the dusty hedges, and the tangles of thorns in the ditches by the side of the road, smelling the faint fragrance from the eucalyptus trees and wondering whether we would ever reach home. Occasionally a horse-drawn tonga passed us, and the women, in their pink or green silks, stared at Premila and me trudging along on the side of the road. A few coolies and a line of women carrying baskets of vegetables on their heads smiled at us. But it was nearing the hottest time of day, and the road was almost deserted. I walked more and more slowly, and shouted to Premila, from time to time, "Wait for me!" with increasing peevishness. She spoke to me only once, and that was to tell me to carry my notebook on my head, because of the sun.

When we got to our house the ayah was just taking a tray of   35
lunch into Mother's room. She immediately started a long, worried

SANTHA RAMA RAU

questioning about what are you children doing back here at this hour of the day.

Mother looked very startled and very concerned, and asked Premila what had happened. 36

Premila said, "We had our test today, and she made me and the other Indians sit at the back of the room, with a desk between each one." 37

Mother said, "Why was that, darling?" 38

"She said it was because Indians cheat," Premila added. "So I don't think we should go back to that school." 39

Mother looked very distant, and was silent a long time. At last she said, "Of course not, darling." She sounded displeased. 40

We all shared the curry she was having for lunch, and afterward I was sent off to the beautifully familiar bedroom for my siesta. I could hear Mother and Premila talking through the open door. 41

Mother said, "Do you suppose she understood all that?" 42

Premila said, "I shouldn't think so. She's a baby." 43

Mother said, "Well, I hope it won't bother her." 44

Of course, they were both wrong. I understood it perfectly, and I remember it all very clearly. But I put it happily away, because it had all happened to a girl called Cynthia, and I never was really particularly interested in her. 45

QUESTIONS

1. Cite five examples the author gives to demonstrate that her attendance at the Anglo-Indian day school was an alien experience for her.

2. According to the author's inferences, what was the effect of British rule on Indian society? How does the headmistress embody this impact?

3. Define these Indian words, preferably from the contexts in which they are used: *kohl* (paragraph 9); *chapatties* (paragraph 17); *ayah* (paragraph 18); *sari* (paragraph 22); *tonga* (paragraph 34).

4. Explain the author's use of sensory language in paragraphs 1, 3, 5, 8, 9, 15, 26, and 34.

5. What is the theme of this narrative essay? How does the author state it?

6. Describe the tone and mood of the essay.

7. What is the utility and value of the author's use of dialogue in the essay?

BY ANY OTHER NAME

8. How do various causal patterns inform the narrative?

9. Although dealing specifically with a colonial situation, the author also illuminates the universal experience of being made to feel different, strange, or alien. Why is this ironic for the author? Why does it remain so vivid in her memory? Do we become more or less conscious of this phenomenon at a later age?

10. a. Write a narrative essay centering on a time when you were made to feel strange or foreign in a social situation.
b. Tell of a time when you felt that someone or some group was trying to change your identity or sense of self.

JAMES THURBER

The Night the Bed Fell

James Thurber (1894–1961), foremost American cartoonist, playwright, and humorist, was from 1927 a lifelong contributer to *The New Yorker.* He demonstrated a distinctive talent for turning his personal experiences into comic renditions of American life in such books as *My Life and Hard Times* (1933) and *The Middle-Aged Man on the Flying Trapeze* (1935). Other significant works include *My World and Welcome to It* (1942), *Fables for Our Time* (1939), and *The Thurber Album* (1952). The comic misadventures that unfold in the following tale are typical of Thurber's approach to human behavior.

suppose that the high-water mark of my youth in   1
Columbus, Ohio, was the night the bed fell on my
father. It makes a better recitation (unless, as some
friends of mine have said, one has heard it five or six
times) than it does a piece of writing, for it is almost necessary to
throw furniture around, shake doors, and bark like a dog, to lend the
proper atmosphere and verisimilitude to what is admittedly a somewhat incredible tale. Still, it did take place.

It happened, then, that my father had decided to sleep in the   2
attic one night, to be away where he could think. My mother opposed
the notion strongly because, she said, the old wooden bed up there
was unsafe; it was wobbly and the heavy headboard would crash
down on father's head in case the bed fell, and kill him. There was no
dissuading him, however, and at a quarter past ten he closed the attic

door behind him and went up the narrow twisting stairs. We later heard ominous creakings as he crawled into bed. Grandfather, who usually slept in the attic bed when he was with us, had disappeared some days before. (On these occasions he was usually gone six or eight days and returned growling and out of temper, with the news that the federal Union was run by a passel of blockheads and that the Army of the Potomac didn't have any more chance than a fiddler's bitch.)

We had visiting us at this time a nervous first cousin of mine named Briggs Beall, who believed that he was likely to cease breathing when he was asleep. It was his feeling that if he were not awakened every hour during the night, he might die of suffocation. He had been accustomed to setting an alarm clock to ring at intervals until morning, but I persuaded him to abandon this. He slept in my room and I told him that I was such a light sleeper that if anybody quit breathing in the same room with me, I would wake instantly. He tested me the first night—which I had suspected he would—by holding his breath after my regular breathing had convinced him I was asleep. I was not asleep, however, and called to him. This seemed to allay his fears a little, but he took the precaution of putting a glass of spirits of camphor on a little table at the head of his bed. In case I didn't arouse him until he was almost gone, he said, he would sniff the camphor, a powerful reviver. Briggs was not the only member of his family who had his crotchets. Old Aunt Melissa Beall (who could whistle like a man, with two fingers in her mouth) suffered under the premonition that she was destined to die on South High Street, because she had been born on South High Street and married on South High Street. Then there was Aunt Sarah Shoaf, who never went to bed at night without the fear that a burglar was going to get in and blow chloroform under her door through a tube. To avert this calamity—for she was in greater dread of anesthetics than of losing her household goods—she always piled her money, silverware, and other valuables in a neat stack just outside her bedroom, with a note reading: "This is all I have. Please take it and do not use your chloroform, as this is all I have." Aunt Gracie Shoaf also had a burglar phobia, but she met it with more fortitude. She was confident that burglars had been getting into her house every night for forty years. The fact that she never missed anything was to her no proof to the contrary. She always claimed that she scared them off before they could take anything, by throwing shoes down the hallway. When she went to bed she piled, where she could get at them handily, all the shoes there were about her house. Five minutes after she had turned off the light, she would sit up in bed and say "Hark!" Her husband, who had learned to ignore the whole situation as long ago as 1903, would either be sound asleep or pretend to be sound asleep. In either case he would not respond to her tugging and pulling, so that presently she would arise, tiptoe to the door, open it slightly and heave a shoe down the hall in one direction, and its mate down the hall in the other direction. Some nights she threw them all, some nights only a couple of pair.

But I am straying from the remarkable incidents that took place during the night that the bed fell on father. By midnight we were all in bed. The layout of the rooms and the disposition of their occupants is important to an understanding of what later occurred. In the front room upstairs (just under father's attic bedroom) were my mother and my brother Herman, who sometimes sang in his sleep, usually "Marching Through Georgia" or "Onward, Christian Soldiers." Briggs Beall and myself were in a room adjoining this one. My brother Roy was in a room across the hall from ours. Our bull terrier, Rex, slept in the hall. 4

My bed was an army cot, one of those affairs which are made wide enough to sleep on comfortably only by putting up, flat with the middle section, the two sides which ordinarily hang down like the sideboards of a drop-leaf table. When these sides are up, it is perilous to roll too far toward the edge, for then the cot is likely to tip completely over, bringing the whole bed down on top of one, with a tremendous banging crash. This, in fact, is precisely what happened, about two o'clock in the morning. (It was my mother who, in recalling the scene later, first referred to it as "the night the bed fell on your father.") 5

Always a deep sleeper, slow to arouse (I had lied to Briggs), I was at first unconscious of what had happened when the iron cot rolled me onto the floor and toppled over on me. It left me still warmly bundled up and unhurt, for the bed rested above me like a canopy. Hence I did not wake up, only reached the edge of consciousness and went back. The racket, however, instantly awakened my mother, in the next room, who came to the immediate conclusion that her worst dread was realized: the big wooden bed upstairs had fallen on father. She therefore screamed, "Let's go to your poor father!" It was this shout, rather than the noise of my cot falling, that awakened Herman, in the same room with her. He thought that mother had become, for no apparent reason, hysterical. "You're all right, Mamma!" he shouted, trying to calm her. They exchanged shout for shout for perhaps ten seconds: "Let's go to your poor father!" and "You're all right!" That woke up Briggs. By this time I was conscious of what was going on, in a vague way, but did not yet realize that I was under my bed instead of on it. Briggs, awakening in the midst of loud shouts of fear and apprehension, came to the quick conclusion that he was suffocating and that we were all trying to 6 "bring him out." With a low moan, he grasped the glass of camphor at the head of his bed and instead of sniffing it poured it over himself. The room reeked of camphor. "Ugf, ahfg," choked Briggs, like a drowning man, for he had almost succeeded in stopping his breath under the deluge of pungent spirits. He leaped out of bed and groped toward the open window, but he came up against one that was closed. With his hand, he beat out the glass, and I could hear it crash and tinkle on the alleyway below. It was at this juncture that I, in trying to get up, had the uncanny sensation of feeling my bed above me! Foggy with sleep, I now suspected, in my turn, that the whole uproar was being made in a frantic endeavor to extricate me from what must be an unheard-of and perilous situation. "Get me out of this!" I bawled. "Get me out!" I think I had the nightmarish belief that I was entombed in a mine. "Gugh," gasped Briggs, floundering in his camphor.

By this time my mother, still shouting, pursued by Herman, still shouting, was trying to open the door to the attic, in order to go up and get my father's body out of the wreckage. The door was stuck, however, and wouldn't yield. Her frantic pulls on it only added to the general banging and confusion. Roy and the dog were now up, the one shouting questions, the other barking. 7

Father, farthest away and soundest sleeper of all, had by this time been awakened by the battering on the attic door. He decided that the house was on fire. "I'm coming, I'm coming!" he wailed in a slow, sleepy voice—it took him many minutes to regain full consciousness. My mother, still believing he was caught under the bed, detected in his "I'm coming!" the mournful, resigned note of one who is preparing to meet his Maker. "He's dying!" she shouted. 8

"I'm all right!" Briggs yelled to reassure her. "I'm all right!" He still believed that it was his own closeness to death that was worrying mother. I found at last the light switch in my room, unlocked the door, and Briggs and I joined the others at the attic door. The dog, who never did like Briggs, jumped for him—assuming that he was the culprit in whatever was going on—and Roy had to throw Rex and hold him. We could hear father crawling out of bed upstairs. Roy pulled the attic door open, with a mighty jerk, and father came down the stairs, sleepy and irritable but safe and sound. My mother began to weep when she saw him. Rex began to howl. "What in the name of God is going on here?" asked father. 9

The situation was finally put together like a gigantic jig-saw puzzle. Father caught a cold from prowling around in his bare feet but there were no other bad results. "I'm glad," said mother, who always looked on the bright side of things, "that your grandfather wasn't here." 10

THE NIGHT THE BED FELL

QUESTIONS

1. Characterize the many participants in this human comedy. How are they similar? What is Thurber's attitude toward them?

2. Trace the sequence of events that throws the Thurber household into confusion.

3. Discuss Thurber's use of action verbs in this narrative.

4. What is the level of diction in this essay?

5. Why is Thurber's digressive technique in the early part of the article a useful strategy?

6. How important is setting in the creation of mood in this selection? How does Thurber create an effective setting? How do mood and tone reinforce each other?

7. Explore Thurber's use of transitions in the essay.

8. Explain the importance of Thurber's conclusion (paragraph 10). What does the conclusion reveal about the theme?

9. Thurber assumes a comic, mildly satirical attitude toward the eccentricity and confusion in his family. What is the value of this comic view in confronting confusing or chaotic situations?

10. Write a narrative account of an amusing moment in the life of your family.

DYLAN THOMAS

A Visit to Grandpa's

Dylan Thomas (1914–1953), Welsh poet and prose writer, had one of the most lyric voices in contemporary literature. Both his poetry and prose are filled with an animated primitivism, forceful sounds and rhythms, and complex patterns of symbolism and imagery. His poetry collections include *Eighteen Poems* (1934), *Twenty-five Poems* (1936), and *In Country Sleep* (1952). The following autobiographical sketch from *Portrait of the Artist as a Young Dog* (1952) contains many of his most expressive techniques.

In the middle of the night I woke from a dream full of   1
whips and lariats as long as serpents, and runaway
coaches on mountain passes, and wide, windy gallops
over cactus fields, and I heard the old man in the next
room crying, "Gee-up!" and "Whoa!" and trotting his tongue on the
roof of his mouth.

It was the first time I had stayed in grandpa's house. The   2
floorboards had squeaked like mice as I climbed into bed, and the
mice between the walls had creaked like wood as though another
visitor was walking on them. It was a mild summer night, but
curtains had flapped and branches beaten against the window. I had
pulled the sheets over my head, and soon was roaring and riding in a
book.

"Whoa there, my beauties!" cried grandpa. His voice sound-   3
ed very young and loud, and his tongue had powerful hooves, and he
made his bedroom into a great meadow. I thought I would see if he
was ill, or had set his bed-clothes on fire, for my mother had said that
he lit his pipe under the blankets, and had warned me to run to his
help if I smelt smoke in the night. I went on tiptoe through the
darkness to his bedroom door, brushing against the furniture and
upsetting a candlestick with a thump. When I saw there was a light in
the room I felt frightened, and as I opened the door I heard grandpa
shout, "Gee-up!" as loudly as a bull with a megaphone.

He was sitting straight up in bed and rocking from side to   4
side as though the bed were on a rough road; the knotted edges of the
counterpane were his reins; his invisible horses stood in a shadow
beyond the bedside candle. Over a white flannel nightshirt he was
wearing a red waistcoat with walnut-sized brass buttons. The over-
filled bowl of his pipe smouldered among his whiskers like a little,
burning hayrick on a stock. At the sight of me, his hands dropped
from the reins and lay blue and quiet, the bed stopped still on a level
road, he muffled his tongue into silence, and the horses drew softly
up.

"Is there anything the matter, grandpa?" I asked, though the   5
clothes were not on fire. His face in the candlelight looked like a
ragged quilt pinned upright on the black air and patched all over with
goat-beards.

He stared at me mildly. Then he blew down his pipe,   6
scattering the sparks and making a high, wet dog-whistle of the stem,
and shouted: "Ask no questions."

After a pause, he said shyly: "Do you ever have nightmares,   7
boy?"

I said: "No."   8

"Oh, yes, you do," he said.   9

I said I was woken by a voice that was shouting to horses.   10

"What did I tell you?" he said. "You eat too much. Who ever 11
heard of horses in a bedroom?"

He fumbled under his pillow, brought out a small, tinkling 12
bag, and carefully untied its strings. He put a sovereign in my hand,
and said "Buy a cake." I thanked him and wished him good night.

As I closed my bedroom door, I heard his voice crying loudly 13
and gaily, "Gee-up! gee-up!" and the rocking of the travelling bed.

In the morning I woke from a dream of fiery horses on a plain 14
that was littered with furniture, and of large, cloudy men who rode
six horses at a time and whipped them with burning bed-clothes.
Grandpa was at breakfast, dressed in deep black. After breakfast he
said, "There was a terrible loud wind last night," and sat in his
arm-chair by the hearth to make clay balls for the fire. Later in the
morning he took me for a walk, through Johnstown village and into
the fields on the Llanstephan road.

A man with a whippet said, "There's a nice morning, Mr 15
Thomas," and when he had gone, leanly as his dog, into the
short-treed green wood he should not have entered because of the
notices, grandpa said: "There, do you hear what he called you?
Mister!"

We passed by small cottages, and all the men who leant on 16
the gates congratulated grandpa on the fine morning. We passed
through the wood full of pigeons, and their wings broke the branches
as they rushed to the tops of the trees. Among the soft, contented
voices and the loud, timid flying, grandpa said, like a man calling
across a field: "If you heard those old birds in the night, you'd wake
me up and say there were horses in the trees."

We walked back slowly, for he was tired, and the lean man 17
stalked out of the forbidden wood with a rabbit held as gently over his
arm as a girl's arm in a warm sleeve.

On the last day but one of my visit I was taken to Llanstephan 18
in a governess cart pulled by a short, weak pony. Grandpa might
have been driving a bison, so tightly he held the reins, so ferociously
cracked the long whip, so blasphemously shouted warning to boys
who played in the road, so stoutly stood with his gaitered legs apart
and cursed the demon strength and wilfulness of his tottering pony.

"Look out, boy!" he cried when we came to each corner, and 19
pulled and tugged and jerked and sweated and waved his whip like a
rubber sword. And when the pony had crept miserably round each
corner, grandpa turned to me with a sighing smile: "We weathered
that one, boy."

When we came to Llanstephan village at the top of the hill, he 20
left the cart by the "Edwinsford Arms" and patted the pony's muzzle
and gave it sugar, saying: "You're a weak little pony, Jim, to pull big
men like us."

DYLAN THOMAS

He had strong beer and I had lemonade, and he paid Mrs 21
Edwinsford with a sovereign out of the tinkling bag; she inquired
after his health, and he said that Llangadock was better for the tubes.
We went to look at the churchyard and the sea, and sat in the wood
called the Sticks, and stood on the concert platform in the middle of
the wood where visitors sang on mid-summer nights and, year by
year, the innocent of the village was elected mayor. Grandpa paused
at the churchyard and pointed over the iron gate at the angelic
headstones and the poor wooden crosses. "There's no sense in lying
there," he said.

We journeyed back furiously: Jim was a bison again. 22

I woke late on my last morning, out of dreams where the 23
Llanstephan sea carried bright sailing-boats as long as liners; and
heavenly choirs in the Sticks, dressed in bards' robes and brass-
buttoned waistcoats, sang in a strange Welsh to the departing sailors.
Grandpa was not at breakfast; he rose early. I walked in the fields
with a new sling, and shot at the Towy gulls and the rooks in the
parsonage trees. A warm wind blew from the summer points of the
weather; a morning mist climbed from the ground and floated among
the trees and hid the noisy birds; in the mist and the wind my pebbles
flew lightly up like hailstones in a world on its head. The morning
passed without a bird falling.

I broke my sling and returned for the midday meal through 24
the parson's orchard. Once, grandpa told me, the parson had bought
three ducks at Carmarthen Fair and made a pond for them in the
centre of the garden; but they waddled to the gutter under the
crumbling doorsteps of the house, and swam and quacked there.
When I reached the end of the orchard path, I looked through a hole
in the hedge and saw that the parson had made a tunnel through the
rockery that was between the gutter and the pond and had set up a
notice in plain writing: "This way to the pond."

The ducks were still swimming under the steps. 25

Grandpa was not in the cottage. I went into the garden, but 26
grandpa was not staring at the fruit-trees. I called across to a man
who leant on a spade in the fields beyond the garden hedge: "Have
you seen my grandpa this morning?"

He did not stop digging, and answered over his shoulder: "I 27
seen him in his fancy waistcoat."

Griff, the barber, lived in the next cottage. I called to him 28
through the open door: "Mr Griff, have you seen my grandpa?"

The barber came out in his shirtsleeves. 29

I said: "He's wearing his best waistcoat." I did not know if it 30
was important, but grandpa wore his waistcoat only in the night.

"Has grandpa been to Llanstephan?" asked Mr Griff anxious- 31
ly.

"We went there yesterday in a little trap," I said.   32

He hurried indoors and I heard him talking in Welsh, and he   33
came out again with his white coat on, and he carried a striped and
coloured walking-stick. He strode down the village street and I ran by
his side.

When we stopped at the tailor's shop, he cried out, "Dan!"   34
and Dan Tailor stepped from his window where he sat like an Indian
priest but wearing a derby hat. "Dai Thomas has got his waistcoat
on," said Mr Griff, "and he's been to Llanstephan."

As Dan Tailor searched for his overcoat, Mr Griff was striding   35
on. "Will Evans," he called outside the carpenter's shop, "Dai
Thomas has been to Llanstephan, and he's got his waistcoat on."

"I'll tell Morgan now," said the carpenter's wife out of the   36
hammering, sawing darkness of the shop.

We called at the butcher's shop and Mr Price's house, and Mr   37
Griff repeated his message like a town crier.

We gathered together in Johnstown square. Dan Tailor had   38
his bicycle, Mr Price his pony-trap. Mr Griff, the butcher, Morgan
Carpenter, and I climbed into the shaking trap, and we trotted off
towards Carmarthen town. The tailor led the way, ringing his bell as
though there were a fire or a robbery, and an old woman by the gate
of a cottage at the end of the street ran inside like a pelted hen.
Another woman waved a bright handkerchief.

"Where are we going?" I asked.   39

Grandpa's neighbours were as solemn as old men with black   40
hats and jackets on the outskirts of a fair. Mr Griff shook his head and
mourned: "I didn't expect this again from Dai Thomas."

"Not after last time," said Mr Price sadly.   41

We trotted on, we crept up Constitution Hill, we rattled down   42
into Lammas Street, and the tailor still rang his bell and a dog ran,
squealing, in front of his wheels. As we clip-clopped over the cobbles
that led down to the Towy bridge, I remembered grandpa's nightly
noisy journeys that rocked the bed and shook the walls, and I saw his
gay waistcoat in a vision and his patchwork head tufted and smiling
in the candlelight. The tailor before us turned round on his saddle,
his bicycle wobbled and skidded. "I see Dai Thomas!" he cried.

The trap rattled on to the bridge, and I saw grandpa there; the   43
buttons of his waistcoat shone in the sun, he wore his tight, black
Sunday trousers and a tall, dusty hat I had seen in a cupboard in the
attic, and he carried an ancient bag. He bowed to us. "Good morning,
Mr Price," he said, "and Mr Griff and Mr Morgan and Mr Evans." To
me, he said, "Good morning, boy."

Mr Griff pointed his coloured stick at him.   44

"And what do you think you are doing on Carmarthen bridge   45 in the middle of the afternoon," he said sternly, "with your best waistcoat and your old hat?"

Grandpa did not answer, but inclined his face to the river 46 wind, so that his beard was set dancing and wagging as though he talked, and watched the coracle men move, like turtles, on the shore.

Mr Griff raised his stunted barber's pole. "And where do you 47 think you are going," he said, "with your old black bag?"

Grandpa said: "I am going to Llangadock to be buried." And 48 he watched the coracle shells slip into the water lightly, and the gulls complain over the fish-filled water as bitterly as Mr Price complained:

"But you aren't dead yet, Dai Thomas." 49

For a moment grandpa reflected, then: "There's no sense in 50 lying dead in Llanstephan," he said. "The ground is comfy in Llangadock; you can twitch your legs without putting them in the sea."

His neighbours moved close to him. They said: "You aren't 51 dead, Mr Thomas."

"How can you be buried, then?" 52

"Nobody's going to bury you in Llanstephan." 53

"Come on home, Mr Thomas." 54

"There's strong beer for tea." 55

"And cake." 56

But grandpa stood firmly on the bridge, and clutched his bag 57 to his side, and stared at the flowing river and the sky, like a prophet who has no doubt.

QUESTIONS

1. What do we learn about Thomas's childhood, his views of himself, his attitude toward his grandfather, and his perceptions of the world?

2. Characterize the personality of Thomas's grandfather. Can we infer whether or not the grandfather will continue his journey at the end of the story? Why or why not?

3. The prose style in this narrative might be termed "poetic." How does Thomas's poetic style influence mood and tone in the essay? What are the components of his style? Isolate five instances of poetic style in the essay and explain their effects.

4. A major motif in the essay is nature imagery. Why is this motif important?

5. How does Thomas use dreams to structure and to inform the essay? In what ways are the dreams symbolic?

 A VISIT TO GRANDPA'S

6. The author uses an episodic technique in the essay, yet he achieves unity and coherence in the presentation of episodes. How? How does he handle proportion?

7. Discuss point of view with regard to the author's relationship to the action and time of the story.

8. Assess the uniqueness of Thomas's conclusion.

9. Thomas presents a microcosm of Welsh society in this essay. What are its contours and cultural points of reference? How do people relate to each other within these social contexts?

10. Relate an episode or series of episodes about a memorable visit to one of your relatives or friends.

MAXINE HONG KINGSTON

The American Father

Maxine Hong Kingston (1940–   ) has written two books on the Chinese-American experience that have established her as a major contemporary prose stylist. *The Woman Warrior* (1976) and *China Men* (1980) are brilliant explorations of personal and ethnic consciousness. This section from her later book is filled with the mysteries, family tales, and legends that the author uses to create the tapestry of her complex cultural identity.

ll I know for sure is that there were mysteries, mysteries   1
about my family—who they were, where they came
from, who they had been in China, how they got
here. . . . And from the time I was little I was always
trying to unravel the mysteries—prying, peeking, snooping, asking.
And like a child, most of the time I got it only half right. For instance,
growing up I thought that:

In 1903 my father was born in San Francisco, where my   2
grandmother had come disguised as a man.

Or, by the magic that Chinese women once had, she gave   3
birth at a distance, my grandfather and father in San Francisco, while
she was in China.

Or, the men of those days had the power to have babies.   4

If my grandparents did no such wonders, my father never- 5
theless turned up in San Francisco an American citizen.

He was also married at a distance. My mother and a few farm 6
women went out into the chickenyard and said words over a
rooster—a fierce rooster, red of comb and feathers—then she went
back inside married, a wife. She laughs, telling this wedding story; he
doesn't say, one way or the other.

When I ask MaMa why she speaks differently from BaBa, she 7
says their parents lived across the river from one another. Maybe his
village was America, the river an ocean, his accent American.

But one of my father's mysteries he showed me. 8

One day he took me walking while I was still young enough 9
to hold his hand, which felt splintery with calluses—"caused by
physical labor," according to MaMa. As we walked, he pointed out
sights, he named plants, told time on the clocks, explained signs, and
I learned the recurring words: "Company. Association. Hui. Tong."
As we walked through the streets of Chinatown BaBa greeted old
men with a finger to his hat. At the candy and tobacco store, BaBa
bought Lucky Strikes and beef jerky and the old men gave me plum
wafers. The tobacconist gave me a cigar box and a candy box. When
we came out, we were not on the busiest Chinatown street but on a
side street across from the park. The mysterious place my father was
taking me to the average pedestrian would have passed by; would
have looked into the barrels and cans in front of the grocery next door
and then walked on to the herbalist's, which had school supplies and
saucers of herbs in the windows. But BaBa stepped between the
grocery store and the herb shop into the kind of sheltered doorway
where Skid Row men sleep and pee and leave their liquor bottles. It
was a place with no business behind its door because no one would
have rented it—it wasn't eye-catching. It might have been a family-
association office. On the glass were dull gold Chinese words, and the
number was the same as our house number. And—delightful!—a big
old orange cat sat dozing in the window; it had pushed aside the
closed Venetian blinds and rested with its fur flat against the glass. I
tapped on the iron grillwork protecting the glass to see whether the
cat was asleep or dead; it blinked.

BaBa found the keys on his chain and unlocked the grating, 10
then the door. Inside was an immense room like a bank or post office.
Suddenly no city street, no noise, no people, no sun. Here was
horizontal and vertical order, counters and tables in cool gray
twilight. It was safe in here. The cat ran across the cement floor. The
place smelled like cat urine or eucalyptus berries. Brass and porcelain
spittoons squatted in the corners. Another cat, a gray one, walked
into the open and I tried following it, but it ran off. I walked under the
tables, which had thick legs.

BaBa filled a bucket with sawdust and water. He and I   11
scattered handfuls of the mixture on the floor and the place smelled
like a carnival. With our push brooms leaving wet streaks, we swept
up the sawdust, which turned gray as it picked up the dirt. BaBa
threw his cigarette butts into it. The cat dirt got picked up too. He
scooped everything into the dustpan he had made out of an oilcan.

We put away our brooms and I followed him to a wall where   12
sheaves of paper hung by their corners, diamond-shaped. "Pigeon
lottery," he called them. "Pigeon lottery tickets." Yes, in the wind of
the paddle fan the soft, thick sheaves ruffled like feathers and wings.

So this was where my father worked and what he did for a   13
living—running a gambling house, keeping track of gamblers' bets!

We were getting the gambling house ready. Tonight the   14
gamblers would come here from the towns and the fields; they would
sail from San Francisco all the way up the river through the delta to
Stockton, which had more gambling than any other city on the coast.
It would be a party tonight. The gamblers would eat the free food and
drink the free whiskey. They'd laugh and exclaim and cheer when
they won.

BaBa gave me a paper punch and let me help by making   15
perfect round holes in the corners of fresh papers so that I could hang
them, like diamonds, like pigeons. I collected round and crescent
confetti in my cigar box.

While I worked on the floor under the table, BaBa sat behind   16
a counter on his tall stool. With black elastic armbands around his
shirt sleeves and an eyeshade on his forehead, he clicked the abacus
fast and steadily, stopping to write the numbers down in ledgers. He
melted red wax in candle flame and made seals. He checked the
pigeon papers and set out fresh stacks of them. Then we twirled the
dials of the safe to make sure the combination was obliterated, wound
the grandfather clock with the long brass pendulum and locked up.
We bought crackly pork on the way home.

According to MaMa, the gambling house belonged to the   17
most powerful Chinese-American in Stockton. He paid my father to
manage it and pretend to be the owner. BaBa took the blame for the
real owner. When the cop on the beat walked in, BaBa gave him a
plate of food, a carton of cigarettes and a bottle of whiskey. Once a
month the police raided with a paddy wagon, and it was also part of
my father's job to be arrested. He never got a record, however,
because he thought up a new name for himself every time. Sometimes it came to him while the city sped past the barred windows.
Sometimes just when the white demon at the desk asked him for it a
new name came to him, one befitting the situation. They never found
out his real names, or that he had an American name at all. "I got
away with aliases," he said, "because the white demons can't tell one

Chinese name from another—or one face from another." He had a hundred dollars ready in an envelope with which he bribed the demon in charge. It might have been a fine, not a bribe, but BaBa saw him pocket the hundred dollars. After that the police let him walk out the door.

But my mother keeps saying those were dismal years. "He 18 worked twelve hours a day, no holidays," she says. "Even on New Year's, no day off. He couldn't come home until two in the morning. He stood on his feet, gambling twelve hours straight."

"I saw a tall stool," I say. 19

"He only got to sit on that when there were no customers. He 20 got paid almost nothing. He was a slave. I was a slave." She is angry, recalling those days.

A few years before, after my father's partners had stolen his 21 New York laundry, the owner of the gambling house, a man from the same village in China, paid my parents' fares to Stockton. The way my mother repaid him was to be a servant to his, the owner's, family. My mother, who had a degree as a medical doctor. She ironed for twelve people and bathed ten children. Bitterly she kept their house.

When their free time coincided, my parents sat with us on 22 apple and orange crates at a tiny table, our knees touching under it. We ate rice and salted fish, which is what peasants in China eat. Everything was nice except what MaMa was saying: "We've turned into slaves. We're slaves to villagers who were nothing when they were in China. I've turned into the servant of a woman who can't read. Maybe we should go back to China." My father said, "No," angry.

Sometimes we waited up until BaBa came home from work. 23 In addition to a table and crates, we had for furniture an ironing board and an army cot, which MaMa unfolded next to the gas stove in wintertime. While she ironed our clothes she sang and talked story, and I sat on the cot, holding one or two of my baby brothers or sisters. When BaBa came home, they got into the cot and pretended they were refugees under a blanket tent.

During World War II a gang of police demons charged into the 24 gambling house with drawn guns. They handcuffed the gamblers and assigned them to paddy wagons and patrol cars that lined the street. The wagons were so full, people had to stand with their hands up against the ceiling to keep their balance. My father was not jailed or deported, but neither he nor the owner worked in gambling again. They went straight. Stockton became a clean town. From outside, the gambling house looked the same closed down as when it had flourished.

My father brought his abacus, the hole punch and extra 25

tickets home, but those were the last presents for a while. A dismal time began for him.

He became a disheartened man. He was always home. He sat 26 in his chair and stared or he sat on the floor and stared. He stopped showing the boys the few kung fu moves he knew. He suddenly turned angry and quiet. For a few days he walked up and down the sidewalk in front of businesses but could not bring himself to enter. He walked right past in his beautiful clothes and acted very busy.

"You're nothing but a gambler," MaMa said, "You're spoiled 27 and won't go looking for a job. . . . It's a wife's duty to scold her husband into working," she explained to us.

My father sat. "You're scared," MaMa accused him. "You're 28 shy. You're lazy. Do something! You never do anything. You let your so-called friends steal your laundry. You let your brothers and the Communists take your land. You have no head for business." She did not understand how it is some of us run down and stop.

BaBa ignored her, stopped shaving and sat in his T shirt from 29 morning to night.

He seemed to have lost his feelings. His own mother wrote 30 asking him for money, and he asked for proof that she was still alive before he would send it. He never said, "I miss her." He sat drinking whiskey. He no longer bought new clothes.

MaMa worked in the fields, picking fruit, digging and har- 31 vesting vegetables. She showed us how to use her new tools, the pitters and curved knives. We tried on her cap pinned with union buttons and her rubber gloves that smelled like rubber tomatoes. She filled her baskets, shopping bags, lunch pail, her apron and scarf, and brought home every kind of vegetable and fruit grown in San Joaquin County. She said she was tired, but kept moving, busy, banging doors, drawers, pots and cleaver, turning faucets off and on with *ka-chunks* in the pipes. Her cleaver banged on the chopping block for an hour straight as she minced pork and steak into patties. Her energy slammed BaBa back into his chair. She took care of every-thing; he did not have a reason to get up. He stared at his toes and fingers. "You've lost your sense of emergency," she said. She kept her sense of emergency every moment.

The one event of the day that made BaBa get out of his easy 32 chair was the newspaper. He looked forward to it. He opened the front door and looked for it hours before the mailman was due. The Gold Mountain News (The Chinese Times, according to the English logo) came from San Francisco in a paper sleeve with his name and address neatly typed. He put on his gold-rimmed glasses and readied his smoking equipment: the 1939 World's Fair ashtray, Lucky Strikes, matches, coffee. He killed several hours reading the paper, scrupu-lously reading everything—the date on each page, the page numbers, the want ads. Then he just sat. "What's wrong?" MaMa would ask. "I'm tired," he would answer, and she would give him the cure for tiredness, which is to hit the inside joints of elbows and knees until red and black dots—the tiredness—appear on the skin.

He screamed in his sleep. "Night sweats," MaMa diagnosed it. "Fear sweats." 33

Finally we children became so wild that we broke BaBa loose from his chair. We goaded him, irked him—and the gravity suddenly let him go. He chased my sister, who locked herself in a bedroom. "Come out!" he shouted, but of course she wouldn't, since he had a wooden coat hanger in his hand ready to hit her. I watched him kick the door; the round mirror fell off the wall and crashed. The door broke open and he beat her. 34

BaBa did not return to sitting. He shaved, put on some good clothes and went out. He found a friend who had opened a new laundry on El Dorado Street. He went inside and chatted, asked if he could help out. The friend said he had changed his mind about owning the laundry; my father bought it and had a Grand Opening. We were proud and quiet as he wrote in gold and black on big red ribbons. The Chinese community brought flowers, mirrors, and pictures of flowers and one of Guan Goong, god of good fortune. BaBa's liveliness returned. Now at last he owned his own house and his own business in America. His loofa and grape vines climbed up ropes to the roof of the house. He planted many kinds of gourds— peas, beans, melons and cabbages—and perennials—tangerines, oranges, grapefruits, almonds, pomegranates, apples, black figs, white figs; and from seed pits, a loquat, peaches, apricots, plums of many varieties—trees that would take years to bear fruit. 35

One morning we found a stack of new coloring books and follow-the-dot books on the floor next to our beds. "BaBa left them," we said. He gave me a picture from the newspaper of redwoods in Yosemite. 36

"This is beautiful," he said. 37

QUESTIONS

1. What is the "mystery" that Kingston's father reveals to her? What other mysteries are in her account?

2. Summarize the history of the author's family. What is the father like? The mother? What does Kingston say about the immigrant experience?

3. In the first paragraph, Kingston used the words "prying, peeking, snooping, asking." What are the connotative shifts in meaning among these words? What other stylistic devices are used in this sentence?

 THE AMERICAN FATHER

4. What words does Kingston emphasize through repetition? Why does she employ this device?

5. What is the theme of this essay? How is it introduced in the first paragraph? How does the conclusion reinforce the theme?

6. Analyze the author's presentation of chronology. List the scenes into which the action is divided. Are there any flashbacks? Is there any way to determine the amount of time that passes? Why or why not?

7. How does the author achieve paragraph variety in this essay?

8. How is the authorial point of view consistent with the dimensions of the story itself?

9. The author speaks of "trying to unravel the mysteries" about her family. Why has this become a preoccupation of contemporary Americans? What do you know about your family's origins or "roots"?

10. a. Write a narrative essay about your family's history.
b. Write a biography of one family member.

MAYA ANGELOU

The Deterioration of My Marriage

Maya Angelou (1928–   ) is an American poet, playwright, television screen writer, actress, and singer. Her autobiographical writing, notably *I Know Why the Caged Bird Sings* (1970), provides one of the fullest accounts of the black female experience in the United States. Fluent in six languages, active in artistic and political affairs, Angelou often presents autobiographical material against the backdrop of larger cultural concerns. Her account of the crisis in her marriage constitutes a chapter in *Singin' and Swingin' and Gettin' Merry Like Christmas* (1976).

he articles in the women's magazines did nothing to   1
help explain the deterioration of my marriage. We had
no infidelity; my husband was a good provider and I
was a good cook. He encouraged me to resume my
dance classes and I listened to him practice the saxophone without
interruption. He came directly home from work each afternoon and

in the evening after my son was asleep I found as much enjoyment in our marital bed as he.

The form was there, but the spirit had disappeared. 2

A bizarre sensation pervades a relationship of pretense. No 3
truth seems true. A simple morning's greeting and response appear loaded with innuendo and fraught with implications.

"How are you?" Does he/she really care? 4

"Fine," I'm not really. I'm miserable, but I'll never tell you. 5

Each nicety becomes more sterile and each withdrawal more 6
permanent.

Bacon and coffee odors mingled with the aseptic aroma of 7
Lifebuoy soap. Wisps of escaping gas, which were as real a part of a fifty-year-old San Francisco house as the fourteen-foot high ceilings and the cantankerous plumbing, solidified my reality. Those were natural morning mists. The sense that order was departing my life was refuted by the daily routine. My family would awaken. I would shower and head for the kitchen to begin making breakfast. Clyde would then take over the shower as Tosh read the newspaper. Tosh would shower while Clyde dressed, collected his crayons and lunch pail for school. We would all sit at breakfast together. I would force unwanted pleasantries into my face. (My mother had taught me: "If you have only one smile in you, give it to the people you love. Don't be surly at home, then go out in the street and start grinning 'Good morning' at total strangers.")

Tosh was usually quiet and amiable. Clyde gabbled about his 8
dreams, which had to do with Roy Rogers as Jesus and Br'er Rabbit as God. We would finish breakfast in a glow of family life and they would both leave me with kisses, off to their separate excitements.

One new morning Tosh screamed from the bathroom, 9
"Where in the hell are the goddamn dry towels?" The outburst caught me as unexpectedly as an upper cut. He knew that I kept the linen closet filled with towels folded as I had seen them photographed in the *Ladies' Home Journal*. More shocking than his forgetfulness, however, was his shouting. Anger generally rendered my husband morose and silent as a stone.

I went to the bathroom and handed him the thickest towel we 10
owned.

"What's wrong, Tosh?" 11

"All the towels in here are wet. You know I hate fucking wet 12
towels."

I didn't know because he had never told me. I went back to 13
the kitchen, not really knowing him, either.

At breakfast, Clyde began a recounting of Roy Rogers on his 14
horse and Red Ryder, riding on clouds up to talk to God about some rustlers in the lower forty.

Tosh turned, looking directly at him, and said, "Shut up, will   15
you. I'd like a little fucking peace and quiet while I eat."

The statement slapped Clyde quiet; he had never been   16
spoken to with such cold anger.

Tosh looked at me. "The eggs are like rocks. Can't you fry a   17
decent goddamn egg? If not, I'll show you."

I was too confounded to speak. I sat, not understanding the   18
contempt. Clyde asked to be excused from the table. I excused him
and followed him to the door.

He whispered, "Is Dad mad at me?"   19

I picked up his belongings, saw him jacketed and told him,   20
"No, not at you. You know grownups have a lot on their minds.
Sometimes they're so busy thinking they forget their manners. It's
not nice, but it happens."

He said, "I'll go back and tell him 'bye."   21

"No, I think you should just go on to school. He'll be in a   22
better mood this evening."

I held the front door open.   23

He shouted, " 'Bye, Dad."   24

There was no answer as I kissed him and closed the door.   25
Fury quickened my footsteps. How could he scream at my son like
that? Who the hell was he? A white-sheeted Grand Dragon of the Ku
Klux Klan? I wouldn't have a white man talk to me in that tone of
voice and I'd slap him with a coffeepot before he could yell at my child
again. The midnight murmuring of soft words was forgotten. His
gentle hands and familiar body had become in those seconds the
shelter of an enemy.

He was still sitting over coffee, brooding. I went directly to   26
the table.

"What do you mean, screaming at us that way?"   27

He said nothing.   28

"You started, first with the towels, then it was Clyde's dream.   29
Then my cooking. Are you going crazy?"

He said, "I don't want to talk about it," still looking down   30
into a half-filled cup of near-cold coffee.

"You sure as hell will talk about it. What have I done to you?   31
What's the matter with you?"

He left the table and headed for the door without looking at   32
me. I followed, raising my protest, hoping to puncture his cloak of
withdrawal.

"I deserve and demand an explanation."   33

He held the door open and turned at last to face me. His voice   34
was soft again and tender. "I think I'm just tired of being married."
He pulled the door closed.

There is a shock that comes so quickly and strikes so deep   35 that the blow is internalized even before the skin feels it. The strike must first reach bone marrow, then ascend slowly to the brain where the slowpoke intellect records the deed.

I went about cleaning my kitchen. Wash the dishes, sweep the floor, swipe the sputtered grease from the stove, make fresh coffee, put a fresh starched cloth on the table. Then I sat down. A sense of loss suffused me until I was suffocating within the vapors. 36

What had I done? I had placed my life within the confines of my marriage. I was everything the magazines said a wife should be. Constant, faithful and clean. I was economical. I was compliant, never offering headaches as excuses for not sharing the marital bed. 37

I had generously allowed Tosh to share my son, encouraging Clyde to think of him as a permanent life fixture. And now Tosh was "tired of being married." 38

Experience had made me accustomed to make quick analyses and quick if often bad decisions. So I expected Tosh, having come to the conclusion that marriage was exhausting, to ask me for a divorce when he returned from work. My tears were for myself and my son. We would be thrown again into a maelstrom of rootlessness. I wept for our loss of security and railed at the brutality of fate. Forgotten were my own complaints of the marriage. Unadmitted was the sense of strangulation I had begun to feel, or the insidious quality of guilt for having a white husband, which surrounded me like an evil aura when we were in public. 39

At my table, immersed in self-pity, I saw my now dying marriage as a union made in heaven, officiated over by St. Peter and sanctioned by God. It wasn't just that my husband was leaving me, I was losing a state of perfection, of grace. 40

My people would nod knowingly. Again a white man had taken a Black woman's body and left her hopeless, helpless and alone. But I couldn't expect their sympathy. I hadn't been ambushed on a dark country lane or raped by a group of randy white toughs. I had sworn to obey the man and had accepted his name. Anger, first at injustice, then at Tosh, stopped my tears. The same words I had used to voice my anguish I now used to fan the fires of rage. I had been a good wife, kind and compliant. And that wasn't enough for him? It was better than he deserved. More than he could reasonably have expected had he married within his own race. Anyway, had he planned to leave me from the first? Had he intended in the beginning to lure me into trust, then break up our marriage and break my heart? Maybe he was a sadist, scheming to inflict pain on poor, unsuspecting me. Well, he didn't know me. I would show him. I was no helpless biddy to be beckoned, then belittled. He was tired of marriage; all right, then I would leave him. 41

I got up from the table and cooked dinner, placed the food in 42 the refrigerator and dressed in my best clothes. I left the dinner pots dirty and my bed unmade and hit the streets.

The noontime bar in the popular hotel on Eddy Street was 43 filled with just-awakened petty gamblers and drowsy whores. Pimps not yet clad in their evening air of exquisite brutality spent the whores' earnings on their fellow parasites. I was recognized by a few drinkers, because I was Clydell and Vivian's daughter, because I had worked at the popular record shop or because I was that girl who had married the white man. I knew nothing about strong liquor except the names of some cocktails. I sat down and ordered a Zombie.

I clung to the long, cold drink and examined my predica- 44 ment. My marriage was over, since I believed the legal bonds were only as good as the emotional desire to make them good. If a person didn't want you, he didn't want you. I could have thrown myself and my son on Tosh's mercy; he was a kind man, and he might have tolerated us in his home and on the edges of his life. But begging had always stuck, resisting, in my throat. I thought women who accepted their husbands' inattention and sacrificed all their sovereignty for a humiliating marriage more unsavory than the prostitutes who were drinking themselves awake in the noisy bar.

A short, thickset man sat down beside me and asked if he 45 could pay for my second Zombie. He was old enough to be my father and reminded me of a kindly old country doctor from sepia-colored B movies. He asked my name and where I lived. I told his soft, near-feminine face that my name was Clara. When I said "No, I'm not married," he grinned and said, "I don't know what these young men are waiting for. If I was a few years younger, I'd give them a run for they money. Yes siree bob." He made me feel comfortable. His Southern accent was as familiar to me as the smell of baking cornbread and the taste of wild persimmons. He asked if I was "a, uh, a ah a fancy lady?"

I said, "No." Desperate, maybe. Fanciful, maybe. Fancy? No. 46

He told me he was a merchant marine and was staying in the 47 hotel and asked would I like to come upstairs and have a drink with him.

I would. 48

I sat on the bed in the close room, sipping the bourbon 49 diluted with tap water. He talked about Newport News and his family as I thought about mine. He had a son and daughter near my age and they were "some kinda good children" and the girl was "some kinda pretty."

He noticed that I was responding to the whiskey, and came 50 near the bed. "Why don't you just stretch out and rest a little while? You'll feel better. I'll rest myself. Just take off your shoes and your clothes. To keep them from wrinkling up on you."

MAYA ANGELOU

My troubles and memories swam around, then floated out   51
the window when I laid my head on the single pillow.

When I awakened, the dark room didn't smell familiar and   52
my head throbbed. Confusion panicked me. I could have been picked
up by an extraterrestrial being and teleported into some funky rocket
ship. I jumped out of bed and fumbled along the walls, bumping
until I found the light switch. My clothes were folded neatly and my
shoes peeked their tidy toes from under the chair. I remembered the
room and the merchant marine. I had no idea what had happened
since I passed out. I examined myself and found no evidence that the
old man had misused my drunkenness.

Dressing slowly, I wondered over the next move. Night had   53
fallen on my affairs, but the sharp edges of rejection were not
softened. There was a note on the dresser. I picked it up to read
under the naked bulb that dangled from the ceiling; it said in effect:

Dear Clara,   54
         I tell you like I tell my own daughter. Be careful of
strangers. Everybody smile at you don't have to mean you no
good. I'll be back in two months from now. You be a good
girl, hear? You'll make some boy a good wife.

                                              Abner Green

I walked through the dark streets to Ivonne's house. After I   55
explained what had happened, she suggested I telephone home.

"Hello, Tosh?"   56

"Marguerite, where are you?" The strain in his voice made   57
me smile.

He asked, "When are you coming home? Clyde hasn't   58
eaten."

I knew that was a lie.   59

"Nor have I. I can't eat," he said. I wasn't concerned about   60
his appetite.

I said, "You're tired of being married. Yes? Well, I'll be home   61
when I get there." I hung up before he could say more.

Ivonne said, "Maya, you're cold. Aren't you worried about   62
Clyde?"

"No. Tosh loves Clyde. He'll look after him. He loves me too,   63
but I gave up too much and gave in too much. Now we'll see."

The thought of his loneliness in the large apartment made my   64
own less acute. I slept badly on Ivonne's sofa.

I went home the next day and we resumed a sort of marriage,   65
but the center of power had shifted. I was no longer the dutiful wife
ready with floors waxed and rugs beaten, with my finger between the

pages of a cookbook and my body poised over the stove or spread-eagled on the bed.

One day my back began to hurt with a sullen ache, the kind usually visited only on the arthritic aged. My head pulsed and my side was punished by short, hot stabs of pain. The doctor advised immediate hospitalization. A simple appendectomy developed complications and it was weeks before I was released. The house was weary with failure—I told my husband that I wanted to go to Arkansas. I would stay with my grandmother until I had fully recovered. I meant in mind, as well as body.   66

He came close and in a hoarse whisper said, "Marguerite. Your grandmother died the day after your operation. You were too sick. I couldn't tell you."   67

Ah, Momma. I had never looked at death before, peered into its yawning chasm for the face of a beloved. For days my mind staggered out of balance. I reeled on a precipice of knowledge that even if I were rich enough to travel all over the world, I would never find Momma. If I were as good as God's angels and as pure as the Mother of Christ, I could never have Momma's rough slow hands pat my cheek or braid my hair.   68

Death to the young is more than that undiscovered country; despite its inevitability, it is a place having reality only in song or in other people's grief.   69

QUESTIONS

1. What does the author absorb from the women's magazines she mentions in the essay? Why does her behavior change? Trace this change through the main episodes in the narrative.

2. Explain the meaning of these sentences:
a. "A bizarre sensation pervades a relationship of pretense" (paragraph 3).
b. "There is a shock that comes so quickly and strikes so deep that the blow is internalized even before the skin feels it" (paragraph 35).
c. "Unadmitted was the sense of strangulation I had begun to feel, or the insidious quality of guilt for having a white husband, which surrounded me like an evil aura when we were in public" (paragraph 40).

3. Define these words: *innuendo* (paragraph 3); *refuted* (paragraph 7); *morose* (paragraph 9); *suffused* (paragraph 6); *compliant* (paragraph 7). Use them in sentences.

4. Analyze the author's handling of language in paragraph 7.

5. What is the function of exposition in this narrative essay? Point to sections in which you think exposition is used effectively and explain why.

6. What is the special quality associated with point of view in the essay?

7. What is the importance of the author's use of dialogue?

8. What is the relationship of the concluding paragraphs to the rest of the essay?

9. Speaking of her marriage, the author states, "The form was there, but the spirit had disappeared" (paragraph 2). Is this a common characteristic of relationships? What causes people to maintain such relationships? Are there solutions to relationships that have reached this point?

10. Write a narrative essay about the deterioration of a relationship in your life or that of a friend or family member.

GEORGE ORWELL

Shooting an Elephant

George Orwell (1903–1950) was the pseudonym of Eric Blair, an English novelist, essayist, and journalist. Orwell served with the Indian Imperial Police from 1922 to 1927 in Burma, fought in the Spanish Civil War, and acquired from his experiences a disdain of totalitarian and imperialistic systems. This attitude is reflected in the satirical fable *Animal Farm* (1945) and in his bleak, futuristic novel, *1984* (1949). In this essay, Orwell invokes personal experience to expose the contradictions inherent in British imperialism.

n Moulmein, in Lower Burma, I was hated by large   1
numbers of people—the only time in my life that I have been important enough for this to happen to me. I was sub-divisional police officer of the town, and in an aimless, petty kind of way anti-European feeling was very bitter. No one had the guts to raise a riot, but if a European woman went through the bazaars alone somebody would probably spit betel juice over her dress. As a police officer I was an obvious target and was baited whenever it seemed safe to do so. When a nimble Burman tripped me up on the football field and the referee (another Burman) looked the other way, the crowd yelled with hideous laughter. This happened more than once. In the end the sneering yellow faces of

young men that met me everywhere, the insults hooted after me when I was at a safe distance, got badly on my nerves. The young Buddhist priests were the worst of all. There were several thousands of them in the town and none of them seemed to have anything to do except stand on street corners and jeer at Europeans.

All this was perplexing and upsetting. For at that time I had 2 already made up my mind that imperialism was an evil thing and the sooner I chucked up my job and got out of it the better. Theoretically—and secretly, of course—I was all for the Burmese and all against their oppressors, the British. As for the job I was doing, I hated it more bitterly than I can perhaps make clear. In a job like that you see the dirty work of Empire at close quarters. The wretched prisoners huddling in the stinking cages of the lock-ups, the grey, cowed faces of the long-term convicts, the scarred buttocks of the men who had been flogged with bamboos—all these oppressed me with an intolerable sense of guilt. But I could get nothing into perspective. I was young and ill-educated and I had had to think out my problems in the utter silence that is imposed on every Englishman in the East. I did not even know that the British Empire is dying, still less did I know that it is a great deal better than the younger empires that are going to supplant it. All I knew was that I was stuck between my hatred of the empire I served and my rage against the evil-spirited little beasts who tried to make my job impossible. With one part of my mind I thought of the British Raj as an unbreakable tyranny, as something clamped down, *in saecula saeculorum,* upon the will of prostrate peoples; with another part I thought that the greatest joy in the world would be to drive a bayonet into a Buddhist priest's guts. Feelings like these are the normal by-products of imperialism; ask any Anglo-Indian official, if you can catch him off duty.

One day something happened which in a roundabout way 3 was enlightening. It was a tiny incident in itself, but it gave me a better glimpse than I had had before of the real nature of imperialism—the real motives for which despotic governments act. Early one morning the sub-inspector at a police station the other end of the town rang me up on the phone and said that an elephant was ravaging the bazaar. Would I please come and do something about it? I did not know what I could do, but I wanted to see what was happening and I got on to a pony and started out. I took my rifle, an old .44 Winchester and much too small to kill an elephant, but I thought the noise might be useful *in terrorem.* Various Burmans stopped me on the way and told me about the elephant's doings. It was not, of course, a wild elephant, but a tame one which had gone "must." It had been chained up as tame elephants always are when their attack of "must" is due, but on the previous night it had broken its chain and escaped. Its mahout, the only person who could manage it when it was in that state, had set out in pursuit, but he had taken the wrong direction and was now twelve hours' journey away, and in the morning the elephant had suddenly reappeared in the town. The Burmese population had no weapons and were quite helpless against it. It had already destroyed somebody's bamboo hut, killed a cow and raided some fruit-stalls and devoured the stock; also it had met the municipal rubbish van, and, when the driver jumped out and took to his heels, had turned the van over and inflicted violence upon it.

The Burmese sub-inspector and some Indian constables were   4 waiting for me in the quarter where the elephant had been seen. It was a very poor quarter, a labyrinth of squalid bamboo huts, thatched with palm-leaf, winding all over a steep hillside. I remember that it was a cloudy stuffy morning at the beginning of the rains. We began questioning the people as to where the elephant had gone, and, as usual, failed to get any definite information. That is invariably the case in the East; a story always sounds clear enough at a distance, but the nearer you get to the scene of events the vaguer it becomes. Some of the people said that the elephant had gone in one direction, some said that he had gone in another, some professed not even to have heard of any elephant. I had almost made up my mind that the whole story was a pack of lies, when we heard yells a little distance away. There was a loud, scandalised cry of "Go away, child! Go away this instant!" and an old woman with a switch in her hand came round the corner of a hut, violently shooing away a crowd of naked children. Some more women followed, clicking their tongues and exclaiming; evidently there was something there that the children ought not to have seen. I rounded the hut and saw a man's dead body sprawling in the mud. He was an Indian, a black Dravidian coolie, almost naked, and he could not have been dead many minutes. The people said that the elephant had come suddenly upon him round the corner of the hut, caught him with its trunk, put its foot on his back and ground him into the earth. This was the rainy season and the ground was soft, and his face had scored a trench a foot deep and a couple of yards long. He was lying on his belly with arms crucified and head sharply twisted to one side. His face was coated with mud, the eyes wide open, the teeth bared and grinning with an expression of unendurable agony. (Never tell me, by the way, that the dead look peaceful. Most of the corpses I have seen looked devilish.) The friction of the great beast's foot had stripped the skin from his back as neatly as one skins a rabbit. As soon as I saw the dead man I sent an orderly to a friend's house nearby to borrow an elephant rifle. I had already sent back the pony, not wanting it to go mad with fright and throw me if it smelled the elephant.

The orderly came back in a few minutes with a rifle and five   5 cartridges, and meanwhile some Burmans had arrived and told us that the elephant was in the paddy fields below, only a few hundred yards away. As I started forward practically the whole population of the quarter flocked out of their houses and followed me. They had seen the rifle and were all shouting excitedly that I was going to shoot the elephant. They had not shown much interest in the elephant when he was merely ravaging their homes, but it was different now that he was going to be shot. It was a bit of fun to them, as it would be to an English crowd; besides, they wanted the meat. It made me vaguely uneasy. I had no intention of shooting the elephant—I had merely sent for the rifle to defend myself if necessary—and it is always unnerving to have a crowd following you. I marched down the hill, looking, and feeling a fool, with the rifle over my shoulder and an ever-growing army of people jostling at my heels. At the bottom, when you got away from the huts, there was a metalled road and beyond that a miry waste of paddy fields a thousand yards across, not yet ploughed but soggy from the first rains and dotted with coarse grass. The elephant was standing eighty yards from the road, his left side towards us. He took not the slightest notice of the crowd's approach. He was tearing up bunches of grass, beating them against his knees to clean them and stuffing them into his mouth.

I had halted on the road. As soon as I saw the elephant I 6 knew with perfect certainty that I ought not to shoot him. It is a serious matter to shoot a working elephant—it is comparable to destroying a huge and costly piece of machinery—and obviously one ought not to do it if it can possibly be avoided. And at a distance, peacefully eating, the elephant looked no more dangerous than a cow. I thought then and I think now that his attack of "must" was already passing off; in which case he would merely wander harmlessly about until the mahout came back and caught him. Moreover, I did not in the least want to shoot him. I decided that I would watch him for a little while to make sure that he did not turn savage again, and then go home.

But at that moment I glanced round at the crowd that had 7 followed me. It was an immense crowd, two thousand at the least and growing every minute. It blocked the road for a long distance on either side. I looked at the sea of yellow faces above the garish clothes—faces all happy and excited over this bit of fun, all certain that the elephant was going to be shot. They were watching me as they would watch a conjuror about to perform a trick. They did not like me, but with the magical rifle in my hands I was momentarily worth watching. And suddenly I realised that I should have to shoot the elephant after all. The people expected it of me and I had got to do it; I could feel their two thousand wills pressing me forward, irresistibly. And it was at this moment, as I stood there with the rifle in my hands, that I first grasped the hollowness, the futility of the

GEORGE ORWELL

white man's dominion in the East. Here was I, the white man with his gun, standing in front of the unarmed native crowd—seemingly the leading actor of the piece; but in reality I was only an absurd puppet pushed to and fro by the will of those yellow faces behind. I perceived in this moment that when the white man turns tyrant it is his own freedom that he destroys. He becomes a sort of hollow, posing dummy, the conventionalised figure of a sahib. For it is the condition of his rule that he shall spend his life in trying to impress the "natives" and so in every crisis he has got to do what the "natives" expect of him. He wears a mask, and his face grows to fit it. I had got to shoot the elephant. I had committed myself to doing it when I sent for the rifle. A sahib has got to act like a sahib; he has got to appear resolute, to know his own mind and do definite things. To come all that way, rifle in hand, with two thousand people marching at my heels, and then to trail feebly away, having done nothing—no, that was impossible. The crowd would laugh at me. And my whole life, every white man's life in the East, was one long struggle not to be laughed at.

But I did not want to shoot the elephant. I watched him 8
beating his bunch of grass against his knees, with that preoccupied grandmotherly air that elephants have. It seemed to me that it would be murder to shoot him. At that age I was not squeamish about killing animals, but I had never shot an elephant and never wanted to. (Somehow it always seems worse to kill a *large* animal.) Besides, there was the beast's owner to be considered. Alive, the elephant was worth at least a hundred pounds; dead, he would only be worth the value of his tusks—five pounds, possibly. But I had got to act quickly. I turned to some experienced-looking Burmans who had been there when we arrived, and asked them how the elephant had been behaving. They all said the same thing: he took no notice of you if you left him alone, but he might charge if you went to close to him.

It was perfectly clear to me what I ought to do. I ought to 9
walk up to within, say, twenty-five yards of the elephant and test his behaviour. If he charged I could shoot, if he took no notice of me it would be safe to leave him until the mahout came back. But also I knew that I was going to do no such thing. I was a poor shot with a rifle and the ground was soft mud into which one would sink at every step. If the elephant charged and I missed him, I should have about as much chance as a toad under a steam-roller. But even then I was not thinking particularly of my own skin, only the watchful yellow faces behind. For at that moment, with the crowd watching me, I was not afraid in the ordinary sense, as I would have been if I had been alone. A white man mustn't be frightened in front of "natives"; and so, in general, he isn't frightened. The sole thought in my mind was that if anything went wrong those two thousand Burmans would see

me pursued, caught, trampled on and reduced to a grinning corpse like that Indian up the hill. And if that happened it was quite probable that some of them would laugh. That would never do. There was only one alternative. I shoved the cartridges into the magazine and lay down on the road to get a better aim.

The crowd grew very still, and a deep, low, happy sigh, as of 10 people who see the theatre curtain go up at last, breathed from innumerable throats. They were going to have their bit of fun after all. The rifle was a beautiful German thing with cross-hair sights. I did not then know that in shooting an elephant one should shoot to cut an imaginary bar running from ear-hole to ear-hole. I ought therefore, as the elephant was sideways on, to have aimed straight at his ear-hole; actually I aimed several inches in front of this, thinking the brain would be further forward.

When I pulled the trigger I did not hear the bang or feel the 11 kick—one never does when a shot goes home—but I heard the devilish roar of glee that went up from the crowd. In that instant, in too short a time, one would have thought, even for the bullet to get there, a mysterious, terrible change had come over the elephant. He neither stirred nor fell, but every line of his body had altered. He looked suddenly stricken, shrunken, immensely old, as though the frightful impact of the bullet had paralysed him without knocking him down. At last, after what seemed a long time—it might have been five seconds, I dare say—he sagged flabbily to his knees. His mouth slobbered. An enormous senility seemed to have settled upon him. One could have imagined him thousands of years old. I fired again into the same spot. At the second shot he did not collapse but climbed with desperate slowness to his feet and stood weakly upright, with legs sagging and head drooping. I fired a third time. That was the shot that did for him. You could see the agony of it jolt his whole body and knock the last remnant of strength from his legs. But in falling he seemed for a moment to rise, for as his hind legs collapsed beneath him he seemed to tower upwards like a huge rock toppling, his trunk reaching skyward like a tree. He trumpeted, for the first and only time. And then down he came, his belly towards me, with a crash that seemed to shake the ground even where I lay.

I got up. The Burmans were already racing past me across the 12 mud. It was obvious that the elephant would never rise again, but he was not dead. He was breathing very rhythmically with long rattling gasps, his great mound of a side painfully rising and falling. His mouth was wide open—I could see far down into caverns of pale pink throat. I waited a long time for him to die, but his breathing did not weaken. Finally I fired my two remaining shots into the spot where I thought his heart must be. The thick blood welled out of him like red velvet, but still he did not die. His body did not even jerk when the

56   GEORGE ORWELL

shots hit him, the tortured breathing continued without a pause. He was dying, very slowly and in great agony, but in some world remote from me where not even a bullet could damage him further. I felt that I had got to put an end to that dreadful noise. It seemed dreadful to see the great beast lying there, powerless to move and yet powerless to die, and not even to be able to finish him. I sent back for my small rifle and poured shot after shot into his heart and down his throat. They seemed to make no impression. The tortured gasps continued as steadily as the ticking of a clock.

In the end I could not stand it any longer and went away. I   13
heard later that it took him half an hour to die. Burmans were arriving with dahs and baskets even before I left, and I was told they had stripped his body almost to the bones by the afternoon.

Afterwards, of course, there were endless discussions about   14
the shooting of the elephant. The owner was furious, but he was only an Indian and could do nothing. Besides, legally I had done the right thing, for a mad elephant has to be killed, like a mad dog, if its owner fails to control it. Among the Europeans opinion was divided. The older men said I was right, the younger men said it was a damn shame to shoot an elephant for killing a coolie, because an elephant was worth more than any damn Coringhee coolie. And afterwards I was very glad that the coolie had been killed; it put me legally in the right and it gave me a sufficient pretext for shooting the elephant. I often wondered whether any of the others grasped that I had done it solely to avoid looking a fool.

QUESTIONS

1. How does the shooting of the elephant give Orwell a better understanding of "the real nature of imperialism—the real motives for which despotic governments act" (paragraph 3)? Why does Orwell kill the elephant? What is his attitude toward the Burmese people?

2. Why does Orwell concentrate on the prolonged death of the elephant? What effect does it have?

3. How would you describe the level of language in the essay? Point to specific words, sentences, and phrases to support your answer.

4. Define *supplant* (paragraph 2); *labyrinth* (paragraph 4); *jostling* (paragraph 5); *conjuror* (paragraph 7); *senility* (paragraph 11).

5. What is the function of the first two paragraphs? Where is the thesis stated in the essay?

6. Analyze Orwell's use of dramatic techniques to develop the narrative.

 SHOOTING AN ELEPHANT

Examine consecutive paragraphs in the essay to determine the author's presentation of action from different perspectives.

7. Select and analyze some of the details in the essay that are designed to impress the reader's senses and emotions. Why does Orwell rely so heavily on the presentation and accumulation of detail in the essay?

8. How is the entire essay structured by irony of situation and paradox? How do these devices relate to the ethical issues raised by Orwell?

9. In this essay, written in 1936, Orwell declares: "I did not even know that the British Empire is dying, still less did I know that it is a great deal better than the younger empires that are going to supplant it" (paragraph 2). In what ways is Orwell's statement prophetic?

10. Write a narrative essay about an episode in your life when you came into conflict with social or political forces.

JAMES BOSWELL

Wednesday, 12 January 1763:
A Man of Pleasure

James Boswell (1740–1795) was a Scottish writer, the major biographer of Samuel Johnson, and one of the world's greatest diarists. In this entry from his *London Journal, 1762–63*, Boswell, cloaking his quest for pleasure in the artifice and courtly wit of the era, recounts his seduction of the beautiful actress, Mrs. Lewis. Boswell's affair resulted subsequently in venereal disease for this "gentleman of pleasure."

ednesday 12 January. Louisa and I agreed that at eight   1
at night she would meet me in the Piazzas of Covent Garden. I was quite elevated, and felt myself able and undaunted to engage in the wars of the Paphian Queen.

   I dined at Sheridan's very heartily. He showed to my convic-   2
tion that Garrick did not play the great scene in the Second Part of *King Henry* with propriety. "People," said he, "in this age know when particular lines or even speeches are well spoke; but they do not study character, which is a matter of the utmost moment, as people of different characters feel and express their feelings very differently. For want of a knowledge of this, Mr. Barry acted the distress of

Othello, the Moorish warrior whose stubborn soul was hard to bend, and that of Castalio, the gentle lover who was all tenderness, in the self-same way. Now Mr. Garrick in that famous scene whines most piteously when he ought to upbraid. Shakespeare has discovered there a most intimate knowledge of human nature. He shows you the King worn out with sickness and so weak that he faints. He had usurped the crown by the force of arms and was convinced that it must be held with spirit. He saw his son given up to low debauchery. He was anxious and vexed to think of the anarchy that would ensue at his death. Upon discovering that the Prince had taken the crown from his pillow, and concluding him desirous of his death, he is fired with rage. He starts up. He cries, 'Go chide him hither!' His anger animates him so much that he throws aside his distemper. Nature furnishes all her strength for one last effort. He is for a moment renewed. He is for a moment the spirited Henry the Fourth. He upbraids him with bitter sarcasm and bold figures. And then what a beautiful variety is there, when, upon young Harry's contrition, he falls on his neck and melts into parental tenderness.''

I yielded this point to Sheridan candidly. But upon his attacking Garrick as a tragedian in his usual way, I opposed him keenly, and declared he was prejudiced; because the world thought him a good tragic actor. "So do I, Sir," said he; "I think him the best I ever saw." BOSWELL. "Except yourself, Mr. Sheridan. But come, we shall take this for granted. The world then think him near equal or as good as you in what you excel in." SHERIDAN. "Sir, I am not a bit prejudiced. I don't value acting. I shall suppose that I was the greatest actor that ever lived and universally acknowledged so, I would not choose that it should be remembered. I would have it erased out of the anecdotes of my life. Acting is a poor thing in the present state of the stage. For my own part, I engaged in it merely as a step to something greater, a just notion of eloquence." This was in a good measure true. But he certainly talked too extravagantly.

An old Irish maid, or rather an Irish old maid (O most hideous character!) dined with us. She was indeed a terrible Job. She was a woman of knowledge and criticism and correct taste. But there came to tea a Miss Mowat who played once on the stage here for a winter or two, a lovely girl. Many an amorous glance did I exchange with her. I was this day quite flashy with love. We often addressed our discourse to each other. I hope to see her again; and yet what have I to do with anybody but dear Louisa?

At the appointed hour of eight I went to the Piazzas, where I sauntered up and down for a while in a sort of trembling suspense, I knew not why. At last my charming companion appeared, and I immediately conducted her to a hackney-coach which I had ready waiting, pulled up the blinds, and away we drove to the destined scene of delight. We contrived to seem as if we had come off a journey, and carried in a bundle our night-clothes, handkerchiefs, and other little things. We also had with us some almond biscuits, or as they call them in London, macaroons, which looked like provision on the road. On our arrival at Hayward's we were shown into the parlour, in the same manner that any decent couple would be. I here thought proper to conceal my own name (which the people of the house had never heard), and assumed the name of Mr. Digges. We were shown up to the very room where he slept. I said my cousin, as I called him, was very well. That Ceres and Bacchus might in moderation lend their assistance to Venus, I ordered a genteel supper and some wine.

Louisa told me she had two aunts who carried her over to France when she was a girl, and that she could once speak French as fluently as English. We talked a little in it, and agreed that we would improve ourselves by reading and speaking it every day. I asked her if we did not just look like man and wife. "No," said she, "we are too fond for married people." No wonder that she may have a bad idea of that union, considering how bad it was for her. She has contrived a pretty device for a seal. A heart is gently warmed by Cupid's flame, and Hymen comes with his rude torch and extinguishes it. She said she found herself quite in a flutter. "Why, really," said I, "reason sometimes has no power. We have no occasion to be frightened, and yet we are both a little so. Indeed, I preserve a tolerable presence of mind." I rose and kissed her, and conscious that I had no occasion to doubt my qualifications as a gallant, I joked about it: "How curious would it be if I should be so frightened that we should rise as we lay down." She reproved my wanton language by a look of modesty. The bells of St. Bride's church rung their merry chimes hard by. I said that the bells in Cupid's court would be this night set a-ringing for joy at our union.

We supped cheerfully and agreeably and drank a few glasses, and then the maid came and put the sheets, well aired, upon the bed. I now contemplated my fair prize. Louisa is just twenty-four, of a tall rather than short figure, finely made in person, with a handsome face and an enchanting languish in her eyes. She dresses with taste. She has sense, good humour, and vivacity, and looks quite a woman in genteel life. As I mused on this elevating subject, I could not help being somehow pleasingly confounded to think that so fine a woman was at this moment in my possession, that without any motives of interest she had come with me to an inn, agreed to be my intimate companion, was to be my bedfellow all night, and to permit me the full enjoyment of her person.

When the servant left the room, I embraced her warmly and begged that she would not now delay my felicity. She declined to undress before me, and begged I would retire and send her one of the maids. I did so, gravely desiring the girl to go up to Mrs. Digges. I then took a candle in my hand and walked out to the yard. The night was very dark and very cold. I experienced for some minutes the rigours of the season, and called into my mind many terrible ideas of hardships, that I might make a transition from such dreary thoughts to the most gay and delicious feelings. I then caused make a bowl of negus, very rich of the fruit, which I caused be set in the room as a reviving cordial.

I came softly into the room, and in a sweet delirium slipped 9 into bed and was immediately clasped in her snowy arms and pressed to her milk-white bosom. Good heavens, what a loose did we give to amorous dalliance! The friendly curtain of darkness concealed our blushes. In a moment I felt myself animated with the strongest powers of love, and, from my dearest creature's kindness, had a most luscious feast. Proud of my godlike vigour, I soon resumed the noble game. I was in full glow of health. Sobriety had preserved me from effeminacy and weakness, and my bounding blood beat quick and high alarms. A more voluptuous night I never enjoyed. Five times was I fairly lost in supreme rapture. Louisa was madly fond of me; she declared I was a prodigy, and asked me if this was not extraordinary for human nature. I said twice as much might be, but this was not, although in my own mind I was somewhat proud of my performance. She said it was what there was no just reason to be proud of. But I told her I could not help it. She said it was what we had in common with the beasts. I said no. For we had it highly improved by the pleasures of sentiment. I asked her what she thought enough. She gently chid me for asking such questions, but said two times. I mentioned the Sunday's assignation, when I was in such bad spirits, told her in what agony of mind I was, and asked her if she would not have despised me for my imbecility. She declared she would not, as it was what people had not in their own power.

She often insisted that we should compose ourselves to sleep 10 before I would consent to it. At last I sunk to rest in her arms and she in mine. I found the negus, which had a fine flavour, very refreshing to me. Louisa had an exquisite mixture of delicacy and wantonness that made me enjoy her with more relish. Indeed I could not help roving in fancy to the embraces of some other ladies which my lively imagination strongly pictured. I don't know if that was altogether fair. However, Louisa had all the advantage. She said she was quite fatigued and could neither stir leg nor arm. She begged I would not despise her, and hoped my love would not be altogether transient. I have painted this night as well as I could. The description is faint; but I surely may be styled a Man of Pleasure.

QUESTIONS

1. Describe Boswell's day up to the time of his appointment with Louisa. What do we learn about his personality in paragraphs 1 to 4?

2. Why does Boswell style himself "a Man of Pleasure" (paragraph 10)? Describe his role playing in this regard. What is Louisa's role? Why are Boswell and Louisa so highly mannered?

3. Identify Boswell's allusions to "the Paphian Queen" (paragraph 1); Sheridan and Garrick (paragraph 2); Ceres, Bacchus, and Venus (paragraph 5); Cupid and Hymen (paragraph 6).

4. Locate and define three words or phrases in the selection that would be considered archaic today.

5. How does the very nature of diary writing dictate the form of this entry? Does Boswell exercise as much craft on his entry as the writer of an autobiographical essay might? Why or why not?

6. Discuss the utility and effectiveness of the introductory paragraph.

7. At what point does Boswell's entry divide into two segments? What relationships do you sense between these segments? Does Boswell maintain proper proportion? Explain.

8. How does the author utilize contrast to develop the narrative action?

9. Boswell seems clearly to be playing a role—that of the man of pleasure—in this selection. How important is role playing and ritualistic behavior in our lives? What roles can we play in the course of a day? At what point might role playing become self-destructive?

10. a. Compose a diary entry for one day in your life, stressing like Boswell one dominant aspect of your personality that lends coherence to events.
b. Write an autobiographical essay describing a role that you played at a certain stage in your life.

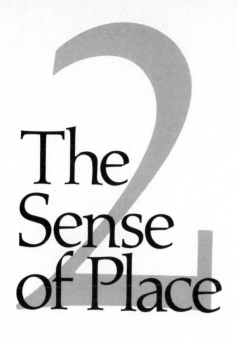

The Sense of Place

HARRY CREWS

Why I Live Where I Live

Harry Crews (1935–   ) is a Southern writer who is a master of the art of the grotesque. His novels include *Karate is a Thing of the Spirit* (1971), *The Gypsy's Curse* (1974), and *A Feast of Snakes* (1976). He contributes regularly to *Playboy, The Sewanee Review, Esquire,* and other publications. In this personal essay, Crews examines the relationship between the writer's surroundings and the creative process.

I can leave the place where I live a couple of hours before   1
daylight and be on a deserted little strip of sand called
Crescent Beach in time to throw a piece of meat on a fire
and then, in a few minutes, lie back sucking on a vodka
bottle and chewing on a hunk of bloody beef while the sun lifts out of
the Atlantic Ocean (somewhat unnerving but also mystically beautiful to a man who never saw a body of water bigger than a pond until
he was grown) and while the sun rises lie on a blanket, brain singing
from vodka and a bellyful of beef, while the beautiful bikinied
children from the University of Florida drift down the beach, their
smooth bodies sweating baby oil and the purest kind of innocent lust
(which of course is the rankest sort) into the bright air. If all that starts
to pall—and what *doesn't* start to pall?—I can leave the beach and be

out on the end of a dock, sitting in the Captain's Table eating hearts-of-palm salad and hot boiled shrimp and sipping on a tall, icy glass of beer while the sun I saw lift out of the Atlantic that morning sinks into the warm, waveless Gulf of Mexico. It makes for a hell of a day. But that isn't really why I live in the north-central Florida town of Gainesville.

Nor do I live in Gainesville because seven blocks from my house there are two enormous libraries filled with the most courteous, helpful people you can imagine, people who, after explaining some of the more intricate mysteries of how the place works, including the purposes of numerous indices, will go ahead and cheerfully find what I cannot: for example, the car capacity of drive-in theaters in Bakersfield, California, in 1950. A man never knows when he may need a bit of information like that, but it isn't enough to keep him living in a little town in Florida as opposed to, say, Ann Arbor, Michigan.

I love the size of Gainesville. I can walk anywhere I want to go, and consequently I have very little to do with that abomination before the Lord, the car. It's a twenty-minute stroll to my two favorite bars, Lillian's Music Store and the Winnjammer; ten minutes to a lovely square of grass and trees called the Plaza of the Americas; less than ten minutes to the house of a young lady who has been hypnotizing me for six years. Some people get analyzed; I get hypnotized. It leaves me with the most astonishing and pleasurable memories. But there must be ten thousand towns like Gainesville in this country, and surely several hundred of them would have good places to drink and talk and at least one house where a young lady lived who would consent to hypnotize me into astonishing and pleasurable memories. So I cannot lean too heavily on walking and memories to justify being where I am.

The reason I live where I do is more complicated than the sorts of things I've been talking about thus far—more complicated and, I expect, ultimately inexplicable. Or, said another way: anyone other than I may find that the explanation does not satisfy. To start, I live right in the middle of town on three acres of land, land thick with pines a hundred feet tall, oak, wild plum trees, and all manner of tangled, unidentifiable underbrush. The only cleared space is the very narrow road leading down to the house. No lawn. (There are many things I absolutely refuse to do in this world, but the three things leading the list are: wash my car, shine my shoes, and mow a lawn.) The back wall of the room I work in at the rear of the house is glass, and when I raise my eyes from the typewriter I look past an enormous bull bay tree through a thin stand of reeds into a tiny creek, the banks of which are thick with the greenest fern God ever made. In my imagination I can follow that little creek upstream to the place

2

3

4

where, after a long, circuitous passage, it joins the Suwannee River, and then follow the dark waters of the Suwannee upriver to the place where it rises in the nearly impenetrable fastness of the Okefenokee Swamp. Okefenokee: Creek Indian word for Land of the Trembling Earth, because most of the islands in the swamp—some of them holding hundreds of huge trees growing so thick that their roots are matted and woven as closely as a blanket—actually float on the water, and when a black bear crashes across one of them, the whole thing trembles.

5   I saw the Okefenokee Swamp long before I saw the Suwannee River, and the Suwannee River long before I saw the little creek I'm looking at as I write this. When I was a boy, I was in the swamp a lot, on the edges of it practically all the time that I was not in the fields working. I went deep into the Okefenokee with T. J., the husband of one of my first cousins. His left leg was cut off at the knee and he wore a peg, but he got along fine with it because we were usually in a flat skiff casting nets for crawfish, which he sold for fish bait at a penny apiece. I did not know enough then and do not know enough now to go into the deep middle swamp, but T. J. did; he knew the twisting maze of sloughs like his back yard, could read every sign of every living thing in the swamp, and made a good living with the crawfish nets and his string of traps and his gun. He sold alligator, wore alligator, and ate alligator. This was long before the federal government made the place a national wildlife refuge.

6   T. J. made his living out of the swamp, and I make mine now out of how the swamp shaped me, how the rhythms and patterns of speech in that time and place are still alive in my mouth today and, more important, alive in my ear. I feed off now and hope always to feed off the stories I heard told in the early dark around fires where coffee boiled while our clothes, still wet from stringing traps all day, slowly dried to our bodies. Even when I write stories not set in Georgia and not at all about anything in the South, that writing is of necessity still informed by my notions of the world and of what it is to be caught in it. Those notions obviously come out of South Georgia and out of everything that happened to me there, or so I believe.

7   Living here in North Florida, I am a little more than a hundred miles from where I was born and raised to manhood. I am just far enough away from the only place that was ever mine to still see it, close enough to the only people to whom I was ever kin in ways deeper than blood to still hear them. I know that what I have just written will sound precious and pretentious to many people. So be it. Let them do their work as they will, and I'll do mine.

8   I've tried to work—that is, to write—in Georgia, but I could not. Even under the best of circumstances, at my mama's farm, for instance, it was all too much for me. I was too deep in it, too close to it

to use it, to make anything out of it. My memory doesn't even seem to work when I'm writing in Georgia. I can't seem to hold a story in my head. I write a page, and five pages later what I wrote earlier has begun to slide out of focus. If this is all symptomatic of some more profound malaise, I don't want to know about it and I certainly don't want to understand it.

Living here in Gainesville seems to give me a kind of geographic and emotional distance I need to write. I can't write if I get too far away. I tried to work on a novel in Tennessee once and after a ruined two months gave it up in despair. I once spent four months near Lake Placid in a beautiful house lent to me by a friend—perfect place to write—and I didn't do a damn thing but eat my guts and look out the window at the mountains. 9

And that, all of it, precious, pretentious, or whatever, is why I live where I live. And unless something happens that I cannot control, I plan to die here. 10

QUESTIONS

1. The author gives uncomplicated reasons to explain why he lives where he does. What are these reasons? Why does he raise them?

2. How does Crews's sense of place relate to his conception of himself as a writer?

3. What are the key words in the first, long sentence of the essay that create a persona for the author? To what extent is the language in this sentence sustained or modified throughout the essay?

4. Locate words and phrases in paragraphs 4 and 5 that convey connotations of mystery and the unknown. What do these words indicate about the theme of the essay?

5. Study Crews's introductory paragraph. What is the effect of the first sentence? Of the parenthetical asides? Of the last two sentences? How does the introduction function in relation to the next two paragraphs?

6. How does description function in relation to the causal patterns that Crews develops?

7. Notice the shift in tone between the first half of the essay (paragraphs 1 to 5) and the second half (paragraphs 6 to 10). Why does the author do this? What does he achieve by "breaking" tonal consistency?

8. Describe the method of development in the concluding paragraph. What new element is introduced? Justify its placement and effectiveness.

9. Crews speaks of "a kind of geographic and emotional distance" that

he needs to work or to create. Why can being too close to a place or neighborhood be harmful? Conversely, how can such closeness be a strength?

10.   a. Write an essay on why you live where you live.
b. Write a paper about the ideal place for you to live if you had the opportunity.

WASHINGTON IRVING

A Sunday in London

Washington Irving (1783–1859), an American author, was a pioneer in the development of the modern short story, writing "Rip Van Winkle," "The Legend of Sleepy Hollow," and other tales. Trained for the law, which he never practiced, he became one of the most famous American writers of his time, and the first person in the United States to succeed as a professional writer. In addition to short fiction, Irving wrote biography, history, and essays. The following essay, a tourist's view of London, is taken from his popular *The Sketch Book* (1820).

I n a preceding paper I have spoken of an English Sunday in the country and its tranquilizing effect upon the landscape; but where is its sacred influence more strikingly apparent than in the very heart of that great Babel, London? On this sacred day the gigantic monster is charmed into repose. The intolerable din and struggle of the week are at an end. The shops are shut. The fires of forges and manufactories are extinguished; and the sun, no longer obscured by murky clouds of smoke, pours down a sober, yellow radiance into the quiet streets. The few pedestrians we meet, instead of hurrying forward with anxious countenances, move leisurely along; their brows are smoothed from the wrinkles of business and care; they have put on their Sunday looks and Sunday manners with their Sunday clothes, and are cleansed in mind as well as in person.

And now the melodious clangor of bells from church towers summons their several flocks to the fold. Forth issues from his mansion the family of the decent tradesman, the small children in the advance; then the citizen and his comely spouse, followed by the grown-up daughters, with small morocco-bound prayerbooks laid in the folds of their pocket handkerchiefs. The housemaid looks after them from the window, admiring the finery of the family and receiving, perhaps, a nod and smile from her young mistresses, at whose toilet she has assisted.

Now rumbles along the carriage of some magnate of the city, peradventure an alderman or a sheriff; and now the patter of many feet announces a procession of charity scholars, in uniforms of antique cut, and each with a prayerbook under his arm. 3

The ringing of bells is at an end; the rumbling of the carriage has ceased; the pattering of feet is heard no more; the flocks are folded in ancient churches, cramped up in by-lanes and corners of the crowded city, where the vigilant beadle keeps watch, like the shepherd's dog, around the threshold of the sanctuary. For a time everything is hushed; but soon is heard the deep, pervading sound of the organ, rolling and vibrating through the empty lanes and courts, and the sweet chanting of the choir making them resound with melody and praise. Never have I been more sensible of the sanctifying effect of church music than when I have heard it thus poured forth, like a river of joy, through the inmost recesses of this great metropolis, elevating it, as it were, from all the sordid pollutions of the week, and bearing the poor, world-worn soul on a tide of triumphant harmony to heaven. 4

The morning service is at an end. The streets are again alive with the congregations returning to their homes, but soon again relapse into silence. Now comes on the Sunday dinner, which, to the city tradesman, is a meal of some importance. There is more leisure for social enjoyment at the board. Members of the family can now gather together, who are separated by the laborious occupations of the week. A schoolboy may be permitted on that day to come to the paternal home; an old friend of the family takes his accustomed Sunday seat at the board, tells over his well-known stories and rejoices young and old with his well-known jokes. 5

On Sunday afternoon the city pours forth its legions to breathe the fresh air and enjoy the sunshine of the parks and rural environs. Satirists may say what they please about the rural enjoyments of a London citizen on Sunday, but to me there is something delightful in beholding the poor prisoner of the crowded and dusty city enabled thus to come forth once a week and throw himself upon the green bosom of nature. He is like a child restored to the mother's breast; and they who first spread out these noble parks and magnificent pleasure grounds which surround this huge metropolis have done at least as much for its health and morality as if they had expended the amount of cost in hospitals, prisons, and penitentiaries. 6

QUESTIONS

1. Describe the typical Sunday in London as Irving presents it.

2. How does the day-to-day London world contrast with its Sundays?

3. Comment on Irving's use of verbs in paragraph 4.

4. Study the author's handling of diction throughout the essay. What level of diction does he strive for? What stylistic techniques does he use?

5. How do the details presented in the introductory paragraph serve to clarify Irving's thesis?

6. How does narration contribute to the unity of the essay?

7. What is the function of the presentation of character types in the essay?

8. Analyze the tone of the concluding paragraph and the means used to achieve it. How does it reinforce the tone implicit in the introductory paragraph?

9. Irving speaks of the "sacred influence" of a certain day upon place. Do certain days still alter our sense of place? Explain your answer.

10. Write an essay describing a typical Sunday in your neighborhood or on your campus.

MARGARET MEAD

A Day in Samoa

Margaret Mead (1901–1979), famed American anthropologist, was curator of ethnology at the American Museum of Natural History and a professor at Columbia University. Her field expeditions to Samoa, New Guinea, and Bali in the 1920s and 1930s produced several major studies, notably *Coming of Age in Samoa* (1928), *Growing Up in New Guinea* (1930), and *Sex and Temperament in Three Primitive Societies* (1935). Her interest in the development of personality in primitive culture is evident in this selection from *Coming of Age in Samoa*.

he life of the day begins at dawn, or if the moon has 1 shown until daylight, the shouts of the young men may be heard before dawn from the hillside. Uneasy in the night, populous with ghosts, they shout lustily to one another as they hasten with their work. As the dawn begins to fall among the soft brown roofs and the slender palm trees stand out against a colourless, gleaming sea, lovers slip home from trysts beneath the palm trees or in the shadow of beached canoes, that the light may find each sleeper in his appointed place. Cocks crow, negligently, and a shrill-voiced bird cries from the breadfruit trees. The insistent roar of the reef seems muted to an undertone for the sounds of a waking village. Babies cry, a few short wails before sleepy mothers give them the breast. Restless little children roll out of their sheets and wander drowsily down to the beach to freshen their faces in the sea. Boys, bent upon an early fishing, start collecting their tackle and go to rouse their more laggard companions. Fires are lit, here and there, the white smoke hardly visible against the paleness of the dawn. The whole village, sheeted and frowsy, stirs, rubs its eyes, and stumbles towards the beach. "Talofa!" "Talofa!" "Will the journey start to-day?" "Is it bonito fishing your lordship is going?" Girls stop to giggle over some young ne'er-do-well who escaped during the night from an angry father's pursuit and to venture a shrewd guess that the daughter knew more about his presence than she told. The boy who is taunted by another, who has succeeded him in his sweetheart's favour, grapples with his rival, his foot slipping in the wet sand. From the other end of the village comes a long drawn-out, piercing wail. A messenger has just brought word of the death of some relative in another village. Half-clad, unhurried women, with babies at their breasts, or astride their hips, pause in their tale of Losa's outraged departure from her father's house to the greater kindness in the home of her uncle, to wonder who is dead. Poor relatives whisper their requests to rich relatives, men make plans to set a fish trap together, a woman begs a bit of yellow dye from a kinswoman, and through the village sounds the rhythmic tattoo which calls the young men together. They gather from all parts of the village, digging sticks in hand, ready to start inland to the plantation. The older men set off upon their more lonely occupations, and each household, reassembled under its peaked roof, settles down to the routine of the morning. Little children, too hungry to wait for the late breakfast, beg lumps of cold taro which they munch greedily. Women carry piles of washing to the sea or to the spring at the far end of the village, or set off inland after weaving materials. The older girls go fishing on the reef, or perhaps set themselves to weaving a new set of Venetian blinds.

In the houses, where the pebbly floors have been swept bare with a stiff long-handled broom, the women great with child and the nursing mothers sit and gossip with one another. Old men sit apart, unceasingly twisting palm husk on their bare thighs and muttering old tales under their breath. The carpenters begin work on the new

MARGARET MEAD

house, while the owner bustles about trying to keep them in good humour. Families who will cook to-day are hard at work; the taro, yams and bananas have already been brought from inland; the children are scuttling back and forth, fetching sea water, or leaves to stuff the pig. As the sun rises higher in the sky, the shadows deepen under the thatched roofs, the sand is burning to the touch, the hibiscus flowers wilt on the hedges, and little children bid the smaller ones, "Come out of the sun." Those whose excursions have been short return to the village, the women with strings of crimson jelly fish, or baskets of shell fish, the men with cocoanuts, carried in baskets slung on a shoulder pole. The women and children eat their breakfasts, just hot from the oven, if this is cook day, and the young men work swiftly in the mid-day heat, preparing the noon feast for their elders.

It is high noon. The sand burns the feet of the little children, 3 who leave their palm leaf balls and their pin-wheels of frangipani blossoms to wither in the sun, as they creep into the shade of the houses. The women who must go abroad carry great banana leaves as sun-shades or wind wet cloths about their heads. Lowering a few blinds against the slanting sun, all who are left in the village wrap their heads in sheets and go to sleep. Only a few adventurous children may slip away for a swim in the shadow of a high rock, some industrious woman continues with her weaving, or a close little group of women bend anxiously over a woman in labour. The village is dazzling and dead; any sound seems oddly loud and out of place. Words have to cut through the solid heat slowly. And then the sun gradually sinks over the sea.

A second time, the sleeping people stir, roused perhaps by 4 the cry of "a boat," resounding through the village. The fishermen beach their canoes, weary and spent from the heat, in spite of the slaked lime on their heads, with which they have sought to cool their brains and redden their hair. The brightly coloured fishes are spread out on the floor, or piled in front of the houses until the women pour water over them to free them from taboo. Regretfully, the young fishermen separate out the "Taboo fish," which must be sent to the chief, or proudly they pack the little palm leaf baskets with offerings of fish to take to their sweethearts. Men come home from the bush, grimy and heavy laden, shouting as they come, greeted in a sonorous rising cadence by those who have remained at home. They gather in the guest house for their evening kava drinking. The soft clapping of hands, the high-pitched intoning of the talking chief who serves the kava echoes through the village. Girls gather flowers to weave into necklaces; children, lusty from their naps and bound to no particular task, play circular games in the half shade of the late afternoon. Finally the sun sets, in a flame which stretches from the mountain

 A DAY IN SAMOA

behind to the horizon on the sea, the last bather comes up from the beach, children straggle home, dark little figures etched against the sky; lights shine in the houses, and each household gathers for its evening meal. The suitor humbly presents his offering, the children have been summoned from their noisy play, perhaps there is an honoured guest who must be served first, after the soft, barbaric singing of Christian hymns and the brief and graceful evening prayer. In front of a house at the end of the village, a father cries out the birth of a son. In some family circles a face is missing, in others little runaways have found a haven! Again quiet settles upon the village, as first the head of the household, then the women and children, and last of all the patient boys, eat their supper.

After supper the old people and the little children are bundled off to bed. If the young people have guests the front of the house is yielded to them. For day is the time for the councils of old men and the labours of youth, and night is the time for lighter things. Two kinsmen, or a chief and his councillor, sit and gossip over the day's events or make plans for the morrow. Outside a crier goes through the village announcing that the communal breadfruit pit will be opened in the morning, or that the village will make a great fish trap. If it is moonlight, groups of young men, women by twos and threes, wander through the village, and crowds of children hunt for land crabs or chase each other among the breadfruit trees. Half the village may go fishing by torchlight and the curving reef will gleam with wavering lights and echo with shouts of triumph or disappointment, teasing words or smothered cries of outraged modesty. Or a group of youths may dance for the pleasure of some visiting maiden. Many of those who have retired to sleep, drawn by the merry music, will wrap their sheets about them and set out to find the dancing. A white-clad, ghostly throng will gather in a circle about the gaily lit house, a circle from which every now and then a few will detach themselves and wander away among the trees. Sometimes sleep will not descend upon the village until long past midnight; then at last there is only the mellow thunder of the reef and the whisper of lovers, as the village rests until dawn.

5

QUESTIONS

1. Trace the daily cycle of Samoan life that Mead presents.

2. At first glance this essay seems to be a superbly crafted description of daily life in Samoa. However, it is more than a mere description. What anthropological inferences does Mead make about Samoan culture?

3. Certain words in the essay are indigenous to Samoan culture and

geography. Locate these words and define them. Can these words be used in American culture?

4. Explain the images and figurative language in paragraph 1.

5. Discuss the effect of the author's lengthy introductory and concluding paragraphs.

6. What is the relationship of description to mood and tone in the essay?

7. How does narrative influence essay structure and theme?

8. Discuss the transitions from paragraph to paragraph in the essay.

9. To what extent do you think that Mead is seduced by primitive or exotic life in her treatment of Samoan culture? Justify your answer.

10. Write your own description of a vivid or memorable place that you have visited and observed.

N. SCOTT MOMADAY

The Way to Rainy Mountain

Navarre Scott Momaday (1934–   ), Pulitzer Prize–winning poet, critic, and academician, is the author of *House Made of Dawn* (1968), *The Way to Rainy Mountain* (1969), *The Names* (1976), and other works. "I am an American Indian (Kiowa), and am vitally interested in American Indian art, history and culture," Momaday has written. In this essay, he elevates personal experience to the realm of poety and tribal myth.

single knoll rises out of the plain in Oklahoma, north   1 and west of the Wichita Range. For my people, the Kiowas, it is an old landmark, and they gave it the name Rainy Mountain. The hardest weather in the world is there. Winter brings blizzards, hot tornadic winds arise in the spring, and in summer the prairie is an anvil's edge. The grass turns brittle and brown, and it cracks beneath your feet. There are green belts along the rivers and creeks, linear groves of hickory and pecan, willow and witch hazel. At a distance in July or August the steaming foliage seems almost to writhe in fire. Great green and yellow grasshoppers are everywhere in the tall grass, popping up like corn to sting the flesh, and tortoises crawl about on the red earth, going nowhere in the plenty of time. Loneliness is an aspect of the land. All things in the plain are isolate; there is no confusion of objects in the eye, but *one* hill or *one* tree or *one* man. To look upon that landscape in the early morning, with the sun at your back, is to lose the sense of proportion. Your imagination comes to life, and this, you think, is where Creation was begun.

I returned to Rainy Mountain in July. My grandmother had died in the spring, and I wanted to be at her grave. She had lived to be very old and at last infirm. Her only living daughter was with her when she died, and I was told that in death her face was that of a child. 2

I like to think of her as a child. When she was born, the Kiowas were living the last great moment of their history. For more than a hundred years they had controlled the open range from the Smoky Hill River to the Red, from the headwaters of the Canadian to the fork of the Arkansas and Cimarron. In alliance with the Comanches, they had ruled the whole of the southern Plains. War was their sacred business, and they were among the finest horsemen the world has ever known. But warfare for the Kiowas was preeminently a matter of disposition rather than of survival, and they never understood the grim, unrelenting advance of the U.S. Cavalry. When at last, divided and ill-provisioned, they were driven onto the Staked Plains in the cold rains of autumn, they fell into panic. In Palo Duro Canyon they abandoned their crucial stores to pillage and had nothing then but their lives. In order to save themselves, they surrendered to the soldiers at Fort Sill and were imprisoned in the old stone corral that now stands as a military museum. My grandmother was spared the humiliation of those high gray walls by eight or ten years, but she must have known from birth the affliction of defeat, the dark brooding of old warriors. 3

Her name was Aho, and she belonged to the last culture to evolve in North America. Her forebears came down from the high country in western Montana nearly three centuries ago. They were a mountain people, a mysterious tribe of hunters whose language has never been positively classified in any major group. In the late seventeenth century they began a long migration to the south and east. It was a journey toward the dawn, and it led to a golden age. Along the way the Kiowas were befriended by the Crows, who gave them the culture and religion of the Plains. They acquired horses, and their ancient nomadic spirit was suddenly free of the ground. They acquired Tai-me, the sacred Sun Dance doll, from that moment the object and symbol of their worship, and so shared in the divinity of the sun. Not least, they acquired the sense of destiny, therefore courage and pride. When they entered upon the southern Plains they 4 had been transformed. No longer were they slaves to the simple necessity of survival; they were a lordly and dangerous society of fighters and thieves, hunters and priests of the sun. According to their origin myth, they entered the world through a hollow log. From one point of view, their migration was the fruit of an old prophecy, for indeed they emerged from a sunless world.

Although my grandmother lived out her long life in the 5 shadow of Rainy Mountain, the immense landscape of the continental interior lay like memory in her blood. She could tell of the Crows, whom she had never seen, and of the Black Hills, where she had never been. I wanted to see in reality what she had seen more perfectly in the mind's eye, and traveled fifteen hundred miles to begin my pilgrimage.

Yellowstone, it seemed to me, was the top of the world, a 6 region of deep lakes and dark timber, canyons and waterfalls. But, beautiful as it is, one might have the sense of confinement there. The skyline in all directions is close at hand, the high wall of the woods and deep cleavages of shade. There is a perfect freedom in the mountains, but it belongs to the eagle and the elk, the badger and the bear. The Kiowas reckoned their stature by the distance they could see, and they were bent and blind in the wilderness.

Descending eastward, the highland meadows are a stairway 7 to the plain. In July the inland slope of the Rockies is luxuriant with flax and buckwheat, stonecrop and larkspur. The earth unfolds and the limit of the land recedes. Clusters of trees, and animals grazing far in the distance, cause the vision to reach away and wonder to build upon the mind. The sun follows a longer course in the day, and the sky is immense beyond all comparison. The great billowing clouds that sail upon it are shadows that move upon the grain like water, dividing light. Farther down, in the land of the Crows and Blackfeet, the plain is yellow. Sweet clover takes hold of the hills and bends upon itself to cover and seal the soil. There the Kiowas paused on their way; they had come to the place where they must change their lives. The sun is at home on the plains. Precisely there does it have the certain character of a god. When the Kiowas came to the land of the Crows, they could see the dark lees of the hills at dawn across the Bighorn River, the profusion of light on the grain shelves, the oldest deity ranging after the solstices. Not yet would they veer southward to the caldron of the land that lay below; they must wean their blood from the northern winter and hold the mountains a while longer in their view. They bore Tai-me in procession to the east.

A dark mist lay over the Black Hills, and the land was like 8 iron. At the top of a ridge I caught sight of Devil's Tower upthrust against the gray sky as if in the birth of time the core of the earth had broken through its crust and the motion of the world was begun.

There are things in nature that engender an awful quiet in the heart of man; Devil's Tower is one of them. Two centuries ago, because they could not do otherwise, the Kiowas made a legend at the base of the rock. My grandmother said:

> Eight children were there at play, seven sisters and their brother. Suddenly the boy was struck dumb; he trembled and began to run upon his hands and feet. His fingers became claws, and his body was covered with fur. Directly there was a bear where the boy had been. The sisters were terrified; they ran, and the bear after them. They came to the stump of a great tree, and the tree spoke to them. It bade them climb upon it, and as they did so it began to rise into the air. The bear came to kill them, but they were just beyond its reach. It reared against the tree and scored the bark all around with its claws. The seven sisters were borne into the sky, and they became the stars of the Big Dipper.

From that moment, and so long as the legend lives, the Kiowas have kinsmen in the night sky. Whatever they were in the mountains, they could be no more. However tenuous their well-being, however much they had suffered and would suffer again, they had found a way out of the wilderness.

My grandmother had a reverence for the sun, a holy regard 9 that now is all but gone out of mankind. There was a wariness in her, and an ancient awe. She was a Christian in her later years, but she had come a long way about, and she never forgot her birthright. As a child she had been to the Sun Dances; she had taken part in those annual rites, and by them she had learned the restoration of her people in the presence of Tai-me. She was about seven when the last Kiowa Sun Dance was held in 1887 on the Washita River above Rainy Mountain Creek. The buffalo were gone. In order to consummate the ancient sacrifice—to impale the head of a buffalo bull upon the medicine tree—a delegation of old men journeyed into Texas, there to beg and barter for an animal from the Goodnight herd. She was ten when the Kiowas came together for the last time as a living Sun Dance culture. They could find no buffalo; they had to hang an old hide from the sacred tree. Before the dance could begin, a company of soldiers rode out from Fort Sill under orders to disperse the tribe. Forbidden without cause the essential act of their faith, having seen the wild herds slaughtered and left to rot upon the ground, the Kiowas backed away forever from the medicine tree. That was July 20, 1890, at the great bend of the Washita. My grandmother was there. Without bitterness, and for as long as she lived, she bore a vision of deicide.

Now that I can have her only in memory, I see my grand- 10

mother in the several postures that were peculiar to her: standing at the wood stove on a winter morning and turning meat in a great iron skillet; sitting at the south window, bent above her beadwork, and afterwards, when her vision failed, looking down for a long time into the fold of her hands; going out upon a cane, very slowly as she did when the weight of age came upon her; praying. I remember her most often at prayer. She made long, rambling prayers out of suffering and hope, having seen many things. I was never sure that I had the right to hear, so exclusive were they of all mere custom and company. The last time I saw her she prayed standing by the side of her bed at night, naked to the waist, the light of a kerosene lamp moving upon her dark skin. Her long, black hair, always drawn and braided in the day, lay upon her shoulders and against her breasts like a shawl. I do not speak Kiowa, and I never understood her prayers, but there was something inherently sad in the sound, some merest hesitation upon the syllables of sorrow. She began in a high and descending pitch, exhausting her breath to silence; then again and again—and always the same intensity of effort, of something that is, and is not, like urgency in the human voice. Transported so in the dancing light among the shadows of her room, she seemed beyond the reach of time. But that was illusion; I think I knew then that I should not see her again.

Houses are like sentinels in the plain, old keepers of the weather watch. There, in a very little while, wood takes on the appearance of great age. All colors wear soon away in the wind and rain, and then the wood is burned gray and the grain appears and the nails turn red with rust. The windowpanes are black and opaque; you imagine there is nothing within, and indeed there are many ghosts, bones given up to the land. They stand here and there against the sky, and you approach them for a longer time than you expect. They belong in the distance; it is their domain. 11

Once there was a lot of sound in my grandmother's house, a lot of coming and going, feasting and talk. The summers there were full of excitement and reunion. The Kiowas are a summer people; they abide the cold and keep to themselves, but when the season turns and the land becomes warm and vital they cannot hold still; an old love of going returns upon them. The aged visitors who came to my grandmother's house when I was a child were made of lean and leather, and they bore themselves upright. They wore great black hats and bright ample shirts that shook in the wind. They rubbed fat upon their hair and wound their braids with strips of colored cloth. Some of them painted their faces and carried the scars of old and cherished enmities. They were an old council of warlords, come to remind and be reminded of who they were. Their wives and daughters served them well. The women might indulge themselves; gossip was at once 12 the mark and compensation of their servitude. They made loud and elaborate talk among themselves, full of jest and gesture, fright and false alarm. They went abroad in fringed and flowered shawls, bright beadwork and German silver. They were at home in the kitchen, and they prepared meals that were banquets.

There were frequent prayer meetings, and great nocturnal 13 feasts. When I was a child I played with my cousins outside, where the lamplight fell upon the ground and the singing of the old people rose up around us and carried away into the darkness. There were a lot of good things to eat, a lot of laughter and surprise. And afterwards, when the quiet returned, I lay down with my grandmother and could hear the frogs away by the river and feel the motion of the air.

Now there is funeral silence in the rooms, the endless wake 14 of some final word. The walls have closed in upon my grandmother's house. When I returned to it in mourning, I saw for the first time in my life how small it was. It was late at night, and there was a white moon, nearly full. I sat for a long time on the stone steps by the kitchen door. From there I could see out across the land; I could see the long row of trees by the creek, the low light upon the rolling plains, and the stars of the Big Dipper. Once I looked at the moon and caught sight of a strange thing. A cricket had perched upon the handrail, only a few inches away from me. My line of vision was such that the creature filled the moon like a fossil. It had gone there, I thought, to live and die, for there, of all places, was its small definition made whole and eternal. A warm wind rose up and purled like the longing within me.

The next morning I awoke at dawn and went out on the dirt 15 road to Rainy Mountain. It was already hot, and the grasshoppers began to fill the air. Still, it was early in the morning, and the birds sang out of the shadows. The long yellow grass on the mountain shone in the bright light, and a scissortail hied above the land. There, where it ought to be, at the end of a long and legendary way, was my grandmother's grave. Here and there on the dark stones were ancestral names. Looking back once, I saw the mountain and came away.

QUESTIONS

1. Why does Momaday return to his grandmother's house and journey to her grave?

2. List the various myths and legends the author mentions in the essay. What subjects do they treat? How are these subjects interrelated?

3. Locate and explain instances of sensory, metaphorical, and symbolic language in the essay. Why are these modes of language consistent with the subject and theme elaborated by Momaday?

4. How does Momaday's use of abstract language affect the concrete vocabulary in the essay?

5. What is the method of development in the first paragraph? How does the introduction serve as a vehicle for the central meanings in the essay?

6. Consider the relationship of narration to description in the organization of the essay. What forms of narrative serve to unify the selection? Are the narrative patterns strictly linear, or do they shift for other purposes? Explain. In what sense is Momaday's descriptive technique cinematic?

7. How do the land, the Kiowas, and Momaday's grandmother serve as reinforcing frames of the essay?

8. Describe in detail the creation of mood in this essay. Explain specifically the mood at the conclusion.

9. Momaday implies that myth is central to his life and the life of the Kiowas. What *is* myth? Do you think that myth is as strong in general American culture as it is in Kiowa culture? In what ways does it operate? How can myth sustain the individual, community, and nation?

10. Write about a person and place that, taken together, hold a special reverence for you.

HENRY DAVID THOREAU

Economy

Henry David Thoreau (1817–1862), author of the masterpiece *Walden* (1854), is one of the most important figures in American thought and literature. A social and political activist, he opposed the Mexican War, protested slavery, and refused to pay his poll taxes. As a naturalist, he believed in the preeminence of individualism and nature over technology, materialism, and nationalism. In 1845, Thoreau went to live at Walden Pond, "living deep and sucking the marrow out of life." *Walden*, describing his life at the pond, is one of the most challenging, exuberant, and innovative works of American literature. This account from Thoreau's masterpiece, tracing the construction of his dwelling, reflects his preoccupation with economy, natural process, and self-reliance.

N ear the end of March, 1845, I borrowed an axe and went down to the woods by Walden Pond, nearest to where I intended to build my house, and began to cut down some tall arrowy white pines, still in their youth, for timber. It is difficult to begin without borrowing, but perhaps it is the most generous course thus to permit your fellow-men to have an interest in your enterprise. The owner of the axe, as he released his hold on it, said that it was the apple of his eye; but I returned it sharper than I received it. It was a pleasant hillside where I worked, covered with pine woods, through which I looked out on the pond, and a small open field in the woods where pines and hickories were springing up. The ice in the pond was not yet dissolved, though there were some open spaces, and it was all dark colored and saturated with water. There were some slight flurries of snow during the days that I worked there; but for the most part when I came out onto the railroad, on my way home, its yellow sand heap stretched away gleaming in the hazy atmosphere, and the rails shone in the spring sun, and I heard the lark and pewee and other birds already come to commence another year with us. They were pleasant spring days, in which the winter of man's discontent was thawing as well as the earth, and the life that had lain torpid began to stretch itself. One day, when my axe had come off and I had cut a green hickory for a wedge, driving it with a stone, and had placed the whole to soak in a pond hole in order to swell the wood, I saw a striped snake run into the water, and he lay on the bottom, apparently without inconvenience, as long as I stayed there, or more than a quarter of an hour; perhaps because he had not yet fairly come out of the torpid state. It appeared to me that for a like reason men remain in their present low and primitive condition; but if they should feel the influence of the spring of springs arousing them, they would of necessity rise to a higher and more ethereal life. I had previously seen the snakes in frosty mornings in my path with portions of their bodies still numb and inflexible, waiting for the sun to thaw them. On the 1st of April it rained and melted the ice, and in the early part of the day, which was very foggy, I heard a stray goose groping about over the pond and cackling as if lost, or like the spirit of the fog.

So I went on for some days cutting and hewing timber, and also studs and rafters, all with my narrow axe, not having many communicable or scholar-like thoughts, singing to myself. 2

HENRY DAVID THOREAU

Men say they know many things;
But lo! they have taken wings—
The arts and sciences,
And a thousand appliances;
The wind that blows
Is all that anybody knows.

I hewed the main timber six inches square, most of the studs on two sides only, and the rafters and floor timbers on one side, leaving the rest of the bark on, so that they were just as straight and much stronger than sawed ones. Each stick was carefully mortised or tenoned by its stump, for I had borrowed other tools by this time. My days in the woods were not very long ones; yet I usually carried my dinner of bread and butter, and read the newspaper in which it was wrapped, at noon, sitting amid the green pine boughs which I had cut off, and to my bread was imparted some of their fragrance, for my hands were covered with a thick coat of pitch. Before I had done I was more the friend than the foe of the pine tree, though I had cut down some of them, having become better acquainted with it. Sometimes a rambler in the wood was attracted by the sound of my axe, and we chatted pleasantly over the chips which I had made.

By the middle of April, for I made no haste in my work, but rather made the most of it, my house was framed and ready for the raising. I had already bought the shanty of James Collins, an Irishman who worked on the Fitchburg Railroad, for boards. James Collins' shanty was considered an uncommonly fine one. When I called to see it he was not at home. I walked about the outside, at first unobserved from within, the window was so deep and high. It was of small dimensions, with a peaked cottage roof, and not much else to be seen, the dirt being raised five feet all around as if it were a compost heap. The roof was the soundest part, though a good deal warped and made brittle by the sun. Doorsill there was none, but a perennial passage for the hens under the door board. Mrs. C. came to the door and asked me to view it from the inside. The hens were driven in by my approach. It was dark, and had a dirt floor for the most part, dank, clammy, and aguish, only here a board and there a board which would not bear removal. She lighted a lamp to show me the inside of the roof and the walls, and also that the board floor extended under the bed, warning me not to step into the cellar, a sort of dust hole two feet deep. In her own words, they were "good boards overhead, good boards all around, and a good window"—of two whole squares originally, only the cat had passed out that way lately. There was a stove, a bed, and a place to sit, an infant in the house where it was born, a silk parasol, gilt-framed looking-glass, and a patent new coffee-mill nailed to an oak sapling, all told. The bargain was soon concluded, for James had in the meanwhile returned. I to pay four dollars and twenty-five cents tonight, he to vacate at five tomorrow morning, selling to nobody else meanwhile: I to take possession at six. It were well, he said, to be there early, and anticipate certain indistinct but wholly unjust claims on the score of ground rent and fuel. This he assured me was the only encumbrance. At six I passed him and his family on the road. One large bundle held their all—bed, coffee-mill, looking-glass, hens—all but the cat; she took to the woods and became a wild cat and, as I learned afterward, trod in a trap set for woodchucks, and so became a dead cat at last.

I took down this dwelling the same morning, drawing the 4 nails, and removed it to the pond side by small cartloads, spreading the boards on the grass there to bleach and warp back again in the sun. One early thrush gave me a note or two as I drove along the woodland path. I was informed treacherously by a young Patrick that neighbor Seeley, an Irishman, in the intervals of the carting, transferred the still tolerable, straight, and drivable nails, staples, and spikes to his pocket, and then stood when I came back to pass the time of day, and look freshly up, unconcerned, with spring thoughts, at the devastation; there being a dearth of work, as he said. He was there to represent spectatordom, and help make this seemingly insignificant event one with the removal of the gods of Troy.

I dug my cellar in the side of a hill sloping to the south, where 5 a woodchuck had formerly dug his burrow, down through sumach and blackberry roots, and the lowest stain of vegetation, six feet square by seven deep, to a fine sand where potatoes would not freeze in any winter. The sides were left shelving, and not stoned; but the sun having never shone on them, the sand still keeps its place. It was but two hours' work. I took particular pleasure in this breaking of ground, for in almost all latitudes men dig into the earth for an equable temperature. Under the most splendid house in the city is still to be found the cellar where they store their roots as of old, and long after the superstructure had disappeared posterity remark its dent in the earth. The house is still but a sort of porch at the entrance of a burrow.

At length, in the beginning of May, with the help of some of 6 my acquaintances, rather to improve so good an occasion for neighborliness than from any necessity, I set up the frame of my house. No man was ever more honored in the character of his raisers than I. They are destined, I trust, to assist at the raising of loftier structures one day. I began to occupy my house on the 4th of July, as soon as it was boarded and roofed, for the boards were carefully feather-edged and lapped, so that it was perfectly impervious to rain, but before boarding I laid the foundation of a chimney at one end, bringing two cartloads of stones up the hill from the pond in my arms. I built the chimney after my hoeing in the fall, before a fire became necessary for warmth, doing my cooking in the meanwhile out of doors on the ground, early in the morning: which mode I still think is in some respects more convenient and agreeable than the usual one. When it stormed before my bread was baked, I fixed a few boards over the fire, and sat under them to watch my loaf, and passed some pleasant hours in that way. In those days, when my hands were much employed, I read but little, but the least scraps of paper which lay on the ground, my holder, or tablecloth, afforded me as much entertainment, in fact answered the same purpose as the Iliad.

QUESTIONS

1. Describe the process by which Thoreau builds his house.

2. What is Thoreau's attitude toward economy in this selection? Which of the details Thoreau has included most successfully reveal this attitude?

3. In paragraph 1, what connotation does the author develop for the word "borrowing"? How do words related to economics serve as a motif in the essay?

4. What is the analogy in paragraph 1?

5. How does Thoreau use process analysis? Why is this rhetorical technique reinforced by the natural processes depicted in the essay?

6. How does Thoreau particularize the generalizations he makes in the essay?

7. What is the tone of the essay? Does an implied thesis for the essay emerge? Justify your answer.

8. What is the relationship of the last two sentences in paragraph 6 to the rest of the selection?

9. Analyze Thoreau's poem in paragraph 2. What is your response to the theme of the poem?

10. Using Thoreau's method, write an essay in which you trace the process of building or creating something that was important to you.

The Big House

Elizabeth Bowen (1899–1973), Irish essayist, novelist, autobiographer, and short story writer, is noted for her portrayals of upper-middle-class society. Influenced by Henry James, she created her most finely delineated portrayal of human sensitivity in *The Death of the Heart* (1938). Another significant novel, set in wartime London, is *The Heat of the Day* (1949). In the following essay, from *Collected Impressions* (1950), Bowen offers an introspective, analytical, and sympathetic defense of a special way of life.

B ig houses in Ireland are, I am told, very isolated. I say "I   1
am told" because the isolation, or loneliness of my own
house is only borne in on me, from time to time, by the
exclamations of travellers when they arive. "Well," they
exclaim, with a hint of denunciation, *"you* are a long way from
everywhere!" I suppose I see this the other way round: everywhere
seems to have placed itself a long way from me—if "everywhere"
means shopping towns, railway stations or Ireland's principal
through roads. But one's own point of departure always seems to one
normal: I have grown up accustomed to seeing out of my windows
nothing but grass, sky, tree, to being enclosed in a ring of almost
complete silence and to making journeys for anything that I want.
Actually, a main road passes my gates (though it is a main road not
much travelled); my post village, which is fairly animated, is just a
mile up the hill, and a daily bus, now, connects this village with Cork.
The motor car demolishes distances, and the telephone and wireless
keep the house knit up, perhaps too much, with the world. The
loneliness of my house, as of many others, is more an effect than a
reality. But it is the effect that is interesting.

When I visit other big houses I *am* struck by some quality that   2
they all have—not so much isolation as mystery. Each house seems to
live under its own spell, and that is the spell that falls on the visitor
from the moment he passes in at the gates. The ring of woods inside
the demesne wall conceals, at first, the whole demesne from the eye:
this looks, from the road, like a *bois dormant,* with a great glade inside.
Inside the gates the avenue often describes loops, to make itself of
still more extravagant length; it is sometimes arched by beeches,
sometimes silent with moss. On each side lie those tree-studded grass
spaces we Anglo-Irish call lawns and English people puzzle us by
speaking of as "the park." On these browse cattle, or there may be

horses out on grass. A second gate—(generally white-painted, so that one may not drive into it in the dark)—keeps these away from the house in its inner circle of trees. Having shut this clanking white gate behind one, one takes the last reach of avenue and meets the faded, dark-windowed and somehow hypnotic stare of the big house. Often a line of mountains rises above it, or a river is seen through a break in woods. But the house, in its silence, seems to be contemplating the swell or fall of its own lawns.

The paradox of these big houses is that often they are not big 3 at all. Those massive detached villas outside cities probably have a greater number of rooms. We have of course in Ireland the *great* houses—houses Renaissance Italy hardly rivals, houses with superb façades, colonnades, pavilions and, inside, chains of plastered, painted saloons. But the houses that I know best, and write of, would be only called "big" in Ireland—in England they would be "country houses," no more. They are of adequate size for a family, its dependants, a modest number of guests. They have few annexes, they do not ramble; they are nearly always compactly square. Much of the space inside (and there is not so much space) has been sacrificed to airy halls and lobbies and to the elegant structure of staircases. Their façades (very often in the Italian manner) are not lengthy, though they may be high. Is it height—in this country of otherwise low buildings—that got these Anglo-Irish houses their "big" name? Or have they been called "big" with a slight inflection— that of hostility, irony? One may call a man "big" with just that inflection because he seems to think the hell of himself.

These houses, however, are certainly not little. Let us say that 4 their size, like their loneliness, is an effect rather than a reality. Perhaps the wide, private spaces they occupy throw a distending reflection on to their walls. And, they were planned for spacious living—for hospitality above all. Unlike the low, warm, ruddy French and English manors, they have made no natural growth from the soil—the idea that begot them was a purely social one. The functional parts of them—kitchens and offices, farm-buildings, outbuildings— were sunk underground, concealed by walls or by trees: only the stables (for horses ranked very highly) emerged to view, as suavely planned as the house. Yet, in another sense, the most ornate, spacious parts of these buildings *were* the most functional—the steps, the halls, the living-rooms, the fine staircases—it was these that contributed to society, that raised life above the exigencies of mere living to the plane of art, or at least style. There was a true bigness, a sort of impersonality, in the manner in which the houses were conceived. After an era of greed, roughness and panic, after an era of camping in charred or desolate ruins (as my Cromwellian ancestors did certainly) these new settlers who had been imposed on Ireland

 THE BIG HOUSE

began to wish to add something to life. The security that they had, by the eighteenth century, however ignobly gained, they did not use quite ignobly. They began to feel, and exert, the European idea—to seek what was humanistic, classic and disciplined.

It is something to subscribe to an idea, even if one cannot live up to it. These country gentlemen liked sport, drink and card-playing very much better than they liked the arts—but they religiously stocked their libraries, set fine craftsmen to work on their ceilings and mantelpieces and interspersed their own family portraits with heroic-ized paintings of foreign scenes. Outdoors there was at first a good deal of negligence, but later one planned and planted demesnes. . . . All this cost money: many of these genial builders died badly in debt and left their families saddled with mansions that they could ill afford. Then, decline set in almost at once. A more modest plan of living would have made, in the end, for very much more peace: big houses that had begun in glory were soon only maintained by struggle and sacrifice. Sons were recalled from college, or never went there; daughters, undowered, stayed unwed; love-marriages had to be interdicted because money was needed to prop the roof. Hus-bands and wives struggled, shoulder to shoulder, to keep the estate anything like solvent, or, in the last issue, to hold creditors off; their children grew up *farouches*, haughty, quite ignorant of the outside world. And in this struggle for life, a struggle that goes on every-where, that may be said, in fact, to *be* life itself, and should not therefore have anything terrible about it, the big house people were handicapped, shadowed and to an extent queered—by their pride, by their indignation at their decline and by their divorce from the countryside in whose heart their struggle was carried on. They would have been surprised to receive pity. I doubt, as a matter of fact, that they ever pitied themselves: they were obsessed, and to a degree exalted. They had begun as conquerors and were not disposed to let that tradition lapse. These big house people admit only one class-distinction: they instinctively "place" a person who makes a poor mouth.

It is, I think, to the credit of big house people that they concealed their struggles with such nonchalance and for so long continued to throw about what did not really amount to much weight. It is to their credit that, with grass almost up to their doors and hardly a sixpence to turn over, they continued to be resented by the rest of Ireland as being the heartless rich. Now this myth has broken down: I think everyone knows that life is not all jam in the big house. Nowadays, what I hear most commented on is the apparent futility of the sacrifice. New democratic Ireland no longer denounces the big house, but seems to marvel at it. Why fight to maintain life in a draughty barrack, in a demesne shorn of most of its other land, a demesne in which one can hardly keep down the thistles, far from neighbours, golf links, tennis clubs, cinemas, buses, railways, shops? "What do you *do* all day? Isn't it very lonely? Do servants stay with you? Can you keep warm in winter? Isn't it very ghostly? How do you do your shopping?"

To most of these questions it would be hard to give a concrete and satisfactory answer. To some few of the big houses wealth and security have returned—or one should say had returned, for the war attacks these again. But in the majority life maintains itself by a series of fortuities. As I have heard many occupants say: "I have no idea how we live, but we do." Such people not only live but enjoy life. To the keeping afloat of the household not only the family but the servants contribute ingenuity and goodwill. As on a ship out at sea, there is a sense of community. There is also—and this, I think, is the strength of such households—a very great feeling of independence: in the big house one does not feel overlooked; one lives by one's own standards, makes one's own laws and does not care, within fairly wide limits, what anybody outside the demesne wall thinks. This may tend to exaggerate, to the point of absurdity, the family's individual point of view: there are a thousand legends of eccentricity. But it does also make for a sort of hardiness and absence of social fear. And ennui, that threat to life in Ireland, is kept at bay by the constant exigencies, some of them unexpected, of the house and place. (This was not so in the more prosperous days—"Beautiful as it is, much as I love it," wrote one of George Moore's ancestors about Moore Hall, "I have not been able to exclude ennui from its precincts.") No, life in the big house, in its circle of trees, is saturated with character: this is, I suppose, the element of the spell. The indefinite ghosts of the past, of the dead who lived here and pursued this same routine of life in these walls add something, a sort of order, a reason for living, to every minute and hour. This is the order, the form of life, the tradition to which big house people still sacrifice much.

From the point of view of the outside Irish world, does the big house justify its existence? I believe it could do so now as never before. As I said, the idea from which these houses sprang was, before everything, a social one. That idea, although lofty, was at first rigid and narrow—but it could extend itself, and it must if the big house is to play an alive part in the alive Ireland of to-day. What is fine about the social idea is that it means the subjugation of the personal to the impersonal. In the interest of good manners and good behaviour people learned to subdue their own feelings. The result was an easy and unsuspicious intercourse, to which everyone brought the best that they had—wit, knowledge, sympathy or personal beauty. Society—or, more simply, the getting-together of people—was meant to be at once a high pleasure and willing discipline, not just an occasion for self-display. The big, or big-seeming, rooms in the big houses are meant for just such pleasures of intercourse. They are meant for something more creative, and gayer, than grumbles, gossip or the tearing to pieces of acquaintances' characters. "Can we not," big, half-empty rooms seem to ask, "be, as never before, sociable? Cannot we scrap the past, with its bitternesses and barriers, and all meet, throwing in what we have?"

There are difficulties—expensive "entertainment," for in- 9
stance, cannot be given now. The distances *are* great—and an impalpable barrier stands between city and country Ireland. But there are buses and there are bicycles; we all eat and drink a good deal less, and would not find it any shame in a host not to offer what he has not got. The world around us is moving so rapidly that it is impossible to be dull-minded; we should all, more than ever, have a great deal to say; every newcomer, with his point of view, becomes an object of quite magnetic interest. Symbolically (though also matter-of-factly) the doors of the big houses stand open all day; it is only regretfully that they are barred up at night. The stranger is welcome, just as much as the friend—the stranger, in fact, *is* the friend if he does not show himself otherwise. But who ever walks in? Is it suspicion, hostility, irony that keep so much of Ireland away from the big house door? If this lasts, we impoverish life all round. Or is it the fear that, if one goes into the big house, one will have to be "polite"? Well, why not *be* polite—are not humane manners the crown of being human at all? Politeness is not constriction; it is a grace: it is really no worse than an exercise of the imagination on other people's behalf. And are we to cut grace quite out of life?

The big house has much to learn—and it must learn if it is to 10
survive at all. But it also has much to give. The young people who are taking on these big houses, who accept the burden and continue the struggle are not content, now, to live for themselves only; they will not be content, either, to live "just for the house." The young cannot afford to be stupid—they expect the houses they keep alive to inherit, in a changed world and under changed conditions, the good life for which they were first built. The good in the new can add to, not destroy, the good in the old. From inside many big houses (and these will be the survivors) barriers are being impatiently attacked. But it must be seen that a barrier has two sides.

QUESTIONS

1. What objections do people give to living in big houses? What connections does Bowen establish between big houses and the social life of a people?

ELIZABETH BOWEN

2. What does Bowen mean in paragraph 4 when she speaks of raising life "above the exigencies of mere living to the plane of art"?

3. List typical words and phrases Bowen uses to describe big houses and discuss the range of connotations.

4. How does Bowen personify the house in paragraph 2? What effect is she seeking?

5. Discuss Bowen's careful development of topic sentences and the material developed from them. What progression do you detect among them?

6. What techniques of persuasion does Bowen utilize to develop the essay?

7. How does the big house function as a symbol of Bowen's social attitudes?

8. What tone emerges from Bowen's defense of the big house? How does it emerge?

9. Bowen states at the start of paragraph 5: "It is something to subscribe to an idea, even if one cannot live up to it." Do Americans, with their fondness for conspicuous consumption, nevertheless abide by set beliefs? What is the American attitude toward bigness? How is this attitude changing?

10. Analyze a particular type of dwelling with which you are familiar: the big house, the farmhouse, the garden apartment, the ranch house. Try to capture the essence of the dwelling and at the same time to persuade the reader to subscribe to your viewpoint.

JOSEPH ADDISON

The Royal Exchange

Joseph Addison (1672–1719) was an essayist, poet, dramatist, statesman, and journalist. As a playwright, he wrote one of the most successful tragedies of the eighteenth century (*Cato*, in 1713). As a statesman, he served as secretary of state under George I. As an essayist, he wrote with reason and wit in *The Tatler* (1709–1711) and *The Spectator* (1711–1712, and 1714). He not only excelled as a statesman and tragedian, but also is often considered one of the best English essayists. In this periodical essay, Addison pays tribute to one of Britain's sacred institutions.

There is no place in the town which I so much love to frequent as the Royal Exchange. It gives me a secret satisfaction, and, in some measure, gratifies my vanity, as I am an Englishman, to see so rich an assembly of countrymen and foreigners consulting together upon the private business of mankind, and making this metropolis a kind of emporium for the whole earth. I must confess I look upon high-change to be a great council, in which all considerable nations have their representatives. Factors in the trading world are what ambassadors are in the politic world; they negotiate affairs, conclude treaties, and maintain a good correspondence between those wealthy societies of men that are divided from one another by seas and oceans, or live on the different extremities of a continent. I have often been pleased to hear disputes adjusted between an inhabitant of Japan and an alderman of London, or to see a subject of the Great Mogul entering into a league with one of the Czar of Muscovy. I am infinitely delighted in mixing with these several ministers of commerce, as they are distinguished by their different walks and different languages: sometimes I am justled among a body of Armenians: sometimes I am lost in a crowd of Jews; and sometimes make one in a group of Dutchmen. I am a Dane, Swede, or Frenchman at different times, or rather fancy myself like the old philosopher, who upon being asked what country-man he was, replied, that he was a citizen of the world.

Though I very frequently visit this busy multitude of people, I am known to nobody there but my friend Sir Andrew, who often smiles upon me as he sees me bustling in the crowd, but at the same time connives at my presence without taking any further notice of me. There is indeed a merchant of Egypt, who just knows me by sight, having formerly remitted me some money to Grand Cairo; but as I am not versed in the modern Coptic, our conferences go no further than a bow and a grimace.

This grand scene of business gives me an infinite variety of solid and substantial entertainments. As I am a great lover of mankind, my heart naturally overflows with pleasure at the sight of a prosperous and happy multitude, insomuch that at many public solemnities I cannot forbear expressing my joy with tears that have stolen down my cheeks. For this reason I am wonderfully delighted to see such a body of men thriving in their own private fortunes, and at the same time promoting the public stock; or in other words, raising estates for their own families, by bringing into their country whatever is wanting, and carrying out of it whatever is superfluous.

Nature seems to have taken a particular care to disseminate her blessings among the different regions of the world, with an eye to this mutual intercourse and traffic among mankind, that the natives

1

2

3

4

JOSEPH ADDISON

of the several parts of the globe might have a kind of dependence upon one another, and be united together by their common interest. Almost every degree produces something peculiar to it. The food often grows in one country, and the sauce in another. The fruits of Portugal are corrected by the products of Barbadoes: the infusion of a China plant sweetened with the pith of an Indian cane. The Philippick Islands give a flavour to our European bowls. The single dress of a woman of quality is often the product of an hundred climates. The muff and the fan come together from the different ends of the earth. The scarf is sent from the torrid zone, and the tippet from beneath the Pole. The brocade petticoat rises out of the mines of Peru, and the diamond necklace out of the bowels of Indostan.

If we consider our own country in its natural prospect, without any of the benefits and advantages of commerce, what a barren uncomfortable spot of earth falls to our share! Natural historians tell us that no fruit grows originally among us, besides hips and haws, acorns and pig-nuts, with other delicacies of the like nature; that our climate of itself, and without the assistances of art, can make no further advances towards a plum than to a sloe, and carries an apple to no greater a perfection than a crab: that our melons, our peaches, our figs, our apricots, and cherries, are strangers among us, imported in different ages, and naturalized in our English gardens; and that they would all degenerate and fall away into the trash of our own country, if they were wholly neglected by the planter, and left to the mercy of our sun and soil. 5

Nor has traffic more enriched our vegetable world than it has improved the whole face of nature among us. Our ships are laden with the harvest of every climate: our tables are stored with spices, and oils, and wines: our rooms are filled with pyramids of China, and adorned with the workmanship of Japan: our morning's-draught comes to us from the remotest corners of the earth: we repair our bodies by the drugs of America, and repose ourselves under Indian canopies. My friend Sir Andrew calls the vineyards of France our gardens; the spice-islands our hot-beds; the Persians our silk-weavers, and the Chinese our potters. Nature indeed furnishes us with the bare necessaries of life, but traffic gives us a great variety of what is useful, and at the same time supplies us with every thing that is convenient and ornamental. Nor is it the least part of this our happiness, that whilst we enjoy the remotest products of the north and south, we are free from those extremities of weather which give them birth; that our eyes are refreshed with the green fields of Britain, at the same time that our palates are feasted with fruits that rise between the tropics. 6

For these reasons there are not more useful members in a 7

THE ROYAL EXCHANGE

commonwealth than merchants. They knit mankind together in a mutual intercourse of good offices, distribute the gifts of nature, find work for the poor, add wealth to the rich, and magnificence to the great. Our English merchant converts the tin of his own country into gold, and exchanges his wool for rubies. The Mahometans are clothed in our British manufacture, and the inhabitants of the frozen zone warmed with the fleeces of our sheep.

When I have been upon the 'Change, I have often fancied one 8 of our old kings standing in person, where he is represented in effigy, and looking down upon the wealthy concourse of people with which that place is every day filled. In this case, how would he be surprized to hear all the languages of Europe spoken in this little spot of his former dominions, and to see so many private men, who in his time would have been the vassals of some powerful baron, negotiating like princes for greater sums of money than were formerly to be met with in the royal treasury! Trade, without enlarging the British territories, has given us a kind of additional empire: it has multiplied the number of the rich, made our landed estates infinitely more valuable than they were formerly, and added to them an accession of other estates as valuable as the lands themselves.

QUESTIONS

1. How is Addison's description of himself as a "citizen of the world" and "lover of mankind" reflected in his attitude toward the Royal Exchange?

2. What is Addison's opinion about merchants? About capitalism? About colonialism? About internationalism?

3. Locate and define these words as they would have been used in Addison's time: *high-change* (paragraph 1); *grimace* (paragraph 2); *Philippick Islands* (paragraph 4); *tippet* (paragraph 4); *concourse* (paragraph 8). Even though these words are out of date, can they be used in contemporary contexts? Try using them in sentences.

4. What words and phrases in the first paragraph set the tone of the essay? How do sentence balance and parallel structure affect the tone? Find other examples of balance and parallel structure in the essay.

5. Show the structural function of Addison's extended metaphor of the Royal Exchange as a "grand scene of business." To what extent is the Royal Exchange itself a symbol? Explain.

6. What types of illustration does Addison use to advance his thesis?

7. Describe the strength or weakness of Addison's logic in paragraphs 4 to 7.

8. What techniques of development appear in Addison's concluding paragraph?

9. Why might Addison be termed a forerunner of today's business booster? What traits does he share with today's apostles of business?

10. Focus on a cultural landmark—the Empire State Building, the Stock Exchange, Golden Gate Park, the Astrodome—and write a speculative essay about it in the manner of Addison.

E. B. WHITE

Once More to the Lake

Elwyn Brooks White (1899–   ), perhaps the finest contemporary American essayist, is at his most distinctive in his treatments of people and nature. A recipient of the National Medal for Literature, and associated for years with *The New Yorker,* White is the author of *One Man's Meat* (1942), *Here Is New York* (1949), and *The Second Tree from the Corner* (1954), among numerous works. He is also one of the most talented writers of literature for children, the author of *Stuart Little* (1945), *Charlotte's Web* (1952), and *The Trumpet of the Swan* (1970). In this essay, White combines narration and description to render a poignant and vivid statement about past and present, youth and age, life and death.

ne summer, along about 1904, my father rented a camp on a lake in Maine and took us all there for the month of August. We all got ringworm from some kittens and had to rub Pond's Extract on our arms and legs night and morning, and my father rolled over in a canoe with all his clothes on; but outside of that the vacation was a success and from then on none of us ever thought there was any place in the world like that lake in Maine. We returned summer after summer—always on August 1st for one month. I have since become a salt-water man, but sometimes in summer there are days when the restlessness of the tides and the fearful cold of the sea water and the incessant wind which blows across the afternoon and into the evening make me wish for the placidity of a lake in the woods. A few weeks ago this feeling got so

 ONCE MORE TO THE LAKE

strong I bought myself a couple of bass hooks and a spinner and returned to the lake where we used to go, for a week's fishing and to revisit old haunts.

I took along my son, who had never had any fresh water up 2 his nose and who had seen lily pads only from train windows. On the journey over to the lake I began to wonder what it would be like. I wondered how time would have marred this unique, this holy spot—the coves and streams, the hills that the sun set behind, the camps and the paths behind the camps. I was sure the tarred road would have found it out and I wondered in what other ways it would be desolated. It is strange how much you can remember about places like that once you allow your mind to return into the grooves which lead back. You remember one thing, and that suddenly reminds you of another thing. I guess I remembered clearest of all the early mornings, when the lake was cool and motionless, remembered how the bedroom smelled of the lumber it was made of and of the wet woods whose scent entered through the screen. The partitions in the camp were thin and did not extend clear to the top of the rooms, and as I was always the first up I would dress softly so as not to wake the others, and sneak out into the sweet outdoors and start out in the canoe, keeping close along the shore in the long shadows of the pines. I remembered being very careful never to rub my paddle against the gunwale for fear of disturbing the stillness of the cathedral.

The lake had never been what you would call a wild lake. 3 There were cottages sprinkled around the shores, and it was in farming country although the shores of the lake were quite heavily wooded. Some of the cottages were owned by nearby farmers, and you would live at the shore and eat your meals at the farmhouse. That's what our family did. But although it wasn't wild, it was a fairly large and undisturbed lake and there were places in it which, to a child at least, seemed infinitely remote and primeval.

I was right about the tar: it led to within half a mile of the 4 shore. But when I got back there, with my boy, and we settled into a camp near a farmhouse and into the kind of summertime I had known, I could tell that it was going to be pretty much the same as it had been before—I knew it, lying in bed the first morning, smelling the bedroom, and hearing the boy sneak quietly out and go off along the shore in a boat. I began to sustain the illusion that he was I, and therefore, by simple transposition, that I was my father. This sensation persisted, kept cropping up all the time we were there. It was not an entirely new feeling, but in this setting it grew much stronger. I seemed to be living a dual existence. I would be in the middle of some simple act, I would be picking up a bait box or laying down a table fork, or I would be saying something, and suddenly it would be not I

E. B. WHITE

but my father who was saying the words or making the gesture. It gave me a creepy sensation.

We went fishing the first morning. I felt the same damp moss covering the worms in the bait can, and saw the dragonfly alight on the tip of my rod as it hovered a few inches from the surface of the water. It was the arrival of this fly that convinced me beyond any doubt that everything was as it always had been, that the years were a mirage and there had been no years. The small waves were the same, chucking the rowboat under the chin as we fished at anchor, and the boat was the same boat, the same color green and the ribs broken in the same place, and under the floor-boards the same fresh-water leavings and débris—the dead hellgrammite, the wisps of moss, the rusty discarded fishhook, the dried blood from yesterday's catch. We stared silently at the tips of our rods, at the dragonflies that came and went. I lowered the tip of mine into the water, tentatively, pensively dislodging the fly, which darted two feet away, poised, darted two feet back, and came to rest again a little farther up the rod. There had been no years between the ducking of this dragonfly and the other one—the one that was part of memory. I looked at the boy, who was silently watching his fly, and it was my hands that held his rod, my eyes watching. I felt dizzy and didn't know which rod I was at the end of. 5

We caught two bass, hauling them in briskly as though they were mackerel, pulling them over the side of the boat in a business-like manner without any landing net, and stunning them with a blow on the back of the head. When we got back for a swim before lunch, the lake was exactly where we had left it, the same number of inches from the dock, and there was only the merest suggestion of a breeze. This seemed an utterly enchanted sea, this lake you could leave to its own devices for a few hours and come back to, and find that it had not stirred, this constant and trustworthy body of water. In the shallows, the dark, water-soaked sticks and twigs, smooth and old, were undulating in clusters on the bottom against the clean ribbed sand, and the track of the mussel was plain. A school of minnows swam by, each minnow with its small individual shadow, doubling the attendance, so clear and sharp in the sunlight. Some of the other campers were in swimming, along the shore, one of them with a cake of soap, and the water felt thin and clear and unsubstantial. Over the years there had been this person with the cake of soap, this cultist, and here he was. There had been no years. 6

Up to the farmhouse to dinner through the teeming, dusty field, the road under our sneakers was only a two-track road. The middle track was missing, the one with the marks of the hooves and the splotches of dried, flaky manure. There had always been three tracks to choose from in choosing which track to walk in; now the 7 choice was narrowed down to two. For a moment I missed terribly the middle alternative. But the way led past the tennis court, and something about the way it lay there in the sun reassured me; the tape had loosened along the backline, the alleys were green with plaintains and other weeds, and the net (installed in June and removed in September) sagged in the dry noon, and the whole place steamed with midday heat and hunger and emptiness. There was a choice of pie for dessert, and one was blueberry and one was apple, and the waitresses were the same country girls, there having been no passage of time, only the illusion of it as in a dropped curtain—the waitresses were still fifteen; their hair had been washed, that was the only difference—they had been to the movies and seen the pretty girls with the clean hair.

Summertime, oh summertime, pattern of life indelible, the 8 fade-proof lake, the woods unshatterable, the pasture with the sweetfern and the juniper forever and ever, summer without end; this was the background, and the life along the shore was the design, the cottagers with their innocent and tranquil design, their tiny docks with the flagpole and the American flag floating against the white clouds in the blue sky, the little paths over the roots of the trees leading from camp to camp and the paths leading back to the outhouses and the can of lime for sprinkling, and at the souvenir counters at the store the miniature birch-bark canoes and the post cards that showed things looking a little better than they looked. This was the American family at play, escaping the city heat, wondering whether the newcomers in the camp at the head of the cove were "common" or "nice," wondering whether it was true that the people who drove up for Sunday dinner at the farmhouse were turned away because there wasn't enough chicken.

It seemed to me, as I kept remembering all this, that those 9 times and those summers had been infinitely precious and worth saving. There had been jollity and peace and goodness. The arriving (at the beginning of August) had been so big a business in itself, at the railway station the farm wagon drawn up, the first smell of the pine-laden air, the first glimpse of the smiling farmer, and the great importance of the trunks and your father's enormous authority in such matters, and the feel of the wagon under you for the long ten-mile haul, and at the top of the last long hill catching the first view of the lake after eleven months of not seeing this cherished body of water. The shouts and cries of the other campers when they saw you, and the trunks to be unpacked, to give up their rich burden. (Arriving was less exciting nowadays, when you sneaked up in your car and parked it under a tree near the camp and took out the bags and in five minutes it was all over, no fuss, no loud wonderful fuss about trunks.)

96

E. B. WHITE

Peace and goodness and jollity. The only thing that was 10
wrong now, really, was the sound of the place, an unfamiliar nervous
sound of the outboard motors. This was the note that jarred, the one
thing that would sometimes break the illusion and set the years
moving. In those other summertimes all motors were inboard; and
when they were at a little distance, the noise they made was a
sedative, an ingredient of summer sleep. They were one-cylinder and
two-cylinder engines, and some were make-and-break and some
were jump-spark, but they all made a sleepy sound across the lake.
The one-lungers throbbed and fluttered, and the twin-cylinder ones
purred and purred, and that was a quiet sound too. But now the
campers all had outboards. In the daytime, in the hot mornings, these
motors made a petulant, irritable sound; at night, in the still evening
when the afterglow lit the water, they whined about one's ears like
mosquitoes. My boy loved our rented outboard, and his great desire
was to achieve singlehanded mastery over it, and authority, and he
soon learned the trick of choking it a little (but not too much), and the
adjustment of the needle valve. Watching him I would remember the
things you could do with the old one-cylinder engine with the heavy
flywheel, how you could have it eating out of your hand if you got
really close to it spiritually. Motor boats in those days didn't have
clutches, and you would make a landing by shutting off the motor at
the proper time and coasting in with a dead rudder. But there was a
way of reversing them, if you learned the trick, by cutting the switch
and putting it on again exactly on the final dying revolution of the
flywheel, so that it would kick back against compression and begin
reversing. Approaching a dock in a strong following breeze, it was
difficult to slow up sufficiently by the ordinary coasting method, and
if a boy felt he had complete mastery over his motor, he was tempted
to keep it running beyond its time and then reverse it a few feet from
the dock. It took a cool nerve, because if you threw the switch a
twentieth of a second too soon you would catch the flywheel when it
still had speed enough to go up past center, and the boat would leap
ahead, charging bull-fashion at the dock.

We had a good week at the camp. The bass were biting well 11
and the sun shone endlessly, day after day. We would be tired at
night and lie down in the accumulated heat of the little bedrooms
after the long hot day and the breeze would stir almost imperceptibly
outside and the smell of the swamp drift in through the rusty screens.
Sleep would come easily and in the morning the red squirrel would be
on the roof, tapping out his gay routine. I kept remembering
everything, lying in bed in the mornings—the small steamboat that
had a long rounded stern like the lip of a Ubangi, and how quietly she
ran on the moonlight sails, when the older boys played their
mandolins and the girls sang and we ate doughnuts dipped in sugar,

ONCE MORE TO THE LAKE 97

and how sweet the music was on the water in the shining night, and what it had felt like to think about girls then. After breakfast we would go up to the store and the things were in the same place—the minnows in a bottle, the plugs and spinners disarranged and pawed over by the youngsters from the boys' camp, the fig newtons and the Beeman's gum. Outside, the road was tarred and cars stood in front of the store. Inside, all was just as it had always been, except there was more Coca-Cola and not so much Moxie and root beer and birch beer and sarsaparilla. We would walk out with a bottle of pop apiece and sometimes the pop would backfire up our noses and hurt. We explored the streams, quietly, where the turtles slid off the sunny logs and dug their way into the soft bottom; and we lay on the town wharf and fed worms to the tame bass. Everywhere we went I had trouble making out which was I, the one walking at my side, the one walking in my pants.

One afternoon while we were there at that lake a thunder- 12 storm came up. It was like the revival of an old melodrama that I had seen long ago with childish awe. The second-act climax of the drama of the electrical disturbance over a lake in America had not changed in any important respect. This was the big scene, still the big scene. The whole thing was so familiar, the first feeling of oppression and heat and a general air around camp of not wanting to go very far away. In midafternoon (it was all the same) a curious darkening of the sky, and a lull in everything that had made life tick; and then the way the boats suddenly swung the other way at their moorings with the coming of a breeze out of the new quarter, and the premonitory rumble. Then the kettle drum, then the snare, then the bass drum and cymbals, then crackling light against the dark, and the gods grinning and licking their chops in the hills. Afterward the calm, the rain steadily rustling in the calm lake, the return of light and hope and spirits, and the campers running out in joy and relief to go swimming in the rain, their bright cries perpetuating the deathless joke about how they were getting simply drenched, and the children screaming with delight at the new sensation of bathing in the rain, and the joke about getting drenched linking the generations in a strong industructible chain. And the comedian who waded in carrying an umbrella.

When the others went swimming my son said he was going 13 in too. He pulled his dripping trunks from the line where they had hung all through the shower, and wrung them out. Languidly, and with no thought of going in, I watched him, his hard little body, skinny and bare, saw him wince slightly as he pulled up around his vitals the small, soggy, icy garment. As he buckled the swollen belt suddenly my groin felt the chill of death.

E. B. WHITE

QUESTIONS

1. What motivates White to return to the lake in Maine? Explain the "simple transposition" that he mentions in paragraph 4. List the illustrations that he gives of this phenomenon. What change does he detect in the lake?

2. Explain the significance of White's last sentence. Where are there foreshadowings of this statement?

3. Describe the author's use of figurative language in paragraphs 2, 10, and 12.

4. Identify those words and phrases that White invokes to establish the sense of mystery about the lake. Why are these words and their connotations important to the nature of the illusion that he describes?

5. Explain the organization of the essay in terms of the following paragraph units: 1 to 4; 5 to 7; 8 to 10; 11 to 13. Explain the function of paragraphs 8 and 12.

6. There are many vivid and unusual descriptive details in this essay—for example, the dragonfly in paragraph 2 and the two-track road in paragraph 7. How does White create symbolic overtones for these descriptive details and others? Why is the lake itself a complex symbol? Explain with reference to paragraph 6.

7. Describe the persona that White creates for himself in the essay. How does this persona function?

8. What is the relation between the introductory and concluding paragraphs, specifically in terms of irony of statement?

9. Discuss the type of nostalgia that White describes in "Once More to the Lake." What are the beauties and the dangers of nostalgia? Can the past ever be recaptured or relived? Justify your answer.

10. Write a descriptive account of a return to a favorite location and of your reaction to the experience. Explore the interrelationship of past and present.

GEORGE ORWELL

Marrakech

George Orwell (1903–1950) was the pseudonym of Eric Blair, an English novelist, essayist, and journalist. Orwell served with the Indian Imperial Police from 1922 to 1927 in Burma, fought in the Spanish Civil War, and acquired from his experiences a disdain of totalitarian and imperialistic systems. This attitude is reflected in the satiric fable *Animal Farm* (1945) and in his bleak, futuristic novel, *1984* (1949). In the following essay, Orwell depicts vividly third world poverty, and criticizes colonial responses to it.

A s the corpse went past the flies left the restaurant 1 table in a cloud and rushed after it, but they came back a few minutes later.

The little crowd of mourners—all men and boys, 2 no women—threaded their way across the market-place between the piles of pomegranates and the taxis and the camels, wailing a short chant over and over again. What really appeals to the flies is that the corpses here are never put into coffins, they are merely wrapped in a piece of rag and carried on a rough wooden bier on the shoulders of four friends. When the friends get to the burying-ground they hack an oblong hole a foot or two deep, dump the body in it and fling over it a little of the dried-up, lumpy earth, which is like broken brick. Nogravestone, no name, no identifying mark of any kind. The burying-ground is merely a huge waste of hummocky earth, like a derelict building-lot. After a month or two no one can even be certain where his own relatives are buried.

When you walk through a town like this—two hundred 3 thousand inhabitants, of whom at least twenty thousand own literally nothing except the rags they stand up in—when you see how people live, and still more how easily they die, it is always difficult to believe that you are walking among human beings. All colonial empires are in reality founded upon that fact. The people have brown faces— besides, there are so many of them! Are they really the same flesh as yourself? Do they even have names? Or are they merely a kind of undifferentiated brown stuff, about as individual as bees or coral insects? They rise out of the earth, they sweat and starve for a few years, and then they sink back into the nameless mounds of the graveyard and nobody notices that they are gone. And even the graves themselves soon fade back into the soil. Sometimes, out for a walk, as you break your way through the prickly pear, you notice that it is rather bumpy underfoot, and only a certain regularity in the bumps tells you that you are walking over skeletons.

I was feeding one of the gazelles in the public gardens. 4

Gazelles are almost the only animals that look good to eat 5 when they are still alive, in fact, one can hardly look at their hindquarters without thinking of mint sauce. The gazelle I was feeding seemed to know that this thought was in my mind, for though it took the piece of bread I was holding out it obviously did

GEORGE ORWELL

not like me. It nibbled rapidly at the bread, then lowered its head and tried to butt me, then took another nibble and then butted again. Probably its idea was that if it could drive me away the bread would somehow remain hanging in mid-air.

An Arab navvy working on the path nearby lowered his 6 heavy hoe and sidled towards us. He looked from the gazelle to the bread and from the bread to the gazelle, with a sort of quiet amazement, as though he had never seen anything quite like this before. Finally he said shyly in French:

"I could eat some of that bread." 7

I tore off a piece and he stowed it gratefully in some secret 8 place under his rags. This man is an employee of the Municipality.

When you go through the Jewish quarters you gather some 9 idea of what the medieval ghettoes were probably like. Under their Moorish rulers the Jews were only allowed to own land in certain restricted areas, and after centuries of this kind of treatment they have ceased to bother about overcrowding. Many of the streets are a good deal less than six feet wide, the houses are completely window- less, and sore-eyed children cluster everywhere in unbelievable numbers, like clouds of flies. Down the centre of the street there is generally running a little river of urine.

In the bazaar huge families of Jews, all dressed in the long 10 black robe and little black skull-cap, are working in dark fly-infested booths that look like caves. A carpenter sits cross-legged at a prehistoric lathe, turning chair-legs at lightning speed. He works the lathe with a bow in his right hand and guides the chisel with his left foot, and thanks to a lifetime of sitting in this position his left leg is warped out of shape. At his side his grandson, aged six, is already starting on the simpler parts of the job.

I was just passing the coppersmiths' booths when somebody 11 noticed that I was lighting a cigarette. Instantly, from the dark holes all round, there was a frenzied rush of Jews, many of them old grandfathers with flowing grey beards, all clamouring for a cigarette. Even a blind man somewhere at the back of one of the booths heard a rumour of cigarettes and came crawling out, groping in the air with his hand. In about a minute I had used up the whole packet. None of these people, I suppose, works less than twelve hours a day, and every one of them looks on a cigarette as a more or less impossible luxury.

As the Jews live in self-contained communities they follow 12 the same trades as the Arabs, except for agriculture. Fruit-sellers, potters, silversmiths, blacksmiths, butchers, leather-workers, tailors, water-carriers, beggars, porters—whichever way you look you see nothing but Jews. As a matter of fact there are thirteen thousand of them, all living in the space of a few acres. A good job Hitler isn't here. Perhaps he is on his way, however. You hear the usual dark rumours about the Jews, not only from the Arabs but from the poorer Europeans.

"Yes, *mon vieux*, they took my job away from me and gave it 13 to a Jew. The Jews! They're the real rulers of this country, you know. They've got all the money. They control the banks, finance— everything."

"But," I said, "isn't it a fact that the average Jew is a labourer 14 working for about a penny an hour?"

"Ah, that's only for show! They're all moneylenders really. 15 They're cunning, the Jews."

In just the same way, a couple of hundred years ago, poor old 16 women used to be burned for witchcraft when they could not even work enough magic to get themselves a square meal.

All people who work with their hands are partly invisible, 17 and the more important the work they do, the less visible they are. Still, a white skin is always fairly conspicuous. In northern Europe, when you see a labourer ploughing a field, you probably give him a second glance. In a hot country, anywhere south of Gibraltar or east of Suez, the chances are that you don't even see him. I have noticed this again and again. In a tropical landscape one's eye takes in everything except the human beings. It takes in the dried-up soil, the prickly pear, the palm-tree and the distant mountain, but it always misses the peasant hoeing at his patch. He is the same colour as the earth, and a great deal less interesting to look at.

It is only because of this that the starved countries of Asia and 18 Africa are accepted as tourist resorts. No one would think of running cheap trips to the Distressed Areas. But where the human beings have brown skins their poverty is simply not noticed. What does Morocco mean to a Frenchman? An orange-grove or a job in govern- ment service. Or to an Englishman? Camels, castles, palm-trees, Foreign Legionnaires, brass trays and bandits. One could probably live here for years without noticing that for nine-tenths of the people the reality of life is an endless, back-breaking struggle to wring a little food out of an eroded soil.

Most of Morocco is so desolate that no wild animal bigger 19 than a hare can live on it. Huge areas which were once covered with forest have turned into a treeless waste where the soil is exactly like broken-up brick. Nevertheless a good deal of it is cultivated, with frightful labour. Everything is done by hand. Long lines of women, bent double like inverted capital Ls, work their way slowly across the fields, tearing up the prickly weeds with their hands, and the peasant gathering lucerne for fodder pulls it up stalk by stalk instead of reaping it, thus saving an inch or two on each stalk. The plough is a wretched wooden thing, so frail that one can easily carry it on one's shoulder, and fitted underneath with a rough iron spike which stirs the soil to a depth of about four inches. This is as much as the strength of the animals is equal to. It is usual to plough with a cow and a donkey yoked together. Two donkeys would not be quite strong enough, but on the other hand two cows would cost a little more to feed. The peasants possess no harrows, they merely plough the soil several times over in different directions, finally leaving it in rough furrows, after which the whole field has to be shaped with hoes into small oblong patches, to conserve water. Except for a day or two after the rare rainstorms there is never enough water. Along the edges of the fields channels are hacked out to a depth of thirty or forty feet to get at the tiny trickles which run through the subsoil.

Every afternoon a file of very old women passes down the road outside my house, each carrying a load of firewood. All of them are mummified with age and the sun, and all of them are tiny. It seems to be generally the case in primitive communities that the women, when they get beyond a certain age, shrink to the size of children. One day a poor old creature who could not have been more than four feet tall crept past me under a vast load of wood. I stopped her and put a five-sou piece (a little more than a farthing) into her hand. She answered with a shrill wail, almost a scream, which was partly gratitude but mainly surprise. I suppose that from her point of view, by taking any notice of her, I seemed almost to be violating a law of nature. She accepted her status as an old woman, that is to say as a beast of burden. When a family is travelling it is quite usual to see a father and a grown-up son riding ahead on donkeys, and an old woman following on foot, carrying the baggage. 20

But what is strange about these people is their invisibility. For several weeks, always at about the same time of day, the file of old women had hobbled past the house with their firewood, and though they had registered themselves on my eyeballs I cannot truly say that I had seen them. Firewood was passing—that was how I saw it. It was only that one day I happened to be walking behind them, and the curious up-and-down motion of a load of wood drew my attention to the human being underneath it. Then for the first time I noticed the poor old earth-coloured bodies, bodies reduced to bones and leathery skin, bent double under the crushing weight. Yet I suppose I had not been five minutes on Moroccan soil before I noticed the overloading of the donkeys and was infuriated by it. There is no question that the donkeys are damnably treated. The Moroccan donkey is hardly bigger than a St. Bernard dog, it carries a load which in the British army would be considered too much for a fifteen-hands mule, and very often its pack-saddle is not taken off its back for weeks together. But what is peculiarly pitiful is that it is the most willing creature on earth, it follows its master like a dog and does not need either bridle 21 or halter. After a dozen years of devoted work it suddenly drops dead, whereupon its master tips it into the ditch and the village dogs have torn its guts out before it is cold.

22   This kind of thing makes one's blood boil, whereas—on the whole—the plight of the human beings does not. I am not commenting, merely pointing to a fact. People with brown skins are next door to invisible. Anyone can be sorry for the donkey with its galled back, but it is generally owing to some kind of accident if one even notices the old woman under her load of sticks.

23   As the storks flew northward the Negroes were marching southward—a long, dusty column, infantry, screw-gun batteries and then more infantry, four or five thousand men in all, winding up the road with a clumping of boots and a clatter of iron wheels.

24   They were Senegalese, the blackest Negroes in Africa, so black that sometimes it is difficult to see whereabouts on their necks the hair begins. Their splendid bodies were hidden in reach-me-down khaki uniforms, their feet squashed into boots that looked like blocks of wood, and every tin hat seemed to be a couple of sizes too small. It was very hot and the men had marched a long way. They slumped under the weight of their packs and the curiously sensitive black faces were glistening with sweat.

25   As they went past a tall, very young Negro turned and caught my eye. But the look he gave me was not in the least the kind of look you might expect. Not hostile, not contemptuous, not sullen, not even inquisitive. It was the shy, wide-eyed Negro look, which actually is a look of profound respect. I saw how it was. This wretched boy, who is a French citizen and has therefore been dragged from the forest to scrub floors and catch syphilis in garrison towns, actually has feelings of reverence before a white skin. He has been taught that the white race are his masters, and he still believes it.

26   But there is one thought which every white man (and in this connection it doesn't matter twopence if he calls himself a Socialist) thinks when he sees a black army marching past. "How much longer can we go on kidding these people? How long before they turn their guns in the other direction?"

27   It was curious, really. Every white man there has this thought stowed somewhere or other in his mind. I had it, so had the other onlookers, so had the officers on their sweating chargers and the white NCOs marching in the ranks. It was a kind of secret which we all knew and were too clever to tell; only the Negroes didn't know it. And really it was almost like watching a flock of cattle to see the long column, a mile or two miles of armed men, flowing peacefully up the road, while the great white birds drifted over them in the opposite direction, glittering like scraps of paper.

QUESTIONS

1. Describe the major scenes that Orwell develops to render his impression of Marrakech. What relationships do you perceive among the scenes? What dominant impression emerges from the presentation of scenes?

2. What is Orwell's attitude toward the misery he describes? What does he say about certain foreign responses to misery and poverty?

3. Orwell uses both subjective and objective language in this essay. Cite examples of both. Why does he combine these two modes? What effect is created?

4. Locate and evaluate Orwell's use of similes, juxtaposed imagery, personification, and onomatopoeia in the essay.

5. How does Orwell's short initial paragraph set the stage for the entire essay?

6. Analyze Orwell's technique of juxtaposition in the presentation of major paragraph units in the essay. What is the effect of his decision not to provide normal transitions between major segments? How are the segments related in terms of theme, tone, and mood? Is there final essay coherence? Why or why not?

7. How does Orwell's persistent use of contrasting elements relate to his treatment of characterization? How does characterization relate to animal life?

8. Account for paragraphs 3, 8, 16, 22, and 27 in terms of their antecedents.

9. Orwell states that it is easy to ignore glaring poverty and to pretend that the poor and exploited do not exist. What explains this behavior? Offer your own examples to confirm or refute it.

10. Write a descriptive essay illuminating your personal encounter with poverty, as you have either observed or experienced it.

PHYLLIS McGINLEY

Suburbia: Of Thee I Sing

Phyllis McGinley (1905–   ) is a Canadian-born essayist, author of children's literature, and poet who lives in the United States. Noted in both her poetry and prose for wit and lightness of tone, McGinley has written that "in times of unrest and fear it is perhaps [the writer's] duty to celebrate, to single out some of the values we can cherish, to talk about some of the few warm things we know in a cold world." In this essay from *The Province of the Heart* (1959), she offers a response to the numerous critics and satirists of suburban living.

wenty miles east of New York City as the New Haven   1
Railroad flies sits a village I shall call Spruce Manor. The Boston Post Road, there, for the length of two blocks, becomes Main Street, and on one side of that thundering thoroughfare are the grocery stores and the drug stores and the Village Spa where teen-agers gather of an afternoon to drink their cokes and speak their curious confidences. There one finds the shoe repairers and the dry cleaners and the second-hand stores which sell "antiques" and the stationery stores which dispense comic books to ten-year-olds and greeting cards and lending library masterpieces to their mothers. On the opposite side stand the bank, the fire house, the public library. The rest of this town of perhaps four or five thousand people lies to the south and is bounded largely by Long Island Sound, curving protectively on three borders. The movie theater (dedicated to the showing of second-run, single-feature pictures) and the grade schools lie north, beyond the Post Road, and that is a source of worry to Spruce Manorites. They are always a little uneasy about the children, crossing, perhaps, before the lights are safely green. However, two excellent policemen—Mr. Crowley and Mr. Lang—station themselves at the intersections four times a day, and so far there have been no accidents.

Spruce Manor in the spring and summer and fall is a pretty   2
town, full of gardens and old elms. (There are few spruces, but the village Council is considering planting a few on the station plaza, out of sheer patriotism.) In the winter, the houses reveal themselves as comfortable, well-kept, architecturally insignificant. Then one can see the town for what it is and has been since it left off being farm and woodland some sixty years ago—the epitome of Suburbia, not the country and certainly not the city. It is a commuter's town, the living center of a web which unrolls each morning as the men swing aboard the locals, and contracts again in the evening when they return. By day, with even the children pent in schools, it is a village of women. They trundle mobile baskets at the A&P, they sit under driers at the hairdressers, they sweep their porches and set out bulbs and stitch up slip covers. Only on weekends does it become heterogeneous and lively, the parking places difficult to find.

Spruce Manor has no country club of its own, though   3
devoted golfers have their choice of two or three not far away. It does

PHYLLIS McGINLEY

have a small yacht club and a beach which can be used by anyone who rents or owns a house here. The village supports a little park with playground equipment and a counselor, where children, unattended by parents, can spend summer days if they have no more pressing engagements.

It is a town not wholly without traditions. Residents will point out the two-hundred-year-old manor house, now a minor museum; and in the autumn they line the streets on a scheduled evening to watch the Volunteer Firemen parade. That is a fine occasion, with so many heads of households marching in their red blouses and white gloves, some with flaming helmets, some swinging lanterns, most of them genially out of step. There is a bigger parade on Memorial Day with more marchers than watchers and with the Catholic priest, the rabbi, and the Protestant ministers each delivering a short prayer when the paraders gather near the War Memorial. On the whole, however, outside of contributing generously to the Community Chest, Manorites are not addicted to municipal get-togethers. 4

No one is very poor here and not many families rich enough to be awesome. In fact, there is not much to distinguish Spruce Manor from any other of a thousand suburbs outside of New York City or San Francisco or Detroit or Chicago or even Stockholm, for that matter. Except for one thing. For some reason, Spruce Manor has become a sort of symbol to writers and reporters familiar only with its name or trivial aspects. It has become a symbol of all that is middle-class in the worst sense, of settled-downness or rootlessness, according to what the writer is trying to prove; of smug and prosperous mediocrity—or even, in more lurid novels, of lechery at the country club and Sunday morning hangovers. 5

To condemn Suburbia has long been a literary cliché, anyhow. I have yet to read a book in which the suburban life was pictured as the good life or the commuter as a sympathetic figure. He is nearly as much a stock character as the old stage Irishman: the man who "spends his life riding to and from his wife," the eternal Babbitt who knows all about Buicks and nothing about Picasso, whose sanctuary is the club locker room, whose ideas spring ready-made from the illiberal newspapers. His wife plays politics at the P.T.A. and keeps up with the Joneses. Or—if the scene is more gilded and less respectable—the commuter is the high-powered advertising executive with a station wagon and an eye for the ladies, his wife a restless baggage given to too many cocktails in the afternoon. 6

These clichés I challenge. I have lived in the country, I have lived in the city. I have lived in an average Middle Western small town. But for the best eleven years of my life I have lived in Suburbia and I like it. 7

"Compromise!" cried our friends when we came here from   8
an expensive, inconvenient, moderately fashionable tenement in
Manhattan. It was the period in our lives when everyone was moving
somewhere. Farther uptown, farther downtown, across town to
Sutton Place, to a half-dozen rural acres in Connecticut or New Jersey
or even Vermont. But no one in our rather rarefied little group was
thinking of moving to the suburbs except us. They were aghast that
we could find anything appealing in the thought of a middle-class
house on a middle-class street in a middle-class village full of
middle-class people. That we were tired of town and hoped for
children, that we couldn't afford both a city apartment and a farm,
they put down as feeble excuses. To this day they cannot understand
us. You see, they read the books. They even write them.

Compromise? Of course we compromise. But compromise, if   9
not the spice of life, is its solidity. It is what makes nations great and
marriages happy and Spruce Manor the pleasant place it is. As for its
being middle-class, what is wrong with acknowledging one's roots?
And how free we are! Free of the city's noise, of its ubiquitous
doormen, of the soot on the windowsill and the radio in the next
apartment. We have released ourselves from the seasonal hegira to
the mountains or the seashore. We have only one address, one house
to keep supplied with paring knives and blankets. We are free from
the snows that block the countryman's roads in winter and his
electricity which always goes off in a thunderstorm. I do not insist
that we are typical. There is nothing really typical about any of our
friends and neighbors here, and therein lies my point. The true
suburbanite needs to conform less than anyone else; much less than
the gentleman farmer with his remodeled salt-box or than the
determined cliff dweller with his necessity for living at the right
address. In Spruce Manor all addresses are right. And since we are
fairly numerous here, we need not fall back on the people nearest us
for total companionship. There is not here, as in a small city away
from truly urban centers, some particular family whose codes must
be ours. And we could not keep up with the Joneses even if we
wanted to, for we know many Joneses and they are all quite different
people leading the most various lives.

The Albert Joneses spend their weekends sailing, the Bertram   10
Joneses cultivate their delphinium, the Clarence Joneses—Clarence
being a handy man with a cello—are enthusiastic about amateur
chamber music. The David Joneses dote on bridge, but neither of the
Ernest Joneses understands it, and they prefer staying home of an
evening so that Ernest Jones can carve his witty caricatures out of
pieces of old fruit wood. We admire each other's gardens, applaud
each other's sailing records; we are too busy to compete. So long as
our clapboards are painted and our hedges decently trimmed, we

PHYLLIS McGINLEY

have fulfilled our community obligations. We can live as anonymously as in a city or we can call half the village by their first names.

On our half-acre or three-quarters, we can raise enough tomatoes for our salads and assassinate enough beetles to satisfy the gardening urge. Or we can buy our vegetables at the store and put the whole place to lawn without feeling that we are neglecting our property. We can have privacy and shade and the changing of the seasons and also the Joneses next door from whom to borrow a cup of sugar or a stepladder. Despite the novelists, the shadow of the country club rests lightly on us. Half of us wouldn't be found dead with a golf stick in our hands, and loathe Saturday dances. Few of us expect to be deliriously wealthy or world-famous or divorced. What we do expect is to pay off the mortgage and send our healthy children to good colleges. 11

For when I refer to life here, I think, of course, of living with children. Spruce Manor without children would be a paradox. The summer waters are full of them, gamboling like dolphins. The lanes are alive with them, the yards overflow with them, they possess the tennis courts and the skating pond and the vacant lots. Their roller skates wear down the asphalt, and their bicycles make necessary the twenty-five-mile speed limit. They converse interminably on the telephones and make rich the dentist and the pediatrician. Who claims that a child and a half is the American middle-class average? A nice medium Spruce Manor family runs to four or five, and we count proudly, but not with amazement, the many solid households running to six, seven, eight, nine, even up to twelve. Our houses here are big and not new, most of them, and there is a temptation to fill them up, let the décor fall where it may. 12

Besides, Spruce Manor seems designed by providence and town planning for the happiness of children. Better designed than the city; better, I say defiantly, than the country. Country mothers must be constantly arranging and contriving for their children's leisure time. There is no neighbor child next door for playmate, no school within walking distance. The ponds are dangerous to young swimmers, the woods full of poison ivy, the romantic dirt roads unsuitable for bicycles. An extra acre or two gives a fine sense of possession to an adult; it does not compensate children for the give-and-take of our village, where there is always a contemporary to help swing the skipping rope or put on the catcher's mitt. Where in the country is the Friday evening dancing class or the Saturday morning movie (approved by the P.T.A.)? It is the greatest fallacy of all time that children love the country as a year-around plan. Children would take a dusty corner of Washington Square or a city sidewalk, even, in preference to the lonely sermons in stones and books in running brooks which their contemporaries cannot share. 13

As for the horrors of bringing up progeny in the city, for all its   14
museums and other cultural advantages (so perfectly within reach of
suburban families if they feel strongly about it), they were summed
up for me one day last winter. The harried mother of one, speaking to
me on the telephone just after Christmas, sighed and said, "It's been
a really wonderful time for me, as vacations go. Barbara has had an
engagement with a child in our apartment house every afternoon this
week. I have had to take her almost nowhere." Barbara is eleven. For
six of those eleven years, I realized, her mother must have dreaded
Christmas vacation, not to mention spring, as a time when Barbara
had to be entertained. I thought thankfully of my own daughters
whom I had scarcely seen since school closed, out with their skis and
their sleds and their friends, sliding down the roped-off hill half a
block away, coming in hungrily for lunch and disappearing again,
hearty, amused, and safe—at least as safe as any sled-borne child can
be.

Spruce Manor is not Eden, of course. Our taxes are higher   15
than we like, and there is always that eight-eleven in the morning to
be caught, and we sometimes resent the necessity of rushing from a
theater to a train on a weekday evening. But the taxes pay for our
really excellent schools and for our garbage collections (so that the
pails of orange peels need not stand in the halls overnight as ours did
in the city) and for our water supply which does not give out every
dry summer as it frequently does in the country. As for the theaters—
they are twenty miles away and we don't get to them more than twice
a month. But neither, I think, do many of our friends in town. The
eight-eleven is rather a pleasant train, too, say the husbands; it gets
them to work in thirty-four minutes and they read the papers
restfully on the way.

"But the suburban mind!" cry our die-hard friends in Man-   16
hattan and Connecticut. "The suburban conversation! The monotony!" They imply that they and I must scintillate or we perish. Let me
anatomize Spruce Manor, for them and for the others who envision
Suburbia as a congregation of mindless housewives and amoral
go-getters.

From my window, now, on a June morning, I have a view. It   17
contains neither solitary hills nor dramatic skyscrapers. But I can see
my roses in bloom, and my foxglove, and an arch of trees over the
lane. I think comfortably of my friends whose houses line this and
other streets rather like it. Not one of them is, so far as I know, doing
any of the things that suburban ladies are popularly supposed to be
doing. One of them, I happen to know, has gone bowling for her
health and figure, but she had already tidied up her house and
arranged to be home before the boys return from school. Some,

undoubtedly, are ferociously busy in the garden. One lady is on her way to Ellis Island, bearing comfort and gifts to a Polish boy—a seventeen-year-old stowaway who did slave labor in Germany and was liberated by a cousin of hers during the war—who is being held for attempting to attain the land of which her cousin told him. The boy has been on the Island for three months. Twice a week she takes this tedious journey, meanwhile besieging courts and immigration authorities on his behalf. This lady has a large house, a part-time maid, and five children.

My friend around the corner is finishing her third novel. She 18 writes daily from nine-thirty until two. After that her son comes back from school and she plunges into maternity; at six, she combs her pretty hair, refreshes her lipstick, and is charming to her doctor husband. The village dancing school is run by another neighbor, as it has been for twenty years. She has sent a number of ballerinas on to the theatrical world as well as having shepherded for many a successful season the white-gloved little boys and full-skirted little girls through their first social tasks.

Some of the ladies are no doubt painting their kitchens or a 19 nursery; one of them is painting the portrait, on assignment, of a very distinguished personage. Some of them are nurses' aides and Red Cross workers and supporters of good causes. But all find time to be friends with their families and to meet the 5:32 five nights a week. They read something besides the newest historical novel, Braque is not unidentifiable to most of them, and their conversation is for the most part as agreeable as the tables they set. The tireless bridge players, the gossips, the women bored by their husbands live perhaps in our suburb, too. Let them. Our orbits need not cross.

And what of the husbands, industriously selling bonds or 20 practicing law or editing magazines or looking through microscopes or managing offices in the city? Do they spend their evenings and their weekends in the gaudy bars of Fifty-second Street? Or are they the perennial householders, their lives a dreary round of taking down screens and mending drains? Well, screens they have always with them, and a man who is good around the house can spend happy hours with the plumbing even on a South Sea island. Some of them cut their own lawns and some of them try to break par and some of them sail their little boats all summer with their families for crew. Some of them are village trustees for nothing a year and some listen to symphonies and some think Milton Berle ought to be President. There is a scientist who plays wonderful bebop, and an insurance salesman who has bought a big old house nearby and with his own hands is gradually tearing it apart and reshaping it nearer to his heart's desire. Some of them are passionate hedge-clippers and some read Plutarch for fun. But I do not know many—though there may be such—who either kiss their neighbor's wives behind doors or whose idea of sprightly talk is to tell you the plot of an old movie.

It is June, now, as I have said. This afternoon my daughters 21 will come home from school with a crowd of their peers at their heels. They will eat up the cookies and drink up the ginger ale and go down for a swim at the beach if the water is warm enough, that beach which is only three blocks away and open to all Spruce Manor. They will go unattended by me, since they have been swimming since they were four, and besides there are lifeguards and no big waves. (Even our piece of ocean is a compromise.) Presently it will be time for us to climb into our very old Studebaker—we are not car-proud in Spruce Manor—and meet the 5:32. That evening expedition is not vitally necessary, for a bus runs straight down our principal avenue from the station to the shore, and it meets all trains. But it is an event we enjoy. There is something delightfully ritualistic about the moment when the train pulls in and the men swing off, with the less sophisticated children running squealing to meet them. The women move over from the driver's seat, surrender the keys, and receive an absent-minded kiss. It is the sort of picture that wakes John Marquand screaming from his sleep. But, deluded people that we are, we do not realize how mediocre it all seems. We will eat our undistinguished meal, probably without even a cocktail to enliven it. We will drink our coffee at the table, not carry it into the living room; if a husband changes for dinner here it is into old and spotty trousers and more comfortable shoes. The children will then go through the regular childhood routine—complain about their homework, grumble about going to bed, and finally accomplish both ordeals. Perhaps later the Gerard Joneses will drop in. We will talk a great deal of unimportant chatter and compare notes on food prices; we will also discuss the headlines and disagree. (Some of us in the Manor are Republicans, some are Democrats, a few lean plainly leftward. There are probably anti-Semites and anti-Catholics and even anti-Americans. Most of us are merely anti-antis.) We will all have one highball, and the Joneses will leave early. Tomorrow and tomorrow and tomorrow the pattern will be repeated. This is Suburbia.

But I think that some day people will look back on our little 22 interval here, on our Spruce Manor way of life, as we now look back on the Currier and Ives kind of living, with nostalgia and respect. In a world of terrible extremes, it will stand out as the safe, important medium.

Suburbia, of thee I sing! 23

PHYLLIS McGINLEY

QUESTIONS

1. Describe the author's attitude toward suburbia. List the illustrations she provides to challenge the clichés about suburban life.

2. On the basis of the examples given in paragraph 10, what generalization can be made about the "Joneses"?

3. Explain the allusion in the title, and also the allusions to "the eternal Babbitt" (paragraph 6), John Marquand, and Shakespeare (paragraph 22).

4. Locate clichés used by the author. Can they be justified and, if so, how? What is their effect on the tone of the essay?

5. How does the author organize the introductory paragraph?

6. Locate the most concise statement of the thesis in the essay. How do the paragraphs preceding the thesis relate to it?

7. Does the author use patterned methods of comparison and contrast or more casual comparative techniques? Explain your answer.

8. Analyze paragraphs 16 to 23. How does the author achieve coherence in paragraphs 16 to 21? How does this unit prepare for the short concluding paragraphs?

9. How convincing is McGinley's argument? Are you persuaded by it, or do you consider it a weak defense? Justify your answer.

10. Write an essay praising the virtues (or criticizing the vices) of suburban, urban, or rural life.

JEAN-PAUL SARTRE

American Cities

Jean-Paul Sartre (1905–1980), French philosopher, novelist, and playwright, was the leading exponent of secular existentialism in the years after World War II. His leftist convictions and commitment to political action, expressed in *Les Temps Modernes,* a journal he and Simone de Beauvoir founded, had enormous impact in France. Similarly, his literary works influenced the antinovel and new wave cinema. His major writing includes *Nausea* (1938), *The Flies* (1943), *Being and Nothingness* (1943), *No Exit* (1945), and *The Condemned of Altona* (1960). The following selection, which Sartre wrote during a trip to the United States in 1945, elevates the travel essay into a critique of American culture.

For the first few days I was lost. My eyes were not 1 accustomed to the skyscrapers and they did not surprise me; they did not seem like man-made, man-inhabited constructions, but rather like rocks and hills, dead parts of the urban landscape one finds in cities built on a turbulent soil and which you pass without even noticing. At the same time, I was continually and vainly looking for something to catch my attention for a moment—a detail, a square, perhaps, or a public building. I did not yet know that these houses and streets should be seen in the mass.

In order to learn to live in these cities and to like them as 2 Americans do, I had to fly over the immense deserts of the west and south. Our European cities, submerged in human countrysides that have been worked over mile by mile, are continuous. And then we are vaguely aware that far away, across the sea, there is the desert, a myth. For the American, this myth is an everyday reality. We flew for hours between New Orleans and San Francisco, over an earth that was dry and red, clotted with verdigris bushes. Suddenly, a city, a little checkerboard flush with the ground, arose and then, again, the red earth, the Savannah, the twisted rocks of the Grand Canyon, and the snows of the Rocky Mountains.

After a few days of this diet, I came to understand that the 3 American city was, originally, a camp in the desert. People from far away, attracted by a mine, a petroleum field or fertile land, arrived one fine day and settled as quickly as possible in a clearing, near a river. They built the vital parts of the town, the bank, the town hall, the church, and then hundreds of one-storey frame houses. The road, if there was one, served as a kind of spinal column to the town, and then streets were marked out like vertebrae, perpendicular to the road. It would be hard to count the American cities that have that kind of parting in the middle.

Nothing has changed since the time of the covered wagons; 4 every year towns are founded in the United States, and they are founded according to the same methods.

Take Fontana, Tennessee, which is situated near one of the 5 great T.V.A. dams. Twelve years ago there were pine-trees growing in the mountain's red soil. As soon as the construction of the dam began, the pines were felled and three towns—two whites ones of 3000 and 5000 inhabitants each, and one Negro town—sprang from the soil. The workers live there with their families; four or five years ago, when work was in full swing, one birth was recorded each day. Half of the village looks like a pile-dwellers' community: the houses are of wood, with green roofs, and have been built on piles to avoid dampness. The other half is made of collapsible dwellings, "prefabricated houses." They too are of wood; they are constructed about 500 miles away and loaded onto trucks: a single team of men can set one up within four hours after its arrival. The smallest costs the employer two thousand dollars, and he rents them to his workers for nineteen dollars a month (thirty-one dollars if they are furnished). The interiors, with their mass-produced furniture, central heating, electric lamps, and refrigerators, remind one of ship cabins. Every square inch of these antiseptic little rooms has been utilized; the walls have clothes-presses and under the beds there are chests of drawers.

One leaves with a slightly depressed feeling, with the feeling   6 of having seen the careful, small-scale reconstitution of a 1944 flat in the year 3000. The moment one steps outside one sees hundreds of houses, all alike, piled up, squashed against the earth, but retaining in their very form some sort of nomadic look. It looks like a caravan graveyard. The pile-dweller community and the caravan cemetery face one another. Between them a wide road climbs toward the pines. There you have a city, or rather the nucleus of an American city, with all its essential parts. Below is the Woolworth's, higher up the hospital, and at the top, a "mixed" church in which what might be called a minimum service—that is, one valid for all creeds—is conducted.

The striking thing is the lightness, the fragility of these   7 buildings. The village has no weight, it seems barely to rest on the soil; it has not managed to leave a human imprint on the reddish earth and the dark forest; it is a temporary thing. And besides, it will soon take to the road; in two years the dam will be finished, the workers will leave, and the prefabricated houses will be taken down and sent to a Texas oil well or a Georgia cotton plantation, to reconstitute another Fontana, under other skies, with new inhabitants.

This roving village is no exception; in the United States,   8 communities are born as they die—in a day. The Americans have no complaint to make; the main thing is to be able to carry their homes with them. These homes are the collections of objects, furnishings, photographs, and souvenirs belonging to them, that reflect their own image and constitute the inner, living landscape of their dwellings. These are their penates. Like Aeneas, they haul them about everywhere.

The "house" is the shell; it is abandoned on the slightest   9 pretext.

We have workers' communities in France. But they are   10
sedentary, and then they never become real cities; on the contrary,
they are the artificial product of neighbouring cities. In America, just
as any citizen can theoretically become President, so each Fontana can
become Detroit or Minneapolis; all that is needed is a bit of luck. And
conversely, Detroit and Minneapolis are Fontanas which have had
luck. To take only one example: in 1905 Detroit had a population of
300,000. Its population is now 1,000,000.

The inhabitants of this city are perfectly aware of this luck;   11
they like to recall in their books and films the time when their
community was only an outpost. And that is why they pass so easily
from city to outpost; they make no distinction between the two.
Detroit and Minneapolis, Knoxville and Memphis were *born temporary*
and have stayed that way. They will never, of course, take to the road
again on the back of a truck. But they remain at the meeting point;
they have never reached an internal temperature of solidification.

Things that would not constitute a change of situation for us   12
are, for the American, occasions for real breaks with his past. There
are many who, on going off to war, have sold their apartments and
everything else, including their suits. What is the point of keeping
something that will be outmoded upon their return? Soldiers' wives
often reduce their scale of living and go to live more modestly in other
neighbourhoods. Thus, sadness and faithfulness to the absent are
marked by a removal.

The removals also indicate fluctuations in American fortunes.   13

It is customary, in the United States, for the fashionable   14
neighbourhoods to slide from the centre to the outskirts of the city;
after five years the centre of town is "polluted." If you walk about
there, you come upon tumble-down houses that retain a pretentious
look beneath their filth; you find a complicated kind of architecture,
one-storey frame houses with entrances formed by peristyles supported by columns, gothic chalets, "colonial houses," etc. These were
formerly aristocratic homes, now inhabited by the poor. Chicago's
lurid Negro section contains some of these Greco-Roman temples;
from the outside they still look well. But inside, twelve rat- and
louse-plagued Negro families are crowded together in five or six
rooms.

At the same time, changes are continually made within the   15
same place. An apartment house is bought to be demolished, and a
larger apartment house is built on the same plot. After five years, the
new house is sold to a contractor who tears it down to build a third
one. The result is that in the States a city is a moving landscape for its
inhabitants, whereas our cities are our shells.

In France, one hears only from very old people what a   16

forty-year-old American said to me in Chicago. "When I was young, this whole neighbourhood was taken up by a lake. But this part of the lake was filled in and built over." And a thirty-five-year-old lawyer who was showing me the Negro section said: "I was born here. Then it was a white section and, apart from servants, you would not have seen a Negro in the streets. Now the white people have left and 250,000 Negroes are crowded into their houses."

M. Verdier, the owner of the "City of Paris" department store 17 in San Francisco, witnessed the earthquake and fire that destroyed three quarters of the city. At that time he was a young man; he remembers the disaster perfectly. He watched the reconstruction of the city which still had an Asiatic look around 1913, and then its rapid Americanization. Thus, he has superimposed memories of three San Franciscos.

We Europeans change within changeless cities, and our 18 houses and neighbourhoods outlive us; American cities change faster than their inhabitants do, and it is the inhabitants who outlive the cities.

I am really visiting the United States in wartime; the vast life 19 of the American city has suddenly become petrified; people hardly change their residences any more. But this stagnation is entirely temporary; the cities have been immobilized like the dancer on the film-screen who stays with his foot suspended in air when the film is stopped; one feels all about one the rising of the sap which will burst open the cities as soon as the war is ended.

First, there are immediate problems; Chicago's Negro section 20 will have to be rebuilt, for instance. The government had begun this before Pearl Harbour. But the government-built apartment houses barely manage to shelter 7000 people. Now, there are 250,000 to be housed. Then the industrialists want to enlarge and transform their factories; the famous abattoirs of Chicago are going to be completely modernized.

Finally, the average American is obsessed by the image of the 21 "modern house" which is considerably publicized and which will be, so we are told, a hundred times more comfortable than the present dwellings and whose construction in huge quantities certainly has its place in the plans for "industrial conversion" which are now springing up almost everywhere.

When the war is over, America will certainly be seized with a 22 real construction fever. Today the American sees his city objectively; he does not dream of finding it ugly, but thinks it really old. If it were even older, like ours, he could find a social past, a tradition in it. We generally live in our grandfathers' houses. Our streets reflect the customs and ways of past centuries; they tend to filter the present;

none of what goes on in the Rue Montorgueil or the Rue Pot-de-Fer is completely of the present. But the thirty-year-old American lives in a house that was built when he was twenty.

These houses that are too young to seem *old* seem merely outdated to them; they lag behind the other tools, the car that can be traded in every two years, the refrigerator or the wireless set. That is why they see their cities without vain sentimentality. They have grown slightly attached to them, as one becomes attached to one's car, but they consider them as instruments, rather than anything else, instruments to be exchanged for more convenient ones. 23

For us a city is, above all, a past; for them it is mainly a future; what they like in the city is everything it has not yet become and everything it can be. 24

What are the impressions of a European who arrives in an American city? First, he thinks he has been taken in. He has heard only about skyscrapers; New York and Chicago have been described to him as "upright cities." Now his first feeling is, on the contrary, that the average height of an American city is noticeably smaller than that of a French one. The immense majority of houses have only two storeys. Even in the very large cities, the five-storey apartment house is an exception. 25

Then he is struck by the lightness of the materials used. In the United States stone is less frequently used than in Europe. The skyscraper consists of a coating of concrete applied to a metal framework, and the other buildings are made of brick or wood. Even in the richest cities and the smartest sections, one often finds frame houses. New Orleans' lovely colonial houses are of wood; many of the pretty chalets belonging to the Hollywood stars and film-directors are made of wood; so are the "California style" cottages in San Francisco. Everywhere you find groups of frame houses crushed between two twenty-storeyed buildings. 26

The brick houses are the colour of dried blood, or, on the contrary, daubed and smeared with bright yellow, green or raw white. In most of the cities, they are roofless cubes or rectangular parallelpipeds, with severely flat façades. All these houses, hastily constructed and made expressly to be hastily demolished, obviously bear a strange resemblance to Fontana's "prefabricated houses." 27

The lightness of these jerry-built houses, their loud colours alternating with the sombre red of the bricks, the extraordinary variety of their decorations which does not manage to conceal the uniformity of their patterns, all give one the feeling, when in the middle of the city, of walking through the suburbs of a watering town, like Trouville or Cabourg or La Baule. Only those ephemeral seaside chalets with their pretentious architectural style and 28 their fragility can convey to those of my French readers who have never seen the States an idea of the American apartment house.

To complete the impression, I should also like to add that sometimes one also thinks of an exposition-city, but an obsolescent, dirty one, like those that ten years later, in some park, survive the celebration that occasioned them. For these shanties quickly grow dirty, particularly in industrial sections. 29

Chicago, blackened by its smoke, clouded by the Lake Michigan fog, is a dark and gloomy red. Pittsburgh is more gloomy still. And there is nothing more immediately striking than the contrast between the formidable power, the inexhaustible abundance of what is called the "American Colossus" and the puny insignificance of those little houses that line the widest roads in the world. But on second thought, there is no clearer indication that America is not finished, that her ideas and plans, her social structure and her cities have only a strictly temporary reality. 30

These perfectly straight cities bear no trace of organization. Many of them have the rudimentary structure of a polypary. Los Angeles, in particular, is rather like a big earthworm that might be chopped into twenty pieces without being killed. If you go through this enormous urban cluster, probably the largest in the world, you come upon twenty juxtaposed cities, strictly identical, each with its poor section, its business streets, night-clubs and smart suburb, and you get the impression that a medium-sized urban centre has schizogenetically reproduced itself twenty times. 31

In America, where the neighbourhoods are added on to each other as the region's prosperity attracts new immigrants, this juxtaposition is the rule. You pass without any transition from a poor street into an aristocratic avenue; a promenade lined with skyscrapers, museums and public monuments and adorned with lawns and trees, suddenly stops short above a smoky station; one frequently discovers at the feet of the largest buildings, along an aristocratic avenue, a "zone" of miserable little kitchen-gardens. 32

This is due to the fact that these cities that move at a rapid rate are not constructed in order to grow old, but move forward like modern armies, encircling the islands of resistance they are unable to destroy; the past does not manifest itself in them as it does in Europe, through public monuments, but through survivals. The wooden bridge in Chicago which spans a canal two steps away from the world's highest skyscrapers is a survival. The elevated railways, rolling noisily through the central streets of New York and Chicago, supported by great iron pillars and cross-girders, nearly touching the façades of houses on either side, are survivals. They are there simply 33 because no one has taken the time to tear them down, and as a kind of indication of work to be done.

You find this disorder in each individual vista. Nowhere have 34 I seen so many empty lots. Of course they do have a definite function; they are used as car parks. But they break the alignment of the street nonetheless sharply for all that. Suddenly it seems as if a bomb had fallen on three or four houses, reducing them to powder, and as if they had just been swept out: this is a "parking space," two hundred square metres of bare earth with its sole ornament, perhaps, a poster on a big hoarding. Suddenly the city seems unfinished, badly assembled; suddenly you rediscover the desert and the big empty site: noticeable at Fontana. I remember this Los Angeles landscape in the middle of the city, two modern apartment houses, two white cubes framing an empty lot with the ground torn up—a parking space. A few abandoned-looking cars were parked there. A palm tree grew like a weed between the cars. Down at the bottom there was a steep grassy hill, rather like the fortification mounds we use for garbage disposal. On top of the mound was a frame house, and a little below this a string stretched between two little trees, with multi-coloured washing hanging out to dry. When one turned around the block of houses, the hill disappeared; its other side had been built up, covered with asphalt, streaked with tar roads, and pierced with a magnificent tunnel.

The most striking aspect of the American city is the vertical 35 disorder. These brick shanties are of varying heights; I noted at random during a walk in Detroit the following successive proportions: one storey, two storeys, one storey, one storey, three storeys. You find the same proportions in Albuquerque or San Antonio, at the other end of the country. In depth, above this irregular crenellation, you see apartment houses of all shapes and dimensions, long cases, thick thirty-storeyed boxes with forty windows to a storey. As soon as there is a bit of fog the colours fade away, and only volumes remain—every variety of polyhedron. Between them, you have enormous empty spaces, empty lots cut out in the sky.

In New York, and even in Chicago, the skyscraper is on home 36 ground, and imposes a new order upon the city. But everywhere else it is out of place; the eye is unable to establish any unity between these tall, gawky things and the little houses that run close to the ground; in spite of itself it looks for that line so familiar in European cities, the sky-line, and cannot find it. That is why the European feels at first as though he were travelling through a rocky chaos that resembles a city—something like Montpellier-le-Vieux—rather than a city.

But the European makes a mistake in visiting American cities 37 as one does Paris or Venice; they are not meant to be seen that way. The streets here do not have the same meaning as our streets. In Europe, a street is half-way between the path of communication and the sheltered "public place." It is on a footing with the cafés, as proved by the use of the "terrasses" that spring up on the sidewalks of the cafés in fine weather. Thus it changes its aspect more than a hundred times a day, for the crowd that throngs the European street changes, and men are its primary element. The American street is a piece of highway. It sometimes stretches over many miles. It does not stimulate one to walk. Ours are oblique and twisting, full of bends and secrets. The American street is a straight line that gives itself away immediately. It contains no mystery. You see the street straight through, from one end to the other no matter what your location in it. And the distances in American cities are too great to permit moving about on foot; in most of them one gets about almost exclusively in cars, on buses and by underground. Sometimes, while going from one appointment to another, I have been carried like a parcel from underground to escalator, from escalator to elevator, from elevator to taxi, from taxi to bus and, again, by metro and elevator, without walking a step.

In certain cities I noticed a real atrophy of the sidewalk. In Los Angeles, for example, on La Cienega, which is lined with bars, theatres, restaurants, antique dealers and private residences, the sidewalks are scarcely more than side-streets that lead customers and guests from the roadway into the house. Lawns have been planted from the façades to the roadway of this luxurious avenue. I followed a narrow path between the lawns for a long time without meeting a living soul, while to my right, cars streaked by on the road; all animation in the street had taken refuge on the high road.   38

New York and Chicago do not have neighbourhoods, but they do have a neighbourhood life; the American is not familiar with his city; once he is ten "blocks" away from his home, he is lost. This does not mean that there are no crowds in the business streets, but they are crowds that do not linger; people shop or emerge from the Underground to go to their offices.   39

I rarely saw an occasional Negro day-dreaming before a shop.   40

Yet one quickly begins to like American cities. Of course they all look alike. And when you arrive at Wichita, Saint Louis or Albuquerque, it is disappointing to realize that, hidden behind these magnificent and promising names, is the same standard checkerboard city with the same red and green traffic lights and the same provincial look. But one gradually learns to tell them apart. Chicago, the noble, lurid city, red as the blood that trickles through its abattoirs, with its canals, the grey water of Lake Michigan and its   41 streets crushed between clumsy and powerful buildings, in no way resembles San Francisco, city of air, salt and sea, built in the shape of an amphitheatre.

And then one finally comes to like their common element, that temporary look. Our beautiful closed cities, full as eggs, are a bit stifling. Our slanting, winding streets run head on against walls and houses; once you are inside the city, you can no longer see beyond it. In America, these long, straight unobstructed streets carry one's glance, like canals, outside the city. You always see mountains or fields or the sea at the end of them, no matter where you may be. 42

Frail and temporary, formless and unfinished, they are haunted by the presence of the immense geographical space surrounding them. And precisely because their boulevards are highways, they always seem to be stopping places on the roads. They are not oppressive, they do not close you in; nothing in them is definitive, nothing is arrested. You feel, from your first glance, that your contact with these places is a temporary one; either you will leave them or they will change around you. 43

Let us beware of exaggerating; I have spent Sundays in the American provinces that were more depressing than Sundays anywhere else; I have seen those suburban "colonial style" inns where, at two dollars a head, middle-class families go to eat shrimp cocktails and turkey with cranberry sauce in silence while listening to the electric organ. One must not forget the heavy boredom that weighs over America. 44

But these slight cities, still so similar to Fontana and the outposts of the Far West, reveal the other side of the United States: their freedom. Here everyone is free—not to criticize or to reform their customs—but to flee them, to leave for the desert or another city. The cities are open, open to the world, and to the future. This is what gives them their adventurous look and, even in their ugliness and disorder, a touching beauty. 45

QUESTIONS

1. Explain in the context of the whole essay Sartre's remark that the American city "is a moving landscape for its inhabitants" (paragraph 15).

2. What comparative points does Sartre draw between European and American cities?

3. Locate and explain the various analogies, metaphors, and similes Sartre employs to illuminate the qualities of American cities.

JEAN-PAUL SARTRE

4. What terms from art, architecture, and mathematics does Sartre use to describe American cities?

5. On what details does the author focus to develop his analysis of the American city?

6. How does Sartre particularize his generalizations about American cities? What is the general thesis that he develops?

7. How does the author combine personal, aesthetic, and social judgments to create the tone of the essay?

8. What is Sartre's method of identification in the essay? How does he use identification to arrive at an informal definition of the American city?

9. Sartre's essay was written in 1945 for *Le Figaro*. Which of his observations still apply? How did he anticipate postwar developments in urban American life? How biased was Sartre in his analysis?

10. a. Write an analysis of American cities, attempting, as Sartre does, to capture their essence.
b. Write about one or more foreign cities from the perspective of a visitor.

ANAÏS NIN

Morocco

Anaïs Nin (1903–1977), diarist, novelist, essayist, and feminist, was an American born in Paris. A student of psychology under Otto Rank, Nin always retained her interest in the inner self and specifically in the consciousness of women. In her words, she wished "to unmask the deeper self that lies hidden behind the self that we present to the world." Her diaries, started as letters to her father in 1931, were published in seven volumes between 1966 and 1980. These diaries, an imposing collection termed by Gunther Stuhlmann "one of the unique literary documents of our century," have been compared in method to the work of Marcel Proust. In the following entry from *The Diaries of Anaïs Nin, 1934–39* (1967), the author reveals her debt to her literary friends Henry Miller and Lawrence Durrell in this remarkable evocation of exotic landscape.

A trip to Morocco. A short but vivid one. I fell in love with   1
Fez. Peace, Dignity. Humility. I have just left the balcony where I stood listening to the evening prayer rising over the white city. A religious emotion roused by the Arabs' lives, by the simplicity of it, the fundamental beauty. Stepping into the labyrinth of their streets, streets like intestines, two yards wide, into the abyss of their dark eyes, into peace. The rhythm affects one first of all. The slowness. Many people on the streets. You touch elbows. They breathe into your face, but with a silence, a gravity, a dreaminess. Only the children cry and laugh and run. The Arabs are silent. The little square room open on the street in which they sit on the ground, on the mud, with their merchandise around them. They are weaving, they are sewing, baking bread, chiseling jewels, repairing knives, making guns for the Berbers in the mountains. They are dying wool in vast cauldrons, big cauldrons full of dye emerald green, violet, Orient blue. They are making sienna earth pottery, weaving rugs, shaving, shampooing and writing legal documents right there, under your eyes. One Arab is asleep over his bag of saffron. Another is praying with his beads while selling herbs. Further, a big tintamarre, the street of copperwork. Little boys are beating copper trays with small hammers, beating a design into them, beating copper lamps, Aladdin's lamps. Little boys and old men do the work. They hold the tray between their legs. The younger men walk down the street in their burnouses, going I know not where, some so beautiful one thinks they are women. The women are veiled. They are going to the mosque, probably. At a certain hour all selling, all work ceases and they all go to the mosque. But first of all they wash their faces, their feet, their sore eyes, their leprous noses, their pock-marked skins at the fountain. They shed their sandals. Some of the old men and old women never leave the mosque. They squat there forever until death overtakes them. Women have their own entrance. They kiss the wall of the mosque as they pass. To make way for a donkey loaded with kindling wood, I step into a dark doorway. A choking stench overwhelms me. This stench is everywhere. It takes a day to get used to it. It makes you feel nauseated at first. It is the smell of excrement, saffron, leather being cured, sandalwood, olive oil being used for frying, nut oil on the bodies, incense, muskrat, so strong that at first you cannot swallow food. There is mud on the white burnous, on the Arab legs. Children's heads shaved, with one tuft of hair left. The women with faces uncovered and tattooed are the primitive Berbers from the mountains, wives of warriors, not civilized. I saw the wives of one Arab, five of them sitting on a divan, like mountains of flesh, enormous, with several chins and several stomachs, and diamonds set in their foreheads.

The streets and houses are inextricably woven, intricately   2 interwoven, by bridges from one house to another, passageways covered with lattice, creating shadows on the ground. They seem to be crossing within a house, you never know when you are out in a street or in a patio, or a passageway, as half of the houses are open on the street, you get lost immediately. Mosques run into a merchant's home, shops into mosques, now you are under a trellised roof covered with rose vines, now walking in utter darkness through a tunnel, behind a donkey raw and bleeding from being beaten, and now you are on a bridge built by the Portuguese. Now admire lacy trelliswork done by the Andalusians, and now look at the square next to the mosque where the poor are allowed to sleep on mats.

Everywhere the Arab squats and waits. Anywhere. An old   3
Arab is teaching a young one a religious chant. Another is defecating carefully, conscientiously. Another is begging, showing all his open sores, standing near the baker baking bread in ovens built in the earth.

The atmosphere is so clear, so white and blue, you feel you   4
can see the whole world as clearly as you see Fez. The birds do not chatter as they do in Paris, they chant, trill with operatic and tropical fervor. The poor are dressed in sackcloths, the semi-poor in sheets and bathtowels, the well-to-do women in silks and muslins. The Jews wear a black burnous. In the streets and in the houses of the poor the floor is of stamped earth. Houses are built of sienna-red earth, sometimes whitewashed. The olive oil is pressed out in the street too, under large wooden wheels.

I had letters of introduction. First I visited Si Boubekertazi.   5
He sat in his patio, on pillows. A beautiful Negro woman, a concubine, brought a copper tray full of delicacies. And tea served in tiny cups without handles.

At the house of Driss Mokri Montasseb I was allowed to visit   6
the harem. Seven wives of various ages, but all of them fat, sat around a low table eating candy and dates. We discussed nail polish. They wanted some of mine, which was pearly. They told me how they made up their eyes. They bought kohl dust at the market, filled their eyes with it. The eyes smart and cry, and so the black kohl marks the edges and gives that heavily accented effect.

Pasha El Glaoui de Marrakesh offered me a military escort to   7
visit the city. He said it was absolutely necessary. He signaled to a soldier standing at his door, who never left me from then on except when I went to my hotel room to sleep.

De Sidi Hassan Benanai received me under the fine spun-   8
gold colonnades. But he had just begun a forty-day fast and prayer, so he sat in silence, counting his beads, and tea was served in silence, and he continued to pray, occasionally smiling at me, and bowing his head, until I left.

 MOROCCO   **125**

From outside, the houses are uniformly plain, with high   9
walls covered with flowers. One cannot tell when one is entering a
luxurious abode. The door may be of beautiful ironwork. There may
be two, or four, or six guards at the door. But inside, the walls are all
mosaics, or painted, and the stucco worked like lace, the ceilings
painted in gold. The pillows are of silk. The Negro women are simply
dressed but always beautiful. One does not see the children or the
wives.

The white burnous is called a *jelabba*.   10

Mystery and labyrinth. Complex streets. Anonymous walls.   11
Secret luxury. Secrecy of these houses without windows on the
streets. The windows and door open on the patio. The patio has a
fountain and lovely plants. There is a labyrinth design in the
arrangement of the gardens. Bushes are placed to form a puzzle so
you might get lost. They love the feeling of being lost. It has been
interpreted as a desire to reproduce the infinite.

Fez. One always, sooner or later, comes upon a city which is   12
an image of one's inner cities. Fez is an image of my inner self. This
may explain my fascination for it. Wearing a veil, full and inexhaustible, labyrinthian, so rich and variable I myself get lost. Passion for
mystery, the unknown, and for the infinite, the uncharted.

With my guide I visited the Quartier Réservé. It lay within   13
medieval walls, guarded at each gate by a French soldier. The houses
were full of prostitutes. Only the poor Arabs go there because the
others have enough wives to satisfy their need of variety. Dark,
dramatic, tortuous streets. Bare cellars which have become cafés.
Arabs slinking in and out. Negroes. Beggars. Arab music heard now
and then. The walls, ceilings covered with shabby rugs and potteries.
Thé à menthe served, or beer. No wine drinking but much drug traffic.
Bare, cellarlike rooms. Doors covered by muslin curtains, or beaded
curtains. Front room is the bar or café where the men sit and the
musicians play. Back room is for the prostitutes. The muslin curtain
was parted and I found myself before Fatima, the queen of the
prostitutes.

Fatima had a beautiful face, straight patrician nose, enormous   14
black velvet eyes, tawny smooth skin, full but firm, and the usual
Arabian attributes of several folds of stomach, several chins. She
could only move with difficulty on her enormous legs. She was both
queenly and magnificent, opulent, and voluptuous. She was dressed
in a wedding costume, a pink chiffon dress embroidered with gold
sequins laid over several layers of other chiffon petticoats. Heavy gold
belt, bracelets, rings, a gold band across her forehead, enormous
dangling gold earrings. Over her glistening black hair she wore a
colored silk turban placed on the back of her head exposing the black
curls. She had four gold teeth, considered beautiful by Arab women.

The coal-black rim around her eyes exaggerated their size, as in Egyptian paintings.

She sat among pillows in a room shaped like many bedrooms ¹⁵ in Fez, long and narrow. At each end of the room she had a brass bed, a sign of luxury and success. They are not used as beds, they are only a symbol of wealth. In between the two brass beds lay all the pillows, rugs, and low divans. (In rich homes the floors are tiled but the brass beds are displayed there too.) Fatima not only collected brass beds but also cuckoo clocks from Switzerland. One wall was covered with them, each one telling a different time. The other walls were covered with flowered cretonne. The atmosphere was heavy with perfume, enclosed and voluptuous, the womb itself. A young girl came in with an atomizer and lifting up my skirt gently atomized my underclothes with rose water. She came once more to throw rose petals around my feet. Then she came carrying a tray with glass tea containers, sheathed in copper holders with handles. We sat cross-legged on vast pillows, Fatima in the center. She never made a vulgar gesture. Two blind, crippled musicians were invited in and played monotonously, but with such a beat that my excitement grew as if I had taken wine. Fatima began to prepare tea on the tray. Then she passed around a bottle of rose water and we perfumed our hands. Then she lit a sandalwood brazier and placed it at my feet. I was duly and thoroughly perfumed and the air grew heavier and richer. The Arab soldier lay back on the pillows. The handsome bodyguard in his white burnous, white turban and blue military costume conversed with Fatima, who could not speak French. He translated my compliments on her beauty. She asked him to translate a question about my nail polish. I promised to send her some. While we sat there dreaming between each phrase, there was a fight outside. A young Arab burst in, his face bleeding. "Aii, Aii, Aiii," he cried. Fatima sent her maid to see what could be done for the young Arab. She never lost her composure. The musicians played louder and faster so I would not notice the commotion and my pleasure would not be spoiled. I spent two hours with Fatima, as it is impolite to hurry here. It is a mortal insult to leave too soon or to seem hurried. It offends them deeply. Relationship does not depend so much on conversation or exchange as in the creation of a propitious, dreamy, meditative, contemplative atmosphere, a mood. Finally, when I was ready to leave, my escort made a parting speech.

It was after midnight. The city, so crowded during the day ¹⁶ that I could hardly move in it, was silent and empty. The night watchman sleeps on the doorsteps. There are gates between different quarters. Six gates had to be opened for us with enormous keys. You are not allowed to circulate at night except by special permission and with a pass which the soldier showed to each watchman.

 MOROCCO

The frogs were croaking in the garden pools behind the walls, 17
the crickets were announcing tomorrow's heat. The smell of roses
won the battle of smells. A window was suddenly opened above me,
an old woman stuck her head out and threw out a big rat she had just
caught, with many curses. It fell at my feet.

Fez is a drug. It enmeshes you. The life of the senses, of 18
poetry (even the poor Arabs who visit a prostitute will find a woman
dressed in a wedding dress like a virgin), of illusion and dream. It
made me passionate, just to sit there on pillows, with music, the
birds, the fountains, the infinite beauty of the mosaic designs, the
teakettle singing, the many copper trays shining, the twelve bottles of
rose perfume and the sandalwood smoking in the brazier, and the
cuckoo clocks chiming in disunion, as they pleased.

The layers of the city of Fez are like the layers and secrecies of 19
the inner life. One needs a guide.

I loved the racial nobility of the Arabs, the pride, the love of 20
sweets instead of alcohol, the gentleness, the peace, the hospitality,
the reserve, pride, love of turquoise and coral colors, dignity of
bearing, their silences. I love the way the men embrace in the street,
proudly and nobly. I love the expression in their eyes, brooding, or
fiery, but deep.

The river under the bridge was foul. Men held hands while 21
talking on the street. A dead Arab was carried on a stretcher, covered
with narrow white bandages like an Egyptian mummy. Over his feet
they had thrown a red rug. Silence and quietism. Contemplation and
chanting. Music. Tea served on copper trays with a samovar kettle.
Glasses have colored tops. On another tray a big silver box with big
rough pieces of rock sugar. Trays with perfume bottles. Trays with
almond cakes covered by a silk handkerchief or copper painted lids.

I met the Arab women walking to their baths. They went 22
there always in groups, and carrying a change of clothes in a basket
over their heads. They walked veiled and laughing, showing only
their eyes and the hennaed tips of their hands holding their veils.
Their full white skirts and heavily embroidered belts made them
heavy and full-looking, like the pillows they liked to sit on. It was
heavy flesh moving in white robes, nourished on sweets and inertia,
on passive watches behind grilled windows. This was one of their few
moments of liberty, one of the few times they appeared in the street.
They walked in groups with their servants, children, and bundles of
fresh clothes, laughing and talking, and dragging their feet in
embroidered mules.

I followed them. When they entered at the mosaic-covered 23
building near the mosque, I entered with them. The first room was
very large and square, all of stone, with stone benches, and rugs on
the floor. Here the women laid down their bundles and began

undressing. This was a long ceremony, for they wore so many skirts, and several blouses, and belts which looked like bandages, so much white muslin, linen, cotton to unroll, unfold, and fold again on the bench. Then there were bracelets to take off, earrings, anklets, and then the long black hair to unwind from the ribbons tressed into the hair. So much white cotton fallen on the floor, a field of white petals, leaves, lace, shed by the full-fleshed women, and as I looked at them I felt they could never be really naked, that all this they wore must cling to them forever, grow with their bodies. I was already undressed and waiting, standing, as I would not sit naked on the stone bench. They were waiting for the children to be undressed by the African maids, waiting for the maids to get undressed.

An old woman was waiting for us, a completely shriveled old 24 woman with only one eye. Her breasts were two long empty gourds hanging almost to the middle of her stomach. She wore a sackcloth around her waist. She gave me a little approving tap on the shoulder and smiled. She pointed to my finger nails and talked but I could not understand, and I smiled.

She opened the door to the steam room, another very large 25 square room all of grey stone. But here there were no benches. All the women were sitting on the floor. The old woman filled pails of water from one of the fountains and occasionally poured one over their heads, after they had finished soaping themselves. The steam filled the room. The women sat on the floor, took their children between their knees and scrubbed them. Then the old woman threw a pail of water over them. This water flowed all around us, and it was dirty. We sat in rivulets of soapy, dirty water. The women did not hurry. They used the soap, then a piece of pumice stone, and then they began to use depilatories with great care and concentration. All of them were enormous. The flesh billowed, curved, folded in tremendous heavy waves. They seemed to be sitting on pillows of flesh of all colors, from the pale Northern Arab skin to the African. I was amazed that they could lift such heavy arms to comb their long hair. I had come to look at them, because the beauty of their faces was legendary, and proved not at all exaggerated. They had absolutely beautiful faces, enormous, jeweled eyes, straight noble noses with wide spaces between the eyes, full and voluptuous mouths, flawless skins, and always a royal bearing. The faces had a quality of statuary rather than painting, because the lines were so pure and clear. I sat in admiration of their faces, and then I noticed that they looked at me. They sat in groups, looking at me and smiling. They mimicked that I should wash my hair and face. I could not explain that I was hurrying through the ritual because I did not like sitting in the darkening waters. They offered me the pumice stone after using it thoroughly all over their ponderous bodies. I tried it but it scratched my face. The

Arab women's skin was tougher. The women chatted in circles while washing themselves and their children. I could not bring myself to wash my face with the soap they all used for their feet and armpits. They laughed at what they must have thought was a European woman who did not know the rules of cleanliness.

They wanted me also to pull out superfluous eyebrows, hair under the arms, and to shave my pubic hair. I finally slipped away to the next room where pails of cooler water were thrown over me.   26

I wanted to see the Arab women clothed again, concealed in yards of white cotton. Such beautiful heads had risen out of these mountains of flesh, heads of incredible perfection, dazzling eyes heavily fringed, sensual features. Sometimes moss-green eyes in dark sienna skins, sometimes coal-black eyes in pale moonlit skins, and always the long heavy black hair, the undulating tresses. But these heads rose from formless masses of flesh, heaving like plants in the sea, swelling, swaying, falling, the breasts like sea anemones, floating, the stomachs of perpetually pregnant women, the legs like pillows, the backs like cushions, the hips with furrows like a mattress.   27

They were all watching me, with friendly nodding of their heads, commenting on my figure. By counting on their fingers they asked was I adolescent? I had no fat on me. I must be a girl. They came around me and we compared skin colors. They seemed amazed by my waist. They could enclose it in their two hands. They wanted to wash my hair. They soaped my face with tenderness. They touched me and talked with volubility. The old woman came with two pails and threw them over me. I was ready to leave, but the Arab women transmitted messages of all kinds with their eyes, smiles, talk. The old woman led me to the third room, which was cooler, and threw cold water over me, and then led me back to the dressing room.   28

QUESTIONS

1. Explain what the author means when she states in paragraph 12, "One always, sooner or later, comes upon a city which is an image of one's inner cities."

2. The Moroccan women dominate the author's description of life in Fez. What is Nin's attitude toward them? In what ways does she romanticize them? How do they contrast with the men?

3. How does the author's use of short sentence fragments, introduced in the first paragraph and woven into the essay, contribute to the mood and tone of the essay?

4. Where does the author use figurative and metaphorical language in

paragraph 27? How are the prose rhythms in this paragraph typical of the essay as a whole?

5. What techniques of development does the author employ in the introductory paragraph? How does this paragraph establish motifs for the entire essay?

6. Which paragraph establishes the thesis for the essay? How is the paragraph prepared for in terms of the structure of the essay?

7. Examine paragraphs 13 to 15, 16 to 21, and 22 to 28. What dominant impression emerges from these paragraphs?

8. What methods does the author use to make point of view so distinctive in this essay?

9. Compare and contrast this essay with Orwell's "Marrakech."

10. Write about a place that has had an overwhelming, almost intoxicating, effect on you.

Manners and Morals

MARYA MANNES

Wasteland

Marya Mannes (1904–   ) has written several novels and some light verse, but she is best known for her essays, which have appeared in *Vogue, McCall's, Harper's,* and *The New Republic.* She has collected her essays in *More In Anger* (1958) and in *The New York I Know* (1961). Mannes has also written on such subjects as suicide and euthanasia in *Last Rights* (1974) and television in *Who Owns the Air?* (1960). Throughout her career, she has always been concerned with and critical of the quality of American life. In "Wasteland," Mannes describes the modern American landscape.

ans. Beer cans. Glinting on the verges of a million miles   1
of roadways, lying in scrub, grass, dirt, leaves, sand, mud, but never hidden. Piels, Rheingold, Ballantine, Schaefer, Schlitz, shining in the sun or picked by moon or the beams of headlights at night; washed by rain or flattened by wheels, but never dulled, never buried, never destroyed. Here is the mark of savages, the testament of wasters, the stain of prosperity.

Who are these men who defile the grassy borders of our   2
roads and lanes, who pollute our ponds, who spoil the purity of our ocean beaches with the empty vessels of their thirst? Who are the

men who make these vessels in millions and then say, "Drink—and discard"? What society is this that can afford to cast away a million tons of metal and to make of wild and fruitful land a garbage heap?

What manner of men and women need thirty feet of steel and two hundred horsepower to take them, singly, to their small destinations? Who demand that what they eat is wrapped so that forests are cut down to make the paper that is thrown away, and what they smoke and chew is sealed so that the sealers can be tossed in gutters and caught in twigs and grass? 3

What kind of men can afford to make the streets of their towns and cities hideous with neon at night, and their roadways hideous with signs by day, wasting beauty; who leave the carcasses of cars to rot in heaps; who spill their trash into ravines and make smoking mountains of refuse for the town's rats? What manner of men choke off the life in rivers, streams and lakes with the waste of their produce, making poison of water? 4

Who is as rich as that? Slowly the wasters and despoilers are impoverishing our land, our nature, and our beauty, so that there will not be one beach, one hill, one lane, one meadow, one forest free from the debris of man and the stigma of his improvidence. 5

Who is so rich that he can squander forever the wealth of earth and water for the trivial needs of vanity or the compulsive demands of greed; or so prosperous in land that he can sacrifice nature for unnatural desires? The earth we abuse and the living things we kill will, in the end, take their revenge; for in exploiting their presence we are diminishing our future. 6

And what will we leave behind us when we are long dead? Temples? Amphora? Sunken treasure? 7

Or mountains of twisted, rusted steel, canyons of plastic containers, and a million miles of shores garlanded, not with the lovely wrack of the sea, but with the cans and bottles and light-bulbs and boxes of a people who conserved their convenience at the expense of their heritage, and whose ephemeral prosperity was built on waste. 8

QUESTIONS

1. What evidence of wastefulness does Mannes give in the essay?

2. How does Mannes relate prosperity to waste?

3. What are the multiple meanings of the title "Wasteland"? How are they represented in the essay?

4. Why does Mannes use fragments in the first paragraph and in para-

graphs 7 and 8? What is the significance of the term "ephemeral prosperity" in the last paragraph?

5.   What is the effect of the author's use of rhetorical questions to structure her essay? Explain the use of irony in Mannes's answers to her questions.

6.   Identify the concrete objects listed in the essay. How does Mannes's selection of objects support her thesis?

7.   How does Mannes describe such things as cars, cigarette wrappers, streetlights, and road signs? Why is her technique, called periphrasis, successful?

8.   Paragraph 6 is made up of a question and a declarative sentence. Although the declarative sentence does not directly answer the question, the two are related. How?

9.   How do you think Americans can become less wasteful?

10.   Describe several objects that, taken as a whole, make a positive or negative statement about pollution, elections, education, or sports.

S. I. HAYAKAWA

Sex Is Not a Spectator Sport

Samuel Ichize Hayakawa (1906–   ) began his career as a professor of linguistics and was the author of numerous books on language, such as *Language in Thought and Action* (1941), *Our Language and Our World* (1959), and *Symbol, Status, and Personality* (1963). When he became president of San Francisco State College, student unrest was at its height. By defending traditional values and, indeed, authority itself, Hayakawa became a national and controversial figure; subsequently, he was elected a senator from California to the United States Congress. In "Sex Is Not a Spectator Sport," he presents a linguist's and conservative's view of pornography.

n current discussions of pornography and obscenity, 1 there is widespread confusion about two matters. First there is sexual behavior and what it means to the participants. Secondly there is the outside observer of that sexual behavior and what it means to him. When a man and a woman make love, enjoying themselves and each other fully and unself-consciously, a rich relationship is reaffirmed and made richer by their lovemaking. However beautiful or sacred that love relationship may be to that man and woman, it would have an entirely different significance to a Peeping Tom, secretly watching the proceedings from outside the window. The sexual behavior is not itself obscene. Obscenity is peculiarly the evaluation of the outside observer. Theoretically the actors may themselves be made the observers. If, for example, unknown to the man and woman, a movie were to be made of their lovemaking, and that movie were to be shown to them later, that lovemaking might take on an entirely different significance. What was performed unself-consciously and spontaneously might be viewed later by the actors themselves with giggling or shame or shock. They might even insist that the film be destroyed—which is entirely different from saying that they would stop making love.

What I am saying is that obscenity and pornography can   2
happen only when sexual events are seen from the outside, from a spectator's point of view. This is the crux of the pornography problem. Pornography is sexual behavior made public through symbolization—by representation in literature, by simulation or enactment in a nightclub act or on stage, by arts such as painting, photography, or the movies. To object to pornographic movies or art is not, as some would have us believe, a result of hang-ups about sex. One may be completely healthy and still object to many of the current representations of sexual acts in the movies and on the stage.

Standards of morality are one thing. Standards of decorum   3
are another. There is nothing immoral about changing one's clothes or evacuating one's bowels. But in our culture people as a rule do not change their clothing in the presence of the other sex, excepting their spouses. Men and women have separate public lavatories, and within them each toilet is in a separate compartment for privacy. Love too needs privacy. Human beings normally make love in private, whether that love is socially sanctioned, as in marriage, or unsanctioned, as in a house of prostitution.

The trouble with sexual intercourse as an object of artistic or   4
literary representation is that its meaning is not apparent in the behavior. Hence serious writers have historically been reticent in their description of sex. In Dante's *Divine Comedy* Francesca tells of her tragic love for Paolo. They were reading an ancient romance, and as they read, their passions suddenly overcame them. What happened? Dante simply has Francesca say, "That day we read no further." The rest is left to the reader's imagination—and the reader cannot help feeling the power of that onrushing, fatal passion.

Men and women couple with each other for a wide variety of   5 reasons. Sometimes the sexual encounter is the fulfillment of true love and respect for each other. Sometimes one of the partners is using sex as an instrument of exploitation or aggression against the other. Sometimes sex is a commercial transaction, with either party being the prostitute. Sometimes sex is the expression of neurosis. Sometimes it is evidence of people getting over their neuroses. However, to the movie camera, as to a Peeping Tom, they are all "doing the same thing." To concentrate on the mechanics of sex is to ignore altogether its human significance.

Today movies do not stop at exhibiting copulation. Every 6 kind of aberrant sexual behavior and sadomasochistic perversion is being shown. The advertisements in the newspaper before me announce such titles as *Nude Encounter, Too Hot to Handle, Deep Throat, The Devil in Miss Jones, The Passion Parlor, Hot Kitten,* and *Honeymoon Suite,* as well as "16 hours of hard-core male stag." The only purpose of movies such as these, from all I can tell from advertisements and reviews, is, as D. H. Lawrence expressed it, "to do dirt on sex." Let the American Civil Liberties Union fight for the right of these movies to be shown. I will not.

QUESTIONS

1. How does Hayakawa define decorum and morality? How are they contrasted with pornography?

2. According to Hayakawa, sex can be evidence to "prove" a variety of things. What are they?

3. Is there connotative language in this essay? Is it used frequently or not? Why or why not?

4. Why does Hayakawa refer to Dante in paragraph 4 rather than to a modern author? Explain the effectiveness of this allusion. Explain the allusion to D. H. Lawrence.

5. Where does Hayakawa use hypothetical examples? Where does he use literal examples? What purposes do they serve?

6. Identify the topic sentence in each paragraph. Why are they so consistently placed? Relate their placement to the movement from general or abstract to specific or concrete in each paragraph.

7. How does Hayakawa use definition in this essay? Why does he use it?

8. What is the tone of the essay? What effect does that tone have upon the way Hayakawa describes sex?

S. I. HAYAKAWA

9. What is your opinion of Hayakawa's proposition that pornography degrades sex?

10. a. Write an extended definition of pornography.
b. Write an essay that uses definition to defend a moral position.

ANN GRACE MOJTABAI

Polygamy

Ann Grace Mojtabai (1938–   ) spent several years living in Iran. She has written three novels: *Mundome* (1974), *A Stopping Place* (1979), and *The Four Hundred Eels of Sigmund Freud* (1976). In the following essay, Mojtabai tries to look clearly at a particularly disturbing—from our perspective—aspect of Iranian culture.

eheran, 1960. A warm evening. The courtyard in which   1
we were sitting was not very beautiful. There was a
narrow strip of ground that ran along the edge of the
wall, spotted with shrubbery and some insignificant
roses; the rest was flagstone surrounding the customary small pool
for ablutions, set like a turquoise in the center.

I had come to Iran expecting nightingales and roses, but had   2
not yet heard a nightingale above the sounds of street hawkers and
traffic, and the famed rose gardens of Persia were nowhere in
evidence; they remained out of sight, if they ever existed, sealed off
by high proprietary walls.

But my interest of the moment was not in the garden; my   3
eyes were fixed on my father-in-law. He was a large, imposing man in
his mid-90's, with high color, still-black eyebrows and the scrub of a
heavy beard. He might have passed for a much younger man and, in
fact, claimed to be in his young, vigorous 70's.

"What do you think of this?" he asked, pointing to his wives,   4
one large, one small, on either side of him. His wives smiled in my
direction, then at each other. My father-in-law continued to stare at
me and to wait; he really wanted to know what I thought.

For the few separate moments it took to translate his question   5
and my reply (with what distortion I shall never know), we gazed
coolly at each other, each an anthropologist confronting opacity—the
mind of a stranger. I thought I could hear him taking notes. I, for my
part, was certainly jotting things down—but only impressions. I

would see; I wasn't going to judge prematurely. My judgment, when it came, wouldn't be narrow, biased or culture-bound. "Customs differ," I said.

Long before meeting my father-in-law, I had been prepared 6 for this—or, rather, I had been briefed, and imagined that I was prepared. It had been a briefing full of history (polygamy as a practical solution to the decimation of the male population in warfare and the resulting disproportionate preponderance of females over males); it had been a briefing on principle as well (the Koranic requirement that the husband distribute his affection equally among the co-wives).

But, of course, I was not ready to confront the live instance— 7 three individuals who would bear an intimate family relation to me. Mother, father and what—aunt? mother-surrogate? I decided that the other party would simply be my Other Mother-in-Law. At that moment, the language barrier turned out to be an opportune cover for, really, I did not know what I thought.

The happy threesome sat cross-legged on a takhte, a low 8 wooden platform, covered with a rug. My particular mother-in-law, the tiny one, was the junior wife, chosen, I later learned, by the older woman as someone agreeable to herself, someone she thought the old man would like, too. The senior wife's passion was for talking, and her husband's silence had long been wearing her down. She wanted someone in the house willing to hear her out and, she hoped, to respond from time to time.

I was left to imagine the precise formalities, but it seemed to 9 me to be a marriage welcome to all the parties concerned. It was an arrangement not without its share of bickerings and quarrels, for however well-disposed the women were to each other, their respective children were rivals, and the wives were partisan for their children.

Still, as marriages go, theirs seemed to be a reasonably happy 10 one.

When it grew chilly, we moved indoors. The sitting room was 11 also my father-in-law's bedroom. He sat on a fine, ancient rug, with bolsters at his back, a bay of windows on his left and, in front of him, an array of small vials: vitamins, elixirs, purges. He didn't believe in modern medicine, but was taking no chances.

Stiff, wooden chairs of mismatching shapes were lined 12 against the walls of the room. I eyed them, but, noticing that they were mantled in dust, furred with a thin, unbroken velvet, decided they were not really for use, and sat on the floor instead. In fact, the chairs were chiefly ceremonial, a reluctant concession to the times, to the imposition of Westernization around the world. Not like the

ANN GRACE MOJTABAI

television set, which was an ecstatic testimony to the march of *universal* human progress, and which held, along with the samovar, pride of place among the old man's possessions.

The wives stepped out to bring refreshments. With a sinking 13 sense, I noticed my husband getting up to speak to his mother in private. I was utterly adrift, alone with my father-in-law, a total stranger. The old man turned to me and said what I later learned was: "When hearts speak, no language is necessary." I recognized none of the words, but I guessed from his face and tone that whatever it was he had said was meant to be comforting and, trusting in a language of gesture and sign, I ventured a smile by way of reply.

Even today, I do not know what I think about polygamy. Or, 14 perhaps, I know what I think—it's only that my feelings are mixed. Abstractly, I oppose the custom. These bonds ought to be reciprocal, one-to-one. Sexual favors *may* be distributed equally as required (a night with A, a night with B), but I doubt whether affection can be distributed so neatly. And, of course, the custom speaks of the poverty of opportunities for women.

On the other hand, the custom of mut'a, or temporary 15 marriage, practiced by Shiites, though not by Sunnites, seems to me to be possessed of some merits and, on the whole, somewhat more enlightened than prostitution, or the vaguely polygamous custom of balancing wife (with legal rights) with mistress (having no rights), which is so widely prevalent in the West.

In the mut'a marriage, a term is stipulated—a night, a year, a 16 decade, an hour, whatever. A set term, a mehr—a wedding endow-ment for the woman—mutual consent and a contract specifying all this are required. The children of such unions are legitimate and entitled to a share of the father's inheritance, although the sigheh, the temporary wife, has no claim to maintenance beyond the initial marriage endowment.

But polygamy is meant to be more than a mere alternative to 17 such clearly deficient institutions as prostitution. And my feelings for polygamy as a true and viable form of marriage remain contrary, held in suspension. My opposition in theory is muffled by my observation of one palpable contrary fact. I saw a polygamous marriage work, and work well. That my mothers-in-law were deeply attached to each other, I have no doubt. I tend to question rather more their devotion to the husband who brought them together.

As for two mothers-in-law in one household, an old proverb 18 would seem to apply: "Better two tigers in one cage than two mistresses in one household." But, in point of fact, the laws of addition don't always apply. After all, one shark and one codfish equal one shark; one raindrop and one raindrop equal one raindrop.

The two women worked off their intensities on each other, with less energy left for me. So, actually, I had one mother-in-law, which, as all the proverbs of all nations attest, was quite sufficient.

QUESTIONS

1. What effects of Westernization appear in the essay? Of which ones do the Iranians approve? Of which ones do they disapprove?

2. What academic-sounding reasons for polygamy has Mojtabai been given? Do they help her to confront the reality of it? Why or why not? What is her final attitude toward polygamy?

3. Identify Iranian words in the essay and explain what they mean.

4. What does Mojtabai mean when she describes her first meeting with her father-in-law as "each an anthropologist confronting opacity" (paragraph 5)? What level of language does that suggest Mojtabai uses in the essay? Can these words be used by Westerners to describe aspects of Western culture?

5. What is the function of the opening narrative? Why is it effective?

6. In this essay, the narrator is both actor and observer. How does this affect the tone of the essay?

7. Why does Mojtabai spend considerable time describing *mut'a?* What elements of contrast does she utilize here? For what purpose?

8. One paragraph is considerably shorter than the others. How does this contribute to the structure and meaning of the essay?

9. Discuss a custom you have confronted that was alien to your own values. Compare your response to Mojtabai's response.

10. a. Write an essay describing your confrontation with an alien custom and your response to it.
b. Write your own evaluation of polygamy.

foolishness

Adult Cruelty and Folly

St. Augustine of Hippo (354–430) was the son of a pagan and a Christian. At the age of 32, he became convinced of the truth of Christianity and subsequently achieved fame as one of the Church's greatest philosophers and polemicists. In his works *The City of God* (413–426) and *The Confessions* (397–398), he addresses the problem of evil in both world history and his own life. In this section from *The Confessions,* we learn that as a child, even a saint stumbles.

God, my God, great was the misery and great the 1
deception that I met with when it was impressed upon me that, to behave properly as a boy, I must obey my teachers. This was all that I might succeed in this world and excel in those arts of speech which would serve to bring honor among men and to gain deceitful riches. Hence I was sent to school to acquire learning, the utility of which, wretched child that I was, I did not know. Yet if I was slow at learning, I was beaten. This method was praised by our forebears, many of whom had passed through this life before us and had laid out the hard paths that we were forced to follow. Thus were both toil and sorrow multiplied for the sons of Adam.

We discovered, Lord, that certain men prayed to you and we 2
learned from them, and imagined you, as far as we could, as some sort of mighty one who could hear us and help us, even though not appearing before our senses. While still a boy, I began to pray to you, my help and my refuge, and in praying to you I broke the knots that tied my tongue. A little one, but with no little feeling, I prayed to you that I would not be beaten at school. When you did not hear me—and it was "not to be reputed folly in me"—my punishments, which were then a huge and heavy evil to me, were laughed at by older men, and even by my own parents who wished no harm to befall me.

Lord, is there any man of so great a soul, who clings to you 3
with so mighty love, is there anyone, I ask you—for indeed a certain type of stolidity is capable of this—is there anyone who so devoutly clings to you and is thus so deeply affected that he deems of little consequence the rack, the hook, and similar tools of torture—to be saved from which men throughout the whole world pray to you with great fear—although he loves those who dread such things most bitterly? If there is such a man, he acts in the way in which our parents laughed at the torments we boys suffered from our teachers.

In no less measure did we fear our punishments, and no less did we beseech you to let us escape.

Yet we sinned by writing, reading, and thinking over our 4 lessons less than was required of us. Lord, there was in us no lack of memory or intelligence, for you willed that we should have them in sufficient measure for our years. Yet we loved to play, and this was punished in us by men who did the same things themselves. However, the trivial concerns of adults are called business, while such things in children are punished by adults. Yet no one has pity on either children or grown-up men, or on both. Perhaps some fine judge of things approves my beatings. For I played ball as a child; by such play I was kept from quickly learning arts by which, as an adult, I would disport myself in a still more unseemly fashion. Did the very man who beat me act different from me? If he was outdone by a fellow teacher in some trifling discussion, he was more tormented by anger and envy than I was when beaten by my playmate in a ball game.

QUESTIONS

1. List some examples of adult cruelty and folly in this essay.

2. Contrast Augustine's youthful attitude toward education with his mature attitude. Why is his attitude toward business crucial to the essay?

3. Augustine makes frequent use of the words "O God, my God" and "Lord" in the essay. Why? What is the effect of such use?

4. How does Augustine use the phrase "sons of Adam" (paragraph 1)?

5. How is the word *yet* used to structure the paragraphs in this essay?

6. Does Augustine use specific or general examples from his childhood? What is the effect?

7. Why does Augustine use rhetorical questions to frame paragraph 3?

8. Locate and explain examples of situational and verbal irony in the essay.

9. According to Augustine, does education truly improve men and women? Do you agree with him? Justify your answer.

10. Write an essay using events from your own life to examine the values of education, punishment, business, or another related subject.

Soul Food

Imamu Amiri Baraka (1934–   ) is a playwright, novelist, editor, poet, essayist, and community leader. Baraka's most famous work, the play *Dutchman* (1964), is about the often destructive relations between black and white Americans. During his career, Baraka has, through the powerful use of the black idiom, introduced the public to the richness of black culture.

1   Recently, a young Negro novelist writing in *Esquire* about the beauties of America mentioned that one of the things wrong with Negroes was that, unlike the Chinese, boots have neither a language of their own nor a characteristic cuisine. And this to me is the deepest stroke, the unkindest cut, of oppression, especially as it has distorted Black Americans. America, where the suppliant, far from rebelling or even disagreeing with the forces that have caused him to suffer, readily backs them up and finally tries to become an honorary oppressor himself.

2   No language? No characteristic food? Oh, man, come on.

3   Maws are things ofays seldom get to peck, nor are you likely ever to hear about Charlie eating a chitterling. Sweet potato pies, a good friend of mine asked recently, "Do they taste anything like pumpkin?" Negative. They taste more like memory, if you're not uptown.

4   All those different kinds of greens (now quick frozen for anyone) once were all Sam got to eat. (Plus the potlikker, into which one slipped some throwed away meat.) Collards and turnips and kale and mustards were not fit for anybody but the woogies. So they found a way to make them taste like something somebody would want to freeze and sell to a Negro going to Harvard as exotic European spinach.

5   The watermelon, friend, was imported from Africa (by whom?) where it had been growing many centuries before it was necessary for some people to deny that they had ever tasted one.

6   Did you ever hear of a black-eyed pea? (Whitey used it for forage, but some folks couldn't.) And all those weird parts of the hog? (After the pig was stripped of its choicest parts, the feet, snout, tail, intestines, stomach, etc., were all left for the "members," who treated them mercilessly.) Is it mere myth that shades are death on chickens? (Deep fat frying, the Dutch found out in 17th century New Amsterdam, was an African speciality: and if you can get hold of a fried

chicken leg, or a fried porgie, you can find out what happened to that tradition.)

I had to go to Rutgers before I found people who thought 7 grits were meant to be eaten with milk and sugar, instead of gravy and pork sausage . . . and that's one of the reasons I left.

Away from home, you must make the trip uptown to get 8 really straight as far as a good grease is concerned. People kill chickens all over the world, but chasing them through the dark on somebody else's property would probably insure, once they went in the big bag, that you'd find some really beautiful way to eat them. I mean, after all the risk involved. The fruit of that tradition unfolds everywhere above 100th Street. There are probably more restaurants in Harlem whose staple is fried chicken, or chicken in the basket, than any other place in the world. Ditto, barbecued ribs—also straight out of the South with the West Indians, *i.e.*, Africans from farther south in the West, having developed the best sauce for roasting whole oxen and hogs, spicy and extremely hot.

Hoppin' John (black-eyed peas and rice), hushpuppies 9 (crusty cornmeal bread cooked in fish grease and best with fried fish, especially fried salt fish, which ought to soak overnight unless you're over fifty and can take all that salt), hoecake (pan bread), buttermilk biscuits and pancakes, fatback, *i.e.*, streak'alean-streak'afat, dumplings, neck bones, knuckles (both good for seasoning limas or string beans), okra (another African importation, other name gumbo), pork chops—some more staples of the Harlem cuisine. Most of the food came North when the people did.

There are hundreds of tiny restaurants, food shops, rib joints, 10 shrimp shacks, chicken shacks, "rotisseries" throughout Harlem that serve "soul food"—say, a breakfast of grits, eggs and sausage, pancakes and Alaga syrup—and even tiny booths where it's at least possible to get a good piece of barbecue, hot enough to make you whistle, or a chicken wing on a piece of greasy bread. You can *always* find a fish sandwich: a fish sandwich is something you walk with, or "Two of those small sweet potato pies to go." The Muslim temple serves bean pies which are really separate. It is never necessary to go to some big expensive place to get a good filling grease. You *can* go to the Red Rooster, or Wells, or Joch's, and get a good meal, but Jennylin's, a little place on 135th near Lenox, is more filling, or some place like the A&A food shop in a basement up in the 140's, and you can really get away. I guess a square is somebody who's in Harlem and eats at Nedicks.

QUESTIONS

1. According to Baraka, what foods and cooking styles originated in African or Afro-American culture?

2. The theme of white oppression and the black response to it recurs frequently in the essay. Identify some of the different ways in which the theme is put forth. Why does the author state and restate the theme?

3. List the various words that come from the black language and define them. There are also several references to "uptown" in the essay, which can be considered examples of metonymy. Explain.

4. Why is slang so effective in this essay?

5. What are the two opinions Baraka sets out to disprove? He uses two different methods of refuting these opinions. What are they?

6. How does the essay use inductive reasoning?

7. Why does Baraka present historical information in parentheses?

8. Analyze the development of Baraka's concluding paragraph.

9. Can you give examples of other systems of ethnic slang? What is the purpose of slang? Why do composition teachers often discourage the use of slang?

10. a. Write an essay that develops your own definition of soul food.
b. Write an argumentative essay on the value of "separate" languages used by some ethnic, social, or professional group.

BENJAMIN FRANKLIN

The Art of Procuring Pleasant Dreams

Benjamin Franklin (1706–1790), statesman, inventor, philanthropist, printer, scientist, diplomat, and author, was founding father not only of the American nation but of American humor, language, and values. His *Poor Richard's Almanack* (1732–1757) and *Autobiography* (written between 1771 and 1789) have had a tremendous influence on American readers and authors. In "The Art of Procuring Pleasant Dreams," Franklin offers some typically practical advice for improving the human condition.

As a great part of our life is spent in sleep during which   1
we have sometimes pleasant and sometimes painful
dreams, it becomes of some consequence to obtain the
one kind and avoid the other; for whether real or
imaginary, pain is pain and pleasure is pleasure. If we can sleep
without dreaming, it is well that painful dreams are avoided. If while
we sleep we can have any pleasing dream, it is, as the French say,
autant de gagné, so much added to the pleasure of life.

To this end it is, in the first place, necessary to be careful in   2
preserving health, by due exercise and great temperance; for, in
sickness, the imagination is disturbed, and disagreeable, sometimes
terrible, ideas are apt to present themselves. Exercise should precede
meals, not immediately follow them; the first promotes, the latter,
unless moderate, obstructs digestion. If, after exercise, we feed
sparingly, the digestion will be easy and good, the body lightsome,
the temper cheerful, and all the animal functions performed agreeable. Sleep, when it follows, will be natural and undisturbed; while
indolence with full feeding, occasions nightmares and horrors inexpressible; we fall from precipices, are assaulted by wild beasts,
murderers, and demons, and experience every variety of distress.
Observe, however, that the quantities of food and exercise are relative
things; those who move much may, and indeed ought to eat more;
those who use little exercise should eat little. In general, mankind,
since the improvement of cookery, eat about twice as much as nature
requires. Suppers are not bad, if we have not dined; but restless
nights naturally follow hearty suppers after full dinners. Indeed, as
there is a difference in constitutions, some rest well after these meals;
it costs them only a frightful dream and an apoplexy, after which they
sleep till doomsday. Nothing is more common in the newspapers,
than instances of people who, after eating a hearty supper, are found
dead abed in the morning.

Another means of preserving health, to be attended to, is the   3
having a constant supply of fresh air in your bedchamber. It has been
a great mistake, the sleeping in rooms exactly closed, and in beds
surrounded by curtains. No outward air that may come in to you is so
unwholesome as the unchanged air, often breathed, of a close
chamber. As boiling water does not grow hotter by longer boiling, if
the particles that receive greater heat can escape; so living bodies do
not putrefy, if the particles, so fast as they become putrid, can be
thrown off. Nature expels them by the pores of the skin and the
lungs, and in a free, open air they are carried off; but in a close room
we receive them again and again, though they become more and
more corrupt. A number of persons crowded into a small room thus
spoil the air in a few minutes, and even render it mortal, as in the
Black Hole at Calcutta. A single person is said to spoil only a gallon of

air per minute, and therefore requires a longer time to spoil a chamber-full; but it is done, however, in proportion, and many putrid disorders hence have their origin. It is recorded of Methusalem, who, being the longest liver, may be supposed to have best preserved his health, that he slept always in the open air; for, when he had lived five hundred years, an angel said to him: "Arise, Methusalem, and build thee an house, for thou shalt live yet five hundred years longer." But Methusalem answered, and said, "If I am to live but five hundred years longer, it is not worth while to build me an house; I will sleep in the air, as I have been used to do." Physicians, after having for ages contended that the sick should not be indulged with fresh air, have at length discovered that it may do them good. It is therefore to be hoped, that they may in time discover likewise, that it is not hurtful to those who are in health, and that we may be then cured of the *aërophobia*, that at present distresses weak minds, and makes them choose to be stifled and poisoned, rather than leave open the window of a bedchamber, or put down the glass of a coach.

Confined air, when saturated with perspirable matter, will   4
not receive more; and that matter must remain in our bodies, and occasion diseases; but it gives some previous notice of its being about to be hurtful, by producing certain uneasiness, slight indeed at first, which as with regard to the lungs is a trifling sensation, and to the pores of the skin a kind of restlessness, which is difficult to describe, and few that feel it know the cause of it. But we may recollect, that sometimes on waking in the night, we have, if warmly covered, found it difficult to get asleep again. We turn often without finding repose in any position. This fidgettiness (to use a vulgar expression for want of a better) is occasioned wholly by an uneasiness in the skin, owing to the retention of the perspirable matter—the bedclothes having received their quantity, and, being saturated, refusing to take any more. To become sensible of this by an experiment, let a person keep his position in the bed, but throw off the bedclothes, and suffer fresh air to approach the part uncovered of his body; he will then feel that part suddenly refreshed; for the air will immediately relieve the skin, by receiving, licking up, and carrying off, the load of perspirable matter that incommoded it. For every portion of cool air that approaches the warm skin, in receiving its part of that vapor, receives therewith a degree of heat that rarefies and renders it lighter, when it will be pushed away with its burthen, by cooler and therefore heavier fresh air, which for a moment supplies its place, and then, being likewise changed and warmed, gives way to a succeeding quantity. This is the order of nature, to prevent animals being infected by their own perspiration. He will now be sensible of the difference between the part exposed to the air and that which, remaining sunk in the bed, denies the air access; for this part now manifests its uneasiness more

distinctly by the comparison, and the seat of the uneasiness is more plainly perceived than when the whole surface of the body was affected by it.

Here, then, is one great and general cause of unpleasing 5 dreams. For when the body is uneasy, the mind will be disturbed by it, and disagreeable ideas of various kinds will in sleep be the natural consequences. The remedies, preventive and curative, follow:

1.   By eating moderately (as before advised for health's sake) less 6 perspirable matter is produced in a given time; hence the bedclothes receive it longer before they are saturated, and we may therefore sleep longer before we are made uneasy by their refusing to receive any more.

2.   By using thinner and more porous bedclothes, which will suffer 7 the perspirable matter more easily to pass through them, we are less incommoded, such being longer tolerable.

3.   When you are awakened by this uneasiness, and find you cannot 8 easily sleep again, get out of bed, beat up and turn your pillow, shake the bedclothes well, with at least twenty shakes, then throw the bed open and leave it to cool; in the meanwhile, continuing undrest, walk about your chamber till your skin has had time to discharge its load, which it will do sooner as the air may be dried and colder. When you begin to feel the cold air unpleasant, then return to your bed, and you will soon fall asleep, and your sleep will be sweet and pleasant. All the scenes presented to your fancy will be too of the pleasing kind. I am often as agreeably entertained with them, as by the scenery of an opera. If you happen to be too indolent to get out of bed, you may, instead of it, lift up your bedclothes with one arm and leg, so as to draw in a good deal of fresh air, and by letting them fall force it out again. This, repeated twenty times, will so clear them of the perspirable matter they have imbibed, as to permit your sleeping well for sometime afterwards. But this latter method is not equal to the former.

Those who do not love trouble, and can afford to have two 9 beds, will find great luxury in rising, when they wake in a hot bed, and going into the cool one. Such shifting of beds would also be of great service to persons ill of a fever, as it refreshes and frequently procures sleep. A very large bed, that will admit a removal so distant from the first situation as to be cool and sweet, may in a degree answer the same end.

One or two observations more will conclude this little piece. 10 Care must be taken, when you lie down, to dispose your pillow so as to suit your manner of placing your head, and to be perfectly easy;

then place your limbs so as not to bear inconveniently hard upon one another, as, for instance, the joints of your ankles; for, though a bad position may at first give but little pain and be hardly noticed, yet a continuance will render it less tolerable, and the uneasiness may come on while you are asleep, and disturb your imagination. These are the rules of the art. But, though they will generally prove effectual in producing the end intended, there is a case in which the most punctual observance of them will be totally fruitless. I need not mention the case to you, my dear friend, but my account of the art would be imperfect without it. The case is, when the person who desires to have pleasant dreams has not taken care to preserve, what is necessary above all things,

A GOOD CONSCIENCE.

QUESTIONS

1. What are the ways to procure pleasant dreams, according to Franklin?

2. Describe the causes of uneasiness at night as Franklin presents them.

3. How is Franklin using the word *art* in his title? Would his use of the word in the eighteenth century differ from present-day usage? In a related matter, the eighteenth-century scientific knowledge of physics and biology was considerably different from our own and was expressed in different terms. Identify and define these terms in Franklin's essay.

4. How does the frequent use of the word *should* contribute to establishing the tone of this essay?

5. Explain Franklin's use of classification to organize the essay.

6. What is the effect of saving "a good conscience" until the end of the essay? How does conscience differ from the other means of procuring good dreams mentioned by Franklin?

7. What is the thesis of this essay? How does its placement in the essay reflect the orderliness of Franklin's reasoning?

8. Identify transitional words that Franklin uses to maintain coherence in his essay. Do some work more effectively than others? Why?

9. Franklin's attitude toward dreams is quite different from Freud's. How do you think a psychologist with a Freudian orientation would respond to his advice?

10. Write an essay listing ways to secure a job, get high grades, or have a successful romance.

Bamama Goes to College

Ellen Holtz Goodman (1941–   ) is an award-winning journalist who writes a syndicated column for *The Boston Globe*.
She is the author of *Close to Home* (1979) and has been a
commentator on television and radio. Goodman is an adept
practitioner of the personal essay. In "Bamama Goes to
College," she takes a jaundiced look at higher education.

B oston—My friend received another degree this month.   1
She became a B.A., M.A., M.A., or as we fondly call
her, a Bamama.

This latest degree raised her academic tempera-   2
ture and the quality of her resume. In fact, my friend Bamama
officially became qualified to be unemployed in yet a better class of
jobs.

Let me explain. When she got a B.A. in philosophy four years   3
ago at the cost of $12,000 (them was the bargain basement days),
Bamama had the choice between becoming an overeducated waitress
or an overeducated office worker. So she became an overeducated
day-camp counselor and went back to school.

The next year, for $4,000, she got a degree in library science.   4
Now, qualified as a librarian, she won a job as an overeducated
part-time library assistant. In her off-hours, she became an overqualified clerk at a cheese counter. Rumors that she arranged the cheddar
according to the Dewey Decimal system were greatly exaggerated.

In any case, her course was clear. Before she entirely coated   5
her brain as well as her arteries with brie, she went back to school.
Now, $5,000 later, she is qualified not only as a librarian, but as a
school librarian, teacher, administrator, etc., for a school system in
need of an efficient, caring, well-educated Bamama. No such luck or,
rather, no such system.

So, Bamama has done the only logical thing: applied for and   6
been accepted for a Ph.D. program. With that degree, Bamamaphd,
three years older and deeper in debt, would be qualified as a college
professor and might therefore be able to find a job as an overqualified
school librarian.

She had, you see, followed the life pattern of Woody Allen,   7
who says that success has meant that he is now turned down for
dates by a better class of women. Bamama may be particularly adroit
at choosing a career track on which 90 percent of the stations have
been closed. But the problem is not uniquely hers.

There are more than one million Americans getting bachelor's   8
degrees this year, more than 300,000 getting master's degrees and
more than 32,000 getting doctorates.

They and/or their parents are up to their ears in debt. The   9
economy is up to its ears in the overeducated underemployed.

Eighty percent of the recent college graduates, we are told,   10
are doing work which was once done quite capably by people without
college degrees. The point is that you don't need the degree to do the
job. But nowadays you do need the degree to get the job.

College graduates may be getting the jobs once filled by   11
nongraduates, but they are not automatically filling the spots once
guaranteed by a degree. There is more educational competition at
every level. In fact, by 1985, 2.5 college graduates will be competing
for every "college" job.

This is the name of the 1980s war game called Defensive   12
Education. As economist Lester Thurow put it: "As the supply of
more highly educated labor increases, individuals find that they must
improve their own education qualification simply to defend their
current income position. If they do not go to college, others will and
they will not find their current job open to them."

This is described as the "tiptoe syndrome" in Michael   13
Harrington's Book, "Decade of Decision." At any parade, the people
in the second row stand on tiptoe to see over the heads of those in the
front row. Then everyone else behind them stands on tiptoe, just to
stay in the same position.

As more and more people go to college, a degree no longer   14
guarantees who will get ahead. But the lack of a degree still can
determine who will fall behind. We keep raising the education
threshold to the job market.

This is the sort of new truth that makes us feel trapped and   15
cynical and furious. Trapped into paying a fortune, not for advance
but for defense. Cynical about the real motivation for "Higher
Education."

Meanwhile, even as we play the game, the gap between our   16
educational level and job level grows and is filled with the discontent
of the "underemployed."

Remember the movie "Goodbye Columbus"? There was a   17
moment when the father who owns a trucking business shakes his
head watching his son work. Finally he sighs, "Four years of college,
and he can't load a truck."

Just a few years ago, that was funny. But at the current rate of   18
the education escalation war, the kid won't even be able to get a
tryout without a Ph.D.

QUESTIONS

1. According to Goodman, how much does it cost to become a Bamama?

2. What does Goodman mean by "Defensive Education"?

3. What is the effect of using the acronym Bamama in the title and in identifying Goodman's friend?

4. Goodman uses two terms to describe modern higher education. Define "tiptoe syndrome" and "education escalation war."

5. What is the effect of repetition in the essay?

6. What different rhetorical strategies are used in paragraph groups 1 to 7, 8 to 11, 12 to 16, and 17 to 18?

7. How does Goodman use humor to forward her argument?

8. In this argumentative essay, what kinds of evidence are given? Why?

9. A second kind of education is alluded to in the essay: practical education. How valuable do you believe education through experience is to your career goals?

10. Statistics are crucial to this essay. Write an argumentative essay that combines anecdote and statistical information. Two possible topics are "Drinking and Driving" and "Teenage Sex."

D. H. LAWRENCE

Do Women Change?

David Herbert Lawrence (1885–1930), novelist, essayist, and poet, wrote in the great tradition of English romanticism. He chafed under the conventions of his age and zealously extended the content and style of the English novel. His novels, such as *Sons and Lovers* (1913), *The Rainbow* (1915), *Women in Love* (1921), *The Plumed Serpent* (1926), and *Lady Chatterley's Lover* (1928), are famous for their often disquieting depictions of love and ambition in the modern world. Lawrence also wrote criticism; his *Studies in Classic American Literature* (1923) is still a revealing, if idiosyncratic, look at American literature. His inventive, powerful use of language is apparent in "Do Women Change?"

hey tell of all the things that are going to happen in the   1
future—babies bred in bottle, all the love-nonsense cut
out, women indistinguishable from men. But it seems to
me bosh. We like to imagine we are something very new
on the face of the earth. But it seems to me we flatter ourselves.
Motor-cars and aeroplanes are something novel, if not something
new—one could draw a distinction. But the people in them are
merely people, and not many steps up, if any, it seems to me, from
the people who went in litters or palanquins or chariots, or who
walked on foot from Egypt to Jordan, in the days of Moses. Humanity
seems to have an infinite capacity for remaining the same—that is,
human.

Of course, there are all kinds of ways of being human; but I   2
expect almost every possible kind is alive and kicking today. There
are little Cleopatras and Zenobias and Semiramises and Judiths and
Ruths, and even Mother Eves, today just the same as in all the
endless yesterdays. Circumstances make them little Cleopatras and
little Semiramises instead of big ones, because our age goes in for
quantity regardless of quality. But sophisticated people are sophisticated people, no matter whether it is Egypt or Atlantis. And sophisticated people are pretty well all alike. All that varies is the proportion
of "modern" people to all the other unmodern sorts, the sophisticated to the unsophisticated. And today there is a huge majority of
sophisticated people. And they are probably very little different from
all the other sophisticated people of all the other civilizations, since
man was man.

And women are just part of the human show. They aren't   3
something apart. They aren't something new on the face of the earth,
like the loganberry or artificial silk. Women are as sophisticated as
men, anyhow, and they were never anything but women, and they
are nothing but women today, whatever they may think of themselves. They say the modern woman is a new type. But is she? I
expect, in fact I am sure, there have been lots of women like ours in
the past, and if you'd been married to one of them, you wouldn't have
found her any different from your present wife. Women are women.
They only have phases. In Rome, in Syracuse, in Athens, in Thebes,
more than two or three thousand years ago, there was the bob-haired,
painted, perfumed Miss and Mrs. of today, and she inspired almost
exactly the feelings that our painted and perfumed Misses and Mrses.
inspire in the men.

I saw a joke in a German paper—a modern young man and a   4
modern young woman leaning on an hotel balcony at night, overlook-
ing the sea. *He:* "See the stars sinking down over the dark restless
ocean!" *She:* "Cut it out! My room number is 32!"

That is supposed to be very modern: the very modern   5

woman. But I believe women in Capri under Tiberias said *"Cut it out"* to their Roman and Campanian lovers in just the same way. And women in Alexandria in Cleopatra's time. Certain phases of history are "modern." As the wheel of history goes round women become "modern," then they become unmodern again. The Roman women of the late Empire were most decidedly "modern"—so were the women of Ptolemaic Egypt. True modern cut-it-out women. Only the hotels were run differently.

Modernity or modernism isn't something we've just invent-   6
ed. It's something that comes at the end of civilizations. Just as leaves in autumn are yellow, so the women at the end of every known civilization—Roman, Greek, Egyptian, etc.—have been modern. They were smart, they were *chic*, they said cut-it-out, and they did as they jolly well pleased.

And then, after all, how deep does modernness go? Even in a   7
woman? You give her a run for her money; and if you don't give it her, she takes it. The sign of modernness in a woman is that she says: Oh, cut it out, boy!—So the boy cuts it out—all the stars and ocean stuff.—My room number's thirty-two!—Come to the point!

But the point, when you come to it, is a very bare little place,   8
a very meagre little affair. It's extraordinary how meagre the point is once you've come to it. It's not much better than a full-stop. So the modern girl comes to the point brutally and repeatedly, to find that her life is a series of full-stops, then a mere string of dots. Cut it out, boy! . . . When she comes to dot number one thousand, she's getting about tired of dots, and of the plain point she's come to. The point is all too plain and too obvious. It is so pointed that it is pointless. Following the series of dots comes a blank—a dead blank. There's nothing left to cut out. Blank-eye!

Then the thoroughly modern girl begins to moan: Oh, boy,   9
do put something in again!—And the thoroughly modern boy, having cut it out so thoroughly that it will never grow again, tunes up with: I can't give you anything but love, Baby!—And the thoroughly modern girl accepts it with unction. She knows it's nothing but a most crestfallen echo from a sentimental past. But when you've cut everything out so that it will never grow again, you are thankful even for echoes from a sentimental past. And so the game begins again. Having cut it out, and brought it down to brass tacks, you find brass tacks are the last thing you want to lie down on.—Oh, boy, aren't you going to do something about it?—And the boy, having cut it all out so that it won't grow again, has no other bright inspiration but to turn the brass tacks round, when lo, they become the brass-headed nails that go around Victorian plush furniture. And there they are, the hyper-modern two.

No, women don't change. They only go through a rather   10

154   D. H. LAWRENCE   3

regular series of phases. They are first the slave; then the obedient helpmeet; then the respected spouse; then the noble matron; then the splendid woman and citizen; then the independent female; then the modern girl, oh, cut-it-out, boy! and when the boy has cut it all out, the mills of God grind on, and having nothing else to grind, they grind the cut-it-out girl down, down, down—back to—we don't know where—but probably to the slave once more, and the whole cycle starts afresh, on and on, till in the course of a thousand years or two we come once more to the really "modern" girl. Oh, cut it out, boy!

A lead-pencil has a point, an argument may have a point, remarks may be pointed, and a man who wants to borrow five pounds from you only comes to the point when he asks you for the fiver. Lots of things have points: especially weapons. But where is the point to life? Where is the point to love? Where, if it comes to the point, is the point to a bunch of violets? There is no point. Life and love are life and love, a bunch of violets is a bunch of violets, and to drag in the idea of a point is to ruin everything. Live and let live, love and let love, flower and fade, and follow the natural curve, which flows on, pointless. ⒒

Now women used to understand this better than men. Men, who were keen on weapons, which all have points, used to insist on putting points to life and love. But women used to know better. They used to know that life is a flow, a soft curving flow, a flowing together and a flowing apart and a flowing together again, in a long subtle motion that has no full-stops and no points, even if there are rough places. Women used to see themselves as a softly flowing stream of attraction and desire and beauty, soft quiet rivers of energy and peace. Then suddenly the idea changes. They see themselves as isolated things, independent females, instruments, instruments for love, instruments for work, instruments for politics, instruments for pleasure, this, that and the other. And as instruments they become pointed and they want everything, even a small child, even love itself, to have a point. When women start coming to the point, they don't hesitate. They pick a daisy, and they say: There must be a point to this daisy, and I'm going to get at it.—So they start pulling off the white petals, till there are none left. Then they pull away the yellow bits of the centre, and come to a mere green part, still without having come to the point. Then in disgust they tear the green base of the flower across, and say: I call that a fool flower. It had no point to it! ⑫

Life is not a question of points, but a question of flow. It's the *flow* that matters. If you come to think of it, a daisy even is like a little river flowing, that never for an instant stops. From the time when the tiny knob of a bud appears down among the leaves, during the slow rising up a stem, the slow swelling and pushing out the white petal-tips from the green, to the full round daisy, white and gold and ⑬ gay, that opens and shuts through a few dawns, a few nights, poised on the summit of her stem, then silently shrivels and mysteriously disappears—there is no stop, no halt, it is a perpetual little streaming of a gay little life out into full radiance and delicate shrivelling, like a perfect little fountain that flows and flows, and shoots away at last into the invisible, even then without any stop.

So it is with life, and especially with love. There is no point. 14 There is nothing you can cut out, except falsity, which isn't love or life. But the love itself is a flow, two little streams of feeling, one from the woman, one from the man, that flow and flow and never stop, and sometimes they twinkle with stars, sometimes they chafe, but still they flow on, intermingling; and if they rise to a floweriness like a daisy, that is part of the flow; and they will inevitably die down again, which is also part of a flow. And one relationship may produce many flowerinesses, as a daisy plant produces many daisies; but they will all die down again as the summer passes, though the green plant itself need not die. If flowers didn't fade they wouldn't be flowers, they'd be artificial things. But there are roots to faded flowers and in the root the flow continues and continues. And only the flow matters; live and let live, love and let love. There is no point to love.

QUESTIONS

1. Describe Lawrence's "cycle of womanhood."

2. According to Lawrence, what is the difference between new and novel? What novel things does he mention? Does he believe that the modern woman fits into either of these categories? Why or why not?

3. The level of language fluctuates radically in this essay. Why? Give some examples of high and low language.

4. Lawrence presents the clichés "cut it out," "down to brass tacks," and "what's the point" as symbols of the modern age. Explain the many different meanings for these terms.

5. There are references to several notable historical women. Who are they? Why does Lawrence choose to cite examples of classical women rather than modern ones? Where does he use general examples? Are they effective?

6. How does Lawrence use the symbols of the river and the flower to explain his view of love? What is the connection between the metaphors *point* and *flow*? What other figurative and implied contrasts serve to structure the essay?

7. What is the significance of the anecdote in paragraph 4 for the structure of the essay?

8. Where does Lawrence state his thesis? How do earlier paragraphs prepare for it? Compare these paragraphs with those that follow the thesis statement.

9. Do you agree with Lawrence that we are at the end of civilization? Why or why not?

10. a. Write one of two essays: "Do Women Change?" or "Do Men Change?"
b. Write an essay in which you examine the levels of meaning of an old cliché. Then show how it symbolizes an aspect of our culture.

CHARLES LAMB

A Bachelor's Complaint

Charles Lamb (1775–1834) was a famous essayist in England in the early nineteenth century. His writings ranged from children's tales to plays, but his forte was the personal essay. In *The Essays of Elia* (*London Magazine*, 1820–1825), Lamb described his friends, himself, and his society in a light, satiric style. In *Specimens of English Dramatic Poets* (1808), he inspired renewed interest in Elizabethan drama. Lamb describes the failures of matrimony under the persona of Elia, an eccentric bachelor, in the following selection, "A Bachelor's Complaint of the Behavior of Married People."

 s a single man, I have spent a good deal of my time in noting down the infirmities of Married People, to console myself for those superior pleasures, which they tell me I have lost by remaining as I am. 1

I cannot say that the quarrels of men and their wives ever made any great impression upon me, or had much tendency to strengthen me in those anti-social resolutions, which I took up long ago upon more substantial considerations. What oftenest offends me at the houses of married persons where I visit, is an error of quite a different description; it is that they are too loving. 2

Not too loving neither: that does not explain my meaning. 3

 A BACHELOR'S COMPLAINT

157

Besides, why should that offend me? The very act of separating themselves from the rest of the world, to have the fuller enjoyment of each other's society, implies that they prefer one another to all the world.

But what I complain of is, that they carry this preference so   4
undisguisedly, they perk it up in the faces of us single people so shamelessly, you cannot be in their company a moment without being made to feel, by some indirect hint or open avowal, that *you* are not the object of this preference. Now there are some things which give no offence, while implied or taken for granted merely; but expressed, there is much offence in them. If a man were to accost the first homely-featured or plain-dressed young woman of his acquaint-ance, and tell her bluntly, that she was not handsome or rich enough for him, and he could not marry her, he would deserve to be kicked for his ill manners; yet no less is implied in the fact, that having access and opportunity of putting the question to her, he has never yet thought fit to do it. The young woman understands this as clearly as if it were put into words; but no reasonable young woman would think of making this the ground of a quarrel. Just as little right have a married couple to tell me by speeches, and looks that are scarce less plain than speeches, that I am not the happy man—the lady's choice. It is enough that I know that I am not: I do not want this perpetual reminding.

The display of superior knowledge or riches may be made   5
sufficiently mortifying; but these admit of a palliative. The knowledge which is brought out to insult me, may accidentally improve me; and in the rich man's houses and pictures, his parks and gardens, I have a temporary usufruct at least. But the display of married happiness has none of these palliatives; it is throughout pure, unrecompensed, unqualified insult.

Marriage by its best title is a monopoly, and not of the least   6
invidious sort. It is the cunning of most possessors of any exclusive privilege to keep their advantage as much out of sight as possible, that their less favored neighbors, seeing little of the benefit, may be less disposed to question the right. But these married monopolists thrust the most obnoxious part of their patent into our faces.

Nothing is to me more distasteful than that entire complacen-   7
cy and satisfaction which beam in the countenances of a new-married couple—in that of the lady particularly; it tells you, that her lot is disposed of in this world: that *you* can have no hopes of her. It is true, I have none; nor wishes either, perhaps; but this is one of those truths which ought, as I said before, to be taken for granted, not expressed.

The excessive airs which those people give themselves,   8
founded on the ignorance of us unmarried people, would be more

offensive if they were less irrational. We will allow them to understand the mysteries belonging to their own craft better than we, who have not had the happiness to be made free of the company: but their arrogance is not content within these limits. If a single person presume to offer his opinion in their presence, though upon the most indifferent subject, he is immediately silenced as an incompetent person. Nay, a young married lady of my acquaintance, who, the best of the jest was, had not changed her condition above a fortnight before, in a question on which I had the misfortune to differ from her, respecting the properest mode of breeding oysters for the London market, had the assurance to ask with a sneer, how such an old Bachelor as I could pretend to know anything about such matters!

But what I have spoken of hitherto is nothing to the airs   9 which these creatures give themselves when they come, as they generally do, to have children. When I consider how little of a rarity children are—that every street and blind alley swarms with them— that the poorest people commonly have them in most abundance— that there are few marriages that are not blest with at least one of these bargains—how often they turn out ill, and defeat the fond hope of their parents, taking to vicious courses, which end in poverty, disgrace, the gallows, &c., I cannot for my life tell what cause for pride there can possibly be in having them. If they were young phoenixes, indeed, that were born but one in a year, there might be a pretext. But when they are so common—

I do not advert to the insolent merit which they assume with   10 their husbands on these occasions. Let *them* look to that. But why *we*, who are not their natural-born subjects, should be expected to bring our spices, myrrh, and incense—our tribute and homage of admiration—I do not see.

"Like as the arrows in the hand of the giant, even so are the   11 young children": so says the excellent office in our Prayer-book appointed for the churching of women. "Happy is the man that hath his quiver full of them": So say I; but then don't let him discharge his quiver upon us that are weaponless; let them be arrows, but not to gall and stick us. I have generally observed that these arrows are double-headed: they have two forks, to be sure to hit with one or the other. As for instance, where you come into a house which is full of children, if you happen to take no notice of them (you are thinking of something else, perhaps, and turn a deaf ear to their innocent caresses), you are set down as untractable, morose, a hater of children. On the other hand, if you find them more than usually engaging—if you are taken with their pretty manners, and set about in earnest to romp and play with them, some pretext or other is sure to be found for sending them out of the room; they are too noisy or boisterous, or Mr.—— does not like children. With one or other of these forks the arrow is sure to hit you.

I could forgive their jealousy, and dispense with toying with their brats, if it gives them any pain; but I think it unreasonable to be called upon to *love* them, where I see no occasion—to love a whole family, perhaps eight, nine, or ten indiscriminately—to love all the pretty dears, because children are so engaging! 12

I know there is a proverb, "Love me, love my dog": that is not always so very practicable, particularly if the dog be set upon you to tease you or snap at you in sport. But a dog, or a lesser thing—any inanimate substance, as a keepsake, a watch or a ring, a tree, or the place where we last parted when my friend went away upon a long absence, I can make shift to love, because I love him, and anything that reminds me of him, provided it be in its nature indifferent, and apt to receive whatever hue fancy can give it. But children have a real character, and an essential being of themselves: they are amiable or unamiable *per se;* I must love or hate them, as I see cause for either in their qualities. A child's nature is too serious a thing to admit of its being regarded as a mere appendage to another being, and to be loved or hated accordingly: they stand with me upon their own stock, as much as men and women do. Oh! but you will say, sure it is an attractive age—there is something in the tender years of infancy that of itself charms us? That is the very reason why I am more nice about them. I know that a sweet child is the sweetest thing in nature, not even excepting the delicate creatures which bear them; but the prettier the kind of a thing is, the more desirable it is that it should be pretty of its kind. One daisy differs not much from another in glory; but a violet should look and smell the daintiest. I was always rather squeamish in my women and children. 13

But this is not the worst: one must be admitted into their familiarity at least, before they can complain of inattention. It implies visits, and some kind of intercourse. But if the husband be a man with whom you have lived on a friendly footing before marriage—if you did not come in on the wife's side—if you did not sneak into the house in her train, but were an old friend in fast habits of intimacy before their courtship was so much as thought on,—look about you—your tenure is precarious—before a twelve-month shall roll over your head, you shall find your old friend gradually grow cool and altered towards you, and at last seek opportunities of breaking with you. I have scarce a married friend of my acquaintance, upon whose firm faith I can rely, whose friendship did not commence *after the period of his marriage.* With some limitations, they can endure that; but that the good man should have dared to enter into a solemn league of friendship in which they were not consulted, though it happened before they knew him,—before they that are now man and wife ever 14 met,—this is intolerable to them. Every long friendship, every old authentic intimacy, must be brought into their office to be new stamped with their currency, as a sovereign prince calls in the good old money that was coined in some reign before he was born or thought of, to be new marked and minted with the stamp of his authority, before he will let it pass current in the world. You may guess what luck generally befalls such a rusty piece of metal as I am in these *new mintings*.

Innumerable are the ways which they take to insult and worm you out of their husbands' confidence. Laughing at all you say with a kind of wonder, as if you were a queer kind of fellow that said good things, *but an oddity*, is one of the ways;—they have a particular kind of stare for the purpose;—till at last the husband, who used to defer to your judgment, and would pass over some excrescenses of understanding and manner for the sake of a general vein of observation (not quite vulgar) which he perceived in you, begins to suspect whether you are not altogether a humorist—a fellow well enough to have consorted with in his bachelor days, but not quite so proper to be introduced to ladies. This may be called the staring way; and is that which has oftenest been put in practice against me. 15

Then there is the exaggerating way, or the way of irony; that is, where they find you an object of especial regard with their husband, who is not so easily to be shaken from the lasting attachment founded on esteem which he has conceived towards you, by never qualified exaggerations to cry up all that you say or do, till the good man, who understands well enough that it is all done in compliment to him, grows weary of the debt of gratitude which is due to so much candor, and by relaxing a little on his part, and taking down a peg or two in his enthusiasm, sinks at length to the kindly level of moderate esteem—that "decent affection and complacent kindness" towards you, where she herself can join in sympathy with him without much stress and violence to her sincerity. 16

Another way (for the ways they have to accomplish so desirable a purpose are infinite) is, with a kind of innocent simplicity, continually to mistake what it was which first made their husband fond of you. If an esteem for something excellent in your moral character was that which riveted the chain which she is to break, upon any imaginary discovery of a want of poignancy in your conversation, she will cry, "I thought, my dear, you described your friend, Mr.——, as a great wit?" If, on the other hand, it was for some supposed charm in your conversation that he first grew to like you, and was content for this to overlook some trifling irregularities in your moral deportment, upon the first notice of any of these she as readily exclaims, "This, my dear, is your good Mr.——!" One good lady whom I took the liberty of expostulating with for not showing 17 me quite so much respect as I thought due to her husband's old friend, had the candor to confess to me that she had often heard Mr.—— speak of me before marriage, and that she had conceived a great desire to be acquainted with me, but that the sight of me had very much disappointed her expectations; for from her husband's representations of me, she had formed a notion that she was to see a fine, tall officer-like-looking man (I use her very words), the very reverse of which proved to be the truth. This was candid; and I had the civility not to ask her in return, how she came to pitch upon a standard of personal accomplishments for her husband's friends which differed so much from his own; for my friend's dimensions as near as possible approximate to mine; he standing five feet five in his shoes, in which I have the advantage of him by about half an inch; and he no more than myself exhibiting any indications of a martial character in his air or countenance.

These are some of the mortifications which I have encoun- 18 tered in the absurd attempt to visit at their houses. To enumerate them all would be a vain endeavor; I shall therefore just glance at the very common impropriety of which married ladies are guilty,—of treating us as if we were their husbands, and *vice versa*. I mean, when they use us with familiarity, and their husbands with ceremony. *Testacea*, for instance, kept me the other night two or three hours beyond my usual time of supping, while she was fretting because Mr.—— did not come home, till the oysters were all spoiled, rather than she would be guilty of the impoliteness of touching one in his absence. This was reversing the point of good manners; for ceremony is an invention to take off the uneasy feeling which we derive from knowing ourselves to be less the object of love and esteem with a fellow-creature than some other person is. It endeavors to make up, by superior attentions in little points, for that invidious preference which it is forced to deny in the greater. Had *Testacea* kept the oysters back for me, and withstood her husband's importunities to go to supper, she would have acted according to the strict rules of proprie-ty. I know no ceremony that ladies are bound to observe to their husbands, beyond the point of a modest behavior and decorum: therefore I must protest against the vicarious gluttony of *Cerasia*, who at her own table sent away a dish of Morellas, which I was applying to with great good-will, to her husband at the other end of the table, and recommended a plate of less extraordinary gooseberries to my unwedded palate in their stead. Neither can I excuse the wanton affront of——

But I am weary of stringing up all my married acquaintance 19 by Roman denominations. Let them amend and change their man-ners, or I promise to record the full-length English of their names, to the terror of all such desperate offenders in future.

CHARLES LAMB

QUESTIONS

1. Lamb labels several ways that women alienate their husbands from their friends. What are the labels and what are the ways?

2. What are the author's complaints about children?

3. What is the effect of using such words as *usufruct, monopoly,* and *patent*? From what field are they derived?

4. Give examples of connotative words used to describe women and children. How do these words reveal the author's attitudes?

5. What is the thesis of the essay? Why is it so surprising?

6. Show where Lamb uses conventional essay techniques such as classification, definition, and exemplification.

7. This essay is part of the series *Essays of Elia;* thus, Lamb does not speak in his own voice. What effect does this have upon your sense of the tone of the essay?

8. What techniques does Lamb use to criticize conventional attitudes toward marriage?

9. Do you think that marriage is overrated? Justify your answer.

10. Write a satiric essay on the supposed "evils" of friendship, motherhood, patriotism, or another, similar convention.

JOSEPH ADDISON

A Superstitious Household

Joseph Addison (1672–1719) was an essayist, poet, dramatist, statesman, and journalist. As a playwright, he wrote one of the most successful tragedies of the eighteenth century (*Cato,* in 1713). As a statesman, he served as secretary of state under George I. As an essayist, he wrote with reason and wit in *The Tatler* (1709–1711) and *The Spectator* (1711–1712, and 1714). Just as he excelled as a statesman and tragedian, he excelled as an essayist; he is often considered one of the best English essayists. Here, Addison examines one of the great foibles of his age—and ours.

Somnia, terrores magicos, miracula, sagas,
Nocturnos, lemures, portentaque Thessala rides?*

Horace

G oing yesterday to dine with an old acquaintance, I had 1
the misfortune to find his whole family very much
dejected. Upon asking him the occasion of it, he told me
that his wife had dreamt a very strange dream the night
before, which they were afraid portended some misfortune to themselves or to their children. At her coming into the room, I observed a
settled melancholy in her countenance, which I should have been
troubled for, had I not heard from whence it proceeded. We were no
sooner sat down, but, after having looked upon me a little while, "My
dear," says she, turning to her husband, "you may now see the
stranger that was in the candle last night." Soon after this, as they
began to talk of family affairs, a little boy at the lower end of the table
told her that he was to go into join-hand on Thursday. "Thursday?"
says she, "no, child, if it please God, you shall not begin upon
Childermas Day, tell your writing master that Friday will be soon
enough." I was reflecting with myself on the oddness of her fancy,
and wondering that anybody would establish it as a rule to lose a day
in every week. In the midst of these my musings, she desired me to
reach her a little salt upon the point of my knife, which I did in such a
trepidation and hurry of obedience, that I let it drop by the way; at
which she immediately startled, and said it fell towards her. Upon
this I looked very blank; and, observing the concern of the whole
table, began to consider myself, with some confusion, as a person
that had brought a disaster upon the family. The lady however
recovering herself, after a little space, said to her husband with a sigh,
"My dear, misfortunes never come single." My friend, I found, acted
but an under part at his table, and being a man of more good nature
than understanding, thinks himself obliged to fall in with all the
passions and humors of his yoke-fellow. "Do not you remember,
child," says she, "that the pigeon-house fell the very afternoon that
our careless wench spilt the salt upon the table?" "Yes," says he, "my
dear, and the next post brought us an account of the battle of
Almanza." The reader may guess at the figure I made, after having
done all this mischief. I despatched my dinner as soon as I could,
with my usual taciturnity; when, to my utter confusion, the lady
seeing me cleaning my knife and fork, and laying them across one
another upon my plate, desired me that I would humor her so far as

---

*"Can you make sport of portents, gipsy crones, Hobgoblins, dreams, raw head and bloody
bones?"

John Conington (translator)

JOSEPH ADDISON   3

to take them out of that figure, and place them side by side. What the absurdity was which I had committed I did not know, but I suppose there was some traditionary superstition in it; and therefore, in obedience to the lady of the house, I disposed of my knife and fork in two parallel lines, which is the figure I shall always lay them in for the future, though I do not know any reason for it.

It is not difficult for a man to see that a person has conceived 2 an aversion to him. For my own part, I quickly found, by the lady's looks, that she regarded me as a very odd kind of fellow, with an unfortunate aspect: for which reason I took my leave immediately after dinner, and withdrew to my own lodgings. Upon my return home, I fell into a profound contemplation on the evils that attend these superstitious follies of mankind; how they subject us to imaginary afflictions, and additional sorrows, that do not properly come within our lot. As if the natural calamities of life were not sufficient for it, we turn the most indifferent circumstances into misfortunes, and suffer as much from trifling accidents as from real evils. I have known the shooting of a star spoil a night's rest; and have seen a man in love grow pale and lose his appetite upon the plucking of a merry-thought. A screech owl at midnight has alarmed a family more than a band of robbers; nay, the voice of a cricket hath struck more terror than the roaring of a lion. There is nothing so inconsiderable, which may not appear dreadful to an imagination that is filled with omens and prognostics. A rusty nail, or a crooked pin, shoot up into prodigies.

I remember I was once in a mixed assembly, that was full of 3 noise and mirth, when on a sudden an old woman unluckily observed there were thirteen of us in company. This remark struck a panic terror into several who were present, insomuch that one or two of the ladies were going to leave the room; but a friend of mine taking notice that one of our female companions was big with child, affirmed there were fourteen in the room, and that, instead of portending one of the company should die, it plainly foretold one of them should be born. Had not my friend found this expedient to break the omen, I question not but half the women in the company would have fallen sick that very night.

An old maid, that is troubled with the vapors, produces 4 infinite disturbances of this kind among her friends and neighbors. I know a maiden aunt of a great family, who is one of these antiquated Sibyls, that forebodes and prophesies from one end of the year to the other. She is always seeing apparitions, and hearing death-watches, and was the other day almost frightened out of her wits by the great house-dog, that howled in the stable at a time when she lay ill of the tooth-ache. Such an extravagant cast of mind engages multitudes of people not only in impertinent terrors, but in supernumerary duties

 A SUPERSTITIOUS HOUSEHOLD

of life; and arises from that fear and ignorance which are natural to the soul of man. The horror with which we entertain the thoughts of death (or indeed of any future evil) and the uncertainty of its approach, fill a melancholy mind with innumerable apprehensions and suspicions, and consequently dispose it to the observation of such groundless prodigies and predictions. For as it is the chief concern of wise men to retrench the evils of life by the reasonings of philosophy; it is the employment of fools to multiply them by the sentiments of superstition.

For my own part, I should be very much troubled were I 5 endowed with this divining quality, though it should inform me truly of every thing that can befall me. I would not anticipate the relish of any happiness, nor feel the weight of any misery, before it actually arrives.

I know but one way of fortifying my soul against these 6 gloomy presages and terrors of mind, and that is, by securing to myself the friendship and protection of that Being who disposes of events, and governs futurity. He sees, at one view, the whole thread of my existence, not only that part of it which I have already passed through, but that which runs forward into all the depths of eternity. When I lay me down to sleep, I recommend myself to his care; when I awake, I give myself up to his direction. Amidst all the evils that threaten me, I will look up to him for help, and question not but he will either avert them, or turn them to my advantage. Though I know neither the time nor the manner of the death I am to die, I am not at all solicitous about it; because I am sure that he knows them both, and that he will not fail to comfort and support me under them.

QUESTIONS

1. Compare the attitude of Addison toward superstition with the attitude of his acquaintance's wife. What is the difference between wise men and fools?

2. Even if he could foretell the future, Addison would choose not to. Why?

3. Who was the Sibyl? Why is the allusion to her in paragraph 4 appropriate? Why does Addison compare elderly, superstitious women to the Sybil?

4. Define these words: *join-hard* (paragraph 1); *Childermas* (paragraph 1); *merry-thought* (paragraph 2); *death-watches* (paragraph 4).

5. How are superstitions examples of the logical fallacy *post hoc ergo propter hoc* in this essay?

166   **JOSEPH ADDISON**

6. Detail shifts of tone in the essay. What function does the difference serve?

7. Contrast Addison's ignorance or knowledge of superstitions in paragraphs 1 and 2 with that in the rest of the essay.

8. What assumptions about reason and superstition underly this essay?

9. What superstitions described in the essay are still prevalent today? Why do you think superstitions remain popular?

10. Write an argumentative essay on the value of superstition. Write it from the first-person point of view and cite examples.

JONATHAN SWIFT

A Treatise on Good Manners and Good Breeding

Jonathan Swift (1667–1745) is best known as the author of three satires: *A Tale of a Tub* (1704), *Gulliver's Travels* (1726), and *A Modest Proposal* (1729). In these satires, he pricks the balloons of many of his contemporaries and our own most cherished prejudices, pomposities, and delusions. Swift was also a famous churchman, an eloquent spokesman for Irish rights, and a political journalist. In this essay, he examines the uses and abuses of "good manners."

ood manners is the art of making those people easy with whom we converse. 1

Whoever makes the fewest persons uneasy is the best bred in the company. 2

As the best law is founded upon reason, so are the best manners. And as some lawyers have introduced unreasonable things into common law, so likewise many teachers have introduced absurd things into common good manners. 3

One principal point of this art is to suit our behaviour to the three several degrees of men; our superiors, our equals, and those below us. 4

For instance, to press either of the two former to eat or drink is a breach of manners; but a farmer or a tradesman must be thus treated, or else it will be difficult to persuade them that they are welcome. 5

Pride, ill nature, and want of sense, are the three great   6
sources of ill manners; without some one of these defects, no man
will behave himself ill for want of experience; or of what, in the
language of fools, is called knowing the world.

I defy any one to assign an incident wherein reason will not   7
direct us what we are to say or do in company, if we are not misled by
pride or ill nature.

Therefore I insist that good sense is the principal foundation   8
of good manners; but because the former is a gift which very few
among mankind are possessed of, therefore all the civilized nations of
the world have agreed upon fixing some rules for common behaviour, best suited to their general customs, or fancies, as a kind of
artificial good sense, to supply the defects of reason. Without which
the gentlemanly part of dunces would be perpetually at cuffs, as they
seldom fail when they happen to be drunk, or engaged in squabbles
about women or play. And, God be thanked, there hardly happens a
duel in a year, which may not be imputed to one of those three
motives. Upon which account, I should be exceedingly sorry to find
the legislature make any new laws against the practice of duelling;
because the methods are easy and many for a wise man to avoid a
quarrel with honour, or engage in it with innocence. And I can
discover no political evil in suffering bullies, sharpers, and rakes, to
rid the world of each other by a method of their own; where the law
hath not been able to find an expedient.

As the common forms of good manners were intended for   9
regulating the conduct of those who have weak understandings; so
they have been corrupted by the persons for whose use they were
contrived. For these people have fallen into a needless and endless
way of multiplying ceremonies, which have been extremely troublesome to those who practise them, and insupportable to everybody
else: insomuch that wise men are often more uneasy at the over
civility of these refiners, than they could possibly be in the conversations of peasants or mechanics.

The impertinencies of this ceremonial behaviour are nowhere   10
better seen than at those tables where ladies preside, who value
themselves upon account of their good breeding; where a man must
reckon upon passing an hour without doing any one thing he has a
mind to; unless he will be so hardy to break through all the settled
decorum of the family. She determines what he loves best, and how
much he shall eat; and if the master of the house happens to be of the
same disposition, he proceeds in the same tyrannical manner to
prescribe in the drinking part: at the same time, you are under the
necessity of answering a thousand apologies for your entertainment.
And although a good deal of this humour is pretty well worn off
among many people of the best fashion, yet too much of it still

remains, especially in the country; where an honest gentleman assured me, that having been kept four days, against his will, at a friend's house, with all the circumstances of hiding his boots, locking up the stable, and other contrivances of the like nature, he could not remember, from the moment he came into the house to the moment he left it, any one thing, wherein his inclination was not directly contradicted; as if the whole family had entered into a combination to torment him.

But, besides all this, it would be endless to recount the many 11 foolish and ridiculous accidents I have observed among these unfortunate proselytes to ceremony. I have seen a duchess fairly knocked down, by the precipitancy of an officious coxcomb running to save her the trouble of opening a door. I remember, upon a birthday at court, a great lady was utterly desperate by a dish of sauce let fall by a page directly upon her head-dress and brocade, while she gave a sudden turn to her elbow upon some point of ceremony with the person who sat next her. Monsieur Buys, the Dutch envoy, whose politics and manners were much of a size, brought a son with him, about thirteen years old, to a great table at court. The boy and his father, whatever they put on their plates, they first offered round in order, to every person in the company; so that we could not get a minute's quiet during the whole dinner. At last their two plates happened to encounter, and with so much violence, that, being china, they broke in twenty pieces, and stained half the company with wet sweetmeats and cream.

There is a pedantry in manners, as in all arts and sciences; 12 and sometimes in trades. Pedantry is properly the overrating any kind of knowledge we pretend to. And if that kind of knowledge be a trifle in itself, the pedantry is the greater. For which reason I look upon fiddlers, dancing-masters, heralds, masters of the ceremony, &c. to be greater pedants than Lipsius, or the elder Scaliger. With these kind of pedants, the court, while I knew it, was always plentifully stocked; I mean from the gentleman usher (at least) inclusive, downward to the gentleman porter; who are, generally speaking, the most insignificant race of people that this island can afford, and with the smallest tincture of good manners, which is the only trade they profess. For being wholly illiterate, and conversing chiefly with each other, they reduce the whole system of breeding within the forms and circles of their several offices; and as they are below the notice of ministers, they live and die in court under all revolutions with great obsequiousness to those who are in any degree of favour or credit, and with rudeness or insolence to everybody else. Whence I have long concluded, that good manners are not a plant of the court growth: for if they were, those people who have understandings directly of a level for such acquirements, and who have served such long apprenticeships to nothing else, would certainly have picked them up. For as to the great officers, who attend the prince's person or councils, or preside in his family, they are a transient body, who have no better a title to good manners than their neighbours, nor will probably have recourse to gentlemen ushers for instruction. So that I know little to be learnt at court upon this head, except in the material circumstance of dress; wherein the authority of the maids of honour must indeed be allowed to be almost equal to that of a favourite actress.

I remember a passage my Lord Bolingbroke told me, that 13 going to receive Prince Eugene of Savoy at his landing, in order to conduct him immediately to the Queen, the prince said, he was much concerned that he could not see her Majesty that night; for Monsieur Hoffman (who was then by) had assured his Highness that he could not be admitted into her presence with a tied-up periwig; that his equipage was not arrived; and that he had endeavoured in vain to borrow a long one among all his valets and pages. My lord turned the matter into a jest, and brought the Prince to her Majesty; for which he was highly censured by the whole tribe of gentlemen ushers; among whom Monsieur Hoffman, an old dull resident of the Emperor's, had picked up this material point of ceremony; and which, I believe, was the best lesson he had learned in five-and-twenty years' residence.

I make a difference between good manners and good breed- 14 ing; although, in order to vary my expression, I am sometimes forced to confound them. By the first, I only understand the art of remembering and applying certain settled forms of general behaviour. But good breeding is of a much larger extent; for besides an uncommon degree of literature sufficient to qualify a gentleman for reading a play, or a political pamphlet, it takes in a great compass of knowledge; no less than that of dancing, fighting, gaming, making the circle of Italy, riding the great horse, and speaking French; not to mention some other secondary, or subaltern accomplishments, which are more easily acquired. So that the difference between good breeding and good manners lies in this, that the former cannot be attained to by the best understandings, without study and labour; whereas a tolerable degree of reason will instruct us in every part of good manners, without other assistance.

I can think of nothing more useful upon this subject, than to 15 point out some particulars, wherein the very essentials of good manners are concerned, the neglect or perverting of which doth very much disturb the good commerce of the world, by introducing a traffic of mutual uneasiness in most companies.

First, a necessary part of good manners, is a punctual 16 observance of time at our own dwellings, or those of others, or at third places; whether upon matter of civility, business, or diversion;

which rule, though it be a plain dictate of common reason, yet the greatest minister I ever knew was the greatest trespasser against it; by which all his business doubled upon him, and placed him in a continual arrear. Upon which I often used to rally him, as deficient in point of good manners. I have known more than one ambassador, and secretary of state with a very moderate portion of intellectuals, execute their offices with good success and applause, by the mere force of exactness and regularity. If you duly observe time for the service of another, it doubles the obligation; if upon your own account, it would be manifest folly, as well as ingratitude, to neglect it. If both are concerned, to make your equal or inferior attend on you, to his own disadvantage, is pride and injustice.

Ignorance of forms cannot properly be styled ill manners; 17 because forms are subject to frequent changes; and consequently, being not founded upon reason, are beneath a wise man's regard. Besides, they vary in every country; and after a short period of time, very frequently in the same; so that a man who travels, must needs be at first a stranger to them in every court through which he passes; and perhaps at his return, as much a stranger in his own; and after all, they are easier to be remembered or forgotten than faces or names.

Indeed, among the many impertinencies that superficial 18 young men bring with them from abroad, this bigotry of forms is one of the principal, and more prominent than the rest; who look upon them not only as if they were matters capable of admitting of choice, but even as points of importance; and are therefore zealous on all occasions to introduce and propagate the new forms and fashions they have brought back with them. So that, usually speaking, the worst bred person in the company is a young traveller just returned from abroad.

QUESTIONS

1. What does Swift say are the differences between good manners and ceremony?

2. According to Swift, what are artificial manners? Why have they developed? What examples of ceremonious manners does Swift offer?

3. Why are the allusions to Lipsius and Scaliger appropriate in paragraph 12?

4. In paragraph 12, Swift defines pedantry. Give examples of his use of hyperbole and connotative language in this paragraph.

5. How does Swift define a gentleman? Give examples from the essay.

6. Analyze Swift's use of comparison to support his thesis.

 A TREATISE ON GOOD MANNERS AND GOOD BREEDING

7. Explain how the anecdote concerning Lord Bolingbroke in paragraph 13 illustrates the general statements in paragraph 12. What other examples of anecdotes supporting assertions are there in the essay?

8. How does the digression in paragraph 8 reveal Swift's attitude toward aristocracy? Is there any contrary evidence in the essay? If so, where?

9. Would we be better off without manners? Have you ever been made uncomfortable by manners? Explain.

10. Write an essay exploring the absurdities of modern manners.

FRANCIS BACON

Of Envy

Francis Bacon (1561–1626), a contemporary of William Shakespeare, Queen Elizabeth, and James I, was a noted author, scientist, and statesman. In *The Advancement of Learning* (1605) and *The Novum Organum* (1620), Bacon argued the superiority of inductive over deductive reasoning. His literary reputation rests on his *Essays* (1597–1625), in which he examines human character and society. "Of Envy" is part of this collection.

here be none of the affections which have been noted to 1 fascinate or bewitch, but love and envy. They both have vehement wishes; they frame themselves readily into imaginations and suggestions; and they come easily into the eye, especially upon the presence of the objects; which are the points that conduce to fascination, if any such thing there be. We see likewise the scripture calleth envy an *evil eye;* and the astrologers call the evil influences of the stars *evil aspects;* so that there seemeth to be acknowledged, in the act of envy, an ejaculation or irradiation of the eye. Nay some have been so curious as to note, that the times when the stroke or percussion of an envious eye doth most hurt, are when the party envied is beheld in glory or triumph; for that sets an edge upon envy; and besides, at such times the spirits of the person envied do come forth most into the outward parts, and so meet the blow.

But leaving these curiosities, (though not unworthy to be 2 thought on in fit place,) we will handle, what persons are apt to envy others; what persons are most subject to be envied themselves; and what is the difference between public and private envy.

A man that hath no virtue in himself, ever envieth virtue in others. For men's minds will either feed upon their own good or upon others' evil; and who wanteth the one will prey upon the other; and whoso is out of hope to attain to another's virtue, will seek to come at even hand by depressing another's fortune. 3

A man that is busy and inquisitive is commonly envious. For to know much of other men's matters cannot be because all that ado may concern his own estate; therefore it must needs be that he taketh a kind of play-pleasure in looking upon the fortunes of others. Neither can he that mindeth but his own business find much matter for envy. For envy is a gadding passion, and walketh the streets, and doth not keep home: *Non est curiosus, quin idem sit malevolus:* [There is no curious man but has some malevolence to quicken his curiosity.] 4

Men of noble birth are noted to be envious towards new men when they rise. For the distance is altered; and it is like a deceit of the eye, that when others come on they think themselves go back. 5

Deformed persons, and eunuchs, and old men, and bastards, are envious. For he that cannot possibly mend his own case will do what he can to impair another's; except these defects light upon a very brave and heroical nature, which thinketh to make his natural wants part of his honour; in that it should be said, that an eunuch, or a lame man, did such great matters; affecting the honour of a miracle; as it was in Narses the eunuch, and Agesilaus and Tamberlanes, that were lame men. 6

The same is the case of men that rise after calamities and misfortunes. For they are as men fallen out with the times; and think other men's harms a redemption of their own sufferings. 7

They that desire to excel in too many matters, out of levity and vain glory, are ever envious. For they cannot want work; it being impossible but many in some one of those things should surpass them. Which was the character of Adrian the Emperor; that mortally envied poets and painters and artificers, in works wherein he had a vein to excel. 8

Lastly, near kinsfolks, and fellows in office, and those that have been bred together, are more apt to envy their equals when they are raised. For it doth upbraid unto them their own fortunes, and pointeth at them, and cometh oftener into their remembrance, and incurreth likewise more into the note of others; and envy ever redoubleth from speech and fame. Cain's envy was the more vile and malignant towards his brother Abel, because when his sacrifice was better accepted there was no body to look on. Thus much for those that are apt to envy. 9

Concerning those that are more or less subject to envy: First, 10 persons of eminent virtue, when they are advanced, are less envied. For their fortune seemeth but due unto them; and no man envieth the payment of a debt, but rewards and liberality rather. Again, envy is ever joined with the comparing of a man's self; and where there is no comparison, no envy; and therefore kings are not envied but by kings. Nevertheless it is to be noted that unworthy persons are most envied at their first coming in, and afterwards overcome it better; whereas contrariwise, persons of worth and merit are most envied when their fortune continueth long. For by that time, though their virtue be the same, yet it hath not the same lustre; for fresh men grow up that darken it.

Persons of noble blood are less envied in their rising. For it 11 seemeth but right done to their birth. Besides, there seemeth not much added to their fortune; and envy is as the sunbeams, that beat hotter upon a bank or steep rising ground than upon a flat. And for the same reason those that are advanced by degrees are less envied than those that are advanced suddenly and *per saltum* [by a leap].

Those that have joined with their honour great travels, cares, 12 or perils, are less subject to envy. For men think that they earn their honours hardly, and pity them sometimes; and pity ever healeth envy. Wherefore you shall observe that the more deep and sober sort of politic persons, in their greatness, are ever bemoaning themselves, what a life they lead; chanting a *quanta patimur* [how we suffer!]. Not that they feel it so, but only to abate the edge of envy. But this is to be understood of business that is laid upon men, and not such as they call unto themselves. For nothing increaseth envy more than an unnecessary and ambitious engrossing of business. And nothing doth extinguish envy more than for a great person to preserve all other inferior officers in their full rights and pre-eminences of their places. For by that means there be so many screens between him and envy.

Above all, those are most subject to envy, which carry the 13 greatness of their fortunes in an insolent and proud manner; being never well but while they are shewing how great they are, either by outward pomp, or by triumphing over all opposition or competition; whereas wise men will rather do sacrifice to envy, in suffering themselves sometimes of purpose to be crossed and overborne in things that do not much concern them. Notwithstanding so much is true, that the carriage of greatness in a plain and open manner (so it be without arrogancy and vain glory) doth draw less envy than if it be in a more crafty and cunning fashion. For in that course a man doth but disavow fortune; and seemeth to be conscious of his own want in worth; and doth but teach others to envy him.

Lastly, to conclude this part; as we said in the beginning that   14
the act of envy had somewhat in it of witchcraft, so there is no other
cure of envy but the cure of witchcraft; and that is, to remove the *lot*
(as they call it) and to lay it upon another. For which purpose, the
wiser sort of great persons bring in ever upon the stage somebody
upon whom to derive the envy that would come upon themselves;
sometimes upon ministers and servants; sometimes upon colleagues
and associates; and the like; and for that turn there are never wanting
some persons of violent and undertaking natures, who, so they may
have power and business, will take it at any cost.

Now, to speak of public envy. There is yet some good in   15
public envy, whereas in private there is none. For public envy is as an
ostracism, that eclipseth men when they grow too great. And
therefore it is a bridle also to great ones, to keep them within bounds.

This envy, being in the Latin word *invidia*, goeth in the   16
modern languages by the name of *discontentment;* of which we shall
speak in handling Sedition. It is a disease in a state like to infection.
For as infection spreadeth upon that which is sound, and tainteth it;
so when envy is gotten once into a state, it traduceth even the best
actions thereof, and turneth them into an ill odour. And therefore
there is little won by intermingling of plausible actions. For that doth
argue but a weakness and fear of envy, which hurteth so much the
more; as it is likewise usual in infections; which if you fear them, you
call them upon you.

This public envy seemeth to beat chiefly upon principal   17
officers or ministers, rather than upon kings and estates themselves.
But this is a sure rule, that if the envy upon the minister be great,
when the cause of it in him is small; or if the envy be general in a
manner upon all the ministers of an estate; then the envy (though
hidden) is truly upon the state itself. And so much of public envy or
discontentment, and the difference thereof from private envy, which
was handled in the first place.

We will add this in general, touching the affection of envy;   18
that of all other affections it is the most importune and continual. For
of other affections there is occasion given but now and then; and
therefore it was well said, *Invidia festos dies non agit:* [Envy keeps no
holidays:] for it is ever working upon some or other. And it is also
noted that love and envy do make a man pine, which other affections
do not, because they are not so continual. It is also the vilest affection,
and the most depraved; for which cause it is the proper attribute of
the devil, who is called *The envious man, that soweth tares amongst the
wheat by night;* as it always cometh to pass, that envy worketh subtilly,
and in the dark; and to the prejudice of good things, such as is the
wheat.

QUESTIONS

1. In what ways does Bacon say love and envy are similar?

2. What steps can one take to minimize envy in others?

3. The -eth suffix appears frequently in this essay. Is there an ending used in modern English to mean the same thing -eth does? What is it?

4. Define the following words as Bacon uses them: *affections* (paragraph 1); *conduce* (paragraph 1); *evil eye* (paragraph 1); *ejaculation* (paragraph 1); *curious* (paragraph 1); *percussion* (paragraph 1); *gadding* (paragraph 4); *natural wants* (paragraph 6); *artificers* (paragraph 8); *importune* (paragraph 18).

5. Bacon uses classification and listing in this essay. Give examples of both.

6. Is Bacon's subject concrete or abstract? How does the nature of his subject affect his use of rhetorical devices?

7. Bacon's essays are well known for their aphorisms. Identify several in this essay.

8. Is this an argumentative or expository essay? Give reasons for your choice.

9. Bacon wrote this essay almost 300 years ago. Are any of his types still relevant? Can you give any contemporary examples of personal and public envy?

10. Write an essay describing a term like *envy*, such as *hatred* or *jealousy*. Divide the body of your essay into two parts: one for those who attract these feelings and one for those who have them.

Human Development and Behavior

VIRGINIA WOOLF

The Death of the Moth

Virginia Woolf (1882–1941), novelist and essayist, was the daughter of Leslie Stephen, a famous critic and writer on economics. An experimental novelist, Woolf attempted to portray consciousness through a poetic, symbolic, and concrete style. Her novels include *Jacob's Room* (1922), *Mrs. Dalloway* (1925), *To the Lighthouse* (1927), and *The Waves* (1931). She was also a perceptive reader and critic, and her criticism appears in *The Common Reader* (1925) and *The Second Common Reader* (1933). The following essay, which demonstrates Woolf's capacity to convey profound meaning even in commonplace events, appeared in *The Death of a Moth and Other Essays* (1948).

oths that fly by day are not properly to be called moths; they do not excite that pleasant sense of dark autumn nights and ivy-blossom which the commonest yellow-underwing asleep in the shadow of the curtain never fails to rouse in us. They are hybrid creatures, neither gay like butterflies nor sombre like their own species. Nevertheless the present specimen, with his narrow hay-coloured wings, fringed with a tassel of the same colour, seemed to be content with life. It was a pleasant morning, mid-September, mild, benignant, yet with a keener breath than that of the summer months. The plough was already scoring the field opposite the window, and where the share had been, the earth was pressed flat and gleamed with moisture. Such vigour came rolling in from the fields and the down beyond that it was difficult to keep the eyes strictly turned upon the book. The rooks too were keeping one of their annual festivities; soaring round the tree tops until it looked as if a vast net with thousands of black knots in it had been cast up into the air; which, after a few moments sank slowly down upon the trees until every twig seemed to have a knot at the end of it. Then, suddenly, the net would be thrown into the air again in a wider circle this time, with the utmost clamour and vociferation, as though to be thrown into the air and settle slowly down upon the tree tops were a tremendously exciting experience.

2   The same energy which inspired the rooks, the ploughmen, the horses, and even, it seemed, the lean bare-backed downs, sent the moth fluttering from side to side of his square of the window-pane. One could not help watching him. One, was, indeed, conscious of a queer feeling of pity for him. The possibilities of pleasure seemed that morning so enormous and so various that to have only a moth's part in life, and a day moth's at that, appeared a hard fate, and his zest in enjoying his meagre opportunities to the full, pathetic. He flew vigorously to one corner of his compartment, and, after waiting there a second, flew across to the other. What remained for him but to fly to a third corner and then to a fourth? That was all he could do, in spite of the size of the downs, the width of the sky, the far-off smoke of houses, and the romantic voice, now and then, of a steamer out at sea. What he could do he did. Watching him, it seemed as if a fibre, very thin but pure, of the enormous energy of the world had been thrust into his frail and diminutive body. As often as he crossed the pane, I could fancy that a thread of vital light became visible. He was little or nothing but life.

3   Yet, because he was so small, and so simple a form of the energy that was rolling in at the open window and driving its way through so many narrow and intricate corridors in my own brain and in those of other human beings, there was something marvellous as well as pathetic about him. It was as if someone had taken a tiny bead of pure life and decking it as lightly as possible with down and feathers, had set it dancing and zigzagging to show us the true nature of life. Thus displayed one could not get over the strangeness of it. One is apt to forget all about life, seeing it humped and bossed and garnished and cumbered so that it has to move with the greatest circumspection and dignity. Again, the thought of all that life might

have been had he been born in any other shape caused one to view his simple activities with a kind of pity.

After a time, tired by his dancing apparently, he settled on the window ledge in the sun, and, the queer spectacle being at an end, I forgot about him. Then, looking up, my eye was caught by him. He was trying to resume his dancing, but seemed either so stiff or so awkward that he could only flutter to the bottom of the window-pane; and when he tried to fly across it he failed. Being intent on other matters I watched these futile attempts for a time without thinking, unconsciously waiting for him to resume his flight, as one waits for a machine, that has stopped momentarily, to start again without considering the reason of its failure. After perhaps a seventh attempt he slipped from the wooden ledge and fell, fluttering his wings, on to his back on the window sill. The helplessness of his attitude roused me. It flashed upon me that he was in difficulties; he could no longer raise himself; his legs struggled vainly. But, as I stretched out a pencil, meaning to help him to right himself, it came over me that the failure and awkwardness were the approach of death. I laid the pencil down again. 4

The legs agitated themselves once more. I looked as if for the enemy against which he struggled. I looked out of doors. What had happened there? Presumably it was midday, and work in the fields had stopped. Stillness and quiet had replaced the previous animation. The birds had taken themselves off to feed in the brooks. The horses stood still. Yet the power was there all the same, massed outside, indifferent, impersonal, not attending to anything in particular. Somehow it was opposed to the little hay-coloured moth. It was useless to try to do anything. One could only watch the extraordinary efforts made by those tiny legs against an oncoming doom which could, had it chosen, have submerged an entire city, not merely a city, but masses of human beings; nothing, I knew had any chance against death. Nevertheless after a pause of exhaustion the legs fluttered again. It was superb this last protest, and so frantic that he succeeded at last in righting himself. One's sympathies, of course, were all on the side of life. Also, when there was nobody to care or to know, this gigantic effort on the part of an insignificant little moth, against a power of such magnitude, to retain what no one else valued or desired to keep, moved one strangely. Again, somehow, one saw life, a pure bead. I lifted the pencil again, useless though I knew it to be. But even as I did so, the unmistakable tokens of death showed themselves. The body relaxed, and instantly grew stiff. The struggle was over. The insignificant little creature now knew death. As I looked at the dead moth, this minute wayside triumph of so great a force over so mean an antagonist filled me with wonder. Just as life 5 had been strange a few minutes before, so death was now as strange. The moth having righted himself now lay most decently and uncomplainingly composed. O yes, he seemed to say, death is stronger than I am.

QUESTIONS

1. Why is Woolf so moved by the moth's death? Why does she call the moth's protest (paragraph 5) "superb"?

2. What, according to Woolf, is the "true nature of life"?

3. Examine Woolf's use of similes in paragraph 1. Where else does she use similes? Are any of them similar to the similes used in paragraph 1?

4. Why does the author personify the moth?

5. What sentences constitute the introduction of this essay? What rhetorical device do they use?

6. Divide the essay into two parts. Why did you divide the essay where you did? How are the two parts different? How are they similar?

7. Explain the importance of description in this essay. Where, particularly, does Woolf describe the setting of her scene? How does that description contribute to the development of her essay? How does she describe the moth, and how does this description affect tone?

8. How is narration used to structure the essay?

9. Woolf implicitly connects insect and human life. What else can we learn about human development by looking at other forms of life?

10. a. Write a detailed description of a small animal. Try to invest it with the importance that Woolf gives this moth.
b. Write a description of a scene, using details and metaphors.

ROLLO MAY

Powerlessness Corrupts

Rollo May (1909–   ) is a writer and psychologist. He was a student of Karen Horney and has written about the growth of the self. His works include *Man's Search for Himself* (1952), *Love and Will* (1969), *Power and Innocence* (1972), and *The*

Meaning of Anxiety (1977). In *Power and Innocence,* from which the following essay is excerpted, May details how violence arises from the individual's perception of his or her powerlessness.

he relationship of powerlessness and psychosis was impressed upon me a number of years ago when I started work as a psychotherapist. In the mentally troubled person psychotherapists are able to see the extremes of the behavior and the experience of us all. It bears out the words of Edgar Z. Friedenberg: "All weakness tends to corrupt, and impotence corrupts absolutely." 1

A young musician, Priscilla, was one of my first patients. 2 According to the person who administered her Rorschach, she had "one foot in schizophrenia and the other on a banana peel." In her sessions with me she would give long, involved comparisons of the colors of the musical notes made by the train from Newark in contrast to those made by the train from New Brunswick. I had not the slightest idea about what she was talking much of the time—and she knew it. But she seemed to need me as a person who listened, wanting and trying to understand her whether I succeeded or not. She was also a woman with considerable dignity and a sense of humor, which helped us immeasurably.

But she could never get angry. Not at me or her parents or 3 anyone else. Her self-esteem was so shaky and vague as to be almost nonexistent. Once a young man in a chorus to which she belonged asked her to go to a concert with him. She accepted. But the next day, in a surge of self-doubts, she phoned him to say: "You don't have to take me if you don't want to." She could not affirm or assert herself enough to conceive that someone might *like* to go to a concert with her. When, at the age of eight or nine, she would play football with a boy slightly older than she, he would run into her hard enough to hurt her. Another child might have yelled at the boy, or started a fight, or cried, or abandoned the game; these are all, good or bad, ways of coping. But Priscilla could utilize none of these methods; she could only sit there on the ground, looking at him and silently thinking that he shouldn't hit her so hard.

When she was exploited, as she often was, sexually and 4 financially, she had no defenses, no way of drawing a line beyond which she could firmly say "no," no anger to support her. (One gets a feeling that such persons almost invite exploitation—it at least gives them some relationship and significance.) Along with her inability to get angry, there went, as a necessary corollary, a deep experience of powerlessness and an almost complete lack of capacity to influence or affect other people in interpersonal relations.

 POWERLESSNESS CORRUPTS 181

But such a person has another side which, as I have confirmed in working with many borderline patients since, is completely different. Priscilla's dreams were of cut-up bodies put in bags, of blood and battles—in short, as *violent* as her conscious life was docile.

Since that time and partly due to this young woman, I have frequently reflected on the relationship between powerlessness and madness. I am purposely stressing both meanings of the word *mad*: its personal sense of enragedness to the point of violence; and its historical psychiatric sense of psychosis. There is a relationship between the two, and this double use of the term may lead us to the center of the problem.

We know that a common characteristic of all mental patients is their powerlessness, and with it goes a constant anxiety which is both cause and effect of the impotence. The patients' insignificance is so firmly assumed by them that they accept it as a given, often going through life making sad and pitiful gestures to get whatever bit of significance they can. An adolescent girl came to consult me in the middle of the day wearing a crinoline evening dress, possibly one of the prettiest things she had, as a gesture of how much she needed my attention and concern, unaware that it was likely to be regarded as out of place.

When a person like Priscilla can no longer support this way of life, something "cracks" within her and she may then move into a state in which she is nothing but mad. The person then seems to be the exact opposite of what she had been. The violence of dreams like Priscilla's then becomes the content of her waking life. The person seems *all* madness, which is surely why psychosis through the centuries was called madness. Mad now at everybody, including herself, the person threatens or attempts suicide, cuts her wrists, smears blood over the doors in hospitals to dramatize her need of the attendants and interns. She does overt violence to herself and whoever gets in the range of her projections.

We see the same movement in other patients. In the autobiographical novel on her own schizophrenia *I Never Promised You a Rose Garden*, Hannah Green was admitted to Chestnut Lodge at sixteen. She was the epitome of docility and placidity, never showing any anger at all. Whenever she needed to, she withdrew into the mythology of her private spirit world and talked with mythical figures. Dr. Frieda Fromm-Reichman, the psychiatrist at Chestnut Lodge who treated her, dealt with this mythology with respect, assuring Hannah that she would not take it away as long as the girl needed it. But when Dr. Fromm-Reichman went to Europe one summer, another, younger doctor was assigned to the girl. He charged in, blithely courageous, to break up her mythological world.

ROLLO MAY

The results were disastrous. In her explosion of violence, the patient set fire to herself and to her belongings at the Lodge, scarring herself for life. The error of the young doctor was that he did not appreciate that the mythology was what gave significance to Hannah's existence. The question was not whether it was theoretically right or wrong, but its function for her. This placid patient, who seemed incapable of any aggressive act, swung from docility into outright violence.

This may seem and feel like power to the hospital attendants, 10 but it is a *pseudopower*, an expression of impotence. The patient may now be spoken of as "mad," which means that she does not fit the accepted criteria in our society which, like all societies, prefers a docile, placid "face." It is important to see that the violence is the end result of repressed anger and rage, combined with constant fear based on the patient's powerlessness. Behind the pseudopower of the madness we can often find a person struggling for some sense of significance, some way of making a difference and establishing some self-esteem.

When Priscilla was in treatment with me, she received a 11 newspaper from her home town in which it was reported that a certain man in her village had committed suicide. She said to me: "If only one other person in that town had known him, he would not have committed suicide." Note that she did not say, "If *he* had known someone," but "if someone had known *him*." She was telling me, I believed, that she would not put a violent end to her life so long as I was related to her. But she was also describing something critically important for a human being—*the necessity of having somebody listen, recognize, know him*. It gives a person the conviction that he counts, that he exists as part of the human race. It also gives him some orientation, a point where he can find meaning in an otherwise meaningless world.

It would be a red-letter day when Priscilla could get angry 12 with me, for I knew that she could then begin to protect herself in her contacts with other people in the wide world. And what is more, she could dare to live out her considerable capacities as an original and lovable as well as loving human being.

QUESTIONS

1. According to May, what is the relationship between madness and powerlessness?

2. According to May, how does violence manifest itself in a psychotic person? Who represses anger?

 POWERLESSNESS CORRUPTS

3. Explain the meanings of the following psychological terms: *psychosis* (paragraph 1); *anxiety* and *schizophrenia* (paragraph 2), *pseudopower* (paragraph 10), and *impotence* (paragraph 10).

4. Explain the allusion in the title and in Friedenberg's quote.

5. Explain how and where May uses cause and effect to develop his thesis.

6. Identify the extended examples in this essay. To what general ideas are they related? How do they contribute to the goals of the essay?

7. Show where and how May describes the process of psychoanalysis and how process analysis contributes to the structuring of the essay.

8. Look at the transition words in this essay. How do they mark the development of the essay?

9. How do most people respond to anger? Does our society encourage us to suppress anger? How do you feel about anger?

10. Using May's insights, describe a moment in your life when you either expressed or repressed anger and explain how it made you feel.

RUTH BENEDICT

The Uses of Cannibalism

Ruth Benedict (1887–1948) was an anthropologist and educator. She began her career as a poet. Later, she studied anthropology under Franz Boas and succeeded him as the chairman of the department of anthropology at Columbia University (1936–1939). In 1934, she wrote *Patterns of Culture;* in 1940, *Race: Science and Politics.* In her work, Benedict attempted to study anthropology through sociology, psychology, and philosophy. As the following essay indicates, she could use irony to disparage some of the worst traits of modern culture.

W e have done scant justice to the reasonableness of cannibalism. There are in fact so many and such excellent motives possible to it that mankind has never been able to fit all of them into one universal scheme, and has accordingly contrived various diverse and contradictory systems the better to display its virtues. 1

The present decade, indeed, is likely to appreciate to an unusual degree the advantages that attach to cannibalism so soon as the matter may be presented. We have already had recourse to many quaint primitive customs our fathers believed outmoded by the progress of mankind. We have watched the dependence of great nations upon the old device of the pogrom. We have seen the rise of demagogues, and even in those countries we consider lost in a mortally dangerous idealism we have watched death dealt out to those who harbor the mildest private opinions. Even in our own country we have come to the point of shooting in the back that familiar harmless annoyance, the strike picketer. It is strange that we have overlooked cannibalism.

Mankind has for many thousands of years conducted experiments in the eating of human flesh, and has not found it wanting. Especially it has been proved to foster the feeling of solidarity within the group and of antipathy toward the alien, providing an incomparable means of gratifying with deep emotion the hatred of one's enemy. Indeed, all the noblest emotions have been found not only compatible with it, but reinforced by its practice. It would appear that we have here rediscovered that specific and sovereign remedy for which we have long perceived statesmen to be groping. It will be well, therefore, to pass the known facts briefly in review.

It is necessary first to place beyond doubt the high moral sentiments with which the custom has been allied. It has been unfortunate that in our solicitude lest heroism, endurance, and self-control should perish from a world so largely devoted to commerce and the pursuit of wealth, we should have overlooked the matter of cannibalism. Certain valiant tribes of the Great Lakes and the prairies long ago made use of it to this purpose. It was to them their supreme gesture of homage to human excellence. It is told by old travelers that of three enemies whose death made the occasion for such celebration of their valor, two were eaten with honor, while the one remaining was passed over and untouched. For at the death, this one had marked himself a coward, and cried out under torture. Of such flesh no one would eat. In the old papers of the Jesuit Fathers we find it stated: "When then the captive had been slain, if so be that he had looked with laughter upon the thongs, the knives and the fire, and had sung songs continually in his torture, they took his heart and divided it among the warriors, that they might imbibe a portion of so great a valor." By this device, therefore, they made certain that nobility should not perish from the earth.

This is of course not the only excellent ethical use to which cannibalism has been put among the peoples of the world. There are tribes to whom it is an expression of tenderness to the most nearly related dead so to dispose of their discarded bodies—a supreme cherishing of those for whom there can be no other remaining act of tenderness. But, indeed, it is not necessary to look upon it in this particular light; eating the dead has also been regarded as sharing in the identical qualities of marriage, and those among whom the relations of lawful wedlock were prohibited were denied also the intimacy of cannibalism. It was incest not only to marry from among them, but also to eat their flesh.

Cannibalism has proved also to be extraordinarily well quali- 6 fied to provide the excitement of an ultimate aggression. This has proved recently to be by no means the frivolous subject that it may appear. Indeed we have been confronted by the problem on such a large scale that, in the interests of progress, it is difficult not to press the matter. Without the infantile ostentations and unfortunate appeals to the hatred of one's fellow beings which characterize our Black Shirts and our Red Shirts, the Indians of Vancouver Island found a heightened excitation, disciplined in endless ritual and taboo, in a ceremonial show of cannibalism. Secret societies of the men were all-important on Vancouver Island; the whole winter was given over to their rites. And they were sufficiently aristocratic; membership was limited to first sons of noble birth. When it was time for such a one to become a member of this society, he retired to the forests or the graveyard, and it was said that the spirits had taken him. Here an almost mummified corpse was prepared and smoked, and at the appointed time, in the midst of great excitement, the noble youth returned to the village with the Spirit of the Cannibal upon him. A member of the society carried the corpse before him, while with violent rhythms and trembling of his tense body, he rendered in dance his seeking for human flesh. He was held by his neck-ring that he might not attack the people, and he uttered a terrible reiterated cannibal cry. But when he had bitten the corpse, the ecstasy left him, and he was "tamed." He drank the emetic, and retired again to solitude in a state of great sacredness, where for months he observed the endless taboos of the newly initiate.

It is obvious that nothing could be more harmless to the 7 community; one useless body per year satisfactorily satisfied the craving for violence which we have clumsily supplied in modern times in the form of oaths, blood-and-thunder, and vows to undertake the death of industrious households. They achieved the highest tension of excitement and aggression without advocating malice toward the minority or arrogantly claiming the prerogatives of a Chosen People.

All these uses of cannibalism are, however, of small moment 8 in comparison with the one we must now consider. It is its service in the cause of patriotism. Nothing, we are well aware, will so hold in check the hostile elements of a nation as a common purpose of revenge. This may be raised to a high degree of utility by various well-known phrases and figures of oratory which picture our determination to "drink the blood of our enemies." It has however been held essential that we pursue this end by the death, in great numbers and with distressing tortures, of young men in sound health and vigor. Nothing could show more lamentably our ignorance of previous human experiments. It is this aspect of cannibalism that has appealed most widely to the human species; it has enabled them to derive the most intense emotional satisfaction from the death, even the accidental death, of one solitary enemy, allowing them to taste revenge in a thoroughgoing and convincing manner, ministering to their faith in his extirpation, root and branch, body and soul.

This practice was perhaps best understood by the head- 9 hunters of certain parts of the Malay Archipelago. They carried on their negotiations of warfare with ritualistic formality; with great punctilio they refrained from seeming to dictate to their honored adversaries either the time or the manner of fighting. They slept peacefully side by side, and whiled away the time in ancient ritual. But at the hour agreed, they joined forces with the fierceness of males in breeding season, hurling their vilest taunts each at the other, till bodies had been secured. All the excitement of the engagement was only the preliminary. When a modest feast had been secured, the fires were lighted, and the angry passion which uncurbed might have killed a hundred enemies was humanely employed in the disposal of a few.

The Maoris of New Zealand, before the feast, took from their 10 enemies the exquisitely tattooed heads which were their incomparable pride, and setting them on posts about them, taunted them after this fashion:

You thought to flee, ha? But my power overtook you.
You were cooked; you were made food for my mouth.
Where is your father? He is cooked.
Where is your brother? He is eaten.
Where is your wife? There she sits, a wife for me!

No one who is familiar with the breakdown of emotional 11 satisfaction in warfare as it is recorded in postwar literature of our time can fail to see in all this a hopeful device for the re-establishment of an emotional complex which shows every sign of disintegration among us. It is obvious that something must be done, and no suggestion seems more hopeful than this drawn from the Maoris of New Zealand.

The serviceability of cannibalism is therefore well established. 12

 THE USES OF CANNIBALISM   **187**

In view of the fact that ends now so widely sought in modern war and its aftermaths can thus be attained by the comparatively innocent method of cannibalism, is it not desirable that we consider seriously the possibility of substituting the one for the other before we become involved in another national propaganda? Our well-proved methods of publicity give us a new assurance in the adoption even of unfamiliar programs; where we might at one time well have doubted the possibility of popularizing a practice so unused, we can now venture more boldly. While there is yet time, shall we not choose deliberately between war and cannibalism?

QUESTIONS

1. Benedict has written a bitterly satirical essay about the supposed advantages of cannibalism. What is her real message about cannibalism? Why does she think the modern world should renew the practice?

2. Identify the five uses of cannibalism Benedict mentions. For each use, what is Benedict's actual point?

3. How does Benedict use connotation to contrast her irony with her intended meaning? Give specific examples of words whose underlying meaning is contrary to their ostensible meaning in the essay.

4. Because this essay was written in 1925, many of its allusions to contemporary events may be unclear. Identify the countries and events referred to in paragraph 2 and paragraph 6.

5. What is the main structural device in the essay? What transition words are used?

6. Benedict frequently uses historical narrative. Identify where this method is used in the essay. What words are used to establish chronology?

7. Describe Benedict's point of view in this essay. How does it relate to her goal to write satire?

8. There is an implied comparison and contrast between modern war and cannibalism and between modern and primitive people. Give evidence for these comparisons. How do they contribute to the author's satire?

9. Since 1925, a great deal has happened in our world. Do you think that Benedict's ironic attack on modern society is still relevant, or is it outdated? Explain.

10. Satire is often used to criticize the morality of an age or culture. Write a satiric essay about modern movies, the arms race, fashions, or marriage.

Remarks Concerning the Savages
of North America

Benjamin Franklin (1706–1790), statesman, inventor, philanthropist, printer, scientist, diplomat, and author, was a founding father of the United States and a seminal figure in the
development of a native American humor, language, and
culture. *Poor Richard's Almanack* (1732–1757) and his
Autobiography (written between 1771 and 1789) have both
had a tremendous influence upon American readers and
authors. In the essay below, Franklin observes the American
Indian with the scientific objectivity he often practiced.

avages we call them, because their Manners differ from   1
ours, which we think the Perfection of Civility; they
think the same of theirs.

Perhaps, if we could examine the Manners of   2
different Nations with Impartiality, we should find no People so rude,
as to be without any Rules of Politeness; nor any so polite, as not to
have some Remains of Rudeness.

The Indian Men, when young, are Hunters and Warriors;   3
when old, Counsellors; for all their Government is by Counsel of the
Sages; there is no Force, there are no Prisons, no Officers to compel
Obedience, or inflict Punishment. Hence they generally study Oratory, the best Speaker having the most Influence. The Indian Women
till the Ground, dress the Food, nurse and bring up the Children, and
preserve and hand down to Posterity the Memory of public Transac-
tions. These Employments of Men and Women are accounted natural
and honourable. Having few artificial Wants, they have abundance of
Leisure for Improvement by Conversation. Our laborious Manner of
Life, compared with theirs, they esteem slavish and base; and the
Learning, on which we value ourselves, they regard as frivolous and
useless. An Instance of this occurred at the Treaty of Lancaster, in
Pennsylvania, *anno* 1744, between the Government of Virginia and
the Six Nations. After the principal Business was settled, the Com-
missioners from Virginia acquainted the Indians by a Speech, that
there was at Williamsburg a College, with a Fund for Educating
Indian youth; and that, if the Six Nations would send down half a
dozen of their young Lads to that College, the Government would
take care that they should be well provided for, and instructed in all
the Learning of the White People. It is one of the Indian Rules of
Politeness not to answer a public Proposition the same day that it is

made; they think it would be treating it as a light matter, and that they show it Respect by taking time to consider it, as of a Matter important. They therefore deferr'd their Answer till the Day following; when their Speaker began, by expressing their deep Sense of the kindness of the Virginia Government, in making them that Offer; "for we know," says he, "that you highly esteem the kind of Learning taught in those Colleges, and that the Maintenance of our young Men, while with you, would be very expensive to you. We are convinc'd, therefore, that you mean to do us Good by your Proposal; and we thank you heartily. But you, who are wise, must know that different Nations have different Conceptions of things; and you will therefore not take it amiss, if our Ideas of this kind of Education happen not to be the same with yours. We have had some Experience of it; Several of our young People were formerly brought up at the Colleges of the Northern Provinces; they were instructed in all your Sciences; but, when they came back to us, they were bad Runners, ignorant of every means of living in the Woods, unable to bear either Cold or Hunger, knew neither how to build a Cabin, take a Deer, or kill an Enemy, spoke our Language imperfectly, were therefore neither fit for Hunters, Warriors, nor Counsellors; they were totally good for nothing. We are however not the less oblig'd by your kind Offer, tho' we decline accepting it; and, to show our grateful Sense of it, if the Gentlemen of Virginia will send us a Dozen of their Sons, we will take great Care of their Education, instruct them in all we know, and make *Men* of them."

Having frequent Occasions to hold public Councils, they have acquired great Order and Decency in conducting them. The old Men sit in the foremost Ranks, the Warriors in the next, and the Women and Children in the hindmost. The Business of the Women is to take exact Notice of what passes, imprint it in their Memories (for they have no Writing), and communicate it to their Children. They are the Records of the Council, and they preserve Traditions of the Stipulations in Treaties 100 Years back; which, when we compare with our Writings, we always find exact. He that would speak, rises. The rest observe a profound Silence. When he has finish'd and sits down, they leave him 5 or 6 Minutes to recollect, that, if he has omitted any thing he intended to say, or has any thing to add, he may rise again and deliver it. To interrupt another, even in common Conversation, is reckon'd highly indecent. How different this is from the conduct of a polite British House of Commons, where scarce a day passes without some Confusion, that makes the Speaker hoarse in calling *to Order*; and how different from the Mode of Conversation in many polite Companies of Europe, where, if you do not deliver your Sentence with great Rapidity, you are cut off in the middle of it by the Impatient Loquacity of those you converse with, and never suffer'd to finish it!

The Politeness of these Savages in Conversation is indeed 5 carried to Excess, since it does not permit them to contradict or deny the Truth of what is asserted in their Presence. By this means they indeed avoid Disputes; but then it becomes difficult to know their Minds, or what Impression you make upon them. The Missionaries who have attempted to convert them to Christianity, all complain of this as one of the great Difficulties of their Mission. The Indians hear with Patience the Truths of the Gospel explain'd to them, and give their usual Tokens of Assent and Approbation; you would think they were convinc'd. No such matter. It is mere Civility.

A Swedish Minister, having assembled the chiefs of the 6 Susquehanah Indians, made a Sermon to them, acquainting them with the principal historical Facts on which our Religion is founded; such as the Fall of our first Parents by eating an Apple, the coming of Christ to repair the Mischief, his Miracles and Suffering, &c. When he had finished an Indian Orator stood up to thank him. "What you have told us," says he, "is all very good. It is indeed bad to eat Apples. It is better to make them all into Cyder. We are much oblig'd by your kindness in coming so far, to tell us these Things which you have heard from your Mothers. In return, I will tell you some of those we have heard from ours. In the Beginning, our Fathers had only the Flesh of Animals to subsist on; and if their Hunting was unsuccessful, they were starving. Two of our young Hunters, having kill'd a Deer, made a Fire in the Woods to broil some Part of it. When they were about to satisfy their Hunger, they beheld a beautiful young Woman descend from the Clouds, and seat herself on that Hill, which you see yonder among the blue Mountains. They said to each other, it is a Spirit that has smelt our broiling Venison, and wishes to eat of it; let us offer some to her. They presented her with the Tongue; she was pleas'd with the Taste of it, and said, 'Your kindness shall be rewarded; come to this Place after thirteen Moons, and you shall find something that will be of great Benefit in nourishing you and your Children to the latest Generations.' They did so, and, to their Surprise, found Plants they had never seen before; but which, from that ancient time, have been constantly cultivated among us, to our great Advantage. Where her right Hand had touched the Ground, they found Maize; where her left hand had touch'd it, they found Kidney-Beans; and where her Backside had sat on it, they found Tobacco." The good Missionary, disgusted with this idle Tale, said, "What I delivered to you were sacred Truths; but what you tell me is mere Fable, Fiction, and Falsehood." The Indian, offended, reply'd, "My brother, it seems your Friends have not done you Justice in your Education; they have not well instructed you in the Rules of common Civility. You saw that we, who understand and practise those Rules, believ'd all your stories; why do you refuse to believe ours?"

 REMARKS CONCERNING THE SAVAGES OF NORTH AMERICA

When any of them come into our Towns, our People are apt to 7
crowd round them, gaze upon them, and incommode them, where
they desire to be private; this they esteem great Rudeness, and the
Effect of the Want of Instruction in the Rules of Civility and good
Manners. "We have," say they, "as much Curiosity as you, and when
you come into our Towns, we wish for Opportunities of looking at
you; but for this purpose we hide ourselves behind Bushes, where
you are to pass, and never intrude ourselves into your Company."

Their Manner of entering one another's village has likewise 8
its Rules. It is reckon'd uncivil in travelling Strangers to enter a
Village abruptly, without giving Notice of their Approach. Therefore,
as soon as they arrive within hearing, they stop and hollow, remaining there till invited to enter. Two old Men usually come out to them,
and lead them in. There is in every Village a vacant Dwelling, called
the Strangers' House. Here they are plac'd, while the old Men go round
from Hut to Hut, acquainting the Inhabitants, that Strangers are
arriv'd, who are probably hungry and weary; and every one sends
them what he can spare of Victuals, and Skins to repose on. When the
Strangers are refresh'd, Pipes and Tobacco are brought; and then, but
not before, Conversation begins, with Enquiries who they are,
whither bound, what News, &c.; and it usually ends with offers of
Service, if the Strangers have occasion of Guides, or any Necessaries
for continuing their Journey; and nothing is exacted for the Entertainment.

The same Hospitality, esteem'd among them as a principal 9
Virtue, is practis'd by private Persons; of which Conrad Weiser, our
Interpreter, gave me the following Instance. He had been naturaliz'd
among the Six Nations, and spoke well the Mohock Language. In
going thro' the Indian Country, to carry a Message from our
Governor to the Council at Onondaga, he call'd at the Habitation of
Canassatego, an old Acquaintance, who embrac'd him, spread Furs
for him to sit on, plac'd before him some boil'd Beans and Venison,
and mix'd some Rum and Water for his Drink. When he was well
refresh'd, and had lit his Pipe, Canassatego began to converse with
him; ask'd how he had far'd the many Years since they had seen each
other; whence he then came; what occasion'd the Journey, &c.
Conrad answered all his Questions; and when the Discourse began to
flag, the Indian, to continue it, said, "Conrad, you have lived long
among the white People, and know something of their Customs; I
have been sometimes at Albany, and have observed, that once in
Seven Days they shut up their Shops, and assemble all in the great
House; tell me what it is for? What do they do there?" "They meet
there," says Conrad, "to hear and learn *good Things.*" "I do not
doubt," says the Indian, "that they tell you so; they have told me the
same; but I doubt the Truth of what they say, and I will tell you my

BENJAMIN FRANKLIN

Reasons. I went lately to Albany to sell my Skins and buy Blankets, Knives, Powder, Rum, &c. You know I us'd generally to deal with Hans Hanson; but I was a little inclin'd this time to try some other Merchant. However, I call'd first upon Hans, and asked him what he would give for Beaver. He said he could not give any more than four Shillings a Pound; 'but,' says he, 'I cannot talk on Business now; this is the Day when we meet together to learn *Good Things,* and I am going to the Meeting.' So I thought to myself, 'Since we cannot do any Business to-day, I may as well go to the meeting too,' and I went with him. There stood up a Man in Black, and began to talk to the People very angrily. I did not understand what he said; but, perceiving that he look'd much at me and at Hanson, I imagin'd he was angry at seeing me there; so I went out, sat down near the House, struck Fire, and lit my Pipe, waiting till the Meeting should break up. I thought too, that the Man had mention'd something of Beaver, and I suspected it might be the Subject of their Meeting. So, when they came out, I accosted my Merchant. 'Well, Hans,' says I, 'I hope you have agreed to give more than four Shillings a Pound.' 'No,' says he, 'I cannot give so much; I cannot give more than three shillings and sixpence.' I then spoke to several other Dealers, but they all sung the same song,—Three and sixpence,—Three and sixpence. This made it clear to me, that my Suspicion was right; and, that whatever they pretended of meeting to learn *good Things,* the real purpose was to consult how to cheat Indians in the Price of Beaver. Consider but a little, Conrad, and you must be of my Opinion. If they met so often to learn *good Things,* they would certainly have learnt some before this time. But they are still ignorant. You know our Practice. If a white Man, in travelling thro' our Country, enters one of our Cabins, we all treat him as I treat you; we dry him if he is wet, we warm him if he is cold, we give him Meat and Drink, that he may allay his Thirst and Hunger; and we spread soft Furs for him to rest and sleep on; we demand nothing in return. But, if I go into a white Man's House at Albany, and ask for Victuals and Drink, they say, 'Where is your Money?' and if I have none, they say, 'Get out, you Indian Dog.' You see they have not yet learned those little *Good Things,* that we need no Meetings to be instructed in, because our Mothers taught them to us when we were Children; and therefore it is impossible their Meetings should be, as they say, for any such purpose, or have any such Effect; they are only to contrive *the Cheating of Indians in the Price of Beaver.*"

NOTE.—It is remarkable that in all Ages and Countries Hospitality has been allow'd as the Virtue of those whom the civiliz'd were pleas'd to call Barbarians. The Greeks celebrated the Scythians for it. The Saracens possess'd it eminently, and it is to this day the reigning Virtue of the wild Arabs. St. Paul, too, in the Relation of his Voyage and Shipwreck on the Island of Melita says the Barbarous People shewed us no little kindness; for they kindled a fire, and received us every one, because of the present Rain, and because of the Cold.—F.

 REMARKS CONCERNING THE SAVAGES OF NORTH AMERICA

QUESTIONS

1. In the course of this letter, Franklin describes some of the customs and values of North American Indians. Describe them. Does he approve or disapprove of them? Why?

2. According to Franklin, what are some of the failings of Indian culture? What are the failings, if any, of white culture?

3. Is this essay written primarily in an objective or subjective style? Give evidence to support your opinion.

4. Locate and analyze examples of Franklin's irony in this essay.

5. Explain the importance of the first two sentences of the essay. What effect does Franklin achieve by making them separate paragraphs?

6. Explain how Franklin uses narrative in the essay. What paragraphs contain narrative examples? What words does he use to establish his chronology?

7. Where does Franklin use comparison and contrast in the essay? How do they support his thesis?

8. How is dialogue used in the essay? What is its function?

9. To a great extent, this essay is about prejudice, which of course is still a problem in America. How do you think Franklin would identify modern race problems? How would he respond to them?

10. Many of us are guilty of or have suffered from prejudice. Write a narrative essay in which you explain how you have suffered from or been guilty of prejudice.

FRANZ BOAS

The Diffusion of Cultural Traits

Franz Boas (1858–1942) was a highly influential anthropologist who was known for his rigorous use of scientific method. His most famous works are *The Mind of Primitive Man* (1911), *Primitive Art* (1927), *Anthropology and Modern Life* (1928), and two volumes of collected essays, *Race, Language, and Culture* (1940) and *Race and Democratic Society* (1945). "The Diffusion of Cultural Traits" shows Boas's wide-ranging cultural expertise and, perhaps more importantly, his humanism.

he study of the types of cultures found the world over 1
gives the impression of an enormous diversity of forms.
The differences are so great that we may be inclined to
think that every one of these cultures developed quite
independently and that the peculiar genius of the people has found
expression in the forms under which they live. This impression is
strengthened by the fact that the people themselves differ in appearance. The African Negro, the Australian, the Siberian native, the
people of the Pacific Islands, each have their own peculiar bodily
build and their own peculiar culture.

Added to this is the observation that the people constituting 2
every one of these societies consider themselves as independent
units, specifically distinct from all their neighbors. This finds its
strongest expression in the fact that many primitive people designate
themselves as human beings, while all their neighbors are designated
by specific names in the same way as animals are designated by
names. Thus the Eskimos call themselves human beings, the Indians
whom they know in some regions only by hearsay are considered as
doglike animals, and the white people with whom they came into
contact in later times are considered as descended from dogs. The
specific differences are keenly felt, while the similarities are neglected.

The objective study of cultures and of types of man shows 3
that notwithstanding all these apparently fundamental differences
cultural strains have passed from one people to the other, that no
culture can be assumed to be self-developed and no type to be pure,
unmixed with foreign strains.

This can be most easily shown by a study of the distribution 4
of languages. The migrations of primitive people in early times
covered whole continents. A few examples will suffice. A certain
American language is spoken in the vast area extending from the
Yukon to Hudson Bay; south of this area live people speaking entirely
different languages, but dialects of the same language which is
spoken in the north reappear locally in Oregon and California and in
the vast territory north and south of the Rio Grande. This can be
understood only on the assumption that at one time these people
migrated over this immense area. In southern Brazil the Carib
language is spoken. It reappears locally north of the Amazon River
and on the West Indian Islands. The Bantu languages spoken in
Africa cover the whole district from south of the Sahara, southward
almost to the extreme southern end of Africa. The language of the
Malay, which is spoken in southeastern Asia, found its way eastward
to all the islands of the Pacific Ocean and is also spoken by the
inhabitants of part of Madagascar.

These inferences based on similarities of languages can also 5

 THE DIFFUSION OF CULTURAL TRAITS   **195**

be proved by historical migrations. The great Arab migration, which started in Arabia and at the time of its greatest extent covered the whole of north Africa and part of Spain, and which also influenced all the languages of the Near East, occurred after Mohammed's time. We know that the so-called Aryans invaded India at a very early time. The Greeks migrated from the north into what later became Greece. The Celts of western Europe migrated eastward as far as Asia Minor. The Teutonic migrations destroyed the Roman Empire, and later on the great Turkish migrations swept over a large part of eastern Europe as well as over a large part of Siberia. Thus we actually see mankind on the move since the very earliest times. The whole settlement of America occurred within a comparatively short period. Evidently the American aborigines lived on the continent not earlier than the beginning of the last warm period before the last ice age, coming presumably over the land bridge which is now Bering Sea, and spreading from there as far as the extreme southern part of South America.

It is not only language that was carried by migrations all over   6
the world; it is also easy to show that inventions and ideas were carried from one area to another, partly by migration, partly by cultural contact. One of the most striking examples is found in the distribution of folk tales. The European folk tale of the couple that escaped a pursuing monster by throwing backwards a number of objects which were transformed into obstacles is well known all over Europe. A comb thrown down becomes an impenetrable thicket, a whetstone an insurmountable mountain, a small amount of oil becomes an extensive lake, all of which detain the pursuer. This complicated story containing all the elements mentioned is found not only all over Europe but all over the Asiatic continent and also in northwestern America reaching as far as California, and eastward even in Greenland and Nova Scotia. In more recent times we find that the most isolated tribes of South America tell tales which were carried by Negro slaves to the coast of Brazil.

Equally striking are certain similarities in political organiza-   7
tion characteristic of the Old World but entirely absent in America and other outlying regions. The whole political organization of Africa shows a high development of administration through kings and their ministers in charge of war, judicial procedure and so on—analogous to the ancient organization of European states. Judicial procedure by means of courts taking evidence, administering the oath and finally ascertaining the truth by ordeal is found in a vast part of the Old World, while it is entirely foreign to people that had never been in contact with the Old World.

Perhaps still more convincing is the distribution of agricul-   8
ture. Wheat and barley are two characteristic plants on which early

agriculture is based all over the temperate zone of the Old World, while rice is characteristic of another extended area. The home of the wild plants from which wheat and barley are derived must be looked for somewhere in western Asia, from where they spread from tribe to tribe. In the same way early American agriculture is based on the use of Indian corn which was developed from a native plant of the western highlands of Mexico, from where it spread southward as far as the Argentine republic and northward to the Great Lakes.

Thus a detailed study of cultural traits proves beyond cavil 9 that there is not a single people in the primitive world that has developed its culture independently.

Much of the diffusion must have been accompanied by actual 10 intermingling of tribes. The people speaking the language of the Yukon River, to whom we referred before and who live now on the Rio Grande, differ in type from the people of the north but are similar in appearance to their neighbors who speak an unrelated language. This would not have happened if they had not intermingled with them at the same time that they adopted many important traits of their culture. In South Africa the intermingling of types is perhaps not equally clear but another striking feature of mutual influence may be seen in a linguistic change. The Bushmen of southern Africa have a peculiarity of speech which does not occur in any other part of the world. They produce sounds not by breathing out but by sucking in. This habit, which is considered an ancient African trait, is found in weak traits on the Gold Coast in equatorial West Africa, but only one of the Bantu tribes, who are neighbors of the Bushmen, have adopted the habit of producing strong sounds by sucking in, as the Bushmen do.

If we want to understand the way in which these fundamen- 11 tal modifications of cultures occur we have to remember that the conditions of contact among primitive tribes are very different from what has occurred in more modern times. Most primitive tribes are small; sometimes the whole number of individuals may not be more than a few hundred. Wars between neighboring groups are common and almost everywhere it is customary for the men to be killed, while the women are taken along as captives. These become the mothers of the following generation, so that it may happen that a large number of children grow up bilinguals, with the cultural habits of the mother having a far-reaching influence upon the behavior of the children.

The study of distribution of cultural traits brings out one very 12 characteristic feature: the details of the culture may be similar among different tribes but the general structure will retain fundamental differences. To give an example, one of the most important ceremonials of our North American Indians is the Sun Dance, an elaborate ceremonial the details of which are widespread over our western plains. The meaning of the ceremonial is quite different in the different areas and it is fitted into the fundamental religious ideas of each tribe. We can perhaps best understand these differences when we consider our own culture. All over Europe, and wherever the white race has gone, the fundamental traits are the same; inventions, religion, fundamental traits of state organization are alike. And nevertheless there are decided national patterns which allow us to differentiate between the cultural life of different areas as well as of different times.

It is interesting to follow the processes of acculturation. 13 Evidently in many cases it is due to war. We have already mentioned the importance of the introduction of foreign women. In many cases conquest leads to the establishment of stratified societies of a class of masters to whom the native population becomes subject. This has been the case in the history of Europe as well as in the history of Africa. In Africa we see that pastoral people conquered agricultural communities and became the nobility to whom the natives became subjects. Such conquests led to economic adjustments, and in many traits the conquerors adopted the customs of the old population while these in turn adopted the traits of the invaders. It must not be assumed that every stratified society originated in this manner, because sometimes internal conditions, family privileges and so on have led to similar results. In other cases economic and social advantages favored the adoption of foreign customs. This was obviously the case in the spread of agriculture both in the Old World and in America. In a similar way new religious ideas which strengthen the emotional energy of the people and awaken them from indifferent attitudes have had a powerful influence in modifying cultural life.

One of the many remarkable changes of culture due to an 14 introduction of foreign invention is the change all over North America which occurred with the introduction of the horse. After the introduction of the horse the pursuit of the buffalo became easier and some of the tribes which had been hunting the buffalo on foot were now able to roam over a wider area and gave up agriculture almost entirely, becoming more or less nomadic hunters. Notwithstanding the readiness with which foreign cultural traits are adopted we may also observe in many cases a strong resistance to changes of life. This occurs particularly when new ideas cannot be fitted into the general cultural habits of the people. As an instance may be mentioned the difficulty of adjusting native tribes to the fundamental idea of capitalism. Very rarely do we find among primitive people that wealth can be used to produce more wealth by utilizing the power it may give over other members of the community. Wealth is of value only in so far as it enables the owner to improve his social standing by liberality, or by making a show with his property. In this lies one of the reasons which make it so difficult to assimilate the American Indians, to whom the idea of capital as producing wealth is entirely foreign.

In modern society the conditions favorable to cultural contact 15 are ever so much greater than those existing in primitive society. First of all, the numbers of individuals constituting each unit are infinitely larger than those occurring in primitive society, and within each group diffusion occurs with the greatest rapidity. Our schools, the commercial exploitation of inventions, are of such a character that new ideas and new objects are distributed with incredible rapidity. Most of these extend beyond national boundaries because international trade and international communication make it impossible for any idea to be confined to a single nation. On the other hand general, structural attitudes find much greater resistance than in the small tribes because the inertia of the enormous masses of the population is much greater than that of a small tribal group. It is less difficult to introduce a new idea into the well established structure of a small group than to break down the habits of thought of millions.

We are too much inclined to consider the development of 16 civilization in Europe as an achievement of Europe alone, and to assume that Europe has always been the giver, not the recipient of new ideas. We are likely to forget that in antiquity the exchange of inventions and ideas extended from China all over the continent to Europe, and that the indirect contact between the Far East and Europe contributed much to the development of European civilization. We are likely to forget the immense service that Arab scientists did to Europe in re-establishing contact with Greek thought. Later on, when contact with the Far East was interrupted by the Turkish invasion of eastern Europe and the development of the Mongolian empire, the need for contact with the East led to maritime discoveries, and the discovery of America brought inventions to Europe which modified life in many parts of the Old World. I need only mention the introduction of Indian corn, which in an incredibly short time found its way to all parts of the Old World that were adapted to its cultivation, or the use of tobacco, which has reached all parts of the inhabitable world.

Peculiar types of cultural assimilation developed with coloni- 17 zation. Greek colonies sprang up on all the shores of the Mediterranean and hand in hand with them went a strong influence of Greek culture upon the surrounding people. Still more effective was Roman colonization, which not only carried the habits of Roman life into outlying provinces but led to Latin becoming the language of these countries, so that the languages of what is now Spain, of France, of

THE DIFFUSION OF CULTURAL TRAITS

what is now Romania disappeared and provincial Latin took their place. During the Middle Ages a similar process occurred in central Europe when German colonists reoccupied the former habitat of German tribes which had been filled by Slavic groups. The process that occurred there may still be observed in Mexico, where Spaniards are still colonizing in Indian territory and where we see the Indian languages gradually giving way to Spanish. There is little doubt that the process of assimilation which occurred in Greek and Roman colonization and later on in Germany was of the same type. In Mexico we see the Spaniards settling in small towns. A hybrid population develops with fair rapidity and the town as a trade center attracts the Indians. Intercourse is first by means of poorly developed Spanish, which is gradually adopted by a large part of the native population. Gradually the influence of the town increases in importance, with the final result that the native language disappears and the natives and the Spaniards form a single community. According to the character of the migrating population there would of course be differences in the resultant social structure. When the colonists are poor and uneducated the native population and colonists may merge into a single community. When the colonists are supported by a central power they may become the masters of the territory and a stratified society results.

It is interesting to compare with this the conditions of immigration into countries which are already more or less settled. We may observe this in our own country as well as in South America, Australia, or South Africa. The immigrants who arrive are drawn from many different countries and form always a minority in a larger and economically stronger group, so that their only hope of success in the new country is based on a gradual assimilation. It is not only economic stress, however, which brings about the assimilation of the new colonists to the new environment but also the strong social influence of the majority among whom they live. An interesting example of this kind was observed about thirty years ago in a New York school in a part of the city which had been inhabited by an Irish population then being replaced by Italians. The school had been for some time Irish, with a sprinkling of Italian children. The Italian children had learned an Irish pronunciation of English, and even when they increased to about ninety per cent of all the children they all spoke English with an Irish accent. By the pressure of the majority all immigrants become assimilated, no matter what nationality they belong to, and their own influence is comparatively slight.

It is of considerable practical interest for us to understand what happens in the process of assimilation, how far old habits are stable and how far they are influenced by their new environment. A number of studies made on American immigrants throw light on this question. It has repeatedly been shown that the physical development of children of immigrants differs from that of their parents. During the last century the stature of Americans and also of Europeans has increased noticeably, but the immigrants who came here during the last seventy years have always belonged to the same economic level and their stature has remained quite stable. Their children, however, follow the general increase which is found in the American population. Furthermore, the form of the body of immigrants' children undergoes certain changes, and though the cause is still obscure the result is that in bodily form they differ from their parents. This does not mean that they tend to approach a general American type, but merely that the new environment and new mode of life influence the bodily build.

The changes in their behavior are much more noticeable. It is 20 not only that they adopt American tastes and language, a process which results from contact between children of many nationalities in school, but their motor habits also change from foreign types to what we might call an American type. The Italians and the Jews accompany speech with characteristic gestures. The Italian describes what he has to say with a wide sweep of motions, while the Jew follows his line of thought with short, rather jerky movements. The assimilated Italians and Jews substitute for these movements the descriptive and emphatic motions which are characteristic of American habits, or when they belong to more sophisticated classes tend to suppress all gestures. Statistics also show that the immigrant becomes adjusted very quickly to American social habits. This becomes particularly striking in criminal statistics. On the whole, crimes against property among the immigrants from Europe are comparatively rare, while they are exceedingly common in our American city population. But the distribution of crime in the second generation, that is, among the descendants of immigrants, is quite similar to that found in the American population of native parentage. All this is merely an expression of the fact that when an individual is exposed to a new environment his descent is almost irrelevant when compared to the stress to which he is exposed in his new mode of life.

A review of all the data which have been summarized here 21 altogether too briefly shows that the assumption that any culture is autonomous, uninfluenced from outside sources, or that each type of man produces a culture which is an expression of the biological make-up of the race to which he belongs, is quite untenable. We see everywhere types of culture which develop historically under the impact of multifarious influences that come from neighboring people or those living far away.

 THE DIFFUSION OF CULTURAL TRAITS **201**

QUESTIONS

1. Does Boas believe that there is such a thing as a purely autonomous culture? What evidence does he give to prove or disprove this thesis?

2. What ways of acculturation does Boas present? What kinds of things are exchanged by cultures?

3. As an early anthropologist, Boas might be expected to write in a scientific style. Is there any reflection in word choice or point of view of a scientific method?

4. Explain Boas's use of the word *invention.* How does it differ from the way we use it? How does the difference reflect his anthropological viewpoint?

5. If you were to divide this essay into three parts, where would you divide it? Why did you divide it where you did?

6. How does Boas use process and analysis to support his thesis?

7. What kinds of evidence does he offer to support his thesis?

8. How does Boas use contrast and comparison? Are they his primary rhetorical methods? If so, why do you think he chose them? If not, why not?

9. All Americans either are immigrants or have forebearers who were. How thoroughly have you been assimilated into the mainstream of American life? Do you believe that assimilation is valuable? Explain.

10. Many of us have had to acclimate ourselves to new cultural settings. When we do that, we are in a small way repeating the acts of nations that Boas describes. Remaining scientifically objective, describe the process of assimilation you underwent when you did one of the following things: (a) went out for your first sports team; (b) moved to a new school, for instance, college; (c) moved into a new neighborhood.

JOAN DIDION

In Bed

Joan Didion (1934–   ) is a novelist and essayist. Her most recent novel is *A Book of Common Prayer* (1977). She has also written two collections of essays, *Slouching Towards Bethlehem* (1968) and *The White Album* (1979). Didion is an intensely introspective writer, and her writing in its very particularity takes on general significance. Here she examines one of the most subjective of experiences—pain.

hree, four, sometimes five times a month, I spend the day in bed with a migraine headache, insensible to the world around me. Almost every day of every month, between these attacks, I feel the sudden irrational irritation and the flush of blood into the cerebral arteries which tell me that migraine is on its way, and I take certain drugs to avert its arrival. If I did not take the drugs, I would be able to function perhaps one day in four. The physiological error called migraine is, in brief, central to the given of my life. When I was 15, 16, even 25, I used to think that I could rid myself of this error by simply denying it, character over chemistry. "Do you have headaches *sometimes? frequently? never?*" the application forms would demand. "Check one." Wary of the trap, wanting whatever it was that the successful circumnavigation of that particular form could bring (a job, a scholarship, the respect of mankind and the grace of God), I would check one. "*Sometimes,*" I would lie. That in fact I spent one or two days a week almost unconscious with pain seemed a shameful secret, evidence not merely of some chemical inferiority but of all my bad attitudes, unpleasant tempers, wrongthink.

For I had no brain tumor, no eyestrain, no high blood pressure, nothing wrong with me at all: I simply had migraine headaches, and migraine headaches were, as everyone who did not have them knew, imaginary. I fought migraine then, ignored the warnings it sent, went to school and later to work in spite of it, sat through lectures in Middle English and presentations to advertisers with involuntary tears running down the right side of my face, threw up in washrooms, stumbled home by instinct, emptied ice trays onto my bed and tried to freeze the pain in my right temple, wished only for a neurosurgeon who would do a lobotomy on house call, and cursed my imagination.

It was a long time before I began thinking mechanistically enough to accept migraine for what it was: something with which I would be living, the way some people lived with diabetes. Migraine is something more than the fancy of a neurotic imagination. It is an essentially hereditary complex of symptoms, the most frequently noted but by no means the most unpleasant of which is a vascular headache of blinding severity, suffered by a surprising number of women, a fair number of men (Thomas Jefferson had migraine, and so did Ulysses S. Grant, the day he accepted Lee's surrender), and by some unfortunate children as young as two years old. (I had my first when I was eight. It came on during a fire drill at the Col-

1

2

3

umbia School in Colorado Springs, Colorado. I was taken first home and then to the infirmary at Peterson Field, where my father was stationed. The Air Corps doctor prescribed an enema.) Almost anything can trigger a specific attack of migraine: stress, allergy, fatigue, an abrupt change in barometric pressure, a contretemps over a parking ticket. A flashing light. A fire drill. One inherits, of course, only the predisposition. In other words I spent yesterday in bed with a headache not merely because of my bad attitudes, unpleasant tempers and wrongthink but because both my grandmothers had migraine, my father has migraine and my mother has migraine.

No one knows precisely what it is that is inherited. The   4 chemistry of migraine, however, seems to have some connection with the nerve hormone named serotonin, which is naturally present in the brain. The amount of serotonin in the blood falls sharply at the onset of migraine, and one migraine drug, methysergide, or Sansert, seems to have some effect on serotonin. Methysergide is a derivative of lysergic acid (in fact Sandoz Pharmaceuticals first synthesized LSD-25 while looking for a migraine cure), and its use is hemmed about with so many contraindications and side effects that most doctors prescribe it only in the most incapacitating cases. Methysergide, when it is prescribed, is taken daily, as a preventive; another preventive which works for some people is old-fashioned ergotamine tartrate, which helps to constrict the swelling blood vessels during the "aura," the period which in most cases precedes the actual headache.

Once an attack is under way, however, no drug touches it.   5 Migraine gives some people mild hallucinations, temporarily blinds others, shows up not only as a headache but as a gastrointestinal disturbance, a painful sensitivity to all sensory stimuli, an abrupt overpowering fatigue, a strokelike aphasia, and a crippling inability to make even the most routine connections. When I am in a migraine aura (for some people the aura lasts fifteen minutes, for others several hours), I will drive through red lights, lose the house keys, spill whatever I am holding, lose the ability to focus my eyes or frame coherent sentences, and generally give the appearance of being on drugs, or drunk. The actual headache, when it comes, brings with it chills, sweating, nausea, a debility that seems to stretch the very limits of endurance. That no one dies of migraine seems, to someone deep into an attack, an ambiguous blessing.

My husband also has migraine, which is unfortunate for him   6 but fortunate for me: perhaps nothing so tends to prolong an attack as the accusing eye of someone who has never had a headache. "Why not take a couple of aspirin," the unafflicted will say from the doorway, or "I'd have a headache, too, spending a beautiful day like this inside with all the shades drawn." All of us who have migraine suffer not only from the attacks themselves but from this common conviction that we are perversely refusing to cure ourselves by taking a couple of aspirins, that we are making ourselves sick, that we "bring it on ourselves." And in the most immediate sense, the sense of why we have a headache this Tuesday and not last Thursday, of course we often do. There certainly is what doctors call a "migraine personality," and that personality tends to be ambitious, inward, intolerant of error, rather rigidly organized, perfectionist. "You don't look like a migraine personality," a doctor once said to me. "Your hair's messy. But I suppose you're a compulsive housekeeper." Actually my house is kept even more negligently than my hair, but the doctor was right nonetheless: perfectionism can also take the form of spending most of a week writing and rewriting and not writing a single paragraph.

But not all perfectionists have migraine, and not all mi- 7 grainous people have migraine personalities. We do not escape heredity. I have tried in most of the available ways to escape my own migrainous heredity (at one point I learned to give myself two daily injections of histamine with a hypodermic needle, even though the needle so frightened me that I had to close my eyes when I did it), but I still have migraine. And I have learned how to live with it, learned when to expect it, and how to outwit it, even how to regard it, when it does come, as more friend than lodger. We have reached a certain understanding, my migraine and I. It never comes when I am in real trouble. Tell me that my house is burned down, my husband has left me, that there is gunfighting in the streets and panic in the banks, and I will not respond by getting a headache. It comes instead when I am fighting not an open but a guerrilla war with my own life, during weeks of small household confusions, lost laundry, unhappy help, canceled appointments, on days when the telephone rings too much and I get no work done and the wind is coming up. On days like that my friend comes uninvited.

And once it comes, now that I am wise in its ways, I no longer 8 fight it. I lie down and let it happen. At first every small apprehension is magnified, every anxiety a pounding terror. Then the pain comes, and I concentrate only on that. Right there is the usefulness of migraine, there in that imposed yoga, the concentration on the pain. For when the pain recedes, ten or twelve hours later, everything goes with it, all the hidden resentments, all the vain anxieties. The migraine has acted as a circuit breaker, and the fuses have emerged intact. There is a pleasant convalescent euphoria. I open the windows and feel the air, eat gratefully, sleep well. I notice the particular nature of a flower in a glass on the stair landing. I count my blessings.

1. What are the physical symptoms of migraine? Identify possible genetic and psychological causes of migraine.

2. What kinds of treatments are available to those who suffer from migraine? How does Didion treat her migraines?

3. Identify the analogies and metaphors Didion uses to describe migraines. How do they help you understand how she feels about migraines?

4. What is the tone of this essay? How does Didion maintain this tone even when she is giving medical information?

5. Didion says that migraine is a "physiological error" (paragraph 1). What rhetorical methods does she use to develop this idea?

6. What paragraphs relate personal experience? How does she use personal experience to structure her essay?

7. What other rhetorical techniques does Didion use to define migraine? Where does she use them?

8. Where and how does Didion use contrast in the essay?

9. Do you think Didion's response to migraine is an admirable one? Have you ever been bedridden or seriously ill? How did you respond?

10. Many people suffer from a disability. Write an essay about a disability you or a friend may have. Use personal experience and medical information to describe and define the disease.

ANAÏS NIN

Notes on Feminism

Anaïs Nin (1903–1977), diarist, novelist, essayist, and feminist, was an American born in Paris. A student of psychology under Otto Rank, Nin always retained her interest in the inner self and specifically in the consciousness of women. In her words, she wished "to unmask the deeper self that lies hidden behind the self that we present to the world." Her diaries, started as letters to her father in 1931, were published in seven volumes between 1966 and 1980. These diaries, an imposing collection termed by Gunther Stuhlmann "one of the unique literary documents of our century," have been compared in method to the work of Marcel Proust. In this essay, Nin writes about the need for women to develop their inner selves.

he nature of my contribution to the Women's Liberation 1
Movement is not political but psychological. I get thousands of letters from women who have been liberated by the reading of my diaries, which are a long study of the psychological obstacles that have prevented woman from her fullest evolution and flowering. I studied the negative influence of religion, of racial and cultural patterns, which action alone and no political slogans can dissolve. I describe in the diaries the many restrictions confining woman. The diary itself was an escape from judgment, a place in which to analyze the truth of woman's situation. I believe that is where the sense of freedom has to begin. I say begin, not remain. A reformation of woman's emotional attitudes and beliefs will enable her to act more effectively. I am not speaking of the practical, economic, sociological problems, as I believe many of them are solvable with clear thinking and intelligence. I am merely placing the emphasis on a confrontation of ourselves because it is a source of strength. Do not confuse my shifting of responsibility with blame. I am not blaming woman. I say that if we take the responsibility for our situation, we can feel less helpless than when we put the blame on society or man. We waste precious energy in negative rebellions. Awareness can give us a sense of captainship over our fate, and to take destiny into our own hands is more inspiring than to expect others to direct our destiny for us. No matter what ideas, psychology, history, or art I learned from man, I learned to convert it into the affirmation of my own identity and my own beliefs, to serve my own growth. At the same time, I loved woman and was fully aware of her problems, and I watched her struggles for development. I believe the lasting revolution comes from deep changes in ourselves which influence our collective life.

Many of the chores women accepted were ritualistic; they 2
were means of expressing love and care and protection. We have to find other ways of expressing these devotions. We cannot solve the problem of freeing ourselves of all chores without first understanding why we accomplished them and felt guilty when we did not. We have to persuade those we love that there are other ways of enriching their lives. Part of these occupations were compensatory. The home was our only kingdom, and it returned many pleasures. We were repaid with love and beauty and a sense of accomplishment. If we want our

energy and strength to go into other channels, we have to work at a transitional solution which may deprive us of a personal world altogether. But I also think we have to cope with our deep-seated, deeply instilled sense of responsibility. That means finding a more creative way of love and collaboration, of educating our children, or caring for a house, and we have to convince those we love that there are other ways of accomplishing these things. The restrictions of women's lives, confined to the personal, also created in us qualities men lost to a degree in a competitive world. I think woman retains a more human relationship to human beings and is not corrupted by the impersonality of powerful interests. I have watched woman in law, in politics, and in education. Because of her gift for personal relationships she deals more effectively with injustice, war, prejudice. I have a dream about woman pouring into all professions a new quality. I want a different world, not the same world born of man's need of power which is the origin of war and injustice. We have to create a new woman.

What of ghettos and poverty? A new kind of human being 3 would not allow them to be born in the first place. It is the quality of human beings I want to see improved, because we already know that drugs, crime, war, and injustice are not curable by a change of system. It is humanism which is lacking in our leaders. I do not want to see women follow in the same pattern. To assert individual qualities and thought was tabooed by puritanism and is now being equally tabooed by militant fanatics. But practical problems are often solved by psychological liberation. The imagination, the skills, the intelligence, are freed to discover solutions. I see so many women in the movement thinking in obsessional circles about problems which are solvable when one is emotionally free to think and act clearly. Undirected, blind anger and hostility are not effective weapons. They have to be converted into lucid action. Each woman has to consider her own problems before she can act effectively within her radius; otherwise she is merely adding the burden of her problems to the collective overburdened majority. Her individual solution, courage, become in turn like cellular growth, organic growth. It is added to the general synthesis. Slogans do not give strength because generalizations are untrue. Many intelligent women, many potentially collaborative men, are alienated by generalizations. To recruit all women for a work for which some are unfit is not effective. The group does not always give strength, because it moves only according to the lowest denominator of understanding. The group weakens the individual will and annihilates the individual contribution. To object to individual growth of awareness in women is to work against the benefit of the collective whose quality is raised by individual research and learning.

Each woman has to know herself, her problems, her obstacles. I ask woman to realize she can be master of her own destiny. This is an inspiring thought. To blame others means one feels helpless. What I liked best about psychology is the concept that destiny is interior, in our own hands. While we wait for others to free us, we will not develop the strength to do it ourselves. When a woman has not solved her personal, intimate defeats, her private hostilities, her failures, she brings the dregs of this to the group and only increases its negative reactions. This is placing liberation on too narrow a basis. Liberation means the power to transcend obstacles. The obstacles are educational, religious, racial, and cultural patterns. These have to be confronted, and there is no political solution which serves them all. The real tyrants are guilt, taboos, educational inheritance—these are our enemies. And we can grapple with them. The real enemy is what we were taught, not always by man, but often by our mothers and grandmothers.

The trouble with anger is that it makes us overstate our case   4
and prevents us from reaching awareness. We often damage our case by anger. It is like resorting to war.

Poverty and injustice and prejudice are not solved by any   5
man-made system. I want them to be solved by a higher quality of human being who, by his own law of valuation upon human life, will not permit such inequalities. In that sense whatever we do for the development of this higher quality will eventually permeate all society. The belief that all of us, untrained, unprepared and un-skilled, can be conscripted for mass action is what has prevented woman from developing, because it is the same old-fashioned asser-tion that the only good we can do is outside of ourselves, salvaging others. When we do this we ignore the fact that the evil comes from individual flaws, undeveloped human beings. We need models. We need heroes and leaders. Out of the many lawyers who came from Harvard, we were given only one Nader. But one Nader has incalculable influence. If we continue in the name of politics to denigrate those who have developed their skills to the maximum pitch as elite, privileged, or exceptional people, we will never be able to help others achieve their potential. We need blueprints for the creation of human beings as well as for architecture.

The attack against individual development belongs to the   6
dark ages of socialism. If I am able to inspire or help women today, it is because I persisted in my development. I was often derailed by other duties, but I never gave up this relentless disciplined creation of my awareness because I realized that at the bottom of every failed system to improve the lot of man lies an imperfect, corruptible human being.

It is inspiring to read of the women who defied the codes and taboos of their period: Ninon de Lenclos in the seventeenth century, Lou Andreas-Salomé in the time of Freud, Nietzsche, and Rilke, and in our time Han Suyin. Or the four heroines of Lesley Blanch's *Wilder Shores of Love.*   7

I see a great deal of negativity in the Women's Liberation Movement. It is less important to attack male writers than to discover and read women writers, to attack male-dominated films than to make films by women. If the passivity of woman is going to erupt like a volcano or an earthquake, it will not accomplish anything but disaster. This passivity can be converted to creative will. If it expresses itself in war, then it is an imitation of man's methods. It would be good to study the writings of women who were more concerned with personal relationships than with the power struggles of history. I have a dream of a more human lawyer, a more human educator, a more human politician. To become man, or like man, is no solution. There is far too much imitation of man in the women's movement. That is merely a displacement of power. Woman's definition of power should be different. It should be based on relationships to others. The women who truly identify with their oppressors, as the cliché phrase goes, are the women who are acting like men, masculinizing themselves, not those who seek to convert or transform man. There is no liberation of one group at the expense of another. Liberation can only come totally and in unison.   8

Group thinking does not give strength. It weakens the will. Majority thinking is oppressive because it inhibits individual growth and seeks a formula for all. Individual growth makes communal living of higher quality. A developed woman will know how to take care of all her social duties and how to act effectively.   9

QUESTIONS

1. What arguments does Nin give against group action? What arguments does she offer for individual growth?

2. According to Nin, what are the main differences between man and woman? Why does this difference make women so important to the development of social justice?

3. Give examples of Nin's hortatory style. Examine particularly her point of view and verb forms.

4. Give examples of Nin's use of psychological vocabulary in this essay. How does the vocabulary reflect the theme?

5. Where in this essay does Nin describe her personal experience? How is this placement important for the development of the essay?

6. Does Nin use such conventional forms of organization as comparison and contrast or classification? If not, what kinds of organizational devices does she use? If she does, detail how.

7. The most explicit criticism of the woman's liberation movement occurs in paragraph 8. Why does Nin defer this criticism until so late in her essay?

8. Nin's conclusion clearly recapitulates most of the points of her essay. Why does she write such a conventional conclusion?

9. Do you agree that personal growth must precede social growth? Explain.

10. Write an essay describing your idea of the new woman.

MARYA MANNES

The New Therapy

Marya Mannes (1904–   ) has written several novels and some light verse, but she is best known for her essays, which have appeared in *Vogue, McCall's, Harpers,* and *The New Republic.* She has collected her essays in *More in Anger* (1958) and in *The New York I Know* (1961). Mannes has also written on television in *Who Owns the Air* (1960). The following essay is taken from *Last Rights* (1974), in which Mannes considers the issues of suicide and euthanasia.

 hen Sigmund Freud at seventy-two accepted young   1
Doctor Schur as his personal internist, he stipulated that
Schur would never lie to him, and then said, "Promise
me. When the time comes, you won't let me suffer
unnecessarily." (About his own dying father, Freud had said years
before: "The unconscious is immortal.")

In 1939, after eleven years of acute suffering and countless   2
operations on his cancerous mouth (added to the horror of Hitler's
rise and Freud's own unremitting work), the time came. Now in

THE NEW THERAPY   **211**

English exile, the great psychoanalyst was not only too pain-racked to read, let alone write, but necrosis of the tissue emanated an odor so foul that his own long-loved dog lay twenty feet away, and even those dearest to him could barely endure to come close.

Freud then gave the word to Schur, and Schur gave him two 3 injections of morphine, one at night and one in the early morning. By contemporary standards they were light doses. But since Freud had refused all pain killers through his many cancerous bouts, the drug brought death.

Schur, as his own brilliant psychobiography of Freud made 4 clear, was constant witness to the struggle in this creative genius between the life force and the death wish.

The same struggle now is widely manifest in those psychia- 5 trists who have to deal with it not only in themselves, but in professional contact with the dying.

They are as yet a relatively small band. The reasons are clear. 6 Their profession is oriented to the healing or strengthening of the psyche so that it can withstand not only the pressures of external life but the anxieties of the inner self. It is aimed toward the patient's fullest realization of self, of his powers as well as his limitations, and toward an acceptance of truth that will free the hitherto shackled or impeded spirit. It is therefore deeply concerned with ongoing life.

Yet with the great lengthening of the human life span, and 7 the growing numbers of the fatally ill suspended in limbo to await their end with little spiritual comfort or support, some psychiatrists now feel impelled to come to their aid, to ease the final transition.

They seem to agree on only three points. One is the need to 8 strengthen the vital force by supporting their patient's sense of identity as an individual. The second (essential to the first) is to listen to them. And the third consensus is that the psychiatrists themselves cannot psychically sustain in their practice more than a few patients near death. "It is a terrible strain," said one of them, "because in order to communicate with the dying, we must ourselves under-stand—and try to feel—the process of dying."

It is because of this, and because the attitudes of the family 9 toward this process can deeply affect the doomed patient, that psychiatrists find the counseling of relatives so important.

They know what it can do to a husband aware of his cancer to 10 have a wife who never mentions it. The physical pain can be tempered by drugs, but for the pain of isolation there is no anodyne.

They know that if close family members cannot bring them- 11 selves to share the truth gently with those they are about to lose, then they must share it with a neutral but compassionate ear.

This ear need not be the psychiatrist's alone. In fact, very few 12 of us can afford his counsel, either in time or money. The psychiatrists themselves lack the firm base of knowledge in the psychic aspects of death that the doctor possesses in biological terms. One of their most eloquent spokesmen, Dr. Avery D. Weisman, concedes that psychosocial data on dying are not only very elusive, but much more difficult to obtain than observations about organic disease. An aged person may live for years in a chronic hospital, but his interests, actions, and ordinary habits are neither observed nor recorded.

Weisman also observes, as I have myself found in chronic and terminal wards, that the higher the professional rank of staff members, the less familiar they are with patients as people. 13

A fascinating sidelight was a study made recently (and surreptitiously) by a young psychologist in the geriatric ward of a big city hospital. Having counseled a patient there, he had acquainted himself with the numbers of the rooms that housed those on the critical list. He spent several hours one night in view of the call-board signaling requests from patients by means of lights used for nursing attention. After comparing these calls with the room numbers on his chart and the time it took for them to be answered, he saw—unequivocally—that the nearer the patient was to death, the longer the wait for nursing response. 14

The floor knew the score. Old Mrs. Jones always called just for company, or some trivial thing. Old Mr. Smith didn't know what he was doing anymore. Miss Schwartz was a chronic complainer. 15

This tardy response from the nurses wasn't deliberate callousness: more a feeling of uselessness at this stage of the game. Those with a chance for life deserved priority. 16

Like many of us, inside and outside of the health professions, psychiatrist Kurt Eissler has noticed that all modern medicine has achieved is to make it more difficult for man to die, "although his preoccupation with his body, his worry about disease have not decreased. It may even have been augmented." 17

It is this worry, this call for help in the night or the day, that the "lower echelons" in the treatment hierarchy of the critically ill are now trying to answer. 18

Again in the death of Ivan Ilych, it was his humble servant Gerasim—holding his aching body, sharing his agony—who gave any comfort or peace. And those who have seen Ingmar Bergman's *Cries and Whispers* know that in this elaborate family mansion, cold and dark with unspoken words and ungiven love, it was the maid who held her cancer-ridden mistress to her breast, rocking and soothing her until the convulsive end. 19

So now, social workers, young aides, and unorthodox ministers sit at the bedside of the near-to-death to listen, to comfort, to 20

 THE NEW THERAPY

pray—if asked to—to touch, to answer. They are also open to bewildered or agonized relatives in need of counsel and direction.

The growing trend is for less specialization, more interde-   21
pendence in this ultimate care. Doctors, interns, and nurses should share their knowledge and observations with their subordinates instead of proceeding in virtual ignorance of each other's decisions and actions.

So far, only one out of a hundred private hospitals immedi-   22
ately involved with catastrophic disease and terminal care have established training courses for this new form of "consciousness raising." For one thing, they go against the grain of the medical hierarchy. For another, they are rejected by the hospital unions, who do not want to join any training program with management.

Since union members die as well as doctors, the familiar and   23
fruitless act of cutting off the nose to spite the face is with us again. Or is it perhaps the territorial imperative? The turf?

Whatever the resistance, courses for this new kind of group   24
counseling are being held under the auspices of the Foundation of Thanatology, Cancer Care, and other institutions dedicated to the study and alleviation of critical or terminal diseases ravishing human beings.

Last year the Foundation of Thanatology, spearheaded by its   25
founder Dr. Austin Kutscher, held a conference at Columbia University devoted largely to this counseling. One session included psychiatrists, priests, nurses, doctors, and social workers.

They appeared to agree on several salient points, among   26
them that city hospitals were largely dumping grounds for training doctors and for dying patients on Medicare and Medicaid, and of necessity often brutalized by their own bureaucracy. To reverse this trend, it was suggested that doctors should regain their philosophic control of hospitals, making them more human and less mechanical.

The conferees could not know that scarcely two months after   27
this discussion the American Hospital Association, based in Chicago, would establish a patient's "Bill of Rights" which would include, among the twelve major points, the right to "obtain from his physician complete, current information concerning his diagnosis, treatment, and prognosis in terms the patient can reasonably hope to understand . . . the right to refuse treatment to the extent permitted by law, and to be informed of the medical consequences of his action . . . and the right to receive from his physician information necessary to give informed consent prior to the start of any procedure and/or treatment."

All these rights, moreover, are to include the guarantee of   28 total privacy between patient, doctor, and hospital staff. Most importantly, copies of these rights are to be given to every patient entering or in the hospital.

Following this patient's Bill of Rights in a matter of days was a statement from the New York State Medical Society which, though prohibiting doctors from authorizing mercy killings, supported a patient's "right" to die with dignity if he so chooses; adding that when "there is irrefutable evidence that biological death is inevitable," this right must be "the joint decision of the patient and/or the immediate family with the approval of the family physician." 29

The door was open at last. But only ajar. 30

QUESTIONS

1. According to Mannes, how do the following types traditionally respond to dying patients: doctors, psychiatrists, nurses, and relatives?

2. Describe the patient's Bill of Rights and explain its effect on the terminally ill.

3. Detail the shifting level of diction in this essay. What effect does Mannes achieve by changing diction?

4. Explain how the style in paragraphs 15 and 19 differs from the general style of the essay. Why does Mannes change style here?

5. What paragraphs constitute the introduction of this essay? How does it help Mannes to develop her theme?

6. This essay is about a developing therapy. Show what methods Mannes uses to demonstrate that she is writing a narrative.

7. Paragraphs 13 and 18 are critical to the development of the essay. Why?

8. What is the purpose of the author's quotation of several people?

9. The right to "die with dignity" is, of course deeply controversial. Do you think that people should have this right? Justify your answer.

10. Write an essay exploring a moral issue such as abortion, capital punishment, or euthanasia.

The Mother Archetype

Carl Gustav Jung (1875–1961) is considered the founder of analytic psychology. He began his psychological career as an associate of Sigmund Freud, but the two men parted company when Jung's *Psychology of the Unconscious* (1912, tr. 1916, rev. 1952) was published. Jung separated the unconscious into two parts—the personal and the collective unconscious—and introduced such terms as extroversion and introversion in *Psychological Types* (1921, tr. 1923) and animus and anima. He maintains that the goal of each person is to bring the conscious and the unconscious into harmony. Jung was a prolific writer. His works include *Modern Man in Search of a Soul* (1933), *The Structure and Dynamics of the Psyche* (tr. 1960), and *Psychology and Religion: West and East* (tr. 1958). Jung here describes various aspects of a key archetype: the mother.

ike any other archetype, the mother archetype appears 1 under an almost infinite variety of aspects. I mention here only some of the more characteristic. First in importance are the personal mother and grandmother, stepmother and mother-in-law; then any women with whom a relationship exists, for example, a nurse or governess or perhaps a remote ancestress. Then there are what might be termed mothers in a figurative sense. To this category belongs the goddess, and especially the Mother of God, the Virgin, and Sophia. Mythology offers many variations of the mother archetype, as for instance the mother who reappears as the maiden in the myth of Demeter and Kore; or the mother who is also the beloved, as in the Cybele-Attis myth. Other symbols of the mother in a figurative sense appear in things representing the goal of our longing for redemption, such as Paradise, the Kingdom of God, the Heavenly Jerusalem. Many things arousing devotion or feelings of awe, as for instance the Church, university, city or country, Heaven, Earth, the woods, the sea or any still waters, matter even, the underworld and the moon, can be mother-symbols. The archetype is often associated with things and places standing for fertility and fruitfulness: the cornucopia, a plowed field, a garden. It can be attached to a rock, a cave, a tree, a spring, a deep well, or to various vessels such as the baptismal font, or to vessel-shaped flowers like the rose or the lotus. Because of the protection it implies, the magic circle or mandala can be a form of mother archetype. Hollow objects such as óvens and cooking vessels are associated with the mother archetype, and, of course, the uterus, *yoni,* and anything of a like shape. Added to this list there are many animals, such as the cow, hare, and helpful animals in general.

All these symbols can have a positive, favorable meaning or a negative, evil meaning. An ambivalent aspect is seen in the goddess of fate (Moira, Graeae, Norns). Evil symbols are the witch, the dragon (or any devouring and entwining animal, such as a large fish or a serpent), the grave, the sarcophagus, deep water, death, nightmares and bogies (Empusa, Lilith, etc.). This list is not, of course, complete; it presents only the most important features of the mother archetype. 2

The qualities associated with it are maternal solicitude and sympathy; the magic authority of the female; the wisdom and spiritual exaltation that transcend reason; any helpful instinct or impulse; all that is benign, all that cherishes and sustains, that fosters growth and fertility. The place of magic transformation and rebirth, together with the underworld and its inhabitants, are presided over by the mother. On the negative side the mother archetype may connote anything secret, hidden, dark; the abyss, the world of the dead, anything that devours, seduces, and poisons, that is terrifying and inescapable like fate. All these attributes of the mother archetype have been fully described and documented in my book *Symbols of Transformation.* There I formulated the ambivalence of these attributes as "the loving and the terrible mother." Perhaps the historical example of the dual nature of the mother most familiar to us is the Virgin Mary, who is not only the Lord's mother, but also according to the medieval allegories, his cross. In India, "the loving and terrible mother" is the paradoxical Kali. Sankhya philosophy has elaborated the mother archetype into the concept of *prakrti* (matter) and assigned to it the three *gunas* or fundamental attributes: *sattva, rajas, tamas:* goodness, passion, and darkness. These are three essential aspects of the mother: her cherishing and nourishing goodness, her orgiastic emotionality, and her Stygian depths. The special feature of the philosophical myth, which shows Prakrti dancing before Purusha in order to remind him of "discriminating knowledge," does not belong to the mother archetype but to the archetype of the anima, which in a man's psychology invariably appears, at first, mingled with the mother-image. 3

Although the figure of the mother as it appears in folklore is more or less universal, this image changes markedly when it appears in the individual psyche. In treating patients one is at first impressed, and indeed arrested, by the apparent significance of the personal 4 mother. This figure of the personal mother looms so large in all personalistic psychologies that, as we know, they never got beyond it, even in theory, to other important etiological factors. My own view differs from that of other medico-psychological theories principally in that I attribute to the personal mother only a limited etiological significance. That is to say, all those influences which the literature describes as being exerted on the children do not come from the mother herself, but rather from the archetype projected upon her, which gives her a mythological background and invests her with authority and numinosity.[1] The etiological and traumatic effects produced by the mother must be divided into two groups: (1) those corresponding to traits of character or attitudes actually present in the mother, and (2) those referring to traits which the mother only seems to possess, the reality being composed of more or less fantastic (i.e., archetypal) projections on the part of the child. Freud himself had already seen that the real etiology of neuroses does not lie in traumatic effects, as he at first suspected, but in a peculiar development of infantile fantasy. This is not to deny that such a development can be traced back to disturbing influences emanating from the mother. I myself make it a rule to look first for the cause of infantile neuroses in the mother, as I know from experience that a child is much more likely to develop normally than neurotically, and that in the great majority of cases definite causes of disturbances can be found in the parents, especially in the mother. The contents of the child's abnormal fantasies can be referred to the personal mother only in part, since they often contain clear and unmistakable allusions which could not possibly have reference to human beings. This is especially true where definitely mythological products are concerned, as is frequently the case in infantile phobias where the mother may appear as a wild beast, a witch, a specter, an ogre, a hermaphrodite, and so on. It must be borne in mind, however, that such fantasies are not always of unmistakably mythological origin, and, even if they are, they may not always be rooted in the unconscious archetype but may have been occasioned by fairy tales or accidental remarks. A thorough investigation is therefore indicated in each case. For practical reasons, such an investigation cannot be made so readily with children as with adults, who almost invariably transfer their fantasies to the physician during treatment— or, to be more precise, the fantasies transfer themselves to him automatically.

When that happens, nothing is gained by brushing them aside as ridiculous, for archetypes are among the inalienable assets of

[1]American psychology can supply us with any amount of examples. A blistering but instructive lampoon on this subject is Philip Wylie's *Generation of Vipers* (New York, 1942).

every psyche. They form the "treasure in the realm of shadowy thoughts" of which Kant spoke, and of which we have ample evidence in the countless treasure motifs of mythology. An archetype as such is in no sense just an annoying prejudice; it becomes so only when it is in the wrong place. In themselves, archetypal images are among the highest values of the human psyche; they have peopled the heavens of all races from time immemorial. To discard them as valueless would be a distinct loss. Our task is not, therefore, to deny the archetype, but to dissolve the projections, in order to restore their contents to the individual who has involuntarily lost them by projecting them outside himself.

QUESTIONS

1. List the positive and negative examples Jung gives of the mother archetype.

2. According to Jung, what is the relationship between mother archetypes and mothers?

3. Define the following psychological terms: *archetype* (paragraph 1); *figurative sense* (paragraph 1); *ambivalent* (paragraph 2); *anima* (paragraph 3); *etiological* (paragraph 4); *numinosity* (paragraph 4); *traumatic* (paragraph 4); *project* (paragraph 4); and *phobias* (paragraph 4).

4. Explain Jung's use of the quote "treasure in the realm of shadowy thoughts." How does this indicate his attitude toward archetypes?

5. Describe the classification used in paragraph 1. How is it qualified later to develop Jung's thesis?

6. Divide this essay into two parts. Why did you divide it where you did?

7. Paragraph 4 uses cause and effect. Identify the elements of this rhetorical type here. How does this paragraph contribute to the development of the essay?

8. How does Jung compare literary examples with archetypes of the unconscious? What words structure that relation?

9. Jung sees many things as symbols of the mother. How does his vision affect the way that you look at the world?

10. a. Keeping Jung's list of symbols in mind, attempt to interpret your neighborhood in terms of those symbols.
b. Write an essay on the father archetype.

 THE MOTHER ARCHETYPE

SIGMUND FREUD

Libidinal Types

Sigmund Freud (1856–1939), founder of psychoanalysis, was an excellent writer. His theories concerning the pleasure principle, repression, and infantile sexuality are still controversial; nevertheless, they have had a profound impact upon culture, education, and art. Some of Freud's psychological works include *The Interpretation of Dreams* (1900), *The Psychopathology of Everyday Life* (1904), and *The Ego and the Id* (1923). He also analyzed the relation of culture and psychology in *Totem and Taboo* (1913) and *Moses and Monotheism* (1939). In the following essay, Freud discusses several character types derived from his theory of the libido.

bservation teaches us that in individual human beings the general features of humanity are embodied in almost infinite variety. If we follow the promptings of a legitimate desire to distinguish particular types in this multiplicity, we must begin by selecting the characteristics to look for and the points of view to bear in mind in making our differentiation. For this purpose physical qualities will be no less useful than mental; it will be most valuable of all if we can make our classification on the basis of a regularly occurring combination of physical and mental characteristics.

It is doubtful whether we are as yet able to discover types of this order, although we shall certainly be able to do so sometime on a basis of which we are still ignorant. If we confine our efforts to defining certain purely psychological types, the libidinal situation will have the first claim to serve as the basis of our classification. It may fairly be demanded that this classification should not merely be deduced from our knowledge or our conjectures about the libido, but that it should be easily verified in actual experience and should help to clarify the mass of our observations and enable us to grasp their meaning. Let it be admitted at once that there is no need to suppose that, even in the psychical sphere, these libidinal types are the only possible ones; if we take other characteristics as our basis of classification we might be able to distinguish a whole series of other psychological types. But there is one rule which must apply to all such types: they must not coincide with specific clinical pictures. On the contrary, they should embrace all the variations which according to our practical standards fall within the category of the normal. In their extreme developments, however, they may well approximate to clinical pictures and so help to bridge the gulf which is assumed to exist between the normal and the pathological.

Now we can distinguish three main libidinal types, according 3 as the subject's libido is mainly allocated to one or another region of the mental apparatus. To name these types is not very easy; following the lines of our depth-psychology, I should be inclined to call them the *erotic*, the *narcissistic* and the *obsessional* type.

The *erotic* type is easily characterized. Erotics are persons 4 whose main interest—the relatively largest amount of their libido—is focused on love. Loving, but above all being loved, is for them the most important thing in life. They are governed by the dread of loss of love, and this makes them peculiarly dependent on those who may withhold their love from them. Even in its pure form this type is a very common one. Variations occur according as it is blended with another type and as the element of aggression in it is strong or weak. From the social and cultural standpoint this type represents the elementary instinctual claims of the id, to which the other psychical agencies have become docile.

The second type is that which I have termed the *obsessional*—a 5 name which may at first seem rather strange; its distinctive characteristic is the supremacy exercised by the super-ego, which is segregated from the ego with great accompanying tension. Persons of this type are governed by anxiety of conscience instead of by the dread of losing love; they exhibit, we might say, an inner instead of an outer dependence; they develop a high degree of self-reliance, from the social standpoint they are the true upholders of civilization, for the most part in a conservative spirit.

The characteristics of the third type, justly called the *narcissistic*, are in the main negatively described. There is no tension between 6 ego and super-ego—indeed, starting from this type one would hardly have arrived at the notion of a super-ego; there is no preponderance of erotic needs; the main interest is focused on self-preservation; the type is independent and not easily overawed. The ego has a considerable amount of aggression available, one manifestation of this being a proneness to activity; where love is in question, loving is preferred to being loved. People of this type impress others as being "personalities"; it is on them that their fellow-men are specially likely to lean; they readily assume the role of leader, give a fresh stimulus to cultural development or break down existing conditions.

These pure types will hardly escape the suspicion of being 7 deduced from the theory of the libido. But we feel that we are on the firm ground of experience when we turn to the mixed types which are to be found so much more frequently than the unmixed. These new types: the *erotic-obsessional,* the *erotic-narcissistic* and the *narcissistic-obsessional* do really seem to provide a good grouping of the individual psychical structures revealed in analysis. If we study these mixed types we find in them pictures of characters with which we have long been familiar. In the *erotic-obsessional* type the preponderance of the instincts is restricted by the influence of the super-ego: dependence on persons who are *contemporary* objects and, at the same time, on the residues of *former* objects—parents, educators and ideal figures—is carried by this type to the furthest point. The *erotic-narcissistic* type is perhaps the most common of all. It combines contrasting characteristics which are thus able to moderate one another; studying this type in comparison with the other two erotic types, we can see how aggressiveness and activity go with a predominance of narcissism. Finally, the *narcissistic-obsessional* type represents the variation most valuable from the cultural standpoint, for it combines independence of external factors and regard for the requirements of conscience with the capacity for energetic action, and it reinforces the ego against the super-ego.

It might be asked in jest why no mention has been made of 8 another mixed type which is theoretically possible: the *erotic-obsessional-narcissistic.* But the answer to this jest is serious: such a type would no longer be a type at all, but the absolute norm, the ideal harmony. We thereupon realize that the phenomenon of different *types* arises just in so far as one or two of the three main modes of expending the libido in the mental economy have been favoured at the cost of the others.

Another question that may be asked is what is the relation of 9 these libidinal types to pathology, whether some of them have a special disposition to pass over into neurosis and, if so, which types lead to which forms of neurosis. The answer is that the hypothesis of these libidinal types throws no fresh light on the genesis of the neuroses. Experience testifies that persons of all these types can live free from neurosis. The pure types marked by the undisputed predominance of a single psychical agency seem to have a better prospect of manifesting themselves as pure character-formations, while we might expect that the mixed types would provide a more fruitful soil for the conditioning factors of neurosis. But I do not think that we should make up our mind on these points until they have been carefully submitted to appropriate tests.

It seems easy to infer that when persons of the erotic type fall 10 ill they will develop hysteria, just as those of the obsessional type will develop obsessional neurosis; but even this conclusion partakes of the uncertainty to which I have just alluded. People of the narcissistic type, who, being otherwise independent, are exposed to frustration from the external world, are peculiarly disposed to psychosis; and their mental composition also contains some of the essential conditioning factors which make for criminality.

We know that we have not as yet exact certainty about the aetiological conditions of neurosis. The precipitating occasions are frustrations and inner conflicts: conflicts between the three great psychical agencies, conflicts arising in the libidinal economy by reason of our bisexual disposition, conflicts between the erotic and the aggressive instinctual components. It is the endeavour of the psychology of the neurosis to discover what imparts a pathogenic character to these processes, which are a part of the normal course of mental life.

11

QUESTIONS

1. According to Freud, what types of individuals uphold society? What are their psychological characteristics?

2. What relationship does Freud see between mental illness and these character types?

3. Freud assumes that the reader is familiar with several psychological terms. Make sure you understand the following: *depth-psychology* (paragraph 3); *id* (paragraph 4); *ego* (paragraph 5); *neuroses* (paragraph 9); *psychosis* (paragraph 10); and *aetiological* (paragraph 11).

4. Is Freud general or specific in this essay? How does his choice here relate to the conclusions he draws in paragraphs 9 to 11?

5. Freud's primary rhetorical technique is classification. Identify his categories and explain the method he uses to classify people.

6. Explain the relations of paragraphs 1 and 2 to the body of the essay.

7. Freud uses definition frequently in this essay. What kinds of definitions does he use? How do they contribute to the structuring of the essay?

8. Explain the importance of paragraph 7 to the essay's structure. What effect does it have on the classification the author has established?

9. Using Freud's "pure" categories, how would you categorize politicians, actors, teachers, religious leaders, and students?

10. There are innumerable ways to classify people. In essay form, devise your own method for classifying a particular group of people.

The Psychological Reactions of Oppressed People

Richard Wright (1908–1960), American author, spoke eloquently about the black experience in America in his novels
and essays. Wright was born on a Mississippi plantation. As a
young man he moved to Chicago, where he joined a
Federal Writers' Project in the 1930s. His experiences in Mississippi and Chicago appear in his early fiction: *Uncle Tom's
Children* (1938) is about racial oppression in the South and
Native Son (1940) is about discrimination and exploitation in
Chicago during the Depression. Wright became an expatri-
ate after World War II. From Paris, he wrote an autobiography,
Black Boy (1945), and two novels, *The Outsider* (1953) and *The
Long Dream* (1958). Wright visited the African Gold Coast
where, as the following essay demonstrates, he observed the
oppression of blacks once more.

Buttressed by their belief that their God had entrusted 1
the earth into their keeping, drunk with power and
possibility, waxing rich through trade in commodities,
human and non-human, with awesome naval and mer-
chant marines at their disposal, their countries filled with human
debris anxious for any adventures, psychologically armed with new
facts, white Western Christian civilization during the fourteenth,
fifteenth, sixteenth, and seventeenth centuries, with a long, slow,
and bloody explosion, hurled itself upon the sprawling masses of
colored humanity in Asia and Africa.

I say to you white men of the West: Don't be too proud of how 2
easily you conquered and plundered those Asians and Africans. You
had unwitting allies in your campaigns; you had Fifth Columns in the
form of indigenous cultures to facilitate your military, missionary,
and mercenary efforts. Your collaborators in those regions consisted
of the mental habits of the people, habits for which they were in no
way responsible, no more than you were responsible for yours. Those
habits constituted corps of saboteurs, of spies, if you will, that worked
in the interests of European aggression. You must realize that it was
not your courage or racial superiority that made you win, nor was it
the racial inferiority or cowardice of the Asians and Africans that
made them lose. This is an important point that you must grasp, or

your concern with this problem will be forever wide of the facts. How, then, did the West, numerically the minority, achieve, during the last four centuries, so many dazzling victories over the body of colored mankind? Frankly, it took you centuries to do a job that could have been done in fifty years! You had the motive, the fire power, the will, the religious spur, the superior organization, but you dallied. Why? You were not aware exactly of what you were doing. You didn't suspect your impersonal strength, or the impersonal weakness on the other side. You were as unconscious, at bottom, as were your victims about what was really taking place.

Your world of culture clashed with the culture-worlds of colored mankind, and the ensuing destruction of traditional beliefs among a billion and a half of black, brown, and yellow men has set off a tide of social, cultural, political, and economic revolution that grips the world today. That revolution is assuming many forms, absolutistic, communistic, fascistic, theocratistic etc.—all marked by unrest, violence, and an astounding emotional thrashing about as men seek new objects about which they can center their loyalties. 3

It is of the reactions, tortured and turbulent, of those Asians and Africans, in the New and Old World, that I wish to speak to you. Naturally I cannot speak for those Asians and Africans who are still locked in their mystical or ancestor-worshiping traditions. They are the voiceless ones, the silent ones. Indeed, I think that they are the doomed ones, men in a tragic trap. Any attempt on their part to wage a battle to protect their outmoded traditions and religions is a battle that is lost before it starts. And I say frankly that I suspect any white man who loves to dote upon those "naked nobles," who wants to leave them as they are, who finds them "primitive and pure," for such mystical hankering is, in my opinion, the last refuge of reactionary racists and psychological cripples tired of their own civilization. My remarks will, of necessity, be confined to those Asians and Africans who, having been partly Westernized, have a quarrel with the West. They are the ones who feel that they are oppressed. In a sense, this is a fight of the West with *itself*, a fight that the West blunderingly began, and the West does not to this day realize that it is the sole responsible agent, the sole instigator. For the West to disclaim responsibility for what it so clearly did is to make every white man alive on earth today a criminal. In history as in law, men must be held strictly responsible for the consequences of their historic actions, whether they intended those consequences or not. For the West to accept its responsibility is to create the means by which white men can liberate themselves from their fears, panic, and terror while they confront the world's colored majority of men who are also striving for liberation from the irrational ties which the West 4

 THE PSYCHOLOGICAL REACTIONS OF OPPRESSED PEOPLE 225

prompted them to disown—ties of which the West has partially robbed them.

Let's imagine a mammoth flying saucer from Mars landing,   5
say, in a peasant Swiss village and debouching swarms of fierce-looking men whose skins are blue and whose red eyes flash lightning bolts that deal instant death. The inhabitants are all the more terrified because the arrival of these men had been predicted. The religious myths of the Western world—the Second Coming of Christ, the Last Judgment, etc., have conditioned Europeans for just such an improbable event. Hence, those Swiss natives will feel that resistance is useless for a while. As long as the blue strangers are casually kind, they are obeyed and served. They become the Fathers of the people. Is this a fragment of paperback science fiction? No. It's more prosaic than that. The image I've sketched above is the manner, by and large, in which white Europe overran Asia and Africa. (Remember the Cortés-Montezuma drama!)

But why did Europe do this? Did it only want gold, power,   6
women, raw materials? It was more complicated than that.

The fifteenth-, sixteenth-, and seventeenth-century neurotic   7
European, sick of his thwarted instincts, restless, filled with self-disgust, was looking for not only spices and gold and slaves when he set out; he was looking for an Arcadia, a Land's End, a Shangri-la, a world peopled by shadow men, a world that would permit free play for his repressed instincts. Stripped of tradition, these misfits, adventurers, indentured servants, convicts and freebooters were the most advanced individualists of their time. Rendered socially superfluous by the stifling weight of the Church and nobility, buttressed by the influence of the ideas of Hume and Descartes, they had been brutally molded toward attitudes of emotional independence and could doff the cloying ties of custom, tradition, and family. The Asian-African native, anchored in family-dependence systems of life, could not imagine why or how these men had left their homelands, could not conceive of the cold, arid emotions sustaining them. . . . Emotional independence was a state of mind not only utterly inconceivable, but an attitude toward life downright evil to the Asian-African native—something to be avoided at all costs. Bound by a charged array of humble objects that made up an emotionally satisfying and exciting world, they, trapped by their limited mental horizon, could not help thinking that the white men invading their lands had been driven forcibly from their homes!

Living in a waking dream, generations of emotionally impov-   8
erished colonial European whites wallowed in the quick gratification of greed, reveled in the cheap superiority of racial domination, slaked their sensual thirst in illicit sexuality, draining off the dammed-up

libido that European morality had condemned, amassing through trade a vast reservoir of economic fat, thereby establishing vast accumulations of capital which spurred the industrialization of the West. Asia and Africa thus became a neurotic habit that Europeans could forgo only at the cost of a powerful psychic wound, for this emotionally crippled Europe had, through the centuries, grown used to leaning upon this black crutch.

But what of the impact of those white faces upon the personalities of the native? Steeped in dependence systems of family life and anchored in ancestor-worshiping religions, the native was prone to identify those powerful white faces falling athwart his existence with the potency of his dead father who had sustained him in the past. Temporarily accepting the invasion, he transferred his loyalties to those white faces, but, because of the psychological, racial, and economic luxury which those faces derived from their domination, the native was kept at bay. 9

Today, as the tide of white domination of the land mass of Asia and Africa recedes, there lies exposed to view a procession of shattered cultures, disintegrated societies, and a writhing sweep of more aggressive, irrational religion than the world has known for centuries. And, as scientific research, partially freed from the blight of colonial control, advances, we are witnessing the rise of a new genre of academic literature dealing with colonial and post-colonial facts from a wider angle of vision than ever possible before. The personality distortions of hundreds of millions of black, brown, and yellow people that are being revealed by this literature are confounding and will necessitate drastic alteration of our past evaluations of colonial rule. In this new literature one enters a universe of menacing shadows where disparate images coalesce—white turning into black, the dead coming to life, the top becoming the bottom—until you think you are seeing Biblical beasts with seven heads and ten horns rising out of the sea. Imperialism turns out to have been much more morally foul a piece of business than even Marx and Lenin imagined! 10

An agony was induced into the native heart, rotting and pulverizing it as it tried to live under a white domination with which it could not identify in any real sense, a white domination that mocked it. The more Westernized that native heart became, the more anti-Western it had to be, for that heart was now weighing itself in terms of white Western values that made it feel degraded. Vainly attempting to embrace the world of white faces that rejected it, it recoiled and sought refuge in the ruins of moldering tradition. But it was too late; it was trapped; it found haven in neither. This is the psychological stance of the elite of the populations, free or still in a 11 state of subjection, of present-day Asia and Africa; this is the profound revolution that the white man cast into the world; this is the revolution (a large part of which has been successfully captured by the Communists) that the white man confronts today with fear and paralysis.

QUESTIONS

1. Whom does Wright blame for the state of oppressed nations? What reasons does he give for blaming them?

2. According to Wright, what are the cultural traits of Western people in the fifteenth, sixteenth, seventeenth, and eighteenth centuries?

3. Explain what Wright means by "advanced individualists" (paragraph 7). What other words does he use to describe Westerners? What connotations do these words tend to have?

4. Give examples of Wright's hortatory style. What other styles of writing appear in this essay?

5. How does Wright develop his history? Is his chronological structure linear? Does he repeat events? How does his choice here reflect the goals of the essay?

6. Explain how contrast is used as a structural device in this essay.

7. What words introduce the hypothetical example in paragraph 5? How does this example contribute to the theme of the essay?

8. Identify an instance of syllogistic reasoning in Wright's argument.

9. In an age of diminishing resources and burgeoning populations, can Americans afford to be concerned with the plight of oppressed peoples? How do you think Wright would answer this question? How do you?

10. a. Write your own essay on the psychological reactions of oppressor nations.
b. Write an essay on the new psychology of third world nations, notably OPEC (Organization of Petroleum Exporting Countries).
c. People often engage in actions whose consequences are damaging. Show how this insight is true in your experience.

The Oedipus Complex

Karen Horney (1885–1952), although a psychologist, believed that neuroses are not strictly biological in origin, that they could be culturally determined. Because of this belief, she also rejected two key aspects of Freudian psychology: the preeminence of the Oedipus complex and pleasure strivings in character formation. Horney wrote several books, including *Our Inner Conflicts* (1945) and *Neuroses and Human Conflict* (1950). The following essay explains in part her criticism of the Oedipus complex.

B y Oedipus complex Freud means sexual attraction to one of the parents with a concomitant jealousy toward the other parent. Freud regards this experience as biologically determined, though in the individual it is engendered by the parents' care of the physical needs of the child. Its numerous variations depend on the individual constellation actually existing in the particular family. Libidinal desires directed toward the parents vary in nature according to the stages of libido development. They culminate in genital desires toward the parents.   1

The assumption that such a constellation is biologically conditioned, and hence ubiquitous, has made two further assumptions necessary for its support. Finding no traces of the Oedipus complex in the majority of healthy adults, Freud assumed that in these persons the complex had been successfully repressed, a conclusion which, as McDougall has already pointed out,[1] is not convincing to those who do not share Freud's belief in the biological nature of the complex. Furthermore, finding many instances in which the major tie occurred between mother and daughter, or father and son, Freud propounded an enlargement of the concept according to which the homosexual—inverted—Oedipus complex is equal in importance to the heterosexual—normal—one; thus, for example, the homosexual tie, in the case of a girl, is a normal precursor of a later attachment to the father.   2

Freud's conviction of the ubiquitous occurrence of the Oedipus complex rests on the presuppositions given by the libido theory, so much so that anyone accepting the libido theory must accept also the doctrine of the universality of the Oedipus complex. As indicated before, according to the libido theory every human relationship is based ultimately on instinctual drives.   3

[1]William McDougall, *Psychoanalysis and Social Psychology* (1936).

When this theory is applied to the child-parent relationship it   4
suggests several conclusions: the wish to be like a parent may be a
derivate of wishes toward oral incorporation; a dependent clinging to
a parent may be the expression of an intensified oral organization;[2]
any kind of submissive devotion to a parent of the same sex is
probably the expression of passive homosexuality or of sexual masochistic trends, while a rebellious rejection of a parent of the same sex
is probably an inner fight against existing homosexual desires; more
generally, any kind of affection or tenderness toward a parent is by
definition aim-inhibited sexuality; fears concern mainly punishment
for forbidden instinctual desires (incestuous desires, masturbation,
jealousy), and the anticipated danger is the prohibition of physical
satisfaction (fear of castration, fear of loss of love); finally, hostility
toward a parent, if not related to the frustration of instinctual drives,
may be understood as the ultimate expression of sexual rivalry.

As some of these feelings or attitudes are present in every   5
child-parent relationship—as they are in every human relationship—
the evidence for an omnipresent Oedipus complex is overwhelming
indeed to anyone accepting the theoretical premise. There is no doubt
that persons who later develop a neurosis or a psychosis may be
closely tied to the parents, whether the nature of this tie be sexual or
not. It is Freud's merit to have seen this in spite of existing social
tabus and to have recognized its implications. The question remains,
however, as to whether fixations on the parents arise in a child for
biological reasons or whether they are the product of describable
conditions. I firmly believe that the latter is true. There are in the
main two series of conditions provoking a stronger attachment to one
of the parents. They may or may not be allied, but both are created by
the parents.

---

[2]To quote Otto Fenichel: "A young girl had suffered as an infant from a gastric affection, on account
of which she had been put on a starvation diet. This engendered in her peculiarly strong oral
cravings. In the period immediately following this illness, she had contracted the habit of throwing
her bottle, when she had finished the milk in it, on the floor and breaking it, a gesture which I
construe as an expression of some such thought as this: What good is an empty bottle to me? I want
a full one! As a little child she was very greedy. *The oral fixation manifested itself in an intense dread of a
loss of love and a passionate clinging to her mother* [italics mine]. It was therefore a great disappointment
to her, at the age of three, when her mother became pregnant" (Otto Fenichel, "The Scopophilic
Instinct and Identification" in *International Journal of Psychoanalysis*, 1937).
 The implicit assumption in the report can only be that the passionate clinging to the
mother, the fear of losing her love, the outbreaks of temper and the hatred of the mother are the
results of a reinforced oral libido. All factors which in my estimation are relevant to the picture are
omitted. While it is possible that the starvation diet was important, in so far as it focused the child's
attention on food, I should like to hear in the first place about the manner in which the mother
treated the child. By analogy I should assume that here was a child in whom, because of the
treatment accorded it, intense anxiety and hostility were engendered, resulting in an enhanced
need for affection and thus in claims for unconditional love, enhanced jealousy and a great fear of
rejection and desertion. Furthermore, I should assume that the hostility appearing in temper
tantrums and in destructive fantasies was partly an expression of the hostility provoked by the
mother and partly an expression of rage because possessive love claims were not fulfilled.

One of them is, briefly, sexual stimulation by the parents. 6
This may consist in a gross sexual approach to the child; it may arise
from sexually-tinged caresses, or from an emotional hothouse atmosphere surrounding all members of the family or including some
members and excluding others who are regarded with animosity.
Such a parental attitude is not only the result of the parents'
emotional or sexual dissatisfaction, but according to my experience it
has also other more complicated causes, which I do not wish to
elaborate here as it would lead us too far astray.

The other series of conditions is entirely different in nature. 7
While in the above group there is a genuinely sexual response to
stimulation, the second group is connected in no way with either
spontaneous or stimulated sexual desires of the child, but with its
anxiety. Anxiety, as we shall see later, is an outcome of conflicting
tendencies or needs. The typical conflict leading to anxiety in a child
is that between dependency on the parents—enhanced by the child's
feelings of being isolated and intimidated—and hostile impulses
against the parents. Hostility may be aroused in a child in many
ways: by the parents' lack of respect for him; by unreasonable
demands and prohibitions; by injustice; by unreliability; by suppres-
sion of criticism; by the parents dominating him and ascribing these
tendencies to love; by misusing children for the sake of prestige or
ambitious goals. If a child, in addition to being dependent on his
parents, is grossly or subtly intimidated by them and hence feels that
any expression of hostile impulses against them endangers his
security, then the existence of such hostile impulses is bound to
create anxiety.[3]

One way to allay this anxiety is to cling to one of the parents, 8
and a child will do so if there is any chance of thus receiving
reassuring affection. Such a hanging-on to a person out of sheer
anxiety is easily confounded with love, and in the child's own mind
seems like love. It does not necessarily take on a sexual coloring, but
it may easily do so. It certainly assumes all the characteristics of a
neurotic need for affection, that is, a need for affection conditioned by
anxiety, as we see it in adult neurotics: dependency, insatiability,
possessiveness, jealousy toward anyone who does or might interfere.

The resulting picture may look exactly like what Freud 9
describes as the Oedipus complex: passionate clinging to one parent
and jealousy toward the other or toward anyone interfering with the
claim of exclusive possession. In my experience the vast majority of
infantile attachments to parents, as they are retrospectively revealed
in the analysis of adult neurotics, belongs to this group. But the

[3]Cf. Lawrence F. Woolley, "The Effect of Erratic Discipline in Childhood on Emotional Tensions" in
Psychiatric Quarterly (1937).

 THE OEDIPUS COMPLEX

dynamic structure of these attachments is entirely different from what Freud conceives as the Oedipus complex. They are an early manifestation of neurotic conflicts rather than a primarily sexual phenomenon.

A comparison between this situation and one primarily 10 determined by a stimulated sexual attachment to the parent shows several significant differences. In the attachment created mainly by anxiety the sexual element is not essential; it may be present, but it may be entirely missing. In the incestuous attachment the goal is love, but in the attachment conditioned by anxiety the main goal is security. Hence, in the first kind, attachment goes to the parent who elicits love or sexual desires; in the second group it usually goes to the parent who is the more powerful or the more awe-inspiring, for the winning of his affection promises the greatest chance of protection. If in the latter case the same clinging attitude a girl had toward a domineering mother reappears in her relation to her husband, this means not that to the girl the husband represents the mother but that for reasons which have to be analyzed the girl is still full of anxiety and tries to allay it in the same way she did in childhood, clinging now to the husband instead of to the mother.

In both groups the attachment to the parents is not a 11 biologically given phenomenon but a response to provocations from the outside. This contention that the Oedipus complex is not of a biological nature seems to be confirmed by anthropological observation, the results of which indicate that the generation of such a complex depends on the whole set of factors operating in family life, such as the role of authority of the parents, seclusion of the family, size of the family, sexual prohibitions and the like.

There still remains the question whether spontaneous sexual 12 feelings for the parents arise at all under "normal" conditions, that is, when there is no special provocation by either stimulation or anxiety. Our knowledge is restricted to neurotic children and adults. But I should be inclined to think that there is no good reason why a child born with its sexual instincts should not have sexual inclinations toward the parents or siblings. It is questionable, however, whether without other factors these spontaneous sexual attractions ever reach an intensity sufficient to meet Freud's description of an Oedipus complex—which is the presence of sexual desire strong enough to arouse so much jealousy and fear that they can be dissolved only by repression.

The theory of the Oedipus complex has greatly influenced 13 present-day education. On the positive side, it has helped to make parents conscious of the lasting harm inflicted on children by exciting them sexually and also by being overindulgent, overprotective and too prohibitive in sexual matters. On the negative side, it has fostered the illusion that it is enough to enlighten children sexually and to refrain from forbidding masturbation, from whipping them, from letting them witness parental intercourse and from attaching them too strongly to parents. The danger lies in the one-sidedness of such suggestions. Even if they are all religiously adhered to, the germs for later neuroses may be laid. Why? The answer is in principle the same as the answer to the charge that psychoanalytical therapy is insufficiently successful: too many factors extremely relevant to a child's growth are regarded as comparatively superficial, and hence are not given the weight they deserve. I am thinking of such parental attitudes as having real interest in a child, real respect for it, giving it real warmth, and of such qualities as reliability and sincerity.

It may be, however, that the actual damage done by a 14 one-sided sexual orientation is less harmful than would appear at first thought. At least the psychoanalytical suggestions to the educator are reasonable and can be followed easily, as they consist mainly in avoiding certain concrete errors. But suggestions concerning more important factors, such as those I have mentioned—factors which create an atmosphere favorable to growth—are infinitely more difficult to follow as they entail changes in character.

The theory of the Oedipus complex is significant mainly 15 because of the bearing the complex is assumed to have on later relationships. Freud believes that later attitudes to people are largely a repetition of the oedipal one. Thus, for example, a man's defiant attitude toward other men would suggest that he is warding off homosexual tendencies which he had toward his father or brother; a woman's incapacity to love her children spontaneously would be interpreted as an identification with her own mother.

The debatable points in this kind of thinking will be discussed 16 in connection with the theory of repetition compulsion. Only this much here: if it is an unwarranted belief that incestuous attachment to parents is a normal incident of childhood, then the validity of interpretations relating later peculiarities to infantile incestuous wishes, and reactions to them, is likewise dubitable. Interpretations of this kind serve mainly to strengthen the interpreter's conviction as to the regular occurrence of the Oedipus complex and its powerful after-effects. But the evidence thus found results from a process of circular reasoning.

If we discard the theoretical implications of the theory, what 17 remains is not the Oedipus complex but the highly constructive finding that early relationships *in their totality* mold the character to an extent which can scarcely be overestimated. Later attitudes to others, then, are not repetitions of infantile ones but emanate from the character structure, the basis of which is laid in childhood.

THE OEDIPUS COMPLEX

QUESTIONS

1. Explain why Karen Horney rejects Freud's definition of the Oedipus complex.

2. According to Horney, what are the main characteristics of Freud's Oedipus complex?

3. As with many authors in this section, Horney is a psychologist using the vocabulary of her profession. Identify the psychological terms used in this essay and define them.

4. Horney is writing an argument, and at times she uses hyperbole and connotation to criticize Freud's theory. Identify and analyze examples of these methods.

5. Identify the thesis in the essay. Why is it located where it is?

6. Explain how Horney uses personal experiences in the essay.

7. Horney employs logic to analyze Freud's theory. Identify those paragraphs organized by logical analysis. What words are used to organize that analysis?

8. Horney also uses contrast to organize parts of this essay. Identify examples of contrast and explain how they are organized.

9. How can you use Horney's description of child-parent relations to help you understand your own relationships with teachers, police officers, or other people of authority?

10. Write an essay defining anxiety or depression, and give examples of experiences in that state.

5
Social Processes and Institutions

E. M. FORSTER

My Wood

Edward Morgan Forster (1879–1970), English essayist, novelist, biographer, and literary critic, wrote several notable works of fiction dealing with the constricting effects of social and national conventions upon human relationships. These novels include *A Room with a View* (1908), *Howards End* (1910), and *A Passage to India* (1924). In addition, his lectures on fiction, collected as *Aspects of the Novel* (1927), remain graceful elucidations of the genre. In "My Wood," taken from his essay collection *Abinger Harvest* (1936), Forster writes with wit and wisdom about the effect of property upon human behavior—notably his own.

A few years ago I wrote a book which dealt in part with the difficulties of the English in India. Feeling that they would have had no difficulties in India themselves, the Americans read the book freely. The more they read it the better it made them feel, and a cheque to the author was the result. I bought a wood with the cheque. It is not a large wood—it contains scarcely any trees, and it is intersected, blast it, by a public footpath. Still, it is the first property that I have owned, so it is right that other people should participate in my shame, and should ask themselves, in accents that will vary in horror, this very important question: What is the effect of property upon the character? Don't let's touch economics; the effect of private ownership upon the community as a whole is another question—a more important question, perhaps, but another one. Let's keep to psychology. If you own things, what's their effect on you? What's the effect on me of my wood?

In the first place, it makes me feel heavy. Property does have   2
this effect. Property produces men of weight, and it was a man of weight who failed to get into the Kingdom of Heaven. He was not wicked, that unfortunate millionaire in the parable, he was only stout; he stuck out in front, not to mention behind, and as he wedged himself this way and that in the crystalline entrance and bruised his well-fed flanks, he saw beneath him a comparatively slim camel passing through the eye of a needle and being woven into the robe of God. The Gospels all through couple stoutness and slowness. They point out what is perfectly obvious, yet seldom realized: that if you have a lot of things you cannot move about a lot, that furniture requires dusting, dusters require servants, servants require insurance stamps, and the whole tangle of them makes you think twice before you accept an invitation to dinner or go for a bathe in the Jordan. Sometimes the Gospels proceed further and say with Tolstoy that property is sinful; they approach the difficult ground of asceticism here, where I cannot follow them. But as to the immediate effects of property on people, they just show straightforward logic. It produces men of weight. Men of weight cannot, by definition, move like the lightning from the East unto the West, and the ascent of a fourteen-stone bishop into a pulpit is thus the exact antithesis of the coming of the Son of Man. My wood makes me feel heavy.

In the second place, it makes me feel it ought to be larger.   3

The other day I heard a twig snap in it. I was annoyed at first,   4
for I thought that someone was blackberrying, and depreciating the value of the undergrowth. On coming nearer, I saw it was not a man who had trodden on the twig and snapped it, but a bird, and I felt pleased. My bird. The bird was not equally pleased. Ignoring the relation between us, it took fright as soon as it saw the shape of my face, and flew straight over the boundary hedge into a field, the property of Mrs. Henessy, where it sat down with a loud squawk. It had become Mrs. Henessy's bird. Something seemed grossly amiss here, something that would not have occurred had the wood been larger. I could not afford to buy Mrs. Henessy out, I dared not murder her, and limitations of this sort beset me on every side. Ahab did not want that vineyard—he only needed it to round off his property, preparatory to plotting a new curve—and all the land around my

wood has become necessary to me in order to round off the wood. A boundary protects. But—poor little thing—the boundary ought in its turn to be protected. Noises on the edge of it. Children throw stones. A little more, and then a little more, until we reach the sea. Happy Canute! Happier Alexander! And after all, why should even the world be the limit of possession? A rocket containing a Union Jack, will, it is hoped, be shortly fired at the moon. Mars. Sirius. Beyond which . . . But these immensities ended by saddening me. I could not suppose that my wood was the destined nucleus of universal dominion—it is so very small and contains no mineral wealth beyond the blackberries. Nor was I comforted when Mrs. Henessy's bird took alarm for the second time and flew clean away from us all, under the belief that it belonged to itself.

In the third place, property makes its owner feel that he 5 ought to do something to it. Yet he isn't sure what. A restlessness comes over him, a vague sense that he has a personality to express—the same sense which, without any vagueness, leads the artist to an act of creation. Sometimes I think I will cut down such trees as remain in the wood, at other times I want to fill up the gaps between them with new trees. Both impulses are pretentious and empty. They are not honest movements towards money-making or beauty. They spring from a foolish desire to express myself and from an inability to enjoy what I have got. Creation, property, enjoyment form a sinister trinity in the human mind. Creation and enjoyment are both very, very good, yet they are often unattainable without a material basis, and at such moments property pushes itself in as a substitute, saying, "Accept me instead—I'm good enough for all three." It is not enough. It is, as Shakespeare said of lust, "The expense of spirit in a waste of shame": it is "Before, a joy proposed; behind, a dream." Yet we don't know how to shun it. It is forced on us by our economic system as the alternative to starvation. It is also forced on us by an internal defect in the soul, by the feeling that in property may lie the germs of self-development and of exquisite or heroic deeds. Our life on earth is, and ought to be, material and carnal. But we have not yet learned to manage our materialism and carnality properly; they are still entangled with the desire for ownership, where (in the words of Dante) "Possession is one with loss."

And this brings us to our fourth and final point: the blackber- 6 ries.

Blackberries are not plentiful in this meagre grove, but they 7 are easily seen from the public footpath which traverses it, and all too easily gathered. Foxgloves, too—people will pull up the foxgloves, and ladies of an educational tendency even grub for toadstools to show them on the Monday in class. Other ladies, less educated, roll down the bracken in the arms of their gentlemen friends. There is paper, there are tins. Pray, does my wood belong to me or doesn't it? And, if it does, should I not own it best by allowing no one else to walk there? There is a wood near Lyme Regis, also cursed by a public footpath, where the owner has not hesitated on this point. He had built high stone walls each side of the path, and has spanned it by bridges, so that the public circulate like termites while he gorges on the blackberries unseen. He really does own his wood, this able chap. Dives in Hell did pretty well, but the gulf dividing him from Lazarus could be traversed by vision, and nothing traverses it here. And perhaps I shall come to this in time. I shall wall in and fence out until I really taste the sweets of property. Enormously stout, endlessly avaricious, pseudo-creative, intensely selfish, I shall weave upon my forehead the quadruple crown of possession until those nasty Bolshies come and take it off again and thrust me aside into the outer darkness.

QUESTIONS

1. List the four effects that property ownership has upon the author.

2. Describe the persona that emerges from the essay. What is the relationship of the last sentence to this persona?

3. What words and phrases does the author use to create a conversational style in the essay?

4. Analyze biblical, historical, and literary allusions in the essay. What is their function?

5. What is the purpose of Forster's reference to Americans at the outset of the essay?

6. How is the thesis reinforced in the first paragraph? How are essay clarity and proper sequence achieved through placement of topic sentences?

7. Analyze the manner in which Forster integrates the analysis of effects with a personal definition of property.

8. Explain the shift in tone, and the movement from concrete to abstract, in paragraph 5.

9. Do you agree with Forster that property ownership is as difficult as he declares it to be? Give the basis of your response and elucidate.

10. Write an essay of definition in which you explain an abstract term in personal, concrete, and carefully organized terms.

E. M. FORSTER

Conserving Old Work
by Adding New

Jane Jacobs (1916–   ), a versatile American author and
editor, began her career as a free-lance writer while working
as a stenographer in New York City. Interested in urban
history, she wrote *The Death and Life of Great American
Cities* (1961) and *The Economy of Cities* (1969), studies considered to be the most significant contribution to the field since
the classic work of Lewis Mumford. In this essay, Jacobs
discusses economic principles of work from an original perspective.

ld products and arts are often retained and put to new   1
uses in economic life after new work has made them
obsolete. The United States probably has more sailboats
than it had in "the age of sail," although their purpose
has changed. When I was a child, in the 1920s, I was urged to
remember carefully the sight of a blacksmith at work shoeing a horse,
for this was work expected to disappear. But in 1960, more people
knew how to shoe horses than in the 1920s, although most of these
were also veterinarians and had learned blacksmithing in veterinary
school.

To put old goods and services to new uses, or to employ them   2
in new combinations of work instead of jettisoning them, might well
be called a "conserving" tendency in an economy. Another expression of this tendency is the "backward" application of new techniques to goods and services that would otherwise be obsolete. The
phonograph is an illustration. It was temporarily eclipsed by radio
and, like the blacksmith, it was supposed to disappear. It almost did
in the early 1930s. But the phonograph itself was changed by
incorporating some of the technology of radio; and the phonograph
in turn brought changes to radio broadcasting. It was conserved to
live another life.

Similarly, as Western dress for women gained favor in Japan,   3
the disappearance of the kimono was predicted. But kimonos have
been changing and, according to the *New York Times*, have been
reinstated as high-fashion formal dress by the most modern young
women in Japan, the students and office and professional workers.
"New simplified designs, the introduction of synthetic fibers and
other new materials and use of zippers and ready-tied obis" have
made the kimono easier to put on, more comfortable and easier to

care for, the *Times* reported, and thus popular again with the young. In short, the kimono is being conserved to live another life.

These are trivial instances, but the economic behavior they illustrate is far from trivial. It is the kind of behavior that seems to permit old crafts like handweaving, fine glassmaking or guitar making to change instead of being dropped, or being arrested and then degenerating. This kind of behavior was obviously at work in Catal Hüyük, where people were combining the new woven clothing with sophisticated versions of the old animal-hide clothing, and trinkets of copper with trinkets of stones and shells, and radically new cultivated foods with old-fashioned wild foods, some of which would in time be cultivated too. 4

This tendency to conserve old goods and services is conspicuously absent in stagnated economies, although we are apt, offhand, to think of stagnation as being synonymous with "conservatism." When white sugar becomes easily available in an Appalachian settlement, sorghum pressing is abandoned. When nylon fishing nets reach a Southeast Asian village, the old net making is dropped. At its most extreme, such profoundly unconserving behavior results in the well-known havoc wrought on the cultures and economies of primitive people by contact with new goods, services and work brought in from outside. 5

A society's ability to conserve old skills or old goods seems to depend upon combining them with new goods or services or new purposes. But how does this happen? A very simple illustration may give a clue. Some artists of my acquaintance who were fighting a proposed expressway in New York decided, as part of the campaign, to paint a huge street banner. A banner of the weight and opacity desired, capable of withstanding the wind without being torn from its ropes, turned out to be impossible to construct until someone remembered an old-fashioned sailmaker in the second story of a loft nearby. He had never made a street banner before, but he made one now, and a good one. Here was a case in which the practitioner of the old work (to which a new purpose was, for the moment, added) was not the one who took the initiative. His work, rather, was seen—by somebody who had a problem—as appropriate work upon which to add something more. In this instance, since the sailmaker produced only this one banner, the addition of new work was ephemeral. 6

But much the same thing can happen on a more permanent basis. A friend of mine, Allen Block, runs a successful sandal-making business in New York. He started by designing sandals, but he did not know how to make them properly. Hence, as he was soon to learn, he did not really know how to design them either. He therefore apprenticed himself to an aged cobbler. The working quarters these two devised were almost a diagram of the act of conserving old work 7

JANE JACOBS

by adding new. From the street, one seemed to see two separate shops: at the left, with its own door and its own sign, was the cobbler's; at the right, with its own door and its own sign, was the sandal maker's. But inside, where the work was being done, the dividing partition had been removed and the two shops were one. The cobbler is dead now, but his "obsolete" skill, having been conserved, is retained in the economy to live another life.

QUESTIONS

1. What is the "economic behavior" that sailboats, blacksmithing, the phonograph, and the kimono illustrate?

2. How does the author define a stagnated economy? What is the way to avoid this economic condition?

3. Explain the way that Jacobs uses economic jargon. How does she make it acceptable and accessible to the reader?

4. Examine Jacobs's use of abstract language. Cite examples. How does she relate key abstractions to the concrete?

5. Identify the thesis of the essay.

6. Analyze the author's use of illustration to develop the essay in paragraphs 1 to 3, 4 to 5, and 6 to 7.

7. Explain the author's use of definition and causal analysis as rhetorical strategies in the essay.

8. How is process analysis reflected in the concluding paragraphs?

9. In what way might the United States be considered a "stagnated economy"? Think of examples to support your opinion.

10. Write an essay on the conservation of old work skills in contemporary American life. Develop illustrations to explain and support your general observations.

An Election

FROM LIEN CHI ALTANGI TO FUM HOAM,
FIRST PRESIDENT OF THE CEREMONIAL
ACADEMY AT PEKIN, IN CHINA.

Oliver Goldsmith (1730–1774), the son of an Anglican curate, was an Anglo-Irish essayist, poet, novelist, dramatist, and journalist. His reputation as an enduring figure in English literature is based on his novel, *The Vicar of Wakefield* (1766); his play *She Stoops to Conquer* (1773); his major poem, *The Deserted Village* (1770); and the essays and satiric letters collected in *The Bee* (1759) and *The Citizen of the World* (1762). In this sample from *The Citizen of the World,* Goldsmith assumes the role of a Chinese visitor to England who is amazed by one of the nation's ritualistic political conventions.

he English are at present employed in celebrating a feast   1
which becomes general every seventh year; the parliament of the nation being then dissolved, and another appointed to be chosen. This solemnity falls infinitely short of our Feast of the Lanterns in magnificence and splendour; it is also surpassed by others of the East in unanimity and pure devotion; but no festival in the world can compare with it for eating. Their eating, indeed, amazes me; had I five hundred heads, and were each head furnished with brains, yet would they all be insufficient to compute the number of cows, pigs, geese, and turkeys which upon this occasion die for the good of their country.

To say the truth, eating seems to make a grand ingredient in   2
all English parties of zeal, business, or amusement. When a church is to be built or a hospital endowed, the directors assemble and, instead of consulting upon it, they eat upon it, by which means the business goes forward with success. When the poor are to be relieved, the officers appointed to dole out public charity assemble and eat upon it. Nor has it ever been known that they filled the bellies of the poor till they had previously satisfied their own. But in the election of magistrates the people seem to exceed all bounds; the merits of a candidate are often measured by the number of his treats; his constituents assemble, eat upon him, and lend their applause, not to his integrity or sense, but to the quantities of his beef and brandy.

And yet I could forgive this people their plentiful meals on   3
this occasion, as it is extremely natural for every man to eat a great

deal when he gets it for nothing; but what amazes me is that all this good living no way contributes to improve their good-humour. On the contrary, they seem to lose their temper as they lose their appetites; every morsel they swallow, and every glass they pour down, serves to increase their animosity. Many an honest man, before as harmless as a tame rabbit, when loaded with a single election dinner has become more dangerous than a charged culverin. Upon one of these occasions I have actually seen a bloody-minded man-milliner sally forth at the head of a mob, determined to face a desperate pastry-cook who was general of the opposite party.

But you must not suppose they are without a pretext for thus 4
beating each other. On the contrary, no man here is so uncivilized as to beat his neighbour without producing very sufficient reasons. One candidate, for instance, treats with gin, a spirit of their own manufacture; another always drinks brandy, imported from abroad. Brandy is a wholesome liquor; gin, a liquor wholly their own. This, then, furnishes an obvious cause of quarrel—whether it be most reasonable to get drunk with gin or get drunk with brandy? The mob meet upon the debate, fight themselves sober, and then draw off to get drunk again, and charge for another encounter. So that the English may now properly be said to be engaged in war; since, while they are subduing their enemies abroad, they are breaking each other's heads at home.

I lately made an excursion to a neighbouring village, in order 5
to be a spectator of the ceremonies practised upon this occasion. I left town in company with three fiddlers, nine dozen of hams, and a corporation poet, which were designed as reinforcements to the gin-drinking party. We entered the town with a very good face; the fiddlers, no way intimidated by the enemy, kept handling their arms up the principal street. By this prudent manoeuvre, they took peaceable possession of their headquarters, amidst the shouts of multitudes, who seemed perfectly rejoiced at hearing their music, but above all at seeing their bacon.

I must own, I could not avoid being pleased to see all ranks of 6
people, on this occasion, levelled into an equality, and the poor, in some measure, enjoying the primitive privileges of nature. If there was any distinction shown, the lowest of the people seemed to receive it from the rich. I could perceive a cobbler with a levee at his door, and a haberdasher giving audience from behind his counter.

But my reflections were soon interrupted by a mob, who 7
demanded whether I was for the distillery or the brewery? As these were terms with which I was totally unacquainted, I chose at first to be silent; however, I know not what might have been the consequence of my reserve, had not the attention of the mob been called off

to a skirmish between a brandy-drinker's cow and a gin-drinker's mastiff, which turned out, greatly to the satisfaction of the mob, in favour of the mastiff.

8   This spectacle, which afforded high entertainment, was at last ended by the appearance of one of the candidates, who came to harangue the mob: he made a very pathetic speech upon the late excessive importation of foreign drams, and the downfall of the distillery; I could see some of the audience shed tears. He was accompanied in his procession by Mrs. Deputy and Mrs. Mayoress. Mrs. Deputy was not in the least in liquor; and as for Mrs. Mayoress, one of the spectators assured me in my ear that—she was a very fine woman before she had the small-pox.

9   Mixing with the crowd, I was now conducted to the hall where the magistrates are chosen: but what tongue can describe this scene of confusion! The whole crowd seemed equally inspired with anger, jealousy, politics, patriotism, and punch. I remarked one figure that was carried up by two men upon this occasion. I at first began to pity his infirmities as natural, but soon found the fellow so drunk that he could not stand; another made his appearance to give his vote, but though he could stand, he actually lost the use of his tongue, and remained silent; a third, who, though excessively drunk, could both stand and speak, being asked the candidate's name for whom he voted, could be prevailed upon to make no other answer but "Tobacco and brandy." In short, an election hall seems to be a theatre, where every passion is seen without disguise; a school where fools may readily become worse, and where philosophers may gather wisdom.—Adieu.

QUESTIONS

1. Summarize Goldsmith's attitude toward English elections.

2. Why does Goldsmith pose as a visiting Chinese? What advantages does the role afford him?

3. Identify and analyze examples of exaggeration and understatement in the essay.

4. Explain the effect of the alliteration in paragraph 9.

5. How does the introductory paragraph alert readers to the ironic and satiric nature of the essay? Cite other examples of irony and satire in the essay.

6. Trace the method whereby the act of eating becomes an extended metaphor in the essay.

7. Examine paragraphs 5 to 8 as a self-contained unit. What key principle of rhetoric does Goldsmith utilize to develop these paragraphs?

8. Where does the author state his thesis most clearly? Evaluate the placement of the thesis.

9. What foibles do you encounter in the American political process that lend themselves to ironic or satiric treatment?

10. Write an essay on some aspect of American political life, treating the subject in a lightly satiric or tongue-in-cheek manner.

J. B. PRIESTLEY

Wrong Ism

John Boynton Priestley (1894–   ), best-selling English novelist and popular dramatist, is also a prolific writer of essays, many of them involving social and political criticism. His work includes *The English Novel* (1927), *The Good Companions* (1929), *Time and the Conways* (1937), *An Inspector Calls* (1946), and *The English* (1973). This selection from *Essays of Five Decades* (1968) offers an astute analysis of contemporary political habits.

here are three isms that we ought to consider very carefully—regionalism, nationalism, internationalism. Of these three the one there is most fuss about, the one that starts men shouting and marching and shooting, the one that seems to have all the depth and thrust and fire, is of course nationalism. Nine people out of ten, I fancy, would say that of this trio it is the one that really counts, the big boss. Regionalism and internationalism, they would add, are comparatively small, shadowy, rather cranky. And I believe all this to be quite wrong. Like many another big boss, nationalism is largely bogus. It is like a bunch of flowers made of plastics. 1

The real flowers belong to regionalism. The mass of people everywhere may never have used the term. They are probably regionalists without knowing it. Because they have been brought up in a certain part of the world, they have formed perhaps quite unconsciously a deep attachment to its landscape and speech, its traditional customs, its food and drink, its songs and jokes. (There are of course always the rebels, often intellectuals and writers, but they 2 are not the mass of people.) They are rooted in their region. Indeed, without this attachment a man can have no roots.

So much of people's lives, from earliest childhood onwards, is deeply intertwined with the common life of the region, they cannot help feeling strongly about it. A threat to it is a knife pointing at the heart. How can life ever be the same if bullying strangers come to change everything? The form and colour, the very taste and smell of dear familiar things will be different, alien, life-destroying. It would be better to die fighting. And it is precisely this, the nourishing life of the region, for which common men have so often fought and died. 3

This attachment to the region exists on a level far deeper than that of any political hocus-pocus. When a man says "my country" with real feeling, he is thinking about his region, all that has made up his life, and not about that political entity, the nation. There can be some confusion here simply because some countries are so small— and ours is one of them—and so old, again like ours, that much of what is national is also regional. Down the centuries, the nation, itself, so comparatively small, has been able to attach to itself the feeling really created by the region. (Even so there is something left over, as most people in Yorkshire or Devon, for example, would tell you.) This probably explains the fervent patriotism developed early in small countries. The English were announcing that they were English in the Middle Ages, before nationalism had arrived elsewhere. 4

If we deduct from nationalism all that it has borrowed or stolen from regionalism, what remains is mostly rubbish. The nation, as distinct from the region, is largely the creation of power-men and political manipulators. Almost all nationalist movements are led by ambitious frustrated men determined to hold office. I am not blaming them. I would do the same if I were in their place and wanted power so badly. But nearly always they make use of the rich warm regional feeling, the emotional dynamo of the movement, while being almost untouched by it themselves. This is because they are not as a rule deeply loyal to any region themselves. Ambition and a love of power can eat like acid into the tissues of regional loyalty. It is hard, if not impossible, to retain a natural piety and yet be for ever playing both ends against the middle. 5

Being itself a power structure, devised by men of power, the nation tends to think and act in terms of power. What would benefit the real life of the region, where men, women and children actually live, is soon sacrificed for the power and prestige of the nation. (And the personal vanity of presidents and ministers themselves, which historians too often disregard.) Among the new nations of our time innumerable peasants and labourers must have found themselves being cut down from five square meals a week to three in order to provide unnecessary airlines, military forces that can only be used 6

J. B. PRIESTLEY

against them and nobody else, great conference halls and official yachts and the rest. The last traces of imperialism and colonialism may have to be removed from Asia and Africa, where men can no longer endure being condemned to a permanent inferiority by the colour of their skins; but even so, the modern world, the real world of our time, does not want and would be far better without more and more nations, busy creating for themselves the very paraphernalia that western Europe is now trying to abolish. You are compelled to answer more questions when trying to spend half a day in Cambodia than you are now travelling from the Hook of Holland to Syracuse.

This brings me to internationalism. I dislike this term, which I   7 used only to complete the isms. It suggests financiers and dubious promoters living nowhere but in luxury hotels; a shallow world of entrepreneurs and impresarios. (Was it Sacha Guitry who said that impresarios were men who spoke many languages but all with a foreign accent?) The internationalism I have in mind here is best described as world civilisation. It is life considered on a global scale. Most of our communications and transport already exist on this high wide level. So do many other things from medicine to meteorology. Our astronomers and physicists (except where they have allowed themselves to be hush-hushed) work here. The UN special agencies, about which we hear far too little, have contributed more and more to this world civilisation. All the arts, when they are arts and not chunks of nationalist propaganda, naturally take their place in it. And it grows, widens, deepens, in spite of the fact that for every dollar, ruble, pound or franc spent in explaining and praising it, a thousand are spent by the nations explaining and praising themselves.

This world civilisation and regionalism can get along togeth-   8 er, especially if we keep ourselves sharply aware of their quite different but equally important values and rewards. A man can make his contribution to world civilisation and yet remain strongly regional in feeling: I know several men of this sort. There is of course the danger—it is with us now—of the global style flattening out the regional, taking local form, colour, flavour, away for ever, disinherit-ing future generations, threatening them with sensuous poverty and a huge boredom. But to understand and appreciate regionalism is to be on guard against this danger. And we must therefore make a clear distinction between regionalism and nationalism.

It is nationalism that tries to check the growth of world   9 civilisation. And nationalism, when taken on a global scale, is more aggressive and demanding now than it has ever been before. This in the giant powers is largely disguised by the endless fuss in public about rival ideologies, now a largely unreal quarrel. What is intensely real is the glaring nationalism. Even the desire to police the world is nationalistic in origin. (Only the world can police the world.) Moreover, the nation-states of today are for the most part far narrower in their outlook, far more inclined to allow prejudice against the foreigner to impoverish their own style of living, than the old imperial states were. It should be part of world civilisation that men with particular skills, perhaps the product of the very regionalism they are rebelling against, should be able to move easily from country to country, to exercise those skills, in anything from teaching the violin to running a new type of factory to managing an old hotel. But nationalism, especially of the newer sort, would rather see everything done badly than allow a few non-nationals to get to work. And people face a barrage of passports, visas, immigration controls, labour permits; and in this respect are worse off than they were in 1900. But even so, in spite of all that nationalism can do—so long as it keeps its nuclear bombs to itself—the internationalism I have in mind, slowly creating a world civilisation, cannot be checked.

Nevertheless, we are still backing the wrong ism. Almost all   10
our money goes on the middle one, nationalism, the rotten meat between the two healthy slices of bread. We need regionalism to give us roots and that very depth of feeling which nationalism unjustly and greedily claims for itself. We need internationalism to save the world and to broaden and heighten our civilisation. While regional man enriches the lives that international man is already working to keep secure and healthy, national man, drunk with power, demands our loyalty, money and applause, and poisons the very air with his dangerous nonsense.

QUESTIONS

1. Define regionalism, nationalism, and internationalism as Priestley presents these terms.

2. Explain Priestley's objections to nationalism. Where does he state these objections in the essay?

3. What striking metaphor does the author develop to capture the essence of nationalism? What is its sensory impact? Analyze another example of metaphorical language in the essay.

4. How does the suffix "-ism" function in the essay?

5. What is Priestley's principle of classification in this essay? How does he maintain proportion in the presentation of categories?

6. Analyze the relationship between definition and classification in the essay.

7. Examine Priestley's use of comparison and contrast.

8. Explain the connection between the introductory and concluding paragraphs.

9. Priestley makes many assumptions about regionalism, nationalism, and internationalism. Which assumptions do you accept? Which assumptions do you reject? Explain.

10. Write a classification essay on at least three related "-isms": capitalism, socialism, and communism; Protestantism, Catholicism, and Judaism; regionalism, nationalism, and internationalism.

ALEXIS DE TOCQUEVILLE

Some Reflections on American Manners

Alexis Charles Henri Clerél de Tocqueville (1805–1859), descended from an aristocratic Norman family, was a French lawyer, politician, statesman, and historian. Sent to the United States in 1831 to study the American penal system, he wrote instead one of the most penetrating inquiries into the nature of the American system, *Democracy in America* (1835). In this chapter from his study, Tocqueville compares and contrasts manners as manifested in the political and social contexts of democracy and aristocracy.

N othing, at first sight, seems less important than the external formalities of human behavior, yet there is nothing to which men attach more importance. They can get used to anything except living in a society which does not share their manners. The influence of the social and political system on manners is therefore worth serious examination.   1

Manners, speaking generally, have their roots in mores; they are also sometimes the result of an arbitrary convention agreed between certain men. They are both natural and acquired.   2

When some see that, without dispute or effort of their own, they stand first in society; when they daily have great aims in view which keep them occupied, leaving details to others; and when they live surrounded by wealth they have not acquired and do not fear to lose, one can see that they will feel a proud disdain for all the petty interests and material cares of life and that there will be a natural   3 grandeur in their thoughts that will show in their words and manners.

In democracies there is generally little dignity of manner, as private life is very petty. Manners are often vulgar, as thoughts have small occasion to rise above preoccupation with domestic interests.   4

True dignity in manners consists in always taking one's proper place, not too high and not too low; that is as much within the reach of a peasant as of a prince. In democracies everybody's status seems doubtful; as a result, there is often pride but seldom dignity of manners. Moreover, manners are never well regulated or well thought out.   5

There is too much mobility in the population of a democracy for any definite group to be able to establish a code of behavior and see that it is observed. So everyone behaves more or less after this own fashion, and a certain incoherence of manners always prevails, because they conform to the feelings and ideas of each individual rather than to an ideal example provided for everyone to imitate.   6

In any case, this is much more noticeable when an aristocracy has just fallen than when it has long been destroyed.   7

New political institutions and new mores then bring together in the same places men still vastly different in education and habits and compel them to a life in common; this constantly leads to the most ill-assorted juxtapositions. There is still some memory of the former strict code of politeness, but no one knows quite what it said or where to find it. Men have lost the common standard of manners but have not yet resolved to do without it, so each individual tries to shape, out of the ruins of former customs, some rule, however arbitrary and variable. Hence manners have neither the regularity and dignity frequent in aristocracies nor the qualities of simplicity and freedom which one sometimes finds in democracies; they are both constrained and casual.   8

But this is not a normal state of things.   9

When equality is complete and old-established, all men, having roughly the same ideas and doing roughly the same things, do not need to come to an understanding or to copy each other in order to behave and talk in the same way; one sees a lot of petty variations in their manners but no great differences. They are never exactly alike, since they do not copy one pattern; they are never very unlike, because they have the same social condition. At first sight one might be inclined to say that the manners of all Americans are exactly alike, and it is only on close inspection that one sees all the variations among them.   10

The English make game of American manners, but it is odd that most of those responsible for those comic descriptions belong themselves to the English middle classes, and the cap fits them very   11

ALEXIS DE TOCQUEVILLE **5**

well too. So these ruthless critics generally themselves illustrate just what they criticize in America; they do not notice that they are abusing themselves, to the great delight of their own aristocracy.

Nothing does democracy more harm than its outward forms 12 of behavior; many who could tolerate its vices cannot put up with its manners.

But I will not admit that there is nothing to praise in 13 democratic manners.

In aristocracies, all within reach of the ruling class are at pains 14 to imitate it, and very absurd and insipid imitations result. Democracies, with no models of high breeding before them, at least escape the necessity of daily looking at bad copies thereof.

In democracies manners are never so refined as among 15 aristocracies, but they are also never so coarse. One misses both the crude words of the mob and the elegant and choice phrases of the high nobility. There is much triviality of manner, but nothing brutal or degraded.

I have already said that a precise code of behavior cannot take 16 shape in democracies. That has its inconveniences and its advantages. In aristocracies rules of propriety impose the same demeanor on all, making every member of the same class seem alike in spite of personal characteristics; they bedizen and conceal nature. Democratic manners are neither so well thought out nor so regular, but they often are more sincere. They form, as it were, a thin, transparent veil through which the real feelings and personal thoughts of each man can be easily seen. Hence there is frequently an intimate connection between the form and the substance of behavior; we see a less decorative picture, but one truer to life. One may put the point this way: democracy imposes no particular manners, but in a sense prevents them from having manners at all.

Sometimes the feelings, passions, virtues, and vices of an 17 aristocracy may reappear in a democracy, but its manners never. They are lost and vanish past return when the democratic revolution is completed. It would seem that nothing is more lasting than the manners of an aristocratic class, for it preserves them for some time after losing property and power, nor more fragile, for as soon as they have gone, no trace of them is left, and it is even difficult to discover what they once were when they have ceased to exist. A change in the state of society works this marvel, and a few generations are enough to bring it about.

The principal characteristics of the aristocracy remain en- 18 graved in history after its destruction, but the slight and delicate forms of its manners are lost to memory almost immediately after its fall. No one can imagine them when they are no longer seen. Their disappearance is unnoted and unfelt. For the heart needs an appren-

ticeship of custom and education to appreciate the refined pleasure
derived from distinguished and fastidious manners; once the habit is
lost, the taste for them easily goes too.

Thus, not only are democratic peoples unable to have aristo-   19
cratic manners, but they cannot even conceive or desire them. As
they cannot imagine them, from their point of view it is as if they had
never existed.

One should not attach too much importance to this loss, but it   20
is permissible to regret it.

I know it has happened that the same men have had very   21
distinguished manners and very vulgar feelings; the inner life of
courts has shown well enough what grand appearances may conceal
the meanest hearts. But though the manners of an aristocracy by no
means create virtue, they may add grace to virtue itself. It was no
ordinary sight to see a numerous and powerful class whose every
gesture seemed to show a constant and natural dignity of feeling and
thought, an ordered refinement of taste and urbanity of manners.

The manners of the aristocracy created a fine illusion about   22
human nature; though the picture was often deceptive, it was yet a
noble satisfaction to look on it.

QUESTIONS

1. How does Tocqueville develop his introductory observation about the
impact of the social and political system on manners?

2. What distinctions does the author draw between manners in aristocracies and manners in democracies?

3. Analyze the relationship between the parallelism of the first sentence in
paragraph 3 and the author's purpose.

4. Show the importance of the connotations that develop around the
author's application of the key words *aristocracy* and *democracy*.

5. What is Tocqueville's main thesis? Analyze the way he develops the
thesis. Explain the tone that emerges from the essay.

6. Analyze the importance of definition in paragraphs 1 to 5.

7. Explain the significance of comparison and contrast and of causal
analysis in the development of the essay. Cite instances of these rhetorical
strategies.

8. Many of Tocqueville's paragraphs are relatively short. Analyze their
length in relation to the topic treated.

9. How valid are Tocqueville's assumptions about manners today? Have

we abandoned manners in modern American democracy? Justify your answer.

10. Write an essay analyzing the manners of modern Americans. You may contrast American manners with the manners of people from other countries or political states.

FRANCES FITZGERALD

America Revised:
HISTORY SCHOOLBOOKS
IN THE TWENTIETH CENTURY

Frances Fitzgerald (1940–   ), winner of the Pulitzer Prize for *Fire in the Lake: The Vietnamese and Americans in Vietnam* (1972), is an American journalist who has contributed to the *Atlantic,* the *New Yorker,* the *New York Times Book Review,* and other magazines. Fitzgerald's interest in contemporary affairs and in the history of modern education resulted in the controversial study *America Revised: History Schoolbooks in the Twentieth Century* (1979), from which this selection is taken.

t is a commonplace to say that the texts of the fifties were superpatriotic—dominated, almost to the exclusion of all else, by the concerns of the Cold War. But it is now hard to remember exactly what this meant, or how it happened. It is interesting, therefore, to watch the ideological drift as it crossed over the subsequent junior-high-school texts of the mid-century. First published in 1931, Casner and Gabriel's *Exploring American History* has had a life span of almost fifty years and was for much of the time a best-selling American history for seventh and eighth graders. Initially, at least, it was the product of a collaboration between a Yale history professor, Ralph Henry Gabriel, and a West Haven, Connecticut, schoolteacher, Mabel B. Casner. According to its first editor, at Harcourt Brace, it did well in the market because of its thematic approach to American history and its "ingenious" teaching strategies.

The first edition is clearly the work of liberals, and it has more than a touch of John Dewey about it. The foreword states that history should be "socially helpful" and should lead to "an understanding of how the life about us has evolved out of the life of the past." The text

AMERICA REVISED

begins by drawing a parallel between a child's exploration of his own world and the wanderings of an imaginary knight over medieval Europe—the point of which is to explain "why did Europeans wait 500 years to discover America again?" It goes on to draw a picture of pre-Colonial North American Indian life in a manner so stylized that it might have been taken from the backdrop of a case in the American Museum of Natural History. The forest is deep, birds are flitting, squirrels are chattering, and so forth. The Indians, so the book says, were "deeply religious," the proof being that they worshipped so many different spirits; their tragedy was that they had no domestic animals, and therefore "could not progress toward a higher way of life." There are a certain number of poor people in the book—Jacob Riis is mentioned and there is a drawing of the immigrant boats—and very little chauvinism. The War of 1812 is said to have been won by no one, and the Mexican War to have occurred because President James Polk wanted to buy some empty land from the Mexicans and the Mexicans, though poor, were too proud to sell it. Such attempts at balance run through the narrative. The book reports that the United States was "drawn into" world affairs before the First World War, and in the title of the last foreign-policy chapter it asks, "What Steps Has the United States Taken Recently to Promote International Peace?" (a question that provides a perfect logical parallel to "When did you stop beating your wife?").

The 1938 edition of Casner and Gabriel has a new title, *The Rise of American Democracy*, and is said to be a complete reworking of the original volume. It has a new rationale. In their foreword, the authors say that democracy is now being challenged by other forms of government, including "swift-striking dictatorships," and that we therefore have to ask, "What does the word, *democracy*, mean?" The book never quite gets around to answering this question, but its focus is more political than that of the first edition, and its tone more urgent. The story of the knight in the first chapter has been condensed, and the American scenery of birds, squirrels, and leafy boughs has largely disappeared. The Indians are now said to have practiced democracy, not religion; they are no longer "deeply religious." Jacob Riis is still around, but the United States government has become a much more positive actor in social reform. Whereas a mid-thirties edition seems to judge some of President Franklin Roosevelt's legislation to have been unconstitutional, this one simply credits him with having helped the country out of the Depression. In foreign policy, too, the government has taken a positive role: it "helps" the Allies in the First World War and "promotes" world peace thereafter, within the limits of its isolationist position. In the last part of the book, "American Democracy Faces a Confused World," the text maintains that Americans now have new ideals, including a balanced

3

FRANCES FITZGERALD

economy, Social Security, and well-being for all citizens. But it ends, rather ominously, "The struggle still goes on. It was never more intense than in our day. The outcome will depend upon the intelligence and alertness of this generation and of future generations."

The 1942 edition, now called *The Story of American Democracy*, has an update on the Second World War and a new preface that refers to the "perilous times" we are living in. Apparently because of this emergency, the Indian sections have been condensed. (They drop out completely in subsequent editions.) In the central part of the book, the titles have changed, and these give a rather different tone to the book. Where once there were "problems" to "challenge democracy," there is now only progress: "American Life Becomes Better for the Common Man," and so on. The Constitutional period is headed "Free Americans Organize a Strong Democratic Nation," and the words "freedom" and "strength" crop up a lot elsewhere. In the last chapter—a completely new one, entitled "The United States Fights for Its Life and for a Free, Democratic World"—there is a photograph caption that reads, "This picture shows citizens enjoying the democratic privilege of free discussion. . . . The leader is helping them to carry on their business in an orderly way." The photograph shows several men on a dais facing a seated audience; it is clearly a meeting of some sort. In contrast to the final worryings of the 1938 edition, this book ends on a note of optimism concerning air travel.

Over the next eight years, the authors—or whoever did the revising of the text—must have felt justified in their optimism, for the 1950 text is a victorious book. The United States now "leads the struggle for democracy"; it has "faced problems," "met challenges"; it has risen "to a position of world leadership" and become "a bastion of the free nations." All of this is, of course, in the twentieth century, but retrospectively the nation has made other gains as well—notably in its nineteenth-century wars. It has not exactly won the War of 1812, but the war is now said to have helped "build the nation." (In earlier editions, the war, less grandly, "develops national feeling.") The Mexican War, which in the first two editions brought the country only empty land, now has brought it vast territories rich in oil and precious metals. In addition, the country has become more prosperous: there are no more poor people or bad social conditions. Pages have been added explaining the superiority of the American democratic system to the Russian police state.

In accordance with the authors' new belief that "perhaps the most important event of the first half of the twentieth century was the rise of the United States to a position of world leadership," the last quarter of the book deals mainly with foreign affairs. These sections portray the United States as playing an essentially benevolent and

4

5

6

pacific role in the world. The nation is always attempting to improve communications with the Soviet Union and to "gain peace by mutual understanding"—this in spite of continual rebuffs. In an echo of the liberal internationalism of the first edition, the book talks about the need for international control of atomic energy and the effort to remove the causes of war through the United Nations. The last section, "Democracy Enriches the Lives of Americans," confidently describes recent "advances" in art, education, and science, and points up the American belief in the importance of the individual, of whatever race or creed.

Five years later, this confidence has evaporated; the book is a bundle of anxieties. In the first place, the authors no longer appear to believe that the United States exerts "world leadership." In their foreword, they say that the United States leads "those people in the world who believe in freedom" (a worrying kind of group), and that it is "locked in a struggle" with "another powerful world leader . . . the Soviet Union." Faced with the need to prepare "young people" for the "struggle" in a "complicated and often dangerous world," the authors propose to compare the Russian and American ways of life—American history apparently being of no use anymore. Later on in the book, the authors fulfill their promise by giving an account of Soviet institutions. In this section, one is told that "Russia" is a police state, where "the leader of the Communist party has absolute power over . . . every person." (The book cautiously does not name this leader; Stalin had died two years before publication.) Russia, one learns, is a "fake democracy" and a "fake republic"; worse yet, its industry is geared not to the production of television sets but to war production. In addition, one learns that Russia is tremendously powerful—perhaps even more powerful than the United States, because, in spite of all the American aid to free nations, Russia has managed to block progress and block the growth of prosperity. It is now threatening the free world. (In this section, there is a map of the world color-coded to show which nations are "Communist," which are "free," and which are "neutral." This map classifies all of Indo-China and all of sub-Sahara Africa as "free" and classifies Saudi Arabia, Iran, and most of Latin America, including Mexico, as "neutral." This assessment is mysterious, since the book appeared a year after Dien Bien Phu, several years before the decolonization of most of Africa, and some time after the C.I.A. had brought the Shah of Iran to power and had overturned the Arbenz government in Guatemala.) Internationally, nothing is safe from the Communists, and the home front is not very secure, either. The United States may be a free country, with "wonderful machines" and a free-enterprise system (over which the government now presides in the much reduced capacity of referee), but the Russians are in the

7

FRANCES FITZGERALD

process of undermining it. They have already stolen American state secrets through Alger Hiss and the Rosenbergs. They lie a lot, and the Communist Party in the United States espouses violent, undemocratic means. The book therefore approves of the Internal Security Act, the Loyalty Board, and the firm hand of J. Edgar Hoover in the F.B.I.

The most surprising thing about this 1955 edition is the attitude that its authors take toward children. In the thirties editions, they had tried to engage their young readers with adventure stories and romance; here they do nothing but lecture—as if the children might turn out to be small subversives. The last page, subheaded "A Citizen's Rights and Duties," is terribly stern. A citizen's duties, they warn, include military service, jury duty, and paying taxes without cheating. The last few pages—usually given over to science and technology—now include a warning against "false news" and "dangerous propaganda." What the authors are referring to here can only be conjectured, since they are no more explicit than they were when they warned in an earlier section against the questionable practices of "some investigating committees of Congress"—surely the House Un-American Activities Committee and Senator Joseph R. McCarthy's subcommittee. But these two things are probably connected, because the authors offer this explicit piece of advice:

> The FBI urges Americans to report directly to its offices any suspicions they may have about Communist activity on the part of their fellow Americans. The FBI is expertly trained to sift out the truth of such reports under the laws of our free nation. When Americans handle their suspicions in this way, rather than by gossip and publicity, they are acting in line with American traditions.

What this paragraph literally says is that an American tradition is that of the police informer. The authors, however, appear to have thought of the F.B.I. as the liberal alternative to the McCarthy subcommittee.

This edition of Casner and Gabriel was not untypical of the texts of the period—certainly in its emphasis on the Communist threat. Virtually all the texts of the mid-fifties made the same estimates of Soviet power and Soviet aggressiveness in foreign policy. Virtually all of them expressed similar doubts about the survival of democracy in this country. The texts of the early forties had not portrayed the Nazis as half so aggressive, or the Second World War as half such a threat to the country. Now the danger was everywhere, invisible. According to Bragdon and McCutchen, one of the most respectable of the high-school texts of the period:

Unquestioning party members are found everywhere. Everywhere they are willing to engage in spying, sabotage, and the promotion of unrest on orders from Moscow.

And

Agents of the worldwide Communist conspiracy have been active inside the United States. Some of them have been trusted officials of the State Department, regularly furnishing information to Russia. Others have passed on atomic secrets; still others have even represented the United States in the UN.

Bragdon and McCutchen were quoting Senator McCarthy and representing his charges as true.

The subversion anxieties of the texts peaked in the mid-   10
fifties, subsiding gradually after that. The early-sixties texts did not repudiate McCarthy except by saying, "Some Americans said there was too much fuss being made about the Communists since there were so relatively few in the United States," or "The struggle divided us when we should have been united." Only now do some texts actually denounce McCarthy's "scare tactics" and take issue with the general assessment of the Soviet Union in the fifties. The aspect of fifties texts that persisted most strongly into the sixties was a certain tone of grimness toward children, and particularly toward young children. It was the junior-high-school books, rather than the high-school ones, that gave such warnings as "Some forces in the world today want to abolish freedom. [But] your heritage as an American provides you with the ideals and faith to give you strength to preserve the rights that are yours as a free American. It is your duty to preserve these rights." And so on. Since these books never defined what they meant by "freedom," the burden they laid on children was truly awesome.

QUESTIONS

1. Trace the changes in the "ideological drift" of the Casner and Gabriel textbook from 1931 to the mid-1950s.

2. What assumptions and inferences does Fitzgerald make about the teaching of American history in the junior high school classroom?

3. Although this is an analytical essay, the diction tends to be informal.

FRANCES FITZGERALD

Point to examples of this informal style. What is the effect of the diction on the analysis itself?

4.   Explain the allusions to John Dewey and Jacob Riis in paragraph 2. Identify the allusion in paragraph 8.

5.   How does the term *ideological drift* serve to structure the entire essay? What type of process analysis is involved in the development? Identify the steps in the process.

6.   Comment on the effectiveness of the author's topic sentences. How do they reinforce the implied thesis in the essay?

7.   Explain how Fitzgerald uses causal analysis. Analyze one paragraph in detail to illuminate this procedure.

8.   What is the author's tone in her analysis of the Casner and Gabriel text? Cite examples to support your position.

9.   Discuss the presentation of American history (or any other subject) in a textbook with which you are familiar. What connections can you make among the text, the author, and the era in which it was written?

10.   Write an analysis of a textbook, dealing with its assumptions, its content, its intended audience, and its purpose. What view of American history, politics, or society does it project?

LEWIS MUMFORD

The Social Concept of the City

Lewis Mumford (1895–   ) is one of the major twentieth-century writers on architecture and the city. His international reputation is based on his studies of the history of architecture and urban planning, notably *Technics and Civilization* (1934), *The Culture of Cities* (1938), *The City in History* (1961), and *Roots of Contemporary Architecture* (1972). A prolific and versatile writer, he is also the author of *Sticks and Stones* (1924), *Herman Melville* (1929), and *The Conduct of Life* (1951). The following essay reflects what Mumford has indicated are his abiding strains of pessimism and optimism concerning man's "participation in the cosmic and historic process."

Much recent housing and city planning has been handi- 1
capped because those who have undertaken the work
have had no clear notion of the social functions of the
city. They sought to derive these functions from a
cursory survey of the activities and interests of the contemporary
urban scene. And they did not, apparently, suspect that there might
be gross deficiencies, misdirected efforts, mistaken expenditures,
here that would not be set straight by merely building sanitary
tenements or widening narrow streets.

The city as a purely physical fact has been subject to numer- 2
ous investigations. But what is the city as a social institution? The
earlier answers to these questions, in Aristotle, Plato, and the
Utopian writers from Sir Thomas More to Robert Owen, have been on
the whole more satisfactory than those of the more systematic
sociologists: most contemporary treatises on "urban sociology" in
America throw no important light upon the problem.

One of the soundest definitions of the city was that framed by 3
John Stow, an honest observer of Elizabethan London, who said:
"Men are congregated into cities and commonwealths for honesty
and utility's sake, these shortly be the commodities that do come by
cities, commonalties, and corporations. First, men by this nearness of
conversation are withdrawn from barbarous feritie and force, to
certain mildness of manners, and to humanity and justice, whereby
they are contented to give and take right, to and from their equals and
inferiors, and to hear and obey their heads and superiors. Also the
doctrine of God is more fitly delivered, and the discipline thereof
more aptly to be executed, in peopled towns than abroad, by reason
of the facility of common and often assembling; and consequently
such inhabitants be better managed in order, and better instructed in
wisdom. . . . Good behavior is yet called *urbanitas* because it is rather
found in cities than elsewhere. In sum, by often hearing, men be
better persuaded in religion, and for that they live in the eyes of
others, they be by example the more easily trained to justice, and by
shame-fastness restrained from injury.

"And whereas commonwealths and kingdoms cannot have, 4
next after God, any surer foundation than the love and good will of
one man towards another, that also is closely bred and maintained in
cities, where men by mutual society and companying together, do
grow to alliances, commonalties, and corporations."

It is with no hope of adding much to the essential insight of 5
this description of the urban process that I would sum up the
sociological concept of the city in the following terms:

The city is a related collection of primary groups and purpos- 6
ive associations: the first, like family and neighborhood, are common
to all communities, while the second are especially characteristic of

LEWIS MUMFORD

city life. These varied groups support themselves through economic organizations that are likewise of a more or less corporate, or at least publicly regulated, character; and they are all housed in permanent structures, within a relatively limited area. The essential physical means of a city's existence are the fixed site, the durable shelter, the permanent facilities for assembly, interchange, and storage; the essential social means are the social division of labor, which serves not merely the economic life but the cultural processes.

The city in its complete sense, then, is a geographic plexus, 7 an economic organization, an institutional process, a theater of social action, and an esthetic symbol of collective unity. On one hand it is a physical frame for the commonplace domestic and economic activities; on the other, it is a consciously dramatic setting for the more significant actions and the more sublimated urges of a human culture. The city fosters art and *is* art; the city creates the theater and *is* the theater. It is in the city, the city as theater, that man's more purposive activities are formulated and worked out, through conflicting and cooperating personalities, events, groups, into more significant culminations.

Without the social drama that comes into existence through 8 the focusing and intensification of group activity there is not a single function performed in the city that could not be performed—and has not in fact been performed—in the open country. The physical organization of the city may deflate this drama or make it frustrate; or it may, through the deliberate efforts of art, politics, and education, make the drama more richly significant, as a stage-set, well-designed, intensifies and underlines the gestures of the actors and the action of the play. It is not for nothing that men have dwelt so often on the beauty or the ugliness of cities: these attributes condition men's social activities. And if there is a deep reluctance, on the part of the true city dweller, to leave his cramped quarters for the physically more benign environment of a suburb—even a model garden suburb!—his instincts are partly justified: in its various and many-sided life, in its very opportunities for social disharmony and conflict, the city creates drama; the suburb lacks it.

One may describe the city, in its social aspect, as a special 9 framework directed toward the creation of differentiated opportunities for a common life and a significant collective drama. As indirect forms of association, with the aid of signs and symbols and specialized organizations, supplement direct face-to-face intercourse, the personalities of the citizens themselves become many-faceted: they reflect their specialized interests, their more intensively trained aptitudes, their finer discriminations and selections: the personality no longer presents a more or less unbroken traditional face to reality as a whole. Here lies the possibility of personal disintegration; and here lies the need for re-integration through wider participations in a concrete and visible collective whole. What men cannot imagine as a vague formless society, they can live through and experience as citizens in a city. Their unified plans and buildings become a symbol of their social relatedness; and when the physical environment itself becomes disordered and incoherent, the social functions that it harbors become more difficult to express.

Before man can become fully humanized, the social man 10 must break up into a thousand parts: so that each grain of aptitude, each streak of intelligence, each fiber of special interest, may take a deeper color by mingling with other grains, streaks, and fibers of the same nature. The undifferentiated common bond of primary association is weakened by these specialized associations; but the cable of civilization itself becomes stronger through such multiform twisting into a more complex and many-colored strand. From simple consciousness of kind in the tribe or family to the developed consciousness of kind that goes with special associations and differentiated groups: from habit to choice: from a fixed mold to a dynamic equilibrium of forces, from taking life as it comes to comprehending it and redesigning it—that is the path of both human and civic development. This transfer of emphasis from the uniformities and common acceptances of the primary group to the critical choices, the purposive associations, and the rational ends of the secondary group is one of the main functions of the city. The city is in fact the physical form of the highest and most complex types of associative life.

One further conclusion follows from this concept of the city: 11 social facts are primary, and the physical organization of a city, its industries and its markets, its lines of communication and traffic, must be subservient to its social needs. Whereas in the development of the city during the last century we expanded the physical plant recklessly and treated the essential social nucleus, the organs of government and education and social service, as mere afterthoughts, today we must treat the social nucleus as the essential element in every valid city plan: the spotting and inter-relationship of schools, libraries, theaters, community centers, is the first task in defining the urban neighborhood and laying down the outlines of an integrated city.

If this is the correct interpretation of the nature of the city, a 12 good part of the work that has been done under the name of city planning must be discounted and discredited: it has no more to do with the essential functions of living in cities than the work of the scene shifter and property man have to do with the development of Hamlet. This is not to deny its use: for scene shifters have their use: but it is to cast a doubt upon its sufficiency. The planning of cities by those who have hitherto called themselves city planners is like having

LEWIS MUMFORD

the play itself written by the property man, or mistaking the stage directions for the lines of the actors.

Though our conception of the physical structure of cities during the last century has been inadequate even in purely physical terms, like the movement of people and the service of industries, people have been even more wantonly inept in their conception of the social structure and the social activities of cities. With their eyes on the purely material changes that are so necessary, even those who have striven most earnestly for improvement have been content to build mere buildings. But buildings do not make a city; and the adequate planning of buildings is only a part of the necessary social schema. 13

From the standpoint of city design, the sociological theory of groups has a direct bearing upon plan. One of the difficulties in the way of political association is that we have not provided it with the necessary physical organs of existence: we have failed to provide the necessary sites, the necessary buildings, the necessary halls, rooms, meeting places: hence in big cities the saloon and the shabby district headquarters, open only to the more sedulous party members, have served. As for industries, the political opportunities for association have been even scantier: in how many factory districts are there well-equipped halls of sufficient size in which the workers can meet? 14

On this point one may well quote the Webbs. "We do not think it is usually understood," they observe, "how greatly the efficiency of trade unionism may be increased, and its very character raised to the height of a service of public utility, merely by the provision of structural accommodation equal in dignity to that of a government department, in which all the several unions in each locality may be worthily housed together." 15

The town meeting of the New England political system had reality because it had dimensions and members: the citizens met face to face in a special building, the town hall: they saw and heard their fellow citizens, and they discussed problems relating to a unit immediately within their grasp and vision. But the peoples of the Western World have sought to live under an abstract and disembodied political democracy without giving its local units any other official organ than the polling booth. We have hitherto lacked the energy or the insight to provide the necessary meeting halls, committee rooms, permanent offices. We have still to organize neighborhoods and corporate organizations as if the political functions of the community were important ones. In the conglomerate masses we have called cities, it is no wonder that political life, as a concrete exercise of duties and functions, has given way to various subtle parasitisms and diversions. And contrariwise, in new communities that have been planned as social units, with visible coherence in the architecture, 16 with a sufficient number of local meeting rooms for group activities, as in Sunnyside Gardens, L. I., a robust political life, with effective collective action and a sense of renewed public responsibility, has swiftly grown up.

The moral should be plain: we must design whole social 17 units: we must design *cities:* and in the order of design the arrangement of the essential social institutes, their adequate provision and servicing, is a key to the rest of the structure. It is on the purely instrumental physical services that we must practice the most stringent economy, even parsimony; it is on the political and educational services that we must spend with a lavish hand. This means a new order of design and a different type of designer: it means that that emphasis will shift progressively from the stage-set to the drama, and that the handling of the social activities and relationships will engage the fuller attention of the planner. In time, this will have the effect of reducing the instrumental arts of town planning to fairly stable routine, while a greater amount of energy and economic support will be set free for the expressive arts: painting and sculpture, drama and music, will again have greater importance than sanitation and sewage and the studious habits of antisepsis.

The elemental unit of planning, then, is no longer the house 18 or the houseblock: the elemental unit is the city, because it is only in terms of this more complex social formation that any particular type of activity or building has significance. And the aim of such planning is not the efficiency of industry by itself, or the diminution of disease by itself, or the spreading of culture by itself: the aim is the adequate dramatization of communal life: the widening of the domain of human significance so that, ultimately, no act, no routine, no gesture will be devoid of human value, or will fail to contribute to the reciprocal support of citizen and community. When this drama is sharply focused and adequately staged, every part of life feels an uprush of social energy: eating, working, mating, sleeping are not less than they were before, but far more: life has, despite its broken moments, the poise and unity of a collective work of art. To create that background, to achieve that insight, to enliven each individual capacity through articulation in an intelligible and esthetically stimulating whole, is the essence of the art of building cities. And less than that is not enough.

QUESTIONS
1. Paraphrase Mumford's sociological concept of the city. Why is the sociological theory of groups central to this concept?

2.   What does Mumford think about urban planning? How is his position reflected in the prescriptions for improvement that he offers?

3.   Explain the metaphorical language in paragraph 10.

4.   Mumford uses an unusual number of colons in this essay. Cite examples of this strategy, and explain the function and effect of the punctuation.

5.   How does the author's analogical reference to the drama influence the substance and structure of the essay?

6.   Analyze paragraph 1 as the introductory base of the essay.

7.   Analyze the techniques and strategies used by Mumford to develop an extended definition of the social concept of the city. What is the thesis behind this extended definition?

8.   Analyze Mumford's topic sentences as guidelines for the abstract and complex reasoning contained in the paragraphs.

9.   Mumford states in paragraph 18 that the "elemental unit of planning . . . is the city." What is he suggesting by this remark? Do you agree or disagree with his premise, and why?

10.   Write your own sociological definition of the city, attempting to explain and analyze the unique characteristics of city life.

W. E. B. DU BOIS

Of the Meaning of Progress

William Edward Burghardt Du Bois (1868–1963) was born in Massachusetts, the descendant of French Huguenots and slaves. He studied at Harvard and Berlin, and was a professor of economics and history at Atlanta University from 1896 to 1910. Emerging as a leader of the militant wing of the black movement in America, Du Bois wrote *The Souls of Black Folk* (1903) and other sociological studies. His increasing militancy moved him toward socialism and communism, culminating in renunciation of American citizenship and residence in Ghana, where he died. In this chapter from *The Souls of Black Folk,* Du Bois presents a highly personalized sociological account of black education in the South.

nce upon a time I taught school in the hills of Tennessee,   1
where the broad dark vale of the Mississippi begins to
roll and crumple to greet the Alleghenies. I was a Fisk
student then, and all Fisk men thought that Tennessee—beyond the Veil—was theirs alone, and in vacation time they
sallied forth in lusty bands to meet the county school-commissioners.
Young and happy, I too went, and I shall not soon forget that
summer, seventeen years ago.

First, there was a Teachers' Institute at the countyseat; and   2
there distinguished guests of the superintendent taught the teachers
fractions and spelling and other mysteries,—white teachers in the
morning, Negroes at night. A picnic now and then, and a supper,
and the rough world was softened by laughter and song. I remember
how—But I wander.

There came a day when all the teachers left the Institute and   3
began the hunt for schools. I learn from hearsay (for my mother was
mortally afraid of firearms) that the hunting of ducks and bears and
men is wonderfully interesting, but I am sure that the man who has
never hunted a country school has something to learn of the
pleasures of the chase. I see now the white, hot roads lazily rise and
fall and wind before me under the burning July sun; I feel the deep
weariness of heart and limb as ten, eight, six miles stretch relentlessly
ahead; I feel my heart sink heavily as I hear again and again, "Got a
teacher? Yes." So I walked on and on—horses were too expensive—
until I had wandered beyond railways, beyond stage lines, to a land
of "varmints" and rattlesnakes, where the coming of a stranger was
an event, and men lived and died in the shadow of one blue hill.

Sprinkled over hill and dale lay cabins and farmhouses, shut   4
out from the world by the forests and the rolling hills toward the east.
There I found at last a little school. Josie told me of it; she was a thin,
homely girl of twenty, with a dark-brown face and thick, hard hair. I
had crossed the stream at Watertown, and rested under the great
willows; then I had gone to the little cabin in the lot where Josie was
resting on her way to town. The gaunt farmer made me welcome, and
Josie, hearing my errand, told me anxiously that they wanted a school
over the hill; that but once since the war had a teacher been there; that
she herself longed to learn—and thus she ran on, talking fast and
loud, with much earnestness and energy.

Next morning I crossed the tall round hill, lingered to look at   5
the blue and yellow mountains stretching toward the Carolinas, then
plunged into the wood, and came out at Josie's home. It was a dull
frame cottage with four rooms, perched just below the brow of the
hill, amid peach-trees. The father was a quiet, simple soul, calmly
ignorant, with no touch of vulgarity. The mother was different,—

strong, bustling, and energetic, with a quick, restless tongue, and an ambition to live "like folks." There was a crowd of children. Two boys had gone away. There remained two growing girls; a shy midget of eight; John, tall awkward, and eighteen; Jim, younger, quicker, and better looking; and two babies of indefinite age. Then there was Josie herself. She seemed to be the centre of the family: always busy at service, or at home, or berrypicking, a little nervous and inclined to scold, like her mother, yet faithful, too, like her father. She had about her a certain fineness, the shadow of an unconscious moral heroism that would willingly give all of life to make life broader, deeper, and fuller for her and hers. I saw much of this family afterwards, and grew to love them for their honest efforts to be decent and comfortable, and for their knowledge of their own ignorance. There was with them no affectation. The mother would scold the father for being so "easy"; Josie would roundly berate the boys for carelessness; and all knew that it was a hard thing to dig a living out of a rocky side-hill.

I secured the school. I remember the day I rode horseback out   6
to the commissioner's house with a pleasant young white fellow who wanted the white school. The road ran down the bed of a stream; the sun laughed and the water jingled, and we rode on. "Come in," said the commissioner,—come in. Have a seat. Yes, that certificate will do. Stay to dinner. What do you want a month?" "Oh," thought I, "this is lucky"; but even then fell the awful shadow of the Veil, for they ate first, then I—alone.

The schoolhouse was a log hut, where Colonel Wheeler used   7
to shelter his corn. It sat in a lot behind a rail fence and thorn bushes, near the sweetest of springs. There was an entrance where a door once was, and within a massive rickety fireplace; great chinks between the logs served as windows. Furniture was scarce. A pale blackboard crouched in the corner. My desk was made of three boards, reinforced at critical points, and my chair, borrowed from the landlady, had to be returned every night. Seats for the children— these puzzled me much. I was haunted by a New England vision of neat little desks and chairs, but, alas! the reality was rough plank benches without backs, and at times without legs. They had the one virtue of making naps dangerous,—possibly fatal, for the floor was not to be trusted.

It was a hot morning late in July when the school opened. I   8
trembled when I heard the patter of little feet down the dusty road, and saw the growing row of dark solemn faces and bright eager eyes facing me. First came Josie and her brothers and sisters. The longing to know, to be a student in the great school at Nashville, hovered like a star above this child-woman amid her work and worry, and she studied doggedly. There were the Dowells from their farm over

toward Alexandria,—Fanny, with her smooth black face and wondering eyes; Martha, brown and dull; the pretty girl-wife of a brother, and the younger brood.

There were the Burkes,—two brown and yellow lads, and a tiny haughty-eyed girl. Fat Reuben's little chubby girl came, with golden face and old-gold hair, faithful and solemn. Thenie was on hand early,—a jolly, ugly, goodhearted girl, who slyly dipped snuff and looked after her little bow-legged brother. When her mother could spare her, Tildy came,—a midnight beauty, with starry eyes and tapering limbs; and her brother, correspondingly homely. And then the big boys,—the hulking Lawrences; and lazy Neills, unfathered sons of mother and daughter; Hickman, with a stoop in his shoulders; and the rest. 9

There they sat, nearly thirty of them, on the rough benches, 10 their faces shading from a pale cream to a deep brown, the little feet bare and swinging, the eyes full of expectation, with here and there a twinkle of mischief, and the hands grasping Webster's blue-back spelling-book. I loved my school, and the fine faith the children had in the wisdom of their teacher was truly marvellous. We read and spelled together, wrote a little, picked flowers, sang, and listened to stories of the world beyond the hill. At times the school would dwindle away, and I would start out. I would visit Mun Eddings, who lived in two very dirty rooms, and ask why little Lugene, whose flaming face seemed ever ablaze with the dark-red hair uncombed, was absent all last week, or why I missed so often the inimitable rags of Mack and Ed. Then the father, who worked Colonel Wheeler's farm on shares, would tell me how the crops needed the boys; and the thin, slovenly mother, whose face was pretty when washed, assured me that Lugene must mind the baby. "But we'll start them again next week." When the Lawrences stopped, I knew that the doubts of the old folks about book-learning had conquered again, and so, toiling up the hill, and getting as far into the cabin as possible, I put Cicero "pro Archia Poeta" into the simplest English with local applications, and usually convinced them—for a week or so.

On Friday nights I often went home with some of the 11 children,—sometimes to Doc Burke's farm. He was a great, loud, thin Black, ever working, and trying to buy the seventy-five acres of hill and dale where he lived; but people said that he would surely fail, and the "white folks would get it all." His wife was a magnificent Amazon, with saffron face and shining hair, uncorseted and barefooted, and the children were strong and beautiful. They lived in a one-and-a-half room cabin in the hollow of the farm, near the spring. The front room was full of great fat white beds, scrupulously neat; and there were bad chromos on the walls, and a tired centre-table. In the tiny back kitchen I was often invited to "take out and help"

W. E. B. DU BOIS

myself to fried chicken and wheat biscuit, "meat" and corn pone, string-beans and berries. At first I used to be a little alarmed at the approach of bedtime in the one lone bedroom, but embarrassment was very deftly avoided. First, all the children nodded and slept, and were stowed away in one great pile of goose feathers; next, the mother and the father discreetly slipped away to the kitchen while I went to bed; then, blowing out the dim light, they retired in the dark. In the morning all were up and away before I thought of awaking. Across the road, where fat Reuben lived, they all went outdoors while the teacher retired, because they did not boast the luxury of a kitchen.

I liked to stay with the Dowells, for they had four rooms and 12 plenty of good country fare. Uncle Bird had a small, rough farm, all woods and hills, miles from the big road; but he was full of tales,—he preached now and then,—and with his children, berries, horses, and wheat he was happy and prosperous. Often, to keep the peace, I must go where life was less lovely; for instance, Tildy's mother was incorrigibly dirty, Reuben's larder was limited seriously, and herds of untamed insects wandered over the Eddingses' beds. Best of all I loved to go to Josie's, and sit on the porch, eating peaches, while the mother bustled and talked: how Josie had bought the sewing-machine; how Josie worked at service in winter, but that four dollars a month was "mighty little" wages; how Josie longed to go away to school, but that it "looked like" they never could get far enough ahead to let her; how the crops failed and the well was yet unfinished; and, finally, how "mean" some of the white folks were.

For two summers I lived in this little world; it was dull and 13 humdrum. The girls looked at the hill in wistful longing, and the boys fretted and haunted Alexandria. Alexandria was "town,"—a straggling, lazy village of houses, churches, and shops, and an aristocracy of Toms, Dicks, and Captains. Cuddled on the hill to the north was the village of the colored folks who lived in three- or four-room unpainted cottages, some neat and homelike, and some dirty. The dwellings were scattered rather aimlessly, but they centered about the twin temples of the hamlet, the Methodist, and the Hard-Shell Baptist churches. These, in turn, leaned gingerly on a sad-colored schoolhouse. Hither my little world wended its crooked way on Sunday to meet other worlds, and gossip, and wonder, and make the weekly sacrifice with frenzied priest at the altar of the "old-time religion." Then the soft melody and mighty cadences of Negro song fluttered and thundered.

I have called my tiny community a world, and so its isolation 14 made it; and yet there was among us but a half-awakened common consciousness, sprung from common joy and grief, at burial, birth, or wedding; from a common hardship in poverty, poor land, and low wages; and, above all, from the sight of the Veil that hung between us and Opportunity. All this caused us to think some thoughts together; but these, when ripe for speech, were spoken in various languages. Those whose eyes twenty-five and more years before had seen "the glory of the coming of the Lord," saw in every present hindrance or help a dark fatalism bound to bring all things right in His own good time. The mass of those to whom slavery was a dim recollection of childhood found the world a puzzling thing: it asked little of them, and they answered with little, and yet it ridiculed their offering. Such a paradox they could not understand, and therefore sank into listless indifference, or shiftlessness, or reckless bravado. There were, however, some—such as Josie, Jim, and Ben—to whom War, Hell, and Slavery were but childhood tales, whose young appetites had been whetted to an edge by school and story and half-awakened thought. Ill could they be content, born without and beyond the World. And their weak wings beat against their barriers,—barriers of caste, of youth, of life; at last, in dangerous moments, against everything that opposed even a whim.

The ten years that follow youth, the years when first the 15 realization comes that life is leading somewhere,—these were the years that passed after I left my little school. When they were past, I came by chance once more to the walls of Fisk University, to the halls of the chapel of melody. As I lingered there in the joy and pain of meeting old school-friends, there swept over me a sudden longing to pass again beyond the blue hill, and to see the homes and the school of other days, and to learn how life had gone with my school-children; and I went.

Josie was dead, and the gray-haired mother said simply, 16 "We've had a heap of trouble since you've been away." I had feared for Jim. With a cultured parentage and a social caste to uphold him, he might have made a venturesome merchant or a West Point cadet. But here he was, angry with life and reckless; and when Farmer Durham charged him with stealing wheat, the old man had to ride fast to escape the stones which the furious fool hurled after him. They told Jim to run away; but he would not run, and the constable came that afternoon. It grieved Josie, and great awkward John walked nine miles every day to see his little brother through the bars of Lebanon jail. At last the two came back together in the dark night. The mother cooked supper, and Josie emptied her purse, and the boys stole away. Josie grew thin and silent, yet worked the more. The hill became steep for the quiet old father, and with the boys away there was little to do in the valley. Josie helped them to sell the old farm, and they moved nearer town. Brother Dennis, the carpenter, built a new house with six rooms; Josie toiled a year in Nashville, and brought back ninety dollars to furnish the house and change it to a home.

When the spring came, and the birds twittered, and the stream ran proud and full, little sister Lizzie, bold and thoughtless, flushed with the passion of youth, bestowed herself on the tempter, and brought home a nameless child. Josie shivered and worked on, with the vision of schooldays all fled, with a face wan and tired,— worked until, on a summer's day, some one married another; then Josie crept to her mother like a hurt child, and slept—and sleeps. 17

I paused to scent the breeze as I entered the valley. The Lawrences have gone,—the father and son forever,—and the other son lazily digs in the earth to live. A new young widow rents out their cabin to fat Reuben. Reuben is a Baptist preacher now, but I fear as lazy as ever, though his cabin has three rooms; and little Ella has grown into a bouncing woman, and is ploughing corn on the hot hillside. There are babies a-plenty, and one half-witted girl. Across the valley is a house I did not know before, and there I found, rocking one baby and expecting another one of my schoolgirls, a daughter of Uncle Bird Dowell. She looked somewhat worried with her new duties, but soon bristled into pride over her neat cabin and the tale of her thrifty husband, and the horse and cow, and the farm they were planning to buy. 18

My log schoolhouse was gone. In its place stood Progress; and Progress, I understand, is necessarily ugly. The crazy foundation stones still marked the former site of my poor little cabin, and not far away, on six weary boulders, perched a jaunty board house, perhaps twenty by thirty feet, with three windows and a door that locked. Some of the window-glass was broken, and part of an old iron stove lay mournfully under the house. I peeped through the window half reverently, and found things that were more familiar. The blackboard had grown by about two feet, and the seats were still without backs. The county owns the lot now, I hear, and every year there is a session of school. As I sat by the spring and looked on the Old and the New I felt glad, very glad, and yet— 19

After two long drinks I started on. There was the great double log-house on the corner. I remembered the broken, blighted family that used to live there. The strong, hard face of the mother, with its wilderness of hair, rose before me. She had driven her husband away, and while I taught school a strange man lived there, big and jovial, and people talked. I felt sure that Ben and Tildy would come to naught from such a home. But this is an odd world; for Ben is a busy farmer in Smith County, "doing well, too," they say, and he had cared for little Tildy until last spring, when a lover married her. A hard life the lad had led, toiling for meat, and laughed at because he was homely and crooked. There was a Sam Carlon, an impudent old skinflint, who had definite notions about "niggers," and hired Ben a summer and would not pay him. Then the hungry boy gathered his 20 sacks together, and in broad daylight went to Carlon's corn; and when the hard-fisted farmer set upon him, the angry boy flew at him like a beast. Doc Burke saved a murder and a lynching that day.

The story reminded me again of the Burkes, and an impa- tience seized me to know who won in the battle, Doc or the seventy-five acres. For it is a hard thing to make a farm out of nothing, even in fifteen years. So I hurried on, thinking of the Burkes. They used to have a certain magnificent barbarism about them that I liked. They were never vulgar, never immoral, but rather rough and primitive, with an unconventionality that spent itself in loud guffaws, slaps on the back, and naps in the corner. I hurried by the cottage of the misborn Neill boys. It was empty, and they were grown into fat, lazy farm-hands. I saw the home of the Hickmans, but Albert, with his stooping shoulders, had passed from the world. Then I came to the Burkes' gate and peered through; the inclosure looked rough and untrimmed, and yet there were the same fences around the old farm save to the left, where lay twenty-five other acres. And Lo! the cabin in the hollow had climbed the hill and swollen to a half-finished six-room cottage.

The Burkes held a hundred acres, but they were still in debt. Indeed, the gaunt father who toiled night and day would scarcely be happy out of debt, being so used to it. Some day he must stop, for his massive frame is showing decline. The mother wore shoes, but the lion-like physique of other days was broken. The children had grown up. Rob, the image of his father, was loud and rough with laughter. Birdie, my school baby of six, had grown to a picture of maiden beauty, tall and tawny. "Edgar is gone," said the mother, with head half bowed,—"gone to work in Nashville; he and his father couldn't agree."

Little Doc, the boy born since the time of my school, took me horseback down the creek next morning toward Farmer Dowell's. The road and the stream were battling for mastery, and the stream had the better of it. We splashed and waded, and the merry boy, perched behind me, chattered and laughed. He showed me where Simon Thompson had bought a bit of ground and a home; but his daughter Lana, a plump, brown, slow girl, was not there. She had married a man and a farm twenty miles away. We wound on down the stream till we came to a gate that I did not recognize, but the boy insisted that it was "Uncle Bird's." The farm was fat with the growing crop. In that little valley was a strange stillness as I rode up; for death and marriage had stolen youth and left age and childhood there. We sat and talked that night after the chores were done. Uncle Bird was grayer, and his eyes did not see so well, but he was still jovial. We talked of the acres bought,—one hundred and twenty-five,—of the new guest-chamber added, of Martha's marrying. Then we talked of death: Fanny and

W. E. B. DU BOIS

Fred were gone; a shadow hung over the other daughter and when it lifted she was to go to Nashville to school. At last we spoke of the neighbors, and as night fell, Uncle Bird told me how, on a night like that, 'Thenie came wandering back to her home over yonder, to escape the blows of her husband. And next morning she died in the home that her little bow-legged brother, working and saving, had bought for their widowed mother.

My journey was done, and behind me lay hill and dale, and Life and Death. How shall man measure Progress there where the dark-faced Josie lies? How many heartfuls of sorrow shall balance a bushel of wheat? How hard a thing is life to the lowly, and yet how human and real! And all this life and love and strife and failure,—is it the twilight of nightfall or the flush of some faint-dawning day? 24

Thus sadly musing, I rode to Nashville in the Jim Crow car. 25

QUESTIONS

1. In general, what is the author's basic attitude toward progress? Where does he state this attitude most clearly?

2. Put into your own words the feelings Du Bois projects in his description of the people he taught in the hills of Tennessee.

3. Would you label the language in the essay subjective or objective? Justify your answer by citing passages from the text.

4. How does the symbolism of "the Veil," first introduced in paragraph 1, influence the tone of the essay? How does the author control mood through shifting patterns of imagery? Cite examples.

5. What are the primary rhetorical patterns employed by the author to develop his definition of progress?

6. The essay divides into two main narrative segments. What are they? Analyze the relationship between these segments. How does Du Bois maintain unity? How does the time element affect the mood and tone that are generated?

7. Analyze the spatial transitions that the author uses in the essay.

8. Assess the effectiveness of the short, concluding paragraph.

9. Discuss the value of personal experience and observation as a sociological method. Why do you think that Du Bois mistrusted scientific objectivity in sociological analysis? Compare and contrast the sociological methods of Du Bois and Mumford.

10. Write a definition of "progress" based on personal experience and observation.

ON THE MEANING OF PROGRESS

The Circle of Governments

Niccolo Machiavelli (1469–1527), Italian patriot, statesman, and writer, is one of the seminal figures in the history of Western political thought. His inquiries into the nature of the state, the amoral quality of political life, and the primacy of power are distinctly modernist in outlook. He began his studies of political and historical issues after being forced to retire from Florentine politics in 1512. Exiled outside the city, Machiavelli wrote *The Prince* (1513), *The Discourses* (1519), *The Art of War* (1519–1520), and *The Florentine History* (1525). The following selection from *The Discourses* (conceived as commentaries by the author on the first ten books of Livy's *History of Rome*) analyzes the varieties of government and their political implications in history.

Having proposed to myself to treat of the kind of government established at Rome, and of the events that led to its perfection, I must at the beginning observe that some of the writers on politics distinguished three kinds of government, vis. the monarchical, the aristocratic, and the democratic; and maintain that the legislators of a people must choose from these three the one that seems to them most suitable. Other authors, wiser according to the opinion of many, count six kinds of governments, three of which are very bad, and three good in themselves, but so liable to be corrupted that they become absolutely bad. The three good ones are those which we have just named; the three bad ones result from the degradation of the other three, and each of them resembles its corresponding original, so that the transition from the one to the other is very easy. Thus monarchy becomes tyranny; aristocracy degenerates into oligarchy; and the popular government lapses readily into licentiousness. So that a legislator who gives to a state which he founds either of these three forms of government, constitutes it but for a brief time; for no precautions can prevent either one of the three that are reputed good from degenerating into its opposite kind; so great are in these the attractions and resemblances between the good and the evil.

Chance has given birth to these different kinds of governments amongst men; for at the beginning of the world the inhabitants were few in number and lived for a time dispersed, like beasts. As the human race increased, the necessity for uniting themselves for defence made itself felt; the better to attain this object they chose the strongest and most courageous from amongst themselves and placed him at their head promising to obey him. Thence they began to know the good and the honest, and to distinguish them from the bad and vicious; for seeing a man injure his benefactor aroused at once two sentiments in every heart, hatred against the ingrate and love for the benefactor. They blamed the first, and on the contrary honoured those the more who showed themselves grateful, for each felt that he in turn might be subject to a like wrong; and to prevent similar evils, they set to work to make laws, and to institute punishments for those who contravened them. Such was the origin of justice. This caused them, when they had afterwards to choose a prince, neither to look to the strongest nor bravest, but to the wisest and most just. But when they began to make sovereignty hereditary and non-elective, the children quickly degenerated from their fathers; and, so far from trying to equal their virtues, they considered that a prince had nothing else to do than to excel all the rest in luxury, indulgence, and every other variety of pleasure. The prince consequently soon drew upon himself the general hatred. An object of hatred, he naturally felt fear; fear in turn dictated to him precautions and wrongs, and thus tyranny quickly developed itself. Such were the beginning and causes of disorders, conspiracies, and plots against the sovereigns, set on foot, not by the feeble and timid, but by those citizens who, surpassing the others in grandeur of soul, in wealth, and in courage, could not submit to the outrages and excesses of their princes.

Under such powerful leaders the masses armed themselves against the tyrant, and after having rid themselves of him, submitted to these chiefs as their liberators. These, abhorring the very name of prince, constituted themselves a new government; and at first bearing in mind the past tyranny, they governed in strict accordance with the laws which they had established themselves; preferring public interests to their own, and to administer and protect with greatest care both public and private affairs. The children succeeded their fathers, and ignorant of the changes of fortune, having never experienced its reverses, and indisposed to remain content with this civil equality, they in turn gave themselves up to cupidity, ambition, libertinage, and violence, and soon caused the aristocratic government to degenerate into an oligarchic tyranny, regardless of all civil rights. They soon, however, experienced the same fate as the first tyrant; the people, disgusted with their government, placed themselves at the command of whoever was willing to attack them, and this disposition soon produced an avenger, who was sufficiently well seconded to destroy them. The memory of the prince and the wrongs committed by him being still fresh in their minds, and having overthrown the oligarchy, the people were not willing to return to the government of a prince. A popular government was therefore resolved upon, and it was so organized that the authority would not again fall into the hands of a prince or a small number of nobles. And as all governments are at first looked up to with some degree of reverence, the popular state also maintained itself for a time, but which was never of long duration, and lasted generally only about as long as the generation that had established it; for it soon ran into that kind of licence which inflicts injury upon public as well as private interests. Each individual only consulted his own passions, and a thousand acts of injustice were daily committed, so that, constrained by necessity, or directed by the counsels of some good man, or for the purpose of escaping from this anarchy, they returned anew to the government of a prince, and from this they generally lapsed again into anarchy, step-by-step, in the same manner and from the same causes as we have indicated.

Such is the circle which all republics are destined to run 4 through. Seldom, however, do they come back to the original form of government, which results from the fact that their duration is not sufficiently long to be able to undergo these repeated changes and preserve their existence. But it may well happen that a republic lacking strength and good counsel in its difficulties becomes subject after a while to some neighbouring state, that is better organized than itself; and if such is not the case, then they will be apt to revolve indefinitely in the circle of revolutions. I say, then, that all kinds of government are defective; those three which we have qualified as good because they are too short-lived, and the three bad ones because of their inherent viciousness. Thus sagacious legislators, knowing the vices of each of these systems of government by themselves, have chosen one that should partake of all of them, judging that to be the most stable and solid. In fact, when there is combined under the same constitution a prince, a nobility, and the power of the people, then these three powers will watch and keep each other reciprocally in check.

QUESTIONS

1. Explain the relation between the author's three forms of government and six forms of government.

2. Describe the "circle which all republics are destined to run through" (paragraph 4).

3. Analyze the definitions Machiavelli provides in context for the key political terms *monarchy, tyranny, aristocracy, oligarchy, democracy,* and *anarchy.*

4. What does the term *justice* mean to the author?

5. The author uses classification as a method of essay development. Analyze the way in which the key categories are introduced and developed.

6. Explain the relationship of the "circle" as a metaphor to the development of the essay. Is the application purely figurative or based on logic? Explain.

7. Explain the use of comparison and contrast as a strategy in the essay.

8. Where does the author present his thesis? How is it reinforced by other materials in the essay?

9. What is your opinion concerning Machiavelli's definition of good or viable government? Are Machiavelli's types of government obsolete, or are they universal? Explain.

10. Write a classification essay on the types of government in the modern world, or on the branches of government or levels of government in the United States.

JONATHAN SWIFT

A Modest Proposal
FOR PREVENTING THE CHILDREN OF POOR PEOPLE IN IRELAND FROM BEING A BURDEN TO THEIR PARENTS OR COUNTRY, AND FOR MAKING THEM BENEFICIAL TO THE PUBLIC

Jonathan Swift (1667–1745) is best known as the author of three satires: *A Tale of a Tub* (1704), *Gulliver's Travels* (1726), and *A Modest Proposal* (1729). In these satires, Swift pricks the balloon of many of his contemporaries' and our own most cherished prejudices, pomposities, and delusions. He was also a famous churchman, an eloquent spokesman for Irish rights, and a political journalist. The following selection, perhaps the most famous satiric essay in the English language, offers modest advice to a nation suffering from poverty, overpopulation, and political injustice.

t is a melancholy object to those who walk through this great town or travel in the country, when they see the streets, the roads, and cabin doors, crowded with beggars of the female-sex, followed by three, four, or six children, all in rags and importuning every passenger for an alms. These mothers, instead of being able to work for their honest livelihood, are forced to employ all their time in strolling to beg sustenance for their helpless infants, who, as they grow up, either turn thieves for want of work, or leave their dear native country to fight for the Pretender in Spain, or sell themselves to the Barbadoes.

I think it is agreed by all parties that this prodigious number of children in the arms, or on the backs, or at the heels of their mothers, and frequently of their fathers, is in the present deplorable state of the kingdom a very great additional grievance; and therefore whoever could find out a fair, cheap, and easy method of making these children sound, useful members of the commonwealth would deserve so well of the public as to have his statue set up for a preserver of the nation.

But my intention is very far from being confined to provide only for the children of professed beggars; it is of a much greater extent, and shall take in the whole number of infants at a certain age who are born of parents in effect as little able to support them as those who demand our charity in the streets.

As to my own part, having turned my thoughts for many years upon this important subject, and maturely weighed the several schemes of other projectors, I have always found them grossly mistaken in their computation. It is true, a child just dropped from its dam may be supported by her milk for a solar year, with little other nourishment; at most not above the value of two shillings, which the mother may certainly get, or the value in scraps, by her lawful occupation of begging; and it is exactly at one year old that I propose to provide for them in such a manner as instead of being a charge upon their parents or the parish, or wanting food and raiment for the rest of their lives, they shall on the contrary contribute to the feeding, and partly to the clothing, of many thousands.

There is likewise another great advantage in my scheme, that it will prevent those voluntary abortions, and that horrid practice of women murdering their bastard children, alas, too frequent among us, sacrificing the poor innocent babes, I doubt, more to avoid the expense than the shame, which would move tears and pity in the most savage and inhuman breast.

The number of souls in this kingdom being usually reckoned one million and a half, of these I calculate there may be about two hundred thousand couple whose wives are breeders; from which number I subtract thirty thousand couples who are able to maintain their own children, although I apprehend there cannot be so many under the present distresses of the kingdom; but this being granted, there will remain an hundred and seventy thousand breeders. I again subtract fifty thousand for those women who miscarry, or whose children die by accident or disease within the year. There only remain an hundred and twenty thousand children of poor parents annually born. The question therefore is, how this number shall be reared and provided for, which, as I have already said, under the present situation of affairs, is utterly impossible by all the methods hitherto proposed. For we can neither employ them in handicraft or agriculture; we neither build houses (I mean in the country) nor cultivate land. They can very seldom pick up a livelihood by stealing till they arrive at six years old, except where they are of towardly parts; although I confess they learn the rudiments much earlier, during which time they can however be looked upon only as probationers, as I have been informed by a principal gentlemen in the county of Cavan, who protested to me that he never knew above one or two instances under the age of six, even in a part of the kingdom so renowned for the quickest proficiency in that art.

I am assured by our merchants that a boy or girl before twelve years old is no salable commodity; and even when they come to this age they will not yield above three pounds, or three pounds and half a crown at most on the Exchange; which cannot turn to account either to the parents or the kingdom, the charge of nutriment and rags having been at least four times that value. 7

I shall now therefore humbly propose my own thoughts, which I hope will not be liable to the least objection. 8

I have been assured by a very knowing American of my acquaintance in London, that a young healthy child well nursed is at a year old a most delicious, nourishing, and wholesome food, whether stewed, roasted, baked or boiled; and I make no doubt that it will equally serve in a fricassee or a ragout. 9

I do therefore humbly offer it to public consideration that of the hundred and twenty thousand children, already computed, twenty thousand may be reserved for breed, whereof only one fourth part to be males, which is more than we allow to sheep, black cattle, or swine; and my reason is that these children are seldom the fruits of marriage, a circumstance not much regarded by our savages, therefore one male will be sufficient to serve four females. That the remaining hundred thousand may at a year old be offered in sale to the persons of quality and fortune through the kingdom, always advising the mother to let them suck plentifully in the last month, so as to render them plump and fat for a good table. A child will make two dishes at an entertainment for friends; and when the family dines alone, the fore or hind quarter will make a reasonable dish, and 10 seasoned with a little pepper or salt will be very good boiled on the fourth day, especially in winter.

I have reckoned upon a medium that a child just born will 11 weigh twelve pounds, and in a solar year if tolerably nursed increaseth to twenty-eight pounds.

I grant this food will be somewhat dear, and therefore very 12 proper for landlords, who, as they have already devoured most of the parents, seem to have the best title to the children.

Infant's flesh will be in season throughout the year, but more 13 plentiful in March, and a little before and after. For we are told by a grave author, an eminent French physician, that fish being a prolific diet, there are more children born in Roman Catholic countries about nine months after Lent than at any other season: therefore, reckoning a year after Lent, the markets will be more glutted than usual, because the number of popish infants is at least three to one in this kingdom; and therefore it will have one other collateral advantage, by lessening the number of Papists among us.

I have already computed the charge of nursing a beggar's 14 child (in which list I reckon all cottagers, laborers, and four fifths of the farmers) to be about two shillings per annum, rags included: and I believe no gentleman would repine to give ten shillings for the carcass of a good fat child, which, as I have said, will make four dishes of excellent nutritive meat, when he hath only some particular friend or his own family to dine with him. Thus the squire will learn to be a good landlord, and grow popular among the tenants; the mother will have eight shillings net profit, and be fit for work till she produces another child.

Those who are more thrifty (as I must confess the times 15 require) may flay the carcass; the skin of which artificially dressed will make admirable gloves for ladies, and summer boots for fine gentlemen.

As to our city of Dublin, shambles may be appointed for this 16 purpose in the most convenient parts of it, and butchers we may be assured will not be wanting; although I rather recommend buying the children alive, and dressing them hot from the knife as we do roasting pigs.

A very worthy person, a true lover of his country, and whose 17 virtues I highly esteem, was lately pleased in discoursing on this matter to offer a refinement upon my scheme. He said that many gentlemen of this kingdom, having of late destroyed their deer, he conceived that the want of venison might be well supplied by the bodies of young lads and maidens, not exceeding fourteen years of age nor under twelve, so great a number of both sexes in every county being now ready to starve for want of work and service; and these to be disposed of by their parents, if alive, or otherwise by their

JONATHAN SWIFT 5

nearest relations. But with due deference to so excellent a friend and so deserving a patriot, I cannot be altogether in his sentiments; for as to the males, my American acquaintance assured me from frequent experience that their flesh was generally tough and lean, like that of our schoolboys, by continual exercise, and their taste disagreeable; and to fatten them would not answer the charge. Then as to the females, it would, I think with humble submission, be a loss to the public, because they soon would become breeders themselves: and besides, it is not improbable that some scrupulous people might be apt to censure such a practice (although indeed very unjustly) as a little bordering upon cruelty; which, I confess, hath always been with me the strongest objection against any project, how well soever intended.

18 But in order to justify my friend, he confessed that this expedient was put into his head by the famous Psalmanazar, a native of the island Formosa, who came from thence to London above twenty years ago, and in conversation told my friend that in his country when any young person happened to be put to death, the executioner sold the carcass to persons of quality as a prime dainty; and that in his time the body of a plump girl of fifteen, who was crucified for an attempt to poison the emperor, was sold to his Imperial Majesty's prime minister of state, and other great mandarins of the court, in joints from the gibbet, at four hundred crowns. Neither indeed can I deny that if the same use were made of several plump young girls in this town, who without one single groat to their fortunes cannot stir abroad without a chair, and appear at the playhouse and assemblies in foreign fineries which they never will pay for, the kingdom would not be the worse.

19 Some persons of a desponding spirit are in great concern about that vast number of poor people who are aged, diseased, or maimed, and I have been desired to employ my thoughts what course may be taken to ease the nation of so grievous an encumbrance. But I am not in the least pain upon that matter, because it is very well known that they are every day dying and rotting by cold and famine, and filth and vermin, as fast as can be reasonably expected. And as to the younger laborers, they are now in almost as hopeful a condition. They cannot get work, and consequently pine away for want of nourishment to a degree that if at any time they are accidentally hired to common labor, they have not strength to perform it; and thus the country and themselves are happily delivered from the evils to come.

20 I have too long digressed, and therefore shall return to my subject. I think the advantages by the proposal which I have made are obvious and many, as well as of the highest importance.

21 For first, as I have already observed, it would greatly lessen the number of Papists, with whom we are yearly overrun, being the

principal breeders of the nation as well as our most dangerous enemies; and who stay at home on purpose to deliver the kingdom to the Pretender, hoping to take their advantage by the absence of so many good Protestants, who have chosen rather to leave their country than to stay at home and pay tithes against their conscience to an Episcopal curate.

22   Secondly, the poorer tenants will have something valuable of their own, which by law may be made liable to distress, and help to pay their landlord's rent, their corn and cattle being already seized and money a thing unknown.

23   Thirdly, whereas the maintenance of an hundred thousand children, from two years old and upwards, cannot be computed at less than ten shillings a piece per annum, the nation's stock will be thereby increased fifty thousand pounds per annum, besides the profit of a new dish introduced to the tables of all gentlemen of fortune in the kingdom who have any refinement in taste. And the money will circulate among ourselves, the goods being entirely of our own growth and manufacture.

24   Fourthly, the constant breeders, besides the gain of eight shillings sterling per annum by the sale of their children, will be rid of the charge of maintaining them after the first year.

25   Fifthly, this food would likewise bring great custom to taverns, where the vinters will certainly be so prudent as to procure the best receipts for dressing it to perfection, and consequently have their houses frequented by all the fine gentlemen, who justly value themselves upon their knowledge in good eating; and a skillful cook, who understands how to oblige his guests, will contrive to make it as expensive as they please.

26   Sixthly, this would be a great inducement to marriage, which all wise nations have either encouraged by rewards or enforced by laws and penalties. It would increase the care and tenderness of mothers toward their children, when they were sure of a settlement for life to the poor babes, provided in some sort by the public, to their annual profit instead of expense. We should see an honest emulation among the married women, which of them could bring the fattest child to the market. Men would become as fond of their wives during the time of their pregnancy as they are now of their mares in foal, their cows in calf, or sows when they are ready to farrow; nor offer to beat or kick them (as is too frequent a practice) for fear of a miscarriage.

27   Many other advantages might be enumerated. For instance, the addition of some thousand carcasses in our exportation of barreled beef, the propagation of swine's flesh, and improvement in the art of making good bacon, so much wanted among us by the great destruction of pigs, too frequent at our tables, which are no way

comparable in taste or magnificence to a well-grown, fat yearling child, which roasted whole will make a considerable figure at a lord mayor's feast or any other public entertainment. But this and many others I omit, being studious of brevity.

Supposing that one thousand families in this city would be 28 constant customers for infants' flesh, besides others who might have it at merry meetings, particularly weddings and christenings, I compute that Dublin would take off annually about twenty thousand carcasses, and the rest of the kingdom (where probably they will be sold somewhat cheaper) the remaining eighty thousand.

I can think of no one objection that will possibly be raised 29 against this proposal, unless it should be urged that the number of people will be thereby much lessened in the kingdom. This I freely own, and it was indeed one principal design in offering it to the world. I desire the reader will observe, that I calculate my remedy for this one individual kingdom of Ireland and for no other that ever was, is, or I think ever can be upon earth. Therefore let no man talk to me of other expedients: of taxing our absentees at five shillings a pound: of using neither clothes nor household furniture except what is of our own growth and manufacture: of utterly rejecting the materials and instruments that promote foreign luxury: of curing the expensiveness of pride, vanity, idleness, and gaming in our women: of introducing a vein of parsimony, prudence, and temperance: of learning to love our country, in the want of which we differ even from Laplanders and the inhabitants of Topinamboo: of quitting our animosities and factions, nor acting any longer like the Jews, who were murdering one another at the very moment their city was taken: of being a little cautious not to sell our country and conscience for nothing: of teaching landlords to have at least one degree of mercy toward their tenants: lastly, of putting a spirit of honesty, industry, and skill into our shopkeepers; who, if a resolution could be now taken to buy only our native goods, would immediately unite to cheat and exact upon us in the price, the measure and the goodness, nor could ever yet be brought to make one fair proposal of just dealing, though often and earnestly invited to it.

Therefore I repeat, let no man talk to me of these and the like 30 expedients, till he hath at least some glimpse of hope that there will ever be some hearty and sincere attempt to put them in practice.

But as to myself, having been wearied out for many years 31 with offering vain, idle, visionary thoughts, and at length utterly despairing of success, I fortunately fell upon this proposal, which, as it is wholly new, so it hath something solid and real, of no expense and little trouble, full in our own power, and whereby we can incur no danger in disobliging England. For this kind of commodity will not bear exportation, the flesh being of too tender a consistence to admit a long continuance in salt, although perhaps I could name a country which would be glad to eat up our whole nation without it.

After all, I am not so violently bent upon my own opinion as to reject any offer proposed by wise men, which shall be found equally innocent, cheap, easy, and effectual. But before something of that kind shall be advanced in contradiction to my scheme, and offering a better, I desire the author or authors will be pleased maturely to consider two points. First, as things now stand, how they will be able to find food and raiment for an hundred thousand useless mouths and backs. And secondly, there being a round million of creatures in human figure throughout this kingdom, whose sole subsistence put into a common stock would leave them in debt two millions of pounds sterling, adding those who are beggars by profession to the bulk of farmers, cottagers, and laborers, with their wives and children who are beggars in effect; I desire those politicians who dislike my overture, and may perhaps be so bold to attempt an answer, that they will first ask the parents of these mortals whether they would not at this day think it a great happiness to have been sold for food at a year old in the manner I prescribe, and thereby have avoided such a perpetual scene of misfortunes as they have since gone through by the oppression of landlords, the impossibility of paying rent without money or trade, the want of common sustenance, with neither house nor clothes to cover them from the inclemencies of the weather, and the most inevitable prospect of entailing the like or greater miseries upon their breed forever. 32

I profess, in the sincerity of my heart, that I have not the least personal interest in endeavoring to promote this necessary work, having no other motive than the public good of my country, by advancing our trade, providing for infants, relieving the poor, and giving some pleasure to the rich. I have no children by which I can propose to get a single penny; the youngest being nine years old, and my wife past childbearing. 33

QUESTIONS

1. Describe the persona in this essay. How is the unusual narrative personality (as distinguished from Swift's personality) revealed by the author in degrees? How can we tell that the speaker's opinions are not shared by Swift?

2. What are the major propositions behind Swift's modest proposal? What are the minor propositions?

3. Explain the importance of the word *modest* in the title.

JONATHAN SWIFT

4. What is the effect of Swift's persistent reference to people as "breeders," "dams," "carcass," and the like? Why does he define children in economic terms? Find other words that contribute to this motif.

5. Analyze the purpose of the relatively long introduction consisting of paragraphs 1 to 7. How does Swift establish his ironic-satiric tone in this initial section?

6. What contrasts and discrepancies are at the heart of Swift's ironic statement in paragraphs 9 and 10? Explain both the subtlety and savagery of the satire in paragraph 12.

7. Paragraphs 13 to 20 develop six advantages of Swift's proposal, while paragraphs 24 to 26 list them in enumerative manner. Analyze the progression of these propositions. What is the effect of the listing? Why is Swift parodying argumentative techniques?

8. How does the author both sustain and suspend the irony in paragraph 29? How is the strategy repeated in paragraph 32? How does the concluding paragraph cap his satiric commentary on human nature?

9. Discuss Swift's social, political, religious, and economic views as they are revealed in the essay.

10. a. Write a modest proposal, advancing an absurd proposition through various argumentative techniques.
b. Write an analysis of the ironic-satiric structure of Swift's essay.

RUTH BENEDICT

Are Families Passé?

Ruth Benedict (1887–1948), an anthropologist and educator, began her career as a poet. Later, she studied anthropology under Franz Boas and succeeded him as chairman of the department of anthropology at Columbia University (1936–1939). In 1934, she wrote *Patterns of Culture;* in 1940 *Race: Science and Politics.* In her work, Benedict attempted to study anthropology through sociology, psychology, and philosophy. The following essay illustrates her ability to work in an interdisciplinary manner in order to illuminate a core American institution.

 ARE FAMILIES PASSÉ?

A great many people today speak as if the family were in some special sort of danger in our times. We hear a great deal about "saving the family" and about "preserving the home." Authors and lecturers describe how the family is threatened by divorce, or by mothers who work outside of the home, or by unemployment, or by lack of religious training of children. Each of them, depending on his experience in his own home and on his observations in the families he knows, selects something which he thinks should be changed—or should be preserved—and says that, if this or that were done, the family would be "saved."

To an anthropologist such phrasings are dangerously misleading. He has studied the family among naked savages and in contemporary civilizations and he knows that it has survived in all human societies known in the record of mankind. Just as surely he knows that the family takes all kinds of different forms. It is not merely that unlettered primitive nomads have family arrangements different from Western industrial nations; even in Western nations around the Atlantic shores the family differs profoundly. The ethics of marriage, the specific close emotional ties which the family fosters, the disciplines and freedoms for the child, the nature of the dependency of the children upon the parents, even the personnel which makes up the family—all these differ in Western civilized nations. The anthropologist knows that the changes taking place in the home in any decade in any country do not mean that the family is now about to disintegrate under our eyes unless we do something about it. The problem as he states it is quite different: how do legal and customary arrangements in the family tally with the arrangements and premises of the whole way of life which is valued in any tribe or nation? If, for instance, the father has a heavy, authoritarian hand upon his children, the anthropologist asks: Is this in keeping with authoritarianism in the state and in industry? Or is it at odds with a society which values non-authoritarianism and the pursuit of happiness? He asks the same kind of question about a nation's laws of inheritance from father to son, about the divorce laws, about the architectural layout of the house, about the reasons that are given to children when they are told to be good.

Customs enshrined in the family in any tribe or nation are likely to be sensitively adjusted to the values and customs of each particular people. This is no mystic correspondence; the persons who make up the family are the same people who are the citizens of that nation—the business men, the farmers, the churchgoers or non-churchgoers, the readers of newspapers, and the listeners to the radio. In all their roles they are molded more or less surely into a people with certain habits, certain hopes, and a certain *espirit de corps*. Americans come to share certain slogans, behavior, and judgments

RUTH BENEDICT

which differ from those of Frenchmen or Czechs. This is inevitable. And in the process the role of the family also becomes different. By the same token, just as economic and political changes occur over a period of time in the United States or in France or in Czechoslovakia, the family also changes.

An anthropologist, therefore, when he reads about the failure 4 of the family, finds in such criticism a somewhat special meaning. He remembers how often the family is made a convenient whipping boy among many peoples who disapprove of the way their world is going. He has seen it in Amazon jungles and on the islands of the Pacific. The author remembers an American Indian tribe which used to talk about the family in a most uncomplimentary fashion. They were a people who, not long before, had roamed over the great plains hunting buffalo and proving their courage by war exploits. Now they lived on a reservation, and tending crops was no adequate substitute for their old way of life. Their old economic arrangements of boastful gift giving, their political life, and their religious practices haid either been destroyed by circumstances or had lost their old meaningfulness. Life had become pointless to them. These men talked with gusto about the failure of the family. They said that in the family the children no longer learned manners, or religion, or generosity, or whatever it was the individual Indian favored as a cure-all. The family, too, weighed a man down, they said; it was a burden to him.

To the anthropologist studying this tribe, however, the family 5 was precisely the best arranged, most trustworthy institution in their whole culture. It was hard beset and it had not escaped the tragic effects of the general disintegration of tribal life, but it was what provided the warm, human ties and the dependable security which were left in that Indian tribe. The children were loved and cared for, the husbands and wives often had comfortable relations with each other, and family hospitality had a graciousness that was absent in more public life. At birth and marriage and death the family still functioned as an effective institution. And there seemed to be no man or woman of childbearing age who was not married or would not have preferred to be.

The writer thinks of this Indian tribe when she hears 6 Americans talk about the decay of the family. Instead of viewing the family with such alarm, suppose we look at it as it exists in this decade in this country and see how it is arranged to fulfill its functions in American schemes of life. Let us leave aside for the moment the questions of whether conditions are provided that would keep it from preventable overstrain and of whether as human beings we are able to get all the satisfaction we might out of this institution; let us consider only the arrangements of the family as we know it and how these fit in with our values and with the way we should like to plan our lives.

Suppose we take marriage first. Marriage sets up the new family, and it seems to make a great deal of difference whether a society dictates that the new home shall be begun in tears and heartache or with rejoicing. Many human societies would not recognize a marriage without a wailing bride and a sullen groom. Often the bride has to be surrounded by her mourning women, who lament her coming lifelong separation from her parents and her brothers and sisters, as well as her future misery as she goes to work for her mother-in-law. Often they cut her long hair and remove her jewelry as a sign that she is now a worker and no longer alluring. The groom's role, too, may be that of an unwilling victim. Often marriages are arranged by the parents without giving the two young people any chance to know each other. 7

All these circumstances are absent in marriage in the United States. The young people are hardly hampered in their choice of a mate; if occasionally parents deplore their choice, public opinion allows the young couple to outface them and expects the parents to accept the inevitable with as much decency as they can muster. We expect that the bride and groom will be in love or will have chosen each other for reasons known to themselves. Whether they marry for love or for money or to show they can win a sought-after mate from a rival, in any case they are making a personal choice and are not acting on command. Because in every field of life American culture puts such a high value on this kind of freedom and so bitterly resents its curtailment in peace time, the fact that young people do make their own choice of a mate is an important and auspicious arrangement. The arranged marriage which is traditional in France or the careful class restrictions which have been observed in Holland would be difficult to manage in the United States. The wide range of choice of a mate and the fact that the young people make their own selection are conditions which could hardly be made more satisfactory for Americans with their particular habits and demands. 8

After marriage, too, the new family has a wide range of choices about where to live, how the wife shall occupy herself, when to start a family, and a host of other important matters. Such freedom is extremely unusual in the world. Sometimes the couple must live with the husband's family, sometimes with the wife's. Often in other countries, until one or two children are born, the young man continues to work for his father and has no say about the farm or the flock and no money which he can control. But in the United States a young couple plans the family budget before the wedding and what they earn is theirs to spend. 9

The way the new family in this country sets up its own 10

separate home makes possible a rare and delightful circumstance: the two of them can have an incomparable privacy. No matter how hard it has been to arrange for privacy before marriage, as soon as the wedding is over everybody expects them to have their own latch key and their own possessions around them. If they cannot manage this, they feel cheated and other people think something is wrong. It is the same if they have to give a home to a parent. In most civilized countries this is a duty to which as a good son and good daughter they are bound, but if it is necessary in the United States their friends and neighbors will regard them as exceptionally burdened. Even the scarcity and high wages of domestic servants give the young family a greater privacy. Considering that they have chosen each other to their own liking, this privacy in the home is made to order to gratify them; the only problem is whether they can use it to their own happiness.

When they cannot, and when they find that their choice of a 11
mate was not fool-proof just because they made it on their own, there is in the United States great freedom to get a divorce. Our growing divorce rate is the subject of much viewing-with-alarm; yet in a culture built as ours is on ever expanding personal choice, an important goal of which is the pursuit of happiness, the right to terminate an unhappy marriage is the other side of the coin of which the fair side is the right to choose one's spouse. Weak and stunted individuals will of course abuse both privileges, yet it is difficult to see how divorce could consistently be denied in a culture like ours. Certainly if we accepted it more honestly as a necessary phase of our way of life, however sorrowful, and put honest effort and sympathy into not penalizing the divorced, we should be acting more appropriately and in our own best interests. At any rate, the high divorce rate in the United States is no attack on marriage, for it is precisely the divorced—those who have failed in one or two attempts—who have the highest rate of marriage. Between the ages of twenty-five and thirty-five not even the unmarried or the widowed marry at so great a rate as the divorced.

Besides free choice and privacy, the American family has 12
unusual potential leisure because of the labor-saving devices, prepared foods, and ready-made clothes available under modern conditions. The basic labor-saver is running water in the sink, and Americans have little idea how many millions of homes in civilized countries do not have it. Thus we are saved an endless round of drudgery that ties down women—and men also—in countries where homes have no running water, no gas and electricity, no farm tools but those which are driven into the earth by human hands or are swung in human arms, and no use of ready-made soaps and foods and clothes. Americans put high value on lessened drudgery, but they deprecate having free spaces of truly leisure time; the more time

they save the more they fill up their days and nights with a round of engagements and complications. They are unwilling to admit that they have leisure, but the schedules of their lives prove clearly how much they have.

Universal schooling in the United States also frees the family 13 of many duties when children have come. It is hard for Americans to imagine the difference which regular school hours make in a mother's role. For a great part of the working day, American children are in the responsibility of the teacher and not of the mother. As nursery schools spread over the country, younger and younger children get trained care outside the home and the mother's labors are correspondingly relieved. As the children grow older the mother's leisure increases until finally she reaches that idle middle age with its round of card parties and clubs and window shopping and movies which engross and waste the energy of so many millions of American women. Her husband is earning more money now than when he was younger, and her children have flown; she has a plethora of privileges and freedom and leisure. In one sense she has everything.

It is obviously unfair to talk about the incomparable freedom 14 from drudgery which the American home offers without emphasizing that interval of a few years when there is no leisure for the mother in the home—the years when the babies are little. In our great cities where each family is strange to all the others, a mother is likely to have to be baby tender every hour of the day, with no one to relieve her. Along with these duties she must do all her cooking and washing and cleaning. And, as all our magazines and women's pages reiterate, she must make efforts to keep her husband. She must keep herself looking attractive, must keep up social contacts, and be a companion to him. To European wives this program looks formidable. "I was always told that American women were so free," a Polish woman said to me, "but when I came here and saw how they had to manage with the babies and the house without any older women of the family to help, and then how they had to play around with their husbands in the evening to keep them happy, I decided I wouldn't change places with them for anything. In Poland a woman doesn't have to 'keep' her husband; it's all settled when they're married."

The striking fact about the nursery years in the United States 15 is that in comparison with those in other countries they are so short and that nevertheless we do not really treat them as an interim. Mothers who are going through this period give remarkably little thought to the leisure that will come soon. They are often vocal enough about the turmoil of their present lives, and sometimes bitter, but the fact that the nursery years last so short a time in the United States and could be treated as an interim—like a professor's going into the government during war time—is all too seldom part of their

RUTH BENEDICT

thinking. No doubt this is due in part to a lag in our culture, since even with our grandparents conditions were different; but in part it is a result of the sentiment which selects this period, no matter how short, as the fulfillment of a woman's chief duty in life. A social engineer looking at the family, however, would certainly put his major effort into better arrangements for the overburdened mother during these years and into thinking about effecting some transition from this period into that next one during which, in the United States, millions of women become idle parasites upon society—and dull and unhappy into the bargain.

Another notable feature of the American family is its peculiar- 16 ly non-authoritarian character. The old rules that a child should be seen and not heard and the adage, "Spare the rod and spoil the child," are anachronistic in the United States; they are dispensed with even in immigrant groups which honored them in their native country. The rule of the father over the family is still a reality in some European nations, but in the United States the mother is the chief responsible agent in bringing up her children; here the father's opinions are something the children are more likely to play off against the mother's, to their own advantage, rather than a court of last authority from which there is no appeal. Children take the noisy center of the stage at the breakfast table and in the living room in a way that is quite impossible in European countries. The fact that they are expected to know right from wrong in their tenderest years and to act upon it on their own is often commented on by European mothers who have lived here. A Dutch mother once spoke to the author about how hard we are on our children because we expect this of them; she said "I don't expect it of my children before they are seven; until then, I am there to see that they act correctly." But an American mother expects a child of three or four to be a responsible moral agent, and she gives him great latitude in which to prove that he can manage his little affairs by himself.

All this lack of strong authoritarianism in American families 17 accords well with the values that are chiefly sought after in this country. No strong father image is compatible with our politics or our economics. We seek the opportunity to prove that we are as good as the next person, and we do not find comfort in following an authoritarian voice—in the state or in the home, from the landowner or the priest—which will issue a command from on high. We learn as children to measure ourselves against Johnny next door, or against Mildred whose mother our mother knows in church, and this prepares us for living in a society with strongly egalitarian ideals. We do not learn the necessity of submitting to unquestioned commands as the children of many countries do. The family in the United States has become democratic.

 ARE FAMILIES PASSÉ?

These free-choice and non-authoritarian aspects of the fami- 18
ly, along with its privacy and potential leisure, evidence only a few of
the many ways in which it has become consistent with major
emphases in our national life. They seem, when one compares them
with arrangements of other civilized nations, to be quite well fitted to
the role the family must play in a culture like the United States. This
does not mean, however, that Americans capitalize to their own
advantage upon all these consistently contrived arrangements which
are institutionalized in the family as we know it. At the beginning of
this essay two subjects were left for later discussion—how well our
society protects the family from dangerous overstrain, and how well
as human beings with special insights and blind spots we are able to
get all the satisfactions we might out of our version of the home.
These two subjects cannot be omitted.

In spite of all our American sentiment about the home and 19
the family, we do not show great concern about buttressing it against
catastrophe. Any well-considered national program must have regard
for the children; if they are housed and fed below a certain minimum,
if their health is not attended to, the nation suffers in the next
generation. The lack of a tolerable economic floor under the family is
especially crucial in a society like that of the United States, where
competition is so thoroughly relied upon as an incentive and where
so few families have anything but the weekly pay envelope to use for
food and doctors' bills. When factories close, when inflation comes,
the family gets little consideration in the United States. Especially in
economic crises it gets the little end of the horn. Today the necessity
of providing tens of thousands of new homes is of the greatest
importance for healthy family life in the United States, but adequate
housing programs are notoriously unsupported. Sickness insurance,
too, which would provide preventive care as well as relieve the family
budget of all expenses in a crisis, needs high priority in a national
program. When one reads about families in trouble, it is clear that
many of the reefs which are threatening shipwreck are avoidable by
intelligent local, state, or national programs. Such programs have
worked satisfactorily in non-communist countries—as, for instance,
in the Scandinavian nations. But they cost money, and Americans
have not been willing to be taxed for the sake of taking the excessive
strain off the family and providing better circumstances for growing
children. It could be done, and if it were done the incidental
disadvantages of our highly competitive and unregulated economic
system would be largely removed; it should be the surest way to
ensure the successful continuance of what is known as the democratic
way of life.

Besides this American political attitude toward the family, 20
there is also a very different difficulty which threatens it. We have

seen how as an institution it is particularly tailored to American ways of living. But the very best suit of clothes may be badly worn by a careless and irresponsible person. So, too, people may abuse a home well designed to suit them. It is no less true of marriage and the family. These exist as institutions remarkably well adjusted to American life. But many Americans are miserably unable to achieve happiness within them.

It is of course easy to say that a culture like that of the United States, which allows individuals so much free choice among alternatives, is asking a great deal of human beings. In social life, as in literature, some of the finest human achievements have been within restrictions as rigid as those of the sonnet form. Our American culture is more like a sprawling novel where every page may deal with a new encounter and with a special choice. We ask a great deal of individuals when we give them such wide latitude and so little respected authority. But the United States is built on the premise that this is possible, and if ever we as a people decide otherwise our nation will change beyond recognition. We shall have lost the very thing we have been trying to build in this country. 21

It must not be imagined that this craving for individual freedom is what prevents Americans from enjoying the family as much as it might be enjoyed. In so far as the family is an overheavy economic burden on some wage earners, a more careful welfare program could take care of this complaint. Certainly women and children have a freedom in the American family which is hard to match elsewhere in the world, and from all portents this will probably increase rather than diminish. 22

The crucial difficulty in American happiness in marriage is, rather, a certain blind spot which is especially fostered in our privileged United States. An extreme instance of this was mentioned in connection with the millions of idle, middle-aged wives in this country. These are women who as a group are well set up and favored beyond any such great numbers of women in any other part of the world. But privilege to them is separate from responsibility. Comparatively few of them feel that it is compatible with their status to do responsible work in which they have had experience in their own households and which must now be done outside their homes, and few take the initiative in getting the training they would need in jobs which they can see need to be done—except in war time. In periods of peace they have a blind spot about what it takes to live happily. For that the motto is *Noblesse oblige,* or "Privilege obligates one to do something in return." 23

It is not only the middle-aged woman who accepts privilege without a sense of obligation. In marriage, the right of both men and women to choose their mates freely is a privilege which carries with 24 it, if they are to live happily, an accompanying conviction that when things go wrong it is doubly their obligation—to themselves as well as to their spouse—to deal tolerantly. Perhaps a young man realizes that his wife is more petulant than he knew; exactly because he chose her, however, she is "a poor thing; but his own." Privileged as he was to choose her, he has a corresponding responsibility.

It is the same with children. In the United States the reason 25 for having children is not, as it is in most of the world, the perpetuation of the family line down many generations. In most countries people have children because there must be someone to till the piece of land in the village where the family has lived for centuries, there must be an heir to inherit the *Hof,* or there must be a son to perform the ancestral rites. In our atomistic American families these motivations seldom arise. We have children, not because our parents are sitting in judgment, not because of the necessity of having an heir, but because we personally want them—whether as company in the home or to show our friends we can have them. It is a privileged phase of parenthood, and if it is to bring us happiness it implies an acceptance of responsibility. Nothing is all pleasure in this life, and bringing up two or three noisy children in our small urban apartments is no exception to the rule. But with us it is based on choice—far more than it is elsewhere in the world—and we can only make the most of a choice if we follow it through wholeheartedly in all its implications.

It is partly because of this blind spot in the American family, 26 this walling off of privilege from responsibility and tolerance, that we so often ask of life an average happiness—as if it could be presented to us on a platter. Full normal happiness only comes to men and women who give as well as take—who, in this instance, give themselves warmly to their family life, and do not merely arrogate to themselves the rights they are so freely allowed in our society. In the United States, if happiness proves impossible they can get a divorce, but, until they have made this decision, they can capitalize on their privileges only if they bind around their arms the motto "Privilege has its obligations."

The family in the United States is an institution remarkably 27 adapted to our treasured way of life. The changes that are occurring in it do not mean that it is decaying and needs to be saved. It offers a long array of privileges. It needs more consideration in political tax-supported programs, by means of which many difficulties that beset it could be eradicated. Finally, Americans, in order to get the maximum happiness out of such a free institution as the family in the United States, need to parallel their privileges with an awakening responsibility. It is hard to live up to being so privileged as we are in the United States, but it is not impossible.

QUESTIONS

1. Why is the anthropological perspective established by Benedict at the outset of the essay important to our understanding of the selection?

2. List the "notable features" about the American family that the author analyzes.

3. How does the writer achieve an informal yet reflective style in presenting her materials?

4. Define the following foreign words used by the author: *esprit de corps* (paragraph 3); *noblesse oblige* (paragraph 23); *Hof* (paragraph 25). Do they conflict with the intent of a popular essay?

5. What rhetorical strategies does Benedict employ in the introductory section, paragraphs 1 to 5? What is the function of paragraph 6? What other paragraph in the essay has a similar function?

6. How does the author's use of comparison and contrast throughout paragraphs 7 to 18 advance her thesis? What are the main comparative topics?

7. Analyze Benedict's presentation of illustration to develop the thesis. What is the unifying principle behind these illustrations? How are they ordered?

8. Explain the techniques in the development of the concluding paragraph.

9. Benedict wrote this essay in 1948. Do any of her observations require reconsideration today? What assumptions does the author make about "our treasured way of life"? Do you agree or disagree with her assumptions? Why?

10. Write an analysis of the relative strength or weakness of the American family today.

BARBARA TUCHMAN

An Inquiry into the Persistence of Unwisdom in Government

Barbara Tuchman (1912–   ), an eminent American historian, twice winner of the Pulitzer Prize, began her career as a research assistant for the Institute of Pacific Relations in 1933. She was a staff writer and correspondent for the *Nation,* covering the Spanish Civil War from 1935 to 1937. Tuchman gained her first significant literary recognition for *The Zimmerman Telegram* (1958); she followed this initial success with *The Guns of August* (1962), *The Proud Tower* (1966), and *Stilwell and the American Experience in China, 1911–45* (1971). This article offers a wide-ranging historical assessment of the causes of failure, mediocrity, and unwisdom in political life.

A problem that strikes one in the study of history, regardless of period, is why man makes a poorer performance of government than of almost any other human activity. In this sphere, wisdom—meaning judgment acting on experience, common sense, available knowledge, and a decent appreciation of probability—is less operative and more frustrated than it should be. Why do men in high office so often act contrary to the way that reason points and enlightened self-interest suggests? Why does intelligent mental process so often seem to be paralyzed?

Why, to begin at the beginning, did the Trojan authorities drag that suspicious-looking wooden horse inside their gates? Why did successive ministries of George III—that "bundle of imbecility," as Dr. Johnson called them collectively—insist on coercing rather than conciliating the Colonies though strongly advised otherwise by many counselors? Why did Napoleon and Hitler invade Russia? Why did the kaiser's government resume unrestricted submarine warfare in 1917 although explicitly warned that this would bring in the United States and that American belligerency would mean Germany's defeat? Why did Chiang Kai-shek refuse to heed any voice of reform or alarm until he woke up to find that his country had slid from under him? Why did Lyndon Johnson, seconded by the best and the brightest, progressively involve this nation in a war both ruinous and halfhearted and from which nothing but bad for our side resulted? Why does the present Administration continue to avoid introducing effective measures to reduce the wasteful consumption of oil while members of OPEC follow a price policy that must bankrupt their customers? How is it possible that the Central Intelligence Agency, whose function it is to provide, at taxpayers' expense, the information necessary to conduct a realistic foreign policy, could remain unaware that discontent in a country crucial to our interests was boiling up to the point of insurrection and overthrow of the ruler upon whom our policy rested? It has been reported that the CIA was ordered *not* to investigate the opposition to the shah of Iran in order to spare him any indication that we took it seriously, but since this sounds more like the theater of the absurd than like responsible government, I cannot bring myself to believe it.

There was a king of Spain once, Philip III, who is said to have 3 died of a fever he contracted from sitting too long near a hot brazier, helplessly overheating himself because the functionary whose duty it was to remove the brazier when summoned could not be found. In the late twentieth century, it begins to appear as if mankind may be approaching a similar stage of suicidal incompetence. The Italians have been sitting in Philip III's hot seat for some time. The British trade unions, in a lunatic spectacle, seem periodically bent on dragging their country toward paralysis, apparently under the impression that they are separate from the whole. Taiwan was thrown into a state of shock by the United States' recognition of the People's Republic of China because, according to one report, in the seven years since the Shanghai Communiqué, the Kuomintang rulers of Taiwan had "refused to accept the new trend as a reality."

Wooden-headedness is a factor that plays a remarkably large 4 role in government. Wooden-headedness consists of assessing a situation in terms of preconceived, fixed notions while ignoring or rejecting any contrary signs. It is acting according to wish while not allowing oneself to be confused by the facts.

A classic case was the French war plan of 1914, which 5 concentrated everything on a French offensive to the Rhine, leaving the French left flank from Belgium to the Channel virtually unguarded. This strategy was based on the belief that the Germans would not use reserves in the front line and, without them, could not deploy enough manpower to extend their invasion through the French left. Reports by intelligence agents in 1913 to the effect that the Germans were indeed preparing their reserves for the front line in case of war were resolutely ignored because the governing spirits in France, dreaming only of their own offensive, did not want to believe in any signals that would require them to strengthen their left at the expense of their march to the Rhine. In the event, the Germans could and did extend themselves around the French left with results that determined a long war and its fearful consequences for our century.

Wooden-headedness is also the refusal to learn from experi- 6 ence, a form in which fourteenth-century rulers were supreme. No matter how often and obviously devaluation of the currency disrupted the economy and angered the people, French monarchs continued to resort to it whenever they were desperate for cash until they provoked insurrection among the bourgeoisie. No matter how often a campaign that depended on living off a hostile country ran into want and even starvation, campaigns for which this fate was inevitable were regularly undertaken.

Still another form is identification of self with the state, as   7
currently exhibited by the ayatollah Khomeini. No wooden-
headedness is so impenetrable as that of a religious zealot. Because he
is connected with a private wire to the Almighty, no idea coming in
on a lesser channel can reach him, which leaves him ill equipped to
guide his country in its own best interests.

Philosophers of government ever since Plato have devoted   8
their thinking to the major issues of ethics, sovereignty, the social
contract, the rights of man, the corruption of power, the balance
between freedom and order. Few—except Machiavelli, who was
concerned with government as it is, not as it should be—bothered
with mere folly, although this has been a chronic and pervasive
problem. "Know, my son," said a dying Swedish statesman in the
seventeenth century, "with how little wisdom the world is governed." More recently, Woodrow Wilson warned, "In public affairs,
stupidity is more dangerous than knavery."

Stupidity is not related to type of regime; monarchy, oligar-   9
chy, and democracy produce it equally. Nor is it peculiar to nation or
class. The working class as represented by the Communist governments functions no more rationally or effectively in power than the
aristocracy or the bourgeoisie, as has notably been demonstrated in
recent history. Mao Tse-tung may be admired for many things, but
the Great Leap Forward, with a steel plant in every backyard, and the
Cultural Revolution were exercises in unwisdom that greatly dam-
aged China's progress and stability, not to mention the chairman's
reputation. The record of the Russian proletariat in power can hardly
be called enlightened, although after sixty years of control it must be
accorded a kind of brutal success. If the majority of Russians are
better off now than before, the cost in cruelty and tyranny has been
no less and probably greater than under the czars.

After the French Revolution, the new order was rescued only   10
by Bonaparte's military campaigns, which brought the spoils of
foreign wars to fill the treasury, and subsequently by his competence
as an executive. He chose officials not on the basis of origin or
ideology but on the principle of "la carrière ouverte aux talents"—the
said talents being intelligence, energy, industry, and obedience. That
worked until the day of his own fatal mistake.

I do not wish to give the impression that men in office are   11
incapable of governing wisely and well. Occasionally, the exception
appears, rising in heroic size above the rest, a tower visible down the
centuries. Greece had her Pericles, who ruled with authority, moderation, sound judgment, and a certain nobility that imposes natural
dominion over others. Rome had Caesar, a man of remarkable
governing talents, although it must be said that a ruler who arouses

opponents to resort to assassination is probably not as smart as he ought to be. Later, under Marcus Aurelius and the other Antonines, Roman citizens enjoyed good government, prosperity, and respect for about a century. Charlemagne was able to impose order upon a mass of contending elements, to foster the arts of civilization no less than those of war, and to earn a prestige supreme in the Middle Ages—probably not equaled in the eyes of contemporaries until the appearance of George Washington.

Possessor of an inner strength and perseverance that enabled   12
him to prevail over a sea of obstacles, Washington was one of those critical figures but for whom history might well have taken a different course. He made possible the physical victory of American indepen-dence, while around him, in extraordinary fertility, political talent bloomed as if touched by some tropical sun. For all their flaws and quarrels, the Founding Fathers, who established our form of govern-ment, were, in the words of Arthur Schlesinger Sr., "the most remarkable generation of public men in the history of the United States or perhaps of any other nation." It is worth noting the qualities Schlesinger ascribes to them: They were fearless, high-principled, deeply versed in ancient and modern political thought, astute and pragmatic, unafraid of experiment, and—this is significant—"convinced of man's power to improve his condition through the use of intelligence." That was the mark of the Age of Reason that formed them, and though the eighteenth century had a tendency to regard men as more rational than they in fact were, it evoked the best in government from these men.

For our purposes, it would be invaluable if we could know   13
what produced this burst of talent from a base of only two million inhabitants. Schlesinger suggests some contributing factors: wide diffusion of education, challenging economic opportunities, social mobility, training in self-government—all these encouraged citizens to cultivate their political aptitudes to the utmost. Also, he adds, with the Church declining in prestige and with business, science, and art not yet offering competing fields of endeavor, statecraft remained almost the only outlet for men of energy and purpose. Perhaps the need of the moment—the opportunity to create a new political system—is what brought out the best.

Not before or since, I believe, has so much careful and   14
reasonable thinking been invested in the creation of a new political system. In the French, Russian, and Chinese revolutions, too much class hatred and bloodshed were involved to allow for fair results or permanent constitutions. The American experience was unique, and the system so far has always managed to right itself under pressure. In spite of accelerating incompetence, it still works better than most.

We haven't had to discard the system and try another after every crisis, as have Italy and Germany, Spain and France. The founders of the United States are a phenomenon to keep in mind to encourage our estimate of human possibilities, but their example, as a political scientist has pointed out, is "too infrequent to be taken as a basis for normal expectations."

15 The English are considered to have enjoyed reasonably benign government during the eighteenth and nineteenth centuries, except for their Irish subjects, debtors, child laborers, and other unfortunates in various pockets of oppression. The folly that lost the American colonies reappeared now and then, notably in the treatment of the Irish and the Boers, but a social system can survive a good deal of folly when circumstances are historically favorable or when it is cushioned by large resources, as in the heyday of the British Empire, or absorbed by sheer size, as in this country during our period of expansion. Today there are no more cushions, which makes folly less affordable.

16 Elsewhere than in government, man has accomplished marvels: invented the means in our time to leave the world and voyage to the moon; in the past, harnessed wind and electricity, raised earthbound stone into soaring cathedrals, woven silk brocades out of the spinnings of a worm, composed the music of Mozart and the dramas of Shakespeare, classified the forms of nature, penetrated the mysteries of genetics. Why is he so much less accomplished in government? What frustrates, in that sphere, the operation of the intellect? Isaac Bashevis Singer, discoursing as a Nobel laureate in mankind, offers the opinion that God had been frugal in bestowing intellect but lavish with passions and emotions. "He gave us," Singer says, "so many emotions and such strong ones that every human being, even if he is an idiot, is a millionaire in emotions."

17 I think Singer has made a point that applies to our inquiry. What frustrates the workings of intellect is the passions and the emotions: ambition, greed, fear, facesaving, the instinct to dominate, the needs of the ego, the whole bundle of personal vanities and anxieties.

18 Reason is crushed by these forces. If the Athenians out of pride and overconfidence had not set out to crush Sparta for good but had been content with moderate victory, their ultimate fall might have been averted. If fourteenth-century knights had not been obsessed by the idea of glory and personal prowess, they might have defeated the Turks at Nicopolis with incalculable consequence for all of Eastern Europe. If the English, 200 years ago, had heeded Chatham's knocking on the door of what he called "this sleeping and confounded Ministry" and his urgent advice to repeal the Coercive

Acts and withdraw the troops before the "inexpiable drop of blood is shed in an impious war with a people contending in the great cause of publick liberty" or, given a last chance, if they had heeded Edmund Burke's celebrated plea for conciliation and his warning that it would prove impossible to coerce a "fierce people" of their own pedigree, we might still be a united people bridging the Atlantic, with incalculable consequence for the history of the West. It did not happen that way, because king and Parliament felt it imperative to affirm sovereignty over arrogant colonials. The alternative choice, as in Athens and medieval Europe, was close to psychologically impossible.

In the case we know best—the American engagement in   19
Vietnam—fixed notions, preconceptions, wooden-headed thinking, and emotions accumulated into a monumental mistake and classic humiliation. The original idea was that the lesson of the failure to halt fascist aggression during the appeasement era dictated the necessity of halting the so-called aggression by North Vietnam, conceived to be the spearhead of international communism. This was applying the wrong model to the wrong facts, which would have been obvious if our policy makers had taken into consideration the history of the people on the spot instead of charging forward wearing the blinkers of the cold war.

The reality of Vietnamese nationalism, of which Ho Chi Minh   20
had been the standard-bearer since long before the war, was certainly no secret. Indeed, Franklin Roosevelt had insisted that the French should not be allowed to return after the war, a policy that we instantly abandoned the moment the Japanese were out: Ignoring the Vietnamese demand for self-government, we first assisted the return of the French, and then, when incredibly, they had been put to rout by the native forces, we took their place, as if Dien Bien Phu had no significance whatever. Policy founded upon error multiplies, never retreats. The pretense that North versus South Vietnam represented foreign aggression was intensified. If Asian specialists with knowledge of the situation suggested a reassessment, they were not persuasive. As a Communist aggressor, Hanoi was presumed to be a threat to the United States, yet the vital national interest at stake, which alone may have justified belligerency, was never clear enough to sustain a declaration of war.

A further, more fundamental, error confounded our policy.   21
This was the nature of the client. In war, as any military treatise or any soldier who has seen active service will tell you, it is essential to know the nature—that is, the capabilities *and* intentions—of the enemy and no less so of an ally who is the primary belligerent. We fatally underestimated the one and foolishly overestimated the other. Placing reliance on, or hope in, South Vietnam was an advanced case

of wooden-headedness. Improving on the Bourbons, who forgot nothing and learned nothing, our policy makers forgot everything and learned nothing. The oldest lesson in history is the futility and, often, fatality of foreign interference to maintain in power a government unwanted or hated at home. As far back as 500 B.C., Confucius stated, "Without the confidence of the people, no government can stand," and political philosophers have echoed him down through the ages. What else was the lesson of our vain support of Chiang Kai-shek, within such recent experience? A corrupt or oppressive government may be maintained by despotic means but not for long, as the English occupiers of France learned in the fifteenth century. The human spirit protests and generates a Joan of Arc, for people will not passively endure a government that is in fact unendurable.

The deeper we became involved in Vietnam during the Johnson era, the greater grew the self-deception, the lies, the false body counts, the cheating on Tonkin Gulf, the military mess, domestic dissent, and all those defensive emotions in which, as a result, our leaders became fixed. Their concern for personal ego, public image, and government status determined policy. Johnson was not going to be the first President to preside over defeat; generals could not admit failure nor civilian advisers risk their jobs by giving unpalatable advice. 22

Males, who so far in history have managed government are obsessed with potency, which is the reason, I suspect, why it is difficult for them to admit error. I have rarely known a man who, with a smile and a shrug, could easily acknowledge being wrong. Why not? *I* can, without any damage to self-respect. I can only suppose the difference is that deep in their psyches, men somehow equate being wrong with being impotent. For a Chief of State, it is almost out of the question, and especially so for Johnson and Nixon, who both seem to me to have had shaky self-images. Johnson's showed in his deliberate coarseness and compulsion to humiliate others in crude physical ways. No self-confident man would have needed to do that. Nixon was a bundle of inferiorities and sense of persecution. I do not pretend to be a psychohistorian, but in pursuit of this inquiry, the psychological factors must be taken into account. Having no special knowledge of Johnson and Nixon, I will not pursue the question other than to say that it was our misfortune during the Vietnam period to have had two Presidents who lacked the self-confidence for a change of course, much less for a grand withdrawal. "Magnanimity in politics," said Edmund Burke, "is not seldom the truest wisdom, and a great Empire and little minds go ill together." 23

An essential component of that "truest wisdom" is the self-confidence to reassess. Congressman Morris Udall made this 24 point in the first few days after the nuclear accident at Three Mile Island. Cautioning against a hasty decision on the future of nuclear power, he said, "We have to go back and reassess. There is nothing wrong about being optimistic or making a mistake. The thing that is wrong, as in Vietnam, is *persisting* in a mistake when you see you are going down the wrong road and are caught in a bad situation."

The test comes in recognizing when persistence has become a 25 fatal error. A prince, says Machiavelli, ought always to be a great asker and a patient hearer of truth about those things of which he has inquired, and he should be angry if he finds that anyone has scruples about telling him the truth. Johnson and Nixon, as far as an outsider can tell, were not great askers; they did not want to hear the truth or to face it. Chiang Kai-shek knew virtually nothing of real conditions in his domain because he lived a headquarters life amid an entourage all of whom were afraid to be messengers of ill report. When, in World War I, a general of the headquarters staff visited for the first time the ghastly landscape of the Somme, he broke into tears, saying, "If I had known we sent men to fight in that, I could not have done it." Evidently he was no great asker either.

Neither, we now know, was the shah of Iran. Like Chiang 26 Kai-shek, he was isolated from actual conditions. He was educated abroad, took his vacations abroad, and toured his country, if at all, by helicopter.

Why is it that the major clients of the United States, a country 27 founded on the principle that government derives its just powers from the consent of the governed, tend to be unpopular autocrats? A certain schizophrenia between our philosophy and our practice afflicts American policy, and this split will always make the policy based on it fall apart. On the day the shah left Iran, an article summarizing his reign said that "except for the generals, he has few friends or allies at home." How useful to us is a ruler without friends or allies at home? He is a kind of luftmensch, no matter how rich or how golden a customer for American business. To attach American foreign policy to a ruler who does not have the acceptance of his countrymen is hardly intelligent. By now, it seems to me, we might have learned that. We must understand conditions—and by conditions, I mean people and history—on the spot. Wise policy can only be made on the basis of *informed*, not automatic, judgments.

When it has become evident to those associated with it that a 28 course of policy is pointed toward disaster, why does no one resign in protest or at least for the peace of his own soul? They never do. In 1917, the German chancellor Bethmann Hollweg pleaded desperately against the proposed resumption of unrestricted submarine warfare, since, by bringing in the United States, it would revive the Allies' resources, their confidence in victory, and their will to endure. When he was overruled by the military, he told a friend who found him sunk in despair that the decision meant "finis Germaniae." When the friend said simply, "You should resign," Bethmann said he could not, for that would sow dissension at home and let the world know he believed Germany would fail.

This is always the refuge. The officeholder tells himself he 29 can do more from within and that he must not reveal division at the top to the public. In fact if there is to be any hope of change in a democratic society, that is exactly what he must do. No one of major influence in Johnson's circle resigned over our Vietnam policy, although several, hoping to play it both ways, hinted their disagreement. Humphrey, waiting for the nod, never challenged the President's policy, although he campaigned afterward as an opponent of the war. Since then, I've always thought the adulation given to him misplaced.

Basically, what keeps officeholders attached to a policy they 30 believe to be wrong is nothing more nor less, I believe, than the lure of office, or Potomac fever. It is the same whether the locus is the Thames or the Rhine or, no doubt, the Nile. When Herbert Lehman ran for a second term as senator from New York after previously serving four terms as governor, his brother asked him why on earth he wanted it. "Arthur," replied the senator, "after you have once ridden behind a motorcycle escort, you are never the same again."

Here is a clue to the question of why our performance in 31 government is worse than in other activities: because government offers power, excites that lust for power, which is subject to emotional drives—to narcissism, fantasies of omnipotence, and other sources of folly. The lust for power, according to Tacitus, "is the most flagrant of all the passions" and cannot really be satisfied except by power over others. Business offers a kind of power but only to the very successful at the very top, and even they, in our day, have to play it down. Fords and Du Ponts, Hearsts and Pulitzers, nowadays are subdued, and the Rockefeller who most conspicuously wanted power sought it in government. Other activities—in sports, science, the professions, and the creative and performing arts—offer various satisfactions but not the opportunity for power. They may appeal to status seeking and, in the form of celebrity, offer crowd worship and limousines and recognition by headwaiters, but these are the trappings of power, not the essence. Of course, mistakes and stupidities occur in nongovernmental activities too, but since these affect fewer people, they are less noticeable than they are in public affairs. Government remains the paramount field of unwisdom because it is there that men seek power over others—and lose it over themselves.

There are, of course, other factors that lower competence in public affairs, among them the pressure of overwork and overscheduling; bureaucracy, especially big bureaucracy; the contest for votes that gives exaggerated influence to special interests and an absurd tyranny to public opinion polls. Any hope of intelligent government would require that the persons entrusted with high office should formulate and execute policy according to their best judgment and the best knowledge available, not according to every breeze of public opinion. But reelection is on their minds, and that becomes the criterion. Moreover, given schedules broken down into fifteen-minute appointments and staffs numbering in the hundreds and briefing memos of never less than thirty pages, policy makers never have time to think. This leaves a rather important vacuum. Meanwhile, bureaucracy rolls on, impervious to any individual or cry for change, like some vast computer that when once penetrated by error goes on pumping it out forever. 32

Under the circumstances, what are the chances of improving the conduct of government? The idea of a class of professionals trained for the task has been around ever since Plato's Republic. Something of the sort animates, I imagine, the new Kennedy School of Government at Harvard. According to Plato, the ruling class in a just society should be men apprenticed to the art of ruling, drawn from the rational and the wise. Since he acknowledged that in natural distribution these are few, he believed they would have to be eugenically bred and nurtured. Government, he said, was a special art in which competence, as in any other profession, could be acquired only by study of the discipline and could not be acquired otherwise. 33

Without reference to Plato, the Mandarins of China were trained, if not bred, for the governing function. They had to pass through years of study and apprenticeship and weeding out by successive examinations, but they do not seem to have developed a form of government much superior to any other, and in the end, they petered out in decadence and incompetence. 34

In seventeenth-century Europe, after the devastation of the Thirty Years' War, the electors of Brandenburg, soon to be combined with Prussia, determined to create a strong state by means of a disciplined army and a trained civil service. Applicants for the civil positions, drawn from commoners in order to offset the nobles' control of the military, had to complete a course of study covering political theory, law and legal philosophy, economics, history, penology, and statutes. Only after passing through various stages of examination and probationary terms of office did they receive definitive appointments and tenure and opportunity for advancement. The 35 higher civil service was a separate branch, not open to promotion from the middle and lower levels.

The Prussian system proved so effective that the state was 36 able to survive both military defeat by Napoleon in 1807 and the revolutionary surge of 1848. By then it had begun to congeal, losing many of its most progressive citizens in emigration to America; nevertheless, Prussian energies succeeded in 1871 in uniting the German states in an empire under Prussian hegemony. Its very success contained the seed of ruin, for it nourished the arrogance and power hunger that from 1914 through 1918 was to bring it down.

In England, instead of responding in reactionary panic to the 37 thunders from the Continent in 1848, as might have been expected, the authorities, with commendable enterprise, ordered an investigation of their own government practices, which were then the virtually private preserve of the propertied class. The result was a report on the need for a permanent civil service to be based on training and specialized skills and designed to provide continuity and maintenance of the long view as against transient issues and political passions. Though heavily resisted, the system was adopted in 1870. It has produced distinguished civil servants but also Burgess, Maclean, Philby, and the fourth man. The history of British government in the last 100 years suggests that factors other than the quality of its civil service determine a country's fate.

In the United States, civil service was established chiefly as a 38 barrier to patronage and the pork barrel rather than in search of excellence. By 1937, a presidential commission, finding the system inadequate, urged the development of a "real career service . . . requiring personnel of the highest order, competent, highly trained, loyal, skilled in their duties by reason of long experience, and assured of continuity." After much effort and some progress, that goal is still not reached, but even if it were, it would not take care of elected officials and high appointments—that is, of government at the top.

I do not know if the prognosis is hopeful or, given the 39 underlying emotional drives, whether professionalism is the cure. In the Age of Enlightenment, John Locke thought the emotions should be controlled by intellectual judgment and that it was the distinction and glory of man to be able to control them. As witnesses of the twentieth century's record, comparable to the worst in history, we have less confidence in our species. Although professionalism can help, I tend to think that fitness of character is what government chiefly requires. How that can be discovered, encouraged, and brought into office is the problem that besets us.

No society has yet managed to implement Plato's design. 40 Now, with money and image-making manipulating our elective

BARBARA TUCHMAN

process, the chances are reduced. We are asked to choose by the packaging, yet the candidate seen in a studio-filmed spot, sincerely voicing lines from the Tele-PrompTer, is not the person who will have to meet the unrelenting problems and crucial decisions of the Oval Office. It might be a good idea if, without violating the First Amendment, we could ban all paid political commercials and require candidates (who accept federal subsidy for their campaigns) to be televised live only.

That is only a start. More profound change must come if we   41
are to bring into office the kind of person our form of government needs if it is to survive the challenges of this era. Perhaps rather than educating officials according to Plato's design, we should concentrate on educating the electorate—that is, ourselves—to look for, recognize, and reward character in our representatives and to reject the ersatz.

QUESTIONS

1. According to Tuchman, what are the causes of the persistence of unwisdom in government?

2. What is the author's attitude toward the French, Russian, Chinese, and Iranian revolutions respectively?

3. How do such phrases as the following contribute to the author's purpose and tone: "theatre of the absurd" (paragraph 2); "lunatic spectacle" (paragraph 3); "the whole bundle of personal vanities and anxieties" (paragraph 17); "charging forward wearing the blinkers of the Cold War" (paragraph 19); "schizophrenia between our philosophy and our practice" (paragraph 27)?

4. Analyze the connotations that develop around Tuchman's use of the word *unwisdom*.

5. How does the author's use of rhetorical questions, notably in the introduction, contribute to the thesis? To the causal analysis?

6. How selective are the author's illustrations? What types of illustration does she use in the essay?

7. Analyze the author's transitions for paragraphs 7 to 8, 14 to 15, 23 to 24, 30 to 31, and 39 to 40.

8. What particulars develop Tuchman's generalizations about the emotional and psychological drives of politicians?

9. A significant part of Tuchman's critique of unwisdom in government

 AN INQUIRY INTO THE PERSISTENCE OF UNWISDOM IN GOVERNMENT   **307**

deals specifically with the problems of men as rulers. What is your response to her emotional and psychological profile of men as political leaders? Would women be less susceptible to these emotional and psychological problems?

10.   a. Write your own inquiry into the persistence of unwisdom in government, using a series of relevant examples to support your generalizations. b. Write an essay on the failures of men as political leaders or, if you wish, on the desirability of having women as political leaders.

Language, Writing, and Communication

HENRY DAVID THOREAU

On Keeping a Private Journal

Henry David Thoreau (1817–1862), author of the masterpiece *Walden* (1854), is one of the most important figures in American thought and literature. A social and political activist, Thoreau opposed the Mexican War, protested slavery, and refused to pay his poll taxes. As a naturalist, he believed in the preeminence of individualism and nature over technology, materialism, and nationalism. In 1845, he went to live at Walden Pond, "living deep and sucking the marrow out of life." Thoreau began writing a journal in 1837, and he used his journals to write his two most famous books, *A Week on the Concord and Merrimack Rivers* (1849) and *Walden.* No wonder that Thoreau, as he explains below at the age of 18, valued journal keeping.

As those pieces which the painter sketches for his own 1 amusement in his leisure hours, are often superior to his most elaborate productions, so it is that ideas often suggest themselves to us spontaneously, as it were, far surpassing in beauty those which arise in the mind upon applying ourselves to any particular subject. Hence, could a machine be invented which would instantaneously arrange on paper each idea as it occurs to us, without any exertion on our part, how extremely useful would it be considered! The relation between this and the practice of keeping a journal is obvious. But yet, the preservation of our scattered thoughts is to be considered an object but of minor importance.

Every one can think, but comparatively few can write, can 2 express their thoughts. Indeed, how often do we hear one complain of his inability to express what he feels! How many have occasion to make the following remark, "I am sensible that I understand this perfectly, but am not able to find words to convey my idea to others".

But if each one would employ a certain portion of each day in 3 looking back upon the time which has passed, and in writing down his thoughts and feelings, in reckoning up his daily gains, that he may be able to detect whatever false coins have crept into his coffers, and, as it were, in settling accounts with his mind, not only would his daily experience be greatly increased, since his feelings and ideas would thus be more clearly defined, but he would be ready to turn over a new leaf, having carefully perused the preceding one, and would not continue to glance carelessly over the same page, without being able to distinguish it from a new one.

Most of us are apt to neglect the study of our own characters, 4 thoughts, and feelings, and for the purpose of forming our own minds, look to others, who should merely be considered as different editions of the same great work. To be sure, it would be well for us to examine the various copies, that we might detect any errors, but yet, it would be foolish for one to borrow a work which he possessed himself, but had not perused.

In fine, if we endeavoured more to improve ourselves by 5 reflection, by making a business of thinking, and giving our thoughts form and expression, we should be led to "read not to contradict and confute, nor to believe and take for granted, nor to find talk and discourse, but to weigh and consider".

QUESTIONS

1. What reasons does Thoreau give for writing a journal?

2. Why does Thoreau value reflection? How does a journal forward that goal?

3. There are several metaphors, excluding the extended metaphor in paragraphs 3 and 4. Identify them. What do they have in common?

4. Do you believe that this essay is written in the typical style of a journal? If not, how does it differ? If so, how is it similar?

5. What evidence can you offer that this is an argumentative or persuasive essay?

6. Explain the analogy that introduces the essay. How does this analogy help Thoreau introduce his subject?

7. An extended metaphor is crucial to the development of this essay. Identify the metaphor and explain how it contributes to the organization of the essay.

8. Divide this essay into two parts. Where did you divide it and why?

9. Do you feel you do your best thinking when you write? What other devices, such as tape recorders, help you think?

10. a. For the next week, write a daily description of your life.
b. Write an essay on the value of keeping a private journal.

JOAN DIDION

On Keeping a Notebook

Joan Didion (1934–   ) is a novelist and essayist. Her most recent novel is *A Book of Common Prayer* (1977). She has also written two collections of essays, *Slouching towards Bethlehem* (1968) and *The White Album* (1979). Didion is an intensely introspective writer, who in her writing attempts to draw general significance from the particulars of her own life. Here she describes one of the sources of her work: her own notebooks.

hat woman Estelle,' " the note reads, " 'is partly the reason why George Sharp and I are separated today.' *Dirty crepe-de-Chine wrapper, hotel bar, Wilmington RR, 9:45 a.m. August Monday morning."*   1

Since the note is in my notebook, it presumably has some meaning to me. I study it for a long while. At first I have only the most general notion of what I was doing on an August Monday morning in the bar of the hotel across from the Pennsylvania Railroad station in Wilmington, Delaware (waiting for a train? missing one? 1960? 1961? why Wilmington?), but I do remember being there. The woman in the dirty crepe-de-Chine wrapper had come down from her room for a beer, and the bartender had heard before the reason why George Sharp and she were separated today. "Sure," he said, and   2 went on mopping the floor. "You told me." At the other end of the bar is a girl. She is talking, pointedly, not to the man beside her but to a cat lying in the triangle of sunlight cast through the open door. She is wearing a plaid silk dress from Peck & Peck, and the hem is coming down.

Here is what it is: the girl has been on the Eastern Shore, and now she is going back to the city, leaving the man beside her, and all she can see ahead are the viscous summer sidewalks and the 3 a.m. long-distance calls that will make her lie awake and then sleep drugged through all the steaming mornings left in August (1960? 1961?). Because she must go directly from the train to lunch in New York, she wishes that she had a safety pin for the hem of the plaid silk dress, and she also wishes that she could forget about the hem and the lunch and stay in the cool bar that smells of disinfectant and malt and make friends with the woman in the crepe-de-Chine wrapper. She is afflicted by a little self-pity, and she wants to compare Estelles. That is what that was all about. 3

Why did I write it down? In order to remember, of course, but exactly what was it I wanted to remember? How much of it actually happened? Did any of it? Why do I keep a notebook at all? It is easy to deceive oneself on all those scores. The impulse to write things down is a peculiarly compulsive one, inexplicable to those who do not share it, useful only accidentally, only secondarily, in the way that any compulsion tries to justify itself. I suppose that it begins or does not begin in the cradle. Although I have felt compelled to write things down since I was five years old, I doubt that my daughter ever will, for she is a singularly blessed and accepting child, delighted with life exactly as life presents itself to her, unafraid to go to sleep and unafraid to wake up. Keepers of private notebooks are a different breed altogether, lonely and resistant rearrangers of things, anxious malcontents, children afflicted apparently at birth with some presentiment of loss. 4

My first notebook was a Big Five tablet, given to me by my mother with the sensible suggestion that I stop whining and learn to amuse myself by writing down my thoughts. She returned the tablet to me a few years ago; the first entry is an account of a woman who believed herself to be freezing to death in the Arctic night, only to find, when day broke, that she had stumbled onto the Sahara Desert, where she would die of the heat before lunch. I have no idea what turn of a five-year-old's mind could have prompted so insistently "ironic" and exotic a story, but it does reveal a certain predilection for the extreme which has dogged me into adult life; perhaps if I were analytically inclined I would find it a truer story than any I might have told about Donald Johnson's birthday party or the day my cousin Brenda put Kitty Litter in the aquarium. 5

So the point of my keeping a notebook has never been, nor is it now, to have an accurate factual record of what I have been doing or thinking. That would be a different impulse entirely, an instinct for reality which I sometimes envy but do not possess. At no point have I ever been able successfully to keep a diary; my approach to daily life ranges from the grossly negligent to the merely absent, and on those few occasions when I have tried dutifully to record a day's events, boredom has so overcome me that the results are mysterious at best. What is this business about "shopping, typing piece, dinner with E, depressed"? Shopping for what? Typing what piece? Who is E? Was this "E" depressed, or was I depressed? Who cares? **6**

In fact I have abandoned altogether that kind of pointless entry; instead I tell what some would call lies. "That's simply not true," the members of my family frequently tell me when they come up against my memory of a shared event. "The party was *not* for you, the spider was *not* a black widow, *it wasn't that way at all*." Very likely they are right, for not only have I always had trouble distinguishing between what happened and what merely might have happened, but I remain unconvinced that the distinction, for my purposes, matters. The cracked crab that I recall having for lunch the day my father came home from Detroit in 1945 must certainly be embroidery, worked into the day's pattern to lend verisimilitude; I was ten years old and would not now remember the cracked crab. The day's events did not turn on cracked crab. And yet it is precisely that fictitious crab that makes me see the afternoon all over again, a home movie run all too often, the father bearing gifts, the child weeping, an exercise in family love and guilt. Or that is what it was to me. Similarly, perhaps it never did snow that August in Vermont; perhaps there never were flurries in the night wind, and maybe no one else felt the ground hardening and summer already dead even as we pretended to bask in it, but that was how it felt to me, and it might as well have snowed, could have did snow. **7**

How it felt to me: that is getting closer to the truth about a notebook. I sometimes delude myself about why I keep a notebook, imagine that some thrifty virtue derives from preserving everything observed. See enough and write it down, I tell myself, and then some morning when the world seems drained of wonder, some day when I am only going through the motions of doing what I am supposed to do, which is write—on that bankrupt morning I will simply open my notebook and there it will all be, a forgotten account with accumulated interest, paid passage back to the world out there: dialogue overheard in hotels and elevators and at the hatcheck counter in Pavillon (one middle-aged man shows his hatcheck to another and says, "That's my old football number"); impressions of Bettina Aptheker and Benjamin Sonnenberg and Teddy ("Mr. Acapulco") **8**

Stauffer; careful *apercus* about tennis bums and failed fashion models and Greek shipping heiresses, one of whom taught me a significant lesson (a lesson I could have learned from F. Scott Fitzgerald, but perhaps we all must meet the very rich for ourselves) by asking, when I arrived to interview her in her orchid-filled sitting room on the second day of a paralyzing New York blizzard, whether it was snowing outside.

9   I imagine, in other words, that the notebook is about other people. But of course it is not. I have no real business with what one stranger said to another at the hat-check counter in Pavillon; in fact I suspect that the line "That's my old football number" touched not my own imagination at all, but merely some memory of something once read, probably "The Eighty-Yard Run." Nor is my concern with a woman in a dirty crepe-de-Chine wrapper in a Wilmington bar. My stake is always, of course, in the unmentioned girl in the plaid silk dress. *Remember what it was to be me:* that is always the point.

10   It is a difficult point to admit. We are brought up in the ethic that others, any others, all others, are by definition more interesting than ourselves; taught to be diffident, just this side of self-effacing. ("You're the least important person in the room and don't forget it," Jessica Mitford's governess would hiss in her ear on the advent of any social occasion; I copied that into my notebook because it is only recently that I have been able to enter a room without hearing some such phrase in my inner ear.) Only the very young and the very old may recount their dreams at breakfast, dwell upon self, interrupt with memories of beach picnics and favorite Liberty lawn dresses and the rainbow trout in a creek near Colorado Springs. The rest of us are expected, rightly, to affect absorption in other people's favorite dresses, other people's trout.

11   And so we do. But our notebooks give us away, for however dutifully we record what we see around us, the common denominator of all we see is always, transparently, shamelessly, the implacable "I." We are not talking here about the kind of notebook that is patently for public consumption, a structural conceit for binding together a series of graceful *pensées*; we are talking about something private, about bits of the mind's string too short to use, an indiscriminate and erratic assemblage with meaning only for its maker.

12   And sometimes even the maker has difficulty with the meaning. There does not seem to be for example, any point in my knowing for the rest of my life that, during 1964, 720 tons of soot fell on every square mile of New York City, yet there it is in my notebook, labeled "FACT." Nor do I really need to remember that Ambrose Bierce liked to spell Leland Stanford's name "£eland $tanford" or that "smart women almost always wear black in Cuba," a fashion hint

without much potential for practical application. And does not the relevance of these notes seem marginal at best?:

In the basement museum of the Inyo County Courthouse in Independence, California, sign pinned to a mandarin coat: "This MANDARIN COAT was often worn by Mrs. Minnie S. Brooks when giving lectures on her TEAPOT COLLECTION." Redhead getting out of car in front of Beverly Wilshire Hotel, chinchilla stole, Vuitton bags with tags reading:

MRS. LOU FOX

HOTEL SAHARA

VEGAS

Well, perhaps not entirely marginal. As a matter of fact, Mrs. Minnie S. Brooks and her MANDARIN COAT pull me back into my own childhood, for although I never knew Mrs. Brooks and did not visit Inyo County until I was thirty, I grew up in just such a world, in houses cluttered with Indian relics and bits of gold ore and ambergris and the souvenirs my Aunt Mercy Farnsworth brought back from the Orient. It is a long way from that world to Mrs. Lou Fox's world, where we all live now, and is it not just as well to remember that? Might not Mrs. Minnie S. Brooks help me to remember what I am? Might not Mrs. Lou Fox help me to remember what I am not?

But sometimes the point is harder to discern. What exactly did I have in mind when I noted down that it cost the father of someone I know $650 a month to light the place on the Hudson in which he lived before the Crash? What use was I planning to make of this line by Jimmy Hoffa: "I may have my faults, but being wrong ain't one of them"? And although I think it interesting to know where the girls who travel with the Syndicate have their hair done when they find themselves on the West Coast, will I ever make suitable use of it? Might I not be better off just passing it on to John O'Hara? What is a recipe for sauerkraut doing in my notebook? What kind of magpie keeps this notebook? *"He was born the night the Titanic went down."* That seems a nice enough line, and I even recall who said it, but is it not really a better line in life than it could ever be in fiction?

But of course that is exactly it: not that I should ever use the line, but that I should remember the woman who said it and the afternoon I heard it. We were on her terrace by the sea, and we were finishing the wine left from lunch, trying to get what sun there was, a California winter sun. The woman whose husband was born the night the *Titanic* went down wanted to rent her house, wanted to go back to her children in Paris. I remember wishing that I could afford the house, which cost $1,000 a month. "Someday you will," she said lazily. "Someday it all comes." There in the sun on her terrace it seemed easy to believe in someday, but later I had a low-grade afternoon hangover and ran over a black snake on the way to the supermarket and was flooded with inexplicable fear when I heard the checkout clerk explaining to the man ahead of me why she was finally divorcing her husband. "He left me no choice," she said over and over as she punched the register. "He has a little seven-month-old baby by her, he left me no choice." I would like to believe that my dread then was for the human condition, but of course it was for me, because I wanted a baby and did not then have one and because I wanted to own the house that cost $1,000 a month to rent and because I had a hangover.

It all comes back. Perhaps it is difficult to see the value in   16
having one's self back in that kind of mood, but I do see it; I think we are well advised to keep on nodding terms with the people we used to be whether we find them attractive company or not. Otherwise they turn up unannounced and surprise us, come hammering on the mind's door at 4 a.m. of a bad night and demand to know who deserted them, who betrayed them, who is going to make amends. We forget all too soon the things we thought we could never forget. We forget the loves and the betrayals alike, forget what we whispered and what we screamed, forget who we were. I have already lost touch with a couple of people I used to be; one of them, a seventeen-year-old, presents little threat, although it would be of some interest to me to know again what it feels like to sit on a river levee drinking vodka-and-orange-juice and listening to Les Paul and Mary Ford and their echoes sing "How High the Moon" on the car radio. (You see I still have the scenes, but I no longer perceive myself among those present, no longer could even improvise the dialogue.) The other one, a twenty-three-year-old, bothers me more. She was always a good deal of trouble, and I suspect she will reappear when I least want to see her, skirts too long, shy to the point of aggravation, always the injured party, full of recriminations and little hurts and stories I do not want to hear again, at once saddening me and angering me with her vulnerability and ignorance, an apparition all the more insistent for being so long banished.

It is a good idea, then, to keep in touch, and I suppose that   17
keeping in touch is what notebooks are all about. And we are all on our own when it comes to keeping those lines open to ourselves: your notebook will never help me, nor mine you. *"So what's new in the whiskey business?"* What could that possibly mean to you? To me it means a blonde in a Pucci bathing suit sitting with a couple of fat men by the pool at the Beverly Hills Hotel. Another man approaches, and they all regard one another in silence for a while. "So what's new in the whiskey business?" one of the fat men finally says by way of

welcome, and the blonde stands up, arches one foot and dips it in the pool, looking all the while at the cabana where Baby Pignatari is talking on the telephone. That is all there is to that, except that several years later I saw the blonde coming out of Saks Fifth Avenue in New York with her California complexion and a voluminous mink coat. In the harsh wind that day she looked old and irrevocably tired to me, and even the skins in the mink coat were not worked the way they were doing them that year, not the the way she would have wanted them done, and there is the point of the story. For a while after that I did not like to look in the mirror, and my eyes would skim the newspapers and pick out only the deaths, the cancer victims, the premature coronaries, the suicides, and I stopped riding the Lexington Avenue IRT because I noticed for the first time that all the strangers I had seen for years—the man with the seeing-eye dog, the spinster who read the classified pages every day, the fat girl who always got off with me at Grand Central—looked older than they once had.

It all comes back. Even that recipe for sauerkraut: even that 18 brings it back. I was on Fire Island when I first made that sauerkraut, and it was raining, and we drank a lot of bourbon and ate the sauerkraut and went to bed at ten, and I listened to the rain and the Atlantic and felt safe. I made the sauerkraut again last night and it did not make me feel any safer, but that is, as they say, another story.

QUESTIONS

1. Why does Didion mention "keeping" a notebook in her title? How is her essay about keeping rather than writing a notebook?

2. What sort of entries does Didion make in her notebooks? How and why does Didion alter the reality of the events she describes in her notebooks?

3. What is the function of the numerous rhetorical questions in the essay?

4. How does the style of Didion's notebooks differ from her regular writing style?

5. How do the introductory quote and other quotes from her notebook help Didion develop the theme of her essay?

6. Repetition is a key device used to unify the essay. Identify examples of important repetitions.

7. Identify topic sentences in the essay. How does Didion prepare us for the thesis through her topic sentences?

 ON KEEPING A NOTEBOOK

8. Analyze causal patterns of development that appear in the essay.

9. To a great degree, Didion is also describing the process of writing fiction in this essay. Do you think fiction is a lie? How is it also true?

10. a. Write an essay about some events that have occurred in your own past that you feel were significant to your growth.
b. Write an essay about trivial objects and events that nevertheless have been important to you.

S. I. HAYAKAWA

Words and Children

Samuel Ichize Hayakawa (1906–   ) began his career as a professor of linguistics and was the author of numerous books on language such as *Language in Thought and Action* (1941), *Our Language and Our World* (1959), and *Symbol, Status, and Personality* (1963). When Hayakawa became president of San Francisco State College, student unrest was at its height. By defending traditional values and, indeed, authority itself, Hayakawa became a national and controversial figure. His notoriety has propelled him into the United States Senate. The present essay reflects his original career as a semanticist.

hose who still believe, after all the writing that semanti-   1
cists have done, that semantics is a science of words, may be surprised to learn that semantics has the effect— at least, it has had on me and on many others—of reducing rather than increasing one's preoccupation with words. First of all, there is that vast area of nonverbal communication with children that we accomplish through holding, touching, rocking, caressing our children, putting food in their mouths, and all of the little attentions that we give them. These are all communication, and we communicate in this way for a long time before the children even start to talk.

Then, after they start to talk, there is always the problem of   2
interpretation. There is a sense in which small children are recent immigrants in our midst. They have trouble both in understanding and in using the language, and they often make errors. Many people (you can notice this in the supermarkets, especially with parents of

two- and three-year-old children) get angry at their children when they don't seem to mind. Anyone standing within earshot of one of these episodes can tell that the child just hasn't understood what the mother said. But the mother feels, "Well, I said it, didn't I? What's wrong with the child that he doesn't understand? It's English, isn't it?" But, as I say, the child is a recent immigrant in our midst and there are things that the child doesn't understand.

There are curious instances. Once, when our daughter was three years old, she found the bath too hot and she said, "Make it warmer." It took me a moment to figure out that she meant, "Bring the water more nearly to the condition we call warm." It makes perfectly good sense looked at that way. Confronted with unusual formulations such as these which children constantly make, many of us react with incredible lack of imagination. Sometimes children are laughed at for making "silly statements," when it only requires understanding their way of abstracting and their way of formulating their abstractions to see that they are not silly at all. 3

Children are newcomers to the language. Learning a language isn't just learning words; rules of the language are learned at the same time. Prove this? Very simple. Little children use a past tense like "I runned all the way to the park and I swimmed in the pool." "Runned" and "swimmed" are words they did not hear. They made them up by analogy from other past tenses they had heard. This means that they learned not only the vocabulary, they learned the rule for making the past tense—except that the English language doesn't follow its own rules. And when the child proves himself to be more logical than the English language, we take it out on the child—which is nonsense. Children's language should be listened to with great attentiveness and respect. 4

Again, when our daughter was three years old, I was pounding away at my typewriter in my study and she was drawing pictures on the floor when she suddenly said, "I want to go see the popentole." 5

I kept typing. 6

Then I stopped and said, "What?!" 7

She said, "I want to see the popentole." 8

"Did you say *popentole*?" 9

I just stopped. It was a puzzle to figure out, but I did. In a few seconds I said, "You mean like last Saturday, you want to go to Lincoln Park and see the totem pole?" 10

She said, "Yes." 11

And what was so warm about this, so wonderful about it, was that having got her point across she played for another twenty minutes singing to herself, happy that she had communicated. I didn't say to her, "Okay, I'll take you next Sunday to see the 12 popentole." The mere fact that she'd made her point and got it registered was a source of satisfaction to her. And I felt very proud of myself at the time for having understood.

One of the things we tend to overlook in our culture is the tremendous value of the acknowledgment of message. Not, "I agree with you" or "I disagree with you" or "That's a wonderful idea" or "That's a silly idea," but just the acknowledgment, "I know exactly what you've said. It goes on the record. You said that." She said, "I want to go see the totem pole." I said, "Okay, you want to go see the totem pole." The acknowledgment of message says in effect, "I know you're around. I know what you're thinking. I acknowledge your presence."   13

There is also a sense in which a child understands far more than we suspect. Because a child doesn't understand words too well (and also because his nervous system is not yet deadened by years spent as a lawyer, accountant, advertising executive, or professor of philosophy), a child attends not only to what we say but to everything about us as we say it—tone of voice, gesture, facial expression, bodily tensions, and so on. A child attends to a conversation between grown-ups with the same amazing absorption. Indeed, a child listening is, I hope, like a good psychiatrist listening— or like a good semanticist listening—because she watches not only the words but also the nonverbal events to which words bear, in all too many cases, so uncertain a relationship. Therefore a child is in some matters quite difficult to fool, especially on the subject of one's true attitude toward her. For this reason many parents, without knowing it, are to a greater or lesser degree in the situation of the worried mother who said to the psychiatrist to whom she brought her child, "I tell her a dozen times a day that I love her, but the brat still hates me. Why, doctor?"   14

"Life in a big city is dangerous," a mother once said to me. "You hear so often of children running thoughtlessly out in the street and being struck by passing cars. They will never learn unless you keep telling them and telling them." This is the communication theory that makes otherwise pleasant men and women into nagging parents: You've got to keep telling them; then you've got to remind them; then tell 'em again. Are there no better ways to teach children not to run out into the street? Of course there are. I think it was done in our family without words.   15

Whenever my wife crossed the street with our boy Alan—he was then about three—she would come to a stop at the curb whether there was any traffic in sight or not, and look up and down the boulevard before crossing. It soon became a habit. One day I absentmindedly started crossing the street without looking up and down—the street was empty. Alan grabbed my coat and pulled me   16

S. I. HAYAKAWA

back on the curb to look up and down before we started out again. Children love to know the right way to do things. They learn by imitation far more than by precept.

17
The uncritical confidence that many people place in words is a matter of constant amazement to me. When we were living in Chicago there was a concrete courtyard behind our apartment house. I heard a great deal of noise and shouting out there one day, and I looked out and saw a father teaching his boy to ride a bicycle. The father was shouting instructions: "Keep your head up. Now push down with your left foot. Now look out, you're running into the wall. Steer away from it. *Steer away from it!* Now push down with your right foot. Don't fall down!" and so on and so on. The poor boy was trying to keep his balance, manage the bicycle, obey his father's instructions all at the same time, and he looked about as totally confused as it is possible for a little boy to get. One thing we learn from general semantics, if we haven't learned it some other way already, is that there are limits to what can be accomplished in words. Learning to ride a bicycle is beyond those limits. Having sensed those limits, we become content to let many things take care of themselves without words. All this makes for a quieter household.

18
The anthropologist Ray Birdwhistell has undertaken a study that he calls "kinesics,"* which is the systematic examination of gesture and body motion in communication; this is a rich area of concern about which many students of human behavior have been much excited. But there is a danger in going too far in this direction— in going overboard to the extent of saying that words are of *no* importance. There are thousands of things children must know and enjoy that it is not possible for them to get *without* words.

19
The sense of what one misses through the lack of words has been brought home to us by the fact that our second boy, Mark, now twenty-nine, is seriously mentally retarded. At the age of six he was hardly able to talk at all. Now he talks quite a bit, but his speech is very difficult to understand; members of the family can understand it about half the time. He was always able to understand words with direct physical referents—watch, glass of water, orange juice, record-player, television, and so on. But there are certain things that exist only in words, like the concept of the future. I remember the following incident when he was six years old. He came across a candy bar at ten minutes to twelve when lunch was just about to be served. I tried to take it away from him and said, "Look, Mark, you can have it right after lunch. Don't eat it now. You can have it right after lunch." Well, when he was six all he could understand was that it was being taken away from him *now,* and the idea that there was a future in

*Ray Birdwhistell, *Kinesics and Context.* Philadelphia: University of Pennsylvania Press, 1970.

which he'd have it back was something he just couldn't get at the time. Of course, the concept of futurity developed later, but it took him much longer to develop it than it took the other children.

For human beings, the future, which exists *only in language,* is a wonderful dimension in which to live. That is, human beings can readily endure and even enjoy postponement; the anticipation of future pleasures is itself a pleasure. But futurity is something that has no physical referent like "a glass of water." It exists only in language. Mark's frequent frustrations and rage when he was younger were a constant reminder to us that all the warmth and richness of nonverbal communication, all that we could communicate by holding him and feeding him and patting his head and playing on the floor with him, were not enough for the purposes of human interaction. Organized games of any kind all have linguistically formulated rules. Take an organized game like baseball. Can there be a baseball without language? No, there can't. What's the difference between a ball and a strike? There are linguistically formulated rules by which we define the difference. All systematic games, even much simpler games that children play, have to have a language to formulate the rules. An enormous amount of human life is possible only with language, and without it one is very much impoverished.

QUESTIONS

1. Hayakawa says that as a semanticist he has learned that we don't only communicate through words. What other ways of communication does he mention?

2. Hayakawa also points out some of the advantages of language as a communicative skill. What are they?

3. Hayakawa uses two metaphors to explain a child's relation to language. What are they?

4. Cite examples of Hayakawa's use of scientific jargon. What does this suggest about the audience for which he is writing?

5. Explain how Hayakawa uses process to develop his essay.

6. Hayakawa makes several statements about communication. What are they? How does he use examples to illustrate these points?

7. Where does Hayakawa use personal examples? How do they contribute to the development of the essay?

8. Explain the importance of paragraphs 3, 14, and 18 to the development of the essay.

S. I. HAYAKAWA

9. Hayakawa introduces the idea that we often communicate without words. What examples beyond the ones he mentions can you think of?

10. a. Write an essay describing how we use a nonverbal form of communication such as signals in sports, streetlights, or arts such as music, ballet, and painting.
b. Write an essay about the language of children based on your personal experience.

Little Red Riding Hood Revisited

Russell Baker (1925–   ), humorist and journalist, has written a syndicated column called "The Observer" since 1962. His humor runs from allegorical satires of American politics and taste to witty criticisms of current jargon and slang. His column has been collected in such books as *An American in Washington* (1961), *No Cause for Panic* (1964), and *Poor Russell's Almanac* (1972).

 n an effort to make the classics accessible to contempo- 1
rary readers, I am translating them into the modern
American language. Here is the translation of "Little
Red Riding Hood":

Once upon a point in time, a small person named Little Red   2
Riding Hood initiated plans for the preparation, delivery and transportation of foodstuffs to her grandmother, a senior citizen residing at
a place of residence in a forest of indeterminate dimension.

In the process of implementing this program, her incursion   3
into the forest was in midtransportation process when it attained
interface with an alleged perpetrator. This individual, a wolf, made
inquiry as to the whereabouts of Little Red Riding Hood's goal as well
as inferring that he was desirous of ascertaining the contents of Little
Red Riding Hood's foodstuffs basket, and all that.

"It would be inappropriate to lie to me," the wolf said,   4
displaying his huge jaw capability. Sensing that he was a mass of
repressed hostility intertwined with acute alienation, she indicated.

"I see you indicating," the wolf said, "but what I don't see is   5
whatever it is you're indicating at, you dig?"

Little Red Riding Hood indicated more fully, making one   6
thing perfectly clear—to wit, that it was to her grandmother's

 LITTLE RED RIDING HOOD REVISITED   **323**

residence and with a consignment of foodstuffs that her mission consisted of taking her to and with.

At this point in time the wolf moderated his rhetoric and 7 proceeded to grandmother's residence. The elderly person was then subjected to the disadvantages of total consumption and transferred to residence in the perpetrator's stomach.

"That will raise the old woman's consciousness," the wolf 8 said to himself. He was not a bad wolf, but only a victim of an oppressive society, a society that not only denied wolves' rights, but actually boasted of its capacity for keeping the wolf from the door. An interior malaise made itself manifest inside the wolf.

"Is that the national malaise I sense within my digestive 9 tract?" wondered the wolf. "Or is it the old person seeking to retaliate for her consumption by telling wolf jokes to my duodenum?" It was time to make a judgment. The time was now, the hour had struck, the body lupine cried out for decision. The wolf was up to the challenge. He took two stomach powders right away and got into bed.

The wolf had adopted the abdominal-distress recovery pos- 10 ture when Little Red Riding Hood achieved his presence.

"Grandmother," she said, "your ocular implements are of an 11 extraordinary order of magnitude."

"The purpose of this enlarged viewing capability," said the 12 wolf, "is to enable your image to register a more precise impression upon my sight systems."

"In reference to your ears," said Little Red Riding Hood, "it is 13 noted with the deepest respect that far from being underprivileged, their elongation and enlargement appear to qualify you for unparalleled distinction."

"I hear you loud and clear, kid," said the wolf, "but what 14 about these new choppers?"

"If it is not inappropriate," said Little Red Riding Hood, "it 15 might be observed that with your new miracle masticating products you may even be able to chew taffy again."

This observation was followed by the adoption of an aggres- 16 sive posture on the part of the wolf and the assertion that it was also possible for him, due to the high efficiency ratio of his jaw, to consume little persons, plus, as he stated, his firm determination to do so at once without delay and with all due process and propriety, notwithstanding the fact that the ingestion of one entire grandmother had already provided twice his daily recommended cholesterol intake.

There ensued flight by Little Red Riding Hood accompanied 17 by pursuit in respect to the wolf and a subsequent intervention on the part of a third party, heretofore unnoted in the record.

Due to the firmness of the intervention, the wolf's stomach 18 underwent ax-assisted aperture with the result that Red Riding Hood's grandmother was enabled to be removed with only minor discomfort.

The wolf's indigestion was immediately alleviated with such effectiveness that he signed a contract with the intervening third party to perform with grandmother in a television commercial demonstrating the swiftness of this dramatic relief for stomach discontent. 19

"I'm going to be on television," cried grandmother. 20

And they all joined her happily in crying, "What a phenomena!" 21

QUESTIONS

1. What difference is there between the conclusion of this tale and that of the traditional fairy tale? Why do you think Baker has changed the ending?

2. What political allusions are made in this essay?

3. Baker uses several flaws of modern language such as repetition, excessive Latinisms, and jargon. Find examples of these flaws.

4. Diction is also a crucial issue in this essay. How does word choice contribute to Baker's satire?

5. What is Baker's thesis? Is it ever explicitly stated? Why, or why not?

6. This essay is, of course, a narrative. Identify those transitional devices that keep the development of the story clear.

7. Although never explicitly stated, this essay compares modern American English with traditional English. Are there any suggestions of this in the essay?

8. Why does Baker introduce fads, political and social, into a satire on modern English? How do they modify the meaning of the essay?

9. Do you think Baker's critique of modern English is correct or snobbish? Explain. Can you give reasons we should write the way we do?

10. a. Write a modern version of another fairy tale, using Baker's satiric methods.
b. Locate a particularly egregious example of modern American English and write a critique of its faults.

Calculating Machine

Elwyn Brooks White (1899–   ), perhaps the finest contemporary American essayist, is at his most distinctive in his treatments of people and nature. A recipient of the National Medal for literature, and associated for years with *The New Yorker,* White is the author of *One Man's Meat* (1942), *Here Is New York* (1949), and *The Second Tree from the Corner* (1954), among numerous works. He is also one of the most talented writers of literature for children, the author of *Stuart Little* (1945), *Charlotte's Web* (1952), and *The Trumpet of the Swan* (1970). Most writers and lovers of language have read and reread his witty, cogent explanation of English grammar in *The Elements of Style* (1959). In the following essay, White demonstrates his abiding interest in language in taking a bemused look at a style machine built by General Motors.

A publisher in Chicago has sent us a pocket calculating machine by which we may test our writing to see whether it is intelligible. The calculator was developed by General Motors, who, not satisfied with giving the world a Cadillac, now dream of bringing understanding to men. The machine (it is simply a celluloid card with a dial) is called the Reading-Ease Calculator and shows four grades of "reading ease"— Very Easy, Easy, Hard, and Very Hard. You count your words and syllables, set the dial, and an indicator lets you know whether anybody is going to understand what you have written. An instruction book came with it, and after mastering the simple rules we lost no time in running a test on the instruction book itself, to see how *that* writer was doing. The poor fellow! His leading essay, the one on the front cover, tested Very Hard. 1

Our next step was to study the first phrase on the face of the calculator: "How to test Reading-Ease of written matter." There is, of course, no such thing as reading ease of written matter. There is the ease with which matter can be read, but that is a condition of the reader, not of the matter. Thus the inventors and distributors of this calculator get off to a poor start, with a Very Hard instruction book and a slovenly phrase. Already they have one foot caught in the brier patch of English usage. 2

Not only did the author of the instruction book score badly on the front cover, but inside the book he used the word "personalize" in an essay on how to improve one's writing. A man who likes the word 3 "personalize" is entitled to his choice, but we wonder whether he should be in the business of giving advice to writers. "Whenever possible," he wrote, "personalize your writing by directing it to the reader." As for us, we would as lief Simonize our grandmother as personalize our writing.

In the same envelope with the calculator, we received another 4 training aid for writers—a booklet called "How to Write Better," by Rudolf Flesch. This, too, we studied, and it quickly demonstrated the broncolike ability of the English language to throw whoever leaps cocksurely into the saddle. The language not only can toss a rider but knows a thousand tricks for tossing him, each more gay than the last. Dr. Flesch stayed in the saddle only a moment or two. Under the heading "Think Before you Write," he wrote "The main thing to consider is your *purpose* in writing. Why are you sitting down to write?" An echo answered: Because, sir, it is more comfortable than standing up.

Communication by the written word is a subtler (and more 5 beautiful) thing than Dr. Flesch and General Motors imagine. They contend that the "average reader" is capable of reading only what tests Easy, and that the writer should write at or below this level. This is a presumptuous and degrading idea. There is no average reader, and to reach down toward this mythical character is to deny that each of us is on the way up, is ascending. ("Ascending," by the way, is a word Dr. Flesch advises writers to stay away from. Too unusual.)

It is our belief that no writer can improve his work until he 6 discards the dulcet notion that the reader is feeble-minded, for writing is an act of faith, not a trick of grammar. Ascent is at the heart of the matter. A country whose writers are following a calculating machine downstairs is not ascending—if you will pardon the expression—and a writer who questions the capacity of the person at the other end of the line is not a writer at all, merely a schemer. The movies long ago decided that a wider communication could be achieved by a deliberate descent to a lower level, and they walked proudly down until they reached the cellar. Now they are groping for the light switch, hoping to find the way out.

We have studied Dr. Flesch's instructions diligently, but we 7 return for guidance in these matters to an earlier American, who wrote with more patience, more confidence. "I fear chiefly," he wrote, "lest my expression may not be *extra-vagant* enough, may not wander far enough beyond the narrow limits of my daily experience, so as to be adequate to the truth of which I have been convinced. . . . Why level downward to our dullest perception always, and praise that as common sense? The commonest sense is the sense of men asleep, which they express by snoring."

Run that through your calculator! It may come out Hard, it 8 may come out Easy. But it will come out whole, and it will last forever.

QUESTIONS

1. Explain the difference in attitude toward language between Rudolf Flesch and General Motors, and the American, Henry David Thoreau, quoted in paragraph 7.

2. What reasons does White give for criticizing Flesch and General Motors' calculator?

3. Give instances of ironic language in the essay.

4. What concrete metaphors for language appear in the essay?

5. Trace the development of the essay. What major division would you make in the essay?

6. Explain the methods White uses to criticize Flesch and General Motors' calculator.

7. Show how in each paragraph White uses specific and concrete statements. What effect does this organization have on the development of the essay?

8. Explain the extended metaphor in paragraph 6. Why is a metaphor particularly useful in this paragraph?

9. What effect would E. B. White's values have on the nature of television writing?

10. Find an example of bad writing in a textbook and analyze it as White does.

MORTIMER J. ADLER

How to Mark a Book

Mortimer Jerome Adler (1902–   ) is the chairman of the editorial board of the *Encyclopaedia Britannica*. He has overseen and written for several collections of popular philosophy and political theory, such as *The Idea of Freedom* (four volumes, 1958–1959), and *The Great Ideas Program* (nine volumes, 1959–1963). Orderly by nature, Adler below carefully analyzes the way he reads a book.

Y ou know you have to read "between the lines" to get the 1 most out of anything. I want to persuade you to do something equally important in the course of your reading. I want to persuade you to "write between the lines." Unless you do, you are not likely to do the most efficient kind of reading.

I contend, quite bluntly, that marking up a book is not an act 2 of mutilation but of love.

You shouldn't mark up a book which isn't yours. Librarians 3 (or your friends) who lend you books expect you to keep them clean, and you should. If you decide that I am right about the usefulness of marking books, you will have to buy them. Most of the world's great books are available today, in reprint editions, at less than a dollar.

There are two ways in which one can own a book. The first is 4 the property right you establish by paying for it, just as you pay for clothes and furniture. But this act of purchase is only the prelude to possession. Full ownership comes only when you have made it a part of yourself, and the best way to make yourself a part of it is by writing in it. An illustration may make the point clear. You buy a beefsteak and transfer it from the butcher's ice-box to your own. But you do not own the beefsteak in the most important sense until you consume it and get it into your bloodstream. I am arguing that books, too, must be absorbed in your bloodstream to do you any good.

Confusion about what it means to own a book leads people to 5 a false reverence for paper, binding, and type—a respect for the physical thing—the craft of the printer rather than the genius of the author. They forget that it is possible for a man to acquire the idea, to possess the beauty, which a great book contains, without staking his claim by pasting his bookplate inside the cover. Having a fine library doesn't prove that its owner has a mind enriched by books; it proves nothing more than that he, his father, or his wife, was rich enough to buy them.

There are three kinds of book owners. The first has all the 6 standard sets and best-sellers—unread, untouched. (This deluded individual owns woodpulp and ink, not books.) The second has a great many books—a few of them read through, most of them dipped into, but all of them as clean and shiny as the day they were bought. (This person would probably like to make books his own, but is restrained by a false respect for their physical appearance.) The third has a few books or many—every one of them dog-eared and dilapidated, shaken and loosened by continual use, marked and scribbled in from front to back. (This man owns books.)

Is it false respect, you may ask, to preserve intact and unblemished a beautifully printed book, an elegantly bound edition? Of course not. I'd no more scribble all over the first edition of *Paradise Lost* than I'd give my baby a set of crayons and an original Rembrandt! I wouldn't mark up a painting or a statue. Its soul, so to speak, is inseparable from its body. And the beauty of a rare edition or of a richly manufactured volume is like that of a painting or a statue. 7

But the soul of a book *can* be separated from its body. A book is more like the score of a piece of music than it is like a painting. No great musician confuses a symphony with the printed sheets of music. Arturo Toscanini reveres Brahms, but Toscanini's score of the C-minor Symphony is so thoroughly marked up that no one but the maestro himself can read it. The reason why a great conductor makes notations on his musical scores—marks them up again and again each time he returns to study them—is the reason why you should mark up your books. If your respect for magnificent binding or typography gets in the way, buy yourself a cheap edition and pay your respects to the author. 8

Why is marking up a book indispensable to reading it? First, it keeps you awake. (And I don't mean merely conscious; I mean wide awake.) In the second place, reading, if it is active, is thinking, and thinking tends to express itself in words, spoken or written. The marked book is usually the thought-through book. Finally, writing helps you remember the thoughts you had, or the thoughts the author expressed. Let me develop these three points. 9

If reading is to accomplish anything more than passing time, it must be active. You can't let your eyes glide across the lines of a book and come up with an understanding of what you have read. Now an ordinary piece of light fiction, like say, *Gone with the Wind*, doesn't require the most active kind of reading. The books you read for pleasure can be read in a state of relaxation, and nothing is lost. But a great book, rich in ideas and beauty, a book that raises and tries to answer great fundamental questions, demands the most active reading of which you are capable. You don't absorb the ideas of John Dewey the way you absorb the crooning of Mr. Vallee. You have to reach for them. That you cannot do while you're asleep. 10

If, when you've finished reading a book, the pages are filled with your notes, you know that you read actively. The most famous *active* reader of great books I know is President Hutchins, of the University of Chicago. He also has the hardest schedule of business activities of any man I know. He invariably reads with a pencil, and sometimes, when he picks up a book and pencil in the evening, he 11 finds himself, instead of making intelligent notes, drawing what he calls "caviar factories" on the margins. When that happens, he puts the book down. He knows he's too tired to read, and he's just wasting time.

But, you may ask, why is writing necessary? Well, the physical act of writing, with your own hand, brings words and sentences more sharply before your mind and preserves them better in your memory. To set down your reaction to important words and sentences you have read, and the questions they have raised in your mind, is to preserve those reactions and sharpen those questions. 12

Even if you wrote on a scratch pad, and threw the paper away when you had finished writing, your grasp of the book would be surer. But you don't have to throw the paper away. The margins (top and bottom, as well as side), the end-papers, the very space between the lines, are all available. They aren't sacred. And, best of all, your marks and notes become an integral part of the book and stay there forever. You can pick up the book the following week or year, and there are all your points of agreement, disagreement, doubt, and inquiry. It's like resuming an interrupted conversation with the advantage of being able to pick up where you left off. 13

And that is exactly what reading a book should be: a conversation between you and the author. Presumably he knows more about the subject than you do; naturally, you'll have the proper humility as you approach him. But don't let anybody tell you that a reader is supposed to be solely on the receiving end. Understanding is a two-way operation; learning doesn't consist in being an empty receptacle. The learner has to question himself and question the teacher. He even has to argue with the teacher, once he understands what the teacher is saying. And marking a book is literally an expression of your differences, or agreements of opinion, with the author. 14

There are all kinds of devices for marking a book intelligently and fruitfully. Here's the way I do it: 15

1. Underlining: Of major points, of important or forceful statements. 16

2. Vertical lines at the margin: To emphasize a statement already underlined. 17

3. Star, asterisk, or other doo-dad at the margin: To be used sparingly, to emphasize the ten or twenty most important statements in the book. (You may want to fold the bottom corner of each page on which you use such marks. It won't hurt the sturdy paper on which most modern books are printed, and you will be able to take the book 18

off the shelf at any time and, by opening it at the folded-corner page, refresh your recollection of the book.)

4. Numbers in the margin: To indicate the sequence of points the 19
author makes in developing a single argument.

5. Numbers of other pages in the margin: To indicate where else in 20
the book the author made points relevant to the point marked; to tie
up the ideas in a book, which, though they may be separated by
many pages, belong together.

6. Circling of key words or phrases. 21

7. Writing in the margin, or at the top or bottom of the page, for the 22
sake of: Recording questions (and perhaps answers) which a passage
raised in your mind; reducing a complicated discussion to a simple
statement; recording the sequence of major points right through the
book. I use the end-papers at the back of the book to make a personal
index of the author's points in the order of their appearance.

The front end-papers are, to me, the most important. Some 23
people reserve them for a fancy bookplate. I reserve them for fancy
thinking. After I have finished reading the book and making my
personal index on the back end-papers, I turn to the front and try to
outline the book, not page by page, or point by point (I've already
done that at the back), but as an integrated structure, with a basic
unity and an order of parts. This outline is, to me, the measure of my
understanding of the work.

If you're a die-hard and anti-book-marker, you may object 24
that the margins, the space between the lines, and the end-papers
don't give you room enough. All right. How about using a scratch
pad slightly smaller than the page-size of the book—so that the edges
of the sheets won't protrude? Make your index, outlines, and even
your notes on the pad, and then insert these sheets permanently
inside the front and back covers of the book.

Or, you may say that this business of marking books is going 25
to slow up your reading. It probably will. That's one of the reasons for
doing it. Most of us have been taken in by the notion that speed of
reading is a measure of our intelligence. There is no such thing as the
right speed for intelligent reading. Some things should be read
quickly and effortlessly, and some should be read slowly and even
laboriously. The sign of intelligence in reading is the ability to read
different things differently according to their worth. In the case of
good books, the point is not to see how many of them you can get
through, but rather how many can get through you—how many you
can make your own. A few friends are better than a thousand

acquaintances. If this be your aim, as it should be, you will not be impatient if it takes more time and effort to read a great book than it does a newspaper.

You may have one final objection to marking books. You can't 26 lend them to your friends because nobody else can read them without being distracted by your notes. Furthermore, you won't want to lend them because a marked copy is a kind of intellectual diary, and lending it is almost like giving your mind away.

If your friend wishes to read your *Plutarch's Lives,* "Shake- 27 speare," or *The Federalist Papers,* tell him gently but firmly, to buy a copy. You will lend him your car or your coat—but your books are as much a part of you as your head or your heart.

QUESTIONS

1. What reasons does Adler give for marking a book?

2. What objections to careful reading does he offer? How does he dispose of them?

3. What is the tone of this essay? What evidence relating to diction, figurative language, and sentence structure can you give to support your view?

4. Several references in this essay reflect its age. What evidence can you find that this essay was not written recently?

5. Where is the thesis in this essay? Explain the effect of placing it where it is.

6. Show how and to what effect Adler uses rhetorical questions and classification.

7. Explain where and how Adler uses process analysis in this essay.

8. Give examples of Adler's use of deductive reasoning. Why does he use this rather than inductive reasoning?

9. Is it practical to follow Adler's advice for reading a book? Explain.

10. Imitating Adler's style, describe how you should watch movies or television shows or listen to records.

Expressive Language

Imamu Amiri Baraka (1934–   ) is a playwright, novelist, editor, essayist, and community leader. His most famous work, the play *Dutchman* (1964), is about the often destructive relations between blacks and whites in America. During his career, Baraka has, through the powerful use of the black idiom, introduced both whites and blacks to the richness of black culture. Here, he explores the causes behind the connotations of particular words in black and white English.

S peech is the effective form of a culture. Any shape or 1
cluster of human history still apparent in the conscious and unconscious habit of groups of people is what I mean by culture. All culture is necessarily profound. The very fact of its longevity, of its being what it is, *culture,* the epic memory of practical tradition, means that it is profound. But the inherent profundity of culture does not necessarily mean that its *uses* (and they are as various as the human condition) will be profound. German culture is profound. Generically. Its uses, however, are specific, as are all uses . . . of ideas, inventions, products of nature. And specificity, as a right and passion of human life, breeds what it breeds as a result of its context.

Context, in this instance, is most dramatically social. And the 2
social, though it must be rooted, as are all evidences of existence, in culture, depends for its impetus for the most part on a multiplicity of influences. Other cultures, for instance. Perhaps, and this is a common occurrence, the reaction or interreaction of one culture on another can produce a social context that will extend or influence any culture in many strange directions.

Social also means *economic*, as any reader of nineteenth- 3
century European philosophy will understand. The economic is part of the social—and in our time much more so than what we have known as the spiritual or metaphysical, because the most valuable canons of power have either been reduced or traduced into stricter economic terms. That is, there has been a shift in the actual meaning of the world since Dante lived. As if Brooks Adams were right. Money does not mean the same thing to me it must mean to a rich man. I cannot, right now, think of one meaning to name. This is not so simple to understand. Even as a simple term of the English language, *money* does not possess the same meanings for the rich man as it does

for me, a lower-middle-class American, albeit of laughably "aristocratic" pretensions. What possibly can "money" mean to a poor man? And I am not talking now about those courageous products of our permissive society who walk knowledgeably into "poverty" as they would into a public toilet. I mean, The Poor.

I look in my pocket; I have seventy cents. Possibly I can buy a   4
beer. A quart of ale, specifically. Then I will have twenty cents with which to annoy and seduce my fingers when they wearily search for gainful employment. I have no idea at this moment what that seventy cents will mean to my neighbor around the corner, a poor Puerto Rican man I have seen hopefully watching my plastic garbage can. But I am certain it cannot mean the same thing. Say to David Rockefeller, "I have money," and he will think you mean something entirely different. That is, if you also dress the part. He would not for a moment think, "Seventy cents." But then neither would many New York painters.

Speech, the way one describes the natural proposition of   5
being alive, is much more crucial than even most artists realize. Semantic philosophers are certainly correct in their emphasis on the final dictation of words over their users. But they often neglect to point out that, after all, it is the actual importance, *power*, of the words that remains so finally crucial. Words have users, but as well, users have words. And it is the users that establish the world's realities. Realities being those fantasies that control your immediate span of life. Usually they are not your own fantasies, *i.e.,* they belong to governments, traditions, etc., which, it must be clear by now, can make for conflict with the singular human life all ways. The fantasy of America might hurt you, but it is what should be meant when one talks of "reality." Not only the things you can touch or see, but the things that make such touching or seeing "normal." Then words, like their users, have a hegemony. Socially—which is final, right now. If you are some kind of artist, you naturally might think this is not so. There is the future. But *immortality* is a kind of drug, I think—one that leads to happiness at the thought of death. Myself, I would rather live forever . . . just to make sure.

The social hegemony, one's position in society, enforces   6
more specifically one's terms (even the vulgar have "pull"). Even to the mode of speech. But also it makes these terms an available explanation of any social hierachy, so that the words themselves become, even informally, laws. And of course they are usually very quickly stitched together to make formal statutes only fools or the faithfully intrepid would dare to question beyond immediate necessity.

The culture of the powerful is very infectious for the sophisti-   7

 EXPRESSIVE LANGUAGE   **335**

cated, and strongly addictive. To be any kind of "success" one must be fluent in this culture. Know the words of the users, the semantic rituals of power. This is a way into wherever it is you are not now, but wish, very desperately, to get into.

Even speech then signals a fluency in this culture. A knowl- 8 edge at least. "He's an educated man," is the barest acknowledgment of such fluency . . . in any time. "He's hip," my friends might say. They connote a similar entrance.

And it is certainly the meanings of words that are most 9 important, even if they are no longer consciously acknowledged, but merely, by their use, trip a familiar lever of social accord. To recreate instantly the understood hierarchy of social, and by doing that, cultural, importance. And cultures are thought by most people in the world to do their business merely by being hierarchies. Certainly this is true in the West, in as simple a manifestation as Xenophobia, the naïve bridegroom of antihuman feeling, or in economic terms, Colonialism. For instance, when the first Africans were brought into the New World, it was thought that it was all right for them to be slaves because "they were heathens." It is a perfectly logical assumption.

And it follows, of course, that slavery would have been an 10 even stranger phenomenon had the Africans spoken English when they first got here. It would have complicated things. Very soon after the first generations of Afro-Americans mastered this language, they invented white people called Abolitionists.

Words' meanings, but also the rhythm and syntax that frame 11 and propel their concatenation, seek their culture as the final reference for what they are describing of the world. An A flat played twice on the same saxophone by two different men does not have to sound the same. If these men have different ideas of what they want this note to do, the note will not sound the same. Culture is the form, the overall structure of organized thought (as well as emotion and spiritual pretension). There are many cultures. Many ways of organizing thought, or having thought organized. That is, the form of thought's passage through the world will take on as many diverse shapes as there are diverse groups of travelers. Environment is one organizer of *groups,* at any level of its meaning. People who live in Newark, New Jersey, are organized, for whatever purpose, as Newarkers. It begins that simply. Another manifestation, at a slightly more complex level, can be the fact that blues singers from the Midwest sing through their noses. There is an explanation past the geographical, but that's the idea in tabloid. And singing through the nose does propose that the definition of singing be altered . . . even if ever so slightly. (At this point where someone's definitions must be changed, we are flitting around at the outskirts of the old city of Aesthetics. A solemn ghost town. Though some of the bones of reason can still be gathered there.)

But we still need definitions, even if there already are many. The dullest men are always satisfied that a dictionary lists everything in the world. They don't care that you may find out something *extra*, which one day might even be valuable to them. Of course, by that time it might even be in the dictionary, or at least they'd hope so, if you asked them directly.

But for every item in the world, there are a multiplicity of definitions that fit. And every word we use *could* mean something else. And at the same time. The culture fixes the use, and usage. And in "pluralistic" America, one should always listen very closely when he is being talked to. The speaker might mean something completely different from what we think we're hearing. "Where is your pot?"

I heard an old Negro street singer last week, Reverend Pearly Brown, singing, "God don't never change!" This is a precise thing he is singing. He does not mean "God does not ever change!" He means "God don't never change!" The difference, and I said it was crucial, is in the final human reference . . . the form of passage through the world. A man who is rich and famous who sings, "God don't never change," is confirming his hegemony and good fortune . . . or merely calling the bank. A blind hopeless black American is saying something very different. He is telling you about the extraordinary order of the world. But he is not telling you about his "fate." Fate is a luxury available only to those fortunate citizens with alternatives. The view from the top of the hill is not the same as that from the bottom of the hill. Nor are most viewers at either end of the hill, even certain that, in fact, there is any other place from which to look. Looking down usually eliminates the possibility of understanding what it must be like to look up. Or try to imagine yourself as not existing. It is difficult, but poets and politicians try every other day.

Being told to "speak proper," meaning that you become fluent with the jargon of power, is also a part of not "speaking proper." That is, the culture which desperately understands that it does not "speak proper," or is not fluent with the terms of social strength, also understands somewhere that its desire to gain such fluency is done at a terrifying risk. The bourgeois Negro accepts such risk as profit. But does *close-ter* (in the context of "jes a close-ter, walk withee") mean the same thing as *closer*? Close-ter, in the term of its user is, believe me, exact. It means a quality of existence, of actual physical disposition perhaps . . . in its manifestation as a *tone* and *rhythm* by which people live, most often in response to common modes of thought best enforced by some factor of environmental

12

13

14

15

emotion that is exact and specific. Even the picture it summons is different, and certainly the "Thee" that is used to connect the implied "Me" with, is different. The God of the damned cannot know the God of the damner, that is, cannot know he is God. As no Blues person can really believe emotionally in Pascal's God, or Wittgenstein's question, "Can the concept of God exist in a perfectly logical language?" Answer: "God don't never change."

Communication is only important because it is the broadest 16 root of education. And all cultures communicate exactly what they have, a powerful motley of experience.

QUESTIONS

1. Why do words have power, according to Baraka? Explain the different ways Baraka says they have power.

2. Explain the different meanings of "money" and "God don't never change." Why, according to Baraka, do these words have different meanings?

3. How does Baraka account for different meanings of words? Give examples of low, slangy, vulgar diction and scholarly diction. What is the effect of both?

4. Identify any sentence fragments in the essay. How do they contribute to Baraka's style?

5. Detail how Baraka uses contrasts between the rich and the poor to explain his thesis.

6. Give three examples that Baraka offers to prove his point. Explain how examples help him to support his thesis.

7. What methods of definition does Baraka use?

8. Explain how Baraka uses allusion and metaphor to support his thesis.

9. Relate Baraka's description of the differences in words to the words that you or your parents use or words that you or your teachers use.

10. Write an expository essay in which you try to define the "social hegemony" of several words of your own choice.

Sight, Sound, and the Fury

Marshall McLuhan (1911–1980) has been called the "oracle of the electronic age." He began his career as a literary scholar, but later shifted his studies from the message to the medium through which the message is transmitted. Beginning with *Understanding Media: The Extensions of Man* (1964) and *The Gutenberg Galaxy: The Making of Typographic Man* (1967), McLuhan attempted to show the influence of the technology of communication upon culture. His later books include *The Medium Is the Message: An Inventory to Effects* (1967) and *From Cliché to Archetype* (1972). The following essay exhibits in brief the interplay of technology, language, and culture that McLuhan investigated in his major work.

O n his recent visit to America, Roy Campbell mentioned that when Dylan Thomas had discovered he could read poetry on the radio, this discovery transformed his later poetry for the better. Thomas discovered a new dimension in his language when he established a new relation with the public.   1

Until Gutenberg, poetic publication meant the reading or singing of one's poems to a small audience. When poetry began to exist primarily on the printed page, in the seventeenth century, there occurred that strange mixture of sight and sound later known as "metaphysical poetry" which has so much in common with modern poetry.   2

American colonization began when the only culture available to most men was that of the printed book. European culture was then, as now, as much an affair of music, painting, sculpture, and communication as it was of literature. So that to this day North Americans associate culture mainly with books. But, paradoxically, it is in North America that the new media of sight and sound have had the greatest popular sway. Is it precisely because we make the widest separation between culture and our new media that we are unable to see the new media as serious culture? Have four centuries of book-culture hypnotized us into such concentration on the content of books and the new media that we cannot see that the very form of any medium of communication is as important as anything that it conveys?   3

Ireland is perhaps the only part of the English-speaking   4 world where the oral tradition of culture has strongly persisted in spite of the printed page. And Ireland has given us Wilde, Shaw, Yeats, Synge, and Joyce in recent years—all of them masters of the magic of the spoken word. A Ballynooley farmer who returned to Ireland from America said to his neighbor: "In three years I didn't meet a man who could sing a ballad, let alone compose one on his feet."

The printed page was itself a highly specialized (and spatia- 5 lized) term of communication. In 1500 A.D. it was revolutionary. And Erasmus was perhaps the first to grasp the fact that the revolution was going to occur above all in the classroom. He devoted himself to the production of textbooks and to the setting up of grammar schools. The printed book soon liquidated two thousand years of manuscript culture. It created the solitary student. It set up the rule of private interpretation against public disputation. It established the divorce between "literature and life." It created a new and highly abstract culture because it was itself a mechanized form of culture. Today, when the textbook has yielded to the classroom project and the classroom as social workshop and discussion group, it is easier for us to notice what was going on in 1500. Today we know that the turn to the visual on one hand, that is, to photography, and to the audi- tory media of radio and public address systems on the other hand, has created a totally new environment for the educational process.

André Malraux has recently popularized the notion of the art 6 revolution of our time in his *Museum Without Walls*. His theme is that the picture book today can embrace a greater range of art than any museum. By bringing such a range of art within portable compass, however, it has changed even the painter's approach to painting. Again, it is not just a question of message, image, or content. The picture book as a museum without walls has for the artist a new technical meaning, just as for the spectator pictorial communication means a large but unconscious shift in his ways of thought and feeling.

We have long been accustomed to the notion that a person's 7 beliefs shape and color his existence. They provide the windows which frame, and through which he views, all events. We are less accustomed to the notion that the shapes of a technological environ- ment are also idea-windows. Every shape (gimmick or metropolis), every situation planned and realized by man's factive intelligence, is a window which reveals or distorts reality. Today when power technology has taken over the entire global environment to be manipulated as the material of art, nature has disappeared with nature-poetry. And the effectiveness of the classroom has diminished

MARSHALL McLUHAN

with the decline of the monopoly of book-culture. If Erasmus saw the classroom as the new stage for the drama of the printing-press, we can see today that the new situation for young and old alike is classrooms without walls. The entire urban environment has become aggressively pedagogic. Everybody and everything has a message to declare, a line to plug.

This is the time of transition from the commercial age, when 8 it was the production and distribution of commodities which occupied the ingenuity of men. Today we have moved from the production of packaged goods to the packaging of information. Formerly we invaded foreign markets with goods. Today we invade whole cultures with packaged information, entertainment, and ideas. In view of the instantaneous global scope of the new media of sight and sound, even the newspaper is slow. But the press ousted the book in the nineteenth century because the book arrived too late. The newspaper page was not a mere enlargement of the book page. It was, like the movie, a new collective art form.

To retrace some of this ground, it will help to recall that in the 9 *Phaedrus,* Plato argued that the new arrival of writing would revolutionize culture for the worse. He suggested that it would substitute reminiscence for thought and mechanical learning for the true dialect of the living quest for truth by discourse and conversation. It was as if he foresaw the library of Alexandria and the unending exegesis upon previous exegesis of the scholiasts and grammarians.

It would seem that the great virtue of writing is its power to 10 arrest the swift process of thought for steady contemplation and analysis. Writing is the translation of the audible into the visual. In large measure it is the spatialization of thought. Yet writing on papyrus and parchment fostered a very different set of mental habits from those we associate with print and books. In the first place silent reading was unknown until the macadamized, streamlined surfaces of the printed page arrived to permit swift traverse of the eye alone. In the second place, difficulty of access to manuscripts impelled students to memorize so far as possible everything they read. This led to encyclopedism, but also to having on tap in oral discourse one's entire erudition.

The child at school in the Middle Ages had first to make his 11 own copies of texts from dictation. He had next to compile his own grammar and lexicon and commonplace book. The arrival of plenty of cheap, uniform, printed texts changed all this. The mechanization of writing by means of the assembly line of movable type speedily expanded the range of available reading and just as quickly reduced the habit of oral discourse as a way of learning. During the sixteenth century, however, a degree of equilibrium persisted between oral and written learning which we associate with the special excellence of Elizabethan drama, sermon, and poetry.

In the reverse direction, much of the vivid energy of American speech and writing in the twentieth century is the result of the movement away from book-culture towards oral communication. This non-literary direction of speech has been felt to a much smaller degree in England and in Europe during the same period. Radio in particular has encouraged the return to the panel discussion and the round-table. But the spontaneous move towards the seminar and class discussion as learning process has been helped by press and photography too, in so far as these have challenged the monopoly of the book.   12

Above all, the habits of the business community in demanding conference and discussion as the swift way of establishing insight into method and procedure in various specialized branches of business—these have prompted the new reliance on speech as a means of discovery. It is significant, for example, that the atomic physicists found that only by daily, face-to-face association could they get on with their tasks during the past war.   13

It has long been a truism that changes in material culture cause shifts in the patterns of the entire culture. The ancient road made possible armies and empires and destroyed the isolated city states of Greece. But the road depended in the first place on writing. Behind the imperial command of great land areas stood the written word in easily transportable form. In the nineteenth century the newspapers, especially after the telegraph, paid for new roads and faster transport by land and sea. The press altered the forms of government, and the telegraph brought secret diplomacy to an end. When events in Egypt or Russia, London, Paris, or New York were known everywhere at once, the time for secret negotiation was reduced to hours and minutes. And the great national populations of the world, altered and emotionalized by the press, could confront one another immediately for a show-down.   14

Printing had from the first fostered nationalism because the vernaculars with their large reading publics were more profitable to commercial publishers than Latin. The press has pushed this nationalism to its ultimate point. There it remains. But photography and movies, like music and painting, are international in their power of appeal. The power of pictures to leap over national frontiers and prejudices is well-known, for good and ill.   15

One aspect of the press deserves special comment in this same respect. The contents of newspapers, their messages and information, have steadily promoted nationalism. But the form of the newspaper page is powerfully inter-cultural and international. The   16 unformulated message of an assembly of news items from every quarter of the globe is that the world today is one city. All war is civil war. All suffering is our own. So that regardless of the political line, or the time or the place, the mere format of the press exerts a single pressure. Basic acceptance of this fact is recorded in the steady weakening of interest in political parties everywhere.

From the point of view of its format, the press as a daily 17 cross-section of the globe is a mirror of the technological instruments of communication. It is the popular daily book, the great collective poem, the universal entertainment of our age. As such it has modified poetic techniques and in turn has already been modified by the newer media of movie, radio, and television. These represent revolutions in communication as radical as printing itself. In fact, they are "magic casements opening on the foam of perilous seas," on which few of us have yet ventured in thought, art or living. If Erasmus was the first to size up and exploit the printing-press as a new force in art and education, James Joyce was the first to seize upon newspaper, radio, movie, and television to set up his "verbivoco-visual" drama in *Finnegans Wake*. Pound and Eliot are, in comparison with Joyce, timid devotees of the book as art form. But most of the difficulties which the ordinary person encounters with the poetry of Pound and Eliot disappear if it is viewed as a historical newsreel of persons, myths, ideas, and events with thematic musical score built in. Joyce had a much greater trust of language and reality than Pound or Eliot. By contrast they give their language and reality the Hollywood glamor treatment. Joyce is closer to a De Sica film with its awareness of the intimate riches of the most ordinary scenes and situations.

But the reader who approaches Pound, Eliot, and Joyce alike 18 as exploiters of the cinematic aspects of language will arrive at appreciation more quickly than the one who unconsciously tries to make sense of them by reducing their use of the new media of communication to the abstract linear forms of the book page.

The basic fact to keep in mind about the movie camera and 19 projector is their resemblance to the process of human cognition. That is the real source of their magical, transforming power. The camera rolls up the external world on a spool. It does this by rapid still shots. The projector unwinds this spool as a kind of magic carpet which conveys the enchanted spectator anywhere in the world in an instant. The camera records and analyzes the daylight world with more than human intensity because of the forty-five degree angle of the camera eye. The projector reveals this daylight world on a dark screen where it becomes a dream world.

The wonderful resemblance in all this to human cognition 20

extends at least this far: in cognition we have to interiorize the exterior world. We have to recreate in the medium of our senses and inner faculties the drama of existence. This is the work of the *logos poietikos*, the agent intellect. In speech we utter that drama which we have analogously recreated within us. In speech we make or *poet* the world even as we may say that the movie parrots the world. Languages themselves are thus the greatest of all works of art. They are the collective hymns to existence. For in cognition itself is the whole of the poetic process. But the artist differs from most men in his power to arrest and then reverse the stages of human apprehension. He learns how to embody the stages of cognition (Aristotle's "plot") in an exterior work which can be held up for contemplation.

21
Even in this respect the movie resembles the cognitive process since the daylight world which the camera rolls up on the spool is reversed and projected to become the magical dream world of the audience. But all media of communication share something of this cognitive character which only a Thomist vision of existence and cognition dare do justice to.

22
Television, for example, differs from the movie in the immediacy with which it picks up and renders back the visible. The TV camera is like the microphone in relation to the voice. The movie has no such immediacy of pick-up and feedback. As we begin to look into the inevitably cognitive character of the various media we soon get over the jitters that come from exclusive concern with any one form of communication.

23
In his *Theory of the Film*, Bela Balazs notes how "the discovery of printing gradually rendered illegible the faces of men. So much could be read from paper that the method of conveying meaning by facial expression fell into desuetude. Victor Hugo wrote once that the printed book took over the part played by the cathedral in the Middle Ages and became the carrier of the spirit of the people. But the thousands of books tore the one spirit. . . . into thousands of opinions . . . tore the church into a thousand books. The visible spirit was thus turned into a legible spirit and visual culture into a culture of concepts."

24
Before printing, a reader was one who discerned and probed riddles. After printing, it meant one who scanned, who skipped along the macadamized surfaces of print. Today at the end of that process we have come to equate reading skill with speed and distraction rather than wisdom. But print, the mechanization of writing, was succeeded in the nineteenth century by photography and then by the mechanization of human gesture in the movie. This was followed by the mechanization of speech in telephone, phonograph and radio. In the talkies, and finally with TV, came the

mechanization of the totality of human expression, of voice, gesture, and human figure in action.

Each of these steps in the mechanization of human expres- 25 sion was comparable in its scope to the revolution brought about by the mechanization of writing itself. The changes in the ways of human association, social and political, were telescoped in time and so hidden from casual observers.

If there is a truism in the history of human communication it 26 is that any innovation in the external means of communication brings in its train shock on shock of social change. One effect of writing was to make possible cities, roads, armies, and empires. The letters of the alphabet were indeed the dragon's teeth. The printed book not only fostered nationalism but made it possible to bring the world of the past into every study. The newspaper is a daily book which brings a slice of all the cultures of the world under our eyes every day. To this extent it reverses the tendency of the printing press to accentuate merely national culture. Pictorial journalism and reportage tend strongly in the same international direction. But is this true of radio? Radio has strengthened the oral habit of communication and extend-ed it, via the panel and round-table, to serious learning. Yet radio seems to be a form which also strengthens the national culture. Merely oral societies, for example, are the ultimate in national exclusiveness.

A group of us recently performed an experiment with a large 27 group of students. We divided them into four sections and assigned each section to a separate communication channel. Each section got the identical lecture simultaneously, but one read it, one heard it as a regular lecture in a studio, one heard it on radio and one heard and saw it as a TV broadcast. Immediately afterwards we administered a quiz to determine apprehension and understanding of this new and difficult material. The TV section came out on top, then the radio section, then the studio, and reading sections at the bottom. This was a totally unexpected result and it is too soon to generalize; but it is quite certain that the so-called mass media are not necessarily ordained to be channels of popular entertainment only.

It is "desirable" in thinking about the new media that we 28 should recall that buildings are mass communications and that the first mechanical medium was print from movable type. In fact, the discovery of movable type was the ancestor of all assembly lines, and it would be foolish to overlook the impact of the technological form involved in print on the psychological life of readers. To overlook this would be as unrealistic as to ignore rhythm and tempo in music. Likewise it is only common sense to recognize that the general situation created by a communicative channel and its audience is a large part of that in which and by which the individuals commune. The encoded message cannot be regarded as a mere capsule or pellet produced at one point and consumed at another. Communication is communication all along the line.

One might illustrate from sports. The best brand of football played before fifty people would lack something of the power to communicate. The large enthusiastic crowd is necessary to represent the community at large, just as the players enact a drama which externalizes certain motivations and tensions in the communal life which would not otherwise be visible or available for audience participation. In India huge crowds assemble to experience *"darshan,"* which they consider to occur when they are massed in the presence of a visible manifestation of their collective life. 29

The new media do something similar for us in the West. Movies, radio, and TV establish certain personalities on a new plane of existence. They exist not so much in themselves but as types of collective life felt and perceived through a mass medium. L'il Abner, Bob Hope, Donald Duck, and Marilyn Monroe become points of collective awareness and communication for an entire society. And as technology increasingly undertakes to submit the entire planet as well as the contents of consciousness to the purposes of man's factive intelligence, it behooves us to consider the whole process of magical transformation involved in the media acutely and extensively. 30

From this point of view it should be obvious, for example, that the framers of the Hollywood morality code were operating with a very inadequate set of perceptions and concepts about the nature of the movie medium. Modern discussions of censorship, in the same way, are helplessly tied to conceptions borrowed from book culture alone. And the defenders of book culture have seldom given any thought to any of the media as art forms, the book least of all. The result is that their "defense" might as well be staged on an abandoned movie lot for all the effect it has on the actual situation. 31

When I wrote *The Mechanical Bride* some years ago I did not realize that I was attempting a defense of book culture against the new media. I can now see that I was trying to bring some of the critical awareness fostered by literary training to bear on the new media of sight and sound. My strategy was wrong, because my obsession with literary values blinded me to much that was actually happening for good and ill. What we have to defend today is not the values developed in any particular culture or by any one mode of communication. Modern technology presumes to attempt a total transformation of man and his environment. This calls in turn for an inspection and defense of all human values. And so far as merely human aid goes, the citadel of this defense must be located in 32 analytical awareness of the nature of the creative process involved in human cognition. For it is in this citadel that science and technology have already established themselves in their manipulation of the new media.

QUESTIONS

1. McLuhan's definition of communication is far broader than most of our definitions of that word. Give some examples of his more unusual applications of the word "communication."

2. According to the author, what effects have writing, printed words, newspapers, radio, and finally television had upon Western culture?

3. There are numerous allusions in this essay. Identify the following: Gutenberg (paragraph 2); Wilde, Shaw, Yeats, Synge, and Joyce (paragraph 4); André Malraux (paragraph 6); Erasmus (paragraph 7); Plato (paragraph 9); the library of Alexandria (paragraph 9); Ezra Pound, Eliot, and De Sica (paragraph 17); Thomist (paragraph 21); and Victor Hugo (paragraph 23). What effect does the range of allusions have on the reader?

4. In his effort to explain his argument, McLuhan uses numerous metaphors. Identify five of them and explain their relevance to McLuhan's discussion.

5. To a great degree, this essay is a "history of human communications." Does McLuhan present this history in a simple linear way? If not, how does he keep order among his historical events? How does his presentation reflect his sense of modern culture?

6. How and where does McLuhan use cause-and-effect analysis?

7. McLuhan uses contrast to develop meaning. Give examples of contrast in the essay.

8. Explain the importance of paragraph 30 in the essay. What sentence here could serve as the essay's thesis? Why does McLuhan defer his thesis for so long?

9. What effect do you think new technologies such as video cassettes, holography, videophones, and computer terminals will have on our culture?

10. a. Write an essay on the new communications systems in our culture.
b. Use McLuhan's ideas to analyze differences between watching movies and reading.

 SIGHT, SOUND, AND THE FURY

Politics and the English Language

George Orwell (1903–1950) was the pseudonym of Eric Blair, an English novelist, essayist, and journalist. Orwell served with the Indian Imperial Police from 1922 to 1927 in Burma, fought in the Spanish Civil War, and acquired from his experiences a disdain of totalitarian and imperialistic systems. This attitude is reflected in the satirical *Animal Farm* (1945) and in the bleak, futuristic novel *1984* (1949). This essay, one of the more famous of the twentieth century, relates sloppy thinking and writing with political oppression.

ost people who bother with the matter at all would admit that the English language is in a bad way, but it is generally assumed that we cannot by conscious action do anything about it. Our civilisation is decadent, and our language—so the argument runs—must inevitably share in the general collapse. It follows that any struggle against the abuse of language is a sentimental archaism, like preferring candles to electric light or hansom cabs to aeroplanes. Underneath this lies the half-conscious belief that language is a natural growth and not an instrument which we shape for our own purposes. 1

Now, it is clear that the decline of a language must ultimately have political and economic causes: it is not due simply to the bad influence of this or that individual writer. But an effect can become a cause, reinforcing the original cause and producing the same effect in an intensified form, and so on indefinitely. A man may take to drink because he feels himself to be a failure, and then fail all the more completely because he drinks. It is rather the same thing that is happening to the English language. It becomes ugly and inaccurate because our thoughts are foolish, but the slovenliness of our language makes it easier for us to have foolish thoughts. The point is that the process is reversible. Modern English, especially written English, is full of bad habits which spread by imitation and which can be avoided if one is willing to take the necessary trouble. If one gets rid of these habits one can think more clearly, and to think clearly is a necessary first step towards political regeneration: so that the fight against bad English is not frivolous and is not the exclusive concern of profession-al writers. I will come back to this presently, and I hope that by that time the meaning of what I have said here will have become clearer. Meanwhile, here are five specimens of the English language as it is now habitually written. 2

These five passages have not been picked out because they 3
are especially bad—I could have quoted far worse if I had chosen—
but because they illustrate various of the mental vices from which we
now suffer. They are a little below the average, but are fairly
representative samples. I number them so that I can refer back to
them when necessary:

1. I am not, indeed, sure whether it is not true to say
that the Milton who once seemed not unlike a seventeenth-
century Shelley had not become, out of an experience ever
more bitter in each year, more alien (sic) to the founder of that
Jesuit sect which nothing could induce him to tolerate.

Professor Harold Laski (Essay in *Freedom of Expression*).

2. Above all, we cannot play ducks and drakes with a
native battery of idioms which prescribes such egregious
collocations of vocables as the Basic *put up with* for *tolerate* or
put at a loss for *bewilder*.

Professor Lancelot Hogben (*Interglossa*).

3. On the one side we have the free personality: by
definition it is not neurotic, for it has neither conflict nor
dream. Its desires, such as they are, are transparent, for they
are just what institutional approval keeps in the forefront of
consciousness; another institutional pattern would alter their
number and intensity; there is little in them that is natural,
irreducible, or culturally dangerous. But *on the other side*, the
social bond itself is nothing but the mutual reflection of these
self-secure integrities. Recall the definition of love. Is not this
the very picture of a small academic? Where is there a place in
this hall of mirrors for either personality or fraternity?

Essay on psychology in *Politics* (New York).

4. All the "best people" from the gentlemen's clubs,
and all the frantic Fascist captains, united in common hatred
of Socialism and bestial horror of the rising tide of the mass
revolutionary movement, have turned to acts of provocation,
to foul incendiarism, to medieval legends of poisoned wells,
to legalise their own destruction to proletarian organisations,
and rouse the agitated petty-bourgeoisie to chauvinistic fervour on behalf of the fight against the revolutionary way out
of the crisis.

Communist pamphlet.

5. If a new spirit *is* to be infused into this old country,
there is one thorny and contentious reform which must be
tackled, and that is the humanisation and galvanisation of the
BBC. Timidity here will bespeak canker and atrophy of the
soul. The heart of Britain may be sound and of strong beat,

for instance, but the British lion's roar at present is like that of Bottom in Shakespeare's *Midsummer Night's Dream*—as gentle as any sucking dove. A virile new Britain cannot continue indefinitely to be traduced in the eyes, or rather ears, of the world by the effete languors of Langham Place, brazenly masquerading as "standard English". When the Voice of Britain is heard at nine o'clock, better far and infinitely less ludicrous to hear aitches honestly dropped than the present priggish, inflated, inhibited, school-ma'amish arch braying of blameless bashful mewing maidens!

Letter in *Tribune*.

Each of these passages has faults of its own, but, quite apart from avoidable ugliness, two qualities are common to all of them. The first is staleness of imagery: the other is lack of precision. The writer either has a meaning and cannot express it, or he inadvertently says something else, or he is almost indifferent as to whether his words mean anything or not. This mixture of vagueness and sheer incompetence is the most marked characteristic of modern English prose, and especially of any kind of political writing. As soon as certain topics are raised, the concrete melts into the abstract and no one seems able to think of turns of speech that are not hackneyed: prose consists less and less of *words* chosen for the sake of their meaning, and more of *phrases* tacked together like the sections of a prefabricated hen-house. I list below, with notes and examples, various of the tricks by means of which the work of prose construction is habitually dodged:

Dying metaphors. A newly invented metaphor assists thought by evoking a visual image, while on the other hand a metaphor which is technically "dead" (e.g. *iron resolution*) has in effect reverted to being an ordinary word and can generally be used without loss of vividness. But in between these two classes there is a huge dump of worn-out metaphors which have lost all evocative power and are merely used because they save people the trouble of inventing phrases for themselves. Examples are: *Ring the changes on, take up the cudgels for, toe the line, ride roughshod over, stand shoulder to shoulder with, play into the hands of, no axe to grind, grist to the mill, fishing in troubled waters, rift within the lute, on the order of the day, Achilles' heel, swan song, hotbed.* Many of these are used without knowledge of their meaning (what is a "rift", for instance?), and incompatible metaphors are frequently mixed, a sure sign that the writer is not interested in what he is saying. Some metaphors now current have been twisted out of their original meaning without those who use them even being aware of the fact. For example, *toe the line* is sometimes written *tow the line.* Another example is *the hammer and the anvil*, now always used

GEORGE ORWELL

with the implication that the anvil gets the worst of it. In real life it is always the anvil that breaks the hammer, never the other way about: a writer who stopped to think what he was saying would be aware of this, and would avoid perverting the original phrase.

Operators, or verbal false limbs.   These save the trouble of picking out 6 appropriate verbs and nouns, and at the same time pad each sentence with extra syllables which give it an appearance of symmetry. Characteristic phrases are: *render inoperative, militate against, prove unacceptable, make contact with, be subjected to, give rise to, give grounds for, have the effect of, play a leading part (rôle) in, make itself felt, take effect, exhibit a tendency to, serve the purpose of,* etc. etc. The keynote is the elimination of simple verbs. Instead of being a single word, such as *break, stop, spoil, mend, kill,* a verb becomes a *phrase,* made up of a noun or adjective tacked on to some general-purposes verb such as *prove, serve, form, play, render.* In addition, the passive voice is wherever possible used in preference to the active, and noun constructions are used instead of gerunds (*by examination of* instead of *by examining*). The range of verbs is further cut down by means of the *-ise* and *de-* formations, and banal statements are given an appearance of profundity by means of the *not un-* formation. Simple conjunctions and prepositions are replaced by such phrases as *with respect to, having regard to, the fact that, by dint of, in view of, in the interests of, on the hypothesis that;* and the ends of sentences are saved from anticlimax by such resounding commonplaces as *greatly to be desired, cannot be left out of account, a development to be expected in the near future, deserving of serious consideration, brought to a satisfactory conclusion,* and so on and so forth.

Pretentious diction.   Words like *phenomenon, element, individual* (as 7 noun), *objective, categorical, effective, virtual, basic, primary, promote, constitute, exhibit, exploit, utilise, eliminate, liquidate,* are used to dress up simple statements and give an air of scientific impartiality to biassed judgements. Adjectives like *epoch-making, epic, historic, unforgettable, triumphant, age-old, inevitable, inexorable, veritable,* are used to dignify the sordid processes of international politics, while writing that aims at glorifying war usually takes on an archaic colour, its characteristic words being: *realm, throne, chariot, mailed fist, trident, sword, shield, buckler, banner, jackboot, clarion.* Foreign words and expressions such as *cul de sac, ancien régime, deus ex machina, mutatis mutandis, status quo, Gleichschaltung, Weltanschauung,* are used to give an air of culture and elegance. Except for the useful abbreviations *i.e., e.g.,* and *etc.,* there is no real need for any of the hundreds of foreign phrases now current in English. Bad writers, and especially scientific, political and sociological writers, are nearly always haunted by the notion that Latin or Greek words are grander than Saxon ones, and unnecessary words like *expedite, ameliorate, predict, extraneous, deracinated, clandestine, sub-aqueous* and hundreds of others constantly gain ground from their Anglo-Saxon opposite numbers.[1] The jargon peculiar to Marxist writing (*hyena, hangman, cannibal, petty bourgeois, these gentry, lacquey, flunkey, mad dog, White Guard*, etc.) consists largely of words and phrases translated from Russian, German or French; but the normal way of coining a new word is to use a Latin or Greek root with the appropriate affix and, where necessary, the *-ise* formation. It is often easier to make up words of this kind (*deregionalise, impermissible, extramarital, non-fragmentatory* and so forth) than to think up the English words that will cover one's meaning. The result, in general, is an increase in slovenliness and vagueness.

Meaningless words. In certain kinds of writing, particularly in art criticism and literary criticism, it is normal to come across long passages which are almost completely lacking in meaning.[2] Words like *romantic, plastic, values, human, dead, sentimental, natural, vitality*, as used in art criticism, are strictly meaningless, in the sense that they not only do not point to any discoverable object, but are hardly even expected to do so by the reader. When one critic writes, "The outstanding features of Mr X's work is its living quality", while another writes, "The immediately striking thing about Mr X's work is its peculiar deadness", the reader accepts this as a simple difference of opinion. If words like *black* and *white* were involved, instead of the jargon words *dead* and *living*, he would see at once that language was being used in an improper way. Many political words are similarly abused. The word *Fascism* has now no meaning except in so far as it signifies "something not desirable". The words *democracy, socialism, freedom, patriotic, realistic, justice*, have each of them several different meanings which cannot be reconciled with one another. In the case of a word like *democracy*, not only is there no agreed definition, but the attempt to make one is resisted from all sides. It is almost universally felt that when we call a country democratic we are praising it: consequently the defenders of every kind of régime claim that it is a democracy, and fear that they might have to stop using the word if it were tied down to any one meaning. Words of this kind are often

[1]An interesting illustration of this is the way in which the English flower names which were in use till very recently are being ousted by Greek ones, *snapdragon* becoming *antirrhinum, forget-me-not* becoming *myosotis*, etc. It is hard to see any practical reason for this change of fashion: it is probably due to an instinctive turning-away from the more homely word and a vague feeling that the Greek word is scientific.

[2]Example: "Comfort's catholicity of perception and image, strangely Whitmanesque in range, almost the exact opposite in aesthetic compulsion, continues to evoke that trembling atmospheric accumulative hinting at a cruel, an inexorably serene timelessness . . . Wrey Gardiner scores by aiming at simple bullseyes with precision. Only they are not so simple, and through this contented sadness runs more than the surface bitter-sweet of resignation." (*Poetry Quarterly*).

GEORGE ORWELL

used in a consciously dishonest way. That is, the person who uses them has his own private definition, but allows his hearer to think he means something quite different. Statements like *Marshal Pétain was a true patriot, The Soviet press is the freest in the world, The Catholic Church is opposed to persecution,* are almost always made with intent to deceive. Other words used in variable meanings, in most cases more or less dishonestly, are: *class, totalitarian, science, progressive, reactionary, bourgeois, equality.*

Now that I have made this catalogue of swindles and perversions, let me give another example of the kind of writing that they lead to. This time it must of its nature be an imaginary one. I am going to translate a passage of good English into modern English of the worst sort. Here is a well-known verse from *Ecclesiastes:* 9

> I returned, and saw under the sun, that the race is not to the swift, nor the battle to the strong, neither yet bread to the wise, nor yet riches to men of understanding, nor yet favour to men of skill; but time and chance happeneth to them all.

Here it is in modern English: 10

> Objective consideration of contemporary phenomena compels the conclusion that success or failure in competitive activities exhibits no tendency to be commensurate with innate capacity, but that a considerable element of the unpredictable must invariably be taken into account.

This is a parody, but not a very gross one. Exhibit 3, above, 11 for instance, contains several patches of the same kind of English. It will be seen that I have not made a full translation. The beginning and ending of the sentence follow the original meaning fairly closely, but in the middle the concrete illustrations—race, battle, bread—dissolve into the vague phrase "success or failure in competitive activities". This had to be so, because no modern writer of the kind I am discussing—no one capable of using phrases like "objective consideration of contemporary phenomena"—would ever tabulate his thoughts in that precise and detailed way. The whole tendency of modern prose is away from concreteness. Now analyse these two sentences a little more closely. The first contains 49 words but only 60 syllables, and all its words are those of everyday life. The second contains 38 words of 90 syllables: 18 of its words are from Latin roots, and one from Greek. The first sentence contains six vivid images, and only one phrase ("time and chance") that could be called vague. The second contains not a single fresh, arresting phrase, and in spite of its 90 syllables it gives only a shortened version of the meaning con-

 POLITICS AND THE ENGLISH LANGUAGE

tained in the first. Yet without a doubt it is the second kind of sentence that is gaining ground in modern English. I do not want to exaggerate. This kind of writing is not yet universal, and outcrops of simplicity will occur here and there in the worst-written page. Still, if you or I were told to write a few lines on the uncertainty of human fortunes, we should probably come much nearer to my imaginary sentence than to the one from *Ecclesiastes*.

As I have tried to show, modern writing at its worst does not consist in picking out words for the sake of their meaning and inventing images in order to make the meaning clearer. It consists in gumming together long strips of words which have already been set in order by someone else, and making the results presentable by sheer humbug. The attraction of this way of writing is that it is easy. It is easier—even quicker, once you have the habit—to say *In my opinion it is a not unjustifiable assumption that* than to say *I think*. If you use ready-made phrases, you not only don't have to hunt about for words; you also don't have to bother with the rhythms of your sentences, since these phrases are generally so arranged as to be more or less euphonious. When you are composing in a hurry—when you are dictating to a stenographer, for instance, or making a public speech—it is natural to fall into a pretentious, latinised style. Tags like *a consideration which we should do well to bear in mind* or *a conclusion to which all of us would readily assent* will save many a sentence from coming down with a bump. By using stale metaphors, similes and idioms, you save much mental effort, at the cost of leaving your meaning vague, not only for your reader but for yourself. This is the significance of mixed metaphors. The sole aim of a metaphor is to call up a visual image. When these images clash—as in *The Fascist octopus has sung its swan song, the jackboot is thrown into the melting-pot*—it can be taken as certain that the writer is not seeing a mental image of the objects he is naming; in other words he is not really thinking. Look again at the examples I gave at the beginning of this essay. Professor Laski (1) uses five negatives in 53 words. One of these is superfluous, making nonsense of the whole passage, and in addition there is the slip *alien* for akin, making further nonsense, and several avoidable pieces of clumsiness which increase the general vagueness. Professor Hogben (2) plays ducks and drakes with a battery which is able to write prescriptions, and, while disapproving of the everyday phrase *put up with*, is unwilling to look *egregious* up in the dictionary and see what it means. (3), if one takes an uncharitable attitude towards it, is simply meaningless: probably one could work out its intended meaning by reading the whole of the article in which it occurs. In (4) the writer knows more or less what he wants to say, but an accumulation of stale phrases chokes him like tea-leaves blocking a sink. In (5) words and meaning have almost parted company. People who write in this manner usually have a general emotional meaning—they dislike one thing and want to express solidarity with another—but they are not interested in the detail of what they are saying. A scrupulous writer, in every sentence that he writes, will ask himself at least four questions, thus: What am I trying to say? What words will express it? What image or idiom will make it clearer? Is this image fresh enough to have an effect? And he will probably ask himself two more: Could I put it more shortly? Have I said anything that is avoidably ugly? But you are not obliged to go to all this trouble. You can shirk it by simply throwing your mind open and letting the ready-made phrases come crowding in. They will construct your sentences for you—even think your thoughts for you, to a certain extent—and at need they will perform the important service of partially concealing your meaning even from yourself. It is at this point that the special connection between politics and the debasement of language becomes clear.

In our time it is broadly true that political writing is bad 13 writing. Where it is not true, it will generally be found that the writer is some kind of rebel, expressing his private opinions, and not a "party line". Orthodoxy, of whatever colour, seems to demand a lifeless, imitative style. The political dialects to be found in pamphlets, leading articles, manifestos, White Papers and the speeches of Under-Secretaries do, of course, vary from party to party, but they are all alike in that one almost never finds in them a fresh, vivid, home-made turn of speech. When one watches some tired hack on the platform mechanically repeating the familiar phrases—*bestial atrocities, iron heel, blood-stained tyranny, free peoples of the world, stand shoulder to shoulder*—one often has a curious feeling that one is not watching a live human being but some kind of dummy: a feeling which suddenly becomes stronger at moments when the light catches the speaker's spectacles and turns them into blank discs which seem to have no eyes behind them. And this is not altogether fanciful. A speaker who uses that kind of phraseology has gone some distance towards turning himself into a machine. The appropriate noises are coming out of his larynx, but his brain is not involved as it would be if he were choosing his words for himself. If the speech he is making is one that he is accustomed to make over and over again, he may be almost unconscious of what he is saying, as one is when one utters the responses in church. And this reduced state of consciousness, if not indispensable, is at any rate favourable to political conformity.

In our time, political speech and writing are largely the 14 defence of the indefensible. Things like the continuance of British rule in India, the Russian purges and deportations, the dropping of the atom bombs on Japan, can indeed be defended, but only by arguments which are too brutal for most people to face, and which do

 POLITICS AND THE ENGLISH LANGUAGE **355**

not square with the professed aims of political parties. Thus political language has to consist largely of euphemism, question-begging and sheer cloudy vagueness. Defenceless villages are bombarded from the air, the inhabitants driven out into the countryside, the cattle machine-gunned, the huts set on fire with incendiary bullets: this is called *pacification*. Millions of peasants are robbed of their farms and sent trudging along the roads with no more than they can carry: this is called *transfer of population* or *rectification of frontiers*. People are imprisoned for years without trial, or shot in the back of the neck or sent to die of scurvy in Arctic lumber camps: this is called *elimination of unreliable elements*. Such phraseology is needed if one wants to name things without calling up mental pictures of them. Consider for instance some comfortable English professor defending Russian totalitarianism. He cannot say outright, "I believe in killing off your opponents when you can get good results by doing so". Probably, therefore, he will say something like this:

> While freely conceding that the Soviet régime exhibits certain features which the humanitarian may be inclined to deplore, we must, I think, agree that a certain curtailment of the right to political opposition is an unavoidable concomitant of transitional periods, and that the rigours which the Russian people have been called upon to undergo have been amply justified in the sphere of concrete achievement.

The inflated style is itself a kind of euphemism. A mass of   15
Latin words falls upon the facts like soft snow, blurring the outlines and covering up all the details. The great enemy of clear language is insincerity. When there is a gap between one's real and one's declared aims, one turns as it were instinctively to long words and exhausted idioms, like a cuttlefish squirting out ink. In our age there is no such thing as "keeping out of politics". All issues are political issues, and politics itself is a mass of lies, evasions, folly, hatred and schizophrenia. When the general atmosphere is bad, language must suffer. I should expect to find—this is a guess which I have not sufficient knowledge to verify—that the German, Russian and Italian languages have all deteriorated in the last ten or fifteen years, as a result of dictatorship.

But if thought corrupts language, language can also corrupt   16
thought. A bad usage can spread by tradition and imitation, even among people who should and do know better. The debased language that I have been discussing is in some ways very convenient. Phrases like *a not unjustifiable assumption, leaves much to be desired, would serve no good purpose, a consideration which we should do well to bear in mind,* are a continuous temptation, a packet of aspirins always at

one's elbow. Look back through this essay, and for certain you will find that I have again and again committed the very faults I am protesting against. By this morning's post I have received a pamphlet dealing with conditions in Germany. The author tells me that he "felt impelled" to write it. I open it at random, and here is almost the first sentence that I see: "(The Allies) have an opportunity not only of achieving a radical transformation of Germany's social and political structure in such a way as to avoid a nationalistic reaction in Germany itself, but at the same time of laying the foundations of a co-operative and unified Europe." You see, he "feels impelled" to write—feels, presumably, that he has something new to say—and yet his words, like cavalry horses answering the bugle, group themselves automatically into the familiar dreary pattern. This invasion of one's mind by ready-made phrases (*lay the foundations, achieve a radical transformation*) can only be prevented if one is constantly on guard against them, and every such phrase anaesthetises a portion of one's brain.

I said earlier that the decadence of our language is probably curable. Those who deny this would argue, if they produced an argument at all, that language merely reflects existing social conditions, and that we cannot influence its development by any direct tinkering with words and constructions. So far as the general tone or spirit of a language goes, this may be true, but it is not true in detail. Silly words and expressions have often disappeared, not through any evolutionary process but owing to the conscious action of a minority. Two recent examples were *explore every avenue* and *leave no stone unturned*, which were killed by the jeers of a few journalists. There is a long list of fly-blown metaphors which could similarly be got rid of if enough people would interest themselves in the job; and it should also be possible to laugh the *not un-* formation out of existence,[3] to reduce the amount of Latin and Greek in the average sentence, to drive out foreign phrases and strayed scientific words, and, in general, to make pretentiousness unfashionable. But all these are minor points. The defence of the English language implies more than this, and perhaps it is best to start by saying what it does *not* imply.

To begin with, it has nothing to do with archaism, with the salvaging of obsolete words and turns of speech, or with the setting-up of a "standard English" which must never be departed from. On the contrary, it is especially concerned with the scrapping of every word or idiom which has outworn its usefulness. It has nothing to do with correct grammar and syntax, which are of no importance so long as one makes one's meaning clear, or with the avoidance of Americanisms, or with having what is called a "good

17

18

---

[3]One can cure oneself of the *not un-* formation by memorising this sentence: *A not unblack dog was chasing a not unsmall rabbit across a not ungreen field.*

 POLITICS AND THE ENGLISH LANGUAGE 357

prose style". On the other hand it is not concerned with fake simplicity and the attempt to make written English colloquial. Nor does it even imply in every case preferring the Saxon word to the Latin one, though it does imply using the fewest and shortest words that will cover one's meaning. What is above all needed is to let the meaning choose the word, and not the other way about. In prose, the worst thing one can do with words is to surrender to them. When you think of a concrete object, you think wordlessly, and then, if you want to describe the thing you have been visualising, you probably hunt about till you find the exact words that seem to fit it. When you think of something abstract you are more inclined to use words from the start, and unless you make a conscious effort to prevent it, the existing dialect will come rushing in and do the job for you, at the expense of blurring or even changing your meaning. Probably it is better to put off using words as long as possible and get one's meaning as clear as one can through pictures or sensations. Afterwards one can choose—not simply *accept*—the phrases that will best cover the meaning, and then switch round and decide what impression one's words are likely to make on another person. This last effort of the mind cuts out all stale or mixed images, all prefabricated phrases, needless repetitions, and humbug and vagueness generally. But one can often be in doubt about the effect of a word or a phrase, and one needs rules that one can rely on when instinct fails. I think the following rules will cover most cases:

i.   Never use a metaphor, simile or other figure of speech which you are used to seeing in print.

ii.   Never use a long word where a short one will do.

iii.   If it is possible to cut a word out, always cut it out.

iv.   Never use the passive where you can use the active.

v.   Never use a foreign phrase, a scientific word or a jargon word if you can think of an everyday English equivalent.

vi.   Break any of these rules sooner than say anything outright barbarous.

These rules sound elementary, and so they are, but they demand a deep change of attitude in anyone who has grown used to writing in the style now fashionable. One could keep all of them and still write bad English, but one could not write the kind of stuff that I quoted in those five specimens at the beginning of this article.

I have not here been considering the literary use of language, 19 but merely language as an instrument for expressing and not for

concealing or preventing thought. Stuart Chase and others have come near to claiming that all abstract words are meaningless, and have used this as a pretext for advocating a kind of political quietism. Since you don't know what Fascism is, how can you struggle against Fascism? One need not swallow such absurdities as this, but one ought to recognise that the present political chaos is connected with the decay of language, and that one can probably bring about some improvement by starting at the verbal end. If you simplify your English, you are freed from the worst follies of orthodoxy. You cannot speak any of the necessary dialects, and when you make a stupid remark its stupidity will be obvious, even to yourself. Political language—and with variations this is true of all political parties, from Conservatives to Anarchists—is designed to make lies sound truthful and murder respectable, and to give an appearance of solidity to pure wind. One cannot change this all in a moment, but one can at least change one's own habits, and from time to time one can even, if one jeers loudly enough, send some worn-out and useless phrase—some *jackboot, Achilles' heel, hotbed, melting pot, acid test, veritable inferno* or other lump of verbal refuse—into the dustbin where it belongs.

QUESTIONS

1. According to Orwell, "thought corrupts language" and "language can also corrupt thought." Give examples of these assertions in the essay.

2. In what ways does Orwell believe that politics and language are related?

3. Orwell himself uses similes and metaphors. Locate five of them and explain their relationship to the author's analysis.

4. Orwell claims that concrete language is superior to abstract language. Give examples of Orwell's attempt to write concretely.

5. One of the most crucial rhetorical devices in this essay is definition. What important concepts does Orwell define? What methods of definition does he tend to use?

6. Identify an example of hypothetical reasoning in the essay. How does it contribute to the thesis of the essay?

7. After having given five examples of bad English, why does Orwell in paragraph 9 give another example? How does this example differ from the others? What does it add to the essay?

8. Explain the use of extended analogy in paragraph 13.

 POLITICS AND THE ENGLISH LANGUAGE

9. Do you think that language has deteriorated even further or has it improved? Explain.

10. a. Write an essay defending the value of simplified English.
b. In an analytical essay, assess the state of language in politics today.

JONATHAN SWIFT

The Art of Political Lying

Jonathan Swift (1667–1745) is best known as the author of three satires: *A Tale of a Tub* (1704), *Gulliver's Travels* (1726), and *A Modest Proposal* (1729). In these satires, he pricks the balloon of many of his contemporaries' and our own most cherished prejudices, pomposities, and delusions. Swift was also a famous churchman, an eloquent spokesman for Irish rights, and a political journalist. In this essay, he examines a characteristic of politicians that apparently has not changed over the years: lying.

W e are told the devil is the father of lies, and was a liar 1 from the beginning; so that, beyond contradiction, the invention is old: and, which is more, his first Essay of it was purely political, employed in undermining the authority of his prince, and seducing a third part of the subjects from their obedience: for which he was driven down from heaven, where (as Milton expresses it) he had been viceroy of a great western province; and forced to exercise his talent in inferior regions among other fallen spirits, poor or deluded men, whom he still daily tempts to his own sin, and will ever do so, till he be chained in the bottomless pit.

But although the devil be the father of lies, he seems, like 2 other great inventors, to have lost much of his reputation by the continual improvements that have been made upon him.

Who first reduced lying into an art, and adapted it to politics, 3 is not so clear from history, although I have made some diligent inquiries. I shall therefore consider it only according to the modern system, as it has been cultivated these twenty years past in the southern part of our own island.

The poets tell us that, after the giants were overthrown by the 4 gods, the earth in revenge produced her last offspring, which was Fame. And the fable is thus interpreted: that when tumults and seditions are quieted, rumours and false reports are plentifully spread through a nation. So that, by this account, lying is the last relief of a routed, earth-born, rebellious party in a state. But here the moderns have made great additions, applying this art to the gaining of power and preserving it, as well as revenging themselves after they have lost it; as the same instruments are made use of by animals to feed themselves when they are hungry, and to bite those that tread upon them.

But the same genealogy cannot always be admitted for political lying; I shall therefore desire to refine upon it, by adding some circumstances of its birth and parents. A political lie is sometimes born out of a discarded statesman's head, and thence delivered to be nursed and dandled by the rabble. Sometimes it is produced a monster, and licked into shape: at other times it comes into the world completely formed, and is spoiled in the licking. It is often born an infant in the regular way, and requires time to mature it; and often it sees the light in its full growth, but dwindles away by degrees. Sometimes it is of noble birth, and sometimes the spawn of a stockjobber. Here it screams aloud at the opening of the womb, and there it is delivered with a whisper. I know a lie that now disturbs half the kingdom with its noise, [of] which, although too proud and great at present to own its parents, I can remember its whisperhood. To conclude the nativity of this monster; when it comes into the world without a sting it is still-born; and whenever it loses its sting it dies. 5

No wonder if an infant so miraculous in its birth should be destined for great adventures; and accordingly we see it has been the guardian spirit of a prevailing party for almost twenty years. It can conquer kingdoms without fighting, and sometimes with the loss of a battle. It gives and resumes employments; can sink a mountain to a mole-hill, and raise a mole-hill to a mountain; has presided for many years at committees of elections; can wash a blackmoor white; make a saint of an atheist, and a patriot of a profligate; can furnish foreign ministers with intelligence, and raise or let fall the credit of the nation. This goddess flies with a huge looking-glass in her hands, to dazzle the crowd, and make them see, according as she turns it, their ruin in their interest, and their interest in their ruin. In this glass you will behold your best friends, clad in coats powdered with *fleurs de lis* and triple crowns; their girdles hung round with chains, and beads, and wooden shoes; and your worst enemies adorned with the ensigns of liberty, property, indulgence, moderation, and a cornucopia in their hands. Her large wings, like those of a flying-fish, are of no use but while they are moist; she therefore dips them in mud, and, soaring aloft, scatters it in the eyes of the multitude, flying with great swiftness; but at every turn is forced to stoop in dirty ways for new supplies. 6

I have been sometimes thinking, if a man had the art of the 7
second sight for seeing lies, as they have in Scotland for seeing
spirits, how admirably he might entertain himself in this town, by
observing the different shapes, sizes, and colours of those swarms of
lies which buzz about the heads of some people, like flies about a
horse's ears in summer; or those legions hovering every afternoon in
Exchange-alley, enough to darken the air; or over a club of discontented grandees, and thence sent down in cargoes to be scattered at
elections.

There is one essential point wherein a political liar differs 8
from others of the faculty, that he ought to have but a short memory,
which is necessary according to the various occasions he meets with
every hour of differing from himself and swearing to both sides of a
contradiction, as he finds the persons disposed with whom he has to
deal. In describing the virtues and vices of mankind, it is convenient,
upon every article, to have some eminent person in our eye, from
whom we copy our description. I have strictly observed this rule, and
my imagination this minute represents before me a certain great man
famous for this talent, to the constant practice of which he owes his
twenty years' reputation of the most skilful head in England for the
management of nice affairs. The superiority of his genius consists in
nothing else but an inexhaustible fund of political lies, which he
plentifully distributes every minute he speaks, and by an unparalleled generosity forgets, and consequently contradicts, the next
half-hour. He never yet considered whether any proposition were
true or false, but whether it were convenient for the present minute
or company to affirm or deny it; so that, if you think fit to refine upon
him by interpreting everything he says, as we do dreams, by the
contrary, you are still to seek, and will find yourself equally deceived
whether you believe or not: the only remedy is to suppose that you
have heard some inarticulate sounds, without any meaning at all; and
besides, that will take off the horror you might be apt to conceive at
the oaths wherewith he perpetually tags both ends of every proposition; although, at the same time, I think he cannot with any justice be
taxed with perjury when he invokes God and Christ, because he has
often fairly given public notice to the world that he believes in
neither.

Some people may think that such an accomplishment as this 9
can be of no great use to the owner, or his party, after it has been
often practised and is become notorious; but they are widely mistak-
en. Few lies carry the inventor's mark, and the most prostitute enemy
to truth may spread a thousand without being known for the author:
besides, as the vilest writer has his readers, so the greatest liar has his
believers; and it often happens that, if a lie be believed only for an

hour, it has done its work, and there is no farther occasion for it. Falsehood flies, and truth comes limping after it, so that when men come to be undeceived it is too late; the jest is over, and the tale has had its effect: like a man who has thought of a good repartee when the discourse is changed or the company parted; or like a physician who has found out an infallible medicine after the patient is dead.

Considering that natural disposition in many men to lie, and in multitudes to believe, I have been perplexed what to do with that maxim so frequent in everybody's mouth, that truth will at last prevail. Here has this island of ours, for the greatest part of twenty years, lain under the influence of such counsels and persons, whose principle and interest it was to corrupt our manners, blind our understanding, drain our wealth, and in time destroy our constitution both in church and state, and we at last were brought to the very brink of ruin; yet, by the means of perpetual misrepresentations, have never been able to distinguish between our enemies and friends. We have seen a great part of the nation's money got into the hands of those who, by their birth, education, and merit, could pretend no higher than to wear our liveries; while others, who, by their credit, quality, and fortune, were only able to give reputation and success to the Revolution, were not only laid aside as dangerous and useless, but loaded with the scandal of Jacobites, men of arbitrary principles, and pensioners to France; while truth, who is said to lie in a well, seemed now to be buried there under a heap of stones. But I remember it was a usual complaint among the Whigs, that the bulk of the landed men was not in their interests, which some of the wisest looked on as an ill omen; and we saw it was with the utmost difficulty that they could reserve a majority, while the court and ministry were on their side, till they had learned those admirable expedients for deciding elections and influencing distant boroughs by powerful motives from the city. But all this was more force and constraint, however upheld by most dexterous artifice and management, until the people began to apprehend their properties, their religion, and the monarchy itself in danger; when we saw them greedily laying hold on the first occasion to interpose. But of this mighty change in the dispositions of the people I shall discourse more at large in some following paper: wherein I shall endeavour to undeceive or discover those deluded or deluding persons who hope or pretend it is only a short madness in the vulgar, from which they may soon recover; whereas, I believe it will appear to be very different in its causes, its symptoms, and its consequences; and prove a great example to illustrate the maxim I lately mentioned, that truth (however sometimes late) will at last prevail.

QUESTIONS

1. According to Swift, what effects can be traced to political lying?

2. According to Swift, why aren't liars discovered and known to be liars?

3. In paragraphs 8 to 10, Swift uses numerous metaphors and similes. Identify and interpret them, and also explain why Swift uses metaphors and allusive language.

4. How does Swift employ ironic language?

5. Swift employs several extended metaphors, almost fables, to describe liars and lying. Identify these metaphors and explain how they characterize the liar. What is the effect of using this method of definition?

6. Which paragraphs constitute the introductory part of Swift's essay? What methods of development does he employ here?

7. At what point does Swift divide his essay into two parts? How are these parts different? How are they similar?

8. Swift frequently uses deductive reasoning in this essay. Give examples and explain how, particularly in paragraphs 8 to 10, deductions further his argument.

9. One effect Swift says political liars hope to achieve is to confuse friends and enemies. Give examples of similar political behavior today.

10. Write an essay on the art of lying as it relates to particular institutions or subjects—college life, business, politics, marriage, or other relevant topics.

JOHN SIMON

The Corruption of English

John Simon (1925–   ) is best known as a demanding, perceptive, often sardonic reviewer of movies and theater in *New York Magazine* and *Esquire.* His reviews have appeared in *Private Screenings: Views of the Cinema of the Sixties* (1967) and *Movies into Films* (1971). Lately, writing in *Esquire* and appearing on television, Simon has criticized with wit and venom what he considers the shoddy state of modern English.

e are all in the gutter, but some of us are looking at the 1
stars," wrote Oscar Wilde about life. The same applies
to language: we all make mistakes (somebody just wrote
me to point out a badly constructed sentence in one of
my columns), but some of us at least try to maintain standards. It is
not easy, and the best may stumble. Thus the worthy Irving Howe
writes, on the front page of the *New York Times Book Review* (April 9,
1978), about "main protagonists." Now, the protagonist is *the* main
actor in something and has, since Greek times, always been in the
singular. "Protagonists" is incorrect (unless you refer to the protagonists of two or more dramas), and "main protagonists" (main main
actors) is redundant to boot. A double-barreled error, but even the
ablest among us, harried by the exigencies of rapid-fire journalism,
are not immune to lapses.

What worries me more is rock-bottom illiteracy: in the gutter 2
and looking at the sewers. David Sheff of *New West* sent me a
good-size National Airlines poster the other day, depicting a charming flight attendant (formerly stewardess) and bearing this caption
emblazoned in mighty letters: "Watch us shine with more flight's to
Houston." Be honest: did your jaw drop when you read that
"flight's"? I showed the poster to a couple of civilized friends, and it
took them some time and quite a bit of prodding to notice the howler.
So there you have it: half the population (I guess) thinks that any
plural ending in *s* requires an apostrophe, and the other half stands
idly by without squirming, if, in fact, it even notices.

Where does it all come from? Who is the chief culprit? Surely, 3
the schools, both lower and higher, and the distemper of the times
that influences them. Let me give you some horrible examples. Jim
Deutsch of Greenville, Mississippi, has just sent me a Xerox of a letter
published in *American Studies International* (Winter 1977), in which
Toby Fulwiler protests what seems to be a fairly obvious plagiarism of
a paper he wrote. But he twice misspells *plagiarize* as *plagerize*, which
the editors duly note with a *sic*. If Mr. Fulwiler is that concerned with
plagiarism, he might at least ascertain how it is spelled, especially
since he is the Director of Freshman English at Michigan Technological University. It is clear, furthermore, that he knows neither Latin
(*plagiārius:* a kidnapper) nor any major modern language in which the
spelling of the word is made manifest by the pronunciation, e.g.,
French (*plagiat*) or German (*Plagiat*). But it may be asking too much of
a contemporary director of freshman English that he know other
languages: English though, should still be part of his competency.

Or need it be? Two readers, no less (Hortense Berman and 4
Thomas A. Long), have sent me identical clippings from *UC This
Week*, a University of Cincinnati faculty and staff newspaper. The May
2 issue summarizes a talk by William Lasher, associate professor of

English, chairman of the committee on linguistics, and director of undergraduate studies in English. Professor Lasher adduced two sentences—"we was at the ball game last night" and "Mary had five card"—calling them clear and logical attempts to simplify the language.

I quote: "In the first example, Lasher says, the speaker has 5 decided that the distinction between 'was' and 'were' is insignificant and has chosen 'was,' no matter if the subject is singular or plural." Note the assumption that the speaker consciously "decided" to make a simplifying choice. How about the supposition that the speaker was an illiterate ignoramus who neither knew nor cared to know better? But to go on: "The second example is what Lasher calls Black English, a social dialect of American English. In it the speaker drops the 's' from 'cards' because the five already indicates more than one." And Lasher proceeded, at least by strong implication, to belittle those who would consider the above speakers ungrammatical just because they violate what he patronizingly called "the experts' rule." For Lasher, "the people who say 'was' for 'were' or drop the 's' have a grammar that describes the relationship between sound and meaning in their cultures."

Why should we consider some, usually poorly educated, 6 subculture's notion of the relationship between sound and meaning? And how could a grammar—any grammar—possibly describe that relationship? Grammar exists mainly to clarify meaning. *Five* does indeed indicate plurality, but the final *s* confirms it. After all, the speaker may have said "a fine card" or "a five card," and it is the final *s* that ensures that we have not misheard him. So, too, we may be uncertain whether we heard, say, *he* or *we* until the *were* dispels our doubt concerning who was at the ball game.

There is more to it, though. Maintaining these alleged nice- 7 ties links our language to that of the giants of the English tongue who preceded us, all those great writers and speakers who were—not was—in the ball game that counts: the great struggle to use English as clearly and beautifully as possible. We do not wish to dissociate ourselves from them, lose familiarity with their mode of utterance on account of ignorant, misguided, or merely lazy creatures for whom making distinctions is an unnecessary effort. When Professor Lasher invokes the lofty principle of "making things easier," he serves up a typically disingenuous historical example: the shifting of *inpossible* to *impossible* from circa 1300 on. Yes, *inp* is harder to say than *imp*; but is *were* more of a strain on the tongue than *was*? Or, to put it differently: should we destroy a beautiful old building because it has decorative elements on its facade and replace it with a square box because that is a simpler structure? Of course, there are people who tear down architectural masterpieces for just such reasons; but whatever they

JOHN SIMON

call themselves, *we* should call them barbarians and fight their vandalism in every way we can.

What this is, masquerading under the euphemism "descriptive linguistics" (and Lasher is far from being an isolated promulgator of it—in fact, he is part of a growing majority), is a benighted and despicable catering to mass ignorance under the supposed aegis of democracy, of being fair to underprivileged minorities, and similar irruptions of politics where it has no business being. 8

Black English, for example, has a perfect right to exist; it just hasn't the right to change Standard English. The Lashers of this world are being illogical. Either Black English is something different from Standard English, in which case it is no more entitled to interfere with it than Portuguese is, or it is—or means to be—part of Standard English, in which case it has to espouse the latter's rules. And it will not do for the Lashers to say that they do not pass judgment, that they merely record changes in the language that may actually make the language "better" as it "adapts to cultural needs." What kind of cultural need is it that demands *we was* for *we were?* An uncultured, indeed anticultural, need, for the supporting of which Lasher deserves five kick in the pant. 9

There is, I believe, a morality of language: an obligation to preserve and nurture the niceties, the fine distinctions, that have been handed down to us. And the Lashers cannot wash their dainty hands and pretend that anyone who uses the term *language deterioration* displays "ignorance of the facts of language change." Well, there may actually be some ignorance at work in that, though not as Lasher perceives it: "deterioration of language" would be better than "language deterioration." 10

The pressure on language to deteriorate does not, however, come merely from below, from the "democratic" levelers. It comes also from above, from the fancy jargonmongers, idle game players, fashionable coteries for second-rate intellectuals. 11

So far, I have discussed corrupting pressures on language from below—from misguidedly democratizing sources. Now, let me consider the attack on language from above: obfuscation in the name of some supposedly higher philosophy, academicism, linguistic or literary arcanum being foisted on language by allegedly exalted authorities. Here I do not mean simply mistakes—as when William Safire, in his commencement address at Syracuse University ("The Decline of the Written Word," May 13, 1978), declares: "We need not degenerate further from written English to verbal signals to sign language." Safire means *oral*, i.e., spoken signals; *verbal* means anything pertaining to words, written or spoken—hence "written English" is also a series of "verbal signals." 12

No, I refer to the so-called superior wisdom destructively 13

THE CORRUPTION OF ENGLISH

inflicted on language in an effort to rise above what "lesser" people consider correct, straightforward, and self-evident. A typical and highly offensive example of this was submitted to me by Philippe Perebinossoff of Plattsburgh, New York. It is a prospectus for a summer seminar being given at Brown University under the sponsorship of the National Endowment for the Humanities. These seminars, as my correspondent quotes, are "for college teachers . . . who are concerned primarily with increasing their knowledge of the subjects they teach."

The case in point is a seminar entitled "Theories of Reading: 14 Fiction and Film," offered by Robert Scholes and Michael Silverman, both members of the Brown faculty. Scholes instructs "in the semiotics of fiction, in semiotic theory [etc.]—all for undergraduate students." Silverman teaches courses in "visual theory and film." The bibliography for the seminar, replete with texts by structuralists and semiologists, also features movies by Robert Altman, Bernardo Bertolucci, and Nick Ray. Lacking space for the whole prospectus, I quote its essence:

> The engagement of reader, text, and culture in the act of reading points to the constant play of two elements over the face of the third; and this play of movement we would see as semiotic activity.
>
> We intend the seminar members to read a number of examples of current theory, to read some prose passages and to see some films. . . . We do not want them to come up with "readings" of stories and films in the traditional sense; the substantive notion of "a reading" is opposed to our more participial sense of reading. . . . We will at all times read a "primary" text *through* a theoretical text. We hope in this to avoid the notion that the theory of reading and the practice of reading can be divorced. [Surely, what professors Scholes and Silverman have joined together, no man would be rash enough to put asunder!] Those not conversant with recent theory of reading will not acquire it in isolation from texts, but will at the very least be led to posit a dialectical relationship between texts. Thus a Lawrence story will be read through Todorov's *Poetics of Prose*, Bertolucci's *Before the Revolution* will be read ["Read any good movies lately?" "No, but I've seen the books."] through Althusser on Brecht.

Now, it may be that this playing of two elements over the face of the third comes down to not much more than viewing films, reading fiction, and also consulting some critical works. But note the horrible obfuscation of this "reading through other readings," these "posit-ings of dialectical relationships between texts." Amid all that "semiot-ic activity" and the embargo on "readings in the traditional sense" will anyone see *through* to the books and movies? But, to go on:

> The aim is not to make the theoretical text a transparent gloss or aid [no danger of that, I daresay] to the understanding of the "primary" text (thus inevitably producing new "read-ings" of the primary text), but to help us situate the text (both theoretical and "primary") within the area of something that can be read, while simultaneously undertaking to question the relationship between texts and our relation to them. Ideally, we would like at the end of eight weeks to have reached the point in our work in which a seminar member might undertake to read Todorov through Lawrence, or to theorize his own position as a reader through an examination of *Before the Revolution*.

Just as there are some people from whom I would not buy a used car, there are certain professors from whom I refuse to buy this second-hand semiology—not that it would be much better new. Even without being able to make sense out of all this tautologizing, highfalutin jargon, obnubilation, and deadwood, I am dead certain that I have nothing to gain from reading Todorov through Todorov, much less through D. H. Lawrence. And whereas I would be happy to assess the artistic value of Bertolucci's second film (in my opinion, minimal), I would not, while in the possession of a shred of sanity, wish to theorize my own position to it as a reader through Althusser. Rather than that, I would even watch the movie through a bunch of women refusing to take off their hats.

Now for a few further caveats from our pundits: "We must stress that we do intend, in any case, to stress the differences between fiction and film . . . there is a clear difference, for example, in [*sic*] reading a novel in one's study and viewing a film in a public place." O profundity! Could one have arrived at this wisdom without viewing it through Todorov and Althusser? I seriously doubt it. But onward with Scholes and Silverman: "Since one of us is a specialist in prose narrative, the other a specialist in film, our approach to the material will not be fully congruent (this would seem to us a distinct advantage)." Perish the thought of anything so unstructuralist as congruence, so unsemiotic as clarity! Rather, the students will be expected to read Scholes through Silverman, and ideally, if one dare hope it after a mere eight weeks, even Silverman through Scholes. Note also that wonderful "We must stress that we do intend . . . to stress. . . ." I wonder: do two stresses equal one distress?

15

 THE CORRUPTION OF ENGLISH

And here at last, as stressed by Scholes and Silverman, is the   16
promised end: "(1) To establish that the reader of fiction must himself
be activated in dramatistic terms, set into motion and theorized; (2)
that the cinematic viewer must give over his passivity, undertake the
more strenuous activity of reading, while analyzing what this does to
his relation to the text; (3) that the use of a by now widespread body
of semiotic material on the place [sic] of the reader-viewer will
facilitate a re-thinking of old critical positions." So in order to view—I
mean, read—an Altman movie or Hemingway story—pardon me,
"primary" text—I must be dramatistically activated, set into motion,
and theorized; I must read while analyzing my relationship to the text
(a bit onerous for someone already spinning like a top from all that
activation); and I must use a widespread body of semiotic material
while dramatistically whirling about in one place—the place allotted
to the reader-viewer. All this will immeasurably facilitate my rethink-
ing (with or without a hyphen) and is sure to jolt me out of any old
position as a sitter-reader or sitter-viewer that I might have eased
myself into in my outmoded and benighted, dramatistically unacti-
vated state.

If I consecrate all this space to Scholes and Silverman, it is   17
because the woods are full of them, various endowments sponsor
them, and your tax dollars and the English language have to pay for
them. In the place of the three R's, the new education has posited the
three S's: structuralism, semiotics, stultification.

Look now at a more obvious disaster wrought by the new   18
higher philosophizing. Mrs. M. C. (I am deeply sorry that legal
reasons forbid my naming names), of a Dade County, Florida,
college, has sent me a Xerox of the memo from her division director
that lists his reasons for denying her tenure as an instructor of
freshman composition. I quote:

> She holds some tenets regarding her role as an English
> teacher which . . . does [sic] not lend itself to freedom of
> thought and exchange [of what?] for students because stu-
> dents are too busy looking for the right answers, i.e. the
> truth. For example: "Language (English) is precise. . . . I
> want my students to be precise when they write. They should
> not use one word when there is a better (more precise) word
> to say what they mean." This principle ignores two basic
> considerations: A. Denotative definitions of English words
> can vary from one to ten (10) or more definitions. Very few
> English words, usually nouns, have less [correctly: fewer]
> than two meanings. [Actually, quite a few leap to mind; for
> example, nincompoop, numskull, ignoramus, cretin, division
> director.] B. Connotative definitions are as many as there are

people. They are functions of our perceptual field, our view of the world, and are based on our experiences and our psychological imprinting. Hardly precise. This belief is a major guiding principle for Mrs. C.

When you get into the higher reaches of semantics, epistemology, textual explication, and semiology, seven or more types of ambiguity doubtless creep into almost every statement. But while you are writing a simple freshman English composition in Dade County, there is no reason for not hitting your simple point Dade center. A teacher must be propaedeutic before turning heuristic; a student must learn precise, unambiguous expression before he can start contemplating the relativity of the universe and all its components. Or, as they used to say in my school days, you must know the rules before you can learn to break them. Breaking them, in any case, is for shrewd and sophisticated writers, usually of fiction. Otherwise, the rules are still the most practical solution.

So, you see, the language is being attacked from above by the relativists and overcomplicators, from below by the democratic levelers. And, of course, there is overlapping: demotic ignorance plays into the hands of pseudoscientific mumbo jumbo, and structural linguistics rushes to the defense of every popular distortion or misconception. Can the beleaguered middle survive? Perhaps, if you will reject the trends, and yield neither to ignorance nor to obfuscation. 19

QUESTIONS
1. Who are the primary objects of Simon's wrath? Why?

2. What reasons does Simon give for the present corruption of English?

3. Simon scathingly attacks what he considers inferior English. One form of attack is word choice. Identify five highly connotative words he uses to describe abusers of English.

4. How does Simon's choice of personal pronouns involve the reader in his discussion?

5. Give examples of how Simon uses deductive reasoning to undercut his opponents' positions.

6. Explain the importance of paragraphs 7 and 8 to the development of the essay.

7. One of the keys to coherence in this essay is transitional devices linking paragraph to paragraph. What transitional devices does Simon use?

 THE CORRUPTION OF ENGLISH   **371**

8. Identify examples that Simon uses. Why are examples important to the development of the essay?

9. Do you think Simon is correct to attack dialect forms of English? Justify your answer.

10. Locate examples of bad English in newspapers, advertisements, magazines, and the speech of figures on television; then write an essay to show the corruption of English.

GENEVA SMITHERMAN

White English in Blackface, or Who Do I Be?

Geneva Smitherman (1940–   ) is currently professor of linguistics and Afro-American literature at Wayne State University. She has written extensively on black dialects, literature, and culture. Her book *Black Language and Culture: Sounds of the Soul* appeared in 1974. She has published numerous articles, including "The Power of the Rap: Black Idiom and the New Black Poetry" (1973). The following article was published in 1973 and demonstrates Smitherman's skill as a scholar and rapper.

B in nothin in a long time lit up the English teaching profession like the current hassle over Black English. One finds beaucoup sociolinguistic research studies and language projects for the "disadvantaged" on the scene in nearly every sizable black community in the country.[1] And educators from K-Grad. School bees debating whether: (1) blacks should learn and use only standard white English (hereafter referred to as WE); (2) blacks should command both dialects, i.e., be bi-dialectal (hereafter BD); (3) blacks should be allowed (??????) to use standard Black English (hereafter BE or BI). The appropriate choice having everything to do with American political reality, which is usually ignored, and nothing to do with the educational process,

---

[1]For examples of such programs see *Non-Standard Dialect,* Board of Education of the City of New York (National Council of Teachers of English, 1968); San-Su C. Lin, *Pattern Practices in the Teaching of Standard English to Students with a Non-Standard Dialect* (USOE Project 1339, 1965); Arno Jewett, Joseph Mersand, Doris Gunderson, *Improving English Skills of Culturally Different Youth in Large Cities* (U.S. Department of Health, Education and Welfare, 1964); *Language Programs for the Disadvantaged* (NCTE, 1965).

which is usually claimed. I say without qualification that we cannot talk about the Black Idiom apart from Black Culture and the Black Experience. Nor can we specify educational goals for blacks apart from considerations about the structure of (white) American society.

And we black folks is not gon take all that weight, for no one has empirically demonstrated that linguistic/stylistic features of BE impede educational progress in communication skills, or any other area of cognitive learning. Take reading. It's don been charged, but not actually verified, that BE interferes with mastery of reading skills.[2] Yet beyond pointing out the gap between the young brother/sistuh's phonological and syntactical patterns and those of the usually-middle-class-WE-speaking-teacher, this claim has not been validated. The distance between the two systems is, after all, short and is illuminated only by the fact that reading is taught *orally*. (Also get to the fact that preceding generations of BE-speaking folks learned to read, despite the many classrooms in which the teacher spoke a dialect different from that of their students.)

For example, a student who reads *den* for *then* probably pronounces initial /th/ as /d/ in most words. Or the one who reads *doing* for *during* probably deletes intervocalic and final /r/ in most words. So it is not that such students can't read, they is simply employing the black phonological system. In the reading classrooms of today, what we bees needin is teachers with the proper attitudinal orientation who thus can distinguish actual reading problems from mere dialect differences. Or take the writing of an essay. The only percentage in writing a paper with WE spelling, punctuation, and usage is in maybe eliciting a positive *attitudinal* response from a prescriptivist middle-class-aspirant-teacher. Dig on the fact that sheer "correctness" does not a good writer make. And is it any point in dealing with the charge of BE speakers being "non-verbal" or "linguistically deficient" in oral communication skills—behind our many Raps who done disproved that in living, vibrant colors?[3]

What linguists and educators need to do at this juncture is to take serious cognizance of the Oral Tradition in Black Culture. The uniqueness of this verbal style requires a language competence/performance model to fit the black scheme of things. Clearly BI speakers possess rich communication skills (i.e., are highly *competent* in using language), but as yet there bees no criteria (evaluative, testing, or

2

3

4

[2]See, for example, Joan Baratz and Roger Shuy, ed., *Teaching Black Children to Read* (Center for Applied Linguistics, 1969); A. L. Davis, ed., *On the Dialects of Children* (NCTE, 1968); Eldonna L. Evertts, ed., *Dimensions of Dialect* (NCTE, 1967).

[3]For the most racist and glaring of these charges, see Fred Hechinger, ed., *Pre-School Education Today* (Doubleday, 1966); for an excellent rebuttal, see William Labov, *Nonstandard English* (NCTE 1970); for a complete overview of the controversy and issues involved as well as historical perspective and rebuttal to the non-verbal claim, see my "Black Idiom and White Institutions," *Negro American Literature Forum*, Fall 1971.

other instrument of measurement), based on black communication patterns, wherein BI speakers can demonstrate they competence (i.e., *performance*). Hence brothers and sisters fail on language performance tests and in English classrooms. Like, to amplify on what Nikki said, that's why we always lose, not only cause we don't know the rules, but it ain't even our game.

We can devise a performance model only after an analysis of the components of BI. Now there do be linguists who supposedly done did this categorization and definition of BE.[4] But the descriptions are generally confining, limited as they are to discrete linguistic units. One finds simply ten to fifteen patterns cited, as for example, the most frequently listed one, the use of *be* as finite verb, contrasting with its deletion: (a) *The coffee be cold* contrasts with (b) *The coffee cold*, the former statement denoting a continuing state of affairs, the latter applying to the present moment only. (Like if you the cook, (a) probably get you fired, and (b) only get you talked about.) In WE no comparable grammatical distinction exists and *The coffee is cold* would be used to indicate both meanings. However, rarely does one find an investigation of the total vitality of black expressive style, a style inextricable from the Black Cultural Universe, for after all, BI connects with Black Soul and niggers is more than deleted copulas.[5]

The Black Idiom should be viewed from two important perspectives: linguistic and stylistic. The linguistic dimension is comprised of the so-called nonstandard features of phonology and syntax (patterns like *dis heah* and *The coffee be cold*), and a lexicon generally equated with "slang" or hip talk. The stylistic dimension has to do with *rapping, capping, jiving*, etc., and with features such as cadence, rhythm, resonance, gestures, and all those other elusive, difficult-to-objectify elements that make up what is considered a writer or speaker's "style." While I am separating linguistic and stylistic features, I have done so only for the purpose of simplifying the discussion since the BI speaker runs the full gamut of both dimensions in any given speech event.

I acknowledge from the bell that we's dealing with a dialect structure which is a subsystem of the English language; thus BE and WE may not appear fundamentally different. Yet, though black folks speak English, it do seem to be an entirely different lingo altogether. But wherein lies the uniqueness? Essentially in language, as in other areas of Black Culture, we have the problem of isolating those

---

[4]The most thorough and scholarly of these, though a bit overly technical, is Walter Wolfram, *Detroit Negro Speech* (Center for Applied Linguistics, 1969).

[5]Kochman is one linguist who done gone this route; see for instance his "Rapping in the Black Ghetto," *Trans-action*, February 1969. However, he makes some black folks mad because of what one of my students called his "superfluity," and others shame cause of his exposure of our "bad" street elements. Kochman's data: jam up with muthafuckas and pussy-copping raps collected from Southside Chicago.

FEATURES SHARED WITH MAINSTREAM AMERICA	FEATURES SHARED WITH ALL OPPRESSED PEOPLES	FEATURES UNIQUE TO BLACK AMERICANS
Linguistic 1. British/American English lexicon 2. Most aspects of British/American English phonology and syntax	*Linguistic* 1. Superimposition of dominant cultures language on native language, yielding 2. Pidginized form of dominant culture's language, subject to becoming extinct, due to 3. Historical evolution, linguistic leveling out in direction of dominant culture's dialect	*Linguistic* Unique meanings attributed to certain English lexical items *Stylistic* Unique communication patterns and rhetorical flourishes

elements indigenous to black folks from those cultural aspects shared with white folks. Anthropologist Johnnetta Cole suggests that Black Culture has three dimensions: (1) those elements shared with mainstream America; (2) those elements shared with all oppressed peoples; (3) those elements peculiar to the black condition in America.[6] Applying her concepts to language, I propose the accompanying schematic representation.

Referring to the first column, contemporary BE is simply one of the many dialects of contemporary American English, and it is most likely the case that the linguistic patterns of BE differ from those of WE in surface structure only. There's no essential linguistic difference between *dis heah* and *this here,* and from a strictly linguistic point of view, *God don't never change* can be written *God doesn't ever change* (though definitely not from a socio-cultural/political perspective, as Baraka quite rightly notes).[7] Perhaps we could make a case for deep structure difference in the BE use of *be* as finite verb (refer to *The coffee be cold* example above), but we be hard pressed to find any other examples, and even in this case, we could posit that the copula exists in the deep structure, and is simply deleted by some low-level phonological deletion rule, dig: The coffee is cold . . . The coffee's cold . . . The coffee cold. My conclusion at this point is that despite the claims of some highly respected Creole linguists (with special propers to bad Sistuh Beryl Bailey),[8] the argument for deep structure

8

[6]Johnnetta B. Cole, "Culture: Negro, Black and Nigger," *The Black Scholar,* June 1970.

[7]Imamu Baraka, "Expressive Language," *Home,* pp. 166–172.

[8]See her "Toward a New Perspective in Negro English Dialectology," *American Speech* (1965); and "Language and Communicative Styles of Afro-American Children in the United States," *Florida FL Reporter 7* (Spring/Summer 1969).

WHITE ENGLISH IN BLACKFACE, OR WHO DO I BE?

differences between contemporary BE and WE syntax can not pass the test of rigorous transformational analysis.

Referring to the second column, we note the psychological 9 tendency of oppressed people to adopt the modes of behavior and expression of their oppressors (also, during the African slave trade, the functional necessity of pidginized forms of European language). Not only does the conqueror force his victims into political subjugation, he also coerces them into adopting his language and doles out special rewards to those among the oppressed who best mimic his language and cultural style. In the initial language contact stage, the victims attempt to assemble the new language into their native linguistic mold, producing a linguistic mixture that is termed *pidgin*. In the next stage, the pidgin may develop into a Creole, a highly systematic, widely used mode of communication among the oppressed, characterized by a substratum of patterns from the victim's language with an overlay of forms from the oppressor's language. As the oppressed people's identification with the victor's culture intensifies, the pidgin/Creole begins to lose its linguistic currency and naturally evolves in the direction of the victor's language. Reconstructing the linguistic history of BE, we theorize that it followed a similar pattern, but due to the radically different condition of black oppression in America, the process of *de-creolization* is nearly complete and has been for perhaps over a hundred years.

The most important features of BI are, of course, those 10 referred to in column three, for they point us toward the linguistic uniqueness and cultural significance of the Oral Tradition in the Black Experience. It should be clear that all along I been talkin bout that Black Experience associated with the grass-roots folks, the masses, the sho-nuff niggers—in short, all those black folks who do not aspire to white middle-class American standards.

Within this tradition, language is used as a teaching/sociali- 11 zing force and as a means of establishing one's reputation via his verbal competence. Black talk is never meaningless cocktail chit-chat but a functional dynamic that is simultaneously a mechanism for acculturation and information-passing and a vehicle for achieving group recognition. Black communication is highly verbal and highly stylized; it is a performance before a black audience who become both observers and participants in the speech event. Whether it be through slapping of hands ("giving five" or "giving skin"), Amen's, or Right on's, the audience influences the direction of a given rap and at the same time acknowledges or withholds its approval, depending on the linguistic skill and stylistic ingenuity of the speaker. I mean like a Brother is only as bad as his rap bees.

I   TOWARD A BLACK LANGUAGE MODEL: LINGUISTIC

While we concede that black people use the vocabulary of the English
language, certain words are always selected out of that lexicon and
given a special black semantic slant. So though we rappin bout the
same language, the reality referents are different. As one linguist has
suggested, the proper question is not what do words mean but what
do the users of the words mean? These words may be associated with
and more frequently used in black street culture but not necessarily.
Muthafucka has social boundaries, but not *nigger*.

Referring to the lexicon of BI, then, the following general
principles obtain:

1.   The words given the special black slant exist in a dynamic state.
The terms are discarded when they move into the white mainstream.
(Example: One no longer speaks of a "hip" brother; now he is a
"togetha" brother.) This was/is necessitated by our need to have a
code that was/is undecipherable by foreigners (i.e., whites).

2.   In BI, the concept of denotation vs. connotation does not
apply.

3.   What does apply is shades of meaning along the connotative
spectrum. For example, depending on contextual environment, the
word *bad* can mean extraordinary; beautiful; good; versatile; or a host
of other terms of positive value. Dig it: after watching a Sammy Davis
performance, a BI speaker testified: "Sammy sho did some *bad* stuff,"
i.e., extraordinary stuff. Or upon observing a beautiful sister: "She
sho is *bad*," i.e., beautiful, pretty, or goodlooking. Or, noticing how a
brother is dressed: "You sho got on some *bad* shit," i.e., *good* shit =
attractively dressed.

Note that the above examples are all in the category of
approbation. It is necessary to rap bout *denigration* as well, since certain
words in the black lexicon can frequently be used both ways.
Consider the word *nigger*, for instance. "He's my main nigger" means
my best friend (hence, approbation); "The nigger ain't shit," means
he's probably lazy, trifling, scheming, wrong-doing, or a host of other
denigrative terms, depending on the total context of the utterance.

4.   Approbation and denigration relate to the semantic level; we can
add two other possible functions of the same word on the grammatical level: *intensification* and *completion*. Slide back to *nigger* for a
minute, and dig that often the word is void of real meaning and
simply supplies the sentence with a subject. "Niggers was getting out
of there left and right, then the niggers was running, and so the

niggers said . . ." etc., etc., my point being that a steady stream of overuse means neither denigration nor approbation. Some excellent illustrations of this function of the word are to be found in *Manchild in the Promised Land*, where you can observe the word used in larger contexts.

To give you a most vivid illustration, consider the use of what WE labels "obscenities." From the streets of Detroit: (a) "That's a bad *muthafucka*." Referring to a Cadillac Eldorado, obviously indicating approval. (b) "He's a no-good *muthafucka*." Referring to a person who has just "put some game" on the speaker, obviously indicating disapproval. (c) "You *muthafuckin* right I wasn't gon let him do that." Emphasizing how correct the listener's assessment is, obviously using the term as a grammatical intensifier, modifying "right." (d) "We wasn't doin nothing, just messin round and *shit*." Though a different "obscenity," the point is nonetheless illustrated, "shit" being used neutrally, as an expletive (filler) to complete the sentence pattern; semantically speaking, it is an empty word in this contextual environment.
19

Where I'm comin from is that the lexicon of BI, consisting of certain specially selected words, requires a unique scheme of analysis to account for the diverse range and multiplicity of meanings attributed to these words. While there do be some dictionaries of Afro-American "slang," they fail to get at the important question: what are the psycho-cultural processes that guide our selection of certain words out of the thousands of possible words in the Anglo-Saxon vocabulary? Like, for instance, Kochman[9] has suggested that we value action in the black community, and so those words that have action implied in them, we take and give positive meanings to, such as *swing, game, hip, hustle*, etc.; whereas words of implied stasis are taken and given negative connotations, such as *lame, square, hung-up, stiffin and jivin*, etc. At any rate, what I've tried to lay here are some suggestions in this particular linguistic dimension; the definitive word on black lexicon is yet to be given.
20

I shall go on to discuss the stylistic dimension of black communication patterns, where I have worked out a more definitive model.
21

II TOWARD A BLACK LANGUAGE MODEL: STYLISTIC

Black verbal style exists on a sacred-secular continuum, as represented by the accompanying scheme. The model allows us to account for
22

[9]See Thomas Kochman, "The Kinetic Element in Black Idiom," paper read at the American Anthropological Association Convention, Seattle, Washington, 1968; also his *Rappin' and Stylin' Out: Communication in Urban Black America*.

SACRED	SECULAR
Political rap style	*Political rap style*
Examples: Jesse Jackson	Examples: Malcolm X
Martin Luther King	Rap Brown
Political literary style	*Political literary style*
Examples: Barbara Ann Teer's	Examples: Don Lee
National Black Theatre	Last Poets
Nikki Giovanni's	
"Truth Is on Its Way"	

the many individual variations in black speech, which can all be located at some point along the continuum.

The sacred style is rural and Southern. It is the style of the **23** black preacher and that associated with the black church tradition. It tends to be more emotive and highly charged than the secular style. It is also older in time. However, though I've called it "sacred," it abounds in secularisms. Black church service tends to be highly informal, and it ain nothin for a preacher to get up in the pulpit and, say, show off what he's wearing: "Y'all didn't notice the new suit I got on today, did y'all? Ain the Lord good to us. . . ."

The secular style is urban and Northern, but since it probably **24** had its beginnings in black folk tales and proverbs, its *roots* are Southern and rural. This is the street culture; the style found in barbershops and on street corners in the black ghettos of American cities. It tends to be more cool, more emotionally restrained sacred style. It is newer and younger in time and only fully evolved as a distinct style with the massive wave of black migration to the cities.

Both sacred and secular styles share the following characteris- **25** tics:

1. *Call and response.* This is basic to black oral tradition. The **26** speaker's solo voice alternates or is intermingled with the audience's response. In the sacred style, the minister is urged on by the congregation's Amen's, That's right, Reverend's, or Preach Reverend's. One also hears occasional Take your time's when the preacher is initiating his sermon, the congregation desiring to savor every little bit of this good message they bout to hear. (In both sacred and secular political rap styles, the "Preach Reverend" is transposed to "Teach Brother.") In the secular style, the response can take the form of a back-and-forth banter between the speaker and various members of the audience. Or the audience might manifest its response in giving skin (fives) when a really down verbal point is scored. Other approval responses include laughter and phrases like "Oh, you mean, nigger," "Get back, nigger," "Git down, baby," etc.

 WHITE ENGLISH IN BLACKFACE, OR WHO DO I BE? **379**

2.   *Rhythmic pattern.*   I refer to cadence, tone, and musical quality.   27
This is a pattern that is lyrical, sonorous, and generally emphasizing
sound apart from sense. It is often established through repetition,
either of certain sounds or words. The preacher will get a rhythm
going, conveying his message through sound rather than depending
on sheer semantic import. "I-I-I-I-I-Oh-I-I-Oh, yeah, Lord-I-I-heard
the voice of Jesus saying. . . ." Even though the secular style is
characterized by rapidity, as in the toasts (narrative tales of bad
niggers and they exploits, like Stag-O-Lee, or bad animals and they
trickeration, like the Signifying Monkey), the speaker's voice tone still
has that rhythmic, musical quality, just with a faster tempo.

3.   *Spontaneity.*   Generally, the speaker's performance is improvisa-   28
tional, with the rich interaction between speaker and audience
dictating and/or directing the course and outcome of the speech
event. Since the speaker does not prepare a formal document, his
delivery is casual, nondeliberate, and uncontrived. He speaks in a
lively, conversational tone, and with an ever-present quality of
immediacy. All emphasis is on process, movement, and creativity of
the moment. The preacher says "Y'all don wont to hear dat, so I'm
gon leave it lone," and his audience shouts, "Naw, tell it Reverend,
tell it!," and he does. Or, like, once Malcolm mentioned the fact of his
being in prison, and sensing the surprise of his audience, he took
advantage of the opportunity to note that all black people were in
prison: "That's what America means: prison."

4.   *Concreteness.*   The speaker's imagery and ideas center around   29
the empirical world, the world of reality, and the contemporary Here
and Now. Rarely does he drift off into esoteric abstractions; his
metaphors and illustrations are commonplace and grounded in
everyday experience. Perhaps because of this concreteness, there is a
sense of identification with the event being described or narrated, as
in the secular style where the toast-teller's identity merges with that
of the protagonist of his tale, and he becomes Stag-O-Lee or Shine; or
when the preacher assumes the voice of God or the personality of a
Biblical character. Even the experience of being saved takes on a
presentness and rootedness in everyday life: "I first met God in
1925. . . ."

5.   *Signifying.*   This is a technique of talking about the entire audi-   30
ence or some member of the audience either to initiate verbal "war"
or to make a point hit home. The interesting thang bout this rhetorical
device is that the audience is not offended and realizes—naw,
expects—the speaker to launch this offensive to achieve his desired

effect. "Pimp, punk, prostitute, Ph.D.—all the P's—you still in slavery!" announces the Reverend Jesse Jackson. Malcolm puts down the nonviolent movement with: "In a revolution, you swinging, not singing." (Notice the characteristic rhythmic pattern in the above examples—the alliterative poetic effect of Jackson's statement and the rhyming device in Malcolm's.)

An analysis of black expressive style, such as presented here, ³¹ should facilitate the construction of a performance instrument to measure the degree of command of the style of any given BI speaker. Linguists and educators sincerely interested in black education might be about the difficult, complex business of devising such a "test," rather than establishing linguistic remediation programs to correct a nonexistent remediation. Like in any other area of human activity, some BI rappers are better than others, and today's most effective black preachers, leaders, politicians, writers are those who rap in the black expressive style, appropriating the ritual framework of the Oral Tradition as vehicle for the conveyance of they political ideologies. Which brings me back to what I said from Jump Street. The real heart of this language controversy relates to/is the underlying political nature of the American educational system. Brother Frantz Fanon is highly instructive at this point. From his "Negro and Language," in *Black Skins, White Masks*:

> I ascribe a basic importance to the phenomenon of language. . . . To speak means . . . above all to assume a culture, to support the weight of a civilization. . . . Every dialect is a way of thinking. . . . And the fact that the newly returned [i.e., from white schools] Negro adopts a language different from that of the group into which he was born is evidence of a dislocation, a separation. . . .

In showing why the "Negro adopts such a position . . . with respect to European languages," Fanon continues:

> It is because he wants to emphasize the rupture that has now occurred. He is incarnating a new type of man that he imposes on his associates and his family. And so his old mother can no longer understand him when he talks to her about his *duds*, the family's *crummy joint*, the *dump* . . . all of it, of course, tricked out with the appropriate accent.
>
> In every country of the world, there are climbers, 'the ones who forget who they are,' and in contrast to them, 'the ones who remember where they came from.' The Antilles Negro who goes home from France expresses himself in the

dialect if he wants to make it plain that nothing has changed.[10]

As black people go moving on up toward separation and cultural nationalism, the question of the moment is not which dialect, but which culture, not whose vocabulary but whose values, not *I am* vs. *I be*, but WHO DO I BE? 32

QUESTIONS

1. According to Smitherman, what are the distinctive qualities of Black English? How does it differ from White English? How does Smitherman account for these differences?

2. Does Smitherman believe blacks should be taught White English? What reasons does she give for or against this idea?

3. The most important illustration of Black English in this essay is Smitherman's own writing. Her use of Black English involves, among other things, grammar and word choice. Identify her use of black grammar and words. What effect does she achieve by using Black English herself?

4. Smitherman's diction and word choice also reflect "standard" English. Cite examples. How well do these two forms work together?

5. Smitherman uses analysis frequently in this essay. Show where and how she uses this technique. How is classification involved? How do these techniques help her organize the essay?

6. Show how the author uses examples, other than in her own style, to prove her assertions.

7. This is a carefully structured essay. Divide the essay into five parts. Justify your decision.

8. Does Smitherman use inductive or deductive reasoning predominantly to establish her principles in paragraphs 13 to 18? Explain.

9. Comment on other ethnic and social groups that have distinctive styles and grammars.

10. Analyze the linguistic and stylistic features of some vernacular with which you are familiar, such as CB radio; college slang; Hispanic, Italian, Jewish, or Irish English.

---

[10]Frantz Fanon, *Black Skin, White Masks*, trans. Charles Lamm Markmann (New York, 1967), pp. 17–40.

Literature, Media, and the Arts

JUDITH VIORST

How Books Helped Shape My Life

Judith Viorst (193? –   ), a contributing editor to *Redbook*, is an American poet, journalist, and writer of children's books. Her work includes *People and Other Aggravations* (1971) and *Yes, Married: A Saga of Love and Complaint* (1972). Measured, witty, and affirmative, Viorst in her typical writing tries to mediate between extremes, seeking wisdom from the ordinary and commonplace. In this essay, Viorst investigates the books and fictive heroines that have molded her personality.

n books I've read since I was young I've searched for   1
heroines who could serve as ideals, as models, as possibilities—some reflecting the secret self that dwelled inside me, others pointing to whole new ways that a woman (if only she dared!) might try to be. The person that I am today was shaped by Nancy Drew; by Jo March, Jane Eyre and Heathcliff's soul mate Cathy; and by other fictional females whose attractiveness or character or audacity for a time were the standards by which I measured myself.

I return to some of these books to see if I still understand the   2
powerful hold that these heroines once had on me. I still understand.

Consider teen-aged Nancy Drew—beautiful, blond-haired,   3
blue-eyed girl detective—who had the most terrific life that I as a
ten-year-old could ever imagine. Motherless (in other words, quite
free of maternal controls), she lived with her handsome indulgent
lawyer father in a large brick house set back from the street with a
winding tree-lined driveway on the outside and a faithful, nonintru-
sive housekeeper Hannah cooking yummy meals on the inside. She
also had a boy friend, a convertible, nice clothes and two close girl
friends—not as perfect as she, but then it seemed to me that no one
could possibly be as perfect as Nancy Drew, who in dozens and
dozens of books (*The Hidden Staircase, The Whispering Statue, The Clue
in the Diary, The Clue of the Tapping Heels*) was resourceful and brave
and intelligent as she went around solving mysteries left and right,
while remaining kind to the elderly and invariably polite and absolutely completely delightfully feminine.

I mean, what else *was* there?   4

I soon found out what else when I encountered the four   5
March sisters of *Little Women,* a sentimental, old-fashioned book
about girls growing up in Civil War time in New England. About
spoiled, vain, pretty Amy. And sickly, saintly Beth. And womanly,
decent Meg. And about—most important of all—gawky, bookworm
Jo. Dear Jo, who wasn't as flawless as the golden Nancy Drew but
who showed me that girls like her—like *us*—could be heroines. Even
if we weren't much to look at. Even if we were clumsy and socially
gauche. And even if the transition into young womanhood often
appeared to our dubious eye to be difficult and scary and even
unwelcome.

Jo got stains on her dress and laughed when she shouldn't   6
and lost her temper and didn't display tact or patience or restraint. Jo
brought a touch of irreverence to the cultural constraints of the world
she lived in. And yet her instincts were good and her heart was pure
and her headstrong ways led always to virtue. And furthermore
Jo—as I yearned to be—was a writer!

In the book the years go by, Beth dies, Meg and Amy marry   7
and Jo—her fierce heart somewhat tamed—is alone. "An old maid,
that's what I'm to be. A literary spinster, with a pen for a spouse, a
family of stories for children, and twenty years hence a morsel of
fame, perhaps!' . . . Jo sighed, as if the prospect was not inviting."

This worried young reader concurred—not inviting at all!   8

And so I was happy to read of Jo's nice suitor, Mr. Bhaer, not   9
handsome or rich or young or important or witty, but possessed of
kindness and dignity and enough intelligence to understand that

JUDITH VIORST

even a girl who wasn't especially pretty, who had no dazzling charms and who wanted to write might make a wonderful wife. And a wonderful mother. And live happily ever after.

What a relief! 10

What Jo and Nancy shared was active participation in life— 11 they went out and *did*; they weren't simply done to—and they taught and promised me (at a time when mommies stayed home and there was no Women's Movement) that a girl could go out and do and still get a man. Jo added the notion that brusque, ungainly girls could go out and do and still get a man. And Jane of *Jane Eyre*, whose author once said, "I will show you a heroine as small and as plain as myself," added the further idea that such women were able to "feel just as men feel" and were capable of being just as passionate.

Orphaned Jane, a governess at stately Thornfield Hall, was a 12 no-nonsense lady, cool and self-contained, whose lonely, painful childhood had ingrained in her an impressive firmness of character, an unwillingness to charm or curry favor and a sense of herself as the equal of any man. Said Jane to Mr. Rochester, the brooding, haughty, haunted master of Thornfield: "Do you think I am an automaton?—a machine without feelings? Do you think, because I am poor, obscure, plain, and little, I am soulless and heartless? You think wrong!—I have as much soul as you, and full as much heart!"

I loved it that such hot fires burned inside so plain a Jane. I 13 loved her for her unabashed intensity. And I loved her for being so pure that when she learned of Mr. Rochester's lunatic wife, she sacrificed romance for honor and left him immediately.

For I think it's important to note that Nancy and Jo and Jane, 14 despite their independence, were basically as good as girls can be: honest, generous, kind, sincere, reliable, respectable, possessed of absolute integrity. They didn't defy convention. They didn't challenge the rules. They did what was right, although it might cause them pain. And their virtue was always rewarded—look at Jane, rich and married at last to her Mr. Rochester. Oh, how I identified with Jane!

But then I read *Wuthering Heights,* a novel of soul-consuming 15 love on the Yorkshire moors, and Catherine Earnshaw totally captured me. And she captured me, not in spite of her dangerous, dark and violent spirit, but *because* of it.

Cathy was as wild as the moors. She lied and connived and 16 deceived. She was insolent, selfish, manipulative and cruel. And by marrying meek, weak Edgar instead of Heathcliff, her destiny, she betrayed a love she described in throbbing, unforgettable prose as . . . elemental:

"My love for Heathcliff resembles the eternal rocks beneath— 17 a source of little visible delight, but necessary. Nelly, I *am* Heathcliff—he's always, always in my mind—not as a pleasure, any more than I am always a pleasure to myself—but as my own being. . . ."

Now who, at the age of 16, could resist such quivering 18 intensity? Who would settle for less than elemental? Must we untamed creatures of passion—I'd muse as I lay awake in my red flannel nightie—submit ourselves to conventional morality? Or could I actually choose not to be a good girl?

Cathy Earnshaw told me that I could. And so did lost Lady 19 Brett, of *The Sun Also Rises*.

Brett Ashley was to me, at 18, free, modern, woman incar- 20 nate, and she dangled alluring new concepts before my eyes:

The value of style: "She wore a slipover jersey sweater and a 21 tweed skirt, and her hair was brushed back like a boy's. She started all that."

The glamour of having a dark and tortured past: "Finally, 22 when he got really bad, he used to tell her he'd kill her. . . . She hasn't had an absolutely happy life."

The excitement of nonconformity: "I've always done just 23 what I wanted."

The importance of (understated) grace under pressure: "Brett 24 was rather good. She's always rather good."

And the thrill of unrepressed sexuality: "Brett's had affairs 25 with men before. She tells me all about everything."

Brett married lovelessly and drank too much and drifted too 26 much and had an irresponsible fling with a bullfighter. But she also had class—and her own morality. She set her bullfighter free—"I'd have lived with him if I hadn't seen it was bad for him." And even though she was broke, she lied and "told him I had scads of it. . . . I couldn't take his money, you know."

Brett's wasn't the kind of morality that my mother was 27 teaching me in suburban New Jersey. But maybe I wasn't meant for suburban life. Maybe—I would muse as I carefully lined my eyes with blue liner—maybe I'm meant for something more . . . emancipated.

I carried Brett's image with me when, after college, I lived for 28 a while in Greenwich Village, in New York. But I couldn't achieve her desperate gallantry. And it struck me that Brett was too lonely and sad, and that Cathy had died too young (and that Scarlett O'Hara got Tara but lost her Rhett), and that maybe I ought to forget about unconventionality if the price was going to be so painfully high. Although I enjoyed my Village fling, I had no wish to live anguishedly ever after. I needed a heroine who, like me, wanted just a small taste of the wild before settling down into happy domesticity.

I found her in *War and Peace*. Her name was Natasha. 29

Natasha, the leading lady of this epic of Russian society 30

JUDITH VIORST

during Napoleon's time, was "poetic . . . charming . . . overflowing with life," an enchanting girl whose sweet eagerness and passionate impulsivity were tempered by historic and private tragedies. Betrothed to the handsome and excellent Prince Andrew, she fell in love with a heel named Anatole, and when she was warned that this foolish and dangerous passion would lead to her ruin, "I'll go to my ruin . . .," she said, "as soon as possible."

It ended badly with Anatole. Natasha tried suicide. Prince   31
Andrew died. Natasha turned pale, thin, subdued. But unlike Brett and Cathy, her breach with convention was mended and, at long last, she married Pierre—a decent, substantial, loving man, the kind of man all our mothers want us to marry.

In marriage Natasha grew stouter and "the old fire very   32
rarely kindled in her face now." She became an exemplary mother, an ideal wife. "She felt that her unity with her husband was maintained not by the poetic feelings that had attracted him to her but by something else—indefinite but firm as the bond between her own body and soul."

It sounded—if not elemental and doomed—awfully nice.   33

I identified with Natasha when, the following year, I married   34
and left Greenwich Village. I too was ready for domesticity. And yet . . . her husband and children became "the subject which wholly engrossed Natasha's attention." She had lost herself—and I didn't want to lose me. What I needed next was a heroine who could reconcile all the warring wants of my nature—for fire and quiet, independence and oneness, ambition and love, and marriage and family.

But such reconciling heroines, in novels and real life, may not   35
yet exist.

Nevertheless Natasha and Jane and Jo, Cathy, Nancy and   36
Brett—each spoke to my heart and stirred me powerfully. On my journey into young womanhood I was fortunate to have them as my companions. They were, they will always remain, a part of me.

QUESTIONS

1. Analyze the process of growth and maturation reflected in the heroines the author was attracted to between the age of 10 and her adult years. What principle of unity does Viorst find in her early heroines?

2. Explain the author's need for "reconciling heroines." What can we infer about her personality from this statement?

3. What do words like "yummy" (paragraph 3) and "nightie" (paragraph 18) contribute to the tone of the essay? How do the conjunctions "and" in paragraphs 5, 9, and elsewhere reinforce this aspect of tone?

HOW BOOKS HELPED SHAPE MY LIFE

4. Locate examples of one of Viorst's favorite techniques—the use of adjectives in series. Explain the purpose of this technique.

5. Analyze the introductory paragraph in terms of its delineation of thesis and its function in establishing the organizing frame for the essay.

6. Discuss the manner in which Viorst integrates rhetorical strategies of illustration, causal analysis, and process analysis in the essay.

7. Find and analyze those paragraphs that rely on comparative methods of development. Why do they contribute to the unity of the essay?

8. What is the relationship between Viorst's use of summary, characterization, and character analysis and her attitude toward the reading audience?

9. Do you accept Viorst's thesis that books shape our lives? Explain your answer.

10. a. Write an essay entitled "How Books Shaped My Life," "How Music Shaped My Life," or "How Television Shaped My Life."
b. Write an essay focusing on one character from literature, radio, or film who had an impact on your life.

SYLVIA PLATH

A Comparison

Sylvia Plath (1932–1963), American poet and novelist, graduated from Smith College and took a master's at Cambridge University. She married the English poet Ted Hughes in 1956. Plath committed suicide at the age of 30. Her best known work is *The Bell-Jar* (1963), a highly autobiographical novel about a young woman overwhelmed by crises and suicidal tendencies. Plath's poetry, often reflecting a fascination with suffering, pain, and death, is collected in *The Colossus* (1960), *Ariel* (1965), *Crossing the Water* (1971), and *Winter Trees* (1972). This essay, written in 1962, is an energetic and highly poetic celebration of the artist's craft.

ow I envy the novelist!   1
I imagine him—better say her, for it is the women I look   2
to for . . . a parallel—I imagine her, then, pruning a
rosebush with a large pair of shears, adjusting her

spectacles, shuffling about among the teacups, humming, arranging ashtrays or babies, absorbing a slant of light, a fresh edge to the weather, and piercing, with a kind of modest, beautiful X-ray vision, the psychic interiors of her neighbors—her neighbors on trains, in the dentist's waiting room, in the corner teashop. To her, this fortunate one, what is there that *isn't* relevant! Old shoes can be used, doorknobs, air letters, flannel nightgowns, cathedrals, nail varnish, jet planes, rose arbors and budgerigars; little mannerisms—the sucking at a tooth, the tugging at a hemline—any weird or warty or fine or despicable thing. Not to mention emotions, motivations—those rumbling, thunderous shapes. Her business is Time, the way it shoots forward, shunts back, blooms, decays and double-exposes itself. Her business is people in Time. And she, it seems to me, has all the time in the world. She can take a century if she likes, a generation, a whole summer.

I can take about a minute. 3

I'm not talking about epic poems. We all know how long *they* 4 can take. I'm talking about the smallish, unofficial garden-variety poem. How shall I describe it?—a door opens, a door shuts. In between you have had a glimpse: a garden, a person, a rainstorm, a dragonfly, a heart, a city. I think of those round glass Victorian paperweights which I remember, yet can never find—a far cry from the plastic mass-productions which stud the toy counters in Woolworth's. This sort of paperweight is a clear globe, self-complete, very pure, with a forest or village or family group within it. You turn it upside down, then back. It snows. Everything is changed in a minute. It will never be the same in there—not the fir trees, nor the gables, nor the faces.

So a poem takes place. 5

And there is really so little room! So little time! The poet 6 becomes an expert packer of suitcases:

> The apparition of these faces in the crowd;
> Petals on a wet black bough.

There it is: the beginning and the end in one breath. How 7 would the novelist manage that? In a paragraph? In a page? Mixing it, perhaps, like paint, with a little water, thinning it, spreading it out.

Now I am being smug, I am finding advantages. 8

If a poem is concentrated, a closed fist, then a novel is relaxed 9 and expansive, an open hand: it has roads, detours, destinations; a heart line, a head line; morals and money come into it. Where the fist excludes and stuns, the open hand can touch and encompass a great deal in its travels.

I have never put a toothbrush in a poem. 10

 A COMPARISON

I do not like to think of all the things, familiar, useful and   11
worthy things, I have never put into a poem. I did, once, put a yew
tree in. And that yew tree began, with astounding egotism, to
manage and order the whole affair. It was not a yew tree by a church
on a road past a house in a town where a certain woman lived . . .
and so on, as it might have been in a novel. Oh, no. It stood squarely
in the middle of my poem, manipulating its dark shades, the voices in
the churchyard, the clouds, the birds, the tender melancholy with
which I contemplated it—everything! I couldn't subdue it. And, in
the end, my poem was a poem about a yew tree. That yew tree was
just too proud to be a passing black mark in a novel.

Perhaps I shall anger some poets by implying that the *poem* is   12
proud. The poem, too, can include everything, they will tell me. And
with far more precision and power than those baggy, disheveled and
undiscriminate creatures we call novels. Well, I concede these poets
their steamshovels and old trousers. I really *don't* think poems should
be all that chaste. I would, I think, even concede a toothbrush, if the
poem was a real one. But these apparitions, these poetical toothbrushes, are rare. And when they do arrive, they are inclined, like my
obstreperous yew tree, to think themselves singled out and rather
special.

Not so in novels.   13

There the toothbrush returns to its rack with beautiful   14
promptitude and is forgot. Time flows, eddies, meanders, and people
have leisure to grow and alter before our eyes. The rich junk of life
bobs all about us: bureaus, thimbles, cats, the whole much-loved,
well-thumbed catalog of the miscellaneous which the novelist wishes
us to share. I do not mean that there is no pattern, no discernment,
no rigorous ordering here.

I am only suggesting that perhaps the pattern does not insist   15
so much.

The door of the novel, like the door of the poem, also shuts.   16

But not so fast, nor with such manic, unanswerable finality.   17

QUESTIONS

1. What distinctions does the author draw between the poem and the
novel? Why does she envy the novelist? What stated and implied prefer-
ences does she have for the poem rather than the novel?

2. Explain the relevance of rosebushes, toothbrushes, and yew trees to
Plath's discussion.

3. The author employs a remarkable variety of poetic techniques in this

SYLVIA PLATH

essay, including metaphors, symbols, allusions, imagery, personification, onomatopoeia, alliteration, consonance, and assonance. Locate and analyze examples of these techniques.

4. Analyze Plath's use of parallelism in paragraphs 2, 4, and 14.

5. Plath uses a series of figurative comparisons to structure the entire essay. Trace and examine the main figurative comparisons that serve to organize the selection.

6. Examine the spatial and rhetorical effects of the numerous one-sentence paragraphs in the essay.

7. What purpose does Plath's method serve in identification and definition of the novelist and poet?

8. Analyze the cumulative use of illustration to achieve emphasis in this essay.

9. Comment on Plath's view that the poem, unlike the novel, closes with "manic, unanswerable finality."

10. Write an essay that compares and contrasts—either figuratively or literally—two forms of literature, art, music, or film.

D. H. LAWRENCE

Why the Novel Matters

David Herbert Lawrence (1885–1930), novelist, essayist, and poet, wrote in the great tradition of English romanticism. He chafed under the conventions of his age and zealously extended the content and style of the English novel. His novels, such as *Sons and Lovers* (1913), *The Rainbow* (1915), *Women in Love* (1921), *The Plumed Serpent* (1926), and *Lady Chatterley's Lover* (1928), are famous for their often disquieting depictions of love and ambition in the modern world. Lawrence also wrote criticism: his *Studies in Classic American Literature* (1923) is still a revealing, if idiosyncratic, look at American literature. In the following essay, what matters for Lawrence is not simply the essay, which he treats with energy and enthusiasm, but life itself.

We have curious ideas of ourselves. We think of ourselves   1
as a body with a spirit in it, or a body with a soul in it, or
a body with a mind in it. *Mens sana in corpore sano.* The
years drink up the wine, and at last throw the bottle
away, the body, of course, being the bottle.

It is a funny sort of superstition. Why should I look at my   2
hand, as it so cleverly writes these words, and decide that it is a mere
nothing compared to the mind that directs it? Is there really any huge
difference between my hand and my brain? Or my mind? My hand is
alive, it flickers with a life of its own. It meets all the strange universe
in touch, and learns a vast number of things, and knows a vast
number of things. My hand, as it writes these words, slips gaily
along, jumps like a grasshopper to dot an *i*, feels the table rather cold,
gets a little bored if I write too long, has its own rudiments of
thought, and is just as much *me* as is my brain, my mind, or my soul.
Why should I imagine that there is a *me* which is more *me* than my
hand is? Since my hand is absolutely alive, me alive.

Whereas, of course, as far as I am concerned, my pen isn't   3
alive at all. My pen *isn't me* alive. Me alive ends at my finger-tips.

Whatever is me alive is me. Every tiny bit of my hands is   4
alive, every little freckle and hair and fold of skin. And whatever is
me alive is me. Only my finger-nails, those ten little weapons
between me and an inanimate universe, they cross the mysterious
Rubicon between me alive and things like my pen, which are not
alive, in my own sense.

So, seeing my hand is all alive, and me alive, wherein is it just   5
a bottle, or a jug, or a tin can, or a vessel of clay, or any of the rest of
that nonsense? True, if I cut it it will bleed, like a can of cherries. But
then the skin that is cut, and the veins that bleed, and the bones that
should never be seen, they are all just as alive as the blood that flows.
So the tin can business, or vessel of clay, is just bunk.

And that's what you learn, when you're a novelist. And that's   6
what you are very liable *not* to know, if you're a parson, or a
philosopher, or a scientist, or a stupid person. If you're a parson, you
talk about souls in heaven. If you're a novelist, you know that
paradise is in the palm of your hand, and on the end of your nose,
because both are alive; and alive, and man alive, which is more than
you can say, for certain, of paradise. Paradise is after life, and I for one
am not keen on anything that is *after* life. If you are a philosopher, you
talk about infinity, and the pure spirit which knows all things. But if
you pick up a novel, you realize immediately that infinity is just a
handle to this self-same jug of a body of mine; while as for knowing, if
I find my finger in fire, I know that fire burns, with a knowledge so
emphatic and vital, it leaves Nirvana merely a conjecture. Oh, yes,
my body, me alive, *knows*, and knows intensely. And as for the sum

D. H. LAWRENCE

of all knowledge, it can't be anything more than an accumulation of all the things I know in the body, and you, dear reader, know in the body.

These damned philosophers, they talk as if they suddenly 7 went off in steam, and were then much more important than they are when they're in their shirts. It is nonsense. Every man, philosopher included, ends in his own finger-tips. That's the end of his man alive. As for the words and thoughts and sighs and aspirations that fly from him, they are so many tremulations in the ether, and not alive at all. But if the tremulations reach another man alive, he may receive them into his life, and his life may take on a new colour, like a chameleon creeping from a brown rock on to a green leaf. All very well and good. It still doesn't alter the fact that the so-called spirit, the message or teaching of the philosopher or the saint, isn't alive at all, but just a tremulation upon the ether, like a radio message. All this spirit stuff is just tremulations upon the ether into new life, that is because you are man alive, and you take sustenance and stimulation into your alive man in a myriad ways. But to say that the message, or the spirit which is communicated to you, is more important than your living body, is nonsense. You might as well say that the potato at dinner was more important.

Nothing is important but life. And for myself, I can absolutely 8 see life nowhere but in the living. Life with a capital L is only man alive. Even a cabbage in the rain is cabbage alive. All things that are alive are amazing. And all things that are dead are subsidiary to the living. Better a live dog than a dead lion. But better a live lion than a live dog. *C'est la vie!*

It seems impossible to get a saint, or a philosopher, or a 9 scientist, to stick to this simple truth. They are all, in a sense, renegades. The saint wishes to offer himself up as spiritual food for the multitude. Even Francis of Assisi turns himself into a sort of angel-cake, of which anyone may take a slice. But an angel-cake is rather less than man alive. And poor St. Francis might well apologize to his body, when he is dying: "Oh, pardon me, my body, the wrong I did you through the years!" It was no wafer, for others to eat.

The philosopher, on the other hand, because he can think, 10 decides that nothing but thoughts matter. It is as if a rabbit, because he can make little pills, should decide that nothing but little pills matter. As for the scientist, he has absolutely no use for me so long as I am man alive. To the scientist, I am dead. He puts under the microscope a bit of dead me, and calls it me. He takes me to pieces, and says first one piece, and then another piece, is me. My heart, my liver, my stomach have all been scientifically me, according to the scientist; and nowadays I am either a brain, or nerves, or glands, or something more up-to-date in the tissue line.

 WHY THE NOVEL MATTERS **393**

Now I absolutely flatly deny that I am a soul, or a body, or a 11
mind, or an intelligence, or a brain, or a nervous system, or a bunch
of glands, or any of the rest of these bits of me. The whole is greater
than the part. And therefore, I, who am man alive, am greater than
my soul, or spirit, or body, or mind, or consciousness, or anything
else that is merely a part of me. I am a man, and alive. I am man alive,
and as long as I can, I intend to go on being man alive.

For this reason I am a novelist. And being a novelist, I 12
consider myself superior to the saint, the scientist, the philosopher,
and the poet, who are all great masters of different bits of man alive,
but never get the whole hog.

The novel is the one bright book of life. Books are not life. 13
They are only tremulations on the ether. But the novel as a tremulation can make the whole man alive tremble. Which is more than
poetry, philosophy, science, or any other book-tremulation can do.

The novel is the book of life. In this sense, the Bible is a great 14
confused novel. You may say, it is about God. But it is really about
man alive. Adam, Eve, Sarai, Abraham, Isaac, Jacob, Samuel, David,
Bath-Sheba, Ruth, Esther, Solomon, Job, Isaiah, Jesus, Mark, Judas,
Paul, Peter: what is it but man alive, from start to finish? Man alive,
not mere bits. Even the Lord is another man alive, in a burning bush,
throwing the tablets of stone at Moses's head.

I do hope you begin to get my idea, why the novel is 15
supremely important, as a tremulation on the ether. Plato makes the
perfect ideal being tremble in me. But that's only a bit of me.
Perfection is only a bit, in the strange make-up of man alive. The
Sermon on the Mount makes the selfless spirit of me quiver. But that,
too, is only a bit of me. The Ten Commandments set the old Adam
shivering in me, warning me that I am a thief and a murderer, unless
I watch it. But even the old Adam is only a bit of me.

I very much like all these bits of me to be set trembling with 16
life and the wisdom of life. But I do ask that the whole of me shall
tremble in its wholeness, some time or other.

And this, of course, must happen in me, living. 17

But as far as it can happen from a communication, it can only 18
happen when a whole novel communicates itself to me. The Bible—
but *all* the Bible—and Homer, and Shakespeare: these are the
supreme old novels. These are all things to all men. Which means
that in their wholeness they affect the whole man alive, which is the
man himself, beyond any part of him. They set the whole tree
trembling with a new access of life, they do not just stimulate growth
in one direction.

I don't want to grow in any one direction any more. And, if I 19
can help it, I don't want to stimulate anybody else into some

D. H. LAWRENCE

particular direction. A particular direction ends in a *cul-de-sac*. We're in a *cul-de-sac* at present.

I don't believe in any dazzling revelation, or in any supreme Word. "The grass withereth, the flower fadeth, but the Word of the Lord shall stand for ever." That's the kind of stuff we've drugged ourselves with. As a matter of fact, the grass withereth, but comes up all the greener for that reason, after the rains. The flower fadeth, and therefore the bud opens. But the Word of the Lord, being man-uttered and a mere vibration on the ether, becomes staler and staler, more and more boring, till at last we turn a deaf ear and it ceases to exist, far more finally than any withered grass. It is grass that renews its youth like the eagle, not any Word.

We should ask for no absolutes, or absolute. Once and for all and for ever, let us have done with the ugly imperialism of any absolute. There is no absolute good, there is nothing absolutely right. All things flow and change, and even change is not absolute. The whole is a strange assembly of apparently incongruous parts, slipping past one another.

Me, man alive, I am a very curious assembly of incongruous parts. My yea! of today is oddly different from my yea! of yesterday. My tears of tomorrow will have nothing to do with my tears of a year ago. If the one I love remains unchanged and unchanging, I shall cease to love her. It is only because she changes and startles me into change and defies my inertia, and is herself staggered in her inertia by my changing, that I can continue to love her. If she stayed put, I might as well love the pepper-pot.

In all this change, I maintain a certain integrity. But woe betide me if I try to put my finger on it. If I say of myself, I am this, I am that!—then, if I stick to it, I turn into a stupid fixed thing like a lamp-post. I shall never know wherein lies my integrity, my individuality, my me. I *can* never know it. It is useless to talk about my ego. That only means that I have made up an *idea* of myself, and that I am trying to cut myself out to pattern. Which is no good. You can cut your cloth to fit your coat, but you can't clip bits off your living body, to trim it down to your idea. True, you can put yourself into ideal corsets. But even in ideal corsets, fashions change.

Let us learn from the novel. In the novel, the characters can do nothing but *live*. If they keep on being good, according to pattern, or bad, according to pattern, or even volatile, according to pattern, they cease to live, and the novel falls dead. A character in a novel has got to live, or it is nothing.

We, likewise, in life have got to live, or we are nothing.

What we mean by living is, of course, just as indescribable as what we mean by *being*. Men get ideas into their heads, of what they mean by Life, and they proceed to cut life out to pattern. Sometimes they go into the desert to seek God, sometimes they go into the desert to seek cash, sometimes it is wine, woman, and song, and again it is water, political reform, and votes. You never know what it will be next: from killing your neighbour with hideous bombs and gas that tears the lungs, to supporting a Foundlings Home and preaching infinite Love, and being co-respondent in a divorce.

In all this wild welter, we need some sort of guide. It's no good inventing Thou Shalt Nots!   27

What then? Turn truly, honourably to the novel, and see wherein you are man alive, and wherein you are dead man in life. You may love a woman as man alive, and you may be making love to a woman as sheer dead man in life. You may eat your dinner as man alive, or as a mere masticating corpse. As man alive you may have a shot at your enemy. But as a ghastly simulacrum of life you may be firing bombs into men who are neither your enemies nor your friends, but just things you are dead to. Which is criminal, when the things happen to be alive.   28

To be alive, to be man alive, to be whole man alive: that is the point. And at its best, the novel, and the novel supremely, can help you. It can help you not to be dead man in life. So much of man walks about dead and a carcass in the street and house, today: so much of women is merely dead. Like a pianoforte with half the notes mute.   29

But in the novel you can see, plainly, when the man goes dead, the woman goes inert. You can develop an instinct for life, if you will, instead of a theory of right and wrong, good and bad.   30

In life, there is right and wrong, good and bad, all the time. But what is right in one case is wrong in another. And in the novel you see one man becoming a corpse, because of his so-called goodness, another going dead because of his so-called wickedness. Right and wrong is an instinct: but an instinct of the whole consciousness in a man, bodily, mental, spiritual at once. And only in the novel are *all* things given full play, or at least, they may be given full play, when we realize that life itself, and not inert safety, is the reason for living. For out of the full play of all things emerges the only thing that is anything, the wholeness of a man, the wholeness of a woman, man alive, and live woman.   31

QUESTIONS

1. According to Lawrence, what is the relationship between life and the novel? Why does the novel matter?

2. What contrasts does Lawrence establish between the novelist and the parson, philosopher, and scientist?

D. H. LAWRENCE

3. Analyze the levels of diction, the very "sound" of Lawrence's prose. Examine the admixture of declarative, interrogative, and exclamatory sentence structures in the essay. Explain the author's use of fragments, his application of figurative language, his use of italics for typographical emphasis. Examine Lawrence's persistent devices of repetition and over-statement in the essay. Evaluate the effect of these numerous strategies on the tone of the essay.

4. What patterns of imagery do you detect in the essay? How do they relate to the thesis?

5. How do the terms "tremulation on the ether" and "bright book of life" serve as structuring principles in the essay?

6. Trace the association of ideas advancing Lawrence's thesis. In the absence of strictly logical development, how unified and coherent is the essay?

7. Analyze patterns of comparison and contrast in the essay.

8. Examine the relation of point of view to theme and tone in the essay.

9. Do you agree with Lawrence's assertion that the novelist is better equipped than the scientist, philosopher, or theologian to capture the wholeness of life? Explain.

10. Write a personalized essay on why music matters; why film matters; why drama matters; or a similar subject.

URSULA K. LeGUIN

American SF and the Other

Ursula Kroeber LeGuin (1929–   ), one of the most impressive writers of science fiction, has won several Nebula and Hugo awards for her work in this genre. Highly imaginative, often richly allegorical, LeGuin is perhaps the best prose stylist among contemporary science fiction writers, and also one of the most provocative in her persistent vision of an ancient race that once populated the galaxy, including Earth. Le-Guin's work includes *The Left Hand of Darkness* (1969), *The Lathe of Heaven* (1971), *The Dispossessed* (1974), *Orsinian Tales* (1976), and *Malafrena* (1979). Also an astute commentator on the theory and practice of science fiction, LeGuin investigates in this essay the relationship of women in the genre to American sexual, racial, social, and political realities.

ne of the great early socialists said that the status of women in a society is a pretty reliable index of the degree of civilization of that society. If this is true, then the very low status of women in SF should make us ponder about whether SF is civilized at all.

The women's movement has made most of us conscious of the fact that SF has either totally ignored women, or presented them as squeaking dolls subject to instant rape by monsters—or old-maid scientists desexed by hypertrophy of the intellectual organs—or, at best, the loyal little wives or mistresses of accomplished heroes. Male elitism has run rampant in SF. But is it only male elitism? Isn't the "subjection of women" in SF merely a symptom of a whole which is authoritarian, power-worshiping, and intensely parochial?

The question involved here is the question of The Other—the being who is different from yourself. This being can be different from you in its sex; or in its annual income; or in its way of speaking and dressing and doing things; or in the color of its skin, or the number of its legs and heads. In other words, there is the sexual Alien, and the social Alien, and the cultural Alien, and finally the racial Alien.

Well, how about the social Alien in SF? How about, in Marxist terms, "the proletariat"? Where are they in SF? Where are the poor, the people who work hard and go to bed hungry? Are they ever *persons*, in SF? No. They appear as vast anonymous masses fleeing from giant slime-globules from the Chicago sewers, or dying off by the billion from pollution or radiation, or as faceless armies being led to battle by generals and statesmen. In sword and sorcery they behave like the walk-on parts in a high-school performance of *The Chocolate Prince*. Now and then there's a busty lass among them who is honored by the attentions of the Captain of the Supreme Terran Command, or in a spaceship crew there's a quaint old cook, with a Scots or Swedish accent, representing the Wisdom of the Common Folk.

The people, in SF, are not people. They are masses, existing for one purpose: to be led by their superiors.

From a social point of view most SF has been incredibly regressive and unimaginative. All those Galactic Empires, taken straight from the British Empire of 1880. All those planets—with 80 trillion miles between them!—conceived of as warring nation-states, or as colonies to be exploited, or to be nudged by the benevolent Imperium of Earth toward self-development—the White Man's Burden all over again. The Rotary Club on Alpha Centauri, that's the size of it.

What about the cultural and the racial Other? This is the Alien 7 everybody recognizes as alien, supposed to be the special concern of SF. Well, in the old pulp SF, it's very simple. The only good alien is a dead alien—whether he is an Aldebaranian Mantis-Man, or a German dentist. And this tradition still flourishes: witness Larry Niven's story "Inconstant Moon" (in *All the Myriad Ways*, 1971) which has a happy ending—consisting of the fact that America, including Los Angeles, was not hurt by a solar flare. Of course a few million Europeans and Asians were fried, but that doesn't matter, it just makes the world a little safer for democracy, in fact. (It is interesting that the female character in the same story is quite brainless; her only function is to say Oh? and Ooooh! to the clever and resourceful hero.)

Then there's the other side of the same coin. If you hold a 8 thing to be totally different from yourself, your fear of it may come out as hatred, or as awe—reverence. So we get all those wise and kindly beings who deign to rescue Earth from her sins and perils. The Alien ends up on a pedestal in a white nightgown and a virtuous smirk— exactly as the "good woman" did in the Victorian Age.

In America, it seems to have been Stanley Weinbaum who 9 invented the sympathetic alien, in *A Martian Odyssey*. From then on, via people like Cyril Kornbluth, Ted Sturgeon, and Cordwainer Smith, SF began to inch its way out of simple racism. Robots—the alien intelligence—begin to behave nicely. With Smith, interestingly enough, the racial alien is combined with the social alien, in the "Underpeople," and they are allowed to have a revolution. As the aliens got more sympathetic, so did the heroes. They began to have emotions, as well as rayguns, Indeed they began to become almost human.

If you deny any affinity with another person or kind of 10 person, if you declare it to be wholly different from yourself—as men have done to women, and class has done to class, and nation has done to nation—you may hate it, or deify it; but in either case you have denied its spiritual equality, and its human reality. You have made it into a thing, to which the only possible relationship is a power relationship. And thus you have fatally impoverished your own reality. You have, in fact, alienated yourself.

This tendency has been remarkably strong in American SF. 11 The only social change presented by most SF has been toward authoritarianism, the domination of ignorant masses by a powerful elite—sometimes presented as a warning, but often quite complacently. Socialism is never considered as an alternative, and democracy is quite forgotten. Military virtues are taken as ethical ones. Wealth is assumed to be a righteous goal and a personal virtue. Competitive free-enterprise capitalism is the economic destiny of the entire Galaxy. In general, American SF has assumed a permanent hierarchy of superiors and inferiors, with rich, ambitious, aggressive males at the top, then a great gap, and then at the bottom the poor, the uneducated, the faceless masses, and all the women. The whole picture is, if I may say so, curiously "un-American." It is a perfect baboon patriarchy, with the Alpha Male on top, being respectfully groomed, from time to time, by his inferiors.

Is this speculation? Is this imagination? Is this extrapolation? I   12
call it brainless regressivism.

I think it's time SF writers—and their readers!—stopped   13
daydreaming about a return to the age of Queen Victoria, and started
thinking about the future. I would like to see the Baboon Ideal
replaced by a little human idealism, and some serious consideration
of such deeply radical, futuristic concepts as Liberty, Equality, and
Fraternity. And remember that about 53 percent of the Brotherhood
of Man is the Sisterhood of Woman.

QUESTIONS

1. Explain the author's concept of the sexual, social, cultural, and racial Alien. How does she relate these categories to the status of women?

2. According to LeGuin, what is the relationship of science fiction (SF) to politics?

3. What does the author's use of the abbreviation SF indicate about the expectations she has of her audience? What level of diction does she employ to address this audience? Cite examples of ironic statement in the treatment of her subject.

4. Analyze the metaphorical language used to identify women in science fiction in this essay.

5. For what purpose does the author use a series of questions in paragraph 2?

6. Analyze LeGuin's pattern of classification. Does she use a logical or a metaphorical pattern of classification in the essay? Explain.

7. How does the author develop causal relationships in the essay?

8. Explain the effectiveness of the author's concluding paragraph.

9. Why is "baboon patriarchy" (paragraph 11) a particularly apt label for the state of science fiction and perhaps of American culture?

10. a. Write an essay on images of women in literature, television, popular music, or film.

b. Classify the types of women found in a typical television program like *Dallas* or *As the World Turns*.

THOMAS DE QUINCEY

On the Knocking at the Gate in *Macbeth*

Thomas de Quincey (1785–1859), famed author of *Confessions of an English Opium-Eater* (1821), was a major critic and essayist, one of the masters of style in English prose. A confirmed opium eater from 1804 until his death, de Quincey revised his confessions in 1856, altering style and perspective to accord more with Victorian conventions. His work was collected in fourteen volumes between 1853 and 1860. De Quincey's literary criticism is among his most important contributions to the art of the essay. The following essay aims at providing literary analysis with what the author termed "a good psychology."

From my boyish days I had always felt a great perplexity on one point in *Macbeth*. It was this: the knocking at the gate, which succeeds to the murder of Duncan, produced to my feelings an effect for which I never could account. The effect was, that it reflected back upon the murderer a peculiar awfulness and a depth of solemnity; yet, however, obstinately I endeavoured with my understanding to comprehend this, for many years I never could see *why* it should produce such an effect.

Here I pause for one moment, to exhort the reader never to pay any attention to his understanding, when it stands in opposition to any other faculty of his mind. The mere understanding, however useful and indispensable, is the meanest faculty in the human mind, and the most to be distrusted; and yet the great majority of people trust to nothing else, which may do for ordinary life, but not philosophical purposes. Of this out of ten thousand instances that I might produce, I will cite one. Ask of any person whatsoever, who is not previously prepared for the demand by a knowledge of the perspective, to draw in the rudest way the commonest appearance which depends upon the laws of that science; as, for instance, to represent the effect of two walls standing at right angles to each other, or the appearance of the houses on each side of a street, as seen by a person looking down the street from one extremity. Now in all cases, unless the person has happened to observe in pictures how it is that artists produce these effects, he will be utterly unable to make the smallest approximation to it. Yet why? For he has actually seen the effect every day of his life. The reason is—that he allows his understanding to overrule his eyes. His understanding, which includes no intuitive knowledge of the laws of vision, can furnish him with no reason why a line which is known and can be proved to be a horizontal line, should not appear a horizontal line; a line that made any angle with the perpendicular, less than a right angle, would seem to him to indicate that his houses were all tumbling down together. Accordingly, he makes the line of his houses a horizontal line, and fails, of course, to produce the effect demanded. Here, then, is one instance out of many, in which not only the understanding is allowed to overrule the eyes, but where the understanding is positively allowed to obliterate the eyes, as it were; for not only does the man believe the evidence of his understanding in opposition to that of his eyes, but (what is monstrous!) the idiot is not aware that his eyes ever gave such evidence. He does not know that he has seen (and therefore *quoad* his consciousness has *not* seen) that which he *has* seen every day of his life.

But to return from this digression, my understanding could furnish no reason why the knocking at the gate in *Macbeth* should produce any effect, direct or reflected. In fact, my understanding said positively that it could *not* produce any effect. But I knew better; I felt that it did; and I waited and clung to the problem until further knowledge should enable me to solve it. At length, in 1812, Mr. Williams made his *début* on the stage of Ratcliffe Highway, and executed those unparalleled murders which have procured for him such a brilliant and undying reputation. On which murders, by the way, I must observe, that in one respect they have had an ill effect, by making the connoisseur in murder very fastidious in his taste, and dissatisfied by anything that has been since done in that line. All other murders look pale by the deep crimson of his; and, as an amateur once said to me in a querulous tone, "There has been absolutely nothing *doing* since his time, or nothing that's worth speaking of." But this is wrong; for it is unreasonable to expect all men to be great artists, and born with the genius of Mr. Williams. Now it will be remembered, that in the first of these murders (that of the Marrs), the same incident (of a knocking at the door, soon after

THOMAS DE QUINCEY

the work of extermination was complete) did actually occur, which the genius of Shakespeare has invented; and all good judges, and the most eminent dilettanti, acknowledged the felicity of Shakespeare's suggestion, as soon as it was actually realized. Here, then, was a fresh proof that I was right in relying on my own feeling, in opposition to my understanding; and I again set myself to study the problem; at length I solved it to my own satisfaction, and my solution is this. Murder in ordinary cases, where the sympathy is wholly directed to the case of the murdered person, is an incident of coarse and vulgar horror; and for this reason, that it flings the interest exclusively upon the natural but ignoble instinct by which we cleave to life; an instinct which, as being indispensable to the primal law of self-preservation, is the same in kind (though different in degree) amongst all living creatures: this instinct, therefore, because it annihilates all distinctions, and degrades the greatest of men to the level of "the poor beetle that we tread on," exhibits human nature in its most abject and humiliating attitude. Such an attitude would little suit the purposes of the poet. What then he must do? He must throw the interest on the murderer. Our sympathy must be with *him* (of course I mean a sympathy of comprehension, a sympathy by which we enter into his feelings, and are made to understand them,—not a sympathy of pity or approbation). In the murdered person, all strife of thought, all flux and reflux of passion and of purpose, are crushed by one overwhelming panic; the fear of instant death smites him "with its petrific mace." But in the murderer, such a murderer as a poet will condescend to, there must be raging some great storm of passion—jealousy, ambition, venegeance, hatred—which will create a hell within him; and into this hell we are to look.

In *Macbeth*, for the sake of gratifying his own enormous and teeming faculty of creation, Shakespeare has introduced two murders: and, as usual in his hands, they are remarkably discriminated: but, though in Macbeth the strife of mind is greater than in his wife, the tiger spirit not so awake, and his feelings caught chiefly by contagion from her,—yet, as both were finally involved in the guilt of murder, the murderous mind of necessity is finally to be presumed in both. This was to be expressed; and on its own account, as well as to make it a more proportionable antagonist to the unoffending nature of their victim, "the gracious Duncan," and adequately to expound "the deep damnation of his taking off," this was to be expressed with peculiar energy. We were to be made to feel that the human nature, i.e., the divine nature of love and mercy, spread through the hearts of all creatures, and seldom utterly withdrawn from man—was gone, vanished, extinct; and that the fiendish nature had taken its place.

4

And, as this effect is marvellously accomplished in the *dialogues* and *soliloquies* themselves, so it is finally consummated by the expedient under consideration; and it is to this that I now solicit the reader's attention. If the reader has ever witnessed a wife, daughter, or sister in a fainting-fit, he may chance to have observed that the most affecting moment in such a spectacle is *that* in which a sigh and a stirring announce the recommencement of suspended life. Or, if the reader has ever been present in a vast metropolis, on the day when some great national idol was carried in funeral pomp to his grave, and chancing to walk near the course through which it passed, has felt powerfully in the silence and desertion of the streets, and in the stagnation of ordinary business, the deep interest which at that moment was possessing the heart of man—if all at once he should hear the death-like stillness broken up by the sound of wheels rattling away from the scene, and making known that the transitory vision was dissolved, he will be aware that at no moment was his sense of the complete suspension and pause in ordinary human concerns so full and affecting, as at that moment when the suspension ceases, and the goings-on of human life are suddenly resumed. All action in any direction is best expounded, measured, and made apprehensible, by reaction. Now apply this to the case of *Macbeth*. Here, as I have said, the retiring of the human heart, and the entrance of the fiendish heart was to be expressed and made sensible. Another world has stepped in; and the murderers are taken out of the region of human things, human purposes, human desires. They are transfigured: Lady Macbeth is "unsexed"; Macbeth has forgot that he was born of woman; both are conformed to the image of devils; and the world of devils is suddenly revealed. But how shall this be conveyed and made palpable? In order that a new world may step in, this world must for a time disappear. The murderers, and the murder must be insulated— cut off by an immeasurable gulf from the ordinary tide and succession of human affairs—locked up and sequestered in some deep recess; we must be made sensible that the world of ordinary life is suddenly arrested—laid asleep—tranced—racked into a dread armistice; time must be annihilated; relation to things without abolished; and all must pass self-withdrawn into a deep syncope and suspension of earthly passion. Hence it is, that when the deed is done, when the work of darkness is perfect, then the world of darkness passes away like a pageantry in the clouds: the knocking at the gate is heard; and it makes known audibly that the reaction has commenced; the human has made its reflux upon the fiendish; the pulses of life are beginning to beat again; and the re-establishment of the goings-on of the world in which we live, first makes us profoundly sensible of the awful parenthesis that has suspended them.

THOMAS DE QUINCEY

O mighty poet! Thy works are not as those of other men, 5
simply and merely great works of art; but are also like the phenomena
of nature, like the sun and the sea, the stars and the flowers; like frost
and snow, rain and dew, hailstorm and thunder, which are to be
studied with entire submission of our own faculties, and in the
perfect faith that in them there can be no too much or too little,
nothing useless or inert—but that, the further we press in our
discoveries, the more we shall see proofs of design and self-
supporting arrangement where the careless eye had seen nothing but
accident!

QUESTIONS

1. What is de Quincey's definition of the understanding? How does this
relate to *Macbeth*? To the act of murder?

2. What is the intended meaning of the author's statement in paragraph
4, "All action in any direction is best expounded, measured, and made
apprehensible, by reaction"?

3. Describe the level of language employed by de Quincey in paragraphs 1 to 4. How does it coincide with the author's main purpose?

4. Analyze style in the final paragraph.

5. Examine the effectiveness of the introductory paragraph in relation to
the function of causal analysis.

6. Analyze the author's selection of examples—both short and extended—
to explore cause-and-effect relationships.

7. What is the main argument or thesis that the author presents in this
critical essay?

8. What is the relationship of the concluding paragraph to the development of the essay?

9. De Quincey implies that we have "a careless eye," that we do not
comprehend things as well as we should. Do you agree with his analysis of
the cause of our incomprehension? Why or why not?

10. a. Analyze any work of literature or art in terms of your feeling toward it
and your understanding of it.
b. Argue for or against the primacy of intuition over reason in the appreciation of art.
c. Recount an episode in which something that seemed complex or
confusing suddenly became clear and understandable.

ON THE KNOCKING AT THE GATE IN *MACBETH*

On Gusto

William Hazlitt (1778–1830), English journalist, lecturer, essayist, and painter, was the acquaintance of Coleridge and Words-worth but their political adversary. Described by Coleridge as "singularly repulsive—brow-hanging, shoe-contemplative, strange," Hazlitt nevertheless combined intellectual brilliance and stylistic mastery to become one of the most distinctive essayists of the nineteenth century. His notable works include *The Round Table* (1817), *Characters in Shakespeare's Plays* (1817), *The Plain Speaker* (1826), and *The Spirit of the Age* (1825). Hazlitt's essay "On Gusto" reflects his interest in painting and argues for intensity in art.

1   Gusto in art is power or passion defining any object.—It is not so difficult to explain this term in what relates to expression (of which it may be said to be the highest degree) as in what relates to things without expression, to the natural appearances of objects, as mere colour or form. In one sense, however, there is hardly any object entirely devoid of expression, without some character of power belonging to it, some precise association with pleasure or pain: and it is in giving this truth of character from the truth of feeling, whether in the highest or the lowest degree, but always in the highest degree of which the subject is capable, that gusto consists.

2   There is a gusto in the colouring of Titian. Not only do his heads seem to think—his bodies seem to feel. This is what the Italians mean by the *morbidezza* of his flesh-colour. It seems sensitive and alive all over; not merely to have the look and texture of flesh, but the feeling in itself. For example, the limbs of his female figures have a luxurious softness and delicacy, which appears conscious of the pleasure of the beholder. As the objects themselves in nature would produce an impression on the sense, distinct from every other object, and having something divine in it, which the heart owns and the imagination consecrates, the objects in the picture preserve the same impression, absolute, unimpaired, stamped with all the truth of passion, the pride of the eye, and the charm of beauty. Rubens makes his flesh-colour like flowers; Albano's is like ivory; Titian's is like flesh, and like nothing else. It is as different from that of other painters, as the skin is from a piece of white or red drapery thrown over it. The blood circulates here and there, the blue veins just appear, the rest is distinguished throughout only by that sort of

tingling sensation to the eye, which the body feels within itself. This is gusto.—Vandyke's flesh-colour, though it has great truth and purity, wants gusto. It has not the internal character, the living principle in it. It is a smooth surface, not a warm, moving mass. It is painted without passion, with indifference. The hand only has been concerned. The impression slides off from the eye, and does not, like the tones of Titian's pencil, leave a sting behind it in the mind of the spectator. The eye does not acquire a taste or appetite for what it sees. In a word, gusto in painting is where the impression made on one sense excites by affinity those of another.

Michael Angelo's forms are full of gusto. They every where 3 obtrude the sense of power upon the eye. His limbs convey an idea of muscular strength, of moral grandeur, and even of intellectual dignity: they are firm, commanding, broad, and massy, capable of executing with ease the determined purposes of the will. His faces have no other expression than his figures, conscious power and capacity. They appear only to think what they shall do, and to know that they can do it. This is what is meant by saying that his style is hard and masculine. It is the reverse of Correggio's, which is effeminate. That is, the gusto of Michael Angelo consists in expressing energy of will. In Correggio's faces as well as figures we see neither bones nor muscles, but then what a soul is there, full of sweetness and of grace—pure, playful, soft, angelical! There is sentiment enough in a hand painted by Correggio to set up a school of history painters. Whenever we look at the hands of Correggio's women or of Raphael's, we always wish to touch them.

Again, Titian's landscapes have a prodigious gusto, both in 4 the colouring and forms. We shall never forget one that we saw many years ago in the Orleans Gallery of Acteon hunting. It had a brown, mellow, autumnal look. The sky was of the colour of stone. The winds seemed to sing through the rustling branches of the trees, and already you might hear the twanging of bows resound through the tangled mazes of the wood. Mr. West, we understand, has this landscape. He will know if this description of it is just. The landscape background of the St. Peter Martyr is another well-known instance of the power of this great painter to give a romantic interest and an appropriate character to the objects of his pencil, where every circumstance adds to the effect of the scene,—the bold trunks of the tall forest trees, the trailing ground plants, with that cold convent spire rising in the distance, admidst the blue sapphire mountains and the golden sky.

Rubens has a great deal of gusto in his Fauns and Satyrs, and 5 in all that expresses motion, but in nothing else. Rembrandt has it in everything; everything in his pictures has a tangible character. If he puts a diamond in the ear of a Burgomaster's wife, it is of the first water; and his furs and stuffs are proof against a Russian winter. Raphael's gusto was only in expression; he had no idea of the character of anything but the human form. The dryness and poverty of his style in other respects is a phenomenon in the art. His trees are like sprigs of grass stuck in a book of botanical specimens. Was it that Raphael never had time to go beyond the walls of Rome? That he was always in the streets, at church, or in the bath? He was not one of the Society of Arcadians.[1]

Claude's landscapes, perfect as they are, want gusto. This is   6
not easy to explain. They are perfect abstractions of the visible images of things; they speak the visible language of nature truly. They resemble a mirror or microscope. To the eye only they are more perfect than any other landscapes that ever were or will be painted; they give more of nature, as cognizable by one sense alone; but they lay an equal stress on all visible impressions; they do not interpret one sense by another; they do not distinguish the character of different objects as we are taught, and can only be taught, to distinguish them by their effect on the different senses. That is, his eye wanted imagination: it did not strongly sympathize with his other faculties. He saw the atmosphere, but he did not feel it. He painted the trunk of a tree or a rock in the foreground as smooth—with as complete an abstraction of the gross, tangible impression, as any other part of the picture; his trees are perfectly beautiful, but quite immoveable; they have a look of enchantment. In short, his landscapes are unequalled imitations of nature, released from its subjection to the elements,—as if all objects were become a delightful fairy vision, and the eye had rarefied and refined away the other senses.

The gusto in the Greek statues is of a very singular kind. The   7
sense of perfect form nearly occupies the whole mind, and hardly suffers it to dwell on any other feeling. It seems enough for them *to be*, without acting or suffering. Their forms are ideal, spiritual. Their beauty is power. By their beauty they are raised above the frailties of pain or passion; by their beauty they are deified.

The infinite quantity of dramatic invention in Shakspeare   8
takes from his gusto. The power he delights to shew is not intense, but discursive. He never insists on any thing as much as he might, except a quibble. Milton has great gusto. He repeats his blow twice;

---

[1]Raphael not only could not paint a landscape; he could not paint people in a landscape. He could not have painted the heads or the figures, or even the dresses of the St. Peter Martyr. His figures have always an *in-door* look, that is, a set, determined, voluntary, dramatic character, arising from their own passions, or a watchfulness of those of others, and want that wild uncertainty of expression, which is connected with the accidents of nature and the changes of the elements. He has nothing *romantic* about him.

WILLIAM HAZLITT

grapples with and exhausts his subject. His imagination has a double relish of its objects, an inveterate attachment to the things he describes, and to the words describing them.

> ——"Or where Chineses drive
> With sails and wind their *cany* waggons *light*."
>
> .   .   .   .
>
> "Wild above rule or art, *enormous* bliss."

There is a gusto in Pope's compliments, in Dryden's satires, and Prior's tales; and among prose-writers, Boccaccio and Rabelais had the most of it. We will only mention one other work which appears to us to be full of gusto, and that is the *Beggar's Opera*. If it is not, we are altogether mistaken in our notions on this delicate subject.

QUESTIONS

1. Explain the author's distinctions between paintings that have gusto and those that "want gusto."

2. What is Hazlitt's purpose, to define "gusto" subjectively or to present it objectively? Cite examples to support your answer.

3. Select one paragraph from the essay and demonstrate how Hazlitt's tone is achieved through word selection.

4. What does the author accomplish through his use of figurative language in the essay? Cite examples of his method.

5. What is the thesis underlying Hazlitt's definition of gusto?

6. Examine the author's use of a pattern of examples and of analysis to develop his definition.

7. How does Hazlitt employ comparison and contrast to enhance his definition?

8. Account for the author's movement away from painting to sculpture and literature in paragraphs 7 and 8. How does this affect the unity and coherence of the essay?

9. Do you agree with Hazlitt that there is a quality called "gusto" in art and literature? Explain.

10. Write a definition of gusto and offer several examples of the way it manifests itself in either art, literature, music, or film.

KATHARINE KUH

Break-up:
THE CORE OF MODERN ART

Katharine W. Kuh (1904 –   ), specialist in modern art, was from 1946 to 1957 associated as curator and editor with the Art Institute of Chicago. Subsequently she was art editor for *Saturday Review*. Kuh is the author of *Art Has Many Faces* (1951), *Leger* (1953), *The Artist's Voice* (1962), *Break-up: The Core of Modern Art* (1965), and *The Open Eye* (1971). In this essay from her fourth book, Kuh examines the stages in and causes of the altered vision and style of modern art.

he art of our century has been characterized by shat- 1
tered surfaces, broken color, segmented compositions, dissolving forms and shredded images. Curiously insistent is this consistent emphasis on break-up. However, dissolution today does not necessarily mean lack of discipline. It can also mean a new kind of discipline, for disintegration is often followed by reconstruction, the artist deliberately smashing his material only to reassemble it in new and unexpected relationships. Moreover, the process of breaking up is quite different from the process of breaking down. And during the last hundred years, every aspect of art has been broken up—color, light, pigment, form, line, content, space, surface and design.

In the nineteenth century, easels were moved out-of-doors 2
and color was broken into relatively minute areas in order to approximate the reality of sunlight and to preserve on canvas nature's own fleeting atmospheric effects. Known as Impressionism, this movement was the first step in a long sequence of experiments that finally banished the Renaissance emphasis on humanism, on three-dimensional form and on a traditional center of interest. Here was the beginning of a gradual but steady tendency toward diffusion in art. A few years later, Vincent Van Gogh transformed broken color into broken pigment. Less interested in realistic light than in his own highly charged emotions, he allowed smashing rhythmic brush-strokes to mirror his personal turbulence. In doing so he foretold twentieth-century Expressionism, that aptly named movement which relied on pitted surfaces, broken outlines, unpredictable color and scarred textures to intensify emotional expression. As the Impressionists were bent on freeing nature from sham, so the Expressionists hoped to liberate their own feelings from all trace of artificiality.

Perhaps the most revolutionary break-up in modern art took 3 place a little more than fifty years ago with the advent of Cubism. It was the Cubists, Picasso, Braque, Duchamp, Picabia, Léger, Delaunay and Juan Gris, who responded to the inordinate multiplicity of present-day life by breaking up and arbitrarily rearranging transparent planes and surfaces so that all sides of an object could be seen at once. As the Cubists broke through the boundaries of conventional form to show multiple aspects simultaneously, their Italian colleagues, the Futurists, hoped to encompass the uninterrupted motion of an object at one time. This they tried to do by a series of overlapping transparent forms illustrating the path of an object as it moved through space.

With Surrealism came still another kind of break-up, the 4 break-up of chronology. Frankly influenced by Freudian discoveries, this movement splintered time sequence with an abandon borrowed from the world of fragmented dreams. Content was purposely unhinged in denial of all rational expression, allowing disconnected episodes to recreate the disturbing life of our unconscious. At the same time, perspective and distance often became severely dislocated. Denying the orderly naturalism of the Renaissance, painters today project space and distance from innumerable eye levels, intentionally segmenting their compositions into conflicting perspectives. We look from above, from below, from diverse angles, from near, from far—all at one and the same time (not an unfamiliar experience for eyes accustomed to air travel). Here again is the Cubist idea of simultaneity, the twentieth-century urge to approach a scene from many different directions in a single condensed encounter.

Finally we come to the total break-up of Abstract Expression- 5 ism, a technique that celebrates the specific act of painting (sometimes appropriately called Action Painting). Now everything is shattered—line, light, color, form, pigment, surface and design. These canvases defy all the old rules as they reveal the immediate spontaneous feelings of the artist in the process of painting. There is no one central idea, no beginning, no end—only an incessant flow and flux where lightning brushstrokes report the artist's impulsive and compulsive reactions. The pigment actually develops a life of its own, almost strong enough to hypnotize the painter. Here break-up turns into both content and form, with the impetuous paint itself telling the full story. No naturalistic image is needed to describe these artists' volatile feelings.

As one looks back over the last hundred years, the history of 6 break-up becomes a key to the history of art. Why painters and sculptors of this period have been so involved with problems of dissolution is a question only partly answered by the obvious impact of modern scientific methods of destruction. One cannot deny that the last two devastating wars and the possibility of a still more devastating one to come do affect our daily thinking. Since the discovery of the atom bomb, science has become almost synonymous with destruction. The influence of contemporary warfare with its colossal explosions and upheavals has unquestionably had much to do with the tendency toward fragmentation in art, but there have been other and earlier causes.

From the beginning, it was science in one form or another   7
that affected modern painting and sculpture. In nineteenth-century Europe the interest in atmospheric phenomena was not an isolated expression limited to the Impressionists. At that time, numerous scientists were experimenting with all manner of optical color laws, writing widely on the subject as they investigated the relationship of color to the human eye. Artists like Monet and Seurat were familiar with these findings and not unnaturally applied them to their paintings. It would be a grave mistake to underestimate the influence of contemporary scientific research on the development of Impressionism. The wonders of natural light became a focus for nineteenth-century artists exactly as the magic of artificial light stimulated painters of the precentury. If the earlier men were more interested in rural landscapes seen out-of-doors in the sunlight, the later artists quite reasonably concentrated on city scenes, preferably at night when man-made luminosity tends to puncture both form and space.

Other scientific investigations also exerted considerable influ-   8
ence on present-day painters and sculptors. Inventions like the microscope and telescope, with their capacity to enlarge, isolate and probe, offer the artist provocative new worlds to explore. These instruments, which break up structures only to examine them more fully, demonstrate how details can be magnified and separated from the whole and operate as new experiences. Repeatedly artists in recent years have exploited this idea, allowing one isolated symbol to represent an entire complex organism. Miró often needs merely part of a woman's body to describe all women, or Léger, one magnified letter of the alphabet to conjure up the numberless printed words that daily bombard us.

As scientists smash the atom, so likewise artists smash   9
traditional forms. For how, indeed, can anyone remain immune to the new mushroom shape that haunts us day and night? The American painter, Morris Graves, put it well recently, "You simply can't keep the world out any longer. Like everyone else, I've been caught in our scientific culture." This is not to say that painters are interested in reproducing realistic scenes of atomic explosions, but rather that they are concerned with the reactions accompanying these disasters. It is just possible that, with their extra-sensitized intuition, artists may have unconsciously predicted the discovery of atomic energy long

before "the bomb" became a familiar household world, for the history of break-up in art antedates the history of nuclear break-up.

Even the invention of the X-ray machine has brought us 10 closer to penetrating form. We no longer think of outer coverings as solid or final; we know they can be visually pierced merely by rendering them transparent. We have also learned from science that space penetrates everything.

The sculptor Gabo claims, "Space is a reality in all of our 11 experiences and it is present in every object. . . . That's what I've tried to show in certain of my stone carvings. When they turn, observe how their curved forms seem interpenetrated by space." For the artist today, nothing is static or permanent. The new popular dances are no more potently kinetic than the new staccato art forms that everywhere confront us.

With the dramatic development of speedier transportation 12 and swifter communication comes a visual overlapping responsible for much of contemporary art. In modern life one is simultaneously subjected to countless experiences that become fragmented, superimposed, and finally rebuilt into new experiences. Speed is a cogent part of our daily life.

How natural, then, that artists reflect this pressure by show- 13 ing all sides of an object, its entire motion, its total psychological content in one concerted impact. It is almost as if the pressures of time had necessitated a visual speed-up not unlike the industrial one associated with the assembly line and mass production. Speed with its multiple overlays transforms our surroundings into jagged, interrupted images.

Modern technology and science have produced a wealth of 14 new materials and new ways of using old materials. For the artist this means wider opportunities. There is no doubt that the limitations of materials and nature of tools both restrict and shape a man's work. Observe how the development of plastics and light metals along with new methods of welding and brazing have changed the direction of sculpture. Transparent plastic materials allow one to look through an object, to see its various sides superimposed on each other (as in Cubism or in an X ray). Today, welding is as prevalent as casting was in the past. This new method encourages open designs, often of great linear agility, where surrounding and intervening space becomes as important as form itself. In fact, it becomes a kind of negative form. While bronze casting and stone carving are techniques more readily adapted to solid volumes, welding permits perforated metal designs of extreme versatility that free sculpture from the static restrictions which for centuries have moored it to the floor.

More ambiguous than other scientific inventions familiar to 15 modern artists, but no less influential, are the psychoanalytic studies of Freud and his followers, discoveries that have infiltrated recent art, especially Surrealism. The Surrealists, in their struggle to escape the monotony and frustrations of everyday life, claimed that dreams were the only hope. Turning to the irrational world of their unconscious, they banished all time barriers and moral judgments to combine disconnected dream experiences from the past, present and intervening psychological states. The Surrealists were concerned with overlapping emotions more than with overlapping forms. Their paintings often become segmented capsules of associative experiences. For them, obsessive and often unrelated images replaced the direct emotional messages of Expressionism. They did not need to smash pigment and texture; they went beyond this to smash the whole continuity of logical thought.

There is little doubt that contemporary art has taken much 16 from contemporary life. In a period when science has made revolutionary strides, artists in their studios have not been unaware of scientists in their laboratories. But this has rarely been a one-way street. Painters and sculptors, though admittedly influenced by modern science, have also molded and changed our world. If break-up has been a vital part of their expression, it has not always been a symbol of destruction. Quite the contrary: it has been used to examine more fully, to penetrate more deeply, to analyze more thoroughly, to enlarge, isolate and make more familiar certain aspects of life that earlier we were apt to neglect. In addition, it sometimes provides rich multiple experiences so organized as not merely to reflect our world, but in fact to interpret it.

QUESTIONS

1. Trace Kuh's theory of breakup from the impressionists to the abstract expressionists.

2. What examples does the author provide to illustrate the effect of science, technology, and psychology on modern painting?

3. Examine the essay and locate synonyms that Kuh employs for breakup. What connotations does she seem to emphasize for her core term?

4. What stylistic characteristics of art criticism—and criticism in general—does the essay reflect?

5. Analyze the development and function of the introductory paragraph.

6. Examine the combined modes of illustration and process analysis in

KATHARINE KUH

paragraphs 2 to 5. What modes of definition does Kuh employ to convey essential information about modern art movements?

7. Describe the pattern of causal analysis employed by Kuh throughout the essay. Examine the role of topic sentences in guiding causal relationships.

8. What strategies for essay conclusions are evident in paragraph 16?

9. Kuh suggests that breakup is not necessarily destruction. What social and political implications do you perceive in her statement?

10. a. Write an essay on the impact of contemporary life on a literary, artistic, or media form.
b. Select one of the artists or art movements mentioned by Kuh and write a paper on the subject.

MARYA MANNES

How Do You Know It's Good?

Marya Mannes (1904–   ) has written several novels and some light verse, but she is best known for her essays, which have appeared in *Vogue, McCall's, Harper's,* and *The New Republic.* She has collected her essays in *More in Anger* (1958) and in *The New York I Know* (1961). Mannes has also written on such subjects as suicide and euthanasia in *Last Rights* (1974) and television in *Who Owns the Air?* (1960). In this essay from *But Will It Sell?* (1964), she establishes standards for judging excellence in the arts.

uppose there were no critics to tell us how to react to a   1
picture, a play, or a new composition of music. Suppose we wandered innocent as the dawn into an art exhibition of unsigned paintings. By what standards, by what values would we decide whether they were good or bad, talented or untalented, successes or failures? How can we ever know that what we think is right?

For the last fifteen or twenty years the fashion in criticism or   2
appreciation of the arts has been to deny the existence of any valid criteria and to make the words "good" or "bad" irrelevant, immaterial, and inapplicable. There is no such thing, we are told, as a set of

standards, first acquired through experience and knowledge and later imposed on the subject under discussion. This has been a popular approach, for it relieves the critic of the responsibility of judgment and the public of the necessity of knowledge. It pleases those resentful of disciplines, it flatters the empty-minded by calling them open-minded, it comforts the confused. Under the banner of democracy and the kind of equality which our forefathers did *not* mean, it says, in effect, "Who are you to tell us what *is* good or bad?" This is the same cry used so long and so effectively by the producers of mass media who insist that it is the public, not they, who decides what it wants to hear and see, and that for a critic to say that *this* program is bad and *this* program is good is purely a reflection of personal taste. Nobody recently has expressed this philosophy more succinctly than Dr. Frank Stanton, the highly intelligent president of CBS television. At a hearing before the Federal Communications Commission, this phrase escaped him under questioning: "One man's mediocrity is another man's good program."

There is no better way of saying "No values are absolute." 3
There is another important aspect to this philosophy of *laissez faire:* It is the fear, in all observers of all forms of art, of guessing wrong. This fear is well come by, for who has not heard of the contemporary outcries against artists who later were called great? Every age has its arbiters who do not grow with their times, who cannot tell evolution from revolution or the difference between frivolous faddism, amateurish experimentation, and profound and necessary change. Who wants to be caught *flagrante delicto* with an error of judgment as serious as this? It is far safer, and certainly easier, to look at a picture or a play or a poem and to say "This is hard to understand, but it may be good," or simply to welcome it as a new form. The word "new"—in our country especially—has magical connotations. What is new must be good; what is old is probably bad. And if a critic can describe the new in language that nobody can understand, he's safer still. If he has mastered the art of saying nothing with exquisite complexity, nobody can quote him later as saying anything.

But all these, I maintain, are forms of abdication from the 4
responsibility of judgment. In creating, the artist commits himself; in appreciating, you have a commitment of your own. For after all, it is the audience which makes the arts. A climate of appreciation is essential to its flowering, and the higher the expectations of the public, the better the performance of the artist. Conversely, only a public ill-served by its critics could have accepted as art and as literature so much in these last years that has been neither. If anything goes, everything goes; and at the bottom of the junkpile lie the discarded standards too.

MARYA MANNES

But what are these standards? How do you get them? How do 5
you know they're the right ones? How can you make a clear pattern
out of so many intangibles, including that greatest one, the very
private I?

Well for one thing, it's fairly obvious that the more you read 6
and see and hear, the more equipped you'll be to practice that art of
association which is at the basis of all understanding and judgment.
The more you live and the more you look, the more aware you are of a
consistent pattern—as universal as the stars, as the tides, as breathing, as night and day—underlying everything. I would call this
pattern and this rhythm an order. Not order—*an* order. Within it
exists an incredible diversity of forms. Without it lies chaos—the wild
cells of destruction—sickness. It is in the end up to you to distinguish
between the diversity that is health and the chaos that is sickness, and
you can't do this without a process of association that can link a bar of
Mozart with the corner of a Vermeer painting, or a Stravinsky score
with a Picasso abstraction; or that can relate an aggressive act with a
Franz Kline painting and a fit of coughing with a John Cage
composition.

There is no accident in the fact that certain expressions of art 7
live for all time and that others die with the moment, and although
you may not always define the reasons, you can ask the questions.
What does an artist say that is timeless; how does he say it? How
much is fashion, how much is merely reflection? Why is Sir Walter
Scott so hard to read now, and Jane Austen not? Why is baroque right
for one age and too effulgent for another?

Can a standard of craftsmanship apply to art of all ages, or 8
does each have its own, and different, definitions? You may have
been aware, inadvertently, that craftsmanship has become a dirty
word these years because, again, it implies standards—something
done well or done badly. The result of this convenient avoidance is a
plentitude of actors who can't project their voices, singers who can't
phrase their songs, poets who can't communicate emotion, and
writers who have no vocabulary—not to speak of painters who can't
draw. The dogma now is that craftsmanship gets in the way of
expression. You can do better if you don't know *how* you do it, let
alone *what* you're doing.

I think it is time you helped reverse this trend by trying to 9
rediscover craft: the command of the chosen instrument, whether it is
a brush, a word, or a voice. When you begin to detect the difference
between freedom and sloppiness, between serious experimentation
and egotherapy, between skill and slickness, between strength and
violence, you are on your way to separating the sheep from the goats,
a form of segregation denied us for quite a while. All you need to
restore it is a small bundle of standards and a Geiger counter that

detects fraud, and we might begin our tour of the arts in an area where both are urgently needed: contemporary painting.

I don't know what's worse: to have to look at acres of bad art 10 to find the little good, or to read what the critics say about it all. In no other field of expression has so much double-talk flourished, so much confusion prevailed, and so much nonsense been circulated: further evidence of the close interdependence between the arts and the critical climate they inhabit. It will be my pleasure to share with you some of this double-talk so typical of our times.

Item one: preface for a catalogue of an abstract painter: 11

"Time-bound meditation experiencing a life; sincere with 12 plastic piety at the threshold of hallowed arcana; a striving for pure ideation giving shape to inner drive; formalized patterns where neural balances reach a fiction." End of quote. Know what this artist paints like now?

Item two: a review in the *Art News:* 13

". . . a weird and disparate assortment of material, but the 14 monstrosity which bloomed into his most recent cancer of aggregations is present in some form everywhere. . . ." Then, later, "A gluttony of things and processes terminated by a glorious constipation."

Item three, same magazine, review of an artist who welds 15 automobile fragments into abstract shapes:

"Each fragment . . . is made an extreme of human exaspera- 16 tion, torn at and fought all the way, and has its rightness of form as if by accident. *Any technique that requires order or discipline would just be the human ego.* No, these must be egoless, uncontrolled, undesigned and different enough to give you a bang—fifty miles an hour around a telephone pole. . . ."

"Any technique that requires order of discipline would just 17 be the human ego." What does he mean—"just be"? What are they really talking about? Is this journalism? Is it criticism? Or is it that other convenient abdication from standards of performance and judgment practiced by so many artists and critics that they, like certain writers who deal only in sickness and depravity, "reflect the chaos about them"? Again, whose chaos? Whose depravity?

I had always thought that the prime function of art was to 18 create order *out* of chaos—again, not the order of neatness or rigidity or convention or artifice, but the order of clarity by which one will and one vision could draw the essential truth out of apparent confusion. I still do. It is not enough to use parts of a car to convey the brutality of the machine. This is as slavishly representative, and just as easy, as arranging dried flowers under glass to convey nature.

Speaking of which, i.e., the use of real materials (burlap, old 19 gloves, bottletops) in lieu of pigment, this is what one critic had to say about an exhibition of Assemblage at the Museum of Modern Art last year:

"Spotted throughout the show are indisputable works of art, accounting for a quarter or even a half of the total display. But the remainder are works of non-art, anti-art, and art substitutes that are the aesthetic counterparts of the social deficiencies that land people in the clink on charges of vagrancy. These aesthetic bankrupts . . . have no legitimate ideological roof over their heads and not the price of a square intellectual meal, much less a spiritual sandwich, in their pockets."

I quote these words of John Canaday of *The New York Times* as an example of the kind of criticism which puts responsibility to an intelligent public above popularity with an intellectual coterie. Canaday has the courage to say what he thinks and the capacity to say it clearly: two qualities notably absent from his profession.

Next to art, I would say that appreciation and evaluation in the field of music is the most difficult. For it is rarely possible to judge a new composition at one hearing only. What seems confusing or fragmented at first might well become clear and organic a third time. Or it might not. The only salvation here for the listener is, again, an instinct born of experience and association which allows him to separate intent from accident, design from experimentation, and pretense from conviction. Much of contemporary music is, like its sister art, merely a reflection of the composer's own fragmentation: an absorption in self and symbols at the expense of communication with others. The artist, in short, says to the public: If you don't understand this, it's because you're dumb. I maintain that you are not. You may have to go part way or even halfway to meet the artist, but if you must go the whole way, it's his fault, not yours. Hold fast to that. And remember it too when you read new poetry, that estranged sister of music.

"A multitude of causes, unknown to former times, are now acting with a combined force to blunt the discriminating powers of the mind, and, unfitting it for all voluntary exertion, to reduce it to a state of almost savage torpor. The most effective of these causes are the great national events which are daily taking place and the increasing accumulation of men in cities, where the uniformity of their occupations produces a craving for extraordinary incident, which the rapid communication of intelligence hourly gratifies. To this tendency of life and manners, the literature and theatrical exhibitions of the country have conformed themselves."

This startlingly applicable comment was written in the year 1800 by William Wordsworth in the preface to his "Lyrical Ballads"; and it has been cited by Edwin Muir in his recently published book "The Estate of Poetry." Muir states that poetry's effective range and influence have diminished alarmingly in the modern world. He believes in the inherent and indestructible qualities of the human mind and the great and permanent objects that act upon it, and suggests that the audience will increase when "poetry loses what obscurity is left in it by attempting greater themes, for great themes have to be stated clearly." If you keep that firmly in mind and resist, in Muir's words, "the vast dissemination of secondary objects that isolate us from the natural world," you have gone a long way toward equipping yourself for the examination of any work of art.

When you come to theatre, in this extremely hasty tour of the arts, you can approach it on two different levels. You can bring to it anticipation and innocence, giving yourself up, as it were, to the life on the stage and reacting to it emotionally, if the play is good, or listlessly, if the play is boring; a part of the audience organism that expresses its favor by silence or laughter and its disfavor by coughing and rustling. Or you can bring to it certain critical faculties that may heighten, rather than diminish, your enjoyment. 25

You can ask yourselves whether the actors are truly in their parts or merely projecting themselves; whether the scenery helps or hurts the mood; whether the playwright is honest with himself, his characters, and you. Somewhere along the line you can learn to distinguish between the true creative act and the false arbitrary gesture; between fresh observation and stale cliché; between the avant-garde play that is pretentious drivel and the avant-garde play that finds new ways to say old truths. 26

Purpose and craftsmanship—end and means—these are the keys to your judgment in all the arts. What is this painter trying to say when he slashes a broad band of black across a white canvas and lets the edges dribble down? Is it a statement of violence? Is it a self-portrait? If it is *one* of these, has he made you believe it? Or is this a gesture of the ego or a form of therapy? If it shocks you, what does it shock you into? 27

And what of this tight little painting of bright flowers in a vase? Is the painter saying anything new about flowers? Is it different from a million other canvases of flowers? Has it any life, any meaning, beyond its statement? Is there any pleasure in its forms or texture? The question is not whether a thing is abstract or representational, whether it is "modern" or conventional. The question, inexorably, is whether it is good. And this is a decision which only you, on the basis of instinct, experience, and association, can make for yourself. It takes independence and courage. It involves, moreover, the risk of wrong decision and the humility, after the passage of time, of recognizing it as such. As we grow and change and learn, our attitudes can change too, and what we once thought obscure or 28 "difficult" can later emerge as coherent and illuminating. Entrenched prejudices, obdurate opinions are as sterile as no opinions at all.

Yet standards there are, timeless as the universe itself. And when you have committed yourself to them, you have acquired a passport to that elusive but immutable realm of truth. Keep it with you in the forests of bewilderment. And never be afraid to speak up. 29

QUESTIONS

1. What examples does Mannes provide of the "abdication from the responsibility of judgment" (paragraph 4)?

2. Explain Mannes's criteria or standards for judging excellence in the arts.

3. Account for the author's use of the pronoun "you" in addressing her audience. How does it affect tone, notably at the end of the essay?

4. Explain Mannes's strategy of formulating questions, starting with the title and moving consistently through the essay to the conclusion.

5. Where does the author's introduction end? Analyze the material presented in the introduction and the rhetorical strategies involved. What paragraphs constitute the conclusion of the essay? Describe the nature of the conclusion.

6. Explain the function of paragraphs 5 to 9.

7. How does Mannes employ illustration to structure paragraphs 10 to 26? Analyze the main stages in the organization of this section.

8. Explain the author's use of process and causal analysis in the essay.

9. Mannes maintains that standards are absolutely necessary in distinguishing good from bad work in the arts. Do you agree or disagree with her premise, and why? What standards do you employ in determining whether an artistic product is good or bad?

10. a. Write your own essay entitled "How Do You Know It's Good?"
b. Evaluate one literary, artistic, or media work, making clear the standards that you are applying.

ROBERT WARSHOW

The Gangster as Tragic Hero

Robert Warshow (1917–1955) attended the University of Michigan and worked for the U.S. Army Security Agency from 1942 to 1946. After the war, he served as an editor of *Commentary*, writing film criticism for this magazine and also for *Partisan Review*. Before his untimely death from a heart attack, Warshow had written several brilliant essays on film and on popular culture. Writing of Warshow, Lionel Trilling observed, "I believe that certain of his pieces establish themselves in the line of Hazlitt, a tradition in which I would place only one other writer of our time, George Orwell." One of these brilliant essays, focusing on the interrelation of film and society, is "The Gangster as Tragic Hero," which appeared in *The Immediate Experience: Movies, Games, Theatre and Other Aspects of Popular Culture* (1962).

merica, as a social and political organization, is committed to a cheerful view of life. It could not be otherwise. The sense of tragedy is a luxury of aristocratic societies, where the fate of the individual is not conceived of as having a direct and legitimate political importance, being determined by a fixed and supra-political—that is, non-controversial—moral order or fate. Modern equalitarian societies, however, whether democratic or authoritarian in their political forms, always base themselves on the claim that they are making life happier; the avowed function of the modern state, at least in its ultimate terms, is not only to regulate social relations, but also to determine the quality and possibilities of human life in general. Happiness thus becomes the chief political issue—in a sense, the only political issue—and for that reason it can never be treated as an issue at all. If an American or a Russian is unhappy, it implies a certain reprobation of his society, and therefore, by a logic of which we can all recognize the necessity, it becomes an obligation of citizenship to be cheerful; if the authorities find it necessary, the citizen may even be compelled to make a public display of his cheerfulness on important occasions, just as he may be conscripted into the army in time of war.

Naturally, this civic responsibility rests most strongly upon the organs of mass culture. The individual citizen may still be permitted his private unhappiness so long as it does not take on political significance, the extent of this tolerance being determined by how large an area of private life the society can accommodate. But every production of mass culture is a public act and must conform with accepted notions of the public good. Nobody seriously questions the principle that it is the function of mass culture to maintain public morale, and certainly nobody in the mass audience objects to having his morale maintained.[1] At a time when the normal condition of the citizen is a state of anxiety, euphoria spreads over our culture like the broad smile of an idiot. In terms of attitudes towards life, there is very little difference between a "happy" movie like *Good News,* which ignores death and suffering, and a "sad" movie like *A Tree Grows in Brooklyn,* which uses death and suffering as incidents in the service of a higher optimism.

But, whatever its effectiveness as a source of consolation and a means of pressure for maintaining "positive" social attitudes, this optimism is fundamentally satisfying to no one, not even to those who would be most disoriented without its support. Even within the area of mass culture, there always exists a current of opposition, seeking to express by whatever means are available to it that sense of desperation and inevitable failure which optimism itself helps to create. Most often, this opposition is confined to rudimentary or semi-literate forms: in mob politics and journalism, for example, or in certain kinds of religious enthusiasm. When it does enter the field of art, it is likely to be disguised or attenuated: in an unspecific form of expression like jazz, in the basically harmless nihilism of the Marx Brothers, in the continually reasserted strain of hopelessness that often seems to be the real meaning of the soap opera. The gangster film is remarkable in that it fills the need for disguise (though not sufficiently to avoid arousing uneasiness) without requiring any serious distortion. From its beginnings, it has been a consistent and astonishingly complete presentation of the modern sense of tragedy.[2]

In its initial character, the gangster film is simply one example of the movies' constant tendency to create fixed dramatic patterns that can be repeated indefinitely with a reasonable expectation of profit. One gangster film follows another as one musical or one Western follows another. But this rigidity is not necessarily opposed to the requirements of art. There have been very successful types of art in the past which developed such specific and detailed conventions as almost to make individual examples of the type interchange-

[1]In her testimony before the House Committee on Un-American Activities, Mrs. Leila Rogers said that the movie *None But the Lonely Heart* was un-American because it was gloomy. Like so much else that was said during the unhappy investigation of Hollywood, this statement was at once stupid and illuminating. One knew immediately what Mrs. Rogers was talking about; she had simply been insensitive enough to carry her philistinism to its conclusion.

[2]Efforts have been made from time to time to bring the gangster film into line with the prevailing optimism and social constructiveness of our culture; *Kiss of Death* is a recent example. These efforts are usually unsuccessful; the reasons for their lack of success are interesting in themselves, but I shall not be able to discuss them here.

able. This is true, for example, of Elizabethan revenge tragedy and Restoration comedy.

For such a type to be successful means that its conventions 5 have imposed themselves upon the general consciousness and become the accepted vehicles of a particular set of attitudes and a particular aesthetic effect. One goes to any individual example of the type with very definite expectations, and originality is to be welcomed only in the degree that it intensifies the expected experience without fundamentally altering it. Moreover, the relationship between the conventions which go to make up such a type and the real experience of its audience or the real facts of whatever situation it pretends to describe is of only secondary importance and does not determine its aesthetic force. It is only in an ultimate sense that the type appeals to its audience's experience of reality; much more immediately, it appeals to previous experience of the type itself: it creates its own field of reference.

Thus the importance of the gangster film, and the nature and 6 intensity of its emotional and aesthetic impact, cannot be measured in terms of the place of the gangster himself or the importance of the problem of crime in American life. Those European movie-goers who think there is a gangster on every corner in New York are certainly deceived, but defenders of the "positive" side of American culture are equally deceived if they think it relevant to point out that most Americans have never seen a gangster. What matters is that the experience of the gangster *as an experience of art* is universal to Americans. There is almost nothing we understand better or react to more readily or with quicker intelligence. The Western film, though it seems never to diminish in popularity, is for most of us no more than the folklore of the past, familiar and understandable only because it has been repeated so often. The gangster film comes much closer. In ways that we do not easily or willingly define, the gangster speaks for us, expressing that part of the American psyche which rejects the qualities and the demands of modern life, which rejects "Americanism" itself.

The gangster is the man of the city, with the city's language 7 and knowledge, with its queer and dishonest skills and its terrible daring, carrying his life in his hands like a placard, like a club. For everyone else, there is at least the theoretical possibility of another world—in that happier American culture which the gangster denies, the city does not really exist; it is only a more crowded and more brightly lit country—but for the gangster there is only the city; he must inhabit it in order to personify it: not the real city, but that dangerous and sad city of the imagination which is so much more important, which is the modern world. And the gangster—though there are real gangsters—is also, and primarily, a creature of the imagination. The real city, one might say, produces only criminals; the imaginary city produces the gangster: he is what we want to be and what we are afraid we may become.

Thrown into the crowd without background or advantages, with only those ambiguous skills which the rest of us—the real people of the real city—can only pretend to have, the gangster is required to make his way, to make his life and impose it on others. Usually, when we come upon him, he has already made his choice or the choice has already been made for him, it doesn't matter which: we are not permitted to ask whether at some point he could have chosen to be something else than what he is. 8

The gangster's activity is actually a form of rational enter-prise, involving fairly definite goals and various techniques for achieving them. But this rationality is usually no more than a vague background; we know, perhaps, that the gangster sells liquor or that he operates a numbers racket; often we are not given even that much information. So his activity becomes a kind of pure criminality: he hurts people. Certainly our response to the gangster film is most consistently and most universally a response to sadism; we gain the double satisfaction of participating vicariously in the gangster's sadism and then seeing it turned against the gangster himself. 9

But on another level the quality of irrational brutality and the quality of rational enterprise become one. Since we do not see the rational and routine aspects of the gangster's behavior, the practice of brutality—the quality of unmixed criminality—becomes the totality of his career. At the same time, we are always conscious that the whole meaning of this career is a drive for success: the typical gangster film presents a steady upward progress followed by a very precipitate fall. Thus brutality itself becomes at once the means to success and the content of success—a success that is defined in its most general terms, not as accomplishment or specific gain, but simply as the unlimited possibility of aggression. (In the same way, film presenta-tions of businessmen tend to make it appear that they achieve their success by talking on the telephone and holding conferences and that success *is* talking on the telephone and holding conferences.) 10

From this point of view, the initial contact between the film and its audience is an agreed conception of human life: that man is a being with the possibilities of success or failure. This principle, too, belongs to the city; one must emerge from the crowd or else one is nothing. On that basis the necessity of the action is established, and it progresses, by inalterable paths to the point where the gangster lies dead and the principle has been modified: there is really only one possibility—failure. The final meaning of the city is anonymity and death. 11

In the opening scene of *Scarface*, we are shown a successful 12

THE GANGSTER AS TRAGIC HERO   **425**

man; we know he is successful because he has just given a party of opulent proportions and because he is called Big Louie. Through some monstrous lack of caution, he permits himself to be alone for a few moments. We understand from this immediately that he is about to be killed. No convention of the gangster film is more strongly established than this: it is dangerous to be alone. And yet the very conditions of success make it impossible not to be alone, for success is always the establishment of an *individual* pre-eminence that must be imposed on others, in whom it automatically arouses hatred; the successful man is an outlaw. The gangster's whole life is an effort to assert himself as an individual, to draw himself out of the crowd, and he always dies *because* he is an individual; the final bullet thrusts him back, makes him, after all, a failure. "Mother of God," says the dying Little Caesar, "is this the end of Rico?"—speaking of himself thus in the third person because what has been brought low is not the undifferentiated *man*, but the individual with a name, the gangster, the success; even to himself he is a creature of the imagination. (T. S. Eliot has pointed out that a number of Shakespeare's tragic heroes have this trick of looking at themselves dramatically; their true identity, the thing that is destroyed when they die, is something outside themselves—not a man, but a style of life, a kind of meaning.)

At bottom, the gangster is doomed because he is under the   13
obligation to succeed, not because the means he employs are unlawful. In the deeper layers of the modern consciousness, *all* means are unlawful, every attempt to succeed is an act of aggression, leaving one alone and guilty and defenseless among enemies: one is *punished* for success. This is our intolerable dilemma: that failure is a kind of death and success is evil and dangerous, is—ultimately—impossible. The effect of the gangster film is to embody this dilemma in the person of the gangster and resolve it by his death. The dilemma is resolved because it is *his* death, not ours. We are safe; for the moment, we can acquiesce in our failure, we can choose to fail.

QUESTIONS

1. Explain the relationship that Warshow establishes between politics, film, and popular culture.

2. What does the author mean by the statement, "In ways that we do not easily or willingly define, the gangster speaks for us, expressing that part of the American psyche which rejects the qualities and demands of modern life, which rejects 'Americanism' itself" (paragraph 6)? Why is this an important observation in the context of the essay?

3. What connotations does the author establish for the word "happiness"?

What words connect with it? What words and phrases serve as antonyms?

4.   Analyze the author's use of punctuation to enhance the effectiveness of his last paragraph.

5.   Why is Warshow's introduction so long? How can it be justified? What forms of logic and reasoning are established in these paragraphs? Evaluate the effectiveness of the last sentence in paragraph 3 as a transitional device.

6.   What forms of comparison and contrast operate in the essay? Of process analysis? Cite examples of each.

7.   Explain the importance and purpose of definition in terms of the thesis and structure of the essay.

8.   Analyze the complex tone of the essay.

9.   Warshow states at the outset of the essay, "America, as a social and political organization is committed to a cheerful view of life. It could not be otherwise." Do you agree or disagree, and why?

10.   Define one type of figure from television or film—the outlaw, the gangster, the monster—in terms of the sense of American life that it projects.

PAULINE KAEL

Movies on Television

Pauline Kael (1919–   ) has been a film critic for *McCall's*, *The New Republic*, and *The New Yorker*, and a frequent contributor to other national publications. Perhaps the best-known and most controversial film critic in the United States today, Kael is the author of *I Lost It at the Movies* (1965), *Kiss Kiss Bang Bang* (1968), *Going Steady* (1970), *Deeper into the Movies* (1973), and *When the Lights Go Down* (1980). The following essay reflects the energy, brilliance, range, and opinionated tone characteristic of her best film interpretation.

 few years ago, a jet on which I was returning to   1
California after a trip to New York was instructed to
delay landing for a half hour. The plane circled above
the San Francisco area, and spread out under me were

the farm where I was born, the little town where my grandparents were buried, the city where I had gone to school, the cemetery where my parents were, the homes of my brothers and sisters, Berkeley, where I had gone to college, and the house where at that moment, while I hovered high above, my little daughter and my dogs were awaiting my return. It was as though my whole life were suspended in time—as though no matter where you'd gone, what you'd done, the past were all still there, present, if you just got up high enough to attain the proper perspective.

Sometimes I get a comparable sensation when I turn from the news programs or the discussion shows on television to the old movies. So much of what formed our tastes and shaped our experiences, and so much of the garbage of our youth that we never thought we'd see again—preserved and exposed to eyes and minds that might well want not to believe that this was an important part of our past. Now these movies are there for new generations, to whom they cannot possibly have the same impact or meaning, because they are all jumbled together, out of historical sequence. Even what may deserve an honorable position in movie history is somehow dishonored by being so available, so meaninglessly present. Everything is in hopeless disorder, and that is the way new generations experience our movie past. In the other arts, something like natural selection takes place: only the best or the most significant or influential or successful works compete for our attention. Moreover, those from the past are likely to be touched up to accord with the taste of the present. In popular music, old tunes are newly orchestrated. A small repertory of plays is continually reinterpreted for contemporary meanings—the great ones for new relevance, the not so great rewritten, tackily "brought up to date," or deliberately treated as period pieces. By contrast, movies, through the accidents of commerce, are sold in blocks or packages to television, the worst with the mediocre and the best, the successes with the failures, the forgotten with the half forgotten, the ones so dreary you don't know whether you ever saw them or just others like them with some so famous you can't be sure whether you actually saw them or only imagined what they were like. A lot of this stuff never really made it with any audience; it played in small towns or it was used to soak up the time just the way TV in bars does.

There are so many things that we, having lived through them, or passed over them, never want to think about again. But in movies nothing is cleaned away, sorted out, purposefully discarded. (The destruction of negatives in studio fires or deliberately, to save space, was as indiscriminate as the preservation and resale.) There's a kind of hopelessness about it: what does not deserve to last lasts, and so it all begins to seem one big pile of junk, and some people say,

"Movies never really were any good—except maybe the Bogarts." If the same things had happened in literature or music or painting—if we were constantly surrounded by the piled-up inventory of the past—it's conceivable that modern man's notions of culture and civilization would be very different. Movies, most of them produced as fodder to satisfy the appetite for pleasure and relaxation, turned out to have magical properties—indeed, to *be* magical properties. This fodder can be fed to people over and over again. Yet, not altogether strangely, as the years wear on it doesn't please their palates, though many will go on swallowing it, just because nothing tastier is easily accessible. Watching old movies is like spending an evening with those people next door. They bore us, and we wouldn't go out of our way to see them; we drop in on them because they're so close. If it took some effort to see old movies, we might try to find out which were the good ones, and if people saw only the good ones maybe they would still respect old movies. As it is, people sit and watch movies that audiences walked out on thirty years ago. Like Lot's wife, we are tempted to take another look, attracted not by evil but by something that seems much more shameful—our own innocence. We don't try to reread the girls' and boys' "series" books of our adolescence—the very look of them is dismaying. The text books we studied in grammar school are probably more "dated" than the movies we saw then, but we never look at the old schoolbooks, whereas we keep seeing on TV the movies that represent the same stage in our lives and played much the same part in them—as things we learned from and, in spite of, went beyond.

Not all old movies look bad now, of course; the good ones are 4 still good—surprisingly good, often, if you consider how much of the detail is lost on television. Not only the size but the shape of the image is changed, and, indeed, almost all the specifically visual elements are so distorted as to be all but completely destroyed. On television, a cattle drive or a cavalry charge or a chase—the climax of so many a big movie—loses the dimensions of space and distance that made it exciting, that sometimes made it great. And since the structural elements—the rhythm, the buildup, the suspense—are also partly destroyed by deletions and commercial breaks and the interruptions incidental to home viewing, it's amazing that the bare bones of performance, dialogue, story, good directing, and (especially important for close-range viewing) good editing can still make an old movie more entertaining than almost anything new on television. (That's why old movies are taking over television—or, more accurately, vice versa.) The verbal slapstick of the newspaper-life comedies—*Blessed Event, Roxie Hart, His Girl Friday*—may no longer be fresh (partly because it has been so widely imitated), but it's still funny. Movies with good, fast, energetic talk seem better than ever on television—still not great but, on television, better than what *is* great. (And as we listen to the tabloid journalists insulting the corrupt politicians, we respond once again to the happy effrontery of that period when the targets of popular satire were still small enough for us to laugh at without choking.) The wit of dialogue comedies like Preston Sturges's *Unfaithfully Yours* isn't much diminished, nor does a tight melodrama like *Double Indemnity* lose a great deal. Movies like Joseph L. Mankiewicz's *A Letter to Three Wives* and *All About Eve* look practically the same on television as in theatres, because they have almost no visual dimensions to lose. In them the camera serves primarily to show us the person who is going to speak the next presumably bright line—a scheme that on television, as in theatres, is acceptable only when the line *is* bright. Horror and fantasy films like Karl Freund's *The Mummy* or Robert Florey's *The Murders in the Rue Morgue*—even with the loss, through miniaturization, of imaginative special effects—are surprisingly effective, perhaps because they are so primitive in their appeal that the qualities of the imagery matter less than the basic suggestions. Fear counts for more than finesse, and viewing horror films is far more frightening at home than in the shared comfort of an audience that breaks the tension with derision.

Other kinds of movies lose much of what made them worth 5 looking at—the films of von Sternberg, for example, designed in light and shadow, or the subtleties of Max Ophuls, or the lyricism of Satyajit Ray. In the box the work of these men is not as lively or as satisfying as the plain good movies of lesser directors. Reduced to the dead grays of a cheap television print, Orson Welles' *The Magnificent Ambersons*—an uneven work that is nevertheless a triumphant conquest of the movie medium—is as lifelessly dull as a newspaper Wirephoto of a great painting. But when people say of a "big" movie like *High Noon* that it has dated or that it doesn't hold up what they are really saying is that their judgment was faulty or has changed. They may have overresponded to its publicity and reputation or to its attempt to deal with a social problem or an idea, and may have ignored the banalities surrounding that attempt; now that the idea doesn't seem so daring, they notice the rest. Perhaps it was a traditional drama that was new to them and that they thought was new to the world; everyone's "golden age of movies" is the period of his first moviegoing and just before—what he just missed or wasn't allowed to see. (The Bogart films came out just before today's college kids started going.)

Sometimes we suspect, and sometimes rightly, that our 6 memory has improved a picture—that imaginatively we made it what we knew it could have been or should have been—and, fearing this, we may prefer memory to new contact. We'll remember it better if we don't see it again—we'll remember what it meant to us. The nostalgia we may have poured over a performer or over our recollections of a movie has a way of congealing when we try to renew the contact. But sometimes the experience of reseeing is wonderful—a confirmation of the general feeling that was all that remained with us from childhood. And we enjoy the fresh proof of the rightness of our responses that reseeing the film gives us. We re-experience what we once felt, and memories flood back. Then movies seem magical—all those *madelines* waiting to be dipped in tea. What looks bad in old movies is the culture of which they were part and which they expressed—a tone of American life that we have forgotten. When we see First World War posters, we are far enough away from their patriotic primitivism to be amused at the emotions and sentiments to which they appealed. We can feel charmed but superior. It's not so easy to cut ourselves off from old movies and the old selves who responded to them, because they're not an isolated part of the past held up for derision and amusement and wonder. Although they belong to the same world as stories in *Liberty*, old radio shows, old phonograph records, an America still divided between hayseeds and city slickers, and although they may seem archaic, their pastness isn't so very past. It includes the last decade, last year, yesterday.

Though in advertising movies for TV the recentness is the lure, for many of us what constitutes the attraction is the datedness, and the earlier movies are more compelling than the ones of the fifties or the early sixties. Also, of course, the movies of the thirties and forties look better technically, because, ironically, the competition with television that made movies of the fifties and sixties enlarge their scope and their subject matter has resulted in their looking like a mess in the box—the sides of the image lopped off, the crowds and vistas a boring blur, the color altered, the epic themes incongruous and absurd on the little home screen. In a movie like *The Robe*, the large-scale production values that were depended on to attract TV viewers away from their sets become a negative factor. But even if the quality of the image were improved, these movies are too much like the ones we can see in theatres to be interesting at home. At home, we like to look at those stiff, carefully groomed actors of the thirties, with their clipped, Anglophile stage speech and their regular, clean-cut features—walking profiles, like the figures on Etruscan vases and almost as remote. And there is the faithless wife—how will she decide between her lover and her husband, when they seem as alike as two wax grooms on a wedding cake? For us, all three are doomed not by sin and disgrace but by history. Audiences of the period may have enjoyed these movies for their action, their story, their thrills, their wit, and all this high living. But through our window on the past we see the actors acting out other dramas as well. The Middle European immigrants had children who didn't speak the king's English and, after the Second World War, didn't even respect it so much. A flick of the dial and we are in the fifties amid the slouchers, with their thick lips, shapeless noses, and shaggy haircuts, waiting to say their lines until they think them out, then mumbling something that is barely speech. How long, O Warren Beatty, must we wait before we turn back to beautiful stick figures like Phillips Holmes?

We can take a shortcut through the hell of many lives, turning   8
the dial from the social protest of the thirties to the films of the same writers and directors in the fifties—full of justifications for blabbing, which they shifted onto characters in oddly unrelated situations. We can see in the films of the forties the displaced artists of Europe—the anti-Nazi exiles like Conrad Veidt, the refugees like Peter Lorre, Fritz Kortner, and Alexander Granach. And what are they playing? Nazis, of course, because they have accents, and so for Americans—for the whole world—they become images of Nazi brutes. Or we can look at the patriotic sentiments of the Second World War years and those actresses, in their orgies of ersatz nobility, giving their lives—or, at the very least, their bodies—to save their country. It was sickening at the time; it's perversely amusing now—part of the spectacle of our common culture.

Probably in a few years some kid watching *The Sandpiper* on   9
television will say what I recently heard a kid say about *Mrs. Miniver:* "And to think they really believed it in those days." Of course, we didn't. We didn't accept nearly as much in old movies as we may now fear we did. Many of us went to see big-name pictures just as we went to *The Night of the Iguana,* without believing a minute of it. The James Bond pictures are not to be "believed," but they tell us a lot about the conventions that audiences now accept, just as the confessional films of the thirties dealing with sin and illegitimacy and motherhood tell us about the sickly-sentimental tone of American entertainment in the midst of the Depression. Movies indicate what the producers thought people would pay to see—which was not always the same as what they *would* pay to see. Even what they enjoyed seeing does not tell us directly what they believed but only indirectly hints at the tone and style of a culture. There is no reason to assume that people twenty or thirty years ago were stupider than they are now. (Consider how *we* may be judged by people twenty years from now looking at today's movies.) Though it may not seem obvious to us now, part of the original appeal of old movies—which we certainly understood and responded to as children—was that, despite their sentimental tone, they helped to form the liberalized modern consciousness. This trash—and most of it was, and is, trash—probably taught us more about the world, and even about values, than our "education" did. Movies broke down barriers of all kinds, opened up the world, helped to make us aware. And they were almost always on the side of the

mistreated, the socially despised. Almost all drama is. And, because movies were a mass medium, they had to be on the side of the poor.

Nor does it necessarily go without saying that the glimpses of something really good even in mediocre movies—the quickening of excitement at a great performance, the discovery of beauty in a gesture or a phrase or an image—made us understand the meaning of art as our teachers in appreciation courses never could. And—what is more difficult for those who are not movie lovers to grasp—even after this sense of the greater and the higher is developed, we still do not want to live only on the heights. We still want the pleasure of discovering things for ourselves; we need the sustenance of the ordinary, the commonplace, the almost-good as part of the anticipatory atmosphere. And though it all helps us to respond to the moments of greatness, it is not only for this that we want it. The educated person who became interested in cinema as an art form through Bergman or Fellini or Resnais is alien to me (and my mind goes blank with hostility and indifference when he begins to talk). There isn't much for the art-cinema person on television; to look at a great movie, or even a poor movie carefully designed in terms of textures and contrasts, on television is, in general, maddening, because those movies lose too much. (Educational television, though, persists in this misguided effort to bring the television viewer movie classics.) There are few such movies anyway. But there are all the not-great movies, which we probably wouldn't bother going to see in museums or in theatre revivals—they're just not that important. Seeing them on television is a different kind of experience, with different values—partly because the movie past hasn't been filtered to conform to anyone's convenient favorite notions of film art. We make our own, admittedly small, discoveries or rediscoveries. There's Dan Dailey doing his advertising-wise number in *It's Always Fair Weather*, or Gene Kelly and Fred Astaire singing and dancing "The Babbitt and the Bromide" in *Ziegfeld Follies*. And it's like putting on a record of Ray Charles singing "Georgia on My Mind" or Frank Sinatra singing "Bim Bam Baby" or Elisabeth Schwarzkopf singing operetta, and feeling again the elation we felt the first time. Why should we deny these pleasures because there are other, more complex kinds of pleasure possible? It's true that these pleasures don't deepen, and that they don't change *us*, but maybe that is part of what makes them seem our own—we realize that we have some emotions and responses that *don't* change as we get older.

People who see a movie for the first time on television don't remember it the same way that people do who saw it in a theatre. Even without the specific visual loss that results from the transfer to another medium, it's doubtful whether a movie could have as intense an impact as it had in its own time. Probably by definition, works that are not truly great cannot be as compelling out of their time. Sinclair Lewis's and Hemingway's novels were becoming archaic while their authors lived. Can *On the Waterfront* have the impact now that it had in 1954? Not quite. And revivals in movie theatres don't have the same kind of charge, either. There's something a little stale in the air, there's a different kind of audience. At a revival, we must allow for the period, or care because of the period. Television viewers seeing old movies for the first time can have very little sense of how and why new stars moved us when they appeared, of the excitement of new themes, of what these movies meant to us. They don't even know which were important in their time, which were "hits."

But they can discover *something* in old movies, and there are few discoveries to be made on dramatic shows produced for television. In comedies, the nervous tic of canned laughter neutralizes everything; the laughter is as false for the funny as for the unfunny and prevents us from responding to either. In general, performances in old movies don't suffer horribly on television except from cuts, and what kindles something like the early flash fire is the power of personality that comes through in those roles that made a star. Today's high school and college students seeing *East of Eden* and *Rebel Without a Cause* for the first time are almost as caught up in James Dean as the first generation of adolescent viewers was, experiencing that tender, romantic, marvelously masochistic identification with the boy who does everything wrong because he cares so much. And because Dean died young and hard, he is not just another actor who outlived his myth and became ordinary in stale roles—he is the symbol of misunderstood youth. He is inside the skin of moviegoing and television-watching youth—even educated youth—in a way that Keats and Shelley or John Cornford and Julian Bell are not. Youth can respond—though not so strongly—to many of our old heroes and heroines: to Gary Cooper, say, as the elegant, lean, amusingly silent romantic loner of his early Western and aviation films. (And they can more easily ignore the actor who sacrificed that character for blubbering righteous bathos.) Bogart found his myth late, and Dean fulfilled the romantic myth of self-destructiveness, so they look good on television. More often, television, by showing us actors before and after their key starring roles, is a myth-killer. But it keeps acting ability alive.

There is a kind of young television watcher seeing old movies for the first time who is surprisingly sensitive to their values and responds almost with the intensity of a moviegoer. But he's different from the moviegoer. For one thing, he's housebound, inactive, solitary. Unlike a moviegoer, he seems to have no need to discuss what he sees. The kind of television watcher I mean (and the ones I've met are all boys) seems to have extreme empathy with the

PAULINE KAEL

material in the box (new TV shows as well as old movies, though rarely news), but he may not know how to enter into a conversation, or even how to come into a room or go out of it. He fell in love with his baby-sitter, so he remains a baby. He's unusually polite and intelligent, but in a mechanical way—just going through the motions, without interest. He gives the impression that he wants to withdraw from this human interference and get back to his real life—the box. He is like a prisoner who has everything he wants in prison and is content to stay there. Yet, oddly, he and his fellows seem to be tuned in to each other; just as it sometimes seems that even a teen-ager locked in a closet would pick up the new dance steps at the same moment as other teen-agers, these television watchers react to the same things at the same time. If they can find more intensity in this box than in their own living, then this box can provide *constantly* what we got at the movies only a few times a week. Why should they move away from it, or talk, or go out of the house, when they will only experience that as a loss? Of course, we can see why they should, and their inability to make connections outside is frighteningly suggestive of ways in which we, too, are cut off. It's a matter of degree. If we stay up half the night to watch old movies and can't face the next day, it's partly, at least, because of the fascination of our own movie past; *they* live in a past they never had, like people who become obsessed by places they have only imaginative connections with—Brazil, Venezuela, Arabia Deserta. Either way, there is always something a little shameful about living in the past; we feel guilty, stupid—as if the pleasure we get needed some justification that we can't provide.

For some moviegoers, movies probably contribute to that   14 self-defeating romanticizing of expectations which makes life a series of disappointments. They watch the same movies over and over on television, as if they were constantly returning to the scene of the crime—the life they were so busy dreaming about that they never lived it. They are paralyzed by longing, while those less romantic can leap the hurdle. I heard a story the other day about a man who ever since his school days had been worshipfully "in love with" a famous movie star, talking about her, fantasizing about her, following her career, with its ups and downs and its stormy romances and marriages to producers and agents and wealthy sportsmen and rich businessmen. Though he became successful himself, it never occurred to him that he could enter her terrain—she was so glamorously above him. Last week, he got a letter from an old classmate, to whom, years before, he had confided his adoration of the star; the classmate—an unattractive guy who had never done anything with his life and had a crummy job in a crummy business—had just married her.

Movies are a combination of art and mass medium, but   15

television is so single in its purpose—selling—that it operates without that painful, poignant mixture of aspiration and effort and compromise. We almost never think of calling a television show "beautiful," or even of complaining about the absence of beauty, because we take it for granted that television operates without beauty. When we see on television photographic records of the past, like the pictures of Scott's Antarctic expedition or those series on the First World War, they seem almost too strong for the box, too pure for it. The past has a terror and a fascination and a beauty beyond almost anything else. We are looking at the dead, and they move and grin and wave at us; it's an almost unbearable experience. When our wonder and our grief are interrupted or followed by a commercial, we want to destroy the ugly box. Old movies don't tear us apart like that. They do something else, which we can take more of and take more easily: they give us a sense of the passage of life. Here is Elizabeth Taylor as a plump matron and here, an hour later, as an exquisite child. That charmingly petulant little gigolo with the skinny face and the mustache that seems the most substantial part of him—can he have developed into the great Laurence Olivier? Here is Orson Welles as a young man, playing a handsome old man, and here is Orson Welles as he has really aged. Here are Bette Davis and Charles Boyer traversing the course of their lives from ingenue and juvenile, through major roles, into character parts—back and forth, endlessly, embodying the good and bad characters of many styles, many periods. We see the old character actors put out to pasture in television serials, playing gossipy neighbors or grumpy grandpas, and then we see them in their youth or middle age, in the roles that made them famous—and it's startling to find how good they were, how vital, after we've encountered them caricaturing themselves, feeding off their old roles. They have almost nothing left of that young actor we responded to—and still find ourselves responding to—except the distinctive voice and a few crotchets. There are those of us who, when we watch old movies, sit there murmuring the names as the actors appear (Florence Bates, Henry Daniell, Ernest Thesiger, Constance Collier, Edna May Oliver, Douglas Fowley), or we recognize them but can't remember their names, yet know how well we once knew them, experiencing the failure of memory as a loss of our own past until we can supply it (Maude Eburne or Porter Hall)—with great relief. After a few seconds, I can always remember them, though I cannot remember the names of my childhood companions or of the prizefighter I once dated, or even of the boy who took me to the senior prom. We are eager to hear again that line we know is coming. We hate to miss anything. Our memories are jarred by cuts. We want to see the movie to the end.

The graveyard of *Our Town* affords such a tiny perspective 16

PAULINE KAEL

compared to this. Old movies on television are a gigantic, panoramic novel that we can tune in to and out of. People watch avidly for a few weeks or months or years and then give up; others tune in when they're away from home in lonely hotel rooms, or regularly, at home, a few nights a week or every night. The rest of the family may ignore the passing show, may often interrupt, because individual lines of dialogue or details of plot hardly seem to matter as they did originally. A movie on television is no longer just a drama in itself; it is part of a huge ongoing parade. To a new generation, what does it matter if a few gestures and a nuance are lost, when they know they can't watch the parade on all the channels at all hours anyway? It's like traffic on the street. The television generation knows there is no end; it all just goes on. When television watchers are surveyed and asked what kind of programming they want or how they feel television can be improved, some of them not only have no answers but can't understand the questions. What they get on their sets is television—that's it.

QUESTIONS

1. According to Kael, which types of movies on television appear most successfully? Which varieties are not reproduced as well?

2. Examine some of the value judgments that the author makes about older and newer movies; about television in general; about the relationship of movies to history and personal experience.

3. Locate and discuss examples of figurative language in paragraphs 3, 7, 8, 12, and 16.

4. Does the author depend on concrete or abstract language? Explain.

5. What rhetorical strategy does Kael employ in her introductory paragraph? What is the connection between this technique and the subject the author investigates? Cite other examples of this strategy in the essay.

6. Trace the chain of causal analysis that Kael develops in the essay. What causes does she cite? How does she handle primary and secondary causes? Where are effects explained?

7. Locate and analyze examples of paragraphs developed by means of moving from one generalization to another; locate paragraphs in which the movement is from general to particular. Which mode of paragraph development—horizontal or vertical—does Kael prefer? Why?

8. What is the relevance of the anecdote in paragraph 14 to the central

meanings of the essay? How does it serve as a transition from the body of the essay to the conclusion?

9. Do you share Kael's preference for movies instead of television? Why or why not?

10. Write an essay on the effects of watching movies or reruns on television, and the causes behind these effects.

JAMES BALDWIN

The Uses of the Blues

James Baldwin (1924–   ), a major American essayist, novelist, short story writer, and playwright, was born and grew up in Harlem, winning a Eugene Saxon Fellowship, and living in Europe from 1948 to 1956. Always an activist in civil rights causes, Baldwin focuses in his essays and fiction on the black search for identity in modern America and on the myth of white superiority. Among his principal works are *Go Tell It on the Mountain* (1953), *Notes of a Native Son* (1955), *Giovanni's Room* (1958), *Nobody Knows My Name* (1960), *Another Country* (1962), and *If Beale Street Could Talk* (1975). One of the finest contemporary essayists, Baldwin has a rare talent for portraying the deepest social and political themes in an intensely personal style, as the following selection indicates.

he title "The Uses of the Blues" does not refer to music; I don't know anything about music. It does refer to the experience of life, or the state of being, out of which the blues come. Now, I am claiming a great deal for the blues; I'm using them as a metaphor—I might have titled this, for example, "The Uses of Anguish" or "The Uses of Pain." But I want to talk about the blues, not only because they speak of this particular experience of life and this state of being, but because they contain the toughness that manages to make this experience articulate. I am engaged, then, in a discussion of craft or, to use a very dangerous word, art. And I want to suggest that the acceptance of this anguish one finds in the blues, and the expression of it, creates, also, however odd this may sound, a kind of joy. Now joy is a true state, it is a reality; it has nothing to do with what most people have in mind when they talk of happiness, which is not a real state and does not really exist.

Consider some of the things the blues are about. They're about work, love, death, floods, lynchings, in fact, a series of disasters which can be summed up under the arbitrary heading "Facts of Life." Bessie Smith, who is dead now, came out of somewhere in the Deep South. I guess she was born around 1898, a great blues singer; died in Mississippi after a very long, hard—not *very* long, but very *hard*—life: pig's feet and gin, many disastrous lovers and a career that first went up, then went down; died on the road on the way from one hospital to another. She was in an automobile accident and one of her arms was wrenched out of its socket; and because the hospital attendants argued whether or not they could let her in because she was colored, she died. Not a story Horatio Alger would write. Well, Bessie saw a great many things, and among those things was a flood. And she talked about it and she said, "It rained five days and the skies turned dark as night," and she repeated it: "It rained five days and the skies turned dark as night." Then, "Trouble take place in the lowlands at night." And she went on:

> Then it thundered and lightnin'd and the wind began to blow
> Then it thundered and lightnin'd and the wind began to blow
> There's thousands of people ain't got no place to go.

As the song makes clear, she was one of those people. But she ended in a fantastic way:

> Backwater blues done caused me to pack my things and go
> Because my house fell down
> And I can't live there no mo'.

Billie Holiday came along a little later and she had quite a story, too, a story which *Life* magazine would never print except as a tough, bittersweet sob-story obituary—in which, however helplessly, the dominant note would be relief. She was a little girl from the South, and she had quite a time with gin, whiskey and dope. She died in New York in a narcotics ward under the most terrifying and—in terms of crimes of the city and the country against her—disgraceful circumstances, and she had something she called "Billie's Blues":

> My man wouldn't give me no dinner
> Wouldn't give me no supper

Squawked about my supper and turned me outdoors
And had the nerve to lay a padlock on my clothes
I didn't have so many, but I had a long, long way to go.

And one more, one more—Bessie Smith had a song called   4
"Gin House Blues." It's another kind of blues, and maybe I should
explain this to you—a Negro has his difficult days, the days when
everything has gone wrong and on top of it, he has a fight with the
elevator man, or the taxi driver, or somebody he never saw before,
who seems to decide to prove he's white and you're black. But this
particular Tuesday it's more than you can take—sometimes, you
know, you can take it. But Bessie didn't this time, and she sat down in
the gin house and sang:

> Don't try me, nobody
> 'Cause you will never win
> I'll fight the Army and the Navy
> Just me and my gin.

Well, you know, that is all very accurate, all very concrete. I   5
know, I watched, I was there. You've seen these black men and
women, these boys and girls; you've seen them on the streets. But I
know what happened to them at the factory, at work, at home, on the
subway, what they go through in a day, and the way they sort of ride
with it. And it's very, very tricky. It's kind of a fantastic tightrope.
They may be very self-controlled, very civilized; I like to think of
myself as being very civilized and self-controlled, but I know I'm not.
And I know that some improbable Wednesday, for no reason whatever, the elevator man or the doorman, the policeman or the landlord,
or some little boy from the Bronx will say something, and it will be the
wrong day to say it, the wrong moment to have it said to me; and God
knows what will happen. I have seen it all, I have seen that much.
What the blues are describing comes out of all this.

"Gin House Blues" is a real gin house. "Backwater Flood" is a   6
real flood. When Billie says, "My man don't love me," she is not
making a fantasy out of it. This is what happened, this is where it is.
This is what it is. Now, I'm trying to suggest that the triumph
here—which is a very un-American triumph—is that the person to
whom these things happen watched with eyes wide open, saw it
happen. So that when Billie or Bessie or Leadbelly stood up and sang
about it, they were commenting on it, a little bit outside it; they were
accepting it. And there's something funny—there's always something a little funny in all our disasters, if one can face the disaster. So
that it's this passionate detachment, this inwardness coupled with
outwardness, this ability to know that, All right, it's a mess, and you

can't do anything about it . . . so, well, you have to do something about it. You can't stay there, you can't drop dead, you can't give up, but all right, OK, as Bessie said, "Picked up my bag, baby, and I tried it again." This made life, however horrible that life was, bearable for her. It's what makes life bearable for any person, because every person, everybody born, from the time he's found out about people until the whole thing is over is certain of one thing: He is going to suffer. There is no way not to suffer.

Now, this brings us to two things. It brings us to the American Negro's experience of life, and it brings us to the American dream or sense of life. It would be hard to find any two things more absolutely opposed. I want to make it clear that when I talk about Negroes in this context, I am not talking about race; I don't know what race means. I am talking about a social fact. When I say Negro, it is a digression; it is important to remember that I am not talking about a people but a person. I am talking about a man who, let's say, was once seventeen and who is now, let's say, forty, who has four children and can't feed them. I am talking about what happens to that man in this time and during this effort. I'm talking about what happens to you if, having barely escaped suicide, or death, or madness, or yourself, you watch your children growing up and no matter what you do, no matter *what* you do, you are powerless, you are really powerless, against the force of the world that is out to tell your child that he has no right to be alive. And no amount of liberal jargon, and no amount of talk about how well and how far we have progressed, does anything to soften or to point out any solution to this dilemma. In every generation, ever since Negroes have been here, every Negro mother and father has had to face that child and try to create in that child some way of surviving this particular world, some way to make the child, who will be despised, not despise himself. I don't know what the Negro problem means to white people, but this is what it means to Negroes. Now, it would seem to me, since this is so, that one of the reasons we talk about the Negro problem in the way we do is in order precisely to avoid any knowledge of this fact. Imagine Doris Day trying to sing:

> Papa may have, Mama may have
> But God bless the child that's got
> his own.

People talk to me absolutely bathed in a bubble bath of self-congratulation. I mean, I walk into a room and everyone there is terribly proud of himself because I managed to get to the room. It proves to him that he is getting better. It's funny, but it's terribly sad. It's sad that one needs this kind of corroboration and it's terribly sad

7

8

THE USES OF THE BLUES

that one can be so self-deluded. The fact that Harry Belafonte makes as much money as, let's say, Frank Sinatra, doesn't really mean anything in this context. Frank can still get a house anywhere, and Harry can't. People go to see Harry and stand in long lines to watch him. They love him onstage, or at a cocktail party, but they don't want him to marry their daughters. This has nothing to do with Harry; this has everything to do with America. All right. Therefore, when we talk about what we call the Negro problem, we are simply evolving means of avoiding the facts of this life. Because in order to face the facts of a life like Billie's or, for that matter, a life like mine, one has got to—the American white has got to—accept the fact that what he thinks he is, he is not. He has to give up, he has to surrender his image of himself and, apparently, this is the last thing white Americans are prepared to do.

But, anyway, it is not a question now of accusing the white 9 American of crimes against the Negro. It is too late for that. Besides, it is irrelevant. Injustice, murder, the shedding of blood, unhappily, are commonplace. These things happen all the time and everywhere. There is always a reason for it. People will always give themselves reasons for it. What I'm much more concerned about is what white Americans have done to themselves; what has been done to me is irrelevant simply because there is nothing more you can do to me. But, in doing it, you've done something to yourself. In evading my humanity, you have done something to your own humanity. We all do this all the time, of course. One labels people; one labels them Jew, one labels them fascist, one labels them Communist, one lables them Negro, one labels them white man. But in the doing of this, you have not described anything—you have not described me when you call me a nigger or when you call me a Negro leader. You have only described yourself. What I think of you says more about me than it can possibly say about you. This is a very simple law and every Negro who intends to survive has to learn it very soon. Therefore, the Republic, among other things, has managed to create a body of people who have very little to lose, and there is nothing more dangerous in any republic, any state, any country, any time, than men who have nothing to lose.

Because you have thus given him his freedom, the American 10 Negro can do whatever he wills; you can no longer do anything to him. He doesn't want anything you've got, he doesn't believe anything you say. I don't know why and I don't know how America arrived at this peculiar point of view. If one examines American history, there is no apparent reason for it. It's a bloody history, as bloody as everybody else's history, as deluded, as fanatical. One has only to look at it from the time we all got here. Look at the Pilgrims, the Puritans—the people who presumably fled oppression in Europe only to set up a more oppressed society here—people who wanted freedom, who killed off the Indians. Look at all the people moving into a new era and enslaving all the blacks. These are the facts of American history as opposed to the legend. We came from Europe, we came from Africa, we came from all over the world. We brought whatever was in us from China or from France. We *all* brought it with us. We were not transformed when we crossed the ocean. Something else happened. Something much more serious. We no longer had any way of finding out, of knowing who we were.

Many people have said in various tones of voice, meaning various things, that the most unlucky thing that happened in America was the presence of the Negro. Freud said, in a kind of rage, that the black race was the folly of America and that it served America right. Well, of course, I don't quite know what Freud had in mind. But I can see that, in one way, it may have been the most unlucky thing that happened to America, since America, unlike any other Western power, had its slaves on the mainland. They were here. We had our slaves at a time, unluckily for us, when slavery was going out of fashion. And after the Bill of Rights. Therefore, it would seem to me that the presence of this black mass here as opposed to all the things we said we believed in and also at a time when the whole doctrine of white supremacy had never even been questioned is one of the most crucial facts of our history. It would be nightmarish now to read the handbooks of colonialists a hundred years ago, even ten years ago, for that matter. But in those days, it was not even a question of black people being inferior to white people. The American found himself in a very peculiar position because he knew that black people were people. Frenchmen could avoid knowing it—they never met a black man. Englishmen could avoid knowing it. But Americans could not avoid knowing it because, after all, here he was and he was, no matter how it was denied, a man, just like everybody else. And the attempt to avoid this, to avoid this fact, I consider one of the keys to what we can call loosely the American psychology. For one thing, it created in Americans a kind of perpetual, hidden, festering and entirely unadmitted guilt. Guilt is a very peculiar emotion. As long as you are guilty about something, no matter what it is, you are not compelled to change it. Guilt is like a warm bath or, to be rude, it is like masturbation—you can get used to it, you can prefer it, you may get to a place where you cannot live without it, because in order to live without it, in order to get past this guilt, you must act. And in order to act, you must be conscious and take great chances and be responsible for the consquences. Therefore, liberals, and people who are not even liberals, much prefer to discuss the Negro problem than to try to deal with what this figure of the Negro really means personally to them. They still prefer to read statistics, charts, Gallup polls, rather than deal with the reality. They still tell me, to console me, how many Negroes bought Cadillacs, Cutty Sark, Coca-Cola and Schweppes, last year; how many more will buy Cadillacs, Cutty Sark, Coca-Cola and Schweppes next year. To prove to me that things are getting better. Now, of course, I think it is a very sad matter if you suppose that you or I have bled and suffered and died in this country in order to achieve Cadillacs, Cutty Sark, Schweppes and Coca-Cola. It seems to me if one accepts this speculation about the luxury of guilt that the second reason must be related to the first. That has to do with the ways in which we manage to project onto the Negro face, because it is so visible, all of our guilts and aggressions and desires. And if you doubt this, think of the legends that surround the Negro to this day. Think, when you think of these legends, that they were not invented by Negroes, but they were invented by the white republic. Ask yourself if Aunt Jemima or Uncle Tom ever existed anywhere and why it was necessary to invent them. Ask yourself why Negroes until today are, in the popular imagination, at once the most depraved people under heaven and the most saintly. Ask yourself what William Faulkner really was trying to say in *Requiem for a Nun*, which is about a nigger, whore, dope addict, saint. Faulkner wrote it. I never met Nancy, the nun he was writing about. He never met her, either, but the question is why was it necessary for him and for us to hold onto this image? We needn't go so far afield. Ask yourself why liberals are so delighted with the movie *The Defiant Ones*. It ends, if you remember, when Sidney Poitier, the black man, having been chained interminably to Tony Curtis, the white man, finally breaks the chain, is on the train, is getting away, but no, he doesn't go, doesn't leave poor Tony Curtis down there on the chain gang. Not at all. He jumps off the train and they go buddy-buddy back together to the same old Jim Crow chain gang. Now, this is a fable. Why? Who is trying to prove what to whom? I'll tell you something. I saw that movie twice. I saw it downtown with all my liberal friends, who were delighted when Sidney jumped off the train. I saw it uptown with my less liberal friends, who were furious. When Sidney jumped off that train, they called him all kinds of unmentionable things. Well, their reaction was at least more honest and more direct. Why is it necessary at this late date, one screams at the world, to prove that the Negro doesn't really hate you, he's forgiven and forgotten all of it. Maybe he has. That's not the problem. *You* haven't. And that *is* the problem:

> I love you baby,
> But can't stand your dirty ways.

There's one more thing I ought to add to this. The final turn of the screw that created this peculiar purgatory which we call

JAMES BALDWIN

12

America is that aspect of our history that is most triumphant. We really did conquer a continent, we have made a lot of money, we're better off materially than anybody else in the world. How easy it is as a person or as a nation to suppose that one's well-being is proof of one's virtue; in fact, a great many people are saying just that right now. You know, we're the best nation in the world because we're the richest nation in the world. The American way of life has proven itself, according to these curious people, and that's why we're so rich. This is called Yankee virtue and it comes from Calvin, but my point is that I think this has again something to do with the American failure to face reality. Since we have all these things, we can't be so bad and, since we have all these things, we are robbed, in a way, of the incentive to walk away from the TV set, the Cadillac, and go into the chaos out of which and only out of which we can create ourselves into human beings.

To talk about these things in this country today is extremely   13
difficult. Even the words mean nothing anymore. I think, for example, what we call the religious revival in America means that more and more people periodically get more and more frightened and go to church in order to make sure they don't lose their investments. This is the only reason that I can find for the popularity of men who have nothing to do with religion at all, like Norman Vincent Peale, for example—only for example; there're lots of others just like him. I think this is very sad. I think it's very frightening. But Ray Charles, who is a great tragic artist, makes of a genuinely religious confession something triumphant and liberating. He tells us that he cried so loud he gave the blues to his neighbor next door.

How can I put it? Let us talk about a person who is no longer   14
very young, who somehow managed to get to, let us say, the age of forty, and a great many of us do, without ever having been touched, broken, disturbed, frightened—ten-year-old virgin, male or female. There is a sense of the grotesque about a person who has spent his or her life in a kind of cotton batting. There is something monstrous about never having been hurt, never having been made to bleed, never having lost anything, never having gained anything because life is beautiful, and in order to keep it beautiful you're going to stay just the way you are and you're not going to test your theory against all the possibilities outside. America is something like that. The failure on our part to accept the reality of pain, of anguish, of ambiguity, of death has turned us into a very peculiar and sometimes monstrous people. It means, for one thing, and it's very serious, that people who have had no experience have no compassion. People who have had no experience suppose that if a man is a thief, he is a thief; but, in fact, that isn't the most important thing about him. The most important thing about him is that he is a man and, furthermore, that

if he's a thief or a murderer or whatever he is, *you* could also be and you would know this, anyone would know this who had really dared to live. Miles Davis once gave poor Billie Holiday $100 and somebody said, "Man, don't you know she's going to go out and spend it on dope?" and Miles said, "Baby, have you ever been sick?"

Now, you don't know that by reading, by looking. You don't 15 know what the river is like or what the ocean is like by standing on the shore. You can't know anything about life and suppose you can get through it clean. The most monstrous people are those who think they are going to. I think this shows in everything we see and do, in everything we read about these peculiar private lives, so peculiar that it is almost impossible to write about them, because what a man *says* he's doing has nothing to do with what he's *really* doing. If you read such popular novelists as John O'Hara, you can't imagine what country he's talking about. If you read *Life* magazine, it's like reading about the moon. Nobody lives in that country. That country does not exist and, what is worse, everybody knows it. But everyone pretends that it does. Now this is panic. And this is terribly dangerous, because it means that when the trouble comes, and trouble always comes, you won't survive it. It means that if your son dies, you may go to pieces or find the nearest psychiatrist or the nearest church, but you won't survive it on your own. If you don't survive your trouble out of your own resources, you have not really survived it; you have merely closed yourself against it. The blues are tooted in the slave songs; the slaves discovered something genuinely terrible, terrible because it sums up the universal challenge, the universal hope, the universal fear:

> The very time I thought I was lost
> My dungeon shook and my chains fell off.

Well, that is almost all I am trying to say. I say it out of great 16 concern. And out of a certain kind of hope. If you can live in the full knowledge that you are going to die, that you are not going to live forever, that if you live with the reality of death, you can live. This is not mystical talk; it is a fact. It is a principal fact of life. If you can't do it, if you spend your entire life in flight from death, you are also in flight from life. For example, right now you find the most unexpected people building bomb shelters, which is very close to being a crime. It is a private panic which creates a public delusion that some of us will be saved by bomb shelters. If we had, as human beings, on a personal and private level, our personal authority, we would know better; but because we are so uncertain of all these things, some of us, apparently, are willing to spend the rest of our lives underground in concrete. Perhaps, if we had a more working relationship with ourselves and with one another, we might be able to turn the tide and eliminate the propaganda for building bomb shelters. People who in some sense know who they are can't change the world always, but they can do something to make it a little more, to make life a little more human. Human in the best sense. Human in terms of joy, freedom which is always private, respect, respect for one another, even such things as manners. All these things are very important, all these old-fashioned things. People who don't know who they are privately, accept, as we have accepted for nearly fifteen years, the fantastic disaster which we call American politics and which we call American foreign policy, and the incoherence of the one is an exact reflection of the incoherence of the other. Now, the only way to change all this is to begin to ask ourselves very difficult questions.

I will stop now. But I want to quote two things. A very great 17
American writer, Henry James, writing to a friend of his who had just lost her husband, said, "Sorrow wears and uses us but we wear and use it, too, and it is blind. Whereas we, after a manner, see." And Bessie said:

> Good mornin' blues.
> Blues, how do you do?
> I'm doin' all right.
> Good mornin'.
> How are you?

QUESTIONS

1. According to the author, why are the blues essential to life? What connections does Baldwin establish between the blues and social experience? What does he mean by the opposition between the "American Negro's experience of life" and "the American dream or sense of life"?

2. Explain Baldwin's attitude toward danger and the reality of death.

3. What connotations does Baldwin establish for the blues? Cite evidence.

4. Analyze specific aspects of Baldwin's style that make it so distinctive.

5. What is the analogy in the introductory paragraph? How does he state the rhetorical method? Why will the topic be complex and paradoxical?

6. Analyze the development of the analogy in paragraphs 2 to 4. Comment on the effectiveness of the author's examples. What is the relationship of paragraphs 5 and 6 to the preceding material? How do these paragraphs prepare for subsequent material?

7. Analyze Baldwin's comparative method in paragraphs 7 to 14. How does this section relate implicitly to the blues analogy? Explain the function of paragraph 15.

8. Assess the method and effectiveness of Baldwin's conclusion in paragraphs 16 and 17.

9. Baldwin declares at the outset of his essay that he is not writing about music. What does he mean? Do you agree or disagree with his assertion? Why or why not?

10. Write an essay, utilizing the method of analogy, in which you discuss the uses of the blues, of rock and roll, of disco music, or of patriotic music as a statement about people and society.

VIRGIL THOMSON

Taste in Music

Virgil Garnett Thomson (1896–   ), the dean of American composers and music critics, graduated from Harvard University in 1923 and studied in Paris. From 1940 to 1954, Thomas was music critic for *The New York Herald Tribune*. His musical compositions include the operas *Four Saints in Three Acts* (1928) and *The Mother of Us All* (1947), for which Gertrude Stein wrote the librettos; and the scores for the documentary films *The River* (1937), *The Plough That Broke the Plains* (1936), and *Louisiana Story* (1948). In this essay, Thomson investigates the nature of taste in music and the manner in which it can be cultivated.

A taste *for* music, a taste for anything, is an ability to 1 consume it with pleasure. Taste *in* music is preferential consumption, a greater liking for certain kinds of it than for others. A broad taste in music involves the ability to consume with pleasure many kinds of it.

(2) Vast numbers of persons, many of them highly intelligent, 2 derive no pleasure at all from organized sound. An even larger number can take it or leave it alone. They find it agreeable for the most part, stimulating to the sentiments and occasionally interesting to the mind. But music is not for them a passional experience, a transport, an auditory universe. Everybody, however, has some kind of taste *in* music, even persons with little or no taste *for* it. No subject,

save perhaps the theory of money, is disputed about so constantly in contemporary life as the divers styles of musical expression, both popular and erudite, their nature and likability.

(3)There are often striking contradictions between what musi- 3 cal people admire and what they like. Admiration, being a judgment, is submissive to reason. But liking is an inspiration, a datum exigent, unreasonable, and impossible by any act of the will to alter. It will frequently alter itself, however, without warning. And loyalty to things we once loved dearly brings tension into everybody's taste. Persons whose musical experience is limited may, indeed, be more loyal to old likings than persons who deal with music all the time. The latter tend to reject and to accept with vehemence; they are choosy. And their choosiness is quite independent of their judgment; it is personal and profoundly capricious. They can switch from Beethoven to boogie-woogie, from Bach to barbershop, with a facility that is possible only to those who take all music for their clothes closet. For practical living, man needs to be free in his thought and responsible in his actions. But in dealing with art, responsibility of thought, which makes for flexibility of taste, constitute the mechanics of vigor.

(4) The development of taste is not a major objective in 4 musical education. What the young need is understanding, that whole paraphernalia of analysis and synthesis whereby a piece is broken up into its component details, mastered, restored to integrity, and possessed. Musical understanding depends not so much on the number of works one has learned in this fashion, provided examples from several schools have been included, as on the completeness with which the procedure has been carried out. Any student can be convinced by study that Mozart is a more accomplished workman than Grieg or Rachmaninoff. If he still likes Grieg and Rachmaninoff better, that is his privilege. Maturity is certain to alter, whatever they may be, his youthful predilections.

(5) Persons unprepared by training to roam the world of 5 music in freedom but who enjoy music and wish to increase that enjoyment are constantly searching for a key, a passport that will hasten their progress. There is none, really, except study. And how far it is profitable to spend time cultivating talent where there is no vocation every man must decide for himself. But if there is any door opener to taste it is knowledge. One cannot know whether one likes, can use, a work unless one has some method beyond mere instinct for tasting it. The only known ways to taste a piece of music are to read it in score or to follow it in performance. And it is quite impossible to follow unfamiliar kinds of music without an analytical method, a set of aids to memory that enables one to discern the pattern of what is taking place.

(6) But an ability to hear is not the whole of musical reception. 6

A vote seems to be required, a yes or no as to whether one desires for the present, further acquaintance. Now, the enjoyment of old musical acquaintance is such a pleasant thing for all and so quite sufficiently absorbing for the unskilled that nearly everybody leans toward a timid conservatism with regard to unfamiliar music. The too old, the too new, the in-any-way strange we resist simply because we do not know how to take them on. The lay public will try anything; but it will be disappointed, on first hearing, in anything it has no method for remembering. We like the idea of being musically progressive, because progress is one of our national ideals; but we do not always know how to conduct a progress.

(7) Well, the way of that is long. It is nothing less, if one wishes to take part in America's musical growing-up, than learning to hear music correctly and learning to know one's mind. Persons who cannot follow music at all do well to admit the fact and let music alone. Persons who really hear it, whom *it* will not let alone, usually improve themselves by one means and another in their ability to hear patterns in sound; and with more and more music thus rendered available to them, they can choose at any moment their personal allegiances with a modicum of liberty. The tolerant but untrained, however, will always be a bit uncertain in their tastes. They will never know, for instance, whether they are entitled to vote publically or not. They will consequently assume the privilege more proudly, more dogmatically, and more irresponsibly than musicians themselves are likely to do. And they will rarely know the difference between their tastes and their opinions.

(8) It is the ignorantly formed and categorically expressed opinions of the amateur, in fact, that make the music world companionable. Professional musicians express, for the most part, responsible opinions; and these show a surprising tendency to approach, within twenty-five years, unanimity. There is not much difference of opinion any more, for instance, about either the nature or the value of Debussy's music, or of Puccini's, or of what Stravinsky wrote before 1914. But musicians' personal likings are eclectic; they imply no agreement of any kind. It is laymen who like to like together. Musicians' opinions influence nothing; they simply recognize, with a certain delay but correctly, the history of music. Lay opinion influences everything—even, at times, creation. And at all times it is the pronouncements of persons who know something about music but not much, and a bit more about what they like but still not too much, that end by creating those modes or fashions in consumption that make up the history of taste.

(9) There is no doubt that lay opinion is in large part organized and directed by knowledgeable persons—by critics, college instructors, conductors, publishers' employees, and leaders of fash-

VIRGIL THOMSON

ion. It is nevertheless not wholly under their control. The leaders of taste can no more create deliberately a mode in music than advertising campaigns can make popular a product that the public doesn't want. They can only manipulate a trend. And trends follow folk patterns. Nobody connected with a trend in music—whether composer, executant, manager, critic, consumer, or even resister—is a free agent with regard to it. That is why unsuccessful or unfashionable music, music that seems to ignore what the rest of world is listening to, is sometimes the best music, the freest, the most original—though there is no rule about that either.

(10) And so, thus caught up on the wheel of fatality, how can anybody really know anything about music, beyond its immediate practice or perception, least of all what he likes? Learning is a precious thing and knowing one's mind is even more so. But let none of us who think we belong to music fancy too highly our opinions about it, since in twenty-five years most of these will have either gone down the drain or become every man's private conviction. And please let none imagine, either, that his personal tastes are unique, indissoluble, and free. Those who think themselves most individual in their likings are most easily trapped by the appeal of chic, since chic is no more than the ability to accept trends in fashion with grace, to vary them ever so slightly, to follow a movement under the sincere illusion that one is being oneself. And those who imagine themselves most independent as judges make up the most predictable public in the world, that known to managements as the university trade, since intellectuals will always pay for the privilege of exercising their intellectual powers. Rarities of any kind, ancient or modern, are merely stones to whet their minds against. You can always sell to the world of learning acquaintance with that which it does not know.

(11) In the long run, such freedom as anybody has is the reward of labor, much study, and inveterate wariness. And the pleasures of taste, at best, are transitory, since nobody, professional or layman, can be sure that what he finds beautiful this year may not be just another piece of music to him next. The best any of us can do about any piece, short of memorizing its actual sounds and storing it away intact against lean musical moments, is to consult his appetite about its immediate consumption, his appetite and his digestive experience. And after consumption to argue about the thing interminably with all his friends. *De gustibus disputandum est.*

QUESTIONS

1. Explain the author's distinction between taste for music and taste in music. How is a sound appreciation of music best developed? Why does

Thomson say that "The development of taste is not a major objective in musical education" (paragraph 4)?

2. What is the importance of "lay opinion"?

3. Is the author interested in the denotative or connotative meaning of the term "taste"? Explain.

4. Explain the significance of the author's last sentence and the wordplay involved.

5. What is the thesis of Thomson's essay?

6. How would you explain the tone achieved by the author in the introductory paragraph? In the essay as a whole?

7. In what sense does the essay involve process analysis? Definition of terms? Explanation of causes and effects?

8. Analyze Thomson's development of paragraphs from his topic sentences, and transitions from paragraph to paragraph.

9. Discuss this comment in paragraph 11: ". . . the pleasures of taste, at best, are transitory, since nobody, professional or layman, can be sure that what he finds beautiful this year may not be just another piece of music to him the next."

10. a. Write an essay on your taste in music.
b. Write an essay on how to acquire taste in music.

Philosophy, Ethics, and Religious Thought

ROBERT COLES

I Listen to My Parents and I Wonder What They Believe

Robert Coles (1929–   ), author and psychologist, won the Pulitzer Prize for his multivolume work, *Children of Crisis*, in which he examines with compassion and intelligence the effects of the controversy over integration on children in the South. Walker Percy has praised Coles because he "spends his time listening to people and trying to understand them." In its final form, *Children of Crisis* has five volumes, and Coles has widened its focus to include the children of the wealthy and poor, the exploited and the exploiters. In collaboration with Jane Coles, he recently completed *Women of Crisis II* (1980). Below, Coles demonstrates his capacity to listen to and to understand children.

ot so long ago children were looked upon in a sentimental fashion as "angels" or as "innocents." Today, thanks to Freud and his followers, boys and girls are understood to have complicated inner lives; to feel love, hate,   1 envy and rivalry in various and subtle mixtures; to be eager participants in the sexual and emotional politics of the home, neighborhood and school. Yet some of us parents still cling to the notion of childhood innocence in another way. We do not see that our children also make ethical decisions every day in their own lives, or realize how attuned they may be to moral currents and issues in the larger society.

2   In Appalachia I heard a girl of eight whose father owns coal fields (and gas stations, a department store and much timberland) wonder about "life" one day: "I'll be walking to the school bus, and I'll ask myself why there's some who are poor and their daddies can't find a job, and there's some who are lucky like me. Last month there was an explosion in a mine my daddy owns, and everyone became upset. Two miners got killed. My daddy said it was their own fault, because they'll be working and they get careless. When my mother asked if there was anything wrong with the safety down in the mine, he told her no and she shouldn't ask questions like that. Then the Government people came and they said it was the owner's fault—Daddy's. But he has a lawyer and the lawyer is fighting the Government and the union. In school, kids ask me what I think, and I sure do feel sorry for the two miners and so does my mother—I know that. She told me it's just not a fair world and you have to remember that. Of course, there's no one who can be sure there won't be trouble; like my daddy says, the rain falls on the just and the unjust. My brother is only six and he asked Daddy awhile back who are the 'just' and the 'unjust,' and Daddy said there are people who work hard and they live good lives, and there are lazy people and they're always trying to sponge off others. But I guess you have to feel sorry for anyone who has a lot of trouble, because it's poured-down, heavy rain."

3   Listening, one begins to realize that an elementary-school child is no stranger to moral reflection—and to ethical conflict. This girl was torn between her loyalty to her particular background, its values and assumptions, and to a larger affiliation—her membership in the nation, the world. As a human being whose parents were kind and decent to her, she was inclined to be thoughtful and sensitive with respect to others, no matter what their work or position in society. But her father was among other things a mineowner, and she had already learned to shape her concerns to suit that fact of life. The result: a moral oscillation of sorts, first toward nameless others all over the world and then toward her own family. As the girl put it later, when she was a year older: "You should try to have 'good thoughts' about everyone, the minister says, and our teacher says that too. But you should honor your father and mother most of all; that's why you should find out what they think and then sort of copy them. But sometimes you're not sure if you're on the right track."

Sort of copy them. There could be worse descriptions of how children acquire moral values. In fact, the girl understood how girls and boys all over the world "sort of" develop attitudes of what is right and wrong, ideas of who the just and the unjust are. And they also struggle hard and long, and not always with success, to find out where the "right track" starts and ends. Children need encouragement or assistance as they wage that struggle.

In home after home that I have visited, and in many classrooms, I have met children who not only are growing emotionally and intellectually but also are trying to make sense of the world morally. That is to say, they are asking themselves and others about issues of fair play, justice, liberty, equality. Those last words are abstractions, of course—the stuff of college term papers. And there are, one has to repeat, those in psychology and psychiatry who would deny elementary-school children access to that "higher level" of moral reflection. But any parent who has listened closely to his or her child knows that girls and boys are capable of wondering about matters of morality, and knows too that often it is their grown-up protectors (parents, relatives, teachers, neighbors) who are made uncomfortable by the so-called "innocent" nature of the questions children may ask or the statements they may make. Often enough the issue is not the moral capacity of children but the default of us parents who fail to respond to inquiries put to us by our daughters and sons—and fail to set moral standards for both ourselves and our children.

Do's and don't's are, of course, pressed upon many of our girls and boys. But a moral education is something more than a series of rules handed down, and in our time one cannot assume that every parent feels able—sure enough of her own or his own actual beliefs and values—to make even an initial explanatory and disciplinary effort toward a moral education. Furthermore, for many of us parents these days it is a child's emotional life that preoccupies us.

In 1963, when I was studying school desegregation in the South, I had extended conversations with Black and white elementary-school children caught up in a dramatic moment of historical change. For longer than I care to remember, I concentrated on possible psychiatric troubles, on how a given child was managing under circumstances of extreme stress, on how I could be of help— with "support," with reassurance, with a helpful psychological observation or interpretation. In many instances I was off the mark. These children weren't "patients"; they weren't even complaining. They were worried, all right, and often enough they had things to say that were substantive—that had to do not so much with troubled emotions as with questions of right and wrong in the real-life dramas taking place in their worlds.

Here is a nine-year-old white boy, the son of ardent segrega- 8
tionists, telling me about his sense of what desegregation meant to
Louisiana in the 1960s: "They told us it wouldn't happen—never. My
daddy said none of us white people would go into schools with the
colored. But then it did happen, and when I went to school the first
day I didn't know what would go on. Would the school stay open or
would it close up? We didn't know what to do; the teacher kept telling
us that we should be good and obey the law, but my daddy said the
law was wrong. Then my mother said she wanted me in school even
if there were some colored kids there. She said if we all stayed home
she'd be a 'nervous wreck.' So I went.

"After a while I saw that the colored weren't so bad. I saw 9
that there are different kinds of colored people, just like with us
whites. There was one of the colored who was nice, a boy who
smiled, and he played real good. There was another one, a boy, who
wouldn't talk with anyone. I don't know if it's right that we all be in
the same school. Maybe it isn't right. My sister is starting school next
year, and she says she doesn't care if there's 'mixing of the races.' She
says they told her in Sunday school that everyone is a child of God,
and then a kid asked if that goes for the colored too and the teacher
said yes, she thought so. My daddy said that it's true, God made
everyone—but that doesn't mean we all have to be living together
under the same roof in the home or the school. But my mother said
we'll never know what God wants of us but we have to try to read His
mind, and that's why we pray. So when I say my prayers I ask God to
tell me what's the right thing to do. In school I try to say hello to the
colored, because they're kids, and you can't be mean or you'll be
'doing wrong,' like my grandmother says."

Children aren't usually long-winded in the moral discussions 10
they have with one another or with adults, and in quoting this boy I
have pulled together comments he made to me in the course of
several days. But everything he said was of interest to me. I was
interested in the boy's changing racial attitudes. It was clear he was
trying to find a coherent, sensible moral position too. It was also
borne in on me that if one spends days, weeks in a given home, it is
hard to escape a particular moral climate just as significant as the
psychological one.

In many homes parents establish moral assumptions, man- 11
dates, priorities. They teach children what to believe in, what not to
believe in. They teach children what is permissible or not permissible—and why. They may summon up the Bible, the flag, history,
novels, aphorisms, philosophical or political sayings, personal
memories—all in an effort to teach children how to behave, what and
whom to respect and for which reasons. Or they may neglect to do
so, and in so doing teach their children *that*—a moral abdication, of

sorts—and in this way fail their children. Children need and long for words of moral advice, instruction, warning, as much as they need words of affirmation or criticism from their parents about other matters. They must learn how to dress and what to wear, how to eat and what to eat; and they must also learn how to behave under X or Y or Z conditions, and why.

All the time, in 20 years of working with poor children and rich children, Black children and white children, children from rural areas and urban areas and in every region of this country, I have heard questions—thoroughly intelligent and discerning questions—about social and historical matters, about personal behavior, and so on. But most striking is the fact that almost all those questions, in one way or another, are moral in nature: Why did the Pilgrims leave England? Why didn't they just stay and agree to do what the king wanted them to do? . . . Should you try to share all you've got or should you save a lot for yourself? . . . What do you do when you see others fighting—do you try to break up the fight, do you stand by and watch or do you leave as fast as you can? . . . Is it right that some people haven't got enough to eat? . . . I see other kids cheating and I wish I could copy the answers too; but I won't cheat, though sometimes I feel I'd like to and I get all mixed up. I go home and talk with my parents, and I ask them what should you do if you see kids cheating—pay no attention, or report the kids or do the same thing they are doing? 12

Those are examples of children's concerns—and surely millions of American parents have heard versions of them. Have the various "experts" on childhood stressed strongly enough the importance of such questions—and the importance of the hunger we all have, no matter what our age or background, to examine what we believe in, are willing to stand up for, and what we are determined to ask, likewise, of our children? 13

Children not only need our understanding of their complicated emotional lives; they also need a constant regard for the moral issues that come their way as soon as they are old enough to play with others and take part in the politics of the nursery, the back yard and the schoolroom. They need to be told what they must do and what they must not do. They need control over themselves and a sense of what others are entitled to from them—co-operation, thoughtfulness, an attentive ear and eye. They need discipline not only to tame their excesses of emotion but discipline also connected to stated and clarified moral values. They need, in other words, something to believe in that is larger than their own appetites and urges and, yes, bigger than their "psychological drives." They need a larger view of the world, a moral context, as it were—a faith that addresses itself to the meaning of this life we all live and, soon enough, let go of. 14

Yes, it is time for us parents to begin to look more closely at what ideas our children have about the world; and it would be well to do so before they become teen-agers and young adults and begin to remind us, as often happens, of how little attention we did pay to their moral development. Perhaps a nine-year-old girl from a well-off suburban home in Texas put it better than anyone else I've met:

"I listen to my parents, and I wonder what they believe in more than anything else. I asked my mom and my daddy once: What's the thing that means most to you? They said they didn't know but I shouldn't worry my head too hard with questions like that. So I asked my best friend, and she said she wonders if there's a God and how do you know Him and what does He want you to do—I mean, when you're in school or out playing with your friends. They talk about God in church, but is it only in church that He's there and keeping an eye on you? I saw a kid steal in a store, and I know her father has a lot of money—because I hear my daddy talk. But stealing's wrong. My mother said she's a 'sick girl,' but it's still wrong what she did. Don't you think?"

There was more—much more—in the course of the months I came to know that child and her parents and their neighbors. But those observations and questions—a "mere child's"—reminded me unforgettably of the aching hunger for firm ethical principles that so many of us feel. Ought we not begin thinking about this need? Ought we not all be asking ourselves more intently what standards we live by—and how we can satisfy our children's hunger for moral values?

QUESTIONS

1. According to Coles, why do parents have difficulty explaining ethics to their children? On what aspects of their children's development to they tend to concentrate? Why?

2. There is an implied contrast between mothers' and fathers' attitudes toward morality in Coles's essay. Explain this contrast and cite examples for your explanation.

3. What point of view does Coles use here? How does that viewpoint affect the tone of the essay?

4. Compare Coles's sentence structure with the sentence structure of the children he quotes. How do they differ?

5. Does this essay present an inductive or deductive argument? Give evidence for your answer.

ROBERT COLES

6. How does paragraph 13 differ from paragraphs 3, 10, and 17? How do all four paragraphs contribute to the development of the essay?

7. Explain the line of reasoning in the first paragraph. Why does Coles allude to Freud? How is that allusion related to the final sentence of the paragraph?

8. What paragraphs constitute the conclusion of the essay? Why? How do they summarize Coles's argument?

9. Coles asserts the need for clear ethical values. Do you feel your parents provided such values? What kind of values will you give your children?

10. a. Write an essay describing conflict between your parents' ethical views and your own.
b. Gather evidence, based upon conversations, from your friends and relatives about an ethical issue such as poverty, world starvation, abortion, or capital punishment. Incorporate their opinions through direct and indirect quotation into your essay.

We Should Seek Our Own Pleasure

Epicurus (341–270 B.C.), Greek philosopher, was a contemporary of Aristotle and is best known for asserting that pleasure is the highest good toward which people can strive. Epicurus himself favored a reclusive, moderate life and urged people to practice prudence, justice, and honesty. Although he was a voluminous writer, only a few fragments of his works have survived. One of the more extensive fragments appears below.

Let no one when young delay to study philosophy, nor when he is old grow weary of his study. For no one can come too early or too late to secure the health of his soul. And the man who says that the age for philosophy has either not yet come or has gone by is like the man who says that the age for happiness is not yet come to him, or has passed away. Wherefore both when young and old a man must study philosophy, that as he grows old he may be young in blessings through the grateful recollection of what has been, and that in youth he may be old as well, since he will know no fear of what is to come. We must then meditate on the things that make our happiness, seeing that when that is with us we have all, but when it is absent we do all to win it.

The things which I used unceasingly to commend to you, 2 these do and practise, considering them to be the first principles of the good life. First of all believe that god is a being immortal and blessed, even as the common idea of a god is engraved on men's minds, and do not assign to him anything alien to his immortality or ill-suited to his blessedness: but believe about him everything that can uphold his blessedness and immortality. For gods there are, since the knowledge of them is by clear vision. But they are not such as the many believe them to be: for indeed they do not consistently represent them as they believe them to be. And the impious man is not he who denies the gods of the many, but he who attaches to the gods the beliefs of the many. For the statements of the many about the gods are not conceptions derived from sensation, but false suppositions, according to which the greatest misfortunes befall the wicked and the greatest blessings the good by the gift of the gods. For men being accustomed always to their own virtues welcome those like themselves, but regard all that is not of their nature as alien.

Become accustomed to the belief that death is nothing to us. 3 For all good and evil consists in sensation, but death is deprivation of sensation. And therefore a right understanding that death is nothing to us makes the mortality of life enjoyable, not because it adds to it an infinite span of time, but because it takes away the craving for immortality. For there is nothing terrible in life for the man who has truly comprehended that there is nothing terrible in not living. So that the man speaks but idly who says that he fears death not because it will be painful when it comes, but because it is painful in anticipation. For that which gives no trouble when it comes, is but an empty pain in anticipation. So death, the most terrifying of ills, is nothing to us, since so long as we exist death is not with us; but when death comes, then we do not exist. It does not then concern either the living or the dead, since for the former it is not, and the latter are no more.

But the many at one moment shun death as the greatest of 4 evils, at another yearn for it as a respite from the evils in life. But the wise man neither seeks to escape life nor fears the cessation of life, for neither does life offend him nor does the absence of life seem to be any evil. And just as with food he does not seek simply the larger share and nothing else, but rather the most pleasant, so he seeks to enjoy not the longest period of time, but the most pleasant.

And he who counsels the young man to live well, but the old 5 man to make a good end, is foolish, not merely because of the desirability of life, but also because it is the same training which teaches to live well and to die well. Yet much worse still is the man who says it is good not to be born, but

> once born make haste to pass the gates of Death. (Theognis, 427)

For if he says this from conviction why does he not pass away out of life? For it is open to him to do so, if he had firmly made up his mind to this. But if he speaks in jest, his words are idle among men who cannot receive them.

We must then bear in mind that the future is neither ours, nor 6 yet wholly not ours, so that we may not altogether expect it as sure to come, nor abandon hope of it, as if it will certainly not come.

We must consider that of desires some are natural, others 7 vain, and of the natural some are necessary and others merely natural; and of the necessary some are necessary for happiness, others for the repose of the body, and others for very life. The right understanding of these facts enables us to refer all choice and avoidance to the health of the body and the soul's freedom from disturbance, since this is the aim of the life of blessedness. For it is to obtain this end that we always act, namely, to avoid pain and fear. And when this is once secured for us, all the tempest of the soul is dispersed, since the living creature has not to wander as though in search of something that is missing, and to look for some other thing by which he can fulfil the good of the soul and the good of the body. For it is then that we have need of pleasure, when we feel pain owing to the absence of pleasure; but when we do not feel pain, we no longer need pleasure. And for this cause we call pleasure the beginning and end of the blessed life. For we recognize pleasure as the first good innate in us, and from pleasure we begin every act of choice and avoidance, and to pleasure we return again, using the feeling as the standard by which we judge every good.

And since pleasure is the first good and natural to us, for this 8 very reason we do not choose every pleasure, but sometimes we pass over many pleasures, when greater discomfort accrues to us as the result of them: and similarly we think many pains better than pleasures, since a greater pleasure comes to us when we have endured pains for a long time. Every pleasure then because of its natural kinship to us is good, yet not every pleasure is to be chosen:

even as every pain also is an evil, yet not all are always of a nature to be avoided. Yet by a scale of comparison and by the consideration of advantages and disadvantages we must form our judgment on all these matters. For the good on certain occasions we treat as bad, and conversely the bad as good.

And again independence of desire we think a great good— 9 not that we may at all times enjoy but a few things, but that, if we do not possess many, we may enjoy the few in the genuine persuasion that those have the sweetest pleasure in luxury who least need it, and that all that is natural is easy to be obtained, but that which is superfluous is hard. And so plain savours bring us a pleasure equal to a luxurious diet, when all the pain due to want is removed; and bread and water produce the highest pleasure, when one who needs them puts them to his lips. To grow accustomed therefore to simple and not luxurious diet gives us health to the full, and makes a man alert for the needful employments of life, and when after long intervals we approach luxuries, disposes us better towards them, and fits us to be fearless of fortune.

When, therefore, we maintain that pleasure is the end, we do 10 not mean the pleasures of profligates and those that consist in sensuality, as is supposed by some who are either ignorant or disagree with us or do not understand, but freedom from pain in the body and from trouble in the mind. For it is not continuous drinkings and revellings, nor the satisfaction of lusts, nor the enjoyment of fish and other luxuries of the wealthy table, which produce a pleasant life, but sober reasoning, searching out the motives for all choice and avoidance, and banishing mere opinions, to which are due the greatest disturbance of the spirit.

Of all this the beginning and the greatest good is prudence. 11 Wherefore prudence is a more precious thing even than philosophy: for from prudence are sprung all the other virtues, and it teaches us that it is not possible to live pleasantly without living prudently and honourably and justly, nor again, to live a life of prudence, honour, and justice without living pleasantly. For the virtues are by nature bound up with the pleasant life, and the pleasant life is inseparable from them. For indeed who, think you, is a better man than he who holds reverent opinions concerning the gods, and is at all times free from fear of death, and has reasoned out the end ordained by nature? He understands that the limit of good things is easy to fulfil and easy to attain, whereas the course of ills is either short in time or slight in pain: he laughs at destiny, whom some have introduced as the mistress of all things. He thinks that with us lies the chief power in determining events, some of which happen by necessity and some by chance, and some are within our control; for while necessity cannot be called to account, he sees that chance is inconstant, but that which is in our control is subject to no master, and to it are naturally attached praise and blame. For, indeed, it were better to follow the myths about the gods than to become a slave to the destiny of the natural philosophers: for the former suggests a hope of placating the gods by worship, whereas the latter involves a necessity which knows no placation. As to chance, he does not regard it as a god as most men do (for in god's acts there is no disorder), nor as an uncertain cause of all things: for he does not believe that good and evil are given by chance to man for the framing of a blessed life, but that opportunities for great good and great evil are afforded by it. He therefore thinks it better to be unfortunate in reasonable action than to prosper in unreason. For it is better in a man's actions that what is well chosen should fail, rather than that what is ill chosen should be successful owing to chance.

Meditate therefore on these things and things akin to them 12 night and day by yourself, and with a companion like to yourself, and never shall you be disturbed waking or asleep, but you shall live like a god among men. For a man who lives among immortal blessings is not like to a mortal being.

QUESTIONS

1. How does Epicurus define "pain," "death," and "pleasure"? Of what kinds of pleasure does Epicurus approve?

2. Why does he believe "independence of desire" is a "great good"?

3. Examine the tone of the essay. Particularly look for evidence of a hortatory style and explain its function.

4. What are the connotations of "the many" and "the wise man"? How many people do you think Epicurus believes will profit from his advice?

5. Explain how Epicurus uses classification to order paragraph 7. Are there other examples of classification in the essay? If so, where do they appear?

6. Does Epicurus tend to use deductive or inductive reasoning? Examine particularly paragraph 3 for evidence. Are there other examples elsewhere in the essay of the kind of reasoning that appears in paragraph 3? If so, where?

7. What is the topic sentence in paragraph 11? How important is this sentence to the development of the thesis of the essay?

 WE SHOULD SEEK OUR OWN PLEASURE

8. Explain the function of paragraph 10 in the essay. What rhetorical method is Epicurus using here?

9. Do you think living according to Epicurus's advice would lead to happiness? What ways of living do you think lead to happiness?

10. a. Write a paper detailing the three major requirements of the good life for you.
b. Write a paper in which you give advice to readers on dating, education, getting along with your parents, or getting along with friends.

EDITH HAMILTON

Roots of Freedom

Edith Hamilton (1867–1963), teacher, writer, and Grecophile, wrote her first book when she was 63. Her initial career was as headmistress of a private girl's school in Maryland. When she retired, she began to write about ancient civilizations, particularly Greek civilization. In 1930, *The Greek Way* was published. In later years, Hamilton also wrote *The Roman Way* (1932) and *The Prophets of Israel* (1936). She retold Greek, Roman, and Norse myths in *Mythology* (1942). At the age of 90, Hamilton visited Greece and was made an honorary citizen. The following essay makes clear why she admired Greek civilization.

Freedom's challenge in the Atomic Age is a sobering 1
topic. We are facing today a strange new world and we are all wondering what we are going to do with it. What are we going to do with one of our most precious possessions, freedom? The world we know, our Western world, began with something as new as the conquest of space.

Some 2,500 years ago Greece discovered freedom. Before that 2
there was no freedom. There were great civilizations, splendid empires, but no freedom anywhere. Egypt, Babylon, Nineveh, were all tyrannies, one immensely powerful man ruling over helpless masses. In Greece, in Athens, a little city in a little country, there were no helpless masses, and a time came when the Athenians were led by a great man who did not want to be powerful. Absolute

obedience to the ruler was what the leaders of the empires insisted on. Athens said no, there must never be absolute obedience to a man except in war. There must be willing obedience to what is good for all. Pericles, the great Athenian statesman, said: "We are a free government, but we obey the laws, more especially those which protect the oppressed, and the unwritten laws which, if broken, bring shame."

Athenians willingly obeyed the written laws which they themselves passed, and the unwritten, which must be obeyed if free men live together. They must show each other kindness and pity and the many qualities without which life would be intolerable except to a hermit in the desert. The Athenians never thought that a man was free if he could do what he wanted. A man was free if he was self-controlled. To make yourself obey what you approved was freedom. They were saved from looking at their lives as their own private affair. Each one felt responsible for the welfare of Athens, not because it was imposed on him from the outside, but because the city was his pride and his safety. The creed of the first free government in the world was liberty for all men who could control themselves and would take responsibility for the state. This was the conception that underlay the lofty reach of Greek genius. 3

But discovering freedom is not like discovering atomic bombs. It cannot be discovered once for all. If people do not prize it, and work for it, it will depart. Eternal vigilance is its price. Athens changed. It was a change that took place unnoticed though it was of the utmost importance, a spiritual change which penetrated the whole state. It had been the Athenians' pride and joy to give to their city. That they could get material benefits from her never entered their minds. There had to be a complete change of attitude before they could look at the city as an employer who paid her citizens for doing her work. Now instead of men giving to the state, the state was to give to them. What the people wanted was a government which would provide a comfortable life for them; and with this as the foremost object, ideas of freedom and self-reliance and responsibility were obscured to the point of disappearing. Athens was more and more looked on as a cooperative business possessed of great wealth in which all citizens had a right to share. 4

She reached the point when the freedom she really wanted was freedom from responsibility. There could be only one result. If men insisted on being free from the burden of self-dependence and responsibility for the common good, they would cease to be free. Responsibility is the price every man must pay for freedom. It is to be had on no other terms. Athens, the Athens of Ancient Greece, refused responsibility; she reached the end of freedom and was never to have it again. 5

But, "the excellent becomes the permanent," Aristotle said.   6
Athens lost freedom forever, but freedom was not lost forever for the
world. A great American statesman, James Madison, in or near the
year 1776 A.D. referred to: "The capacity of mankind for self-
government." No doubt he had not an idea that he was speaking
Greek. Athens was not in the farthest background of his mind, but
once a great and good idea has dawned upon man, it is never
completely lost. The Atomic Age cannot destroy it. Somehow in this
or that man's thought such an idea lives though unconsidered by the
world of action. One can never be sure that it is not on the point of
breaking out into action only sure that it will do so sometime.

QUESTIONS

1. What were the Greeks' conceptions of freedom? Why, according to Hamilton, did they lose their freedom?

2. What similarities does Hamilton see between Athens and America?

3. Explain the allusions to Pericles in paragraph 2 and James Madison in paragraph 6.

4. Is Hamilton's tone hopeful or pessimistic? What evidence can you give to support your opinion?

5. Narrative is an important rhetorical device in this essay. How is chronology developed in this essay? What transition words are used to mark the progress of the narrative? What paragraphs contain elements of narrative?

6. Where does Hamilton make explicit her comparison between America and Athens? Why does she defer this idea until so late in her essay? What evidence can you find that she intends us to note this comparison before this point?

7. In paragraph 5 how much of the paragraph is narrative? What other rhetorical methods appear here?

8. What is the purpose of paragraph 1? How do paragraphs 1 and 6 frame the essay?

9. Do you think our present ideas of freedom and country are similar to those of the early or the late Greeks? What can we do to maintain or improve the situation?

10. Narrate a personal experience that can illustrate an abstraction such as freedom—for example, tyranny, honesty, or ambition.

The Allegory of the Cave

Plato (427?–347 B.C.), pupil and friend of Socrates, was one of the greatest philosophers of the ancient world. Plato's surviving works are all dialogues, many of them purporting to be conversations of Socrates and his disciples. Two key aspects of his philosophy are the dialectical method, represented by the questioning, probing of the particular event to reveal the general truth; and the existence of Forms. Plato's best-known works include *Phaedo, Symposium, Phaedrus,* and *Timaeus.* The following selection, from *The Republic,* is an early description of the nature of Forms.

A nd now, I said, let me show in a figure how far our   1
nature is enlightened or unenlightened: Behold! human beings living in an underground den, which has a mouth open towards the light and reaching all along the den; here they have been from their childhood, and have their legs and necks chained so that they cannot move, and can only see before them, being prevented by the chains from turning round their heads. Above and behind them a fire is blazing at a distance, and between the fire and the prisoners there is a raised way; and you will see, if you look, a low wall built along the way, like the screen which marionette players have in front of them, over which they show the puppets.

I see.   2

And do you see, I said, men passing along the wall carrying   3
all sorts of vessels, and statues and figures of animals made of wood and stone and various materials, which appear over the wall? Some of them are talking, others silent.

You have shown me a strange image, and they are strange   4
prisoners.

Like ourselves, I replied; and they see only their own shad-   5
ows, or the shadows of one another, which the fire throws on the opposite wall of the cave?

True, he said; how could they see anything but the shadows if   6
they were never allowed to move their heads?

And of the objects which are being carried in like manner   7
they would only see the shadows?

Yes, he said.   8

And if they were able to converse with one another, would   9 they not suppose that they were naming what was actually before them?

Very true. 10

And suppose further that the prison had an echo which came 11 from the other side, would they not be sure to fancy when one of the passers-by spoke that the voice which they heard came from the passing shadow?

No question, he replied. 12

To them, I said, the truth would be literally nothing but the 13 shadows of the images.

That is certain. 14

And now look again, and see what will naturally follow if the 15 prisoners are released and disabused of their error. At first, when any of them is liberated and compelled suddenly to stand up and turn his neck round and walk and look towards the light, he will suffer sharp pains; the glare will distress him and he will be unable to see the realities of which in his former state he had seen the shadows; and then conceive some one saying to him, that what he saw before was an illusion, but that now, when he is approaching nearer to being and his eye is turned towards more real existence, he has a clearer vision—what will be his reply? And you may further imagine that his instructor is pointing to the objects as they pass and requiring him to name them—will he not be perplexed? Will he not fancy that the shadows which he formerly saw are truer than the objects which are now shown to him?

Far truer. 16

And if he is compelled to look straight at the light, will he not 17 have a pain in his eyes which will make him turn away to take refuge in the objects of vision which he can see, and which he will conceive to be in reality clearer than the things which are now being shown to him?

True, he said. 18

And suppose once more, that he is reluctantly dragged up a 19 steep and rugged ascent, and held fast until he is forced into the presence of the sun himself, is he not likely to be pained and irritated? When he approaches the light his eyes will be dazzled and he will not be able to see anything at all of what are now called realities.

Not all in a moment, he said. 20

He will require to grow accustomed to the sight of the upper 21 world. And first he will see the shadows best, next the reflections of men and other objects in the water, and then the objects themselves; then he will gaze upon the light of the moon and the stars and the spangled heaven; and he will see the sky and the stars by night better than the sun or the light of the sun by day?

Certainly. 22

Last of all he will be able to see the sun, and not mere reflections of him in the water, but he will see him in his own proper place, and not in another; and he will contemplate him as he is.   23

Certainly.   24

He will then proceed to argue that this is he who gives the season and the years, and is the guardian of all that is in the visible world, and in a certain way the cause of all things which he and his fellows have been accustomed to behold?   25

Clearly, he said, he would first see the sun and then reason about him.   26

And when he remembered his old habitation, and the wisdom of the den and his fellow-prisoners, do you not suppose that he would felicitate himself on the change, and pity them?   27

Certainly, he would.   28

And if they were in the habit of conferring honors among themselves on those who were quickest to observe the passing shadows and to remark which of them went before, and which followed after, and which were together; and who were therefore best able to draw conclusions as to the future, do you think that he would care for such honors and glories, or envy the possessors of them? Would he not say with Homer,   29

Better to be the poor servant of a poor master,

and to endure anything, rather than think as they do and live after their manner?

Yes, he said, I think that he would rather suffer anything than entertain these false notions and live in this miserable manner.   30

Imagine once more, I said, such an one coming suddenly out of the sun to be replaced in his old situation; would he not be certain to have his eyes full of darkness?   31

To be sure, he said.   32

And if there were a contest, and he had to compete in measuring the shadows with the prisoners who had never moved out of the den, while his sight was still weak, and before his eyes had become steady (and the time which would be needed to acquire this new habit of sight might be very considerable) would he not be ridiculous? Men would say of him that up he went and down he came without his eyes; and that it was better not even to think of ascending; and if any one tried to loose another and lead him up to the light, let them only catch the offender, and they would put him to death.   33

No question, he said.   34

This entire allegory, I said, you may now append, dear Glaucon, to the previous argument; the prison-house is the world of   35 sight, the light of fire is the sun, and you will not misapprehend me if you interpret the journey upwards to be the ascent of the soul into the intellectual world according to my poor belief, which, at your desire, I have expressed—whether rightly or wrongly God knows. But, whether true or false, my opinion is that in the world of knowledge the idea of good appears last of all, and is seen only with an effort; and, when seen, is also inferred to be the universal author of all things beautiful and right, parent of light and of the lord of light in this visible world, and the immediate source of reason and truth in the intellectual; and that this is the power upon which he who would act rationally either in public or private life must have his eye fixed.

I agree, he said, as far as I am able to understand you.   36

Moreover, I said, you must not wonder that those who attain   37
to this beatific vision are unwilling to descend to human affairs; for their souls are ever hastening into the upper world where they desire to dwell; which desire of theirs is very natural, if our allegory may be trusted.

Yes, very natural.   38

And is there anything surprising in one who passes from   39
divine contemplations to the evil state of man, misbehaving himself in a ridiculous manner; if, while his eyes are blinking and before he has become accustomed to the surrounding darkness, he is com- pelled to fight in courts of law, or in other places, about the images or the shadows of images of justice, and is endeavouring to meet the conceptions of those who have never yet seen absolute justice?

Anything but surprising, he replied.   40

Any one who has common sense will remember that the   41
bewilderments of the eyes are of two kinds, and arise from two causes, either from coming out of the light or from going into the light, which is true of the mind's eye, quite as much as of the bodily eye; and he who remembers this when he sees any one whose vision is perplexed and weak, will not be too ready to laugh; he will first ask whether that soul of man has come out of the brighter life, and is unable to see because unaccustomed to the dark, or having turned from darkness to the day is dazzled by excess of light. And he will count the one happy in his condition and state of being, and he will pity the other; or, if he have a mind to laugh at the soul which comes from below into the light, there will be more reason in this than in the laugh which greets him who returns from above out of the light into the den.

That, he said, is a very just distinction.   42

QUESTIONS

1. According to Plato, do human beings typically perceive reality? To what does he compare the world?

2. According to Plato, what often happens to people who develop a true idea of reality? How well do they compete with others? Who is usually considered superior? Why?

3. Is the conversation portrayed here realistic? How effective is this conversational style at conveying information?

4. How do you interpret such details of this allegory as the chains, the cave, and the fire? What connotations do such symbols have?

5. How does Plato use conversation to develop his argument? What is Glaucon's role in the conversation?

6. Note examples of transition words that mark contrasts between the real and the shadow world. How does Plato use contrast to develop his idea of the true real world?

7. Plato uses syllogistic reasoning to derive human behavior from his allegory. Trace his line of reasoning, noting transitional devices and the development of idea in paragraphs 5 to 14. Find and describe a similar line of reasoning.

8. In what paragraph does Plato explain his allegory? Why do you think he locates his explanation where he does?

9. Are Plato's ideas still influencing contemporary society? How do his ideas affect our evaluation of materialism, sensuality, sex, and love?

10. Write an allegory based upon a sport, business, or space flight to explain how we act in the world.

IMMANUEL KANT

The Ethical Systems of the Ancients

Immanuel Kant (1724–1804), famous German philosopher, was professor of logic and metaphysics at Konigsberg. Founder of "critical" or Kantian philosophy, Kant set out to examine the origin, extent, and limits of human knowledge. In *Critique of Pure Reason* (1781) and *Critique of Practical Reason* (1788), he moves from a dogmatic assertion of the primacy of the sensory world to a belief in the immortality of the soul and the existence of God. In this essay from his lectures on ethics, Kant provides an overview of the beliefs of the ancients, while at the same time asserting a truer system of ethical belief.

he ethical systems of the ancients are all based on the 1 question of what constitutes the *summum bonum*—the Supreme Good—and it is in their answers to this question that is to be found the difference between their various systems. We may call this *summum bonum* an idea, that is, the highest conceivable standard by which everything is to be judged and weighed. To form a judgment of anything we must first sketch a pattern by which to judge it. The *summum bonum* is scarcely possible of attainment and is only an ideal—that is, the pattern, the idea, the archetype for all our concepts of the Good.

What constitutes the Supreme Good? The supreme created 2 good is the most perfect world, that is, a world in which all rational beings are happy and are worthy of happiness.

The ancients realized that mere happiness could not be the 3 one highest good. For if all men were to obtain this happiness without distinction of just and unjust, the highest good would not be realized, because though happiness would indeed exist, worthiness of it would not.

In mankind, therefore, we have to look both for happiness 4 and for merit. The combination of the two will be the highest good. Man can hope to be happy only in so far as he makes himself worthy of being happy, for this is the condition of happiness which reason itself proposes.

They further realized that happiness sprang from man's 5 freedom of will, from his intention to make use of everything with which nature so richly endows him. Of the wealthy man we ask to what use he intends to put all those treasures which he has in plenty. Thus the nature and perfectness of the free will, in which dwells the ground of the worthiness to be happy, constitutes ethical perfection. The physical good or well-being, for which health and wealth are requisite, is not by itself the greatest good; the ethical good, right conduct, worthiness of being happy, must be added to the former, and we then have the Supreme Good. Let us imagine a world inhabited by intelligent beings, all of whom behaved well, and so deserved to be happy, but were destitute and lived in the most wretched circumstances. Such beings would have no happiness, and there would, therefore, be no Supreme Good in these conditions. If, on the other hand, all beings were happy but not well-behaved and not worthy of being happy, we should again have no Supreme Good in such circumstances.

The ancients recognized three forms of the ideal of the 6 *summum bonum*:

1. The Cynic ideal of the school of Diogenes.

2. The Epicurean ideal.

3. The Stoic ideal of the school of Zeno.

The Cynic is the ideal of innocence, or rather of simplicity. 7 Diogenes taught that the highest good is to be found in simplicity, in the sober enjoyment of happiness.

The Epicureans set up the ideal of prudence. Epicurus's 8 doctrine was that the highest good was happiness and that well-doing was but a means to happiness.

The ideal of the Stoics was that of wisdom, and is in contrast 9 with the ideal of Epicurus. Zeno taught that the highest good is to be found only in morality, in merit (and thus in well-doing), and that happiness is a consequence of morality. Whoever conducts himself well is happy.

The Cynics argued that the Supreme Good springs from 10 nature and not from art. Diogenes sought it by negative means. He argued that man is by nature satisfied with little; he has no wants by nature and therefore does not feel privation (that is, the lack of means), and so it is in conditions of privation that he finds happiness. There is much in this argument; for the more plentiful nature's gifts and the greater our store of the world's goods the greater are our wants. With growing wealth we acquire fresh wants, and the more we satisfy them the keener becomes our appetite for more. So our hearts are restless for ever. That refined Diogenes, Rousseau, holds that our will is by nature good, but that we ourselves become more and more corrupt; that nature provides us with all necessaries, but that we create wants for ourselves, and he would have children educated on negative lines. Hume disagrees with these views, and argues that the Supreme Good is a thing of art, and not of nature.

Diogenes teaches that we can be happy without abundance, 11 and moral without virtue. His philosophy is the shortest cut to happiness, for, if we are content with life, it is no hardship to do without things, and we can live happily; and it is likewise the shortest cut to morality, because if we have no wants we have no desires, and in that case our actions conform to morality. To be honest involves no sacrifice; so virtue would be merely an idea. Simplicity is thus the shortest cut to morality.

The Epicureans taught that the Supreme Good was a matter   12
of art, and not of nature, and they thus placed themselves in exact
opposition to the Cynics. It is true, said Epicurus, that we have by
nature no vices, but we nevertheless have an inclination to vice, and
innocence and simplicity cannot, therefore, be secured without the
assistance of art. Zeno was in agreement with Epicurus in thus
regarding virtue as a matter of art. If, for instance, a simple country
girl is free of the usual vices, she is so merely because she has no
opportunity of going astray; and if a peasant makes do and is quite
content with poor fare, he does not do so because it is all the same to
him whether his food is simple or sumptuous, but because it is his lot,
and if he had an opportunity of living on a higher scale he would take
it. Simplicity, therefore, is only a negative thing. For this reason
Epicurus and Zeno accepted art, although in different senses.

The Supreme Good consists of the physical good and the   13
moral good—of well-being and well-doing. Inasmuch as all philosophy strives to bring unity into knowledge and to reduce its first
principles to a minimum, attempts have been made to combine into
one these two principles of well-being and well-doing. Now, it is the
end, and not the means, which determines what we call anything. So,
according to the notion of Epicurus, happiness was the end and merit
only a means, which would make morality a consequence of happiness. Zeno also sought to unite the two principles, and according to
his notion it was morality which was the end, virtue and merit were
in themselves the Supreme Good, and happiness was merely a
consequence of morality.

For their ideal, their pattern, Diogenes took the natural man,   14
and Epicurus the man of the world. Zeno's pattern or *Idea archetypon*
is the sage. The sage is happy in himself, he possesses all things, he
has within himself the source of cheerfulness and righteousness, he
is a king because he is lord of himself and, being his own master, he
cannot be mastered. Such perfection could be attained only by
strength in overcoming obstacles, and so a sage was regarded as even
greater than the gods themselves, because a god has no temptations
to withstand and no obstacles to overcome.

We can also conceive a mystical ideal, in which the Supreme   15
Good consists in this: that man sees himself in communion with the
highest being. This is the Platonic ideal, a visionary ideal.

The Christian ideal is that of holiness, and its pattern is   16
Christ. Christ is also merely an ideal, a standard of moral perfection
which is holy by divine aid. This ideal ought not to be confused with
those who call themselves Christians. These only seek to come nearer
to their ideal pattern.

Epicurus taught that virtue had a motive, namely happiness;   17
Zeno took away the motive. Epicurus saw value in merit, but none in

virtue, while Zeno exalted the intrinsic value of virtue. Epicurus placed the Supreme Good in happiness, Zeno in virtue. Both were at fault.

Happiness, in the case of Epicurus, was synonymous with 18 pleasure, by which he meant a contented disposition and a cheerful heart; but his philosophy was not, as it has wrongly been taken to be, one of sensual pleasure. He taught that we must so act as to be safe from reproaches from ourselves and from others, and a letter has come down to us in which he invites a guest to dinner with the intimation that he has nothing better to offer than a cheerful heart and a meal of polenta, poor fare indeed for an "epicure". His was the pleasure of a sage, and while he denied worth to virtue, he made morality the means to happiness.

Zeno inverted the position. To him happiness had value, but 19 virtue no motive. Motives are springs of the will which are drawn from the senses. If a man is conscious of deserving happiness, that is not sufficient to appease his desires, and if his desires are unsatisfied he is not happy, even though he feels himself worthy. Virtue pleases uniquely but it does not satisfy; if it did, all men would be virtuous. His very virtue intensifies a man's yearning for happiness. The more virtuous and the less happy a man is, the more painful is the feeling that he is not happy, though deserving happiness. Such a man is satisfied with his conduct, but not with his condition.

Epicurus taught that man would be satisfied with himself if 20 he saw to it that his condition was happy; Zeno, that man would be satisfied with his condition if he so conducted himself that he was satisfied with himself.

A man can be satisfied or dissatisfied with himself either 21 pragmatically or ethically, but he very often mistakes the one type of satisfaction or dissatisfaction for the other. He often mistakes for remorse what is, in fact, a fear of the tribunal of prudence. If, for instance, we slight someone in public we may reproach ourselves in the privacy of our home, but these are the reproaches of the Judge of Prudence within us, since we must suppose that we have made an enemy. The reproach for an action through which damage arises is always a reproach of prudence. If we knew that the other did not notice the offence given we should be satisfied. It follows, therefore, that what we feel is a reproof of prudence which we take for a reproof of morality. Epicurus, however, taught that if we so conduct ourselves as to deserve no reproaches, either from ourselves or from others, we are happy.

The ideal of holiness is, philosophically, the most perfect in 22 that it is the ideal of the highest pure and moral perfection; but, as it is humanly unattainable, it bases itself on the belief in divine aid. Not only does the notion of deserving happiness acquire in this ideal its highest moral perfection, but the ideal itself contains the most potent motive, that of happiness beyond this world. Thus the ideal of the Gospels contains the purest morality as well as the strongest motive— that of happiness or blessedness.

The ancients had no conception of any higher moral perfec- 23 tion than such as could emanate from human nature. But as human nature is very imperfect, their ethical principles were imperfect. Thus their system of ethics was not pure; it accommodated virtue to man's weakness, and was, therefore, incomplete. But the ideal of the Gospels is complete in every respect. Here we have the greatest purity and the greatest happiness. It sets out the principles of morality in all their holiness. It commands man to be holy, but as he is imperfect it gives him a prop—namely, divine aid.

QUESTIONS

1. What philosophical schools did Diogenes, Epicurus, and Zeno represent, respectively? What is Kant's attitude toward each of these schools?

2. Explain Kant's concept of the Supreme Good. How does it relate to the Platonic ideal? What is the relevance of the Gospels to the Supreme Good?

3. Identify and analyze those words and phrases Kant employs that alert readers to the fact that he is engaging in logical methods of discourse.

4. In what other ways is this essay an example of "philosophical" writing?

5. Analyze Kant's use of logic in paragraphs 1 to 5 and 21 to 23.

6. List and describe Kant's schemes of classification in the essay.

7. How does Kant utilize comparison and contrast in the essay?

8. Explain the function of definition as Kant uses it in the essay.

9. Would you agree or disagree with Kant's thesis that the Gospels offer a better ethical system than the philosophical systems of the ancients? Justify your response.

10. a. Write a philosophical essay on the best way to achieve the Supreme Good.
b. Write a classification essay discussing ways to arrive at moral perfection.

IMMANUEL KANT

JOSEPH WOOD KRUTCH

The New Immorality

Joseph Wood Krutch (1893–1970), American journalist, naturalist, and literary critic, is best known for *The Desert Year* (1952) and *The Modern Temper* (1956). The following essay, first published in 1960, reflects Krutch's concern for the contemporary condition. In it, he argues against an immoral society and criticizes what he terms "the paradox of our age."

he provost of one of our largest and most honored   1
institutions told me not long ago that a questionnaire
was distributed to his undergraduates and that 40
percent refused to acknowledge that they believed
cheating on examinations to be reprehensible.

Recently a reporter for a New York newspaper stopped six   2
people on the street and asked them if they would consent to take
part in a rigged television quiz for money. He reported that five of the
six said yes. Yet most of these five, like most of the college cheaters,
would probably profess a strong social consciousness. They may
cheat, but they vote for foreign aid and for enlightened social
measures.

These two examples exhibit a paradox of our age. It is often   3
said, and my observation leads me to believe it true, that our
seemingly great growth in social morality has oddly enough taken
place in a world where private morality—a sense of the supreme
importance of purely personal honor, honesty, and integrity—seems
to be declining. Beneficent and benevolent social institutions are
administered by men who all too frequently turn out to be accepting
"gifts." The world of popular entertainment is rocked by scandals.
College students put on their honor, cheat on examinations. Candidates for the Ph.D. hire ghost writers to prepare their theses.

But, one may object, haven't all these things always been   4
true? Is there really any evidence that personal dishonesty is more
prevalent than it always was?

I have no way of making a historical measurement. Perhaps   5
these things are not actually more prevalent. What I do know is that
there is an increasing tendency to accept and take for granted such
personal dishonesty. The bureaucrat and disk jockey say, "Well, yes,
I took presents, but I assure you that I made just decisions anyway."
The college student caught cheating does not even blush. He shrugs
his shoulders and comments: "Everybody does it, and besides, I can't
see that it really hurts anybody."

Jonathan Swift once said: "I have never been surprised to find   6
men wicked, but I have often been surprised to find them not
ashamed." It is my conviction that though men may be no more
wicked than they always have been, they seem less likely to be
ashamed. If anybody does it, it must be right. Honest, moral, decent
mean only what is usual. This is not really a wicked world, because
morality means mores or manners and usual conduct is the only
standard.

The second part of the defense, "it really doesn't hurt   7
anybody," is equally revealing. "It doesn't hurt anybody" means it
doesn't do that abstraction called society any harm. The harm it did
the bribe-taker and the cheater isn't important; it is purely personal.
And personal as opposed to social decency doesn't count for much.
Sometimes I am inclined to blame sociology for part of this paradox.
Sociology has tended to lay exclusive stress upon social morality, and
tended too often to define good and evil as merely the "socially
useful" or its reverse.

What social morality and social conscience leave out is the   8
narrower but very significant concept of honor—as opposed to what
is sometimes called merely "socially desirable conduct." The man of
honor is not content to ask merely whether this or that will hurt
society, or whether it is what most people would permit themselves
to do. He asks, and he asks first of all, would it hurt him and his
self-respect? Would it dishonor him personally?

It was a favorite and no doubt sound argument among early   9
twentieth-century reformers that "playing the game" as the gentleman was supposed to play it was not enough to make a decent
society. They were right: it is not enough. But the time has come to
add that it is indeed inevitable that the so-called social conscience
unsupported by the concept of personal honor will create a corrupt
society. But suppose that it doesn't? Suppose that no one except the
individual suffers from the fact that he sees nothing wrong in doing
what everybody else does? Even so, I still insist that for the individual
himself nothing is more important than this personal, interior sense
of right and wrong and his determination to follow that rather than to
be guided by what everybody does or merely the criterion of "social
usefulness." It is impossible for me to imagine a good society
composed of men without honor.

We hear it said frequently that what present-day men most   10
desire is security. If that is so, then they have a wrong notion of what
the real, the ultimate, security is. No one who is dependent on
anything outside himself, upon money, power, fame, or whatnot, is
or ever can be secure. Only he who possesses himself and is content
with himself is actually secure. Too much is being said about the
importance of adjustment and "participation in the group." Even

cooperation, to give this thing its most favorable designation, is no more important than the ability to stand alone when the choice must be made between the sacrifice of one's own integrity and adjustment to or participation in group activity.

No matter how bad the world may become, no matter how much the mass man of the future may lose such of the virtues as he still has, one fact remains. If one person alone refuses to go along with him, if one person alone asserts his individual and inner right to believe in and be loyal to what his fellow men seem to have given up, then at least he will still retain what is perhaps the most important part of humanity. 11

QUESTIONS

1. According to Krutch, what is the paradox of our age? What is unique about this paradox in terms of history?

2. What are the standard defenses and assumptions concerning the new immorality? How does Krutch respond to them?

3. Krutch employs highly connotative language in this essay. What are some of these words? How does the author both control and exploit connotative language in advancing his analysis and argument?

4. Why is the allusion to Jonathan Swift especially appropriate?

5. Explain the patterns of development in paragraphs 1 to 4, 5 to 7, and 8 to 11.

6. Does Krutch present an inductive or deductive argument in this essay? Explain your answer by reference to the text.

7. In what ways do causal analysis and extended definition enter into the development of the essay?

8. Analyze the last paragraph of the essay and evaluate its effectiveness.

9. Do you accept Krutch's premise that a good society depends on people of honor? Why or why not? Cite examples to support your contention.

10. Write an argumentative essay on personal immorality and the condition of modern American society.

MICHAEL NOVAK

Sports: A Sense of Evil

Michael Novak (1933–   ) is an author and educator. His
interests, though principally in religion, also touch upon politics, sports, and popular culture. Novak's books include *The
Tiber Was Silver* (1961), *The Open Church* (1964), *The Rise of
the Unmeltable Ethnics* (1972), and *Choosing Our King* (1976).
The following essay, which perceptively reveals America's
schizoid view of sports, appeared in *The Joy of Sports* (1976).

T he mythic tissue surrounding sports has always sug-   1
gested that sports are "clean" and "All-American." This
mythic world owes much both to Great Britain and to
the Anglo-American spiritual sensitivity. The "fair
play" of the playing fields of Eton, but also the scouting movement,
the Temperance Leagues, the Chatauqua camps, and other American
movements of individualism, self-improvement, and progressive
thinking—these sanctified certain ideal types as truly American,
compared to others. In the stories of Frank Merriwell, Garry Grayson,
Tom Swift, and other heroes for red-blooded American boys, the most
highly prized qualities were wit, pluck, clean-living, and implacable
enmity against ever-present "bullies." Sports were imagined to be a
realm of muscular Christianity—of maleness on the one hand and
purity of heart on the other. If in other climes a certain shiftiness,
sensuality, sheer physical aggression, duplicity, and trickiness were
deemed appropriate, the true American hero was pure of heart,
candid, straight, true, plucky, modest, and full of boyish charm and
manly courage.

These traditions were not, be it noted, precisely British. The   2
British are an older, wiser culture, given to a certain matter-of-fact
toughness and pragmatic amorality. By contrast, those of the British
who came to New England tended to be enthusiasts, dissidents,
saints, passionately religious. The Anglo-American is quite different
from the Briton: more democratic, more active, rougher, less formal.
"Phlegmatic" would not be an apt description of his national character. "Moral" would be closer.

In a peculiar way, as a result, the American mythology of   3
sports has moved on two separate levels. On the higher plane march
Frank Merriwell and all the legions of straight-shooters and Christian
athletes, self-effacing, gutsy, and victorious: the clean-living, true-
blue gentlemen athletes. On the lower plane carouse the avaricious,
sexy, aggressive, hedonistic Texans of *North Dallas Forty* and *Semi-*

tough—the heavy-drinking, womanizing, masculine hell-raisers of the early days of baseball history, and of today: men like Max McGee, Paul Hornung, Joe Namath, and the horny hero-villains of contemporary sports fiction. In Babe Ruth, the high road and the low road ran as parallel as a modern urban street with elevated highway overhead: Babe Ruth visiting the orphans in a tuberculosis asylum in the newspaper story, and carousing late at night with the prostitutes in the parlor car, unknown to the public.

The moral pretenses of Anglo-American civilization demand   4
a public standard of rectitude, while permitting a private standard of individual choice. Attacks upon "hypocrisy" are one of the most consistent patterns of our cultural life. "Muckraking" is possible only because the public rectitude is prescriptive rather than descriptive, and the gap between the two is never closed. We are not even sure we want it closed. We hate Puritans. Yet our allergies inflict on us Puritan itches.

Liberal, radical, and (in general) progressive thinkers com-   5
monly undertake a double mission. First, they engage with gusto in the unmasking of hypocrisies. They attempt to reduce the gap between public myth and private practise by a stream of steamy exposés. Thus, they scratch the itch. Second, they hold aloft new standards of moral progress, idealism, and moral striving. "See," they say, "many athletes are horny, vulgar, racist, sexist hedonists. Frankness and candor are required of a truthful generation. Debunk the myths. For our society must *not* be racist, sexist, or nihilist. It must be just, egalitarian, brave, self-sacrificing, generous and truthful. It must live up to its ideals." Our muckrakers are not immoralists. On the contrary, they are busy setting up a new mythology which their children, carrying the endless project forward, will then debunk. Whatever we are allergic to, they inject into the nation's system. Saintly to the bitter end.

But the true practice of sport goes on, beneath the moralistic   6
mythology of virtue and clean-living. Basketball without deception could not survive. Football without aggression, holding, slugging, and other violations—only a few of which the referees actually will censure—could not be played. Baseball without cunning, trickery, and pressing for advantage would scarcely be a contest. Our sports are lively with the sense of evil. The evil in them is, to be certain, ritualized, controlled, and channeled. But it is silly to deny that the disciplines of sport include learning how to cope with the illegal aggressions and unbounded passions of one's opponent and oneself. Sports provide an almost deliberate exercise in pushing the psyche to cheat and take advantage, to be ruthless, cruel, deceitful, vengeful, and aggressive. It is "good sportsmanship" not to let such passions dominate; it is naïve not to see them operate in others and oneself.

In football, defensive players hold, illegally, on almost every play. In basketball, a "non-contact game," the violence under the boards is fierce. In baseball, intimidation by pitchers, baserunners, and defensive players is straightforward and expectable. Morality on the athletic field is not a Pollyanna morality. It is controlled by more rules and referees than is any other part of life. Coaches devise ways to get around the rules (players change jerseys; feign injuries to stop the clock; call signals to draw the other team offsides, etc.). The many roles of bluff, feint, intimidation and trickery are so important in sports that they are codified and rendered classical. (There are similar codes and classic moves in scholarship, journalism, politics, and every other field.)

Sports, then, are no escape from evil and immorality. They are designed to teach us how to live in a world that is less than moral. That, too, is one of sport's pleasures. To be an American is to be obliged to indulge in certain moral pretenses. The "American way" is to be decent, moral, trustworthy, law-abiding, tolerant, just, egalitarian, and so forth. Which is fairly heavy. To give a fellow an elbow when the referee isn't looking, just before the ball comes off the rim, is profoundly satisfying to the un-American, unregenerate, unsaintly self.

It is "good sportsmanship" to see to it that the basic structure and procedures of the contest are fair. A good contest, by its nature, requires fairness. The outcome should hang uncertainly between evenly matched opponents, playing under similar rules. A false conception of good sportsmanship, however, prevents many players from giving themselves fully to the competition. Instead of concentrating on the excellence of their own performance, many amateurs, in particular, begin to worry about the psyche of their opponents; they hold back. They lack the instinct for the jugular. They don't want to "humiliate" their opponents. Their condescension toward the frail ego (as they imagine it) of their opponents prevents them from playing as well as they might. They "let up." When they do, commitment and fire leave the contest. The true morality of sport is absent.

It is necessary to be objective about games—to play every one as thought it were one's last, seriously, with purpose, at full alert. The point of games is to propel oneself into a more intense mode of being. Not to play hard is to kill time, but not to transcend it. To concentrate on the game is, in a sense, to be indifferent about one's opponent or oneself. It is to refuse to be distracted by wayward passions. If an opponent plays unfairly, the sweetest revenge is not revenge but victory; one avoids striking back in kind in order to concentrate on the one thing necessary: perfect execution. Concentration on the game itself is the best safeguard against indulgence in ugly, errant passions. It is the highest form of sportsmanship. It is not so much a moral as an ontological attitude. One isn't trying to "be good," but to act perfectly.

Recently, the moralistic impulse has uncovered homosexuality in sports. Muckrakers have informed us that homosexuals appear in professional sports at about the same frequency as elsewhere in our society. Writers used to leer about fanny-patting, celibate training camps, nudity and team showering, and wrestling matches on the soapy floor. The new muckrakers seem to want to give a double message: "See, the world of sports is corrupt and hollow, a world of fake machismo, infested by gays. But it's all right to be gay, it's great, it's fine." They want it both ways. In the pagan world, in Greece and in Nazi Germany, athleticism and homosexuality went (so to speak) hand-in-hand. As did art and homosexuality. Machismo and homosexuality are not opposites. Sport favors neither one. 11

Sports are natural religions. All things human are proper to them. In pushing humans to extremities, they push virtues and vices to extremities, too. The world of sports is no escape from virtue, excellence, and grace. In sports, we meet our humanity. Assuming one begins with limited hopes, there is more to admire in sports—and in our humanity, and in our nation—than to despise. 12

QUESTIONS

1. Explain what Novak means when he says, "Sports are natural religions."

2. Why does Novak believe that hypocrisy and muckraking are American obsessions?

3. Give examples of Novak's use of philosophical vocabulary.

4. How does the use of slang affect the tone of the essay? How does it complement the use of philosophical terms?

5. How does Novak's comparison in paragraph 2 contribute to the development of the essay?

6. Give examples of Novak's use of deduction in this essay.

7. Explain the organization of paragraphs 5 and 6. What rhetorical techniques are used in each paragraph? How are the two paragraphs related?

8. Novak uses examples frequently in the essay. Examine their use in paragraphs 1 and 10. How do these kinds of examples differ? How do they contribute to the development of the essay?

9. Novak says that the contrast between high and low planes in American sports exists elsewhere. Discuss how the contrast appears in politics, college life, and literature.

10. a. Write an essay about your own experience as a player or spectator in sports when you confronted the conflict between ideals and reality.
b. Write an essay analyzing other ambiguities in American life, such as the image of politicians, astronauts, or business people.

ALBERT CAMUS

The Myth of Sisyphus

Albert Camus (1913–1960), French author and philosopher, was one of the most important thinkers of the twentieth century. During World War II, he joined the French underground movement against the Germans and was the principal editor of the underground newspaper *Combat*. After the war, he became well known for his theories on the absurdity of life. Camus believed that men and women should respond to absurdity with courage and decency, not with despair. His theories are dramatized in *The Stranger* (1942) and in such later works as *The Plague* (1948) and the plays *Caligula* (1944), *State of Siege* (1948), and *The Just Assassins* (1950). Camus was awarded the 1957 Nobel Prize in Literature. *The Myth of Sisyphus* (1942), from which this essay is taken, is often considered the foundation of his absurdist philosophy.

he gods had condemned Sisyphus to ceaselessly rolling   1
a rock to the top of a mountain, whence the stone would
fall back of its own weight. They had thought with some
reason that there is no more dreadful punishment than
futile and hopeless labor.

If one believes Homer, Sisyphus was the wisest and most   2
prudent of mortals. According to another tradition, however, he was
disposed to practice the profession of highwayman. I see no contradiction in this. Opinions differ as to the reasons why he became the
futile laborer of the underworld. To begin with, he is accused of a
certain levity in regard to the gods. He stole their secrets. Aegina, the

daughter of Aesopus, was carried off by Jupiter. The father was shocked by that disappearance and complained to Sisyphus. He, who knew of the abduction, offered to tell about it on condition that Aesopus would give water to the citadel of Corinth. To the celestial thunderbolts he preferred the benediction of water. He was punished for this in the underworld. Homer tells us also that Sisyphus had put Death in chains. Pluto could not endure the sight of his deserted, silent empire. He dispatched the god of War, who liberated Death from the hands of her conqueror.

It is said also that Sisyphus, being near to death, rashly   3
wanted to test his wife's love. He ordered her to cast his unburied body into the middle of the public square. Sisyphus woke up in the underworld. And there, annoyed by an obedience so contrary to human love, he obtained from Pluto permission to return to earth in order to chastise his wife. But when he had seen again the face of this world, enjoyed water and sun, warm stones and the sea, he no longer wanted to go back to the infernal darkness. Recalls, signs of anger, warnings were of no avail. Many years more he lived facing the curve of the gulf, the sparkling sea, and the smiles of earth. A decree of the gods was necessary. Mercury came and seized the impudent man by the collar and, snatching him from his joys, led him forcibly back to the underworld, where his rock was ready for him.

You have already grasped that Sisyphus is the absurd hero.   4
He *is*, as much through his passions as through his torture. His scorn of the gods, his hatred of death, and his passion for life won him that unspeakable penalty in which the whole being is exerted toward accomplishing nothing. This is the price that must be paid for the passions of this earth. Nothing is told us about Sisyphus in the underworld. Myths are made for the imagination to breathe life into them. As for this myth, one sees merely the whole effort of a body straining to raise the huge stone, to roll it and push it up a slope a hundred times over; one sees the face screwed up, the cheek tight against the stone, the shoulder bracing the claycovered mass, the foot wedging it, the fresh start with arms outstretched, the wholly human security of two earth-clotted hands. At the very end of this long effort measured by skyless space and time without depth, the purpose is achieved. Then Sisyphus watches the stone rush down in a few moments toward that lower world whence he will have to push it up again toward the summit. He goes back down to the plain.

It is during that return, that pause, that Sisyphus interests   5
me. A face that toils so close to stones is already stone itself! I see that man going back down with a heavy yet measured step toward the torment of which he will never know the end. That hour like a breathing-space which returns as surely as his suffering, that is the hour of consciousness. At each of those moments when he leaves the

heights and gradually sinks toward the lairs of the gods, he is superior to his fate. He is stronger than his rock.

If this myth is tragic, that is because its hero is conscious. Where would his torture be, indeed, if at every step the hope of succeeding upheld him? The workman of today works every day in his life at the same tasks, and this fate is no less absurd. But it is tragic only at the rare moments when it becomes conscious. Sisyphus, proletarian of the gods, powerless and rebellious, knows the whole extent of his wretched condition: it is what he thinks of during his descent. The lucidity that was to constitute his torture at the same time crowns his victory. There is no fate that cannot be surmounted by scorn. 6

If the descent is thus sometimes performed in sorrow, it can also take place in joy. This word is not too much. Again I fancy Sisyphus returning toward his rock, and the sorrow was in the beginning. When the images of earth cling too tightly to memory, when the call of happiness becomes too insistent, it happens that melancholy rises in man's heart: this is the rock's victory, this is the rock itself. The boundless grief is too heavy to bear. These are our nights of Gethsemane. But crushing truths perish from being acknowledged. Thus, Oedipus at the outset obeys fate without knowing it. But from the moment he knows, his tragedy begins. Yet at the same moment, blind and desperate, he realizes that the only bond linking him to the world is the cool hand of a girl. Then a tremendous remark rings out: "Despite so many ordeals, my advanced age and the nobility of my soul make me conclude that all is well." Sophocles' Oedipus, like Dostoevsky's Kirilov, thus gives the recipe for the absurd victory. Ancient wisdom confirms modern heroism. 7

One does not discover the absurd without being tempted to write a manual of happiness. "What! by such narrow ways—?" There is but one world, however. Happiness and the absurd are two sons of the same earth. They are inseparable. It would be a mistake to say that happiness necessarily springs from the absurd discovery. It happens as well that the feeling of the absurd springs from happiness. "I conclude that all is well," says Oedipus, and that remark is sacred. It echoes in the wild and limited universe of man. It teaches that all is not, has not been, exhausted. It drives out of this world a god who had come into it with dissatisfaction and a preference for futile sufferings. It makes of fate a human matter, which must be settled among men. 8

All Sisyphus' silent joy is contained therein. His fate belongs to him. His rock is his thing. Likewise, the absurd man, when he contemplates his torment, silences all the idols. In the universe suddenly restored to its silence, the myriad wondering little voices of the earth rise up. Unconscious, secret calls, invitations from all the 9 faces, they are the necessary reverse and price of victory. There is no sun without shadow, and it is essential to know the night. The absurd man says yes and his effort will henceforth be unceasing. If there is a personal fate, there is no higher destiny, or at least there is but one which he concludes is inevitable and despicable. For the rest, he knows himself to be the master of his days. At that subtle moment when man glances backward over his life, Sisyphus returning toward his rock, in that slight pivoting he contemplates that series of unrelated actions which becomes his fate, created by him, combined under his memory's eye and soon sealed by his death. Thus, convinced of the wholly human origin of all that is human, a blind man eager to see who knows that the night has no end, he is still on the go. The rock is still rolling.

I leave Sisyphus at the foot of the mountain! One always finds one's burden again. But Sisyphus teaches the higher fidelity that negates the gods and raises rocks. He too concludes that all is well. This universe henceforth without a master seems to him neither sterile nor futile. Each atom of that stone, each mineral flake of that night-filled mountain, in itself forms a world. The struggle itself toward the heights is enough to fill a man's heart. One must imagine Sisyphus happy.

10

QUESTIONS

1. What does Camus mean when he says, "Myths are made for the imagination to breathe life into them" (paragraph 4)?

2. Why does Camus think Sisyphus is such an appropriate symbol of people today?

3. Explain the style Camus uses to describe Sisyphus in paragraph 4. How does this narration differ in style from the preceding paragraphs?

4. Explain the connotations of such words as "tragic" (paragraph 6), "proletarian" (paragraph 6), "absurd" (paragraph 4), and "myth" (paragraph 4).

5. Why does Camus begin his essay with an analysis of the myth of Sisyphus?

6. Explain the organization of paragraph 4. Why does Camus end the narration where he does? How does this end lead to the next paragraph?

7. How does paragraph 8 differ from the paragraphs before it? How does it affect our sense of Sisyphus?

 THE MYTH OF SISYPHUS 487

8. What crucial comparison is made in this essay? In what paragraphs does it appear? What transition words mark the development of the comparison?

9. Can you think of any other myths from the ancient world that help to explain our nature? Why do you think myths make such effective symbols of human nature?

10. a. Write an essay comparing yourself to a Greek hero such as Hercules, Jason, Medea, Odysseus, or Penelope. How do their histories relate to your own?
b. Write your own analysis of absurdity and the conditions of modern life.

HANNAH ARENDT

The Human Condition

Hannah Arendt (1906–1975), scholar, political theorist, and writer, was born in Hanover, Germany, but was forced to flee because of the Nazi persecution of Jews in the 1930s. She came to the United States in 1940. Many of her works concern the nature of totalitarianism, such as *The Origins of Totalitarianism* (1951), *On Revolution* (1963), and *Eichmann in Jerusalem* (1963). Writing of Arendt, Mary McCarthy has said that she combines "tremendous intellectual power with great common sense." In the following selection, which is from *The Human Condition* (1958), Arendt analyzes three of the major qualities of human beings.

With the term *vita activa*, I propose to designate three 1 fundamental human activities: labor, work, and action. They are fundamental because each corresponds to one of the basic conditions under which life on earth has been given to man.

Labor is the activity which corresponds to the biological 2 process of the human body, whose spontaneous growth, metabolism, and eventual decay are bound to the vital necessities produced and fed into the life process by labor. The human condition of labor is life itself.

488   HANNAH ARENDT

Work is the activity which corresponds to the unnaturalness 3
of human existence, which is not imbedded in, and whose mortality
is not compensated by, the species' ever-recurring life cycle. Work
provides an "artificial" world of things, distinctly different from all
natural surroundings. Within its borders each individual life is
housed, while this world itself is meant to outlast and transcend them
all. The human condition of work is worldliness.

Action, the only activity that goes on directly between men 4
without the intermediary of things or matter, corresponds to the
human condition of plurality, to the fact that men, not Man, live on
the earth and inhabit the world. While all aspects of the human
condition are somehow related to politics, this plurality is specifically
the condition—not only the *conditio sine qua non*, but the *conditio per
quam*—of all political life. Thus the language of the Romans, perhaps
the most political people we have known, used the words "to live"
and "to be among men" (*inter homines esse*) or "to die" and "to cease
to be among men" (*inter homines esse desinere*) as synonyms. But in its
more elementary form, the human condition of action is implicit even
in Genesis. ("Male and female created He *them*"), if we understand
that this story of man's creation is distinguished in principle from the
one according to which God originally created Man (*adam*), "him"
and not "them," so that the multitude of human beings becomes the
result of multiplication.[1] Action would be an unnecessary luxury, a
capricious interference with general laws of behavior, if men were
endlessly reproducible repetitions of the same model, whose nature
or essence was the same for all and as predictable as the nature or
essence of any other thing. Plurality is the condition of human action
because we are all the same, that is, human, in such a way that
nobody is ever the same as anyone else who ever lived, lives, or will
live.

All three activities and their corresponding conditions are 5
intimately connected with the most general condition of human
existence: birth and death, natality and mortality. Labor assures not

---

[1]In the analysis of postclassical political thought, it is often quite illuminating to find out which of
the two biblical versions of the creation story is cited. Thus it is highly characteristic of the difference
between the teaching of Jesus of Nazareth and of Paul that Jesus, discussing the relationship
between man and wife, refers to Genesis 1:27: "Have ye not read, that he which made *them* at the
beginning made them male and female" (Matt. 19:4), whereas Paul on a similar occasion insists that
the woman was created "of the man" and hence "for the man," even though he then somewhat
attenuates the dependence: "neither is the man without the woman, neither the woman without
the man" (I Cor. 11:8–12). The difference indicates much more than a different attitude to the role of
woman. For Jesus, faith was closely related to action; for Paul, faith was primarily related to
salvation. Especially interesting in this respect is Augustine (*De civitate Dei* xii. 21), who not only
ignores Genesis 1:27 altogether but sees the difference between man and animal in that man was
created *unum ac singulum*, whereas all animals were ordered "to come into being several at once"
(*plura simul iussit exsistere*). To Augustine, the creation story offers a welcome opportunity to stress
the species character of animal life as distinguished from the singularity of human existence.

  THE HUMAN CONDITION   **489**

only individual survival, but the life of the species. Work and its product, the human artifact, bestow a measure of permanence and durability upon the futility of mortal life and the fleeting character of human time. Action, in so far as it engages in founding and preserving political bodies, creates the condition for remembrance, that is, for history. Labor and work, as well as action, are also rooted in natality in so far as they have the task to provide and preserve the world for, to foresee and reckon with, the constant influx of newcomers who are born into the world as strangers. However, of the three, action has the closest connection with the human condition of natality; the new beginning inherent in birth can make itself felt in the world only because the newcomer possesses the capacity of beginning something anew, that is, of acting. In this sense of initiative, an element of action, and therefore of natality, is inherent in all human activities. Moreover, since action is the political activity par excellence, natality, and not mortality, may be the central category of political, as distinguished from metaphysical, thought.

The human condition comprehends more than the conditions   6 under which life has been given to man. Men are conditioned beings because everything they come in contact with turns immediately into a condition of their existence. The world in which the *vita activa* spends itself consists of things produced by human activities; but the things that owe their existence exclusively to men nevertheless constantly condition their human makers. In addition to the conditions under which life is given to man on earth, and partly out of them, men constantly create their own, self-made conditions, which, their human origin and their variability notwithstanding, possess the same conditioning power as natural things. Whatever touches or enters into a sustained relationship with human life immediately assumes the character of a condition of human existence. This is why men, no matter what they do, are always conditioned beings. Whatever enters the human world of its own accord or is drawn into it by human effort becomes part of the human condition. The impact of the world's reality upon human existence is felt and received as a conditioning force. The objectivity of the world—its object- or thing-character—and the human condition supplement each other; because human existence is conditioned existence, it would be impossible without things, and things would be a heap of unrelated articles, a non-world, if they were not the conditioners of human existence.

To avoid misunderstanding: the human condition is not the   7 same as human nature, and the sum total of human activities and capabilities which correspond to the human condition does not constitute anything like human nature. For neither those we discuss

HANNAH ARENDT

here nor those we leave out, like thought and reason, and not even the most meticulous enumeration of them all, constitute essential characteristics of human existence in the sense that without them this existence would no longer be human. The most radical change in the human condition we can imagine would be an emigration of men from the earth to some other planet. Such an event, no longer totally impossible, would imply that man would have to live under man-made conditions, radically different from those the earth offers him. Neither labor nor work nor action nor, indeed, thought as we know it would then make sense any longer. Yet even these hypothetical wanderers from the earth would still be human; but the only statement we could make regarding their "nature" is that they still are conditioned beings, even though their condition is now self-made to a considerable extent.

The problem of human nature, the Augustinian *quaestio mihi factus sum* ("a question have I become for myself"), seems unanswerable in both its individual psychological sense and its general philosophical sense. It is highly unlikely that we, who can know, determine, and define the natural essences of all things surrounding us, which we are not, should ever be able to do the same for ourselves—this would be like jumping over our own shadows. Moreover, nothing entitles us to assume that man has a nature or essence in the same sense as other things. In other words, if we have a nature or essence, then surely only a god could know and define it, and the first prerequisite would be that he be able to speak about a "who" as though it were a "what."[2] The perplexity is that the modes of human cognition applicable to things with "natural" qualities, including ourselves to the limited extent that we are specimens of the most highly developed species of organic life, fail us when we raise the question: And *who* are we? This is why attempts to define human nature almost invariably end with some construction of a deity, that is, with the god of the philosophers, who, since Plato, has revealed

[2]Augustine, who is usually credited with having been the first to raise the so-called anthropological question in philosophy, knew this quite well. He distinguishes between the questions of "Who am I?" and "What am I?" the first being directed by man at himself ("And I directed myself at myself and said to me: You, who are you? And I answered: A man"—*tu, quis es?* [*Confessiones* x. 6]) and the second being addressed to God ("What then am I, my God? What is my nature?"—*Quid ergo sum, Deus meus? Quae natura sum?* [x. 17]). For in the "great mystery," the *grande profundum*, which man is (iv. 14), there is "something of man [*aliquid hominis*] which the spirit of man which is in him itself knoweth not. But Thou, Lord, who has made him [*fecisti eum*] knowest everything of him [*eius omnia*]" (x. 5). Thus, the most familiar of these phrases which I quoted in the text, the *quaestio mihi factus sum*, is a question raised in the presence of God, "in whose eyes I have become a question for myself" (x. 33). In brief, the answer to the question "Who am I?" is simply: "You are a man—whatever that may be"; and the answer to the question "What am I?" can be given only by God who made man. The question about the nature of man is no less a theological question than the question about the nature of God; both can be settled only within the framework of a divinely revealed answer.

 THE HUMAN CONDITION 491

himself upon closer inspection to be a kind of Platonic idea of man. Of course, to demask such philosophic concepts of the divine as conceptualizations of human capabilities and qualities is not a demonstration of, not even an argument for, the non-existence of God; but the fact that attempts to define the nature of man lead so easily into an idea which definitely strikes us as "superhuman" and therefore is identified with the divine may cast suspicion upon the very concept of "human nature."

On the other hand, the conditions of human existence—life 9 itself, natality and mortality, worldliness, plurality, and the earth—can never "explain" what we are or answer the question of who we are for the simple reason that they never condition us absolutely. This has always been the opinion of philosophy, in distinction from the sciences—anthropology, psychology, biology, etc.—which also concern themselves with man. But today we may almost say that we have demonstrated even scientifically that, though we live now, and probably always will, under the earth's conditions, we are not mere earth-bound creatures. Modern natural science owes its great triumphs to having looked upon and treated earth-bound nature from a truly universal viewpoint, that is, from an Archimedean standpoint taken, wilfully and explicitly, outside the earth.

QUESTIONS

1. What does Arendt mean when she says, "The human condition is not the same as human nature"?

2. According to Arendt, why do people interpret their nature in terms of a deity? Does she agree with this idea? If so, why? If not, why not?

3. Explain the function of the allusions to Augustine, Plato, and the Bible. Why are references to such figures appropriate to Arendt's subject?

4. Does Arendt tend to write abstractly or concretely? Give examples of the style she uses most frequently.

5. Explain how Arendt uses classification to organize her essay. How many categories does Arendt give? What is the basis of her classification?

6. Definition is an important rhetorical device in this essay. Give five examples of definition and explain how they contribute to the development of the essay.

7. Explain the nature of the example in paragraph 7. How does it follow from the topic sentence of the paragraph?

8. Explain Arendt's syllogistic reasoning in paragraph 5. Give other examples of such reasoning elsewhere.

9. Arendt says we are "not mere earth-bound creatures" (paragraph 9). What does she mean by that? Do you agree? Do we, indeed, have souls?

10. Write an essay categorizing the three most important qualities of being one of the following—a parent, a student, or a teenager.

JOHN DONNE

No Man Is an Island

John Donne (1572–1631), English poet and priest, was a master of wit and devotion. Ben Jonson called him "the first poet in the world in some things." Donne's early career was threatened constantly by poverty, until he became dean of St. Paul's in 1621. He wrote richly complex poetry and sermons. Most of his works were published after his death by his son. Collections of his sermons appeared in 1640, 1649, and 1661; a collection of his poetry appeared in 1633. Donne was a superb inventor of metaphors, as the following essay, called a meditation, indicates.

Perchance he for whom this bell tolls may be so ill, as that he knows not it tolls for him; and perchance I may think myself so much better than I am, as that they who are about me, and see my state, may have caused it to toll for me, and I know not that. The church is Catholic, universal, so are all her actions; all that she does belongs to all. When she baptizes a child, that action concerns me; for that child is thereby connected to that body which is my head too, and ingrafted into that body whereof I am a member. And when she buries a man, that action concerns me: all mankind is of one author, and is one volume; when one man dies, one chapter is not torn out of the book, but translated into a better language; and every chapter must be so translated; God employs several translators; some pieces are translated by age, some by sickness, some by war, some by justice; but God's hand is in every translation, and his hand shall bind up all our scattered leaves again for that library where every book shall lie open to one another. As therefore the bell that rings to a sermon calls not upon the preacher only, but upon the congregation to come, so this bell calls us all; but how much more me, who am brought so near the door by this sickness. There was a contention as far as a suit (in which both poetry and dignity, religion and estimation, were mingled), which of the religious orders should ring to prayers first in the morning; and it was determined, that they should ring first that rose earliest. If we understand aright the dignity of this bell that tolls for our evening prayer, we would be glad to make it ours by rising early, in that application, that it might be ours as well as his, whose indeed it is. The bell doth toll for him that thinks it doth; and though it intermit again, yet from that minute that that occasion wrought upon him, he is united to God. Who casts not up his eye to the sun when it rises? but who takes off his eye from a comet when that breaks out? Who bends not his ear to any bell which upon any occasion rings? but who can remove it from that bell which is passing a piece of himself out of this world? No man is an island, entire of itself; every man is a piece of the continent, a part of the main. If a clod be washed away by the sea, Europe is the less, as well as if a promontory were, as well as if a manor of thy friend's or of thine own were: any man's death diminishes me, because I am involved in mankind, and therefore never send to know for whom the bell tolls; it tolls for thee. Neither can we call this a begging of misery, or a borrowing of misery, as though we were not miserable enough of ourselves, but must fetch in more from the next house, in taking upon us the misery of our neighbors. Truly it were an excusable covetousness if we did, for affliction is a treasure, and scarce any man hath enough of it. No man hath affliction enough that is not matured and ripened by it, and made fit for God by that affliction. If a man carry treasure in bullion, or in a wedge of gold, and have none coined into current money, his treasure will not defray him as he travels. Tribulation is treasure in the nature of it, but it is not current money in the use of it, except we get nearer and nearer our home, heaven, by it. Another man may be sick too, and sick to death, and this affliction may lie in his bowels, as gold in a mine, and be of no use to him; but this bell, that tells me of his affliction, digs out and applies that gold to me: if by this consideration of another's danger I take mine own into contemplation, and so secure myself, by making my recourse to my God, who is our only security.

QUESTIONS

1. Specify Donne's reasons for being moved by a church's mourning bell. How do his religious beliefs enter into his reasoning?

2.   What objection to meditating on death does Donne raise toward the end of his essay? How does he refute these objections?

3.   Give three examples of periodic sentences in this essay. Are such sentences typical of Donne's style? Why?

4.   Despite the seriousness of the meditation, Donne puns in this essay. Identify two puns; what are their meanings? How do they affect the seriousness of the meditation?

5.   What is the thesis of this meditation? Why does it appear where it does?

6.   Donne uses two extended metaphors: the individual is a book and affliction is a treasure. Explain what these metaphors mean and their relation to Donne's thesis.

7.   What transitional devices does Donne use to organize and to structure his paragraph?

8.   How does Donne use association to develop his essay? How is the meditation genre reflected in the development of ideas in this association?

9.   In our very different age, should we be moved by the deaths of strangers? If we are, how will that emotion affect our lives?

10.   Take a common sound or sight—one that you hear or see frequently—and write a meditation about it. Relate the event to some crucial religious or moral concern.

Can Religion Cure Our Troubles?

Bertrand Arthur William Russell (1872–1970) was one of the great philosophers, mathematicians, liberal political theorists, and authors of the twentieth century. His works are legion and range from abstruse explanations of mathematical theory to often bawdy memoirs. From the early *Principles of Mathematics* (1903) through *An Inquiry into Meaning and Truth* (1940), to his three-volume *Autobiography* (1967–1969), Russell demonstrated his multivarious talents as a writer and

CAN RELIGION CURE OUR TROUBLES?   495

I

Mankind is in mortal peril, and fear now, as in the past, is   1
inclining men to seek refuge in God. Throughout the
West there is a very general revival of religion. Nazis
and Communists dismissed Christianity and did things
which we deplore. . . . It is easy to conclude that the repudiation of
Christianity by Hitler and the Soviet Government is at least in part the
cause of our troubles and that if the world returned to Christianity,
our international problems would be solved. I believe this to be a
complete delusion born of terror. And I think it is a dangerous
delusion because it misleads men whose thinking might otherwise be
fruitful and thus stands in the way of a valid solution.

The question involved is not concerned only with the present   2
state of the world. It is a much more general question, and one which
has been debated for many centuries. It is the question whether
societies can practise a sufficient modicum of morality if they are not
helped by dogmatic religion. I do not myself think that the dependence of morals upon religion is nearly as close as religious people
believe it to be. I even think that some very important virtues are
more likely to be found among those who reject religious dogmas
than among those who accept them. I think this applies especially to
the virtue of truthfulness or intellectual integrity. I mean by intellectual integrity the habit of deciding vexed questions in accordance
with the evidence, or the leaving them undecided where the evidence
is inconclusive. This virtue, though it is underestimated by almost all
adherents of any system of dogma, is to my mind of the very greatest
social importance and far more likely to benefit the world than
Christianity or any other system of organized beliefs.

Let us consider for a moment how moral rules have come to   3
be accepted. Moral rules are broadly of two kinds: there are those
which have no basis except in a religious creed; and there are those
which have an obvious basis in social utility. In the Greek Orthodox
Church, two godparents of the same child must not marry. For this
rule, clearly, there is only a theological basis; and, if you think the
rule important, you will be quite right in saying that the decay of
religion is to be deprecated because it will lead to the rule being
infringed. But it is not this kind of moral rule that is in question. The
moral rules that are in question are those for which there is a social
justification independently of theology.

Let us take theft, for example. A community in which   4

everybody steals is inconvenient for everybody, and it is obvious that most people can get more of the sort of life they desire if they live in a community where theft is rare. But in the absence of laws and morals and religion a difficulty arises: for each individual, the ideal community would be one in which everybody else is honest and he alone is a thief. It follows that a social institution is necessary if the interest of the individual is to be reconciled with that of the community. This is effected more or less successfully by the criminal law and the police. But criminals are not always caught, and the police may be unduly lenient to the powerful. If people can be persuaded that there is a God who will punish theft, even when the police fail, it would seem likely that this belief would promote honesty. Given a population that already believes in God, it will readily believe that God has prohibited theft. The usefulness of religion in this respect is illustrated by the story of Naboth's vineyard where the thief is the king, who is above earthly justice.

I will not deny that among semi-civilized communities in the   5 past such considerations may have helped to promote socially desirable conduct. But in the present day such good as may be done by imputing a theological origin to morals is inextricably bound up with such grave evils that the good becomes insignificant in comparison. As civilization progresses, the earthly sanctions become more secure and the divine sanctions less so. People see more and more reason to think that if they steal they will be caught and less and less reason to think that if they are not caught God will nevertheless punish them. Even highly religious people in the present day hardly expect to go to hell for stealing. They reflect that they can repent in time, and that in any case hell is neither so certain nor so hot as it used to be. Most people in civilized communities do not steal, and I think the usual motive is the great likelihood of punishment here on earth. This is borne out by the fact that in a mining camp during a gold rush, or in any such disorderly community, almost everybody does steal.

But, you may say, although the theological prohibition of   6 theft may no longer be very necessary, it at any rate does no harm since we all wish people not to steal. The trouble is, however, that as soon as men incline to doubt received theology it comes to be supported by odious and harmful means. If a theology is thought necessary to virtue and if candid inquirers see no reason to think the theology true, the authorities will set to work to discourage candid inquiry. In former centuries, they did so by burning the inquirers at the stake. In Russia they still have methods which are little better; but in Western countries the authorities have perfected somewhat milder forms of persuasion. Of these, schools are perhaps the most important: the young must be preserved from hearing the arguments in favour of the opinions which the authorities dislike, and those who nevertheless persist in showing an inquiring disposition will incur social displeasure and, if possible, be made to feel morally reprehensible. In this way, any system of morals which has a theological basis becomes one of the tolls by which the holders of power preserve their authority and impair the intellectual vigour of the young.

I find among many people at the present day an indifference 7 to truth which I cannot but think extremely dangerous. When people argue, for example, in defence of Christianity, they do not, like Thomas Aquinas, give reasons for supposing that there is a God and that He has expressed His will in the Scriptures. They argue instead that, if people think this, they will act better than if they do not. We ought not therefore—so these people contend—to permit ourselves to speculate as to whether God exists. If, in an unguarded moment, doubt rears its head, we must suppress it vigorously. If candid thought is a cause of doubt we must eschew candid thought. If the official exponents of orthodoxy tell you that it is wicked to marry your deceased wife's sister, you must believe them lest morals collapse. If they tell you that birth control is sin, you must accept their dictum however obvious it may be to you that without birth control disaster is certain. As soon as it is held that any belief, no matter what, is important for some other reason than that it is true, a whole host of evils is ready to spring up. Discouragement of inquiry, which I spoke of before, is the first of these, but others are pretty sure to follow. Positions of authority will be open to the orthodox. Historical records must be falsified if they throw doubt on received opinions. Sooner or later unorthodoxy will come to be considered a crime to be dealt with by the stake, the purge, or the concentration camp. I can respect the men who argue that religion is true and therefore ought to be believed, but I can only feel profound moral reprobation for those who say that religion ought to be believed because it is useful, and that to ask whether it is true is a waste of time.

It is customary among Christian apologists to regard Com- 8 munism as something very different from Christianity and to contrast its evils with the supposed blessings enjoyed by Christian nations. This seems to me a profound mistake. The evils of Communism are the same as those that existed in Christianity during the Ages of Faith. The Ogpu differs only quantitatively from the Inquisition. Its cruelties are of the same sort, and the damage that it does to the intellectual and moral life of Russians is of the same sort as that which was done by the Inquisitors wherever they prevailed. The Communists falsify history, and the Church did the same until the Renaissance. If the Church is not now as bad as the Soviet Government, that is due to the influence of those who attacked the Church; from the Council of Trent to the present day whatever improvements it has effected have been due to its enemies. There are many who object to the Soviet Government because they dislike the Communist economic doctrine, but this the Kremlin shares with the early Christians, the Franciscans, and the majority of medieval Christian heretics. Nor was the Communist doctrine confined to heretics: Sir Thomas More, an orthodox martyr, speaks of Christianity as Communistic and says that this was the only aspect of the Christian religion which commended it to the Utopians. It is not Soviet doctrine in itself that can be justly regarded as a danger. It is the way in which the doctrine is held. It is held as sacred and inviolable truth, to doubt which is sin and deserving of the severest punishment. The Communist, like the Christian, believes that his doctrine is essential to salvation, and it is this belief which makes salvation possible for him. It is the similarities between Christianity and Communism that make them incompatible with each other. When two men of science disagree, they do not invoke the secular arm; they wait for further evidence to decide the issue, because as men of science, they know that neither is infallible. But when two theologians differ, since there are no criteria to which either can appeal, there is nothing for it but mutual hatred and an open or covert appeal to force. Christianity, I will admit, does less harm than it used to do; but that is because it is less fervently believed. Perhaps, in time, the same change will come over Communism; and, if it does, that creed will lose much of what now makes it obnoxious. But if in the West the view prevails that Christianity is essential to virtue and social stability, Christianity will once again acquire the vices which it had in the Middle Ages; and, in becoming more and more like Communism, will become more and more difficult to reconcile with it. It is not along this road that the world can be saved from disaster.

II

In my first article I was concerned with the evils resulting from any system of dogmas presented for acceptance, not on the ground of truth, but on the ground of social utility. What I had to say applies equally to Christianity, Communism, Islam, Buddhism, Hinduism and all theological systems, except in so far as they rely upon grounds making a universal appeal of the sort that is made by men of science. There are, however, special arguments which are advanced in favour of Christianity on account of its supposed special merits. These have been set forth eloquently and with a show of erudition by Herbert Butterfield, Professor of Modern History in the University of Cambridge,[1] and I shall take him as spokesman of the large body of opinion to which he adheres.

[1]*Christianity and History* (London, 1950.)

 CAN RELIGION CURE OUR TROUBLES?   **499**

Professor Butterfield seeks to secure certain controversial advantages by concessions that make him seem more open-minded than in fact he is. He admits that the Christian Church has relied upon persecution and that it is pressure from without that has led it to abandon this practice in so far as it has been abandoned. He admits that the present tension between Russia and the West is a result of power politics such as might have been expected even if the Government of Russia had continued to adhere to the Greek Orthodox Church. He admits that some of the virtues which he regards as distinctively Christian have been displayed by some free-thinkers and have been absent in the behaviour of many Christians. But, in spite of these concessions, he still holds that the evils from which the world is suffering are to be cured by adherence to Christian dogma, and he includes in the necessary minimum of Christian dogma not only belief in God and immortality, but also belief in the Incarnation. He emphasizes the connection of Christianity with certain historical events, and he accepts these events as historical on evidence which would certainly not convince him if it were not connected with his religion. I do not think the evidence for the Virgin Birth is such as would convince any impartial inquirer it it were presented outside the circle of theological beliefs he was accustomed to. There are innumerable such stories in Pagan mythology, but no one dreams of taking them seriously. Professor Butterfield, however, in spite of being an historian, appears to be quite uninterested in questions of historicity wherever the origins of Christianity are concerned. His argument, robbed of his urbanity and his deceptive air of broad-mindedness, may be stated crudely but accurately as follows: "It is not worth while to inquire whether Christ really was born of a Virgin and conceived of the Holy Ghost because, whether or not this was the case, the belief that it was the case offers the best hope of escape from the present troubles of the world." Nowhere in Professor Butterfield's work is there the faintest attempt to prove the truth of any Christian dogma. There is only the pragmatic argument that belief in Christian dogma is useful. There are many steps in Professor Butterfield's contention which are not stated with as much clarity and precision as one could desire, and I fear the reason is that clarity and precision make them implausible. I think the contention, stripped of inessentials, is as follows: it would be a good thing if people loved their neighbours, but they do not show much inclination to do so; Christ said they ought to, and if they believe that Christ was God, they are more likely to pay attention to His teachings on this point than if they do not; therefore, men who wish people to love their neighbours will try to persuade them that Christ was God.

The objections to this kind of argumentation are so many that it is difficult to know where to begin. In the first place, Professor Butterfield and all who think as he does are persuaded that it is a good thing to love your neighbour, and their reasons for holding this view are not derived from Christ's teaching. On the contrary, it is because they already hold this view that they regard Christ's teaching as evidence of His divinity. They have, that is to say, not an ethic based on theology, but a theology based upon their ethic. They apparently hold, however, that the non-theological grounds which make them think it a good thing to love your neighbour are not likely to make a wide appeal, and they therefore proceed to invent other arguments which they hope will be more effective. This is a very dangerous procedure. Many Protestants used to think it as wicked to break the Sabbath as to commit murder. If you persuaded them it was not wicked to break the Sabbath, they might infer that it was not wicked to commit murder. Every theological ethic is in part such as can be defended rationally, and in part a mere embodiment of superstitious taboos. The part which can be defended rationally should be so defended, since otherwise those who discover the irrationality of the other part may rashly reject the whole.

But has Christianity, in fact, stood for a better morality than 12
that of its rivals and opponents? I do not see how any honest student of history can maintain that this is the case. Christianity has been distinguished from other religions by its greater readiness for persecution. Buddhism has never been a persecuting religion. The Empire of the Caliphs was much kinder to Jews and Christians than Christian States were to Jews and Mohammedans. It left Jews and Christians unmolested, provided they paid tribute. Anti-Semitism was promoted by Christianity from the moment when the Roman Empire became Christian. The religious fervour of the Crusades led to pogroms in Western Europe. It was Christians who unjustly accused Dreyfus, and free-thinkers who secured his final rehabilitation. Abominations have in modern times been defended by Christians not only when Jews were the victims, but also in other connections. The abominations of King Leopold's government of the Congo were concealed or minimized by the Church and were ended only by an agitation conducted mainly by free-thinkers. The whole contention that Christianity has had an elevating moral influence can only be maintained by wholesale ignoring or falsification of the historical evidence.

The habitual answer is that the Christians who did things 13
which we deplore were not *true* Christians in the sense that they did not follow the teachings of Christ. One might of course equally well argue that the Soviet Government does not consist of true Marxists,

x

for Marx taught that Slavs are inferior to Germans and this doctrine is not accepted in the Kremlin. The followers of a teacher always depart in some respects from the doctrine of the master. Those who aim at founding a Church ought to remember this. Every church develops an instinct of self-preservation and minimizes those parts of the founder's doctrine which do not minister to that end. But in any case what modern apologists call 'true' Christianity is something depending upon a very selective process. It ignores much that is to be found in the Gospels: for example, the parable of the sheep and the goats, and the doctrine that the wicked will suffer eternal torment in hell-fire. It picks out certain parts of the Sermon on the Mount, though even these it often rejects in practice. It leaves the doctrine of non-resistance, for example, to be practised only by non-Christians such as Gandhi. The precepts that it particularly favours are held to embody such a lofty morality that they must have had a divine origin. And yet Professor Butterfield must know that these precepts were all uttered by Jews before the time of Christ. They are to be found, for example, in the teaching of Hillel and in the "Testaments of the Twelve Patriarchs", concerning which the Rev. Dr R. H. Charles, a leading authority in this matter, says: "The Sermon on the Mount reflects in several instances the spirit and even reproduces the very phrases of our text: many passages in the Gospels exhibit traces of the same, and St Paul seems to have used the book as a *vade-mecum*." Dr Charles is of the opinion that Christ must have been acquainted with this work. If, as we are sometimes told, the loftiness of the ethical teaching proves the divinity of its author, it is the unknown writer of these Testaments who must have been divine.

That the world is in a bad way is undeniable, but there is not the faintest reason in history to suppose that Christianity offers a way out. Our troubles have sprung, with the inexorability of Greek tragedy, from the First World War, of which the Communists and the Nazis were products. The First World War was wholly Christian in origin. The three Emperors were devout, and so were the more warlike of the British Cabinet. Opposition to the war came, in Germany and Russia, from the Socialists, who were anti-Christian; in France, from Juarès, whose assassin was applauded by earnest Christians; in England, from John Morley, a noted atheist. The most dangerous features of Communism are reminiscent of the medieval Church. They consist of fanatical acceptance of doctrines embodied in a Sacred Book, unwillingness to examine these doctrines critically, and savage persecution of those who reject them. It is not to a revival of fanaticism and bigotry in the West that we must look for a happy issue. Such a revival, if it occurs, will only mean that the hateful

14

BERTRAND RUSSELL

features of the Communist régime have become universal. What the world needs is reasonableness, tolerance, and a realization of the interdependence of the parts of the human family. This interdependence has been enormously increased by modern inventions, and the purely mundane arguments for a kindly attitude to one's neighbour are very much stronger than they were at any earlier time. It is to such considerations that we must look, and not to a return to obscurantist myths. Intelligence, it might be said, has caused our troubles; but it is not unintelligence that will cure them. Only more and wiser intelligence can make a happier world.

QUESTIONS

1. Russell divides religious moral rules into two categories. Which kind does he think are legitimate rules? Which kind are not? Why?

2. What similarities does Russell see between communism and Christianity?

3. How does word choice reflect Russell's attitude toward religion? Find evidence of words that reflect his attitude.

4. Explain the following allusions: Naboth's vineyard (paragraph 4), Thomas Aquinas (paragraph 7), the Inquisition (paragraph 8), and Sir Thomas More (paragraph 8).

5. Trace the line of reasoning from paragraph 4 through paragraph 7. What transition words mark the line Russell's reasoning takes?

6. How does the example given about mining camps at the end of paragraph 5 differ from the preceding examples in the paragraph? How does this kind of example help corroborate Russell's argument?

7. What is the subject of paragraphs 9 to 11? What purpose do they serve for the development of Russell's argument? How do they differ from paragraphs 12 and 13?

8. Explain how Russell uses paragraph 14 to conclude his essay.

9. How do you think Russell would respond to the resurgence of evangelical Protestant religion in America? Do you think such a movement threatens or supports morality?

10. a. Write an essay in which you refute the claims of an editorial in your local newspaper.
b. Write a paper explaining why religion can or cannot help you become a better person.

Aes Triplex

Robert Louis Stevenson (1850–1894), poet, novelist, and journalist, was born in Scotland and spent a great part of his life traveling through Europe and the South Pacific. He is best known for his children's novel, *Treasure Island* (1881), his collection of children's poetry, *A Children's Garden of Verses* (1885), *Kidnapped* (1886), and *Dr. Jekyll and Mr. Hyde* (1886). Stevenson's love of adventure and his distaste for conventions influenced his opinions, as the following essay demonstrates.

he changes wrought by death are in themselves so 1
sharp and final, and so terrible and melancholy in their consequences, that the thing stands alone in man's experience and has no parallel upon earth. It outdoes all other accidents because it is the last of them. Sometimes it leaps suddenly upon its victims, like a Thug; sometimes it lays a regular siege and creeps upon their citadel during a score of years. And when the business is done, there is sore havoc made in other people's lives, and a pin knocked out by which many subsidiary friendships hung together. There are empty chairs, solitary walks, and single beds at night. Again, in taking away our friends, death does not take them away utterly, but leaves behind a mocking, tragical, and soon intolerable residue, which must be hurriedly concealed. Hence a whole chapter of sights and customs striking to the mind, from the pyramids of Egypt to the gibbets and jule trees of medieval Europe. The poorest persons have a bit of pageant going towards the tomb; memorial stones are set up over the least memorable; and, in order to preserve some show of respect for what remains of our old loves and friendships, we must accompany it with much grimly ludicrous ceremonial, and the hired undertaker parades before the door. All this, and much more of the same sort, accompanied by the eloquence of poets, has gone a great way to put humanity in error; nay, in many philosophies the error has been embodied and laid down with every circumstance of logic; although in real life the bustle and swiftness, in leaving people little time to think, have not left them time enough to go dangerously wrong in practice.

As a matter of fact, although few things are spoken of with 2
more fearful whisperings than this prospect of death, few have less influence on conduct under healthy circumstances. We have all heard of cities of South America built upon the side of fiery mountains, and how, even in this tremendous neighborhood, the inhabitants are not

a jot more impressed by the solemnity of moral conditions than if they were delving gardens in the greenest corner of England. There are serenades and suppers and much gallantry among the myrtles overhead; and meanwhile the foundation shudders underfoot, the bowels of the mountain growl, and at any moment living ruin may leap sky-high into the moonlight, and tumble man and his merry-making in the dust. In the eyes of very young people, and very dull old ones, there is something indescribably reckless and desperate in such a picture. It seems not credible that respectable married people, with umbrellas, should find appetite for a bit of supper within quite a long distance of a fiery mountain; ordinary life begins to smell of high-handed debauch when it is carried on so close to a catastrophe; and even cheese and salad, it seems, could hardly be relished in such circumstances without something like a defiance of the Creator. It should be a place for nobody but hermits dwelling in prayer and maceration, or mere born-devils drowning care in a perpetual carouse.

And yet, when one comes to think upon it calmly, the situation of these South American citizens forms only a very pale figure for the state of ordinary mankind. This world itself, traveling blindly and swiftly in overcrowded space, among a million other worlds traveling blindly and swiftly in contrary directions, may very well come by a knock that would set it into explosion like a penny squib. And what, pathologically looked at, is the human body with all its organs, but a mere bagful of petards? The least of these is as dangerous to the whole economy as the ship's powder-magazine to the ship; and with every breath we breathe, and every meal we eat, we are putting one more of them in peril. If we clung as devotedly as some philosophers pretend we do to the abstract idea of life, or were half as frightened as they make out we are, for the subversive accident that ends it all, the trumpets might sound by the hour and no one would follow them into battle—the blue-peter might fly at the truck, but who would climb into a sea-going ship? Think (if these philosophers were right) with what a preparation of spirit we should affront the daily peril of the dinner-table: a deadlier spot than any battle-field in history, where the far greater proportion of our ancestors have miserably left their bones! What woman would ever be lured into marriage, so much more dangerous than the wildest sea? And what would it be to grow old? For, after a certain distance, every step we take in life we find the ice growing thinner below our feet, and all around us and behind us we see our contemporaries going through. By the time a man gets well into the seventies, his continued existence is a mere miracle; and when he lays his old bones in bed for the night, there is an overwhelming probability that he will never see the day. Do the old men mind it, as a matter of fact? Why, no. They

AES TRIPLEX

were never merrier; they have their grog at night, and tell the raciest stories; they hear of the death of people about their own age, or even younger, not as if it was a grisly warning, but with a simple childlike pleasure at having outlived some one else; and when a draft might puff them out like a guttering candle, or a bit of a stumble shatter them like so much glass, their old hearts keep sound and un-affrighted, and they go on, bubbling with laughter, through years of man's age compared to which the valley at Balaklava was as safe and peaceful as a village cricket-green on Sunday. It may fairly be questioned (if we look at the peril only) whether it was a much more daring feat for Curtius to plunge into the gulf than for any old gentleman of ninety to doff his clothes and clamber into bed.

Indeed, it is a memorable subject for consideration, with what unconcern and gaiety mankind pricks on along the Valley of the Shadow of Death. The whole way is one wilderness of snares; and the end of it, for those who fear the last pinch, is irrevocable ruin. And yet we go spinning through it all, like a party for the Derby. Perhaps the reader remembers one of the humorous devices of the deified Caligula: how he encouraged a vast concourse of holiday-makers on to his bridge over Baiae bay, and, when they were in the height of their enjoyment, turned loose the Pretorian guards among the company, and had them tossed into the sea. This is no bad miniature of the dealings of nature with the transitory race of man. Only, what a checkered picnic we have of it, even while it lasts! and into what great waters, not to be crossed by any swimmer, God's pale Pretorian throws us over in the end! 4

We live the time that a match flickers; we pop the cork of a ginger-beer bottle, and the earthquake swallows us on the instant. Is it not odd, is it not incongruous, is it not in the highest sense of human speech, incredible, that we should think so highly of the ginger-beer and regard so little the devouring earthquake? The love of Life and the fear of Death are two famous phrases that grow harder to understand the more we think about them. It is a well-known fact that an immense proportion of boat accidents would never happen if people held the sheet in their hands instead of making it fast; and yet, unless it be some martinet of a professional mariner or some landsman with shattered nerves, every one of God's creatures makes it fast. A strange instance of man's unconcern and brazen boldness in the face of death! 5

We confound ourselves with metaphysical phrases, which we import into daily talk with noble inappropriateness. We have no idea of what death is, apart from its circumstances and some of its consequences to others; and although we have some experience of living, there is not a man on earth who has flown so high into abstraction as to have any practical guess at the meaning of the word 6

ROBERT LOUIS STEVENSON 8

life. All literature, from Job and Omar Khayam to Thomas Carlyle or Walt Whitman, is but an attempt to look upon the human state with such largeness of view as shall enable us to rise from the consideration of living to the Definition of Life. And our sages give us about the best satisfaction in their power when they say that it is a vapor, or a show, or made out of the same stuff with dreams. Philosophy, in its more rigid sense, has been at the same work for ages; and after a myriad bald heads have wagged over the problem, and piles of words have been heaped one upon another into dry and cloudy volumes without end, philosophy has the honor of laying before us, with modest pride, her contribution towards the subject: that life is a Permanent Possibility of Sensation. Truly a fine result! A man may very well love beef, or hunting, or a woman; but surely, surely, not a Permanent Possibility of Sensation! He may be afraid of a precipice, or a dentist, or a large enemy with a club, or even an undertaker's man; but not certainly of abstract death. We may trick with the word life in its dozen senses until we are weary of tricking; we may argue in terms of all the philosophies on earth; but one fact remains true throughout—that we do not love life, in the sense that we are greatly preoccupied about its conservation; that we do not, properly speaking, love life at all, but living. Into the views of the least careful there will enter some degree of providence; no man's eyes are fixed entirely on the passing hour; but although we have some anticipation of good health, good weather, wine, active employment, love, and self-approval, the sum of these anticipations does not amount to anything like a general view of life's possibilities and issues; nor are those who cherish them most vividly, at all the most scrupulous of their personal safety. To be deeply interested in the accidents of our existence, to enjoy keenly the mixed texture of human experience, rather leads a man to disregard precautions, and risk his neck against a straw. For surely the love of living is stronger in an Alpine climber roping over a peril, or a hunter riding merrily at a stiff fence, than in a creature who lives upon a diet and walks a measured distance in the interest of his constitution.

There is a great deal of very vile nonsense talked upon both sides of the matter; tearing divines reducing life to the dimensions of a mere funeral procession, so short as to be hardly decent; and melancholy unbelievers yearning for the tomb as if it were a world too far away. Both sides must feel a little ashamed of their performances now and again, when they draw in their chairs to dinner. Indeed, a good meal and a bottle of wine is an answer to most standard works upon the question. When a man's heart warms to his viands, he forgets a great deal of sophistry, and soars into a rosy zone of contemplation. Death may be knocking at the door, like the Commander's statue; we have something else in hand, thank God, and let

7

him knock. Passing bells are ringing the world over. All the world over, and every hour, some one is parting company with all his aches and ecstasies. For us also the trap is laid. But we are so fond of life that we have no leisure to entertain the terror of death. It is a honeymoon with us all through, and none of the longest. Small blame to us if we give our whole hearts to this glowing bride of ours—to the appetites, to honor, to the hungry curiosity of the mind, to the pleasure of the eyes in nature, and the pride of our own nimble bodies.

We all of us appreciate the sensations; but as for caring about   8
the Permanence of the Possibility, a man's head is generally very bald, and his senses very dull, before he comes to that. Whether we regard life as a lane leading to a dead wall—a mere bag's end, as the French say—or whether we think of it as a vestibule or gymnasium, where we wait our turn and prepare our faculties for some more noble destiny; whether we thunder in a pulpit, or pule in little atheistic poetry-books, about its vanity and brevity; whether we look justly for years of health and vigor, or are about to mount into a bath-chair, as a step towards the hearse; in each and all of these views and situations there is but one conclusion possible: that a man should stop his ears against paralyzing terror, and run the race that is set before him with a single mind. No one surely could have recoiled with more heartache and terror from the thought of death than our respected lexicographer; and yet we know how little it affected his conduct, how wisely and boldly he walked, and in what a fresh and lively vein he spoke of life. Already an old man, he ventured on his Highland tour; and his heart, bound with triple brass, did not recoil before twenty-seven individual cups of tea. As courage and intelligence are the two qualities best worth a good man's cultivation, so it is the first part of intelligence to recognize our precarious estate in life, and the first part of courage to be not at all abashed before the fact. A frank and somewhat headlong carriage, not looking too anxiously before, not dallying in maudlin regret over the past, stamps the man who is well armored for this world.

And not only well armored for himself, but a good friend and   9
a good citizen to boot. We do not go to cowards for tender dealing; there is nothing so cruel as panic; the man who has least fear for his own carcase, has most time to consider others. That eminent chemist who took his walks abroad in tin shoes, and subsisted wholly upon tepid milk, had all his work cut out for him in considerate dealings with his own digestion. So soon as prudence has begun to grow up in the brain, like a dismal fungus, it finds its first expression in a paralysis of generous acts. The victim begins to shrink spiritually; he develops a fancy for parlors with a regulated temperature, and takes his morality on the principle of tin shoes and tepid milk. The care of one important body or soul becomes so engrossing that all the noises

of the outer world begin to come thin and faint into the parlor with the regulated temperature; and the tin shoes go equably forward over blood and rain. To be otherwise is to ossify; and the scruple-monger ends by standing stock still. Now the man who has his heart on his sleeve, and a good whirling weathercock of a brain, who reckons his life as a thing to be dashingly used and cheerfully hazarded, makes a very different acquaintance of the world, keeps all his pulses going true and fast, and gathers impetus as he runs, until, if he be running towards anything better than wildfire, he may shoot up and become a constellation in the end. Lord look after his health, Lord have a care of his soul, says he; and he has at the key of the position, and swashes through incongruity and peril towards his aim. Death is on all sides of him with pointed batteries, as he is on all sides of all of us; unfortunate surprises gird him round; mim-mouthed friends and relations hold up their hands in quite a little elegiacal synod about his path: and what cares he for all this? Being a true lover of living, a fellow with something pushing and spontaneous in his inside, he must, like any other soldier, in any other stirring, deadly warfare, push on at his best pace until he touch the goal. "A peerage or Westminister Abbey!" cried Nelson in his bright, boyish, heroic manner. These are great incentives; not for any of these, but for the plain satisfaction of living, of being about their business in some sort or other, do the brave, serviceable men of every nation tread down the nettle danger, and pass flying over all the stumbling-blocks of prudence. Think of the heroism of Johnson, think of that superb indifference to mortal limitation that set him upon his dictionary, and carried him through triumphantly until the end! Who, if he were wisely considerate of things at large, would ever embark upon any work much more considerable than a halfpenny postcard? Who would project a serial novel, after Thackeray and Dickens had each fallen in mid-course? Who would find heart enough to begin to live, if he dallied with the consideration of death?

And, after all, what sorry and pitiful quibbling all this is! To forgo all the issues of living, in a parlor with a regulated temperature—as if that were not to die a hundred times over, and for ten years at a stretch! As if it were not to die in one's own lifetime, and without even the sad immunities of death! As if it were not to die, and yet to be the patient spectators of our own pitiable change! The Permanent Possibility is preserved, but the sensations carefully held at arm's length, as if one kept a photographic plate in a dark chamber. It is better to lose health like a spendthrift than to waste it like a miser. It is better to live and be done with it, than to die daily in the sick room. By all means begin your folio; even if the doctor does not give you a year, even if he hesitates about a month, make one brave push and see what can be accomplished in a week. It is not only in finished undertakings that we ought to honor useful labor. A spirit goes out of the man who means execution, which outlives the most untimely ending. All who have meant good work with their whole hearts, have done good work, although they may die before they have the time to sign it. Every heart that has beat strong and cheerfully has left a hopeful impulse behind it in the world, and bettered the tradition of mankind. And even if death catch people, like an open pitfall, and in mid-career, laying out vast projects, and planning monstrous foundations, flushed with hope, and their mouths full of boastful language, they should be at once tripped up and silenced: is there not something brave and spirited in such a termination? and does not life go down with a better grace, foaming in full body over a precipice, than miserably straggling to an end in sandy deltas? When the Greeks made their fine saying that those whom the gods love die young, I cannot help believing they had this sort of death also in their eye. For surely, at whatever age it overtake the man, this is to die young. Death has not been suffered to take so much as an illusion from his heart. In the hot-fit of life, a-tiptoe on the highest point of being, he passes at a bound on to the other side. The noise of the mallet and chisel is scarcely quenched, the trumpets are hardly done blowing, when, trailing with him clouds of glory, this happy-starred, full-blooded spirit shoots into the spiritual land.

QUESTIONS

1. Why does Stevenson say, "The love of Life and the fear of Death are two famous phrases that grow harder to understand the more we think about them"?

2. For what kinds of people does Stevenson feel contempt? Why?

3. There are numerous instances of irony in this essay. Give five examples of Stevenson's use of hyperbole for ironic purposes.

4. Stevenson often uses allusions and expressions that no longer are common in our language. Explain the following: "the blue-peter might fly at the truck" (paragraph 3), "Curtius" (paragraph 3), "a party for the Derby" (paragraph 4), "the humorous devices of the deified Caligula" (paragraph 4), "like the Commander's statue" (paragraph 7), and "our respected lexicographer" (paragraph 8).

5. Stevenson says "A man may very well love beef, or hunting, or a woman; but surely, not a Permanent Possibility of Sensation!" How does Stevenson use this phrase as an organizing device? What is the difference between the two categories?

6. Explain the use of the analogy in paragraph 2. How is it interpreted? Give two other examples of extended analogies in this essay.

7. Most philosophers frequently use abstractions. Stevenson, of course, is critical of most philosophers. How does he use language to complement his thesis? Give examples of concrete language in this essay.

8. Divide this essay into three parts and explain why you divided it where you did. How are transitions used to mark the shifts you identified?

9. Stevenson believes that it is better to die bravely. Do you agree? Do you agree with his contempt for caution?

10. Write an essay using analogies and metaphors to describe love, beauty, life, or evil.

Mathematics, Science, and Technology

T. H. HUXLEY

We Are All Scientists

Thomas Henry Huxley (1825–1895) was one of the nineteenth century's most brilliant adventurers, educators, polemicists, and scientists. He defended Charles Darwin's theory of evolution to an often hostile English scientific community. He reformed the organization of the English elementary school. He labored incessantly to explain science to Britain's middle and working classes. Most of Huxley's works were republished in his *Collected Essays* (nine volumes, 1894–1908). In the following selection, Huxley dispels the popular belief that scientists think differently from the rest of us.

he method of scientific investigation is nothing but the expression of the necessary mode of working of the human mind. It is simply the mode at which all phenomena are reasoned about, rendered precise and exact. There is no more difference, between the mental operations of a man of science and those of an ordinary person, than there is between the operations and methods of a baker or of a butcher weighing out his goods in common scales, and the operations of a chemist in performing a difficult and complex analysis by means of his balance and finely graduated weights. It is not that the action of the scales in the one case, and the balance in the other, differ in the principles of their construction or manner of working; but the beam of one is set on an infinitely finer axis than the other, and of course turns by the addition of a much smaller weight.

You will understand this better, perhaps, if I give you some 2
familiar example. You have all heard it repeated, I dare say, that men of science work by means of induction and deduction, and that by the help of these operations, they, in a sort of sense, wring from Nature certain other things, which are called natural laws, and causes, and that out of these, by some cunning skill of their own, they build up hypotheses and theories. And it is imagined by many that the operations of the common mind can be by no means compared with these processes, and that they have to be acquired by a sort of special apprenticeship to the craft. To hear all these large words, you would think that the mind of a man of science must be constituted differently from that of his fellow men; but if you will not be frightened by terms, you will discover that you are quite wrong, and that all these terrible apparatus are being used by yourselves every day and every hour of your lives.

There is a well-known incident in one of Molière's plays, 3
when the author makes the hero express unbounded delight on being told that he had been talking prose during the whole of his life. In the same way I trust that you will take comfort, and be delighted with yourselves, on the discovery that you have been acting on the principles of inductive and deductive philosophy during the same period. Probably there is not one here who has not in the course of the day had occasion to set in motion a complex train of reasoning, of the very same kind, though differing of course in degree, as that which a scientific man goes through in tracing the causes of natural phenomena.

A very trivial circumstance will serve to exemplify this. 4
Suppose you go into a fruiterer's shop, wanting an apple—you take up one, and, on biting it, you find it is sour; you look at it, and see that it is hard and green. You take up another one, and that too is hard, green, and sour. The shopman offers you a third; but, before biting it, you examine it, and find that it is hard and green, and you immediately say that you will not have it, as it must be sour, like that you have already tried.

Nothing can be more simple than that, you think; but if you 5
will take the trouble to analyze and trace out into its logical elements what has been done by the mind, you will be greatly surprised. In the first place, you have performed the operation of induction. You found that, in two experiences, hardness and greenness in apples went

 WE ARE ALL SCIENTISTS   **513**

together with sourness. It was so in the first case, and it was confirmed by the second. True, it is a very small basis, but still it is enough to make an induction from; you generalize the facts, and you expect to find sourness in apples where you get hardness and greenness. You found upon that a general law, that all hard and green apples are sour; and that, so far as it goes, is a perfect induction. Well, having got your natural law in this way, when you are offered another apple which you find is hard and green, you say, "All hard and green apples are sour; this apple is hard and green, therefore this apple is sour." That train of reasoning is what logicians call a syllogism, and has all its various parts and terms—its major premise, its minor premise, and its conclusion. And, by the help of further reasoning, which, if drawn out, would have to be exhibited in two or three other syllogisms, you arrive at your final determination, "I will not have that apple." So that, you see, you have, in the first place, established a law by induction, and upon that you have founded a deduction, and reasoned out the special conclusion of the particular case. Well now, suppose, having got your law, that at some time afterwards, you are discussing the qualities of apples with a friend: you will say to him, "It is a very curious thing but I find that all hard and green apples are sour!" Your friend says to you, "But how do you know that?" You at once reply, "Oh, because I have tried them over and over again, and have always found them to be so." Well, if we were talking science instead of common sense, we should call that an experimental verification. And, if still opposed, you go further, and say, "I have heard from the people in Somersetshire and Devonshire, where a large number of apples are grown, that they have observed the same thing. It is also found to be the case in Normandy, and in North America. In short, I find it to be the universal experience of mankind wherever attention has been directed to the subject." Whereupon, your friend, unless he is a very unreasonable man, agrees with you, and is convinced that you are quite right in the conclusion you have drawn. He believes, although perhaps he does not know he believes it, that the more extensive verifications are—that the more frequently experiments have been made, and results of the same kind arrived at—that the more varied the conditions under which the same results are attained, the more certain is the ultimate conclusion, and he disputes the question no further. He sees that the experiment has been tried under all sorts of conditions, as to time, place, and people, with the same result; and he says with you, therefore, that the law you have laid down must be a good one, and he must believe it.

In science we do the same thing; the philosopher exercises precisely the same faculties, though in a much more delicate manner. In scientific inquiry it becomes a matter of duty to expose a supposed

T. H. HUXLEY

6

law to every possible kind of verification, and to take care, moreover, that this is done intentionally, and not left to a mere accident, as in the case of the apples. And in science, as in common life, our confidence in a law is in exact proportion to the absence of variation in the result of our experimental verifications. For instance, if you let go your grasp of an article you may have in your hand, it will immediately fall to the ground. That is a very common verification of one of the best established laws of nature—that of gravitation. The method by which men of science establish the existence of that law is exactly the same as that by which we have established the trivial proposition about the sourness of hard and green apples. But we believe it in such an extensive, thorough, and unhesitating manner because the universal experience of mankind verifies it, and we can verify it ourselves at any time; and that is the strongest possible foundation on which any natural law can rest.

So much, then, by way of proof that the method of establish- 7
ing laws in science is exactly the same as that pursued in common life. Let us now turn to another matter (though really it is but another phase of the same question), and that is the method by which, from the relations of certain phenomena, we prove that some stand in the position of causes towards the others.

I want to put the case clearly before you, and I will therefore 8
show you what I mean by another familiar example. I will suppose that one of you, on coming down in the morning to the parlor of your house, finds that a teapot and some spoons which had been left in the room on the previous evening are gone—the window is open, and you observe the mark of a dirty hand on the window frame, and perhaps, in addition to that, you notice the impress of a hobnailed shoe on the gravel outside. All these phenomena have struck your attention instantly, and before two seconds have passed you say, "Oh, somebody has broken open the window, entered the room, and run off with the spoons and the teapot!" That speech is out of your mouth in a moment. And you will probably add, "I know he has; I am quite sure of it!" You mean to say exactly what you know; but in reality you are giving expression to what is, in all essential particulars, an hypothesis. You do not *know* it at all; it is nothing but an hypothesis rapidly framed in your own mind. And it is an hypothesis founded on a long train of inductions and deductions.

What are those inductions and deductions, and how have 9
you got at this hypothesis? You have observed, in the first place, that the window is open; but by a train of reasoning involving many inductions and deductions, you have probably arrived long before at the general law—and a very good one it is—that windows do not open of themselves; and you therefore conclude that something has opened the window. A second general law that you have arrived at in

WE ARE ALL SCIENTISTS

the same way is, that teapots and spoons do not go out of a window spontaneously, and you are satisfied that, as they are not now where you left them, they have been removed. In the third place, you look at the marks on the window sill, and the shoe-marks outside, and you say that in all previous experience the former kind of mark has never been produced by anything else but the hand of a human being; and the same experience shows that no other animal but man at present wears shoes with hobnails in them such as would produce the marks in the gravel. I do not know, even if we could discover any of those "missing links" that are talked about,that they would help us to any other conclusion! At any rate the law which states our present experience is strong enough for my present purpose. You next reach the conclusion that as these kinds of marks have not been left by any other animals than men, or are liable to be formed in any other way than by a man's hand and shoe, the marks in question have been formed by a man in that way. You have, further, a general law, founded on observation and experience, and that, too is, I am sorry to say, a very universal and unimpeachable one—that some men are thieves; and you assume at once from all these premises—and that is what constitutes your hypothesis—that the man who made the marks outside and on the window sill, opened the window, got into the room, and stole your teapot and spoons. You have now arrived at a *vera causa;* you have assumed a cause, which it is plain, is competent to produce all the phenomena you have observed. You can explain all these phenomena only by the hypothesis of a thief. But that is a hypothetical conclusion, of the justice of which you have no absolute proof at all; it is only rendered highly probable by a series of inductive and deductive reasonings.

I suppose your first action, assuming that you are a man of   10
ordinary common sense, and that you have established this hypothesis to your own satisfaction, will very likely be to go off for the police, and set them on the track of the burglar, with the view to the recovery of your property. But just as you are starting with this object, some person comes in, and on learning what you are about, says, "My good friend, you are going on a great deal too fast. How do you know that the man who really made the marks took the spoons? It might have been a monkey that took them and the man may have merely looked in afterwards." You would probably reply, "Well, that is all very well, but you see it is contrary to all experience of the way teapots and spoons are abstracted; so that, at any rate, your hypothesis is less probable than mine." While you are talking the thing over in this way, another friend arrives, one of that good kind of people that I was talking of a little while ago. And he might say, "Oh, my dear sir, you are certainly going on a great deal too fast. You are most presumptuous. You admit that all these occurrences took place when

you were fast asleep, at a time when you could not possibly have known anything about what was taking place. How do you know that the laws of Nature are not suspended during the night? It may be that there has been some kind of supernatural interference in this case." In point of fact, he declares that your hypothesis is one of which you cannot at all demonstrate the truth, and that you are by no means sure that the laws of Nature are the same when you are asleep as when you are awake.

Well, now, you cannot at the moment answer that kind of reasoning. You feel that your worthy friend has you somewhat at a disadvantage. You will feel perfectly convinced in your own mind, however, that you are quite right, and you say to him, "My good friend, I can only be guided by the natural probabilities of the case, and if you will be kind enough to stand aside and permit me to pass, I will go and fetch the police." Well, we will suppose that your journey is successful, and that by good luck you meet with a policeman; that eventually the burglar is found with your property on his person, and the marks correspond to his hand and to his boots. Probably any jury would consider those facts a very good experimental verification of your hypothesis, touching the cause of the abnormal phenomena observed in your parlor, and would act accordingly. 11

Now, in this suppositious case, I have taken phenomena of a very common kind, in order that you might see what are the different steps in an ordinary process of reasoning, if you will only take the trouble to analyze it carefully. All the operations I have described, you will see, are involved in the mind of any man of sense in leading him to a conclusion as to the course he should take in order to make good a robbery and punish the offender. I say that you are led, in that case, to your conclusion by exactly the same train of reasoning as that which a man of science pursues when he is endeavoring to discover the origin and laws of the most occult phenomena. The process is, and always must be, the same; and precisely the same mode of reasoning was employed by Newton and Laplace in their endeavors to discover and define the causes of the movements of the heavenly bodies as you, with your own common sense, would employ to detect a burglar. The only difference is that the nature of the inquiry being more abstruse, every step has to be most carefully watched, so that there may not be a single crack or flaw in your hypothesis. A flaw or crack in many of the hypotheses of daily life may be of little or no moment as affecting the general correctness of the conclusions at which we may arrive; but, in a scientific inquiry, a fallacy, a great or small, is always of importance, and is sure to be in the long run constantly productive of mischievous, if not fatal results. 12

Do not allow yourselves to be misled by the common notion that an hypothesis is untrustworthy simply because it is an hypothe- 13 sis. It is often urged, in respect to some scientific conclusion, that, after all, it is only an hypothesis. But what more have we to guide us in nine-tenths of the most important affairs of daily life than hypotheses, and often very ill-based ones? So that in science, where the evidence of a hypothesis is subjected to the most rigid examination, we may rightly pursue the same course. You may have hypotheses and hypotheses. A man may say, if he likes, that the moon is made of green cheese: that is an hypothesis. But another man, who has devoted a great deal of time and attention to the subject, and availed himself of the most powerful telescopes and the results of the observations of others, declares that in his opinion it is probably composed of materials very similar to those of which our own earth is made up: and that is also only an hypothesis. But I need not tell you that there is an enormous difference in the value of the two hypotheses. That one which is based on sound scientific knowledge is sure to have a corresponding value; and that which is a mere hasty random guess is likely to have but little value. Every great step in our progress in discovering causes has been made in exactly the same way as that which I have detailed to you. A person observing the occurrence of certain facts and phenomena asks, naturally enough, what process, what kind of operation known to occur in Nature applied to the particular case, will unravel and explain the mystery? Hence you have the scientific hypothesis; and its value will be proportionate to the care and completeness with which its basis has been tested and verified. It is in these matters as in the commonest affairs of practical life: the guess of the fool will be folly, while the guess of the wise man will contain wisdom. In all cases, you see that the value of the result depends on the patience and faithfulness with which the investigator applies to his hypothesis every possible kind of verification.

QUESTIONS

1. Describe the process of reasoning that, according to Huxley, people use when they are deciding to eat green apples.

2. Why does Huxley reject the reasoning of "some person" in paragraph 10?

3. Huxley uses several "large words," particularly in paragraphs 2 and 5. What are these words and what do they mean?

4. Huxley uses both the second- and first-person pronouns in this essay. How does this affect the tone of the essay?

5. What is the thesis of this essay? Where is it expressed for the first time?

6. How does Huxley use coordinating conjunctions to maintain coherence?

7. Huxley employs two long examples to support and clarify his thesis. Identify these examples and show how Huxley relates them to his thesis.

8. How does paragraph 2 map out the structure of the essay?

9. Do you agree with Huxley's thesis? Why or why not?

10. Write a paper using examples to show how you use inductive and deductive reasoning in everyday life.

ALBERT EINSTEIN

The Common Language of Science

Albert Einstein (1879–1955), one of the greatest scientists who ever lived, was born in Germany. Einstein spent the early years of his career working in the Swiss patent office in Bern. In 1905, while working there, he published the first of many papers on the theory of relativity. These papers revolutionized physics. In 1933, with the advent of nazism, Einstein fled to the United States, where he continued his theoretical work and spoke out for peace in the world. His works range from the scientific *Relativity: The Special and General Theory* (1918), to the personal *The World as I See It* (1934). In the following essay, Einstein discusses the origin of scientific language.

the first step towards language was to link acoustically   1
or otherwise commutable signs to sense-impressions. Most likely all sociable animals have arrived at this primitive kind of communication—at least to a certain degree. A higher development is reached when further signs are introduced and understood which establish relations between those other signs designating sense-impression. At this stage it is already possible to report somewhat complex series of impressions; we can say that language has come to existence. If language is to lead at all to understanding, there must be rules concerning the relations between the signs on the one hand and on the other hand there must be a stable correspondence between signs and impressions. In their childhood individuals connected by the same language grasp these rules

and relations mainly by intuition. When man becomes conscious of the rules concerning the relations between signs the so-called grammar of language is established.

In an early stage the words may correspond directly to impressions. At a later stage this direct connection is lost insofar as some words convey relations to perceptions only if used in connection with other words (for instance such words as: "is," "or," "thing"). Then word-groups rather than single words refer to perceptions. When language becomes thus partially independent from the background of impressions a greater inner coherence is gained.

Only at this further development where frequent use is made of so-called abstract concepts, language becomes an instrument of reasoning in the true sense of the word. But it is also this development which turns language into a dangerous source of error and deception. Everything depends on the degree to which words and word-combinations correspond to the world of impression.

What is it that brings about such an intimate connection between language and thinking? Is there no thinking without the use of language, namely in concepts and concept-combinations for which words need not necessarily come to mind? Has not everyone of us struggled for words although the connection between "things" was already clear?

We might be inclined to attribute to the act of thinking complete independence from language if the individual formed or were able to form his concepts without the verbal guidance of his environment. Yet most likely the mental shape of an individual, growing up under such conditions, would be very poor. Thus we may conclude that the mental development of the individual and his way of forming concepts depend to a high degree upon language. This makes us realize to what extent the same language means the same mentality. In this sense thinking and language are linked together.

What distinguishes the language of science from language as we ordinarily understand the word? How is it that scientific language is international? What science strives for is an utmost acuteness and clarity of concepts as regards their mutual relation and their correspondence to sensory data. As an illustration let us take the language of Euclidian geometry and Algebra. They manipulate with a small number of independently introduced concepts, respectively symbols, such as the integral number, the straight line, the point, as well as with signs which designate the fundamental operations, that is the connections between those fundamental concepts. This is the basis for the construction, respectively definition of all other statements and concepts. The connection between concepts and statements on the one hand and the sensory data on the other hand is established

ALBERT EINSTEIN

through acts of counting and measuring whose performance is sufficiently well determined.

The super-national character of scientific concepts and scientific language is due to the fact that they have been set up by the best brains of all countries and all times. In solitude and yet in cooperative effort as regards the final effect they created the spiritual tools for the technical revolutions which have transformed the life of mankind in the last centuries. Their system of concepts have served as a guide in the bewildering chaos of perceptions so that we learned to grasp general truths from particular observations. 7

What hopes and fears does the scientific method imply for mankind? I do not think that this is the right way to put the question. Whatever this tool in the hand of man will produce depends entirely on the nature of the goals alive in this mankind. Once these goals exist, the scientific method furnishes means to realize them. Yet it cannot furnish the very goals. The scientific method itself would not have led anywhere, it would not even have been born without a passionate striving for clear understanding. 8

Perfections of means and confusion of goals seem—in my opinion—to characterize our age. If we desire sincerely and passionately the safety, the welfare and the free development of the talents of all men, we shall not be in want of the means to approach such a state. Even if only a small part of mankind strives for such goals, their superiority will prove itself in the long run. 9

QUESTIONS

1. According to Einstein, when in the development of language does scientific language appear? How is it different from and similar to nonscientific language?

2. Why does Einstein say that language can "turn" into a dangerous source of error and deception?

3. Explain the use of rhetorical questions in this essay.

4. What is the point of view of this essay? How does this viewpoint complement the diction and tone of the essay?

5. What paragraphs use narrative? What words indicate the development of the narrative?

6. Give reasons and evidence for saying this essay uses extended definition.

7. Why is paragraph 6 important to the development of this essay? What rhetorical technique is used here?

8. Explain the relation of paragraphs 8 and 9 to the rest of the essay. What is the topic of paragraph 9?

9. If the language of science cannot define goals, what kinds of language can? Can we trust science to solve our problems? Explain.

10. a. Write an essay distinguishing means from goals in education, religion, or business.
b. Describe a particular kind of language—academic, political, or religious—and explain how it functions in relation to language in general.

LEWIS THOMAS

On Societies as Organisms

Lewis Thomas (1913–   ) has been the president of the Memorial Sloan-Kettering Cancer Center since 1973. He first came to public attention when his collection of essays, *Lives of a Cell* (1974), appeared. Because of his eloquent capacity to extract metaphors from the discoveries of modern biology and because of his optimism, Thomas's essays have attracted a large and enthusiastic following. Another collection of his essays, *The Medusa and the Snail,* was published in 1979. Thomas can discover an almost magical value in the most humble activities, as the essay below demonstrates.

Viewed from a suitable height, the aggregating clusters of   1
medical scientists in the bright sunlight of the board-
walk at Atlantic City, swarmed there from everywhere
for the annual meetings, have the look of assemblages
of social insects. There is the same vibrating, ionic movement,
interrupted by the darting back and forth of jerky individuals to touch
antennae and exchange small bits of information; periodically, the
mass casts out, like a trout-line, a long single file unerringly toward
Child's. If the boards were not fastened down, it would not be a
surprise to see them put together a nest of sorts.

It is permissible to say this sort of thing about humans. They   2
do resemble, in their most compulsively social behavior, ants at a
distance. It is, however, quite bad form in biological circles to put it
the other way round, to imply that the operation of insect societies
has any relation at all to human affairs. The writers of books on insect
behavior generally take pains, in their prefaces, to caution that insects

are like creatures from another planet, that their behavior is absolutely foreign, totally unhuman, unearthly, almost unbiological. They are more like perfectly tooled but crazy little machines, and we violate science when we try to read human meanings in their arrangements.

It is hard for a bystander not to do so. Ants are so much like human beings as to be an embarrassment. They farm fungi, raise aphids as livestock, launch armies into wars, use chemical sprays to alarm and confuse enemies, capture slaves. The families of weaver ants engage in child labor, holding their larvae like shuttles to spin out the thread that sews the leaves together for their fungus gardens. They exchange information ceaselessly. They do everything but watch television. 3

What makes us most uncomfortable is that they, and the bees and termites and social wasps, seem to live two kinds of lives: they are individuals, going about the day's business without much evidence of thought for tomorrow, and they are at the same time component parts, cellular elements, in the huge, writhing, ruminating organism of the Hill, the nest, the hive. It is because of this aspect, I think, that we most wish for them to be something foreign. We do not like the notion that there can be collective societies with the capacity to behave like organisms. If such things exist, they can have nothing to do with us. 4

Still, there it is. A solitary ant, afield, cannot be considered to have much of anything on his mind; indeed, with only a few neurons strung together by fibers, he can't be imagined to have a mind at all, much less a thought. He is more like a ganglion on legs. Four ants together, or ten, encircling a dead moth on a path, begin to look more like an idea. They fumble and shove, gradually moving the food toward the Hill, but as though by blind chance. It is only when you watch the dense mass of thousands of ants, crowded together around the Hill, blackening the ground, that you begin to see the whole beast, and now you observe it thinking, planning, calculating. It is an intelligence, a kind of live computer, with crawling bits for its wits. 5

At a stage in the construction, twigs of a certain size are needed, and all the members forage obsessively for twigs of just this size. Later, when outer walls are to be finished, thatched, the size must change, and as though given new orders by telephone, all the workers shift the search to the new twigs. If you disturb the arrangement of a part of the Hill, hundreds of ants will set it vibrating, shifting, until it is put right again. Distant sources of food are somehow sensed, and long lines, like tentacles, reach out over the ground, up over walls, behind boulders, to fetch it in. 6

Termites are even more extraordinary in the way they seem to accumulate intelligence as they gather together. Two or three termites in a chamber will begin to pick up pellets and move them from place 7

 ON SOCIETIES AS ORGANISMS **523**

to place, but nothing comes of it; nothing is built. As more join in, they seem to reach a critical mass, a quorum, and the thinking begins. They place pellets atop pellets, then throw up columns and beautiful, curving, symmetrical arches, and the crystalline architecture of vaulted chambers is created. It is not known how they communicate with each other, how the chains of termites building one column know when to turn toward the crew on the adjacent column, or how, when the time comes, they manage the flawless joining of the arches. The stimuli that set them off at the outset, building collectively instead of shifting things about, may be pheromones released when they reach committee size. They react as if alarmed. They become agitated, excited, and then they begin working, like artists.

Bees live lives of organisms, tissues, cells, organelles, all at 8 the same time. The single bee, out of the hive retrieving sugar (instructed by the dancer: "south-southeast for seven hundred meters, clover—mind you make corrections for the sundrift") is still as much a part of the hive as if attached by a filament. Building the hive, the workers have the look of embryonic cells organizing a developing tissue; from a distance they are like the viruses inside a cell, running off row after row of symmetrical polygons as though laying down crystals. When the time for swarming comes, and the old queen prepares to leave with her part of the population, it is as though the hive were involved in mitosis. There is an agitated moving of bees back and forth, like granules in cell sap. They distribute themselves in almost precisely equal parts, half to the departing queen, half to the new one. Thus, like an egg, the great, hairy, black and golden creature splits in two, each with an equal share of the family genome.

The phenomenon of separate animals joining up to form an 9 organism is not unique in insects. Slime-mold cells do it all the time, of course, in each life cycle. At first they are single amebocytes swimming around, eating bacteria, aloof from each other, untouching, voting straight Republican. Then, a bell sounds, and acrasin is released by special cells toward which the others converge in stellate ranks, touch, fuse together, and construct the slug, solid as a trout. A splendid stalk is raised, with a fruiting body on top, and out of this comes the next generation of amebocytes, ready to swim across the same moist ground, solitary and ambitious.

Herring and other fish in schools are at times so closely 10 integrated, their actions so coordinated, that they seem to be functionally a great multi-fish organism. Flocking birds, especially the seabirds nesting on the slopes of offshore islands in Newfoundland, are similarly attached, connected, synchronized.

Although we are by all odds the most social of all social 11 animals—more interdependent, more attached to each other, more

LEWIS THOMAS

inseparable in our behavior than bees—we do not often feel our conjoined intelligence. Perhaps, however, we are linked in circuits for the storage, processing, and retrieval of information, since this appears to be the most basic and universal of all human enterprises. It may be our biological function to build a certain kind of Hill. We have access to all the information of the biosphere, arriving as elementary units in the stream of solar photons. When we have learned how these are rearranged against randomness, to make, say, springtails, quantum mechanics, and the late quartets, we may have a clearer notion how to proceed. The circuitry seems to be there, even if the current is not always on.

The system of communications used in science should pro- 12
vide a neat, workable model for studying mechanisms of information-building in human society. Ziman, in a recent *Nature* essay, points out, "the invention of a mechanism for the systematic publication of *fragments* of scientific work may well have been the key event in the history of modern science." He continues:

> A regular journal carries from one research worker to another the various . . . observations which are of common interest. . . . A typical scientific paper has never pretended to be more than another little piece in a larger jigsaw—not significant in itself but as an element in a grander scheme. *This technique, of soliciting many modest contributions to the store of human knowledge, has been the secret of Western science since the seventeenth century, for it achieves a corporate, collective power that is far greater than any one individual can exert.* [italics mine].

With some alteration of terms, some toning down, the 13
passage could describe the building of a termite nest.

It is fascinating that the word "explore" does not apply to the 14
searching aspect of the activity, but has its origins in the sounds we make while engaged in it. We like to think of exploring in science as a lonely, meditative business, and so it is in the first stages, but always, sooner or later, before the enterprise reaches completion, as we explore, we call to each other, communicate, publish, send letters to the editor, present papers, cry out on finding.

QUESTIONS
1. Describe the insects that Thomas says have humanlike behavior.

2. Why do writers of books about insects avoid using personification in their descriptions? Why does Thomas purposely use it?

 ON SOCIETIES AS ORGANISMS **525**

3.   Thomas tends to use words that are not generally used; therefore, define "genome," "ionic," "amebocytes," "mitosis," "acrasin," "ganglion," "stellate," and "organism."

4.   Thomas uses metaphors frequently and imaginatively. List seven metaphors in the essay and describe how they are used.

5.   Paragraph 4 is crucial to the organization of the essay. What two methods of classification does it introduce?

6.   What is the difference between solitary and collective behavior among the social insects? Thomas compares this behavior to certain kinds of human behavior. What are the details of this comparison?

7.   What is the etymology of the word "explore" according to your dictionary? How does Thomas use this etymology?

8.   Thomas extends his discussion in paragraph 9 beyond insects. What effect does he achieve by doing this?

9.   Do you find it reassuring or disturbing to compare human behavior to insect behavior? Do you find it difficult to consider human society an organism? Why do you think Thomas finds this encouraging?

10.   a. Divide human behavior into groups (school, sports, business) and compare solitary and collective behavior within one or more groups.
b. Write an essay comparing your pet's behavior to human behavior.

BENJAMIN FRANKLIN

Lead Poisoning

Benjamin Franklin (1706–1790), statesman, inventor, philanthropist, printer, scientist, diplomat, and author, was a founding father not only of the American nation but of American humor, language, and values. *Poor Richard's Almanack* (1732–1757) and his *Autobiography* (written between 1771 and 1789) have both had a tremendous influence on American readers and authors. In this letter, Franklin appears in the role of scientist and displays two classic qualities of a scientist: objective observation and communication of information.

DEAR FRIEND,

I recollect, that, when I had the great pleasure of seeing you at Southampton, now a 12month since, we had some conversation on the bad effects of lead taken inwardly; and that at your request I promis'd to send you in writing a particular account of several facts I then mention'd to you, of which you thought some good use might be made. I now sit down to fulfil that promise.

The first thing I remember of this kind was a general discourse in Boston, when I was a boy, of a complaint from North Carolina against New England rum, that it poison'd their people, giving them the dry bellyach, with a loss of the use of their limbs. The distilleries being examin'd on the occasion, it was found that several of them used leaden still-heads and worms, and the physicians were of opinion, that the mischief was occasioned by that use of lead. The legislature of Massachusetts thereupon pass'd an Act, prohibiting under severe penalties the use of such still-heads and worms thereafter. Inclos'd I send you a copy of the Act, taken from my printed law-book.

In 1724, being in London, I went to work in the printing-house of Mr. Palmer, Bartholomew Close, as a compositor. I there found a practice, I had never seen before, of drying a case of types (which are wet in distribution) by placing it sloping before the fire. I found this had the additional advantage, when the types were not only dry'd but heated, of being comfortable to the hands working over them in cold weather. I therefore sometimes heated my case when the types did not want drying. But an old workman, observing it, advis'd me not to do so, telling me I might lose the use of my hands by it, as two of our companions had nearly done, one of whom that us'd to earn his guinea a week, could not then make more than ten shillings, and the other, who had the dangles, but seven and sixpence. This, with a kind of obscure pain, that I had sometimes felt, as it were in the bones of my hand when working over the types made very hot, induced me to omit the practice. But talking afterwards with Mr. James, a letter-founder in the same Close, and asking him if his people, who work'd over the little furnaces of melted metal, were not subject to that disorder; he made light of any danger from the effluvia, but ascribed it to particles of the metal swallow'd with their food by slovenly workmen, who went to their meals after handling the metal, without well washing their fingers, so that some of the metalline particles were taken off by their bread and eaten with it. This appeared to have some reason in it. But the pain I had experienc'd made me still afraid of those effluvia.

LEAD POISONING

Being in Derbyshire at some of the furnaces for smelting of   4
lead ore, I was told, that the smoke of those furnaces was pernicious
to the neighbouring grass and other vegetables; but I do not recollect
to have heard any thing of the effect of such vegetables eaten by
animals. It may be well to make the enquiry.

In America I have often observ'd, that on the roofs of our   5
shingled houses, where moss is apt to grow in northern exposures, if
there be any thing on the roof painted with white lead, such as
balusters, or frames of dormant windows, etc., there is constantly a
streak on the shingles from such paint down to the eaves, on which
no moss will grow, but the wood remains constantly clean and free
from it. We seldom drink rain water that falls on our houses; and if we
did, perhaps the small quantity of lead, descending from such paint,
might not be sufficient to produce any sensible ill effect on our bodies.
But I have been told of a case in Europe, I forgot the place, where a
whole family was afflicted with what we call the dry bellyach, or
Colica Pictonum, by drinking rain-water. It was at a country-seat,
which, being situated too high to have the advantage of a well,
was supply'd with water from a tank, which received the water
from the leaded roofs. This had been drunk several years without mischief; but some young trees planted near the house growing up
above the roof, and shedding their leaves upon it, it was suppos'd
that an acid in those leaves had corroded the lead they cover'd
and furnish'd the water of that year with its baneful particles and
qualities.

When I was in Paris with Sir John Pringle in 1767, he visited   6
La Charité, a hospital particularly famous for the cure of that malady,
and brought from thence a pamphlet containing a list of the names of
persons, specifying their professions or trades, who had been cured
there. I had the curiosity to examine that list, and found that all the
patients were of trades, that, some way or other, use or work in lead;
such as plumbers, glaziers, painters, etc., excepting only two kinds,
stonecutters and soldiers. These I could not reconcile to my notion,
that lead was the cause òf that disorder. But on my mentioning this
difficulty to a physician of that hospital, he inform'd me that the
stonecutters are continually using melted lead to fix the ends of iron
balustrades in stone; and that the soldiers had been employ'd by
painters, as labourers, in grinding of colours.

This, my dear friend, is all I can at present recollect on the   7
subject. You will see by it, that the opinion of this mischievous effect
from lead is at least above sixty years old; and you will observe with
concern how long a useful truth may be known and exist, before it is
generally receiv'd and practis'd on.

I am, ever, yours most affectionately,
B. FRANKLIN

QUESTIONS

1. Franklin gives several examples of lead poisoning. When and where did the poisoning occur?

2. Identify the two symptoms among people that Franklin attributes to lead poisoning. What effects does lead have on plant life?

3. Franklin uses certain expressions that may be unfamiliar to the modern reader. Define "effluvia," "mischief," "the dangles," "the dry bellyache," and "pernicious."

4. How does this letter differ in style and tone from letters you write to your friends?

5. Does Franklin use inductive or deductive reasoning in this essay? Explain.

6. What is the effect of using personal experience in paragraph 3?

7. Explain why the evidence in paragraph 6 is particularly effective.

8. What conclusion does Franklin draw from his evidence? Does his conclusion surprise you?

9. In the past few years, many children have contracted lead poisoning. Would Franklin be surprised by this? If we have known for 200 years that lead is poisonous, why was it still being used in paints until about ten years ago?

10. Franklin accumulates different kinds of evidence to link a particular cause to particular effects. Write an essay in which you cite evidence you have gathered to relate a cause to an effect.

LOREN EISELEY

How Natural Is Natural?

Loren Eiseley (1907–1977) was an educator, anthropologist, poet, and author. He is best known for his books *The Immense Journey* (1957), *Darwin's Century* (1958), *The Firmament of Time* (1960), and *The Night Country* (1971). His books wonderfully combine poetic imagination with scientific objectivity. In the following essay, Eiseley shows his capacity for seeing profoundly into the most common scenes.

In the more obscure scientific circles which I frequent 1
there is a legend circulating about a late distinguished
scientist who, in his declining years, persisted in wearing enormous padded boots much too large for him. He
had developed, it seems, what to his fellows was a wholly irrational
fear of falling through the interstices of that largely empty molecular
space which common men in their folly speak of as the world. A stroll
across his living-room floor had become, for him, something as
dizzily horrendous as the activities of a window washer on the
Empire State Building. Indeed, with equal reason he could have
passed a ghostly hand through his own ribs.

The quivering network of his nerves, the awe-inspiring 2
movement of his thought had become a vague cloud of electrons
interspersed with the light-year distances that obtain between us and
the farther galaxies. This was the natural world which he had helped
to create, and in which, at last, he had found himself a lonely and
imprisoned occupant. All around him the ignorant rushed on their
way over the illusion of substantial floors, leaping, though they did
not see it, from particle to particle, over a bottomless abyss. There
was even a question as to the reality of the particles which bore them
up. It did not, however, keep insubstantial newspapers from being
sold, or insubstantial love from being made.

Not long ago I became aware of another world perhaps 3
equally natural and real, which man is beginning to forget. My
thinking began in New England under a boat dock. The lake I speak
of has been pre-empted and civilized by man. All day long in the
vacation season high-speed motorboats, driven with the reckless
abandon common to the young Apollos of our society, speed back
and forth, carrying loads of equally attractive girls. The shores echo to
the roar of powerful motors and the delighted screams of young
Americans with uncounted horsepower surging under their hands.
In truth, as I sat there under the boat dock, I had some desire to swim
or to canoe in the older ways of the great forest which once lay about
this region. Either notion would have been folly. I would have been
gaily chopped to ribbons by teen-age youngsters whose eyes were
always immutably fixed on the far horizons of space, or upon the
dials which indicated the speed of their passing. There was another
world, I was to discover, along the lake shallows and under the boat
dock, where the motors could not come.

As I sat there one sunny morning when the water was 4
peculiarly translucent, I saw a dark shadow moving swiftly over the
bottom. It was the first sign of life I had seen in this lake, whose
shores seemed to yield little but washed-in beer cans. By and by the
gliding shadow ceased to scurry from stone to stone over the bottom.
Unexpectedly, it headed almost directly for me. A furry nose with

LOREN EISELEY

gray whiskers broke the surface. Below the whiskers green water foliage trailed out in an inverted V as long as his body. A muskrat still lived in the lake. He was bringing in his breakfast.

I sat very still in the strips of sunlight under the pier. To my surprise the muskrat came almost to my feet with his little breakfast of greens. He was young, and it rapidly became obvious to me that he was laboring under an illusion of his own, and that he thought animals and men were still living in the Garden of Eden. He gave me a friendly glance from time to time as he nibbled his greens. Once, even, he went out into the lake again and returned to my feet with more greens. He had not, it seemed, heard very much about men. I shuddered. Only the evening before I had heard a man describe with triumphant enthusiasm how he had killed a rat in the garden because the creature had dared to nibble his petunias. He had even showed me the murder weapon, a sharp-edged brick. 5

On this pleasant shore a war existed and would go on until nothing remained but man. Yet this creature with the gray, appealing face wanted very little: a strip of shore to coast up and down, sunlight and moonlight, some weeds from the deep water. He was an edge-of-the-world dweller, caught between a vanishing forest and a deep lake preempted by unpredictable machines full of chopping blades. He eyed me nearsightedly, a green leaf poised in his mouth. Plainly he had come with some poorly instructed memory about the lion and the lamb. 6

"You had better run away now," I said softly, making no movement in the shafts of light. "You are in the wrong universe and must not make this mistake again. I am really a very terrible and cunning beast. I can throw stones." With this I dropped a little pebble at his feet. 7

He looked at me half blindly, with eyes much better adjusted to the wavering shadows of his lake bottom than to sight in the open air. He made almost as if to take the pebble up into his forepaws. Then a thought seemed to cross his mind—a thought perhaps telepathically received, as Freud once hinted, in the dark world below and before man, a whisper of ancient disaster heard in the depths of a burrow. Perhaps after all this was not Eden. His nose twitched carefully; he edged toward the water. 8

As he vanished in an oncoming wave, there went with him a natural world, distinct from the world of girls and motorboats, distinct from the world of the professor holding to reality by some great snowshoe effort in his study. My muskrat's shore-line universe was edged with the dark wall of hills on one side and the waspish drone of motors farther out, but it was a world of sunlight he had taken down into the water weeds. It hovered there, waiting for my disappearance. I walked away, obscurely pleased that darkness had 9

 HOW NATURAL IS NATURAL?

not gained on life by any act of mine. In so many worlds, I thought, how natural is "natural"—and is there anything we can call a natural world at all?

QUESTIONS

1. Describe the three "worlds" mentioned in this essay by Eiseley.

2. Why is Eiseley surprised that a muskrat still lives in the lake? Cite specific details that might threaten a muskrat in the lake's world.

3. The phrases "sunlight world" and "darkness" (paragraph 9) are meant to be taken figuratively. What do they mean?

4. Explain the allusions to "Apollos" (paragraph 3); "the Garden of Eden" (paragraph 5); and Freud (paragraph 8).

5. Explain the relation between paragraphs 1 to 2 and 3 to 9. What rhetorical technique do both groups use?

6. How does Eiseley use narration and description in his essay? Cite examples of both.

7. What details does Eiseley use in contrasting the muskrat's world to the typical American's world?

8. Analyze the way Eiseley develops his concluding paragraph.

9. Why does Eiseley despair at the disappearance of the other world? Why should we protect wildlife and wilderness if it means limiting our own growth?

10. Write an essay in which you contrast aspects of the natural world with the artificial world. Use details to support your contrast. For example, you can describe the life of a bird in the city, of a raccoon in the suburbs, or a deer or bear in a state park.

RACHEL CARSON

The Changing Year

Rachel Carson (1907–1964) could write with eloquence and sensitivity even as she presented the reader with a rigorous, often demanding, scientific scrutiny of nature. Carson's most famous works are *The Sea around Us* (1951) and *The Silent*

Spring (1962). The former book won her the National Book Award. The latter, an early study of the danger of pesticides to our environment, influenced President John Kennedy to appoint a commission to study her allegations. The following essay, a chapter from *The Sea around Us,* illustrates her knowledge as a scientist and her skill as a writer.

> *Thus with the year seasons return.*
> MILTON

For the sea as a whole, the alternation of day and night, the passage of the seasons, the procession of the years, are lost in its vastness, obliterated in its own changeless eternity. But the surface waters are different. The face of the sea is always changing. Crossed by colors, lights, and moving shadows, sparkling in the sun, mysterious in the twilight, its aspects and its moods vary hour by hour. The surface waters move with the tides, stir to the breath of the winds, and rise and fall to the endless, hurrying forms of the waves. Most of all, they change with the advance of the seasons. Spring moves over the temperate lands of our Northern Hemisphere in a tide of new life, of pushing green shoots and unfolding buds, all its mysteries and meanings symbolized in the northward migration of the birds, the awakening of sluggish amphibian life as the chorus of frogs rises again from the wet lands, the different sound of the wind which stirs the young leaves where a month ago it rattled the bare branches. These things we associate with the land, and it is easy to suppose that at sea there could be no such feeling of advancing spring. But the signs are there, and seen with understanding eye, they bring the same magical sense of awakening. 1

In the sea, as on land, spring is a time for the renewal of life. During the long months of winter in the temperate zones the surface waters have been absorbing the cold. Now the heavy water begins to sink, slipping down and displacing the warmer layers below. Rich stores of minerals have been accumulating on the floor of the continental shelf—some freighted down the rivers from the lands; some derived from sea creatures that have died and whose remains have drifted down to the bottom; some from the shells that once encased a diatom, the streaming protoplasm of a radiolarian, or the transparent tissues of a pteropod. Nothing is wasted in the sea; every particle of material is used over and over again, first by one creature, then by another. And when in spring the waters are deeply stirred, the warm bottom water brings to the surface a rich supply of minerals, ready for use by new forms of life. 2

Just as land plants depend on minerals in the soil for their 3

 THE CHANGING YEAR **533**

growth, every marine plant, even the smallest, is dependent upon the nutrient salts or minerals in the sea water. Diatoms must have silica, the element of which their fragile shells are fashioned. For these and all other microplants, phosphorus is an indispensable mineral. Some of these elements are in short supply and in winter may be reduced below the minimum necessary for growth. The diatom population must tide itself over this season as best it can. It faces a stark problem of survival, with no opportunity to increase, a problem of keeping alive the spark of life by forming tough protective spores against the stringency of winter, a matter of existing in a dormant state in which no demands shall be made on an environment that already withholds all but the most meager necessities of life. So the diatoms hold their place in the winter sea, like seeds of wheat in a field under snow and ice, the seeds from which the spring growth will come.

These, then, are the elements of the vernal blooming of the 4 sea: the "seeds" of the dormant plants, the fertilizing chemicals, the warmth of the spring sun.

In a sudden awakening, incredible in its swiftness, the 5 simplest plants of the sea begin to multiply. Their increase is of astronomical proportions. The spring sea belongs at first to the diatoms and to all the other microscopic plant life of the plankton. In the fierce intensity of their growth they cover vast areas of ocean with a living blanket of their cells. Mile after mile of water may appear red or brown or green, the whole surface taking on the color of the infinitesimal grains of pigment contained in each of the plant cells.

The plants have undisputed sway in the sea for only a short 6 time. Almost at once their own burst of multiplication is matched by a similar increase in the small animals of the plankton. It is the spawning time of the copepod and the glassworm, the pelagic shrimp and the winged snail. Hungry swarms of these little beasts of the plankton roam through the waters, feeding on the abundant plants and themselves falling prey to larger creatures. Now in the spring the surface waters become a vast nursery. From the hills and valleys of the continent's edge lying far below, and from the scattered shoals and banks, the eggs or young of many of the bottom animals rise to the surface of the sea. Even those which, in their maturity, will sink down to a sedentary life on the bottom, spend the first weeks of life as freely swimming hunters of the plankton. So as spring progresses new batches of larvae rise into the surface each day, the young of fishes and crabs and mussels and tube worms, mingling for a time with the regular members of the plankton.

Under the steady and voracious grazing, the grasslands of 7 the surface are soon depleted. The diatoms become more and more scarce, and with them the other simple plants. Still there are brief explosions of one or another form, when in a sudden orgy of cell division it comes to claim whole areas of the sea for its own. So, for a time each spring, the waters may become blotched with brown, jellylike masses, and the fishermen's nets come up dripping a brown slime and containing no fish, for the herring have turned away from these waters as though in loathing of the viscid, foul-smelling algae. But in less time than passes between the full moon and the new, the spring flowering of Phaeocystis is past and the waters have cleared again.

In the spring the sea is filled with migrating fishes, some of 8 them bound for the mouths of great rivers, which they will ascend to deposit their spawn. Such are the spring-run chinooks coming in from the deep Pacific feeding grounds to breast the rolling flood of the Columbia, the shad moving in to the Chesapeake and the Hudson and the Connecticut, the alewives seeking a hundred coastal streams of New England, the salmon feeling their way to the Penobscot and the Kennebec. For months or years these fish have known only the vast spaces of the ocean. Now the spring sea and the maturing of their own bodies lead them back to the rivers of their birth.

Other mysterious comings and goings are linked with the 9 advance of the year. Capelin gather in the deep, cold water of the Barents Sea, their shoals followed and preyed upon by flocks of auks, fulmars, and kittiwakes. Cod approach the banks of Lofoten, and gather off the shores of Iceland. Birds whose winter feeding territory may have encompassed the whole Atlantic or the whole Pacific converge upon some small island, the entire breeding population arriving within the space of a few days. Whales suddenly appear off the slopes of the coastal banks where the swarms of shrimplike krill are spawning, the whales having come from no one knows where, by no one knows what route.

With the subsiding of the diatoms and the completed spawn- 10 ing of many of the plankton animals and most of the fish, life in the surface waters slackens to the slower pace of midsummer. Along the meeting places of the currents the pale moon jelly Aurelia gathers in thousands, forming sinuous lines or windrows across miles of sea, and the birds see their pale forms shimmering deep down in the green water. By midsummer the large red jellyfish Cyanea may have grown from the size of a thimble to that of an umbrella. The great jellyfish moves through the sea with rhythmic pulsations, trailing long tentacles and as likely as not shepherding a little group of young cod or haddock, which find shelter under its bell and travel with it.

A hard, brilliant, coruscating phosphorescence often illumi- 11 nates the summer sea. In waters where the protozoa Noctiluca is abundant it is the chief source of this summer luminescence, causing fishes, squids, or dolphins to fill the water with racing flames and to

 THE CHANGING YEAR

clothe themselves in a ghostly radiance. Or again the summer sea may glitter with a thousand thousand moving pinpricks of light, like an immense swarm of fireflies moving through a dark wood. Such an effect is produced by a shoal of the brilliantly phosphorescent shrimp Meganyctiphanes, a creature of cold and darkness and of the places where icy water rolls upward from the depths and bubbles with white ripplings at the surface.

Out over the plankton meadows of the North Atlantic the dry 12 twitter of the phalaropes, small brown birds, wheeling and turning, dipping and rising, is heard for the first time since early spring. The phalaropes have nested on the arctic tundras, reared their young, and now the first of them are returning to the sea. Most of them will continue south over the open water far from land, crossing the equator into the South Atlantic. Here they will follow where the great whales lead, for where the whales are, there also are the swarms of plankton on which these strange little birds grow fat.

As the fall advances, there are other movements, some in the 13 surface, some hidden in the green depths, that betoken the end of summer. In the fog-covered waters of Bering Sea, down through the treacherous passes between the islands of the Aleutian chain and southward into the open Pacific, the herds of fur seals are moving. Left behind are two small islands, treeless bits of volcanic soil thrust up into the waters of Bering Sea. The islands are silent now, but for the several months of summer they resounded with the roar of millions of seals come ashore to bear and rear their young—all the fur seals of the eastern Pacific crowded into a few square miles of bare rock and crumbling soil. Now once more the seals turn south, to roam down along the sheer underwater cliffs of the continent's edge, where the rocky foundations fall away steeply into the deep sea. Here, in a blackness more absolute than that of arctic winter, the seals will find rich feeding as they swim down to prey on the fishes of this region of darkness.

Autumn comes to the sea with a fresh blaze of phosphores- 14 cence, when every wave crest is aflame. Here and there the whole surface may glow with sheets of cold fire, while below schools of fish pour through the water like molten metal. Often the autumnal phosphorescence is caused by a fall flowering of the dinoflagellates, multiplying furiously in a short-lived repetition of their vernal blooming.

Sometimes the meaning of the glowing water is ominous. Off 15 the Pacific coast of North America, it may mean that the sea is filled with the dinoflagellate Gonyaulax, a minute plant that contains a poison of strange and terrible virulence. About four days after Gonyaulax comes to dominate the coastal plankton, some of the fishes and shellfish in the vicinity become toxic. This is because, in their normal feeding, they have strained the poisonous plankton out of the water. Mussels accumulate the Gonyaulax toxins in their livers, and the toxins react on the human nervous system with an effect similar to that of strychnine. Because of these facts, it is generally understood along the Pacific coast that it is unwise to eat shellfish taken from coasts exposed to the open sea where Gonyaulax may be abundant, in summer or early fall. For generations before the white men came, the Indians knew this. As soon as the red streaks appeared in the sea and the waves began to flicker at night with the mysterious blue-green fires, the tribal leaders forbade the taking of mussels until these warning signals should have passed. They even set guards at intervals along the beaches to warn inlanders who might come down for shellfish and be unable to read the language of the sea.

But usually the blaze and glitter of the sea, whatever its   16
meaning for those who produce it, implies no menace to man. Seen from the deck of a vessel in open ocean, a tiny, man-made observation point in the vast world of sea and sky, it has an eerie and unearthly quality. Man, in his vanity, subconsciously attributes a human origin to any light not of moon or stars or sun. Lights on the shore, lights moving over the water, mean lights kindled and controlled by other men, serving purposes understandable to the human mind. Yet here are lights that flash and fade away, lights that come and go for reasons meaningless to man, lights that have been doing this very thing over the eons of time in which there were no men to stir in vague disquiet.

On such a night of phosphorescent display Charles Darwin   17
stood on the deck of the *Beagle* as she plowed southward through the Atlantic off the coast of Brazil.

> The sea from its extreme luminousness presented a wonderful and most beautiful appearance [he wrote in his diary]. Every part of the water which by day is seen as foam, glowed with a pale light. The vessel drove before her bows two billows of liquid phosphorus, and in her wake was a milky train. As far as the eye reached the crest of every wave was bright; and from the reflected light, the sky just above the horizon was not so utterly dark as the rest of the Heavens. It was impossible to behold this plain of matter, as it were melted and consuming by heat, without being reminded of Milton's description of the regions of Chaos and Anarchy.*

*From *Charles Darwin's Diary of the Voyage of H.M.S. Beagle*, edited by Nora Barlow, 1934 edition, Cambridge University Press, p. 107.

 THE CHANGING YEAR

Like the blazing colors of the autumn leaves before they wither and fall, the autumnal phosphorescence betokens the approach of winter. After their brief renewal of life the flagellates and the other minute algae dwindle away to a scattered few; so do the shrimps and the copepods, the glassworms and the comb jellies. The larvae of the bottom fauna have long since completed their development and drifted away to take up whatever existence is their lot. Even the roving fish schools have deserted the surface waters and have migrated into warmer latitudes or have found equivalent warmth in the deep, quiet waters along the edge of the continental shelf. There the torpor of semi-hibernation descends upon them and will possess them during the months of winter. 18

The surface waters now become the plaything of the winter gales. As the winds build up the giant storm waves and roar along their crests, lashing the water into foam and flying spray, it seems that life must forever have deserted this place. 19

For the mood of the winter sea, read Joseph Conrad's description: 20

> The greyness of the whole immense surface, the wind furrows upon the faces of the waves, the great masses of foam, tossed about and waving, like matted white locks, give to the sea in a gale an appearance of hoary age, lustreless, dull, without gleams, as though it had been created before light itself.*

But the symbols of hope are not lacking even in the grayness and bleakness of the winter sea. On land we know that the apparent lifelessness of winter is an illusion. Look closely at the bare branches of a tree, on which not the palest gleam of green can be discerned. Yet, spaced along each branch are the leaf buds, all the spring's magic of swelling green concealed and safely preserved under the insulating, overlapping layers. Pick off a piece of the rough bark of the trunk; there you will find hibernating insects. Dig down through the snow into the earth. There are the eggs of next summer's grasshoppers; there are the dormant seeds from which will come the grass, the herb, the oak tree. 21

So, too, the lifelessness, the hopelessness, the despair of the winter sea are an illusion. Everywhere are the assurances that the cycle has come to the full, containing the means of its own renewal. There is the promise of a new spring in the very iciness of the winter 22

*From *The Mirror of the Sea*, Kent edition, 1925, Doubleday-Page, p. 71.

RACHEL CARSON

sea, in the chilling of the water, which must, before many weeks, become so heavy that it will plunge downward, precipitating the overturn that is the first act in the drama of spring. There is the promise of new life in the small plantlike things that cling to the rocks of the underlying bottom, the almost formless polyps from which, in spring, a new generation of jellyfish will bud off and rise into the surface waters. There is unconscious purpose in the sluggish forms of the copepods hibernating on the bottom, safe from the surface storms, life sustained in their tiny bodies by the extra store of fat with which they went into this winter sleep.

Already, from the gray shapes of cod that have moved, 23 unseen by man, through the cold sea to their spawning places, the glassy globules of eggs are rising into the surface waters. Even in the harsh world of the winter sea, these eggs will begin the swift divisions by which a granule of protoplasm becomes a living fishlet.

Most of all, perhaps, there is assurance in the fine dust of life 24 that remains in the surface waters, the invisible spores of the diatoms, needing only the touch of warming sun and fertilizing chemicals to repeat the magic of spring.

QUESTIONS

1. What kinds of sea life appear in each season?

2. In her description, Carson indirectly describes the aquatic food chain. Describe that chain.

3. Carson frequently uses metaphors in this essay. Many of them concern human feelings, agriculture, and commerce. Identify them and explain their utility to the essay. Explain also the allusions to Joseph Conrad and Charles Darwin in paragraphs 17 and 20. Why are allusions to them especially appropriate?

4. Identify unfamiliar animals and places in the essay. What effect does Carson achieve by listing the names of unfamiliar creatures and places?

5. How does Carson develop her introductory paragraph?

6. In Carson's description of the cycle of the seasons, time is a crucial structural device. Identify temporal transitional devices in this essay.

7. How does the image of time presented in the essay contribute to Carson's conclusion?

8. How does Carson use analogies to explain the seasons?

9. Because the life of the sea has been deeply threatened by pollution in

 THE CHANGING YEAR

recent years, can you share Carson's view of the cycle of life in the sea? What can we do to protect the sea?

10. Our lives are full of cycles. Write an essay describing one of the following cycles: a college semester, a sports year, or a television season.

BERTRAND RUSSELL

The Study of Mathematics

Bertrand Arthur William Russell (1872–1970) was one of the great philosophers, mathematicians, liberal political theorists, and authors of the twentieth century. His works are legion. From the early *Principles of Mathematics* (1903) to his *An Inquiry into Meaning and Truth* (1940) and finally to his three-volume *Autobiography* (1967–1969), Russell demonstrated his multivarious talents as a writer and thinker. He was awarded the Nobel Prize in Literature in 1950. One aspect of Russell's career—his desire to explain science to lay people—is represented in the following essay.

in regard to every form of human activity it is necessary   1
that the question should be asked from time to time, What is its purpose and ideal? In what way does it contribute to the beauty of human existence? As respects those pursuits which contribute only remotely, by providing the mechanism of life, it is well to be reminded that not the mere fact of living is to be desired, but the art of living in the contemplation of great things. Still more in regard to those avocations which have no end outside themselves, which are to be justified, if at all, as actually adding to the sum of the world's permanent possessions, it is necessary to keep alive a knowledge of their aims, a clear prefiguring vision of the temple in which creative imagination is to be embodied.

Although tradition has decreed that the great bulk of educat-   2
ed men shall know at least the elements of the subject [of mathematics], the reasons for which the tradition arose are forgotten, buried beneath a great rubbish-heap of pedantries and trivialities. To those who inquire as to the purpose of mathematics, the usual answer will be that it facilitates the making of machines, the travelling from place to place, and the victory over foreign nations, whether in war or commerce. If it be objected that these ends—all of which are of

doubtful value—are not furthered by the merely elementary study imposed upon those who do not become expert mathematicians, the reply, it is true, will probably be that mathematics trains the reasoning faculties. Yet the very men who make this reply are, for the most part, unwilling to abandon the teaching of definite fallacies, known to be such, and instinctively rejected by the unsophisticated mind of every intelligent learner. And the reasoning faculty itself is generally conceived, by those who urge its cultivation, as merely a means for the avoidance of pitfalls and a help in the discovery of rules for the guidance of practical life. All these are undeniably important achievements to the credit of mathematics; yet it is none of these that entitles mathematics to a place in every liberal education.

Mathematics, rightly viewed, possesses not only truth, but 3 supreme beauty—a beauty cold and austere, like that of sculpture, without appeal to any part of our weaker nature, without the gorgeous trappings of painting or music, yet sublimely pure, and capable of a stern perfection such as only the greatest art can show. The true spirit of delight, the exaltation, the sense of being more than man, which is the touchstone of the highest excellence, is to be found in mathematics as surely as in poetry. What is best in mathematics deserves not merely to be learnt as a task, but to be assimilated as a part of daily thought, and brought again and again before the mind with ever-renewed encouragement. Real life is, to most men, a long second-best, a perpetual compromise between the ideal and the posssible; but the world of pure reason knows no compromise, no practical limitations, no barrier to the creative activity embodying in splendid edifices the passionate aspiration after the perfect from which all great work springs. Remote from human passions, remote even from the pitiful facts of nature, the generations have gradually created an ordered cosmos, where pure thought can dwell as in its natural home, and where one, at least, of our nobler impulses can escape from the dreary exile of the actual world.

So little, however, have mathematicians aimed at beauty, that 4 hardly anything in their work has had this conscious purpose. Much, owing to irrepressible instincts, which were better than avowed beliefs, has been moulded by an unconscious taste; but much also has been spoilt by false notions of what was fitting. The characteristic excellence of mathematics is only to be found where the reasoning is rigidly logical: the rules of logic are to mathematics what those of structure are to architecture. In the most beautiful work, a chain of argument is presented in which every link is important on its own account, in which there is an air of ease and lucidity throughout, and the premises achieve more than would have been thought possible, by means which appear natural and inevitable. Literature embodies what is general in particular circumstances whose universal significance shines through their individual dress; but mathematics endeavours to present whatever is most general in its purity, without any irrelevant trappings.

QUESTIONS

1. In this essay, Russell compares and contrasts several disciplines or vocations to mathematics. Of which one does he approve? Of which ones does he disapprove?

2. According to Russell, what are the reasons for studying mathematics?

3. Identify examples of connotative language in this essay.

4. How many specific details appear in this essay? How does this affect the style of the essay?

5. Describe the structure of this four-paragraph essay.

6. Why does Russell compare mathematics to the arts? How is mathematics superior?

7. What assumptions about the world of nature and human beings and of the mind underlie the essay?

8. In paragraph 4, what method of definition does Russell use?

9. How would you define beauty, as Russell uses the word? Does your own idea of beauty differ from Russell's? How about your idea of mathematics?

10. Imitate the structure of this essay to organize your definition of engineering, literature, or medicine. Use specific details and examples from the field to clarify your extended definition.

J. B. S. HALDANE

On Being the Right Size

John Burdon Saunderson Haldane (1892–1964) was a geneticist, biologist, and writer of science books for the lay reader. His best-known work is *Animal Biology* (1927), written in collaboration with John S. Huxley. He also wrote *Adventures of a Biologist* (1940) and *Everything Has a History* (1951), a collection of essays. Haldane was famous for his ability to explain the abstract, often abstruse, ideas of modern science with concrete examples. "On Being the Right Size," which mixes mathematics and physics with insects and elephants, exemplifies Haldane's skill.

The most obvious differences between different animals are differences of size, but for some reason the zoologists have paid singularly little attention to them. In a large textbook of zoology before me I find no indication that the eagle is larger than the sparrow, or the hippopotamus bigger than the hare, though some grudging admissions are made in the case of the mouse and the whale. But yet it is easy to show that a hare could not be as large as a hippopotamus, or a whale as small as a herring. For every type of animal there is a most convenient size, and a large change in size inevitably carries with it a change of form.

Let us take the most obvious of possible cases, and consider a giant man sixty feet high—about the height of Giant Pope and Giant Pagan in the illustrated *Pilgrim's Progress* of my childhood. These monsters were not only ten times as high as Christian, but ten times as wide and ten times as thick, so that their total weight was a thousand times his, or about eighty to ninety tons. Unfortunately the cross sections of their bones were only a hundred times those of Christian, so that every square inch of giant bone had to support ten times the weight borne by a square inch of human bone. As the human thigh-bone breaks under about ten times the human weight, Pope and Pagan would have broken their thighs every time they took a step. This was doubtless why they were sitting down in the picture I remember. But it lessens one's respect for Christian and Jack the Giant Killer.

To turn to zoology, suppose that a gazelle, a graceful little creature with long thin legs, is to become large, it will break its bones unless it does one of two things. It may make its legs short and thick, like the rhinoceros, so that every pound of weight has still about the same area of bone to support it. Or it can compress its body and stretch out its legs obliquely to gain stability, like the giraffe. I mention these two beasts because they happen to belong to the same order as the gazelle, and both are quite successful mechanically, being remarkably fast runners.

Gravity, a mere nuisance to Christian, was a terror to Pope, Pagan, and Despair. To the mouse and any smaller animal it presents practically no dangers. You can drop a mouse down a thousand-yard mine shaft; and, on arriving at the bottom, it gets a slight shock and walks away, provided that the ground is fairly soft. A rat is killed, a man is broken, a horse splashes. For the resistance presented to movement by the air is proportional to the surface of the moving object. Divide an animal's length, breadth, and height each by ten; its weight is reduced to a thousandth, but its surface only to a hundredth. So the resistance to falling in the case of the small animal is relatively ten times greater than the driving force.

An insect, therefore, is not afraid of gravity; it can fall without danger, and can cling to the ceiling with remarkably little trouble. It can go in for elegant and fantastic forms of support like that of the daddy-longlegs. But there is a force which is as formidable to an insect as gravitation to a mammal. This is surface tension. A man coming out of a bath carries with him a film of water of about one-fiftieth of an inch in thickness. This weighs roughly a pound. A wet mouse has to carry about its own weight of water. A wet fly has to lift many times its own weight and, as everyone knows, a fly once wetted by water or any other liquid is in a very serious position indeed. An insect going for a drink is in as great danger as a man leaning out over a precipice in search of food. If it once falls into the grip of the surface tension of the water—that is to say, gets wet—it is likely to remain so until it drowns. A few insects, such as water-beetles, contrive to be unwettable; the majority keep well away from their drink by means of a long proboscis. 5

Of course tall land animals have other difficulties. They have to pump their blood to greater heights than a man, and therefore, require a larger blood pressure and tougher blood-vessels. A great many men die from burst arteries, especially in the brain, and this danger is presumably still greater for an elephant or a giraffe. But animals of all kinds find difficulties in size for the following reason. A typical small animal, say a microscopic worm or rotifer, has a smooth skin through which all the oxygen it requires can soak in, a straight gut with sufficient surface to absorb its food, and a single kidney. Increase its dimensions tenfold in every direction, and its weight is increased a thousand times, so that if it is to use its muscles as efficiently as its miniature counterpart, it will need a thousand times as much food and oxygen per day and will excrete a thousand times as much of waste products. 6

Now if its shape is unaltered its surface will be increased only a hundredfold, and ten times as much oxygen must enter per minute through each square millimetre of skin, ten times as much food through each square millimetre of intestine. When a limit is reached to their absorptive powers their surface has to be increased by some special device. For example, a part of the skin may be drawn out into tufts to make gills or pushed in to make lungs, thus increasing the oxygen-absorbing surface in proportion to the animal's bulk. A man, for example, has a hundred square yards of lung. Similarly, the gut, 7

J. B. S. HALDANE

instead of being smooth and straight, becomes coiled and develops a velvety surface, and other organs increase in complication. The higher animals are not larger than the lower because they are more complicated. They are more complicated because they are larger. Just the same is true of plants. The simplest plants, such as the green algae growing in stagnant water or on the bark of trees, are mere round cells. The higher plants increase their surface by putting out leaves and roots. Comparative anatomy is largely the story of the struggle to increase surface in proportion to volume.

Some of the methods of increasing the surface are useful up to a point, but not capable of a very wide adaptation. For example, while vertebrates carry the oxygen from the gills or lungs all over the body in the blood, insects take air directly to every part of their body by tiny blind tubes called tracheae which open to the surface at many different points. Now, although by their breathing movements they can renew the air in the outer part of the tracheal system, the oxygen has to penetrate the finer branches by means of diffusion. Gases can diffuse easily through very small distances, not many times larger than the average length travelled by a gas molecule between collisions with other molecules. But when such vast journeys—from the point of view of a molecule—as a quarter of an inch have to be made, the process becomes slow. So the portions of an insect's body more than a quarter of an inch from the air would always be short of oxygen. In consequence hardly any insects are much more than half an inch thick. Land crabs are built on the same general plan as insects, but are much clumsier. Yet like ourselves they carry oxygen around in their blood, and are therefore able to grow far larger than any insects. If the insects had hit on a plan for driving air through their tissues instead of letting it soak in, they might well have become as large as lobsters, though other considerations would have prevented them from becoming as large as man.

Exactly the same difficulties attach to flying. It is an elementary principle of aeronautics that the minimum speed needed to keep an aeroplane of a given shape in the air varies as the square root of its length. If its linear dimensions are increased four times, it must fly twice as fast. Now the power needed for the minimum speed increases more rapidly than the weight of the machine. So the larger aeroplane, which weighs sixty-four times as much as the smaller, needs one hundred and twenty-eight times its horsepower to keep up. Applying the same principle to the birds, we find that the limit to their size is soon reached. An angel whose muscles developed no more power weight for weight than those of an eagle or a pigeon would require a breast projecting for about four feet to house the muscles engaged in working its wings, while to economize in weight, its legs would have to be reduced to mere stilts. Actually a large bird

 ON BEING THE RIGHT SIZE

such as an eagle or kite does not keep in the air mainly by moving its wings. It is generally to be seen soaring, that is to say balanced on a rising column of air. And even soaring becomes more and more difficult with increasing size. Were this not the case eagles might be as large as tigers and as formidable to man as hostile aeroplanes.

But it is time that we pass to some of the advantages of size. 10 One of the most obvious is that it enables one to keep warm. All warm-blooded animals at rest lose the same amount of heat from a unit area of skin, for which purpose they need a food-supply proportional to their surface and not to their weight. Five thousand mice weigh as much as a man. Their combined surface and food or oxygen consumption are about seventeen times a man's. In fact a mouse eats about one quarter its own weight of food every day, which is mainly used in keeping it warm. For the same reason small animals cannot live in cold countries. In the arctic regions there are no reptiles or amphibians, and no small mammals. The smallest mammal in Spitzbergen is the fox. The small birds fly away in winter, while the insects die, though their eggs can survive six months or more of frost. The most successful mammals are bears, seals, and walruses.

Similarly, the eye is a rather inefficient organ until it reaches a 11 large size. The back of the human eye on which an image of the outside world is thrown, and which corresponds to the film of a camera, is composed of a mosaic of "rods and cones" whose diameter is little more than a length of an average light wave. Each eye has about a half a million, and for two objects to be distinguishable their images must fall on separate rods or cones. It is obvious that with fewer but larger rods and cones we should see less distinctly. If they were twice as broad two points would have to be twice as far apart before we could distinguish them at a given distance. But if their size were diminished and their number increased we should see no better. For it is impossible to form a definite image smaller than a wavelength of light. Hence a mouse's eye is not a small-scale model of a human eye. Its rods and cones are not much smaller than ours, and therefore there are far fewer of them. A mouse could not distinguish one human face from another six feet away. In order that they should be of any use at all the eyes of small animals have to be much larger in proportion to their bodies than our own. Large animals on the other hand only require relatively small eyes, and those of the whale and elephant are little larger than our own.

For rather more recondite reasons the same general principle 12 holds true of the brain. If we compare the brain-weights of a set of very similar animals such as the cat, cheetah, leopard, and tiger, we find that as we quadruple the body-weight the brain-weight is only doubled. The larger animal with proportionately larger bones can economize on brain, eyes, and certain other organs.

Such are a very few of the considerations which show that for every type of animal there is an optimum size. Yet although Galileo demonstrated the contrary more than three hundred years ago, people still believe that if a flea were as large as a man it could jump a thousand feet into the air. As a matter of fact the height to which an animal can jump is more nearly independent of its size than proportional to it. A flea can jump about two feet, a man about five. To jump a given height, if we neglect the resistance of the air, requires an expenditure of energy proportional to the jumper's weight. But if the jumping muscles form a constant fraction of the animal's body, the energy developed per ounce of muscle is independent of the size, provided it can be developed quickly enough in the small animal. As a matter of fact an insect's muscles, although they can contract more quickly than our own, appear to be less efficient; as otherwise a flea or grasshopper could rise six feet into the air. 13

QUESTIONS

1. List people's adaptations to the problems of their size.

2. What are the effects of size on insects and mice?

3. Cite examples of personification in the essay. Why does Haldane use them?

4. Haldane is an adept practitioner of parallel structure. Cite examples of parallel structure in paragraphs 4 and 5.

5. Describe the simple dichotomy Haldane uses to organize his essay.

6. Because Haldane is describing neither a scene nor an event, he cannot use temporal or spatial transitional devices to make his essay coherent. Identify the transitional devices he employs.

7. Many of Haldane's explanations involve mathematical formulas. Give specific examples of how he helps his reader understand his math.

8. Where does Haldane use hypothetical examples? Why are they effective?

9. Based on Haldane's discussion of size, speculate on how the size of a country, of a business, of a family, or of a college might have limits.

10. a. Write an essay on the effect of size on a human institution.
b. Although explaining mathematical and physical laws is difficult, Haldane is successful. Write an essay in which you try to explain a physical law.

To Clone or Not to Clone

Art Buchwald (1925–   ), journalist and humorist, has written a syndicated column, which now appears in almost 400 newspapers, since 1962. Collections of his columns are periodically published in book form, such as *Art Buchwald's Paris* (1953), *Son of the Great Society* (1966), and *The Buchwald Stops Here* (1978). With good-natured mischievousness, Buchwald portrays and mocks the absurdities of American society. In the following essay, he fantasizes about the effects of cloning, a recent development of genetic biology.

1   For some reason, which is hard to explain, my mind keeps wandering these days to cloning. I guess it all started when I read about the book revealing that an anonymous multimillionaire had paid to have a child cloned in his own image.

2   The author of the book says the millionaire, a lifelong bachelor, wanted to leave a son to posterity, but had found no woman whose genes he considered worthy of his own. He hired a scientist who took one of the man's own cells, had it hatched by a woman, cleansed it of all the woman's genetic material and then produced an identical likeness of the rich man. (I'm not making this up—it's all in the book.)

3   Reputable scientists have scoffed at the story, and so far neither the author nor the publisher has produced any proof that it really happened.

4   My concern is that perhaps it didn't this time, but who is to say in the future that it couldn't? Cloning could soon become as common as the Asian Flu. Once we have the knowledge to reproduce exact duplicates of ourselves, with just one cell, it's a whole new ball game as far as the human race is concerned.

5   I wouldn't mind reproducing a thousand persons just like myself, because I think the world needs them. But I definitely would be against one more Codsmather. He lives down the block and he's really a mess. He never washes his car, he lets his dog wander all over the neighborhood, his kids skateboard in the middle of the street, and from the empty bottles in his garbage, he's really into gin.

6   There is something wrong with Codsmather's genes, and if we permitted his cells to be cloned the neighborhood would really go to hell.

7   On the other hand there's Sara Lee, who works down the hall from my office. Sara Lee is beautiful, bright and a joy to behold.

Everyone on the floor has always said that it was a pity that there was only one Sara Lee to go around.

Columnist Robert Novak just told us the other day during a coffee break, "Wouldn't it be wonderful if there was a Sara Lee for everybody?"   8

I told him, "Some day when they get cloning down pat there will be."   9

Our coffee steamed with the thought.   10

But there are many things that enter into the moral aspects of cloning which we all must take into consideration.   11

If there was more than one Reggie Jackson would baseball be as interesting? Can the world afford two Ilie Nastases? Or, for that matter, two Robert Novaks? Would Farrah Fawcett Majors mean as much to all of us if there were 500 of her walking around at the same time? Is there a limit to the number of Billy Carters the country will put up with?   12

Once cloning becomes the "in" thing, teen-agers are going to want to try it. I don't know of any parents who could survive with an exact duplicate of the teen-ager they have now.   13

Another worrisome thing is that in the beginning, cloning is going to be very expensive and only rich people will be capable of duplicating themselves. Therefore, until they get the price down, all we'll be able to reproduce wholesale will be oil and gas tycoons who, as they multiply, will lobby for higher and higher prices, with the excuse that they have so many more mouths to feed.   14

Once the middle class can afford cloning they will probably get Congress to pass laws forbidding poor people from doing it, because they won't want to pay the extra welfare costs.   15

The whole thing will be a shambles unless we start thinking it out today. Each person must search his own heart and ask, "Do I want an exact duplicate of myself to take my place when I'm gone, or am I willing to abort my cells for the good of mankind?"   16

QUESTIONS

1. What is Buchwald's attitude toward humanity? Give examples.

2. Buchwald is particularly worried how certain groups will act if they can clone themselves. Identify these groups and explain why Buchwald is worried.

3. What effects does Buchwald achieve by using names such as "Godsmother" and "Sara Lee"?

 TO CLONE OR NOT TO CLONE   **549**

4. What effect does Buchwald achieve by comparing cloning to the Asian flu?

5. Explain the relation between paragraphs 5 to 10 and 11 to 16.

6. What are Codsmather's failings? Are they proof of bad genes? Is Buchwald's reasoning scientific here?

7. What two arguments against cloning are presented through questions? What kinds of questions appear in paragraph 12?

8. Give evidence that this is a topical essay.

9. If you had the choice, would you clone yourself? Do you think people should have the right to clone themselves?

10. Cloning can be considered a new invention. All sorts of new inventions affect our lives. Write an essay in which you try to describe the effect of fusion energy, holography, or videophones on the way Americans live. Write it in a style similar to Buchwald's.

ALDOUS HUXLEY

Time and the Machine

Aldous Leonard Huxley (1894–1963) was a grandson of T. H. Huxley. He is most famous as the author of *Point Counter Point* (1928) and *Brave New World* (1932). Unlike his grandfather, Aldous Huxley felt that science could threaten human individuality and dignity. In "Time and the Machine," Huxley shows, indeed, how modern technology has transformed our view of time.

ime, as we know it, is a very recent invention. The 1 modern time-sense is hardly older than the United States. It is a by-product of industrialism—a sort of psychological analogue of synthetic perfumes and aniline dyes.

Time is our tyrant. We are chronically aware of the moving 2 minute hand, even of the moving second hand. We have to be. There are trains to be caught, clocks to be punched, tasks to be done in specified periods, records to be broken by fractions of a second, machines that set the pace and have to be kept up with. Our consciousness of the smallest units of time is now acute. To us, for example, the moment 8.17 A.M. means something—something very important, if it happens to be the starting time of our daily train. To our ancestors, such an odd eccentric instant was without significance—did not even exist. In inventing the locomotive, Watt and Stevenson were part inventors of time.

Another time-emphasizing entity is the factory and its dependent, the office. Factories exist for the purpose of getting certain quantities of goods made in a certain time. The old artisan worked as it suited him with the result that consumers generally had to wait for the goods they had ordered from him. The factory is a device for making workmen hurry. The machine revolves so often each minute; so many movements have to be made, so many pieces produced each hour. Result: the factory worker (and the same is true, *mutatis mutandis,* of the office worker) is compelled to know time in its smallest fractions. In the hand-work age there was no such compulsion to be aware of minutes and seconds. 3

Our awareness of time has reached such a pitch of intensity that we suffer acutely whenever our travels take us into some corner of the world where people are not interested in minutes and seconds. The unpunctuality of the Orient, for example, is appalling to those who come freshly from a land of fixed meal-times and regular train services. For a modern American or Englishman, waiting is a psychological torture. An Indian accepts the blank hours with resignation, even with satisfaction. He has not lost the fine art of doing nothing. Our notion of time as a collection of minutes, each of which must be filled with some business or amusement, is wholly alien to the Oriental, just as it was wholly alien to the Greek. For the man who lives in a pre-industrial world, time moves at a slow and easy pace; he does not care about each minute, for the good reason that he has not been made conscious of the existence of minutes. 4

This brings us to a seeming paradox. Acutely aware of the smallest constituent particles of time—of time, as measured by clock-work and train arrivals and the revolutions of machines— industrialized man has to a great extent lost the old awareness of time in its larger divisions. The time of which we have knowledge is artificial, machine-made time. Of natural, cosmic time, as it is measured out by sun and moon, we are for the most part almost wholly unconscious. Pre-industrial people know time in its daily, monthly and seasonal rhythms. They are aware of sunrise, noon and sunset of the full moon and the new; of equinox and solstice; of spring and summer, autumn and winter. All the old religions, including Catholic Christianity, have insisted on this daily and seasonal rhythm. Pre-industrial man was never allowed to forget the majestic movement of cosmic time. 5

Industrialism and urbanism have changed all this. One can 6
live and work in a town without being aware of the daily march of the
sun across the sky; without ever seeing the moon and stars. Broadway and Piccadilly are our Milky Way; our constellations are outlined
in neon tubes. Even changes of season affect the townsman very
little. He is the inhabitant of an artificial universe that is, to a great
extent, walled off from the world of nature. Outside the walls, time is
cosmic and moves with the motion of sun and stars. Within, it is an
affair of revolving wheels and is measured in seconds and minutes—
at its longest, in eight-hour days and six-day weeks. We have a new
consciousness; but it has been purchased at the expense of the old
consciousness.

QUESTIONS

1. According to Huxley, what lengths of time were most important to our
ancestors? What lengths of time are most important to us? Why does Huxley
say that Watt and Stevenson were "part inventors of time" (paragraph 2)?

2. Identify the time-emphasizing machines Huxley mentions.

3. Explain the analogy in paragraph 1, and the metaphor in paragraph
6.

4. Huxley calls time "our tyrant" (paragraph 1), "machine made" (paragraph 5), "artificial" (paragraph 6), and waiting "a psychological torture"
(paragraph 4). He calls time for preindustrial people "majestic" and
"natural" (paragraph 5). Explain the connotations of these words, and
explain how they contribute to Huxley's thesis.

5. What is the thesis of the essay? Where is it stated?

6. How does Huxley organize his contrast of types of time?

7. How does the example of time in the Orient differ from Huxley's other
examples? How does this example complement Huxley's theme?

8. Explain the pattern of causal analysis in paragraphs 2 to 6.

9. How much of your life is determined by schedules? How would you feel
living in a world in which cosmic time predominates?

10. Write an essay describing how you are a victim of the tyrant, time.

ARTHUR C. CLARKE

The Planets Are Not Enough

Arthur Charles Clarke (1917–   ), astronomer, science fiction novelist, and essayist, has been a full-time writer since 1951. Since then, over 5 million copies of his books have appeared in twenty languages. His most famous science fiction novels are *Childhood's End* (1953), *2001 Space Odyssey* (1972, with Stanley Kubrick), and *Rendezvous with Rama* (1978). His most recent collection of essays is *The View from Serendip* (1978). In fiction and essays, Clarke has considered humanity's possibly humble status in the cosmos. In the following essay, published in *Report from Planet 3* (1972), he speculates on ways of exploring the universe.

A ltogether apart from its scientific value, space travel has   1
one justification that transcends all others. It is probably the only way we can hope to answer one of the supreme questions of philosophy: Is Man alone in the Universe? It seems incredible that ours should be the only inhabited planet among the millions of worlds that must exist among the stars, but we cannot solve this problem by speculating about it. If it can be solved at all, it will be by visiting other planets to see for ourselves.

The Solar System, comprising the nine known worlds of our   2
Sun and their numerous satellites, is a relatively compact structure, a snug little celestial oasis in an endless desert. It is true that millions of miles separate Earth from its neighbors, but such distances are cosmically trivial. They will even be trivial in terms of human engineering before another hundred years—a mere moment in historical time—have elapsed. However, the distances that sunder us from the possible worlds of other stars are of a totally different order of magnitude, and there are fundamental reasons for thinking that nothing—no scientific discovery or technical achievement—will ever make *them* trivial.

When today's chemical fuels have been developed to the   3
ultimate, and such tricks as refueling in space have been fully exploited, we will have spaceships which can attain speeds of about ten miles a second. That means that the Moon will be reached in two or three days and the nearer planets in about half a year. (I am deliberately rounding these numbers off, and anyone who tries to check my arithmetic had better remember that spaceships will never travel in straight lines or at uniform speeds.) The remoter planets, such as Jupiter and Saturn, could be reached only after many years of travel, and so the trio Moon-Mars-Venus marks the practical

limit of exploration for chemically propelled spaceships. Even for these cases, it is all too easy to demonstrate that hundreds of tons of fuel would be needed for each ton of payload that would make the round trip.

This situation, which used to depress the pre-atomic-energy astronauts, will not last for long. Since we are not concerned here with engineering details, we can take it for granted that eventually nuclear power, in some form or other, will be harnessed for the purposes of space flight. With energies a millionfold greater than those available from chemical fuels, speeds of hundreds, and ultimately thousands of miles a second will be attainable. Against such speeds, the Solar System will shrink until the inner planets are no more than a few hours apart, and even Pluto will be only a week or two from Earth. Moreover, there should be no reasonable limit to the amount of equipment and material that could be taken on an interplanetary expedition. Anyone who doubts this may ponder the fact that the energy released by a single H-bomb is sufficient to carry about a million tons to Mars. It is true that we cannot as yet tap even a fraction of that energy for such a purpose, but there are already hints of how this may be done.

The short-lived Uranium Age will see the dawn of space flight; the succeeding era of fusion power will witness its fulfillment. But even when we can travel among the planets as freely as we now travel over this Earth, it seems that we will be no nearer to solving the problem of man's place in the Universe. That is a secret that will still lie hidden in the stars.

All the evidence indicates that we are alone in the Solar System. True, there is almost certainly some kind of life on Mars, and possibly on Venus—perhaps even on the Moon. (The slight evidence for lunar vegetation comes from the amateur observers who actually *look* at the Moon, and is regarded skeptically by professional astronomers, who could hardly care less about a small slag heap little more than a light-second away.) Vegetation, however, can provide little intellectual companionship. Mars may be a paradise for the botanist, but it may have little to interest the zoologist—and nothing at all to lure the anthropologist and his colleagues across some scores of millions of miles of space.

This is likely to disappoint a great many people and to take much of the zest out of space travel. Yet it would be unreasonable to expect anything else; the planets have been in existence for several billion years, and only during the last .0001 per cent of that time has the human race been slightly civilized. Even if Mars and Venus have been (or will be) suitable for higher forms of life, the chances are wildly against our encountering beings anywhere near our cultural or intellectual level at this particular moment of time. If rational creatures exist on the planets, they will be millions of years ahead of us in development—or millions of years behind us. We may expect to meet apes or angels, but never men.

The angels can probably be ruled out at once. If they existed, 8 then surely they would already have come here to have a look at us. Some people, of course, think that this is just what they are doing. I can only say that they are going about it in a very odd manner.

We had better assume, therefore, that neither on Mars nor 9 Venus, nor on any other of the planets, will explorers from Earth encounter intelligent life. We are the only castaways upon the tiny raft of the Solar System, as it drifts forever along the Gulf Streams of the Galaxy.

This, then, is the challenge that sooner or later the human 10 spirit must face, when the planets have been conquered and all their secrets brought home to Earth. The nearest of the stars is a million times farther away than the closest of the planets. The spaceships we may expect to see a generation from now would take about a hundred thousand years to reach Proxima Centauri, our nearest stellar neighbor. Even the hypothetical nuclear-powered spaceships which a full century of atomic engineering may produce could hardly make the journey in less than a thousand years.

The expressive term "God's quarantine regulations" has been 11 used to describe this state of affairs. At first sight, it appears that they are rigorously enforced. There may be millions of inhabited worlds circling other suns, harboring beings who to us would seem godlike, with civilizations and cultures beyond our wildest dreams. But we shall never meet them, and they for their part will never know of our existence.

So run the conclusions of most astronomers, even those who 12 are quite convinced that mere common or garden interplanetary flight is just around the corner. But it is always dangerous to make negative predictions, and though the difficulties of *interstellar* travel are stupendous, they are not insuperable. It is by no means certain that man must remain trapped in the Solar System for eternity, never to know if he is a lonely freak of no cosmic significance.

There are two ways in which we might gain direct knowledge 13 of other stellar systems without ever leaving our own. Rather surprisingly, it can be shown that radio communication would be perfectly feasible across interstellar space, if very slow-speed telegraphy were employed. However, we can hardly assume that anyone would be listening in at the precise frequency with a receiver tuned to the extremely narrow band that would have to be employed. And even if they were, it would be extremely tedious learning to talk to them with no initial knowledge of their language—and having to wait many years for any acknowledgment of our own signals, as the radio

 THE PLANETS ARE NOT ENOUGH

waves came limping back across the light-years. If we sent a question to Proxima Centauri, it would be almost nine years before any answer could reach Earth.

A more practical, though at first sight more startling, solution would be to send a survey ship—unmanned. This would be a gigantic extrapolation of existing techniques, but it would not involve anything fundamentally new. Imagine an automatic vessel, crammed with every type of recording instrument and controlled by an electronic brain with preset instructions. It would be launched out across space, aimed at a target it might not reach for a thousand years. But at last one of the stars ahead would begin to dominate the sky, and a century or so later, it would have grown into a sun, perhaps with planets circling around it. Sleeping instruments would wake, the tiny ship would check its speed, and its sense organs would start to record their impressions. It would circle world after world, following a program set up to cover all possible contingencies by men who had died a thousand years before. Then, with the priceless knowledge it had gained, it would begin the long voyage home. 14

This type of proxy exploration of the universe would be slow and uncertain and would demand long-range planning beyond the capacity of our age. Yet if there is no other way of contacting the stars, this is how it might be done. One millennium would make the investment in technical skill so that the next would reap the benefit. It would be as if Archimedes were to start a research project which could produce no results before the time of Einstein. 15

If men, and not merely their machines, are ever to reach the planets of other suns, problems of much greater difficulty will have to be solved. Stated in its simplest form, the question is this: How can men survive a journey which may last for several thousand years? It is rather surprising to find that there are at least five different answers which must be regarded as theoretical possibilities—however far they may be beyond the scope of today's science. 16

Medicine may provide two rather obvious solutions. There appears to be no fundamental reason why men should die when they do. It is certainly not a matter of the body "wearing out" in the sense that an inanimate piece of machinery does, for in the course of a single year almost the entire fabric of the body is replaced by new material. When we have discovered the details of this process, it may be possible to extend the life span indefinitely if so desired. Whether a crew of immortals, however well balanced and psychologically adjusted, could tolerate each other's company for several centuries in rather cramped quarters is an interesting subject for speculation. 17

Perhaps a better answer is that suggested by the story of Rip Van Winkle. Suspended animation (or, more accurately, a drastic slowing down of the body's metabolism) for periods of a few hours is 18

ARTHUR C. CLARKE 9

now, of course, a medical commonplace. It requires no great stretch of the imagination to suppose that, with the aid of low temperatures and drugs, men may be able to hibernate for virtually unlimited periods. We can picture an automatic ship with its oblivious crew making the long journey across the interstellar night until, when a new sun was looming up, the signal was sent out to trigger the mechanisms which would revive the sleepers. When their survey was completed, they would head back to Earth and slumber again until the time came to awake once more, and to greet a world which would regard them as survivors from the distant past.

The third solution was, to the best of my knowledge, suggest- 19
ed over thirty years ago by Professor J. D. Bernal in a long out-of-print essay, *The World, the Flesh, and the Devil*, which must rank as one of the most outstanding feats of scientific imagination in literature. Even today, many of the ideas propounded in this little book have never been fully developed, either in or out of science fiction. (Any requests from fellow authors to borrow my copy will be flatly ignored.)

Bernal imagined entire societies launched across space, in 20
gigantic arks which would be closed, ecologically balanced systems. They would, in fact, be miniature planets, upon which generations of men would live and die so that one day their remote descendants would return to Earth with the record of their celestial Odyssey.

The engineering, biological and sociological problems in- 21
volved in such an enterprise would be of fascinating complexity. The artificial planets (at least several miles in diameter) would have to be completely self-contained and self-supporting, and no material of any kind could be wasted. Commenting on the implications of such closed systems, *Time* magazine's able, erudite science editor Jonathan Leonard once hinted that cannibalism would be compulsory among interstellar travelers. This would be a matter of definition; we crew members of the two-billion-man spaceship Earth do not consider ourselves cannibals despite the fact that every one of us must have absorbed atoms which once formed part of Caesar and Socrates, Shakespeare and Solomon.

One cannot help feeling that the interstellar ark on its 22
thousand-year voyages would be a cumbersome way of solving the problem, even if all the social and psychological difficulties could be overcome. (Would the fiftieth generation still share the aspirations of their Pilgrim Fathers who set out from Earth so long ago?) There are, however, more sophisticated ways of getting men to the stars than the crude, brute-force methods outlined above. After the hardheaded engineering of the last few paragraphs, what follows may appear to verge upon fantasy. It involves, in the most fundamental sense of the word, the storage of human beings. And by that I do not mean anything as naïve as suspended animation.

 THE PLANETS ARE NOT ENOUGH

A few months ago, in an Australian laboratory, I was   23
watching what appeared to be perfectly normal spermatozoa wrig-
gling across the microscope field. They *were* perfectly normal, but
their history was not. For three years, they had been utterly immobile
in a deep freeze, and there seemed little doubt that they could be kept
fertile for centuries by the same technique. What was still more
surprising, there had been enough successes with the far larger and
more delicate ova to indicate that they too might survive the same
treatment. If this proves to be the case, reproduction will eventually
become independent of time.

The social implications of this make anything in *Brave New*   24
World seem like child's play, but I am not concerned here with the
interesting results which might have been obtained by, for example,
uniting the genes of Cleopatra and Newton, had this technique been
available earlier in history. (When such experiments are started,
however, it would be as well to remember Shaw's famous rejection of
a similar proposal: "But suppose, my dear, it turns out to have my
beauty and your brains?")*

The cumbersome interstellar ark, with its generations of   25
travelers doomed to spend their entire lives in empty space, was
merely a device to carry germ cells, knowledge, and culture from one
sun to another. How much more efficient to send only the cells, to
fertilize them automatically some twenty years before the voyage was
due to end, to carry the embryos through to birth by techniques
already foreshadowed in today's biology labs, and to bring up the
babies under the tutelage of cybernetic nurses who would teach them
their inheritance and their destiny when they were capable of
understanding it.

These children, knowing no parents, or indeed anyone of a   26
different age from themselves, would grow up in the strange artificial
world of their speeding ship, reaching maturity in time to explore the
planets ahead of them—perhaps to be the ambassadors of humanity
among alien races, or perhaps to find, too late, that there was no
home for them there. If their mission succeeded, it would be their
duty (or that of their descendants, if the first generation could not
complete the task) to see that the knowledge they had gained was
someday carried back to Earth.

Would any society be morally justified, we may well ask, in   27
planning so onerous and uncertain a future for its unborn—indeed
unconceived—children? That is a question which different ages may
answer in different ways. What to one era would seem a cold-blooded
sacrifice might to another appear a great and glorious adventure.

*We have Shaw's word for it that the would-be geneticist was a complete stranger and not, as
frequently stated, Isadora Duncan.

There are complex problems here which cannot be settled by instinctive, emotional answers.

So far, we have assumed that all interstellar voyages must of necessity last for many hundreds or even thousands of years. The nearest star is more than four light-years away; the Galaxy itself—the island Universe of which our Sun is one insignificant member—is hundreds of thousands of light-years across; and the distances *between* the galaxies are of the order of a million light-years. The speed of light appears to be a fundamental limit to velocity; in this sense it is quite different from the now outmoded "sound barrier," which is merely an attribute of the particular gases which happen to constitute our atmosphere. 28

Even if we could reach the speed of light, therefore, interstellar journeys would still require many years of travel, and only in the case of the very nearest stars would it appear possible for a voyager to make the round trip in a single lifetime, without resort to such techniques as suspended animation. However, as we shall see, the actual situation is a good deal more complex than this. 29

First of all, is it even theoretically possible to build spaceships capable of approaching the speed of light? (That is, 186,000 miles a second or 670,000,000 miles per hour.) The problem is that of finding a sufficient source of energy and applying it. Einstein's famous quotation $E = mc^2$ gives an answer—on paper—which a few centuries of technology may be able to realize in terms of engineering. If we can achieve the *total* annihilation of matter—not the conversion of a mere fraction of a per cent of it into energy—we can approach as near to the speed of light as we please. We can never reach it, but a journey at 99.9 per cent of the speed of light would, after all, take very little longer than one at exactly the speed of light, so the difference would hardly seem of practical importance. 30

Complete annihilation of matter is still as much a dream as atomic energy itself was thirty years ago. However, the discovery of the anti-proton (which engages in mutual suicide on meeting a normal proton) may be the first step on the road to its realization. 31

Traveling at speeds approaching that of light, however, involves us at once in one of the most baffling paradoxes which spring from the theory of relativity—the so-called "time-dilation effect." It is impossible to explain *why* this effect occurs without delving into very elementary yet extremely subtle mathematics. (There is nothing difficult about basic relativity math: most of it is simple algebra. The difficulty lies in the underlying concepts.) Nevertheless, even if the explanation must be skipped, the results of the time-dilation effect can be stated readily enough in nontechnical language. 32

Time itself is a variable quantity; the rate at which it flows depends upon the speed of the observer. The difference is infinitesi- 33 mal at the velocities of everyday life, and even at the velocities of normal astronomical bodies. It is all-important as we approach to within a few per cent of the speed of light. To put it crudely, the faster one travels, the more slowly time will pass. At the speed of light, time would cease to exist; the moment "Now" would last forever.

Let us take an extreme example to show what this implies. If a spaceship left Earth for Proxima Centauri at the speed of light, and came back at once at the same velocity, it would have been gone for some eight and one-half years according to all the clocks and calendars of Earth. *But the people in the ship, and all their clocks, would have recorded no lapsed time at all.* 34

At a physically attainable speed, say 95 per cent of the velocity of light, the inhabitants of the ship would think that the round trip had lasted about three years. At 99 per cent, it would have seemed little more than a year to them. In each case, however, they would return more than eight years—Earth time—after they had departed. (No allowance has been made here for stopping and starting, which would require additional time.) 35

If we imagine a more extensive trip, we get still more surprising results. The travelers might be gone for a thousand years, from the point of view of Earth, having set out for a star five hundred light-years away. If their ship had averaged 99.9 per cent of the speed of light, they would be fifty years older when they returned to an Earth—*where ten centuries had passed away!** 36

It should be emphasized that this effect, incredible though it appears to be, is one of the natural consequences of Einstein's theory. The equation connecting mass and energy once appeared to be equally fantastic and remote from any practical application. It would be very unwise, therefore, to assume that the equation linking time and velocity will never be of more than theoretical interest. Anything which does not violate natural laws must be considered a possibility—and the events of the last few decades have shown clearly enough that things which are possible will always be achieved if the incentive is sufficiently great. 37

Whether the incentive will be sufficient here is a question which only the future can answer. The men of five hundred or a thousand years from now will have motivations very different from ours, but if they are men at all they will still burn with that restless curiosity which has driven us over this world and which is about to take us into space. Sooner or later we will come to the edge of the 38

*The physical reality of the time-dilation effect has been the subject of unusually acrimonious debate in recent years. Very few scientists now have any doubt of its existence, but its magnitude may not have the values quoted above. My figures are based on special relativity, which is too unsophisticated to deal with the complexities of an actual flight.

ARTHUR C. CLARKE

Solar System and will be looking out across the ultimate abyss. Then we must choose whether we reach the stars—or whether we wait until the stars reach us.

QUESTIONS

1. What are the three general means of propulsion? Which is the most advanced method?

2. What are the means of gathering information?

3. Clarke occasionally uses metaphors to enliven his prose. Identify such metaphors. Why would a popularizer of science want to use metaphors?

4. Clarke declares that he is writing in "nontechnical language" (paragraph 32). What evidence of this do you find?

5. Describe the different viewpoints from which Clarke looks at intervals of time and space.

6. How does Clarke utilize illustration in this essay?

7. Explain the structural importance of paragraphs 13, 16, and 29.

8. Analyze the relationship between the author's introductory and concluding paragraphs.

9. For what reasons do you agree or disagree with Clarke that space travel is of crucial importance? What other goals do you think humanity should achieve before space travel?

10. Arthur Clarke presumes that space travel is a critical goal for humanity, and he speculates on ways to achieve it. Write an essay describing another general goal for humanity and ways to achieve it.

KENNETH B. CLARK

The Science of Human Morality

Kenneth Bancroft Clark (1914–   ) is an emeritus professor of psychology at the City College of New York. He is best known for his studies on racism, which helped convince the U.S. Supreme Court in 1954 that segregation was inherently inequitable. Clark has continued to study and sometimes to condemn eloquently the detrimental effects of racism, class, and ignorance upon individual development. Clark's book *The Dark Ghetto* (1965) is a classic critique of the effects of racism in America. The following essay, advocating a scientific method for the social sciences, appeared in *The Pathos of Power* (1974).

Man's successive victories over ignorance and superstition 1
have postponed the probability that the physical environment will destroy him. But he now confronts the reality that the seeds of destruction are inherent in the fruits of knowledge.

This is the significant dilemma of modern man: to control 2
social and psychological forces is as essential to his survival as control of the forces of the physical universe. To fail in this will be a prelude to tragedy. Each new development in science has negative as well as positive potentialities, but the consequences of human conflicts and social tensions become increasingly catastrophic as man gains mastery over his physical universe.

The technological achievement of transforming matter into 3
energy through atomic fission is, for man, the absolute realization of the paradox. Atomic fission offers a challenge and a hope, but it is an instrument of ultimate destruction, filling man's heart and mind with guilt and terror.

Which alternative will dominate cannot be determined by 4
amoral physical science itself. Science will not limit itself or deliberately retard its progress or destroy its findings. The question whether the destructive or constructive potentials will dominate must be answered not by less science, but by more.

The major threat to the stability and security of human 5
society in the contemporary world is the marked discrepancy between the achievements of physical science and technology and the retardation in the development of the social sciences. It is imperative that the social sciences now develop the same objectivity and exactness most modern physical science has achieved.

A truly scientific social science will seek to understand the 6
processes of social and individual interaction—the nature and dynamics of social relations—so it can reach a more valid prediction and control of social phenomena and, at the same time, conserve the dignity and integrity of individual personality. Inherent in this basic goal is the assumption that social stability is meaningless—if not impossible—independent of the stability and dignity of human beings. An asserted dichotomy between social stability and individual security would be clearly incompatible with meaningful social science.

KENNETH B. CLARK

The social and psychological sciences must be determined by a tough-minded search for facts, free from prejudice and stultifying preconceptions. The social scientist must be free to search for his facts unfettered by the biases of myths, mysticism, and the pleadings of special privilege, guided only by his own intelligence and integrity and a dedication to the search for truth. A socially realistic social science would recognize, however, that the quest for fact and truth of social phenomena, unlike the quest in the physical sciences, cannot proceed on the premise of the basic amorality of scientific fact. Fact in the physical universe seems to be empirically amoral, but, precisely, therefore, discoveries of such fact appear to man as two-headed monsters, capable of either destructive or constructive use. A scientific social science can lead to constructive technological advances only as it works within a stable and moral conceptual framework. To be "constructive," "socially desirable," and "beneficial" is, inescapably, to be moral.   7

Instead of seeking to ape the physical sciences in an assumption of amorality the social sciences may be forced to recognize that they are essentially the sciences of human morality. They can contribute to human social stability; they can counter the threat inherent in advance in the physical sciences.   8

A scientific exploitation of social phenomena would require analysis of social tensions and a determination of their causes. Some relevant questions to be answered are these: 9

What is the relationship between social tension and individual adjustment?   10

What forms of social tension most influence personal adjustment?   11

Through what media do social tensions impinge upon the individual and influence his adjustment?   12

What are the effects of personal motivations and the characteristics of the individual on the structure and stability of society?   13

In what ways, if any, are intergroup conflicts, international crises, and wars understandable in terms of disturbances in the personalities of specific individuals—for example, leaders—or in terms of characteristics common to many?   14

Such questions imply a set of moral values and principles, whether articulated or inarticulate. The terms "social tension" and "individual adjustment" would, indeed, be meaningless except in reference to a basic sense of values that suggests that social stability is a positive state of society and social tension a negative one. But, by what processes does stability deteriorate into tension? Stability in itself may be a symptom of social stagnation and potential decadence. If so, social tension would be seen in a more positive light as a symptom of the dynamics of social change and as an inevitable factor   15

 THE SCIENCE OF HUMAN MORALITY   **563**

in social progress. The biological concepts of emergent evolution provide some support for this speculation. The common view that mere stability is a positive state of society and tension a negative symptom must, in consequence, be re-examined. The apparent antithesis may be reconciled by differentiating static stability from dynamic stability, one an index of stagnation and decadence, the other a necessary condition for positive development of the society. Conflicts, potential violence, and eventual extinction threaten a society in stasis, but the tensions in a society of dynamic stability would be symptomatic of positive change and progress.

A socially responsible social science would, then, be required   16
to determine how to channelize social tensions to support dynamic growth and stability and how to prevent undirected tensions from reaching the critical point of frustration and deterioration. Social tension results in and is itself a consequence of profound individual needs and frustrations. This cyclic relationship tends to reinforce itself until a critical point when a pattern of friction, conflict, or spasmodic violent aggressions emerges.

Social stability may reflect balance within the social organism   17
or the equilibrium of potential competing forces. Social tension may begin as pre-violent conflict and competition for priority in the satisfaction of needs. It may be seen as a state of disequilibrium, with competing forces struggling for additional power or dominance, threatening an increase in frustration of others and disturbing the functional equilibrium of the social organism.

A scientific study of social tensions would not only explore   18
the statics and dynamics of the power structure within a society, but also—what seems to be even more fundamental—the psychology of human motivation. A logical and systematic transition into more empirical research on the problem would be to determine the objective indices of detrimental tension. In the more overt symptoms of social disorganization, already recognized, in the family, in the community, the nation, and the international community, social scientists may find a place to begin. For example:

1.   The instability of family relations, reflected in divorce rates, abandonment statistics, and child-welfare problems, seems related to social tensions.

2.   Crime, juvenile delinquency, neuroses, and psychoses may be manifestations of disintegration of the personality that result from, among other causes, the bombardment of social pressures upon the individual.

3.   Intergroup conflicts, such as racial and religious friction, labor-management problems, intense political conflicts, seem to be well

KENNETH B. CLARK

recognized as symptoms of basic pathology or emergent social changes. But, whether such conflicts are symptoms of deterioration or of eventual positive change may be related to the nature and structure of the society as a whole. Their existence in a society marked by striking, crystallized differences in privileges among social, economic, and political groups—approaching the rigidity of a caste system—suggests pathology. It is a reasonable assumption that social tensions reflect profound systemic disturbance and not imminent positive social change when some in a society have more than enough to satisfy their basic material needs and needs for status and prestige while others lack even the minimal requirements of human living.

4. Chronic competitions for power internationally also indicate a fundamental and increasingly significant social tension. If such crises are permitted to develop lawlessly, without control, they will end inevitably in the catastrophe of war, the most dramatic manifestation of man's ignorance of, and inability to control, those psychological and social forces that threaten his existence.

Understanding of the nature of tensions does not, however, provide an understanding of their dynamics or their genesis, yet such understanding is probably necessary to resolution. Social scientists must relate what they have learned in one field to what they know in another if the origin and nature of social tensions are to be understood. 19

Are the dynamics of social stability and social tensions related to principles that have primary relevance to the motivation and adjustment of the individual? 20

Attempts to understand and interpret social phenomena in terms of individual motivation did increase after the rise of Fascism, an unmistakable manifestation of the pathological potentials of human society. Although the struggle and competition for national or international power may not be explained wholly and simply as analogous to the power drive in personal relations, the personal may provide significant insights into the political. 21

Social psychologists no longer find a dichotomy between the individual and the group tenable as a significant hypothesis. Sufficient evidence is available to suggest a basic similarity in the dynamics of each. The transition from individual adjustment and interpersonal relations to an understanding of social interaction and the nature of social tension is not possible or fruitful on a simple linear level. A difference in degree exists, but the same basic principles may work, nevertheless, in a simple or more complex configurational pattern. 22

 THE SCIENCE OF HUMAN MORALITY

The social scientist's next job is to engage in pure research in   23
the problems of human behavior. Social science has, for example,
minimal reliable information on the characteristics of leaders and
their effect on the stability of society, yet leaders are capable of
exerting tremendous power. The existence of millions is immediately
affected by their judgment. Given this obvious fact, the tremendous
ignorance of leadership behavior is shocking. We have no objective
information on such simple dimensions as the criteria of maturity of
personality and intellect required for stable leadership. We do not
even know whether or not some of the facets of personality structure
which are important in achieving leadership are detrimental to social
stability. It could be possible that an individual can become a leader
only if he is insensitive to certain realities on which social stability
itself depends. Lack of knowledge on such a problem seems no longer
tolerable. For psychiatrists, psychologists, and others interested in
society and stability, this would seem a key immediate problem.

It is crucial also for social science to study the degree of   24
impact of social forces on the personality, on the nature of motives,
their genesis, their control, the degree to which similar patterns of
disturbances in personal motivation in large numbers of people in
turn determine social processes and social tensions. It is not enough
to generalize on these problems; if the social sciences are to achieve
their goal of control, it is important to determine such questions with
exactness. One would want to know the specific relationships among
these factors:

1.   Minority status and personal values and attitudes. What is the
effect of the socially accepted dehumanization of the individual on his
attitudes toward the stability of the overall society? How does his
personal attitude toward the society that debases him affect the
stability of that society?

2.   The effect of overt social tensions such as wars on the emerging
and developing personalities of children. How do such inevitable
dislocations affect the personal stability of the child? What are the
consequences, if any, for the child's later personality—could they be
conducive to continuing wars or could they result in the inability of
individuals to tolerate and permit wars?

3.   Exact knowledge of social explosions, such as riots, as they occur
or immediately after their occurrence. It would be important to know
the personality structure of individuals involved in such social chaos.
Is there a significant peculiarity of their personalities that is related to
the personalities of individuals not involved? Are there any significant differences between an individual who participates in a lynch

mob or a race riot and one who does not or cannot? There is very little information on this significant social problem.

The hope for a dynamically stable, progressive, and construc- 25 tive society lies in the ability of the social scientist to attack these and related problems with a vigor, a tough-mindedness, and a scrupulous regard for scientific integrity and freedom. It is the bias of science that answers to such important questions can be discovered by scientific methods. There is little doubt that social science has the ability to maintain a strict scientific direction. There is no doubt that scientific techniques and methods to study social phenomena are available and usable. The only doubt is whether swiftly moving social changes will permit the use of independent science or whether power and privilege will dominate, destroying man's freedom to think and to search for truth.

QUESTIONS

1. What are the crucial distinctions between the social and natural sciences according to Clark?

2. What does Clark mean by detrimental tension? What examples does he give of this concept?

3. Locate and explain the function of figurative language in the essay.

4. How does Clark's word choice reveal his tone? How would you characterize that tone?

5. Explain the importance of paragraphs 6 and 15 to the structure of the essay.

6. How does the comparative method serve to structure parts of Clark's essay?

7. Does this article tend to be general or specific, abstract or concrete? What effect does this have on the essay?

8. There are three lists in this essay. Why does Clark use lists? Why are they usually lists of questions?

9. How does Clark's description of a pathological society relate to American society? What is your response to the idea that our society is pathological?

10. In paragraph 9, Clark introduces a list of relevant questions for social science to pursue. In an essay, give concrete examples of the problems these questions describe.

THE SCIENCE OF HUMAN MORALITY

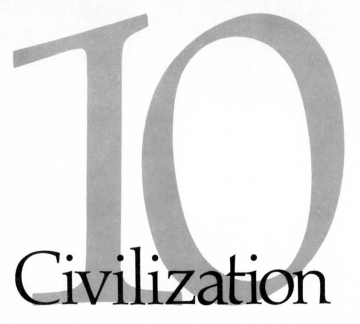

10

Civilization

OLIVER GOLDSMITH

National Prejudices

Oliver Goldsmith (1730–1774), the son of an Anglican curate, was an Anglo-Irish essayist, poet, novelist, dramatist, and journalist. His reputation as an enduring figure in English literature is based on his novel, *The Vicar of Wakefield* (1766); his play *She Stoops to Conquer* (1773); his major poem, *The Deserted Village* (1770); and the essays and satiric letters collected in *The Bee* (1759) and *The Citizen of the World* (1762). In this essay, Goldsmith argues quietly for a new type of citizen who can transcend the xenophobia governing national behavior.

A s I am one of that sauntering tribe of mortals, who   1
spend the greatest part of their time in taverns, coffee-
houses, and other places of public resort, I have thereby
an opportunity of observing an infinite variety of characters, which, to a person of a contemplative turn, is a much higher
entertainment than a view of all the curiosities of art or nature. In one
of these, my late rambles, I accidentally fell into the company of half a
dozen gentlemen, who were engaged in a warm dispute about some
political affair; the decision of which, as they were equally divided in
their sentiments, they thought proper to refer to me, which naturally
drew me in for a share of the conversation.

Amongst a multiplicity of other topics, we took occasion to   2
talk of the different characters of the several nations of Europe; when
one of the gentlemen, cocking his hat, and assuming such an air of
importance as if he had possessed all the merit of the English nation
in his own person, declared that the Dutch were a parcel of avaricious
wretches; the French a set of flattering sycophants; that the Germans
were drunken sots, and beastly gluttons; and the Spaniards proud,
haughty, and surly tyrants; but that in bravery, generosity, clemency,
and in every other virtue, the English excelled all the rest of the
world.

This very learned and judicious remark was received with a   3
general smile of approbation by all the company—all, I mean, but
your humble servant; who, endeavoring to keep my gravity as well as
I could, and reclining my head upon my arm, continued for some
time in a posture of affected thoughtfulness, as if I had been musing
on something else, and did not seem to attend to the subject of
conversation; hoping by these means to avoid the disagreeable
necessity of explaining myself, and thereby depriving the gentleman
of his imaginary happiness.

But my pseudo-patriot had no mind to let me escape so   4
easily. Not satisfied that his opinion should pass without contradiction, he was determined to have it ratified by the suffrage of every
one in the company; for which purpose addressing himself to me
with an air of inexpressible confidence, he asked me if I was not of the
same way of thinking. As I am never forward in giving my opinion,
especially when I have reason to believe that it will not be agreeable;
so, when I am obliged to give it, I always hold it for a maxim to speak
my real sentiments. I therefore told him that, for my own part, I
should not have ventured to talk in such a peremptory strain, unless I
had made the tour of Europe, and examined the manners of these
several nations with great care and accuracy: that, perhaps, a more
impartial judge would not scruple to affirm that the Dutch were more
frugal and industrious, the French more temperate and polite, the
Germans more hardy and patient of labour and fatigue, and the
Spaniards more staid and sedate, than the English; who, though
undoubtedly brave and generous, were at the same time rash,
headstrong, and impetuous; too apt to be elated with prosperity, and
to despond in adversity.

I could easily perceive that all the company began to regard   5
me with a jealous eye before I had finished my answer, which I had
no sooner done, that the patriotic gentleman observed, with a
contemptuous sneer, that he was greatly surprised how some people
could have the conscience to live in a country which they did not
love, and to enjoy the protection of a government, to which in their
hearts they were inveterate enemies. Finding that by this modest

declaration of my sentiments I had forfeited the good opinion of my companions, and given them occasion to call my political principles in question, and well knowing that it was in vain to argue with men who were so very full of themselves, I threw down my reckoning and retired to my own lodgings, reflecting on the absurd and ridiculous nature of national prejudice and prepossession.

Among all the famous sayings of antiquity, there is none that 6 does greater honour to the author, or affords greater pleasure to the reader (at least if he be a person of a generous and benevolent heart), than that of the philosopher, who, being asked what "countryman he was," replied, that he was, "a citizen of the world."—How few are there to be found in modern times who can say the same, or whose conduct is consistent with such a profession!—We are now become so much Englishmen, Frenchmen, Dutchmen, Spaniards, or Germans, that we are no longer citizens of the world; so much the natives of one particular spot, or members of one petty society, that we no longer consider ourselves as the general inhabitants of the globe, or members of that grand society which comprehends the whole human kind.

Did these prejudices prevail only among the meanest and 7 lowest of the people, perhaps they might be excused, as they have few, if any, opportunities of correcting them by reading, travelling, or conversing with foreigners; but the misfortune is, that they infect the minds, and influence the conduct, even of our gentlemen; of those, I mean, who have every title to this appellation but an exemption from prejudice, which however, in my opinion, ought to be regarded as the characteristical mark of a gentleman; for let a man's birth be ever so high, his station ever so exalted, or his fortune ever so large, yet if he is not free from national and other prejudices, I should make bold to tell him, that he had a low and vulgar mind, and had no just claim to the character of a gentleman. And in fact, you will always find that those are most apt to boast of national merit, who have little or no merit of their own to depend on; than which, to be sure, nothing is more natural: the slender vine twists around the sturdy oak, for no other reason in the world but because it has not strength sufficient to support itself.

Should it be alleged in defence of national prejudice, that it is 8 the natural and necessary growth of love to our country, and that therefore the former cannot be destroyed without hurting the latter, I answer, that this is a gross fallacy and delusion. That it is the growth of love to our country, I will allow; but that it is the natural and necessary growth of it, I absolutely deny. Superstition and enthusiasm too are the growth of religion; but who ever took it in his head to affirm that they are the necessary growth of this noble principle?

They are, if you will, the bastard sprouts of this heavenly plant, but not its natural and genuine branches, and may safely enough be lopped off, without doing any harm to the parent stock: nay, perhaps, till once they are lopped off, this goodly tree can never flourish in perfect health and vigour.

Is it not very possible that I may love my own country, without hating the natives of other countries? that I may exert the most heroic bravery, the most undaunted resolution, in defending its laws and liberty, without despising all the rest of the world as cowards and poltroons? Most certainly it is; and if it were not—But why need I suppose what is absolutely impossible?—But if it were not, I must own, I should prefer the title of the ancient philosopher, viz. a citizen of the world, to that of an Englishman, a Frenchman, a European, or to any other appellation whatever.

QUESTIONS

1. Why does Goldsmith maintain that he is "a citizen of the world"? According to the author, could such an individual also be a patriot? Explain.

2. What connection does Goldsmith establish between national prejudices and the conduct of gentlemen? Why does he allude to the manners of gentlemen?

3. Locate in the essay examples of the familiar style in writing. What is the relationship between this style and the tone and substance of the essay?

4. Explain the metaphors at the end of paragraphs 7 and 8.

5. What is the relevance of the introductory narrative, with its description of characters, to the author's declaration of thesis? Where does the author state his proposition concerning national prejudices?

6. Analyze the function of classification and contrast in paragraphs 2 to 5. How does the entire essay serve as a pattern of definition?

7. Examine the pattern of reasoning involved in the author's presentation of his argument in the essay, notably in paragraphs 6 to 8. What appeals to emotion and to reason does he make?

8. Assess the rhetorical effectiveness of Goldsmith's concluding paragraph.

9. Why has it been difficult to eliminate the problem that Goldsmith posed in 1765? Are we better able today to function as citizens of the world? In

 NATIONAL PREJUDICES

what ways? What role does the United Nations play in this issue? What factors contribute to a new world citizenry?

10. a. Write an argumentative essay on the desirability of world government, or on the need to be a citizen of the world.
b. Write a paper on contemporary national prejudices.

JOHN STEINBECK

Americans and the Land

John Steinbeck (1902–1968) was born in California, the setting for some of his best fiction. Steinbeck's fiction of the 1930s, including *The Pastures of Heaven* (1932), *Tortilla Flat* (1935), *In Dubious Battle* (1936), *Of Mice and Men* (1937), and the Pulitzer Prize–winning epic *The Grapes of Wrath* (1939), offers one of the best imaginative presentations of the American Depression. Steinbeck won the Nobel Prize in Literature in 1962, for "realistic and imaginative writings, distinguished as they are by a sympathetic humor and a social perception." In this section from *America and Americans* (1966), Steinbeck offers a probing, critical appraisal of American social development.

I have often wondered at the savagery and thoughtless- 1
ness with which our early settlers approached this rich continent. They came at it as though it were an enemy, which of course it was. They burned the forests and changed the rainfall; they swept the buffalo from the plains, blasted the streams, set fire to the grass, and ran a reckless scythe through the virgin and noble timber. Perhaps they felt that it was limitless and could never be exhausted and that a man could move on to new wonders endlessly. Certainly there are many examples to the contrary, but to a large extent the early people pillaged the country as though they hated it, as though they held it temporarily and might be driven off at any time.

This tendency toward irresponsibility persists in very many 2
of us today; our rivers are poisoned by reckless dumping of sewage and toxic industrial wastes, the air of our cities is filthy and dangerous to breathe from the belching of uncontrolled products from combus-

tion of coal, coke, oil, and gasoline. Our towns are girdled with wreckage and the debris of our toys—our automobiles and our packaged pleasures. Through uninhibited spraying against one enemy we have destroyed the natural balances our survival requires. All these evils can and must be overcome if America and Americans are to survive; but many of us still conduct ourselves as our ancestors did, stealing from the future for our clear and present profit.

Since the river-polluters and the air-poisoners are not crimi- 3 nal or even bad people, we must presume that they are heirs to the early conviction that sky and water are unowned and that they are limitless. In the light of our practices here at home it is very interesting to me to read of the care taken with the carriers of our probes into space to make utterly sure that they are free of pollution of any kind. We would not think of doing to the moon what we do every day to our own dear country.

When the first settlers came to America and dug in on the 4 coast, they huddled in defending villages hemmed in by the sea on one side and by endless forests on the other, by Red Indians and, most frightening, the mystery of an unknown land extending nobody knew how far. And for a time very few cared or dared to find out. Our first Americans organized themselves and lived in a state of military alertness; every community built its blockhouse for defense. By law the men went armed and were required to keep their weapons ready and available. Many of them wore armor, made here or imported; on the East Coast, they wore the cuirass and helmet, and the Spaniards on the West Coast wore both steel armor and heavy leather to turn arrows.

On the East Coast, and particularly in New England, the 5 colonists farmed meager lands close to their communities and to safety. Every man was permanently on duty for the defense of his family and his village; even the hunting parties went into the forest in force, rather like raiders than hunters, and their subsequent quarrels with the Indians, resulting in forays and even massacres, remind us that the danger was very real. A man took his gun along when he worked the land, and the women stayed close to their thick-walled houses and listened day and night for the signal of alarm. The towns they settled were permanent, and most of them exist today with their records of Indian raids, of slaughter, of scalpings, and of punitive counter-raids. The military leader of the community became the chief authority in time of trouble, and it was a long time before danger receded and the mystery could be explored.

After a time, however, brave and forest-wise men drifted 6 westward to hunt, to trap, and eventually to bargain for the furs which were the first precious negotiable wealth America produced for trade and export. Then trading posts were set up as centers of

 AMERICANS AND THE LAND

573

collection and the exploring men moved up and down the rivers and crossed the mountains, made friends for mutual profit with the Indians, learned the wilderness techniques, so that these explorer-traders soon dressed, ate, and generally acted like the indigenous people around them. Suspicion lasted a long time, and was fed by clashes sometimes amounting to full-fledged warfare; but by now these Americans attacked and defended as the Indians did.

For a goodly time the Americans were travelers, moving   7 about the country collecting its valuables, but with little idea of permanence; their roots and their hearts were in the towns and the growing cities along the eastern edge. The few who stayed, who lived among the Indians, adopted their customs and some took Indian wives and were regarded as strange and somehow treasonable creatures. As for their half-breed children, while the tribe sometimes adopted them they were unacceptable as equals in the eastern settlements.

Then the trickle of immigrants became a stream, and the   8 population began to move westward—not to grab and leave but to settle and live, they thought. The newcomers were of peasant stock, and they had their roots in a Europe where they had been landless, for the possession of land was the requirement and the proof of a higher social class than they had known. In America they found beautiful and boundless land for the taking—and they took it.

It is little wonder that they went land-mad, because there was   9 so much of it. They cut and burned the forests to make room for crops; they abandoned their knowledge of kindness to the land in order to maintain its usefulness. When they had cropped out a piece they moved on, raping the country like invaders. The topsoil, held by roots and freshened by leaf-fall, was left helpless to the spring freshets, stripped and eroded with the naked bones of clay and rock exposed. The destruction of the forests changed the rainfall, for the searching clouds could find no green and beckoning woods to draw them on and milk them. The merciless nineteenth century was like a hostile expedition for loot that seemed limitless. Uncountable buffalo were killed, stripped of their hides, and left to rot, a reservoir of permanent food supply eliminated. More than that, the land of the Great Plains was robbed of the manure of the herds. Then the plows went in and ripped off the protection of the buffalo grass and opened the helpless soil to quick water and slow drought and the mischievous winds that roamed through the Great Central Plains. There has always been more than enough desert in America; the new settlers, like overindulged children, created even more.

The railroads brought new hordes of land-crazy people, and   10 the new Americans moved like locusts across the continent until the western sea put a boundary to their movements. Coal and copper and

                                                                    JOHN STEINBECK

gold drew them on; they savaged the land, gold-dredged the rivers to skeletons of pebbles and debris. An aroused and fearful government made laws for the distribution of public lands—a quarter section, one hundred and sixty acres, per person—and a claim had to be proved and improved; but there were ways of getting around this, and legally. My own grandfather proved out a quarter section for himself, one for his wife, one for each of his children, and, I suspect, acreage for children he hoped and expected to have. Marginal lands, of course, suitable only for grazing, went in larger pieces. One of the largest land-holding families in California took its richest holdings by a trick: By law a man could take up all the swamp or water-covered land he wanted. The founder of this great holding mounted a scow on wheels and drove his horses over thousands of acres of the best bottom land, then reported that he had explored it in a boat, which was true, and confirmed his title. I need not mention his name; his descendants will remember.

Another joker with a name still remembered in the West 11 worked out a scheme copied many times in after years. Proving a quarter section required a year of residence and some kind of improvement—a fence, a shack—but once the land was proved the owner was free to sell it. This particular princely character went to the stews and skid rows of the towns and found a small army of hopeless alcoholics who lived for whiskey and nothing else. He put these men on land he wanted to own, grubstaked them and kept them in cheap liquor until the acreage was proved, then went through the motions of buying it from his protégés and moved them and their one-room shacks on sled runners to new quarter sections. Bums of strong constitution might prove out five or six homesteads for this acquisitive hero before they died of drunkenness.

It was full late when we began to realize that the continent 12 did not stretch out to infinity; that there were limits to the indignities to which we could subject it. Engines and heavy mechanical equipment were allowing us to ravage it even more effectively than we had with fire, dynamite, and gang plows. Conservation came to us slowly, and much of it hasn't arrived yet. Having killed the whales and wiped out the sea otters and most of the beavers, the market hunters went to work on game birds; ducks and quail were decimated, and the passenger pigeon eliminated. In my youth I remember seeing a market hunter's gun, a three-gauge shotgun bolted to a frame and loaded to the muzzle with shingle nails. Aimed at a lake and the trigger pulled with a string, it slaughtered every living thing on the lake. The Pacific Coast pilchards were once the raw material for a great and continuing industry. We hunted them with aircraft far at sea until they were gone and the canneries had to be closed. In some of the valleys of the West, where the climate makes several crops a

 AMERICANS AND THE LAND **575**

year available, which the water supply will not justify, wells were driven deeper and deeper for irrigation, so that in one great valley a million acre feet more of water was taken out than rain and melting snow could replace, and the water table went down and a few more years may give us a new desert.

The great redwood forests of the western mountains early 13 attracted attention. These ancient trees, which once grew everywhere, now exist only where the last Ice Age did not wipe them out. And they were found to have value. The Sempervirens and the Gigantea, the two remaining species, make soft, straight-grained timber. They are easy to split into planks, shakes, fenceposts, and railroad ties, and they have a unique virtue: they resist decay, both wet and dry rot, and an inherent acid in them repels termites. The loggers went through the great groves like a barrage, toppling the trees—some of which were two thousand years old—and leaving no maidens, no seedlings or saplings on the denuded hills.

Quite a few years ago when I was living in my little town on 14 the coast of California a stranger came in and bought a small valley where the Sempervirens redwoods grew, some of them three hundred feet high. We used to walk among these trees, and the light colored as though the great glass of the Cathedral at Chartres had strained and sanctified the sunlight. The emotion we felt in this grove was one of awe and humility and joy; and then one day it was gone, slaughtered, and the sad wreckage of boughs and broken saplings left like nonsensical spoilage of the battle-ruined countryside. And I remember that after our rage there was sadness, and when we passed the man who had done this we looked away, because we were ashamed for him.

From early times we were impressed and awed by the 15 fantastic accidents of nature, like the Grand Canyon and Yosemite and Yellowstone Park. The Indians had revered them as holy places, visited by the gods, and all of us came to have somewhat the same feeling about them. Thus we set aside many areas of astonishment as publicly owned parks; and though this may to a certain extent have been because there was no other way to use them as the feeling of preciousness of the things we had been destroying grew in Americans, more and more areas were set aside as national and state parks, to be looked at but not injured. Many people loved and were in awe of the redwoods; societies and individuals bought groves of these wonderful trees and presented them to the state for preservation.

No longer do we Americans want to destroy wantonly, but 16 our new-found sources of power—to take the burden of work from our shoulders, to warm us, and cool us, and give us light, to transport us quickly, and to make the things we use and wear and eat—these power sources spew pollution on our country, so that the rivers

JOHN STEINBECK

and streams are becoming poisonous and lifeless. The birds die
for the lack of food; a noxious cloud hangs over our cities that
burns our lungs and reddens our eyes. Our ability to conserve has
not grown with our power to create, but this slow and sullen poisoning is no longer ignored or justified. Almost daily, the pressure of
outrage among Americans grows. We are no longer content to destroy our beloved country. We are slow to learn; but we learn.
When a super-highway was proposed in California which would
trample the redwood trees in its path, an outcry arose all over the
land, so strident and fierce that the plan was put aside. And we no
longer believe that a man, by owning a piece of America, is free
to outrage it.

But we are an exuberant people, careless and destructive as   17
active children. We make strong and potent tools and then have to
use them to prove that they exist. Under the pressure of war
we finally made the atom bomb, and for reasons which seemed jus-
tifiable at the time we dropped it on two Japanese cities—and I
think we finally frightened ourselves. In such things, one must
onsult himself because there is no other point of reference. I
did not know about the bomb, and certainly I had nothing to do
with its use, but I am horrified and ashamed; and nearly everyone
I know feels the same thing. And those who loudly and angrily justify Hiroshima and Nagasaki—why, they must be the most ashamed of all.

QUESTIONS

1. According to Steinbeck, how did the American attitude toward the
land evolve?

2. Does Steinbeck think that the American attitude toward the land can
be changed? Cite evidence from the essay to support your answer.

3. Analyze Steinbeck's use of figurative language in paragraphs 1, 2, 9,
and 14.

4. Locate images and vocabulary relating to "rape" and destruction in
the essay. What is the relevance of this motif to the development of
Steinbeck's thesis?

5. How does Steinbeck use examples in paragraphs 1 and 2 to establish
the subject and thesis of his essay?

6. Analyze the relationship between the patterns of description and
example in the essay. What types of illustration does Steinbeck employ?
How does he achieve concreteness through examples? Where does he

employ extended example? Does he use examples subjectively or objectively? Explain.

7. How does Steinbeck employ process analysis to highlight his thesis?

8. Explain the relationship between paragraph 16 and paragraph 17 in the essay.

9. Compare and contrast Steinbeck's essay with "Wasteland" by Marya Mannes (see pages 132–133).

10. a. Write an essay entitled "Americans and the Land," using examples to support your thesis.
b. Write an essay on the relationship between ecology and the state of civilization.

WILLIAM FAULKNER

Address upon Receiving the Nobel Prize for Literature

William Faulkner (1897–1962), winner of the Nobel Prize in Literature, is conceivably the greatest American novelist of this century. Born in Oxford, Mississippi, Faulkner erected in such major novels as *The Sound and the Fury* (1929), *As I Lay Dying* (1930), *Light in August* (1932), and *Absalom, Absalom!* (1936) a chronicle of Yoknapatawpha County, his metaphor for the American South, that stands as one of the most brilliant sustaining visions in contemporary literature. Preoccupied in his novels and short fiction with human destiny, Faulkner conveyed basic ethical issues concerning the fate of civilization in his acceptance speech for the Nobel Prize in 1950.

feel that this award was not made to me as a man, but to   1
my work—a life's work in the agony and sweat of the human spirit, not for glory and least of all for profit, but to create out of the materials of the human spirit something which did not exist before. So this award is only mine in trust. It will not be difficult to find a dedication for the money part of it commensurate with the purpose and significance of its origin. But I would like to do the same with the acclaim too, by using this moment as a pinnacle from which I might be listened to by the young men and

women already dedicated to the same anguish and travail, among whom is already that one who will some day stand here where I am standing.

Our tragedy today is a general and universal physical fear so long sustained by now that we can even bear it. There are no longer problems of the spirit. There is only the question: When will I be blown up? Because of this, the young man or woman writing today has forgotten the problems of the human heart in conflict with itself which alone can make good writing because only that is worth writing about, worth the agony and the sweat.

He must learn them again. He must teach himself that the basest of all things is to be afraid; and, teaching himself that, forget it forever, leaving no room in his workshop for anything but the old verities and truths of the heart, the old universal truths lacking which any story is ephemeral and doomed—love and honor and pity and pride and compassion and sacrifice. Until he does so, he labors under a curse. He writes not of love but of lust, of defeats in which nobody loses anything of value, of victories without hope and, worst of all, without pity or compassion. His griefs grieve on no universal bones, leaving no scars. He writes not of the heart but of the glands.

Until he relearns these things, he will write as though he stood among and watched the end of man. I decline to accept the end of man. It is easy enough to say that man is immortal simply because he will endure: that when the last ding-dong of doom has clanged and faded from the last worthless rock hanging tideless in the last red and dying evening, that even then there will still be one more sound: that of his puny inexhaustible voice, still talking. I refuse to accept this. I believe that man will not merely endure: he will prevail. He is immortal, not because he alone among creatures has an inexhaustible voice, but because he has a soul, a spirit capable of compassion and sacrifice and endurance. The poet's, the writer's, duty is to write about these things. It is his privilege to help man endure by lifting his heart, by reminding him of the courage and honor and hope and pride and compassion and pity and sacrifice which have been the glory of his past. The poet's voice need not merely be the record of man, it can be one of the props, the pillars to help him endure and prevail.

QUESTIONS

1. What is Faulkner's view of the contemporary human condition? Cite evidence to support your response.

2. According to Faulkner, what is the responsibility of the writer?

3. Analyze Faulkner's celebrated sentence style—length, type, structure—in the essay.

4. Explain Faulkner's use of "heart" as a metaphor in paragraph 2. Locate other examples of figurative language.

5. Account for the complexity of tone in the essay.

6. What causal connection does Faulkner establish in the introduction and body of the essay?

7. Analyze methods of transition and techniques of emphasis between and within paragraphs 2 through 4.

8. What techniques of persuasion does Faulkner use in the essay, especially in the concluding paragraph?

9. Offer your own evaluation of the tragic sense of life that Faulkner perceives in modern life.

10. a. Write an essay about the role of the artist in addressing the contemporary human condition.
b. Write an argumentative or persuasive essay on the need to restore qualities of the human heart and spirit to modern civilization.
c. Define in your own words "our tragedy today."

JAMES BALDWIN

Stranger in the Village

James Baldwin (1924–   ), a major American essayist, novelist, short story writer, and playwright, was born and grew up in Harlem, winning a Eugene Saxon Fellowship, and living in Europe from 1948 to 1956. Always an activist in civil rights causes, Baldwin focuses in his essays and fiction on the black search for identity in modern America and on the myth of white superiority. Among his principal works are *Go Tell It on the Mountain* (1953), *Notes of a Native Son* (1955), *Giovanni's Room* (1958), *Nobody Knows My Name* (1960), *Another Country* (1962), and *If Beale Street Could Talk* (1975). One of the finest contemporary essayists, Baldwin has a rare talent for portraying the deepest concerns about civilization in an intensely personal style, as the following essay indicates.

From all available evidence no black man had ever set   1
foot in this tiny Swiss village before I came. I was told
before arriving that I would probably be a "sight" for the
village; I took this to mean that people of my complexion were rarely seen in Switzerland, and also that city people are
always something of a "sight" outside of the city. It did not occur to
me—possibly because I am an American—that there could be people
anywhere who had never seen a Negro.

It is a fact that cannot be explained on the basis of the   2
inaccessibility of the village. The village is very high, but it is only
four hours from Milan and three hours from Lausanne. It is true that
it is virtually unknown. Few people making plans for a holiday would
elect to come here. On the other hand, the villagers are able,
presumably, to come and go as they please—which they do: to
another town at the foot of the mountain, with a population of
approximately five thousand, the nearest place to see a movie or go to
the bank. In the village there is no movie house, no bank, no library,
no theater; very few radios, one jeep, one station wagon; and, at the
moment, one typewriter, mine, an invention which the woman next
door to me here had never seen. There are about six hundred people
living here, all Catholic—I conclude this from the fact that the
Catholic church is open all year round, whereas the Protestant
chapel, set off on a hill a little removed from the village, is open only
in the summertime when the tourists arrive. There are four or five
hotels, all closed now, and four or five *bistros,* of which, however,
only two do any business during the winter. These two do not do a
great deal, for life in the village seems to end around nine or ten
o'clock. There are a few stores, butcher, baker, *épicerie,* a hardware
store, and a money-changer—who cannot change travelers' checks,
but must send them down to the bank, an operation which takes two
or three days. There is something called the *Ballet Haus,* closed in the
winter and used for God knows what, certainly not ballet, during the
summer. There seems to be only one schoolhouse in the village, and
this for the quite young children; I suppose this to mean that their
older brothers and sisters at some point descend from these mountains in order to complete their education—possibly, again, to the
town just below. The landscape is absolutely forbidding, mountains
towering on all four sides, ice and snow as far as the eye can reach. In
this white wilderness, men and women and children move all day,
carrying washing, wood, buckets of milk or water, sometimes skiing
on Sunday afternoons. All week long boys and young men are to be
seen shoveling snow off the rooftops, or dragging wood down from
the forest in sleds.

The village's only real attraction, which explains the tourist   3
season, is the hot spring water. A disquietingly high proportion of

these tourists are cripples, or semi-cripples, who come year after year—from other parts of Switzerland, usually—to take the waters. This lends the village, at the height of the season, a rather terrifying air of sanctity, as though it were a lesser Lourdes. There is often something beautiful, there is always something awful, in the spectacle of a person who has lost one of his faculties, a faculty he never questioned until it was gone, and who struggles to recover it. Yet people remain people, on crutches or indeed on deathbeds; and wherever I passed, the first summer I was here, among the native villagers or among the lame, a wind passed with me—of astonishment, curiosity, amusement, and outrage. That first summer I stayed two weeks and never intended to return. But I did return in the winter, to work; the village offers, obviously, no distractions whatever and has the further advantage of being extremely cheap. Now it is winter again, a year later, and I am here again. Everyone in the village knows my name, though they scarcely ever use it, knows that I come from America—though, this, apparently they will never really believe: black men come from Africa—and everyone knows that I am the friend of the son of a woman who was born here, and that I am staying in their chalet. But I remain as much a stranger today as I was the first day I arrived, and the children shout *Neger! Neger!* as I walk along the streets.

It must be admitted that in the beginning I was far too   4
shocked to have any real reaction. In so far as I reacted at all, I reacted by trying to be pleasant—it being a great part of the American Negro's education (long before he goes to school) that he must make people "like" him. This smile-and-the-world-smiles-with-you routine worked about as well in this situation as it had in the situation for which it was designed, which is to say that it did not work at all. No one, after all, can be liked whose human weight and complexity cannot be, or has not been, admitted. My smile was simply another unheard-of phenomenon which allowed them to see my teeth—they did not, really, see my smile and I began to think that, should I take to snarling, no one would notice any difference. All of the physical characteristics of the Negro which had caused me, in America, a very different and almost forgotten pain were nothing less than miraculous—or infernal—in the eyes of the village people. Some thought my hair was the color of tar, that it had the texture of wire, or the texture of cotton. It was jocularly suggested that I might let it all grow long and make myself a winter coat. If I sat in the sun for more than five minutes some daring creature was certain to come along and gingerly put his fingers on my hair, as though he were afraid of an electric shock, or put his hand on my hand, astonished that the color did not rub off. In all of this, in which it must be conceded there was the charm of genuine wonder and in which there was certainly no

element of intentional unkindness, there was yet no suggestion that I was human: I was simply a living wonder.

I knew that they did not mean to be unkind, and I know it now; it is necessary, nevertheless, for me to repeat this to myself each time I walk out of the chalet. The children who shout *Neger!* have no way of knowing the echoes this sound raises in me. They are brimming with good humor and the more daring swell with pride when I stop to speak with them. Just the same, there are days when I cannot pause and smile, when I have no heart to play with them; when, indeed, I mutter sourly to myself, exactly as I muttered on the streets of a city these children have never seen, when I was no bigger than these children are now: *Your* mother *was a nigger*. Joyce is right about history being a nightmare—but it may be the nightmare from which no one *can* awaken. People are trapped in history and history is trapped in them.

There is a custom in the village—I am told it is repeated in many villages—of "buying" African natives for the purpose of converting them to Christianity. There stands in the church all year round a small box with a slot for money, decorated with a black figurine, and into this box the villagers drop their francs. During the *carnaval* which precedes Lent, two village children have their faces blackened—out of which bloodless darkness their blue eyes shine like ice—and fantastic horsehair wigs are placed on their blond heads; thus disguised, they solicit among the villagers for money for the missionaries in Africa. Between the box in the church and the blackened children, the village "bought" last year six or eight African natives. This was reported to me with pride by the wife of one of the *bistro* owners and I was careful to express astonishment and pleasure at the solicitude shown by the village for the souls of black folk. The *bistro* owner's wife beamed with a pleasure far more genuine than my own and seemed to feel that I might now breathe more easily concerning the souls of at least six of my kinsmen.

I tried not to think of these so lately baptized kinsmen, of the price paid for them, or the peculiar price they themselves would pay, and said nothing about my father, who having taken his own conversion too literally never, at bottom, forgave the white world (which he described as heathen) for having saddled him with a Christ in whom, to judge at least from their treatment of him, they themselves no longer believed. I thought of white men arriving for the first time in an African village, strangers there, as I am a stranger here, and tried to imagine the astounded populace touching their hair and marveling at the color of their skin. But there is a great difference between being the first white man to be seen by Africans and being the first black man to be seen by whites. The white man takes the astonishment as tribute, for he arrives to conquer and to convert the

5

6

7

natives, whose inferiority in relation to himself is not even to be questioned; whereas I, without a thought of conquest, find myself among a people whose culture controls me, has even, in a sense, created me, people who have cost me more in anguish and rage than they will ever know, who yet do not even know of my existence. The astonishment with which I might have greeted them, should they have stumbled into my African village a few hundred years ago, might have rejoiced their hearts. But the astonishment with which they greet me today can only poison mine.

And this is so despite everything I may do to feel differently, 8 despite my friendly conversations with the *bistro* owner's wife, despite their three-year-old son who has at last become my friend, despite the *saluts* and *bonsoirs* which I exchange with people as I walk, despite the fact that I know that no individual can be taken to task for what history is doing, or has done. I say that the culture of these people controls me—but they can scarcely be held responsible for European culture. America comes out of Europe, but these people have never seen America nor have most of them seen more of Europe than the hamlet at the foot of their mountain. Yet they move with an authority which I shall never have; and they regard me, quite rightly, not only as a stranger in their village but as a suspect latecomer, bearing no credentials, to everything they have—however unconsciously—inherited.

For this village, even were it incomparably more remote and 9 incredibly more primitive, is the West, the West onto which I have been so strangely grafted. These people cannot be, from the point of view of power, strangers anywhere in the world; they have made the modern world, in effect, even if they do not know it. The most illiterate among them is related, in a way that I am not, to Dante, Shakespeare, Michelangelo, Aeschylus, Da Vinci, Rembrandt, and Racine; the cathedral at Chartres says something to them which it cannot say to me, as indeed would New York's Empire State Building, should anyone here ever see it. Out of their hymns and dances come Beethoven and Bach. Go back a few centuries and they are in their full glory—but I am in Africa, watching the conquerors arrive.

The rage of the disesteemed is personally fruitless, but it is 10 also absolutely inevitable; this rage, so generally discounted, so little understood even among the people whose daily bread it is, is one of the things that makes history. Rage can only with difficulty, and never entirely, be brought under the domination of the intelligence and is therefore not susceptible to any arguments whatever. This is a fact which ordinary representatives of the *Herrenvolk*, having never felt this rage and being unable to imagine it, quite fail to understand. Also, rage cannot be hidden, it can only be dissembled. This dissembling deludes the thoughtless, and strengthens rage and adds, to rage, contempt. There are, no doubt, as many ways of coping with the resulting complex of tensions as there are black men in the world, but no black man can hope ever to be entirely liberated from this internal warfare—rage, dissembling, and contempt having inevitably accompanied his first realization of the power of white men. What is crucial here is that, since white men represent in the black man's world so heavy a weight, white men have for black men a reality which is far from being reciprocal; and hence all black men have toward all white men an attitude which is designed, really, either to rob the white man of the jewel of his naïveté, or else to make it cost him dear.

The black man insists, by whatever means he finds at his 11 disposal, that the white man cease to regard him as an exotic rarity and recognize him as a human being. This is a very charged and difficult moment, for there is a great deal of will power involved in the white man's naïveté. Most people are not naturally reflective any more than they are naturally malicious, and the white man prefers to keep the black man at a certain human remove because it is easier for him thus to preserve his simplicity and avoid being called to account for crimes committed by his forefathers, or his neighbors. He is inescapably aware, nevertheless, that he is in a better position in the world than black men are, nor can he quite put to death the suspicion that he is hated by black men therefore. He does not wish to be hated, neither does he wish to change places, and at this point in his uneasiness he can scarcely avoid having recourse to those legends which white men have created about black men, the most usual effect of which is that the white man finds himself enmeshed, so to speak, in his own language which describes hell, as well as the attributes which lead one to hell, as being as black as night.

Every legend, moreover, contains its residuum of truth, and 12 the root function of language is to control the universe by describing it. It is of quite considerable significance that black men remain, in the imagination, and in overwhelming numbers in fact, beyond the disciplines of salvation; and this despite the fact that the West has been "buying" African natives for centuries. There is, I should hazard, an instantaneous necessity to be divorced from this so visibly unsaved stranger, in whose heart, moreover, one cannot guess what dreams of vengeance are being nourished; and, at the same time, there are few things on earth more attractive than the idea of the unspeakable liberty which is allowed the unredeemed. When, beneath the black mask, a human being begins to make himself felt one cannot escape a certain awful wonder as to what kind of human being it is. What one's imagination makes of other people is dictated, of course, by the laws of one's own personality and it is one of the ironies of black-white relations that, by means of what the white man imagines the black man to be, the black man is enabled to know who the white man is.

I have said, for example, that I am as much a stranger in this 13 village today as I was the first summer I arrived, but this is not quite true. The villagers wonder less about the texture of my hair than they did then, and wonder rather more about me. And the fact that their wonder now exists on another level is reflected in their attitudes and in their eyes. There are the children who make those delightful, hilarious, sometimes astonishingly grave overtures of friendship in the unpredictable fashion of children; other children, having been taught that the devil is a black man, scream in genuine anguish as I approach. Some of the older women never pass without a friendly greeting, never pass, indeed, if it seems that they will be able to engage me in conversation; other women look down or look away or rather contemptuously smirk. Some of the men drink with me and suggest that I learn how to ski—partly, I gather, because they cannot imagine what I would look like on skis—and want to know if I am married, and ask questions about my *métier*. But some of the men have accused *le sale nègre*—behind my back—of stealing wood and there is already in the eyes of some of them that peculiar, intent, paranoiac malevolence which one sometimes surprises in the eyes of American white men when, out walking with their Sunday girl, they see a Negro male approach.

There is a dreadful abyss between the streets of this village 14 and the streets of the city in which I was born, between the children who shout *Neger!* today and those who shouted *Nigger!* yesterday— the abyss is experience, the American experience. The syllable hurled behind me today expresses, above all, wonder: I am a stranger here. But I am not a stranger in America and the same syllable riding on the American air expresses the war my presence has occasioned in the American soul.

For this village brings home to me this fact: that there was a 15 day, and not really a very distant day, when Americans were scarcely Americans at all but discontented Europeans, facing a great uncon- quered continent and strolling, say, into a marketplace and seeing black men for the first time. The shock this spectacle afforded is suggested, surely, by the promptness with which they decided that these black men were not really men but cattle. It is true that the necessity on the part of the settlers of the New World of reconciling their moral assumptions with the fact—and the necessity—of slavery enhanced immensely the charm of this idea, and it is also true that this idea expresses, with a truly American bluntness, the attitude which to varying extents all masters have had toward all slaves.

But between all former slaves and slave-owners and the 16 drama which begins for Americans over three hundred years ago at Jamestown, there are at least two differences to be observed. The American Negro slave could not suppose, for one thing, as slaves in past epochs had supposed and often done, that he would ever be able to wrest the power from his master's hands. This was a supposition which the modern era, which was to bring about such vast changes in the aims and dimensions of power, put to death; it only begins, in unprecedented fashion, and with dreadful implications, to be resurrected today. But even had this supposition persisted with undiminished force, the American Negro slave could not have used it to lend his condition dignity, for the reason that this supposition rests on another: that the slave in exile yet remains related to his past, has some means—if only in memory—of revering and sustaining the forms of his former life, is able, in short, to maintain his identity.

This was not the case with the American Negro slave. He is 17 unique among the black men of the world in that his past was taken from him, almost literally, at one blow. One wonders what on earth the first slave found to say to the first dark child he bore. I am told that there are Haitians able to trace their ancestry back to African kings, but any American Negro wishing to go back so far will find his journey through time abruptly arrested by the signature on the bill of sale which served as the entrance paper for his ancestor. At the time—to say nothing of the circumstances—of the enslavement of the captive black man who was to become the American Negro, there was not the remotest possibility that he would ever take power from his master's hands. There was no reason to suppose that his situation would ever change, nor was there, shortly, anything to indicate that his situation had ever been different. It was his necessity, in the words of E. Franklin Frazier, to find a "motive for living under American culture or die." The identity of the American Negro comes out of this extreme situation, and the evolution of this identity was a source of the most intolerable anxiety in the minds and the lives of his masters.

For the history of the American Negro is unique also in this: 18 that the question of his humanity, and of his rights therefore as a human being, became a burning one for several generations of Americans, so burning a question that it ultimately became one of those used to divide the nation. It is out of this argument that the venom of the epithet *Nigger!* is derived. It is an argument which Europe has never had, and hence Europe quite sincerely fails to understand how or why the argument arose in the first place, why its effects are so frequently disastrous and always so unpredictable, why it refuses until today to be entirely settled. Europe's black possessions remained—and do remain—in Europe's colonies, at which remove they represented no threat whatever to European identity. If they posed any problem at all for the European conscience, it was a problem which remained comfortingly abstract: in effect, the black man, *as a man*, did not exist for Europe. But in America, even as a slave, he was an inescapable part of the general social fabric and no American could escape having an attitude toward him. Americans attempt until today to make an abstraction of the Negro, but the very nature of these abstractions reveals the tremendous effects the presence of the Negro has had on the American character.

When one considers the history of the Negro in America it is   19
of the greatest importance to recognize that the moral beliefs of a person, or a people, are never really as tenuous as life—which is not moral—very often causes them to appear; these create for them a frame of reference and a necessary hope, the hope being that when life has done its worst they will be enabled to rise above themselves and to triumph over life. Life would scarcely be bearable if this hope did not exist. Again, even when the worst has been said, to betray a belief is not by any means to have put oneself beyond its power; the betrayal of a belief is not the same thing as ceasing to believe. If this were not so there would be no moral standards in the world at all. Yet one must also recognize that morality is based on ideas and that all ideas are dangerous—dangerous because ideas can only lead to action and where the action leads no man can say. And dangerous in this respect: that confronted with the impossibility of becoming free of them, one can be driven to the most inhuman excesses. The ideas on which American beliefs are based are not, though Americans often seem to think so, ideas which originated in America. They came out of Europe. And the establishment of democracy on the American continent was scarcely as radical a break with the past as was the necessity, which Americans faced, of broadening this concept to include black men.

This was, literally, a hard necessity. It was impossible, for   20
one thing, for Americans to abandon their beliefs, not only because these beliefs alone seemed able to justify the sacrifices they had endured and the blood that they had spilled, but also because these beliefs afforded them their only bulwark against a moral chaos as absolute as the physical chaos of the continent it was their destiny to conquer. But in the situation in which Americans found themselves, these beliefs threatened an idea which, whether or not one likes to think so, is the very warp and woof of the heritage of the West, the idea of white supremacy.

Americans have made themselves notorious by the shrillness   21
and the brutality with which they have insisted on this idea, but they did not invent it; and it has escaped the world's notice that those very excesses of which Americans have been guilty imply a certain,

unprecedented uneasiness over the idea's life and power, if not, indeed, the idea's validity. The idea of white supremacy rests simply on the fact that white men are the creators of civilization (the present civilization, which is the only one that matters; all previous civilizations are simply "contributions" to our own) and are therefore civilization's guardians and defenders. Thus it was impossible for Americans to accept the black man as one of themselves, for to do so was to jeopardize their status as white men. But not so to accept him was to deny his human reality, his human weight and complexity, and the strain of denying the overwhelmingly undeniable forced Americans into rationalizations so fantastic that they approached the pathological.

At the root of the American Negro problem is the necessity of the American white man to find a way of living with the Negro in order to be able to live with himself. And the history of this problem can be reduced to the means used by Americans—lynch law and law, segregation and legal acceptance, terrorization and concession— either to come to terms with this necessity, or to find a way around it, or (most usually) to find a way of doing both these things at once. The resulting spectacle, at once foolish and dreadful, led someone to make the quite accurate observation that "the Negro-in-America is a form of insanity which overtakes white men." 22

In this long battle, a battle by no means finished, the unforeseeable effects of which will be felt by many future generations, the white man's motive was the protection of his identity; the black man was motivated by the need to establish an identity. And despite the terrorization which the Negro in America endured and endures sporadically until today, despite the cruel and totally inescapable ambivalence of his status in his country, the battle for his identity has long ago been won. He is not a visitor to the West, but a citizen there, an American; as American as the Americans who despise him, the Americans who fear him, the Americans who love him—the Americans who became less than themselves, or rose to be greater than themselves by virtue of the fact that the challenge he represented was inescapable. He is perhaps the only black man in the world whose relationship to white men is more terrible, more subtle, and more meaningful than the relationship of bitter possessed to uncertain possessor. His survival depended, and his development depends, on his ability to turn his peculiar status in the Western world to his own advantage and, it may be, to the very great advantage of that world. It remains for him to fashion out of his experience that which will give him sustenance, and a voice. 23

The cathedral at Chartres, I have said, says something to the people of this village which it cannot say to me; but it is important to 24 understand that this cathedral says something to me which it cannot say to them. Perhaps they are struck by the power of the spires, the glory of the windows; but they have known God, after all, longer than I have known him, and in a different way, and I am terrified by the slippery bottomless well to be found in the crypt, down which heretics were hurled to death, and by the obscene, inescapable gargoyles jutting out of the stone and seeming to say that God and the devil can never be divorced. I doubt that the villagers think of the devil when they face a cathedral because they have never been identified with the devil. But I must accept the status which myth, if nothing else, gives me in the West before I can hope to change the myth.

Yet, if the American Negro has arrived at his identity by 25 virtue of the absoluteness of his estrangement from his past, American white men still nourish the illusion that there is some means of recovering the European innocence, of returning to a state in which black men do not exist. This is one of the greatest errors Americans can make. The identity they fought so hard to protect has, by virtue of that battle, undergone a change: Americans are as unlike any other white people in the world as it is possible to be. I do not think, for example, that it is too much to suggest that the American vision of the world—which allows so little reality, generally speaking, for any of the darker forces in human life, which tends until today to paint moral issues in glaring black and white—owes a great deal to the battle waged by Americans to maintain between themselves and black men a human separation which could not be bridged. It is only now beginning to be borne in on us—very faintly, it must be admitted, very slowly, and very much against our will—that this vision of the world is dangerously inaccurate, and perfectly useless. For it protects our moral high-mindedness at the terrible expense of weakening our grasp of reality. People who shut their eyes to reality simply invite their own destruction, and anyone who insists on remaining in a state of innocence long after that innocence is dead turns himself into a monster.

The time has come to realize that the interracial drama acted 26 out on the American continent has not only created a new black man, it has created a new white man, too. No road whatever will lead Americans back to the simplicity of this European village where white men still have the luxury of looking on me as a stranger. I am not, really, a stranger any longer for any American alive. One of the things that distinguishes Americans from other people is that no other people has ever been so deeply involved in the lives of black men, and vice versa. This fact faced, with all its implications, it can be seen that the history of the American Negro problem is not merely shameful, it is also something of an achievement. For even when the worst has been said, it must also be added that the perpetual challenge posed by this problem was always, somehow, perpetually met. It is precisely this black-white experience which may prove of indispensable value to us in the world we face today. This world is white no longer, and it will never be white again.

QUESTIONS

1. What connections between Europe, Africa, and America emerge from this essay? What is the relevance of the Swiss village to this frame of reference?

2. In the context of the essay, explain what Baldwin means by his statement, "People are trapped in history and history is trapped in them" (paragraph 5).

3. Analyze the effect of Baldwin's repetition of "there is" and "there are" constructions in paragraph 2. What does the parallelism at the start of paragraph 8 accomplish? Locate other examples of parallelism in the essay.

4. Analyze the figure of speech "wind" in paragraph 3 and its relation to the rest of the essay.

5. Where in the essay is Baldwin's complex thesis condensed for the reader? What does this placement of thesis reveal about the logical method of development in the essay?

6. How does Baldwin create his introduction? What is the focus? What key motifs does the author present that will inform the rest of the essay? What is the relationship of paragraph 5 to paragraph 6?

7. What paragraphs constitute the second section of the essay? What example serves to unify this section? What major shift in emphasis occurs in the third part of the essay? Explain the cathedral at Chartres as a controlling motif between these two sections.

8. What comparisons and contrasts help to structure and unify the essay?

9. Discuss the paradox implicit in Baldwin's statement in the last paragraph that the American Negro problem is "something of an achievement."

10. a. Write an essay on civilization based on the last sentence in Baldwin's essay.
b. Describe a time when you felt yourself a "stranger" in a certain culture.

 STRANGER IN THE VILLAGE 591

My Speech to the Graduates

Allen Stewart Konigsberg (1935–   ), legally renamed Heywood Allen and known popularly as Woody Allen, is a comedian, actor, director, and writer for television, film, drama, and such national publications as *Playboy, New Yorker,* and *Esquire.* His notable screenplays include *What's New, Pussycat?* (1965), *Bananas* (1970), *Play It Again, Sam* (1972), *Sleeper* (1973), and *Annie Hall* (1977), a film that won the Academy Award, with Allen also taking honors for best director and, with Marshall Brickman, for best original screenplay. Allen's books, filled with the same comic genius as his best films, include *Getting Even* (1971), *Without Feathers* (1975), and *Side Effects* (1980). This essay from his latest collection is a parody of one graduation ritual as well as a satire on present civilization.

1　More than any other time in history, mankind faces a crossroads. One path leads to despair and utter hopelessness. The other, to total extinction. Let us pray we have the wisdom to choose correctly. I speak, by the way, not with any sense of futility, but with a panicky conviction of the absolute meaninglessness of existence which could easily be misinterpreted as pessimism. It is not. It is merely a healthy concern for the predicament of modern man. (Modern man is here defined as any person born after Nietzche's edict that "God is dead," but before the hit recording "I Wanna Hold Your Hand.") This "predicament" can be stated in one of two ways, though certain linguistic philosophers prefer to reduce it to a mathematical equation where it can be easily solved and even carried around in the wallet.

2　Put in its simplest form, the problem is: How is it possible to find meaning in a finite world given my waist and shirt size? This is a very difficult question when we realize that science has failed us. True, it has conquered many diseases, broken the genetic code, and even placed human beings on the moon, and yet when a man of 80 is left in a room with two 18-year-old cocktail waitresses nothing happens. Because the real problems never change. After all, can the human soul be glimpsed through a microscope? Maybe—but you'd definitely need one of those very good ones with two eyepieces. We know that the most advanced computer in the world does not have a brain as sophisticated as that of an ant. True, we could say that of many of our relatives but we only have to put up with them at weddings or special occasions. Science is something we depend on all the time. If I develop a pain in the chest I must take an X-ray. But what if the radiation from the X-ray causes me deeper problems? Before I know it, I'm in for surgery. Naturally, while they're giving me oxygen an intern decides to light on a cigarette. The next thing you know I'm rocketing over the World Trade Center in bedclothes. Is this science? True, science has taught us how to pasteurize cheese. And true, this can be fun in mixed company—but what of the H-bomb? Have you ever seen what happens, when one of those things falls off a desk accidentally? And where is science when one ponders the eternal riddles? How did the cosmos originate? How long has it been around? Did matter begin with an explosion or by the word of God? And if by the latter, could He not have begun it just two weeks earlier to take advantage of some of the warmer weather? Exactly what do we mean when we say man is mortal? Obviously it's not a compliment.

Religion, too, has unfortunately let us down. Miguel de   3 Unamuno writes blithely of the "eternal persistence of consciousness," but that is no easy feat. Particularly when reading Thackeray. I often think how comforting life must have been for early man because he believed in a powerful, benevolent Creator who looked after all things. Imagine his disappointment when he saw his wife putting on weight. Contemporary man, of course, has no such peace of mind. He finds himself in the midst of a crisis of faith. He is what we fashionably call "alienated." He has seen the ravages of war, he has known natural catastrophes, he has been to singles bars. My good friend Jacques Monod spoke often of the randomness of the cosmos. He believed everything in existence occurred by pure chance with the possible exception of his breakfast, which he felt certain was made by his housekeeper. Naturally belief in a divine intelligence inspires tranquillity. But this does not free us from our human responsibilities. Am I my brother's keeper? Yes. Interestingly, in my case I share that honor with the Prospect Park Zoo. Feeling godless then, what we have done is made technology God. And yet can technology really be the answer when a brand new Buick, driven by my close associate, Nat Persky, winds up in the window of Chicken Delight causing hundreds of customers to scatter? My toaster has never once worked properly in four years. I follow the instructions and push two slices of bread down in the slots and seconds later they rifle upward. Once they broke the nose of a woman I loved very dearly. Are we counting on nuts and bolts and electricity to solve our problems? Yes, the telephone is a good thing—and the refrigerator—and the air conditioner. But not every air conditioner. Not my sister Henny's, for instance. Hers makes a loud noise and still doesn't cool. When the man comes over to fix it, it gets worse. Either that or he tells her she needs a new one. When she complains, he says not to bother him. This man is truly alienated. Not only is he alienated but he can't stop smiling.

The trouble is, our leaders have not adequately prepared us 4 for a mechanized society. Unfortunately our politicians are either incompetent or corrupt. Sometimes both on the same day. The Government is unresponsive to the needs of the little man. Under five-seven, it is impossible to get your Congressman on the phone. I am not denying that democracy is still the finest form of government. In a democracy at least, civil liberties are upheld. No citizen can be wantonly tortured, imprisoned, or made to sit through certain Broadway shows. And yet this is a far cry from what goes on in the Soviet Union. Under their form of totalitarianism, a person merely caught whistling is sentenced to 30 years in a labor camp. If, after 15 years, he still will not stop whistling they shoot him. Along with this brutal fascism we find its handmaiden, terrorism. At no other time in history has man been so afraid to cut into his veal chop for fear that it will explode. Violence breeds more violence and it is predicted that by 1990 kidnapping will be the dominant mode of social interaction. Overpopulation will exacerbate problems to the breaking point. Figures tell us there are already more people on earth than we need to move even the heaviest piano. If we do not call a halt to breeding, by the year 2000 there will be no room to serve dinner unless one is willing to set the table on the heads of strangers. Then they must not move for an hour while we eat. Of course energy will be in short supply and each car owner will be allowed only enough gasoline to back up a few inches.

Instead of facing these challenges we turn to distractions like 5 drugs and sex. We live in far too permissive a society. Never before has pornography been this rampant. And those films are lit so badly! We are a people who lack defined goals. We have never learned to love. We lack leaders and coherent programs. We have no spiritual center. We are adrift in the cosmos wreaking monstrous violence on one another out of frustration and pain. Fortunately, we have not lost our sense of proportion. Summing up, it is clear the future holds great opportunities. It also holds pitfalls. The trick will be to avoid the pitfalls, seize the opportunities, and get back home by six o'clock.

QUESTIONS

1. Explain the author's comic attitude toward science, religion, and politics. What specific subjects does he ridicule?

2. Beneath the surface of comedy in the essay, we can infer that Allen is

WOODY ALLEN

concerned with the modern "predicament." Cite examples to support this judgment.

3. What purpose does the author's allusion to Nietzche, Unamuno, and Monod serve?

4. Does the author use understatement or overstatement in his ironic language? Explain by reference to the essay.

5. What is the relationship of the title to the substance of the essay? Does the author in his introduction give any appearance of writing seriously? How does the introduction echo standard speeches to graduates? How does Allen approach such standard speeches?

6. What role does logic, either inductive or deductive, play within the pattern of the essay?

7. In what manner does the pattern of cause and effect heighten the irony in the essay?

8. Examine the substance and structure of Allen's "summing up" in the last paragraph.

9. Compare and contrast Faulkner's acceptance speech for the Nobel Prize (see pages 578–579) on the state of civilization with Allen's speech to the graduates.

10. a. Write your own comic speech to the graduates.
b. Satirize one aspect of the modern dilemma.

ARNOLD TOYNBEE

Why I Dislike Western Civilization

Arnold Joseph Toynbee (1889–1975), noted English historian, posited in his twelve-volume *A Study of History* (1934–1961) a cyclical theory of the development and decline of civilizations that has elicited considerable contemporary controversy. A professor at the London School of Economics from 1925 until the time of his retirement in 1956, Toynbee was a prolific author of studies on history, international relations, contemporary wars, world religions, Western civilization, and travel. This *essay reflects his main contention that the proper subject for the study of history is civilization itself.*

W
hen I say baldly that I dislike contemporary Western   1
civilization, I am, of course, saying this partly to tease
my fellow Westerners. The stand that I take is partly a
joke, but it is also partly serious.

My dislike of the West, though genuine as far as it goes,   2
cannot really be unmitigated. If it were, I should not feel lost—as I
know that I should—if I did not have a *pied-à-terre* in London. I am a
Londoner born and bred, but I have not reacted against my native
city; and, though I dislike the congestion of the mechanized traffic
there, I know that this pest is just as bad in all the other great cities of
the postwar world.

If I were to be hounded out of London by some (nonexistent)   3
British counterpart of the House Committee on Un-American Activities, I expect I could make myself at home in Edinburgh or Melbourne
or Rome or Hamburg or Boston, Mass. (my great-grandfather's farm
was in sight of Boston Stump, the tapering tower of St. Botolph's
Church in Boston, England). I should not feel at home as a permanent
resident in New York or Chicago or Pittsburgh or Glasgow or
Manchester or Milan. And I do not suppose that I could strike root in
Kyoto or in Damascus or in Istanbul or even in Athens, though I love
and admire each of these beautiful non-Western cities.

In ancient Greece, the navel of the earth was marked by a   4
monolith at Delphi. The navel of my earth is not in Greece (though
my heart and mind reside there). My world-navel is the Albert
Memorial in Kensington Gardens. This British monument may be
comically ugly but, to me, it is reassuringly familiar. I used to play
around its steps when I was a tiny child. Its frieze taught me the
names of the great poets, artists and thinkers of the past; the group of
figures at the four corners put the four continents on the map for me.

Yes, one is a prisoner of one's time and place. I belong to the   5
presyncopation age. Classical Western music is music for my ears.
When I hear jazz, I become uneasy and turn hostile. I feel my
traditional world being victoriously invaded by tropical Africa. Politi-
cally, I am on the side of Africa against the Western colonial powers,
but when it comes to music, Africa's cultural colonialism makes me
cherish the West's pre-African musical past.

To be the prisoner of one's time and place is one of our   6
human limitations. A human being has roots, like a tree, and these
roots tether him—though, unlike a tree's roots, they are emotional
and intellectual roots. However, it is characteristic of our human
nature that we rebel against our human limitations and try to
transcend them. I myself, besides being human, happen to be a

596   ARNOLD TOYNBEE historian, and a historian's special form of human rebellion is to try to shake himself free of his own parochial blood and soil (to use Hitler's hateful but expressive words). A historian's métier is to move freely through time and space.

What a bore one's own native civilization is. It is dull just 7 because it is familiar. I had the good fortune to be educated in Greek and Latin. This education served me as a magic carpet on which I wafted myself from the twentieth century of the Christian era to the third century B.C., and from the North Atlantic to the Eastern Mediterranean. I hated having to learn the names and dates of the Kings of England. The kings of Israel and Judah were almost as bad, since the Old Testament in the King James version has become virtually part of English literature. But I enjoyed finding my way among the Ptolemies and the Seleucuses. English constitutional history? One glance at the syllabus of the Oxford school of medieval and modern history was enough to put me off reading for that. But the history of Islam, the history of Buddhism—these opened up fascinating new worlds.

Contemporary Western civilization annoys me, not because it 8 is Western, but because it is mine and because I am a historian. If I had happened to be born in 1889 in China instead of England, no doubt I should be annoyed today with the China of Pu Yi and Chiang Kai-shek and Chou En-lai. But being, as I am, a Western historian, I am inevitably annoyed by the contemporary West. It holds me fast entangled in its coils. It prevents me from getting back behind the machine age and from getting out into Russia, Dar-el-Islam, the Hindu world, Eastern Asia. My inescapable Westernness makes it impossible for me to become culturally acclimatized in any of these other contemporary civilizations. This is a limitation on my human freedom that I resent.

However, I have a more formidable reason for disliking the 9 West than any that I have mentioned so far. Since I have been grown-up (I am now turned 75), the West has produced two world wars; it has produced Communism, Fascism and National Socialism; it has produced Mussolini and Hitler and McCarthy. These Western enormities make me, as a Westerner, feel insecure. Now that my German fellow-Westerners have murdered six million Jews, how can I be certain that my English fellow-countrymen might not do something equally criminal? We did murder some thousands of defenseless civilians at Port Said in 1956. What might we not go on to do after that? What might I not be capable of doing myself, if this contemporary Western criminal lunacy were to waylay me?

I shiver and shake. Old-fashioned Christian humility, please 10 come to my rescue. Please save me from contemporary post-Christian Western self-complacent sinfulness. I should feel my spirits rise if,

 WHY I DISLIKE WESTERN CIVILIZATION

instead of being Hitler's fellow-Westerner—as I am—I could be Gandhi's fellow-Hindu. Yes, I believe I could even stomach Benares as the price of being liberated from Hitler's company. But I cannot escape Hitler. This fellow-Westerner of mine (of the same age to within a week) is going to haunt me for the rest of my West-bound life.

Apart from contemporary Western crimes, there are other blemishes on contemporary Western life that I find repulsive. Though I dislike the former enslavement of the individual to the community in Japan, I also dislike, and this perhaps even more, the lengths to which contemporary Western individualism has gone. The contemporary West is callous toward the aged. This is, I believe, the first civilization, so far, in which the aged have not had a place, as a matter of course, in their adult children's homes. Looking at this Western callousness with de-Westernized eyes, I find it shocking. 11

I also dislike the contemporary Western advertising business. It has made a fine art out of taking advantage of human silliness. It rams unwanted material goods down surfeited throats when two-thirds of all human beings now alive are in desperate need of the bare necessities of life. This is an ugly aspect of the affluent society; and, if I am told that advertising is the price of affluence, I reply without hesitation, that affluence has been bought too dear. Another item in the price of affluence is the standardization of mass-produced goods and services. This is, in itself, a deplorable impoverishment of the material side of human culture, and it brings spiritual standardization with it, which is still worse. 12

Looking back into the past history of the West—a past which was still present when I was a child—I admire the nineteenth-century West's success in postponing the age of sexual awakening, of sexual experience and sexual infatuation far beyond the age of physical puberty. You may tell me that this was against nature; but to be human consists precisely in transcending nature—in overcoming the biological limitations that we have inherited from our prehuman ancestors. 13

All human societies overcome death by creating and maintaining institutions that are handed on from one generation to another. Sex is a still more awkward feature of our biological inheritance than death, and our nineteenth-century Western society handled sex with relative success. By postponing the age of sexual awakening, it prolonged the length of the period of education. It is this, together with the seventeenth-century Western achievement of learning to think for oneself instead of taking tradition on trust, that accounts for the West's preeminence in the world during the last few centuries. 14

ARNOLD TOYNBEE

Nineteenth-century Westerners condemned with justice the   15
Hindu institution of child-marriage, and they deplored, also with
justice, the spectacle of an intellectually promising Moslem boy being
allowed to commit intellectual suicide by sexual indulgence at the age
of puberty. The twentieth-century West is now imitating the non-
Western habits that the nineteenth-century West rightly—though
perhaps self-righteously—condemned.

Our irrational contemporary Western impatience and our   16
blind adulation of speed for speed's sake are making havoc, today, of
the education of our children. We force their growth as if they were
chicks in a pullet factory. We drive them into a premature awareness
of sex even before physical puberty has overtaken them. In fact, we
deprive our children of the human right of having a childhood. This
forcing of sex-consciousness started in the United States; it has spread
to Britain, and who knows how many other Western countries this
perverse system of miseducation is going to invade and demoralize?

Our whole present policy in the upbringing of the young is   17
paradoxical. While we are lowering the age of sexual awareness—and
frequently the age of sexual experience, too—to a veritably Hindu
degree, we are at the same time prolonging the length of education.
We force our boys and girls to become sex-conscious at twelve or
thirteen, and then we ask them to prolong their postgraduate studies
till they are nearly thirty. How are they to be expected to give their
minds to education during those last sixteen or seventeen sex-
haunted years?

We are proud of ourselves for providing secondary educa-   18
tion, college education, postgraduate education for everybody. But
we shall be plowing the sands if we do not simultaneously revert to
our grandparents' practice of prolonging the age of sexual innocence.
If we persist, in this vital matter, on our present Hindu course, our
brand-new would-be institutions for higher education will become, in
practice, little more than social clubs for sexual mating.

This relapse into precocious sexuality is one of the moral   19
blemishes of the contemporary Western civilization. One of its
intellectual blemishes is its insistence on splitting up the universe into
smaller and smaller splinters. It has split up the human race into a
host of sovereign independent national states. It has split up knowledge and understanding into a host of separate watertight "disciplines." I dislike nationalism and I dislike specialization, and both are
characteristically Western aberrations.

When I was about sixteen years old, I stayed with an uncle   20
who was a specialist on Dante, while his wife was a specialist on
Horace Walpole. Their library was less specialized than they themselves were, and I browsed in it with excitement and delight. When I

was due to leave, my uncle said to me: "Arnold, your aunt and I think you are allowing your interest to be too general. You ought to specialize." I said nothing, but I was instantaneously certain that I was not going to follow this advice; and, in fact, I have consistently done the opposite throughout the sixty years that have passed since then.

What a world to find oneself born into. Since as early as I first 21 became conscious of my native Western environment, Western technology has been inventing new and ever more complicated machines. I did learn to ride a bicycle. How can one be expected, in just one lifetime, to go on to learn to ride a motorcycle or to drive a car? I started shaving in the age of the cutthroat razor, and Mr. Gillette's invention came as a great relief to me. But how can I be expected to go on to use an electric razor? How could I know about volts and ohms and transformers? An American friend did give me an electric razor. This lies safely tucked away in a drawer, and whenever I unearth it, it alarms me.

I do now travel about the world in cars and airplanes. The 22 better these get at covering the distance, the worse they get at allowing an inquisitive passenger to see the view. I did my first traveling in Greece in 1911–12. I did it on foot with a rucksack on my back. I was as free as a bird. I could go where even mules could not go. I could see the world as I pleased. I have never traveled so satisfactorily as that since then.

The other day, I had a three-hour mule ride from an airstrip 23 to the rock-cut churches at Lalibela in Ethiopia. Once again I was seeing the real world, the unmechanized pre-Western world in which I feel truly at home. Machinery perplexes and dismays me, and I have been born into the Western machine age. Why was I not born in the third-century-B.C. Syria or seventh-century-A.D. China? I should not then have been harassed by machinery as I am in the contemporary West. I heartily dislike this side of contemporary Western life, and, in the eyes of the rest of the world, mechanization is what the contemporary West stands for.

Well, these are some of the reasons why I dislike the 24 contemporary Western civilization. But, as I have said at the beginning of this article, my dislike is not undiluted. My grandchildren, after all, are Westerners, and I certainly like them. Moreover, I want them, in their turn, to have grandchildren who will have grandchildren. I should be desolated if I believed that Western man was going to commit mass suicide by engaging in a third world war that, this time, would be fought with atomic weapons.

To discover the existence of the atom and to go on to discover 25 how to split it has been the *chef d'oeuvre* of Western science and

ARNOLD TOYNBEE

technology. I do not love Western science for having made these deadly inventions; but I have just enough faith in Western man's political commonsense to expect that he will not liquidate himself. So perhaps, after all, I do not rate my native Western civilization so low as I fancy that I do in my moments of acute exasperation at the West's more uncongenial vagaries.

QUESTIONS

1. List the reasons Toynbee dislikes Western civilization.

2. What are some of the features of non-Western civilization that appeal to Toynbee?

3. Identify the allusions in paragraphs 7 to 9. Why is the broad range of allusion throughout the essay an important aspect of Toynbee's subject and thesis?

4. Explain the following figures of speech: "world-navel" (paragraph 4); "A human being has roots, like a tree . . ." (paragraph 6); "This education served me as a magic carpet . . ." (paragraph 7); "It holds me fast entangled in its coils" (paragraph 8); "spiritual standardization" (paragraph 12); "to commit intellectual suicide by sexual indulgence . . ." (paragraph 15); ". . . the *chef d'oeuvre* of Western science and technology" (paragraph 25).

5. Analyze the way in which Toynbee moves from a defense of Western civilization to a preliminary criticism of it in paragraphs 1 to 8.

6. Examine the validity and authenticity of the premises upon which Toynbee bases his argument. What supporting evidence does he offer for his assumptions?

7. How does the essay employ the comparative method?

8. How does Toynbee inject appeals to emotion into the essay? What is the effect of this strategy on tone?

9. Toynbee writes that "it is characteristic of our human nature that we rebel against our human limitations and try to transcend them" (paragraph 6). How does this relate to his argument? Do you agree or disagree with his assertion? Explain.

10. a. Write an essay explaining why you like or dislike Western civilization.
b. Write an essay explaining why you like or dislike American civilization.

The Lessons of the Past

Edith Hamilton (1867–1963), teacher, writer, and Grecophile, wrote her first book when she was 63. Her initial career was as headmistress of a private girl's school in Maryland. When she retired, she began to write about ancient civilizations, particularly Greek civilization. In 1930, *The Greek Way* was published. In later years, Hamilton also wrote *The Roman Way* (1932) and *The Prophets of Israel* (1936). She retold Greek, Roman, and Norse myths in *Mythology* (1942). At the age of 90, Hamilton visited Greece and was made an honorary citizen. This essay focuses on Greek civilization in order to illuminate the problems confronting the modern era.

s there an ever-present past? Are there permanent truths which are forever important for the present? Today we are facing a future more strange and untried than any other generation has faced. The new world Columbus opened seems small indeed beside the illimitable distances of space before us, and the possibilities of destruction are immeasurably greater than ever. In such a position can we afford to spend time on the past? That is the question I am often asked. Am I urging the study of the Greeks and Romans and their civilizations for the atomic age? 1

Yes; that is just what I am doing. I urge it without qualifications. We have a great civilization to save—or to lose. The greatest civilization before ours was the Greek. They challenge us and we need the challenge. They, too, lived in a dangerous world. They were a little, highly civilized people, the only civilized people in the west, surrounded by barbarous tribes and with the greatest Asiatic power, Persia, always threatening them. In the end they succumbed, but the reason they did was not that the enemies outside were so strong, but that their own strength, their spiritual strength, had given way. While they had it they kept Greece unconquered and they left behind a record in art and thought which in all the centuries of human effort since has not been surpassed. 2

The point which I want to make is not that their taste was superior to ours, not that the Parthenon was their idea of church architecture nor that Sophocles was the great drawing card in the theaters, nor any of the familiar comparisons between fifth-century Athens and twentieth-century America, but that Socrates found on every street corner and in every Athenian equivalent of the baseball field people who were caught up by his questions into the world of 3 thought. To be able to be caught up into the world of thought—that is to be educated.

How is that great aim to be reached? For years we have eagerly discussed ways and means of education, and the discussion still goes on. William James once said that there were two subjects which if mentioned made other conversation stop and directed all eyes to the speaker. Religion was one and education the other. Today Russia seems to come first, but education is still emphatically the second. In spite of all the articles we read and all the speeches we listen to about it, we want to know more; we feel deeply its importance.

There is today a clearly visible trend toward making it the aim of education to defeat the Russians. That would be a sure way to defeat education. Genuine education is possible only when people realize that it has to do with persons, not with movements.

When I read educational articles it often seems to me that this important side of the matter, the purely personal side, is not emphasized enough; that fact that it is so much more agreeable and interesting to be an educated person than not. The sheer pleasure of being educated does not seem to be stressed. Once long ago I was talking with Prof. Basil L. Gildersleeve of Johns Hopkins University, the greatest Greek scholar our country has produced. He was an old man and he had been honored everywhere, in Europe as well as in America. He was just back from a celebration held for him in Oxford. I asked him what compliment received in his long life had pleased him most. The question amused him and he laughed over it, but he thought too. Finally he said, "I believe it was when one of my students said, 'Professor, you have so much fun with your own mind.'" Robert Louis Stevenson said that a man ought to be able to spend two or three hours waiting for a train at a little country station when he was all alone and had nothing to read, and not be bored for a moment.

What is the education which can do this? What is the furniture which makes the only place belonging absolutely to each one of us, the world within, a place where we like to go? I wish I could answer that question. I wish I could produce a perfect decorator's design warranted to make any interior lovely and interesting and stimulating; but, even if I could, sooner or later we would certainly try different designs. My point is only that while we must and should change the furniture, we ought to throw away old furniture very cautiously. It may turn out to be irreplaceable. A great deal was thrown away in the last generation or so, long enough ago to show some of the results. Furniture which had for centuries been foremost, we lightly, in a few years, discarded. The classics almost vanished from our field of education. That was a great change. Along with it

THE LESSONS OF THE PAST

603

came another. There is a marked difference between the writers of the past and the writers of today who have been educated without benefit of Greek and Latin. Is this a matter of cause and effect? People will decide for themselves, but I do not think anyone will question the statement that clear thinking is not the characteristic which distinguishes our literature today. We are more and more caught up by the unintelligible. People like it. This argues an inability to think, or, almost as bad, a disinclination to think.

Neither disposition marked the Greeks. They had a passion 8 for thinking things out, and they loved unclouded clarity of statement as well as of thought. The Romans did, too, in their degree. They were able to put an idea into an astonishingly small number of words without losing a particle of intelligibility. It is only of late, with a generation which has never had to deal with a Latin sentence, that we are being submerged in a flood of words, words, words. It has been said that Lincoln at Gettysburg today would have begun in some such fashion as this: "Eight and seven-tenths decades ago the pioneer workers in this continental area implemented a new group based on an ideology of free boundaries and initial equality," and might easily have ended, "That political supervision of the integrated units, for the integrated units, by the integrated units, shall not become null and void on the superficial area of this planet." Along with the banishment of the classics, gobbledegook has come upon us—and the appalling size of the Congressional Record, and the overburdened mail service.

Just what the teaching in the schools was which laid the 9 foundation of the Greek civilization we do not know in detail; the result we do know. Greek children were taught, Plato said, to "love what is beautiful and hate what is ugly." When they grew up their very pots and pans had to be pleasant to look at. It was part of their training to hate clumsiness and awkwardness; they loved grace and practiced it. "Our children," Plato said, "will be influenced for good by every sight and sound of beauty, breathing in, as it were, a pure breeze blowing to them from a good land."

All the same, the Athenians were not, as they showed 10 Socrates when he talked to them, preoccupied with enjoying lovely things. The children were taught to think. Plato demanded a stiff examination, especially in mathematics, for entrance to his Academy. The Athenians were a thinking people. Today the scientists are bearing away the prize for thought. Well, a Greek said that the earth went around the sun, sixteen centuries before Copernicus thought of it. A Greek said if you sailed out of Spain and kept to one latitude, you would come at last to land, seventeen hundred years before Columbus did it. Darwin said, "We are mere schoolboys in scientific thinking compared to old Aristotle." And the Greeks did not have a great legacy from the past as our scientists have; they thought science out from the beginning.

The same is true of politics. They thought that out, too, from the beginning, and they gave all the boys a training to fit them to be thinking citizens of a free state that had come into being through thought. 11

Basic to all the Greek achievement was freedom. The Athenians were the only free people in the world. In the great empires of antiquity—Egypt, Babylon, Assyria, Persia—splendid though they were, with riches beyond reckoning and immense power, freedom was unknown. The idea of it never dawned in any of them. It was born in Greece, a poor little country, but with it able to remain unconquered no matter what manpower and what wealth were arrayed against her. At Marathon and at Salamis overwhelming numbers of Persians had been defeated by small Greek forces. It has been proved that one free man was superior to many submissively obedient subjects of a tyrant. Athens was the leader in that amazing victory, and to the Athenians freedom was their dearest possession. Demosthenes said that they would not think it worth their while to live if they could not do so as free men, and years later a great teacher said, "Athenians, if you deprive them of their liberty, will die." 12

Athens was not only the first democracy in the world, it was also at its height an almost perfect democracy—that is, for men. There was no part in it for women or foreigners or slaves, but as far as the men were concerned it was more democratic than we are. The governing body was the Assembly, of which all citizens over eighteen were members. The Council of Five Hundred which prepared business for the Assembly and, if requested, carried out what had been decided there, was made up of citizens who were chosen by lot. The same was true of the juries. Minor officials also were chosen by lot. The chief magistrates and the highest officers in the army were elected by the Assembly. Pericles was a general, very popular, who acted for a long time as if he were head of the state, but he had to be elected every year. Freedom of speech was the right the Athenians prized most and there has never been another state as free in that respect. When toward the end of the terrible Peloponnesian War the victorious Spartans were advancing upon Athens, Aristophanes caricatured in the theater the leading Athenian generals and showed them up as cowards, and even then as the Assembly opened, the herald asked, "Does anyone wish to speak?" 13

There was complete political equality. It was a government of the people, by the people, for the people. An unregenerate old aristocrat in the early fourth century, B.C., writes: "If you *must* have a democracy, Athens is the perfect example. I object to it because it is based on the welfare of the lower, not the better, classes. In Athens 14 the people who row the vessels and do the work have the advantage. It is their prosperity that is important." All the same, making the city beautiful was important too, as were also the great performances in the theater. If, as Plato says, the Assembly was chiefly made up of cobblers and carpenters and smiths and farmers and retail-business men, they approved the construction of the Parthenon and the other buildings on the Acropolis, and they crowded the theater when the great tragedies were played. Not only did all free men share in the government; the love of the beautiful and the desire to have a part in creating it were shared by the many, not by a mere chosen few. That has happened in no state except Athens.

But those free Greeks owned slaves. What kind of freedom   15 was that? The question would have been incomprehensible to the ancient world. There had always been slaves; they were a first necessity. The way of life everywhere was based upon them. They were taken for granted; no one ever gave them a thought. The very best Greek minds, the thinkers who discovered freedom and the solar system, had never an idea that slavery was evil. It is true that the greatest thinker of them all, Plato, was made uncomfortable by it. He said that slaves were often good, trustworthy, doing more for a man than his own family would, but he did not follow his thought through. The glory of being the first one to condemn it belongs to a man of the generation before Plato, the poet Euripides. He called it, "That thing of evil," and in several of his tragedies showed its evil for all to see. A few centuries later the great Greek school of the Stoics denounced it. Greece first saw it for what it is. But the world went on in the same way. The Bible accepts it without comment. Two thousand years after the Stoics, less than a hundred years ago, the American Republic accepted it.

Athens treated her slaves well. A visitor to the city in the   16 early fourth century, B.C., wrote: "It is illegal here to deal a slave a blow. In the street he won't step aside to let you pass. Indeed you can't tell a slave by his dress; he looks like all the rest. They can go to the theater too. Really, the Athenians have established a kind of equality between slaves and free men." They were never a possible source of danger to the state as they were in Rome. There were no terrible slave wars and uprisings in Athens. In Rome, crucifixion was called "the slave's punishment." The Athenians did not practice crucifixion, and had no so-called slave's punishment. They were not afraid of their slaves.

In Athens' great prime Athenians were free. No one told   17 them what they must do or what they should think—no church or political party or powerful private interests or labor unions. Greek schools had no donors of endowments they must pay attention to, no government financial backing which must be made secure by acting as the government wanted. To be sure, the result was that they had to take full responsibility, but that is always the price for full freedom. The Athenians were a strong people, they could pay the price. They were a thinking people; they knew what freedom means. They knew—not that they were free because their country was free, but that their country was free because they were free.

A reflective Roman traveling in Greece in the second century A.D. said, "None ever throve under democracy save the Athenians; *they* had sane self-control and were law-abiding." He spoke truly. That is what Athenian education aimed at, to produce men who would be able to maintain a self-governed state because they were themselves self-governed, self-controlled, self-reliant. Plato speaks of "the education in excellence which makes men long to be perfect citizens, knowing both how to rule and be ruled." "We are a free democracy," Pericles said. "We do not allow absorption in our own affairs to interfere with participation in the city's; we yield to none in independence of spirit and complete self-reliance, but we regard him who holds aloof from public affairs as useless." They called the useless man a "private" citizen, *idiotes,* from which our word "idiot" comes. 18

They had risen to freedom and to ennoblement from what Gilbert Murray calls "effortless barbarism"; they saw it all around them; they hated its filth and fierceness; nothing effortless was among the good things they wanted. Plato said, "Hard is the good," and a poet hundreds of years before Plato said, 19

> Before the gates of Excellence the high gods have placed sweat.
> Long is the road thereto and steep and rough at the first,
> But when the height is won, then is there ease.

When or why the Greeks set themselves to travel on that road we do not know, but it led them away from habits and customs accepted everywhere that kept men down to barbaric filth and fierceness. It led them far. One example is enough to show the way they took. It was the custom—during how many millenniums, who can say?—for a victor to erect a trophy, a monument of his victory. In Egypt, where stone was plentiful, it would be a slab engraved with his glories. Farther east, where the sand took over, it might be a great heap of severed heads, quite permanent objects; bones last a long time. But in Greece, though a man could erect a trophy, it must be made of wood and it could never be repaired. Even as the victor set it up he would see in his mind how soon it would decay and sink into 20 ruin, and there it must be left. The Greeks in their onward pressing along the steep and rough road had learned a great deal. They knew the victor might be the vanquished next time. There should be no permanent records of the manifestly impermanent. They had learned a great deal.

An old Greek inscription states that the aim of mankind should be "to tame the savageness of man and make gentle the life of the world." Aristotle said that the city was built first for safety, but then that men might discover the good life and lead it. So the Athenians did according to Pericles. Pericles said that Athens stood for freedom and for thought and for beauty, but in the Greek way, within limits, without exaggeration. The Athenians loved beauty, he said, but with simplicity; they did not like the extravagances of luxury. They loved the things of the mind, but they did not shrink from hardship. Thought did not cause them to hesitate, it clarified the road to action. If they had riches they did not make a show of them, and no one was ashamed of being poor if he was useful. They were free because of willing obedience to law, not only the written, but still more the unwritten, kindness and compassion and unselfishness and the many qualities which cannot be enforced, which depend on a man's free choice, but without which men cannot live together. 21

If ever there is to be a truly good and great and enduring republic it must be along these lines. We need the challenge of the city that thought them out, wherein for centuries one genius after another grew up. Geniuses are not produced by spending money. We need the challenge of the way the Greeks were educated. They fixed their eyes on the individual. We contemplate millions. What we have undertaken in this matter of education has dawned upon us only lately. We are trying to do what has never been attempted before, never in the history of the world—educate all the young in a nation of 170 millions; a magnificent idea, but we are beginning to realize what are the problems and what may be the results of mass production of education. So far, we do not seem appalled at the prospect of exactly the same kind of education being applied to all the school children from the Atlantic to the Pacific, but there is an uneasiness in the air, a realization that the individual is growing less easy to find; an idea, perhaps, of what standardization might become when the units are not machines, but human beings. 22

Here is where we can go back to the Greeks with profit. The Athenians in their dangerous world needed to be a nation of independent men who could take responsibility, and they taught their children accordingly. They thought about every boy. Someday he would be a citizen of Athens, responsible for her safety and her glory, "each one," Pericles said, "fitted to meet life's chances and 23 changes with the utmost versatility and grace." To them education was by its very nature an individual matter. To be properly educated a boy had to be taught music; he learned to play a musical instrument. He had to learn poetry, a great deal of it, and recite it—and there were a number of musical instruments and many poets; though, to be sure, Homer was the great textbook.

That kind of education is not geared to mass production. It does not produce people who instinctively go the same way. That is how Athenian children lived and learned while our millions learn the same lessons and spend hours before television sets looking at exactly the same thing at exactly the same time. For one reason and another we are more and more ignoring differences, if not trying to obliterate them. We seem headed toward a standardization of the mind, what Goethe called "the deadly commonplace that fetters us all." That was not the Greek way. 24

The picture of the Age of Pericles drawn by the historian Thucydides, one of the greatest historians the world has known, is of a state made up of people who are self-reliant individuals, not echoes or copies, who want to be let alone to do their own work, but who are also closely bound together by a great aim, the commonweal, each one so in love with his country—Pericles' own words—that he wants most of all to use himself in her service. Only an ideal? Ideals have enormous power. They stamp an age. They lift life up when they are lofty; they drag down and make decadent when they are low—and then, by that strange fact, the survival of the fittest, those that are low fade away and are forgotten. The Greek ideals have had a power of persistent life for twenty-five hundred years. 25

Is it rational that now when the young people may have to face problems harder than we face, is it reasonable that with the atomic age before them, at this time we are giving up the study of how the Greeks and Romans prevailed magnificently in a barbaric world; the study, too, of how that triumph ended, how a slackness and softness finally came over them to their ruin? In the end, more than they wanted freedom, they wanted security, a comfortable life, and they lost all—security and comfort and freedom. 26

Is not that a challenge to us? Is it not true that into our education have come a slackness and softness? Is hard effort prominent? The world of thought can be entered in no other way. Are we not growing slack and soft in our political life? When the Athenians finally wanted not to give to the state, but the state to give to them, when the freedom they wished most for was freedom from responsibility, then Athens ceased to be free and was never free again. Is not that a challenge? 27

Cicero said, "To be ignorant of the past is to remain a child." 28

 THE LESSONS OF THE PAST **609**

Santayana said, "A nation that does not know history is fated to repeat it." The Greeks can help us, help us as no other people can, to see how freedom is won and how it is lost. Above all, to see in clearest light what freedom is. The first nation in the world to be free sends a ringing call down through the centuries to all who would be free. Greece rose to the very height, not because she was big, she was very small; not because she was rich, she was very poor; not even because she was wonderfully gifted. So doubtless were others in the great empires of the ancient world who have gone their way leaving little for us. She rose because there was in the Greeks the greatest spirit that moves in humanity, the spirit that sets men free.

Plato put into words what that spirit is. "Freedom" he says, "is no matter of laws and constitutions; only he is free who realizes the divine order within himself, the true standard by which a man can steer and measure himself." True standards, ideals that lift life up, marked the way of the Greeks. Therefore their light has never been extinguished.

"The time for extracting a lesson from history is ever at hand for them who are wise." Demosthenes.

QUESTIONS

1. According to Hamilton, what is the relationship between Greek civilization and the quality of American education?

2. How does the author seek to justify Greek democracy, even though, as she admits, slaves, women, and foreigners were not free or equal?

3. Explain the analogy in paragraph 7.

4. Analyze the elements of style in paragraph 28.

5. What is the author's thesis? How does the first paragraph prepare for it?

6. How does the author order her main topics in the essay?

7. What causal patterns of development appear in the essay? Where is comparison and contrast used as a rhetorical strategy? How does she use rhetorical questions as an argumentative tactic?

8. Explain the significance of definition as a pattern of development in Hamilton's essay.

9. Speaking of the Greeks, Hamilton writes: "In the end, more than they wanted freedom, they wanted security, a comfortable life, and they lost it all—security and comfort and freedom" (paragraph 26). What is the relevance of Hamilton's observation to the state of modern American

civilization? In this connection, do you believe that there is an ever-present past? Explain.

10. a. Write an essay on the lessons that modern nations can learn from the past.
b. Define freedom in terms of the American experience.
c. Analyze freedom in the modern world.

F. M. ESFANDIARY

The Mystical West Puzzles the Practical East

Fereidoun M. Esfandiary (1930–   ) was born in Tehran, Iran, the son of a diplomat, and has lived largely in the United States since 1952. He is the author of three novels—*Day of Sacrifice* (1959), *The Beggar* (1965), and *Identity Card* (1966) —all of which offer critiques of politics and bureaucratic absurdities in the modern Middle East. Esfandiary has also written many essays for *The New York Times, The Nation, The Saturday Review,* and other publications. In this essay, he utilizes his own experience of two cultures to investigate the contradictions and paradoxes governing the ways that East and West view each other.

An American couple recently spent two weeks in the Middle East crawling in and out of archeological sites, visiting the Pyramids, the Sphinx, the ruins of Baalbek, the ruins of Jerash and Petra, and many "holy" places. In Jordan they met a Middle Easterner who urged them to visit a camp of squatters in Old Jerusalem. Sprawled within a stone's throw of stately temples, churches and mosques, it is one of the world's most horrifying shantytowns. Several thousand Arabs, some of them refugees, fester in dark, damp hovels that are no more than holes in the ground. Families of five, eight or 10 live huddled together in cells with hardly room enough for three or four. The stench of urine permeates the trapped air. There are sick and old people down there who have not seen the light of day in months; they lie rotting on damp floors, waiting for death to deliver them. Children, naked and cadaverous, cower in dingy corners or rummage in garbage heaps for food.

The Middle Easterner led the American couple to one of the

openings in the ground and asked them to follow him down. The Americans stared at the steep stairs and the darkness below and refused to go. "These stairs look dangerous," the American woman said. "Besides, there is nothing to see down below."

"If you had been told that two or three thousand years ago   3
people lived down there, you would have crawled on your hands and knees just to have a glimpse of the place, but because people live there now, you refuse to see it."

"But what is there to see anyway?"   4

"You would have seen some of the poverty and misery of   5
these people."

"I'm not so sure these people are all that miserable," the   6
American interposed. "They look peaceful enough to me. They are probably a lot happier than some Americans we know back home." He stopped, looked about and with memorable inattention to logic, added: "In fact, there is something spiritual, something Biblical, about the way these people live."

Westerners have this dispiriting propensity for contorting   7
reality, for weaving fantasies. They have a childlike need to idolize and romanticize. Self-proclaimed prophets, LSD zealots, Black Muslims, beat poets and artists, students, intellectuals and others have all turned to what they call the Wisdom of the East. Today Buddhism, Hinduism, Zen, Yoga, Islam, Baha'iism are attracting countless followers in America and Western Europe. A mass of literature glorifies the East and the past, but books which attempt to deal realistically with its under-developed countries are largely ignored. If reality threatens to obtrude, it is tampered with until it miraculously fits in with cherished fantasies.

This might seem harmless enough but for the fact that in   8
refusing to see things as they are, in reviving stale philosophies and romanticizing the past, the West is helping to perpetuate Eastern backwardness. It encourages those in our own cultures who resist progress, and it is the peoples of the East who must finally endure the suffering and the destitution.

After they have uttered their empty praises, Westerners run   9
back to New York and Beverly Hills and languish in their comfortable apartments while benefiting from all the social and economic amenities of the 20th century—the 20th century which so many of them claim to despise.

The East they glorify is a famished, ailing man sprawled on   10
the side of the road who is struggling to arise while they stand around congratulating him and his ancestors on being spiritual, and living so close to the earth.

There are Americans and Europeans who know every rose   11
petal that dropped from the mouth of a Buddha or a Confucius, who

know every stone of the Pyramids or the Taj Mahal, yet who know nothing of the peoples living in Eastern lands today, nothing of their needs and sorrows, their struggles and hopes. Can this preoccupation with the romanticized past help us understand or in any way alter the sad fact that today, this very day, millions are hungry and homeless and suffering from agonizing maladies of body and mind?

This same unrealism is reflected in Western foreign policy, 12 which refuses to acknowledge, much less support, the genuine revolutionary aspirations of disadvantaged peoples all over the world, which sometimes even refuses to acknowledge the existence of governments and peoples whose orientation is different from its own. The Washington officials who support reactionary regimes in backward countries are rendering the same disservice, perpetuating the same ills, as the beat poet who revives the archaic philosophies of a Lao-Tze or a Buddha.

The American and Western European Underground, which 13 considers itself avant-garde, is in fact pathetically regressive. It does not look ahead; it looks back. It is romantic and mawkish. Bearded zealots, sitting cross-legged on the ground, wallowing in Haiku poetry, Bhagavad-Gitas and Zen in an atmosphere saturated with the exoticisms of incense, opiates and lanterns—the "scene," in short, smacks of a Dr. Fu Manchu melodrama. The dialogue of the Underground, like its poetry, is heavily spiced with pretentious allusions to Nirvana, Karma, Satori. . . . Its idols are the swami, the guru, the mystic and other high priests of Eastern occultism who go about murmuring such profound revelations as, "Life is like a fountain."

In Greenwich Village, as in other bohemias of the Western 14 world, one can often see displayed in cafes and shop windows posters of some swami or yogi. The large head, dark piercing eyes, benign smile and flowing gray beard bear a disquieting resemblance to the popular ideas of the Judeo-Christian God. Looking at these posters, I cannot help wondering if Western man, who has just come back from the highly publicized burial of his late God, is not now fervently looking for a new one.

In the big cities, there is a noticeable restlessness, a groping, a 15 desperation to believe in something. In New York and Los Angeles, Chicago and San Francisco, innumerable cults, religions and spiritual groups flourish and win fanatic adherents. It is appalling to see bright, educated city-dwellers swallow the nonsense that these soothsayers, clairvoyants, spiritualists, prophets, dish out. There is something pathetic about this hunger for fairy tales.

Consciously or unconsciously, the West does not want the 16 old societies to change. It would rather they remained languid and inert—what it calls spiritual. It would rather the Easterner remained cross-legged and contemplative. The West needs this vision to nourish and titillate its fantasies, while it goes on building better homes, richer economies, better societies for itself.

But young revolutionary Asians and Africans do not want to 17 play the spiritual buffoon for the West. They are not amused by suffering and destitution. They are apprehensive of their backwardness and see in it no beauty, no dignity, no spirituality, nothing sacred or worth holding. They are struggling to disembarrass themselves of the very philosophies which a section of the West is striving to regenerate.

These ancient teachings, for the most part, encouraged 18 passivity, withdrawal, involvement with self, submission. They instilled the belief that fate or reincarnation decided everything; that suffering and affliction were rewards or punishment or irreversible destiny and that all effort, all merit, all endeavor was therefore futile. Through the centuries these teachings have seeped into the fabric of Eastern cultures, infecting our economies, our politics, our social and familial institutions, our very self-image.

Twenty-five hundred years ago, Buddha, like other Eastern 19 philosophers before and after him, said: "He who sits still, wins." Asia, then immobilized in primitive torpor, had no difficulty responding. It sat still. What it won for sitting still was the perpetuation of famines and terrorizing superstitions, oppression of children, subjugation of women, emasculation of men, fratricidal wars, persecutions, mass-killings. The history of Asia, like the history of all mankind, is a horrendous account of human suffering.

Thus when life was a relentless cycle of anguish, it was 20 probably inevitable that some, in their desperation and helplessness, should reject reality and withdraw. Their resignation and submission were defenses against suffering. When Lao-Tze, Solomon—even Rousseau centuries later—exhorted their fellow men to go back to nature or spend their lives in contemplation, they were reacting to a world that was hostile and unmanageable, a world that generated anxiety and terror, a sense of nihilism and alienation.

But times have changed. Man is no longer helpless; his 21 problems no longer insurmountable. Ancient exhortations to asceticism and self-renunciation are irrelevant in our modern world. Buddhism, Zen, Sufiism, Islam, Judaism—indeed, all the theologies and philosophies of the past—have nothing to teach modern man. Ahead of *their* time, they are far behind ours. Do not kill; do not hate; love your neighbor; love your fellow man—these were revolutionary concepts at one time. Today they are platitudes—though easier said than done.

The injunction against killing cows, noble in itself, did not 22 deter people from killing one another. The religionist who spoke of the brotherhood of man had no difficulty persecuting members of other religions. But now that man is slowly reaching adulthood, he does not need to be reminded of the teachings of his childhood—he must find ways to implement them.

Americans and Western Europeans, in their sensitivity to 23
lingering problems around them, tend to make science and progress their scapegoats. There is a belief that progress has precipitated widespread unhappiness, anxieties and other social and emotional problems. Science is viewed as a cold mechanical discipline having nothing to do with human warmth and the human spirit.

But to many of us from the nonscientific East, science does 24
not have such repugnant associations. We are not afraid of it, nor are we disappointed by it. We know all too painfully that our social and emotional problems festered long before the age of technology. To us, science is warm and reassuring. It promises hope. It is helping us at long last gain some control over our persecutory environments, alleviating age-old problems—not only physical but also, and especially, problems of the spirit.

Shiraz, for example, a city in southern Iran, has long been 25
renowned for its rose gardens and nightingales; its poets, Sadi and Hafiz, and its mystical, ascetic philosophy, Sufiism. Much poetry has been written in glorification of the spiritual attributes of this oasis city. And to be sure, Shiraz is a green, picturesque town, with a quaint bazaar and refreshing gardens. But in this "romantic" city thousands of emotionally disturbed and mentally retarded men, women and children were, until recently, kept in chains in stifling prison cells and lunatic asylums.

Every now and again, some were dragged, screaming and 26
pleading, to a courtyard and flogged for not behaving "normally." But for the most part, they were made to sit against damp walls, their hands and feet locked in chains, and thus immobilized, without even a modicum of affection from their helpless families and friends, they sat for weeks and months and years—often all their lives. Pictures of these wretched men, women and children can still be seen in this "city of poetry," this "city with the spiritual way of life."

It was only recently that a wealthy young Shirazi who, 27
against the admonitions of his family, had studied psychology at the University of Teheran and foreign universities, returned to Shiraz and after considerable struggle with city officials succeeded in opening a psychiatric clinic, the first in those regions. After still more struggle, he arranged to have the emotionally disturbed and the mentally retarded transferred from prison to their homes, to hospitals and to his clinic, where he and his staff now attend them.

They are fortunate. All over Asia and other backward areas, 28
emotionally disturbed men and women are still incarcerated in these
medieval dungeons called lunatic asylums. The cruel rejection and
punishment are intended to teach them a lesson or help exorcise evil
spirits.

The West, however, still bogged down in its ridiculous 29
romanticism, would like to believe that emotional disturbances, dope
addiction, delinquency are all modern problems brought on by
technological progress, and that backward societies are too spiritual
and beautiful to need the ministrations of science. But while the West
can perhaps afford to think this way, the people of backward lands
cannot.

Young Middle Eastern men and women are daily flouting the 30
devitalizing repressions and fatalism of Islam. India is valiantly
straining to extricate itself from the dead weight of social traditions
whose corrosive nihilism and spiritualism the realist Nehru dis-
dained. Japan's new industrialism and pragmatism are obvious
renunciations of the debilitating influences of Zen. China's revolutionary leaders are prodding their people to reject the ancient
traditions and philosophies which had helped perpetuate the country's backwardness and misery, making it prey to incessant foreign
rapacities.

If at times these struggles have been erratic and violent, it is 31
only because the obstacles are awesome, the inertia too entrenched,
the people's suffering too anguished, their impatience too eruptive.
Moreover, the total cultural reorganizations such as Asia and Africa
are undergoing inevitably engender their own temporary dislocations and confusions. But the goals, the direction remain constant.
We are on the move, however awkwardly at first, to a saner, better
world.

It is precisely this new voice of Asia, this new spirit, that the 32
West must heed and, where necessary, uphold. It is encouraging that
in the Western world today, particularly in America, university
professors, teachers, students, artists, writers, Negroes, housewives
and others who traditionally were uninvolved in politics are now
more and more asserting their rights, making their voices heard. The
increasing numbers of people who travel each year are also helping
all societies to outgrow their insularity, their provincialism, their
social, economic and political traditions.

In spite of colossal obstacles, man has come a long way. Let 33
him not be afraid to believe that he will go still farther; that he will
remake the world—that, indeed, he *is* remaking the world.

If man has to believe in something, let him believe in his own 34
infinite potential, his own future.

QUESTIONS

1. Explain the paradox that is central to Esfandiary's essay.

2. What examples does the author give of the "mystical West" and the "practical East"? How are Western religions different from Eastern religions?

3. Explain the purpose of the figurative language in paragraph 10.

4. Locate examples of the author's presentation of details and items in series. What is the effect of this stylistic strategy?

5. Analyze the relationship of the anecdote to the statement of thesis in paragraphs 1 to 9. What tone emerges from this opening section?

6. What key patterns of comparison and contrast govern the development of the essay?

7. Analyze the rhetorical patterns of development in paragraphs 10 to 15, 16 to 18, 19 to 22, 23 to 28, and 29 to 31.

8. Analyze and evaluate the conclusion of the essay.

9. Discuss Esfandiary's views on religion and the past. Where do you find him biased? How does his view of the past contrast with Edith Hamilton's in the preceding essay?

10. a. Write an essay on conflicts between the East and the West, or between the industrialized nations and the third world at the present time.
b. Define the romantic impulse in American foreign policy.

MARGARET MEAD

One Vote for This Age of Anxiety

Margaret Mead (1901–1979), famed American anthropologist, was curator of ethnology at the American Museum of Natural History and a professor at Columbia University. Her field expeditions to Samoa, New Guinea, and Bali in the 1920s and 1930s produced several major studies, notably *Coming of Age in Samoa* (1928), *Growing Up in New Guinea* (1930), and *Sex and Temperament in Three Primitive Societies* (1935). Her interest in contemporary society is evident in this essay.

When critics wish to repudiate the world in which we live today, one of their familiar ways of doing it is to castigate modern man because anxiety is his chief problem. This, they say, in W. H. Auden's phrase, is the age of anxiety. That is what we have arrived at with all our vaunted progress, our great technological advances, our great wealth—everyone goes about with a burden of anxiety so enormous that, in the end, our stomachs and our arteries and our skins express the tension under which we live. Americans who have lived in Europe come back to comment on our favorite farewell which, instead of the old goodbye (God be with you), is now "Take it easy," each American admonishing the other not to break down from the tension and strain of modern life. 1

Whenever an age is characterized by a phrase, it is presumably in contrast to other ages. If we are the age of anxiety, what were the other ages? And here the critics and carpers do a very amusing thing. First, they give us lists of the opposites of anxiety: security, trust, self-confidence, self-direction. Then, without much further discussion, they let us assume that other ages, other periods of history, were somehow the ages of trust or confident direction. 2

The savage who, on his South Sea island, simply sat and let breadfruit fall into his lap, the simple peasant, at one with the fields he ploughed and the beasts he tended, the craftsman busy with his tools and lost in the fulfillment of the instinct of workmanship—these are the counter-images conjured up by descriptions of the strain under which men live today. But no one who lived in those days has returned to testify how paradisiacal they really were. 3

Certainly if we observe and question the savages or simple peasants in the world today, we find something quite different. The untouched savage in the middle of New Guinea isn't anxious; he is seriously and continually *frightened*—of black magic, of enemies with spears who may kill him or his wives and children at any moment, while they stoop to drink from a spring, or climb a palm tree for a coconut. He goes warily, day and night, taut and fearful. 4

As for the peasant populations of a great part of the world, they aren't so much anxious as hungry. They aren't anxious about whether they will get a salary raise, or which of the three colleges of their choice they will be admitted to, or whether to buy a Ford or Cadillac, or whether the kind of TV set they want is too expensive. They are hungry, cold and, in many parts of the world, they dread that local warfare, bandits, political coups may endanger their homes, their meager livelihoods and their lives. But surely they are not anxious. 5

For anxiety, as we have come to use it to describe our 6

characteristic state of mind, can be contrasted with the active fear of hunger, loss, violence and death. Anxiety is the appropriate emotion when the immediate personal terror—of a volcano, an arrow, the sorcerer's spell, a stab in the back and other calamities, all directed against one's self—disappears.

This is not to say that there isn't plenty to worry about in our   7
world of today. The explosion of a bomb in the streets of a city whose name no one had ever heard before may set in motion forces which end up by ruining one's carefully planned education in law school, half a world away. But there is still not the personal, immediate, active sense of impending disaster that the savage knows. There is rather the vague anxiety, the sense that the future is unmanageable.

The kind of world that produces anxiety is actually a world of   8
relative safety, a world in which no one feels that he himself is facing sudden death. Possibly sudden death may strike a certain number of unidentified other people—but not him. The anxiety exists as an uneasy state of mind, in which one has a feeling that something unspecified and undeterminable may go wrong. If the world seems to be going well, this produces anxiety—for good times may end. If the world is going badly—it may get worse. Anxiety tends to be without locus; the anxious person doesn't know whether to blame himself or other people. He isn't sure whether it is the current year or the Administration or a change in climate or the atom bomb that is to blame for this undefined sense of unease.

It is clear that we have developed a society which depends on   9
having the *right* amount of anxiety to make it work. Psychiatrists have been heard to say, "He didn't have enough anxiety to get well," indicating that, while we agree that too much anxiety is inimical to mental health, we have come to rely on anxiety to push and prod us into seeing a doctor about a symptom which may indicate cancer, into checking up on that old life-insurance policy which may have out-of-date clauses in it, into having a conference with Billy's teacher even though his report card looks all right.

People who are anxious enough keep their car insurance up,   10
have the brakes checked, don't take a second drink when they have to drive, are careful where they go and with whom they drive on holidays. People who are too anxious either refuse to go into cars at all—and so complicate the ordinary course of life—or drive so tensely and overcautiously that they help cause accidents. People who aren't anxious enough take chance after chance, which increases the terrible death toll of the roads.

On balance, our age of anxiety represents a large advance   11
over savage and peasant cultures. Out of a productive system of

 ONE VOTE FOR THIS AGE OF ANXIETY

technology drawing upon enormous resources, we have created a nation in which anxiety has replaced terror and despair, for all except the severely disturbed. The specter of hunger means something only to those Americans who can identify themselves with the millions of hungry people on other continents. The specter of terror may still be roused in some by a knock at the door in a few parts of the South, or in those who have just escaped from a totalitarian regime or who have kin still behind the Curtains.

But in this twilight world which is neither at peace nor at war, and where there is insurance against certain immediate, downright, personal disasters, for most Americans there remains only anxiety over what may happen, might happen, could happen.   12

This is the world out of which grows the hope, for the first time in history, of a society where there will be freedom from want and freedom from fear. Our very anxiety is born of our knowledge of what is now possible for each and for all. The number of people who consult psychiatrists today is not, as is sometimes felt, a symptom of increasing mental ill health, but rather the precursor of a world in which the hope of genuine mental health will be open to everyone, a world in which no individual feels that he need be hopelessly brokenhearted, a failure, a menace to others or a traitor to himself.   13

But if, then, our anxieties are actually signs of hope, why is there such a voice of discontent abroad in the land? I think this comes perhaps because our anxiety exists without an accompanying recognition of the tragedy which will always be inherent in human life, however well we build our world. We may banish hunger, and fear of sorcery, violence or secret police; we may bring up children who have learned to trust life and who have the spontaneity and curiosity necessary to devise ways of making trips to the moon; we cannot—as we have tried to do—banish death itself.   14

Americans who stem from generations which left their old people behind and never closed their parents' eyelids in death, and who have experienced the additional distance from death provided by two world wars fought far from our shores are today pushing away from them both a recognition of death and a recognition of the tremendous significance—for the future—of the way we live our lives. Acceptance of the inevitability of death, which, when faced, can give dignity to life, and acceptance of our inescapable role in the modern world, might transmute our anxiety about making the right choices, taking the right precautions, and the right risks into the sterner stuff of responsibility, which ennobles the whole face rather than furrowing the forehead with the little anxious wrinkles of worry.   15

Worry in an empty context means that men die daily little deaths. But good anxiety—not about the things that were left undone long ago, but which return to haunt and harry men's minds, but active, vivid anxiety about what must be done and that quickly—binds men to life with an intense concern. 16

This is still a world in which too many of the wrong things happen somewhere. But this is a world in which we now have the means to make a great many more of the right things happen everywhere. For Americans, the generalization which a Swedish social scientist made about our attitudes on race relations is true in many other fields: anticipated change which we feel is right and necessary but difficult makes us unduly anxious and apprehensive, but such change, once consummated, brings a glow of relief. We are still a people who—in the literal sense—believe in making good. 17

QUESTIONS

1. What varieties of anxiety does Mead discuss in this essay? What distinguishes healthy anxiety from unhealthy anxiety? What are the causes of modern anxiety? Why does she give her vote to this age of anxiety?

2. What is Mead's vision of America and the world?

3. Analyze the parallelism in paragraphs 1, 10, and 14.

4. Discuss the connotations Mead develops for the core word "anxiety."

5. What is the function of Mead's opening paragraph?

6. Explain the purpose behind the author's use of contrast in paragraphs 3 to 6.

7. Examine the author's use of such conventional rhetorical techniques as illustration, definition, and causal analysis in the essay.

8. What pattern of logic does Mead employ in arriving at her conclusion? What are the stages in this pattern?

9. Mead wrote this essay in 1965. Are her observations still relevant? Explain. Are there new sources of anxiety today, and if so, what are the causes? Reread Woody Allen's essay in light of Mead's thesis on anxiety. How does anxiety work itself out in the world portrayed by Allen?

10. a. Write your own essay for or against this age of anxiety.
b. Analyze the cultural causes of anxiety in your own life.

MARY BEARD

Women and Civilization

Mary Beard (1876–1958), American author, collaborated with her husband Charles Beard on many books, notably the two-volume *Rise of American Civilization* (1927) and *America in Midpassage* (1939). Combining economics, politics, and history from a Madisonian perspective, she argued for a true internationalism in her writing. In this essay from *On Understanding Women* (1931), Beard offers an overview of and a radical argument for the central position of women in the development of civilization.

L ooking backward toward the horizon of dawning socie-   1
ty, what do we see standing clearly against the sky?
Woman—assuming chief responsibility for the continuance and care of life. We are in the presence of a force so
vital and so powerful that anthropologists can devise no meter to
register it and the legislator no rein strong enough to defeat it.
Whether woman possesses sex or is possessed by it may be left to
masculine metaphysicians for debate. Its reality however cannot be
escaped. To an extent not yet gauged by historians, hunting, wars,
states and institutions have been shaped to meet the supreme
exigency of continuing life and must be if mankind is to go on living
at all. Whether it is the primitive woman bringing a mate to her
house, Henry VIII breaking with the Pope, or Napoleon rearranging
the alliances of Europe with reference to his dynasty, the final
necessity is always present. Otherwise human life and everything
built upon it would perish from the earth. Church fathers may curse
it, woman brought to death's door in childbirth may wonder with
Erasmus at her "folly," and man caught in the institutions of support
may rage at his "chains," but while life remains it must be continually
recreated, nourished and esteemed. From this elemental force in the
rise and development of civilisation there is no escape and more of
human history can be written in its terms than any of Clio's disciples
have yet imagined. If the whole story is ever told, it will probably be
necessary to bring in a new Doctor Bowdler to get it past the censor.

But sex itself has been only one segment of woman's life, far   2
less important than the collaterals issuing from it in connection with
the care of life once created. Thus we see primitive women as the
inventors of the domestic arts—cooking, spinning, weaving, garner-
ing, guarding, doctoring, providing comforts and conveniences, and
making beginnings in the decorative arts. They are launching civilisa-

tion. Other animals have sex and continue life but none surround it with such artificial supports which, examined closely, are found to form the prime substance of culture. Woman, by means of these domestic innovations, lifted her low-browed male companion above the wild beasts that he hunted with stone and club and devoured in the raw. Under all the social forms and transformations that have existed since primitive times, activities connected with food, clothing and shelter, woman's first interest, have continued, setting commerce in train, spurring invention, establishing systems of economy more amazing. When men acquired responsibility for weaving garments, the manufacture of soap, and the confection of lingerie, women remained workers, designers, arbiters of taste, and beneficiaries of profits. Amusing as it may seem, it is primitive woman's interest that is now the prime concern of the civilised men. War for war's sake is no longer openly celebrated by the male, however zealously he cherishes in secret his passion for battle. Modern societies—bourgeois, democratic, fascist and communist—all agree in declaring that their fundamental end is the manufacture and wide distribution of those commodities which the old Romans of the republican era declared tend to effeminacy—the conveniences and luxuries that give ease and satisfaction in the continuance and care of life—primitive woman's burden and one that will abide while mankind endures.

After the great State was founded on primitive societies by the sword, when kings, priests and noble classes were established to engage the attention of historians, women merely dropped out of the pen portraits. They remained in the actuality. They were members of all the castes from the slave stratum at the bottom to the ruling families at the top and, even where restrictions were the tightest, took part in nearly everything that went on in the world. Whether it is Aspasia lecturing to Pericles and friends, Sappho "teaching" Socrates, Roman women participating in senatorial conflicts and battles over the succession to the imperial throne, queens contending for their patrimonies, the daughters of the rich setting fleets and caravans in motion to bring them luxuries of the East, or the wife of Pythagoras interpreting and spreading a faith, the truth that women have always been in or near the center of things is illustrated. They have shared in the burdens and privileges of their respective classes, have joined in wars, have owned and managed vast estates, have insisted on dominance in disputes among ruling families, have displayed the lusts of men, have served the temples, and have been deified as gods. If the formalities, such as exclusion from public gatherings in Athens and from the senate in Rome, are penetrated and realities are kept in mind, the energies and influence of women are easily discerned. There was no great historical contest in politics in which they did not appear somewhere. There was no religious cult which they did not affect. There were no exercises in intellectualism which they did not practice. If poets from Ovid to Molière made fun of learned women, these women were no funnier than most of the men who crowded the salons, as the court jester was fair enough to indicate, and some of them spoke with authority on poetry, mathematics, science, philosophy and ethics.

For a time after the dissolution of the Roman Empire, if most 4 of the histories ring true, women retired in favor of the sword, but the retirement was certainly temporary if not illusory. They early appeared in the Middle Ages as managers in the families of barbarian conquerors and their princely retainers, as heads of convents and schools, as restorers of the arts, as manipulators in the papal politics of Italy, as theologians and saints, as the symbol of virtue divinely typified in Mary the Mother of God. They labored with men in the fields providing the economic goods on which the upper structure of mediaeval civilisation rested. They worked in the crafts around which were built the guilds and urban liberties. They suffered as witches, died as heretics, and furnished a military leader in Jeanne d'Arc. The whole art of chivalry, whatever may have been its civilising influence, developed around woman. The writers of canon law and its administrators were endlessly harassed by her conduct. Again and again women of the upper classes shone as the literate wives of illiterate lords and knights, thus sharing with the clergy the world of written wisdom. Exclusion from Oxford and Cambridge did not condemn English ladies to total ignorance; what a complete survey would reveal no one knows but the guess may be hazarded that the women of the upper classes, in fact of all classes, were about as well educated as the men of their circles. Even the famous abstract speculator, Abelard, had to have an intellectual companion, Heloise, as a foil; and Francis of Assisi, critic of scholasticism and learning, the girl Clare as counselor and friend. Although the law of property ran inevitably in favor of the fighter, so constantly exigent was defense, it did not run against woman as such nor did it in practice prevent thousands of women from holding and controlling property, from devoting it to the patronage of religion and the arts as well as to the intrigues and uses of their class.

In the modern age there have been changes in form rather 5 than in substance. Women patronised and assisted directly in the development of the new learning—the recovery and enlargement of ancient secular wisdom. It was a woman, Queen Isabella of Spain, who was chiefly responsible for the underwriting that sent Columbus forth on the voyage of discovery destined to open a new epoch in the history.of Europe and reveal to it the smallness of its empire; after a Queen had dared, kings were prepared to support other voyagers. When secular learning widened out into natural science, women acted as promoters, critics, and creative thinkers and workers. They faced all the hardships involved in the conquest and settlement of the New World, standing steadfastly beside the men under the wintry clouds at Plymouth and beneath the sunny skies of Virginia. The Catholic fathers had scarcely reached the frontiers of Quebec when dauntless nuns appeared to carry forward the task of evangelisation. When natural science was touched with humanism and became an instrument in formulating the concept of Progress, it was mainly by the salons of French women that ideas were patronised, tried out, and set in circulation. In this age, no more than in mediaeval times, did a general exclusion from universities mean ignorance among women; the very notion is based upon an exaggerated view of the rôle of institutions in the origin and diffusion of learning. It is yet to be known whether institutions help rather than hinder thought.

With the rise of machine industry and the multiplication of occupations, the restrictions of all inherited law were found irksome, attacked and broken down, after many a stubborn battle to be sure but with surprising speed considering the herd capacities of the human race. In the rise of political democracy, women were belligerent—Mary Wollstonecraft joining Tom Paine in vindicating the rights of man—a favor reciprocated when the rights of woman were also to be vindicated. Finally, women have been identified with the ideas and movements of social amelioration from the sixteenth century to the latest hour, as thinkers, experimenters, propagandists and administrators.

    6

And now that the long trail has been trod to this point, what of the life ahead of us? What are its possibilities and probabilities? There exists the assumption that what is called the bourgeois, or capitalist, order of things, lately acquired, will endure, if not forever, at least indefinitely. At the present moment it seems to be shaky in Franch, bewildered in England, disturbed in the United States, questioned in Spain, and distressed in Japan. But its current troubles may pass. If the established economic mill keeps running, then the future before various women is clear. They will acquire through inheritance, transfer, or their own efforts more property with all the rights and privileges thereunto attached. The number of professions and employments open to women will increase. The thousands of workers engaged in supplying luxuries to the plutocracy will grow and the gainful occupations of women will become more gainful. Into the great games of business, advertising, selling and speculating, they will enter with expanding zest, with profit to themselves and economic security. Hundreds of callings, though bearing a dubious relation to the care of life in the large, will give them personal independence. The learning of the schools and the facilities of the laboratories will be placed at their disposal in enlarging measure. The

    7

parasitic women of the bourgeois circle will spend, patronise, dabble and entertain and occasionally, very occasionally, play with fire like Marie Antoinette. In other words, those who sit at the feast will continue to enjoy themselves even though the veil that separates them from the world of toiling reality below has been lifted by mass revolts and critics. While this state of affairs lasts, no great thought will be imperative, on the part of women or of men within the prosperous circle, and the repetition of conventional formulas about the Kingdom, the Reich, the Republic, or Democracy, will suffice as in Cicero's day for wisdom and for statecraft.

But other contingencies enter into speculations. The free and easy political democracy of early capitalism may be turned into a middle class dictatorship, as in Italy, managed by men who naturally will look out for themselves in the distribution of economic plums. Supported by arms, dominated by a small self-appointed clique, and bent on the perpetuation of its power, the fascist régime is a menace to the liberties of women. And yet fascism is in the process of evolution. So far it has been able to steer a zig-zag course between capital and labor, closer to the interests of the former than the latter but not completed by any means. In Russia another type of dictatorship is in vogue, autocratic in its form of government but communist in economic theory and to some degree in practice. There the privileges and luxuries of the bourgeois are materially curtailed, if not extirpated, with corresponding effects upon the position of the women formerly belonging to the upper classes or serving them as caterers and retainers. Hence in Russia the bourgeois form of marriage is in process of dissolution, if marriages and families remain. The emphasis in communism, if its ideal is realised, will be on woman as a worker, and the opportunities for a life of leisure, patronage, noblesse oblige, religious service, and idle curiosity will vanish. What that will produce in terms of culture, the future alone can say. After traveling a long and strange road, women of the upper orders in Russia are back where all women began in primitive days, to the prime concern with labor and the care of life, where the vast majority of women in all times and places have stayed through the changing fortunes of politics.

Amid the hopes for bourgeois endurance and the contingences of change, the eternal battle between the State and the Family promises to continue. The State, originally built on the family, is confronted as of old with family loyalties inimical to the public service and to the common life and the common good. In a sense it is true, as political and social critics of the family have long contended, that men and women struggling to advance the family in status and satisfactions often act as enemies of the State, willing to resort to chicanery in economics and corruption in politics in order to augment the proper-

8

9

ty of their group. Thus Ritchie insists that "no real or positive equality in social conditions can be secured so long as individuals are looked at in any respect as members of families and not in every respect as members of the State alone. Suppose two workmen receive equal wages but the one has no children and the other has six, all too young to earn anything, where is the equality in the social condition of the individuals supported out of these wages? Even under the system of a compulsory minimum of education, has the child of incapable or vicious parents—quite apart from his hereditary disadvantages—an equal opportunity given him, in any true sense, with the child who has grown up in a careful and regular household?" To the problem of equality, political dictatorship may provide a better answer perhaps than individualist economics and family politics. The State may try to iron out handicaps of birth and domestic neglect. Even in an individualist nation like the United States, the family is invaded from two directions—one political and the other economic. The State insists upon domestic changes favorable to civic stability, and bourgeois marriage dissolves with amazing swiftness owing to the shift in forms of property and the individualisation of women in the arena where goods are produced.

If the State, bourgeois or communist, continues to apply to 10 family property and nurture strong astringents in the interests of individualism or equality, what then? There seem to be two possibilities, judging by the experience at hand. The family may resist invasion, as it did in Rome, may withdraw more loyalty from the State, disintegrate its authority by opposition and by the refusal of public service, preferring ease and luxury to the severe régime of sacrifice, and dissolving order again into the chaos of family feudalism—for that was the essence of feudalism. On the other hand, the State may defeat this antagonism and press deeper and deeper into the family association, reducing its advantages of property and nurture.

What would be the outcome of State supremacy it may be 11 impossible for any one to forecast though there have been in the past a few brilliant cases of insight into the future. Some speculators see the end of monogamy. But this is an assumption. Monogamy has always been one form of sex relations, surrounded by many others. It is conceivable that the aggression of the State upon the family may mean that monogamy will at last be tried on its merits, certainly with less and possibly with no economic incidence, surviving the storm for reasons deeply fixed in human nature and experience. Though the State may take over more of the education and nurture of children, it will still find that women must be employed in the operation of caring for life. Perhaps by the route of trial and error along new lines, with birth control, humanity will decide that amenities of the home are more conducive to the fundamental mores upon which civilisation depends in final analysis than any abstract loyalties that it can generate through politics and economics alone.

If this analysis of history is approximately sound and if the 12 future like the past is to be crowded with changes and exigencies, then it is difficult to believe that the feminism of the passing generation, already hardened into dogma and tradition, represents the completed form of woman's relations to work, interests and society. In so far as it is a sex antagonism, even though based on legitimate grievances against exclusions or discriminations in employment, it is and has been partial and one-phased, not fundamental. The converse is true with respect to man's hostility to the presence of women at the center of every sort of activity. Women have always been alive to everything that was going on in the world. They always will be. If, as our engineering writers are constantly telling us, society is to be increasingly technical in nature, then competence, not sex, will be the basis of selection and women will have to stand that test with men. Feminism as sex antagonism bearing the wounds of many honorable battles may then drop out of sight. Masculinism as sex monopoly may then yield to concepts of expertness.

The ordinary woman who has functioned in accordance with 13 nature's laws does not hate man or exaggerate his importance; most of the time she is as indifferent to him as he is to her; but with respect to the amenities and enjoyments of life the sexes are one. Love, joy, and beauty are bound up in their relations. As Aristophanes could say twenty-three centuries ago, "there is no pleasure for a man unless the woman shares it," so the modern feminist will soon discover if she has not already, that there is no pleasure for a woman unless the man shares it. Yet if the feminism of the older generation passes, the eternal feminine will be here at the center of all things— that is, the care of life—and, unless the growth of positive knowledge and the humane applications of science during the past three hundred years are a delusion and a mistake, governments and economic institutions, all the arts of comfort and delight, will revolve around the care of life, renewing themselves at that fountain of eternal youth whence come healing waters for despair and cynicism—the enduring belief that it is good to live, to love, to suffer and to labor.

QUESTIONS

1. What is the point of Beard's essay? Is it merely to describe a specific historical process, or is it to investigate a more significant concept? Explain.

MARY BEARD

2. What are the historical periods dealt with by the author? Which period does she emphasize? Explain Beard's attitude toward the status of modern women, as she perceived it writing in 1930. Explain what she means by the eternal battle between the family and the state. What is her attitude toward "sex antagonism"?

3. Examine the author's use of figurative language in the introductory paragraph.

4. What is the connection between the author's language and her subject?

5. How does the author develop her pattern of process analysis? Which paragraphs treat specific stages in the process? What subdivisions exist? Analyze the transitions employed to link major stages in the process.

6. Explain the effectiveness of the author's introductory paragraph. What is unique about paragraphs 4 and 5?

7. How does the author use causal relationships to clarify her thesis and to reinforce the process pattern?

8. How do the substance and tone of the concluding paragraph reinforce the author's introduction?

9. Beard speaks of the "eternal feminine," of the very special role of women in caring for the life of civilization. Do you accept her thesis? Why or why not?

10. a. Write an analysis of the role of women in the development of civilization.
b. Trace the process whereby women have gained increasing rights and equality with men in modern times.

HENRY ADAMS

The Dynamo and the Virgin

Henry Adams (1838–1918), American historian and author, the descendant of the United States presidents John Adams and John Quincy Adams, was one of the most important observers of the rapidly accelerating forces shaping modern life at the start of the twentieth century. A critic of the modernist impulse toward disunity, he investigated in two of his later books, *Mont-Saint-Michel and Chartres* (1905) and *The Edu-*

cation of Henry Adams (1907), the uses of power in relationship to society. In this famous chapter from *The Education*, Adams contrasts medieval civilization, with its achievement of order, and the modern age, lacking the center that he so earnestly sought throughout his adult life.

U ntil the Great Exposition of 1900 closed its doors in November, Adams haunted it, aching to absorb knowledge, and helpless to find it. He would have liked to know how much of it could have been grasped by the best-informed man in the world. While he was thus meditating chaos, Langley came by, and showed it to him. At Langley's behest, the Exhibition dropped its superfluous rags and stripped itself to the skin, for Langley knew what to study, and why, and how; while Adams might as well have stood outside in the night, staring at the Milky Way. Yet Langley said nothing new, and taught nothing that one might not have learned from Lord Bacon, three hundred years before; but though one should have known the "Advancement of Science" as well as one knew the "Comedy of Errors," the literary knowledge counted for nothing until some teacher should show how to apply it. Bacon took a vast deal of trouble in teaching King James I and his subjects, American or other, towards the year 1620, that true science was the development or economy of forces; yet an elderly American in 1900 knew neither the formula nor the forces; or even so much as to say to himself that his historical business in the exposition concerned only the economies or developments of force since 1893, when he began the study at Chicago.

Nothing in education is so astonishing as the amount of ignorance it accumulates in the form of inert facts. Adams had looked at most of the accumulations of art in the storehouses called Art Museums; yet he did not know how to look at the art exhibits of 1900. He had studied Karl Marx and his doctrines of history with profound attention, yet he could not apply them at Paris. Langley, with the ease of a great master of experiment, threw out of the field every exhibit that did not reveal a new application of force, and naturally threw out, to begin with, almost the whole art exhibit. Equally, he ignored almost the whole industrial exhibit. He led his pupil directly to the forces. His chief interest was in new motors to make his airship feasible, and he taught Adams the astonishing complexities of the new Daimler motor, and of the automobile, which, since 1893, had become a nightmare at a hundred kilometres an hour, almost as destructive as the electric train which was only ten years older; and threatening to become as terrible as the locomotive steam-engine itself, which was almost exactly Adams's own age.

Then he showed his scholar the great hall of dynamos, and 3
explained how little he knew about electricity or force of any kind,
even of his own special sun, which spouted heat in inconceivable
volume, but which, as far as he knew, might spout less or more, at
any time, for all the certainty he felt in it. To him, the dynamo itself
was but an ingenious channel for conveying somewhere the heat
latent in a few tons of poor coal hidden in a dirty engine-house
carefully kept out of sight; but to Adams the dynamo became a
symbol of infinity. As he grew accustomed to the great gallery of
machines, he began to feel the forty-foot dynamos as a moral force,
much as the early Christians felt the Cross. The planet itself seemed
less impressive, in its old-fashioned, deliberate, annual or daily
revolution, than this huge wheel, revolving within arm's-length at
some vertiginous speed, and barely murmuring—scarcely humming
an audible warning to stand a hair's-breadth further for respect of
power—while it would not wake the baby lying close against its
frame. Before the end, one began to pray to it; inherited instinct
taught the natural expression of man before silent and infinite force.
Among the thousand symbols of ultimate energy, the dynamo was
not so human as some, but it was the most expressive.

Yet the dynamo, next to the steam-engine, was the most 4
familiar of exhibits. For Adams's objects its value lay chiefly in its
occult mechanism. Between the dynamo in the gallery of machines
and the engine-house outside, the break of continuity amounted to
abysmal fracture for a historian's objects. No more relation could he
discover between the steam and the electric current than between the
Cross and the cathedral. The forces were interchangeable if not
reversible, but he could see only an absolute *fiat* in electricity as in
faith. Langley could not help him. Indeed, Langley seemed to be
worried by the same trouble, for he constantly repeated that the new
forces were anarchical, and specially that he was not responsible for
the new rays, that were little short of parricidal in their wicked spirit
towards science. His own rays, with which he had doubled the solar
spectrum, were altogether harmless and beneficent; but Radium
denied its God—or, what was to Langley the same thing, denied the
truths of his Science. The force was wholly new.

A historian who asked only to learn enough to be as futile as 5
Langley or Kelvin, made rapid progress under this teaching, and
mixed himself up in the tangle of ideas until he achieved a sort of
Paradise of ignorance vastly consoling to his fatigued senses. He
wrapped himself in vibrations and rays which were new, and he
would have hugged Marconi and Branly had he met them, as he
hugged the dynamo; while he lost his arithmetic in trying to figure
out the equation between the discoveries and the economies of force.
The economies, like the discoveries, were absolute, supersensual,

 THE DYNAMO AND THE VIRGIN**631**

occult; incapable of expression in horse-power. What mathematical equivalent could he suggest as the value of a Branly coherer? Frozen air, or the electric furnace, had some scale of measurement, no doubt, if somebody could invent a thermometer adequate to the purpose; but X-rays had played no part whatever in man's consciousness, and the atom itself had figured only as a fiction of thought. In these seven years man had translated himself into a new universe which had no common scale of measurement with the old. He had entered a supersensual world, in which he could measure nothing except by chance collisions of movements imperceptible to his senses, perhaps even imperceptible to his instruments, but perceptible to each other, and so to some known ray at the end of the scale. Langley seemed prepared for anything, even for an indeterminable number of universes interfused—physics stark mad in metaphysics.

Historians undertake to arrange sequences—called stories, or 6 histories—assuming in silence a relation of cause and effect. These assumptions, hidden in the depths of dusty libraries, have been astounding, but commonly unconscious and childlike; so much so, that if any captious critic were to drag them to light, historians would probably reply, with one voice, that they had never supposed themselves required to know what they were talking about. Adams, for one, had toiled in vain to find out what he meant. He had even published a dozen volumes of American history for no other purpose than to satisfy himself whether, by the severest process of stating, with the least possible comment, such facts as seemed sure, in such order as seemed rigorously consequent, he could fix for a familiar moment a necessary sequence of human movement. The result had satisfied him as little as at Harvard College. Where he saw sequence, other men saw something quite different, and no one saw the same unit of measure. He cared little about his experiments and less about his statesmen, who seemed to him quite as ignorant as himself and, as a rule, no more honest; but he insisted on a relation of sequence, and if he could not reach it by one method, he would try as many methods as science knew. Satisfied that the sequence of men led to nothing and that the sequence of their society could lead no further, while the mere sequence of time was artificial, and the sequence of thought was chaos, he turned at last to the sequence of force; and thus it happened that, after ten years' pursuit, he found himself lying in the Gallery of Machines at the Great Exposition of 1900, his historical neck broken by the sudden irruption of forces totally new.

Since no one else showed much concern, an elderly person 7 without other cares had no need to betray alarm. The year 1900 was not the first to upset schoolmasters. Copernicus and Galileo had broken many professorial necks about 1600; Columbus had stood the world on its head towards 1500; but the nearest approach to the

HENRY ADAMS

revolution of 1900 was that of 310, when Constantine set up the Cross. The rays that Langley disowned, as well as those which he fathered, were occult, supersensual, irrational; they were a revelation of mysterious energy like that of the Cross; they were what, in terms of mediaeval science, were called immediate modes of the divine substance.

The historian was thus reduced to his last resources. Clearly 8 if he was bound to reduce all these forces to a common value, this common value could have no measure but that of their attraction on his own mind. He must treat them as they had been felt; as convertible, reversible, interchangeable attractions on thought. He made up his mind to venture it; he would risk translating rays into faith. Such a reversible process would vastly amuse a chemist, but the chemist could not deny that he, or some of his fellow physicists, could feel the force of both. When Adams was a boy in Boston, the best chemist in the place had probably never heard of Venus except by way of scandal, or of the Virgin except as idolatry; neither had he heard of dynamos or automobiles or radium; yet his mind was ready to feel the force of all, though the rays were unborn and the women were dead.

Here opened another totally new education, which promised 9 to be by far the most hazardous of all. The knife-edge along which he must crawl, like Sir Lancelot in the twelfth century, divided two kingdoms of force which had nothing in common but attraction. They were as different as a magnet is from gravitation, supposing one knew what a magnet was, or gravitation, or love. The force of the Virgin was still felt at Lourdes, and seemed to be as potent as X-rays: but in America neither Venus nor Virgin ever had value as force—at most as sentiment. No American had ever been truly afraid of either.

This problem in dynamics gravely perplexed an American 10 historian. The Woman had once been supreme; in France she still seemed potent, not merely as a sentiment, but as a force. Why was she unknown in America? For evidently America was ashamed of her, and she was ashamed of herself, otherwise they would not have strewn fig-leaves so profusely all over her. When she was a true force, she was ignorant of fig-leaves, but the monthly-magazine-made American female had not a feature that would have been recognized by Adam. The trait was notorious, and often humorous, but any one brought up among Puritans knew that sex was sin. In any previous age, sex was strength. Neither art nor beauty was needed. Every one, even among Puritans, knew that neither Diana of the Ephesians nor any of the Oriental goddesses was worshipped for her beauty. She was goddess because of her force; she was the animated dynamo; she was reproduction—the greatest and most mysterious of all energies; all she needed was to be fecund. Singularly enough, not one of Adams's many schools of education had ever drawn his attention to the opening lines of Lucretius, though they were perhaps the finest in all Latin literature, where the poet invoked Venus exactly as Dante invoked the Virgin:—

"Quae quoniam rerum naturam *sola* gubernas."

The Venus of Epicurean philosophy survived in the Virgin of the Schools:—

"Donna, sei tanto grande, e tanto vali,
Che qual vuol grazia, e a te non ricorre,
Sua disianza vuol volar senz' ali."

All this was to American thought as though it had never existed. The true American knew something of the facts, but nothing of the feelings; he read the letter, but he never felt the law. Before this historical chasm, a mind like that of Adams felt itself helpless; he turned from the Virgin to the Dynamo as though he were a Branly coherer. On one side, at the Louvre and at Chartres, as he knew by the record of work actually done and still before his eyes, was the highest energy ever known to man, the creator of four-fifths of his noblest art, exercising vastly more attraction over the human mind than all the steam-engines and dynamos ever dreamed of; and yet this energy was unknown to the American mind. An American Virgin would never dare command; an American Venus would never dare exist.

The question, which to any plain American of the nineteenth century seemed as remote as it did to Adams, drew him almost violently to study, once it was posed; and on this point Langleys were as useless as though they were Herbert Spencers or dynamos. The idea survived only as art. There one turned as naturally as though the artist were himself a woman. Adams began to ponder, asking himself whether he knew of any American artist who had ever insisted on the power of sex, as every classic had always done; but he could think only of Walt Whitman; Bret Harte, as far as the magazines would let him venture; and one or two painters, for the flesh-tones. All the rest had used sex for sentiment, never for force; to them, Eve was a tender flower, and Herodias an unfeminine horror. American art, like the American language and American education, was as far as possible sexless. Society regarded this victory over sex as its greatest triumph, and the historian readily admitted it, since the moral issue, for the moment, did not concern one who was studying the relations of unmoral force. He cared nothing for the sex of the dynamo until he could measure its energy.

Vaguely seeking a clue, he wandered through the art exhibit, 12 and, in his stroll, stopped almost every day before St. Gaudens's General Sherman, which had been given the central post of honor. St. Gaudens himself was in Paris, putting on the work his usual interminable last touches, and listening to the usual. contradictory suggestions of brother sculptors. Of all the American artists who gave to American art whatever life it breathed in the seventies, St. Gaudens was perhaps the most sympathetic, but certainly the most inarticulate. General Grant or Don Cameron had scarcely less instinct of rhetoric than he. All the others—the Hunts, Richardson, John La Farge, Stanford White—were exuberant; only St. Gaudens could never discuss or dilate on an emotion, or suggest artistic arguments for giving to his work the forms that he felt. He never laid down the law, or affected the despot, or became brutalized like Whistler by the brutalities of his world. He required no incense; he was no egoist; his simplicity of thought was excessive; he could not imitate, or give any form but his own to the creations of his hand. No one felt more strongly than he the strength of other men, but the idea that they could affect him never stirred an image in his mind.

This summer his health was poor and his spirits were low. For 13 such a temper, Adams was not the best companion, since his own gaiety was not *folle;* but he risked going now and then to the studio on Mont Parnasse to draw him out for a stroll in the Bois de Boulogne, or dinner as pleased his moods, and in return St. Gaudens sometimes let Adams go about in his company.

Once St. Gaudens took him down to Amiens, with a party of 14 Frenchmen, to see the cathedral. Not until they found themselves actually studying the sculpture of the western portal, did it dawn on Adams's mind that, for his purposes, St. Gaudens on that spot had more interest to him than the cathedral itself. Great men before great monuments express great truths, provided they are not taken too solemnly. Adams never tired of quoting the supreme phrase of his idol Gibbon, before the Gothic cathedrals: "I darted a contemptuous look on the stately monuments of superstition." Even in the footnotes of his history, Gibbon had never inserted a bit of humor more human than this, and one would have paid largely for a photograph of the fat little historian, on the background of Notre Dame of Amiens, trying to persuade his readers—perhaps himself—that he was darting a contemptuous look on the stately monument, for which he felt in fact the respect which every man of his vast study and active mind always feels before objects worthy of it; but besides the humor, one felt also the relation. Gibbon ignored the Virgin, because in 1789 religious monuments were out of fashion. In 1900 his remark sounded fresh and simple as the green fields to ears that had heard a hundred years of other remarks, mostly no more fresh and certainly less simple.

Without malice, one might find it more instructive than a whole lecture of Ruskin. One sees what one brings, and at that moment Gibbon brought the French Revolution. Ruskin brought reaction against the Revolution. St. Gaudens had passed beyond all. He liked the stately monuments much more than he liked Gibbon or Ruskin; he loved their dignity; their unity; their scale; their lines; their lights and shadows; their decorative sculpture; but he was even less conscious than they of the force that created it all—the Virgin, the Woman—by whose genius "the stately monuments of superstition" were built, through which she was expressed. He would have seen more meaning in Isis with the cow's horns, at Edfoo, who expressed the same thought. The art remained, but the energy was lost even upon the artist.

Yet in mind and person St. Gaudens was a survival of the 15 1500's; he bore the stamp of the Renaissance, and should have carried an image of the Virgin round his neck, or stuck in his hat, like Louis XI. In mere time he was a lost soul that had strayed by chance into the twentieth century, and forgotten where it came from. He writhed and cursed at his ignorance, much as Adams did at his own, but in the opposite sense. St. Gaudens was a child of Benvenuto Cellini, smothered in an American cradle. Adams was a quintessence of Boston, devoured by curiosity to think like Benvenuto. St. Gaudens's art was starved from birth, and Adams's instinct was blighted from babyhood. Each had but half of a nature, and when they came together before the Virgin of Amiens they ought both to have felt in her the force that made them one; but it was not so. To Adams she became more than ever a channel of force; to St. Gaudens she remained as before a channel of taste.

For a symbol of power, St. Gaudens instinctively preferred 16 the horse, as was plain in his horse and Victory of the Sherman monument. Doubtless Sherman also felt it so. The attitude was so American that, for at least forty years, Adams had never realized that any other could be in sound taste. How many years had he taken to admit a notion of what Michael Angelo and Rubens were driving at? He could not say; but he knew that only since 1895 had he begun to feel the Virgin or Venus as force, and not everywhere even so. At Chartres—perhaps at Lourdes—possibly at Cnidos if one could still find there the divinely naked Aphrodite of Praxiteles—but otherwise one must look for force to the goddesses of Indian mythology. The idea died out long ago in the German and English stock. St. Gaudens at Amiens was hardly less sensitive to the force of the female energy than Matthew Arnold at the Grande Chartreuse. Neither of them felt goddesses as power—only as reflected emotion, human expression, beauty, purity, taste, scarcely even as sympathy. They felt a railway train as power; yet they, and all other artists, constantly complained that the power embodied in a railway train could never be embodied in art. All the steam in the world could not, like the Virgin, build Chartres.

Yet in mechanics, whatever the mechanicians might think, 17 both energies acted as interchangeable forces on man, and by action on man all known force may be measured. Indeed, few men of science measured force in any other way. After once admitting that a straight line was the shortest distance between two points, no serious mathematician cared to deny anything that suited his convenience, and rejected no symbol, unproved or unproveable, that helped him to accomplish work. The symbol was force, as a compass needle or a triangle was force, as the mechanist might prove by losing it, and nothing could be gained by ignoring their value. Symbol or energy, the Virgin had acted as the greatest force the Western world ever felt, and had drawn man's activities to herself more strongly than any other power, natural or supernatural, had ever done; the historian's business was to follow the track of the energy; to find where it came from and where it went to; its complex source and shifting channels; its values, equivalents, conversions. It could scarcely be more complex than radium; it could hardly be deflected, diverted, polarized, absorbed more perplexingly than other radiant matter. Adams knew nothing about any of them, but as a mathematical problem of influence on human progress, though all were occult, all reacted on his mind, and he rather inclined to think the Virgin easiest to handle.

The pursuit turned out to be long and tortuous, leading at last 18 into the vast forests of scholastic science. From Zeno to Descartes, hand in hand with Thomas Aquinas, Montaigne, and Pascal, one stumbled as stupidly as though one were still a German student of 1860. Only with the instinct of despair could one force one's self into this old thicket of ignorance after having been repulsed at a score of entrances more promising and more popular. Thus far, no path had led anywhere, unless perhaps to an exceedingly modest living. Forty-five years of study had proved to be quite futile for the pursuit of power; one controlled no more force in 1900 than in 1850, although the amount of force controlled by society had enormously increased. The secret of education still hid itself somewhere behind ignorance, and one fumbled over it as feebly as ever. In such labyrinths, the staff is a force almost more necessary than the legs; the pen becomes a sort of blind-man's dog, to keep him from falling into the gutters. The pen works for itself, and acts like a hand, modelling the plastic material over and over again to the form that suits it best. The form is never arbitrary, but is a sort of growth like crystallization, as any artist knows too well; for often the pencil or pen runs into side-paths and shapelessness, loses its relations, stops or is bogged. Then it has to return on its trail, and recover, if it can, its line of force. The result of a year's work depends more on what is struck out than on what is left in; on the sequence of the main lines of thought, than on their play or variety. Compelled once more to lean heavily on this support, Adams covered more thousands of pages with figures as formal as though they were algebra, laboriously striking out, altering, burning, experimenting, until the year had expired, the Exposition had long been closed, and winter drawing to its end, before he sailed from Cherbourg, on January 19, 1901, for home.

QUESTIONS

1. Explain Adams's philosophy of history and his attitude toward civilization. Why does he prefer medieval to modern times?

2. What does the author say about the process of his own education?

3. Adams develops many striking figures of speech to illuminate and reinforce abstract concepts and propositions in this essay. Locate examples of this interrelation of figurative and abstract language.

4. Identify the allusions to Langley (paragraph 1), Daimler (paragraph 2), Marconi and Branly (paragraph 5), and St. Gaudens (paragraph 12). What is the purpose of these allusions? What set of allusions is juxtaposed against them?

5. Explain the way the twin symbols of the Virgin and the dynamo create meaning, coherence, and unity in Adams's essay. What subject links these twin symbols? How do they dictate patterns of comparison and contrast?

6. Why does Adams, writing his autobiography, refer to himself in the third person? What is the effect? How does this strategy reinforce the overall tone of the essay?

7. Analyze the author's presentation of causal analysis in the essay.

8. Why does Adams emphasize St. Gaudens in paragraphs 12 through 16? How does this section prepare for the concluding two paragraphs?

9. Comment on Adams's declaration, "Nothing in education is so astonishing as the amount of ignorance it accumulates in the form of inert facts" (paragraph 2).

10. a. Write an essay investigating what you have learned about civilization from the process of your education.
b. Analyze the role of education in dealing with the forces of modern civilization.

After Civilization, What?

Kenneth Ewart Boulding (1910–   ), born in England and a naturalized American citizen since 1948, was for many years a professor of economics at the University of Michigan and a director of the Center for Research and Conflict Resolution. Currently he is director of the Institute of Behavioral Science at the University of Colorado. The author of *Economic Analysis* (1941), *The Organizational Revolution* (1953), *The Image* (1956), *Disarmament and the Economy* (1963), and other books, Boulding has been interested persistently in the problems of contemporary civilization. In this essay, he sets out to classify civilizations past, present, and future, and to analyze the problems and prospects inherent in all stages of civilization.

We are living in what I call the second great change in the state of man. The first is the change from pre-civilized to civilized societies. The first five hundred thousand years or so of man's existence on earth were relatively uneventful. Compared with his present condition, he puttered along in an astonishingly stationary state. There may have been changes in language and culture which are not reflected in the artifacts, but if there were, these changes are lost to us. The evidence of the artifacts, however, is conclusive. Whatever changes they were, they were almost unbelievably slow. About ten thousand years ago, we begin to perceive an acceleration in the rate of change. This becomes very noticeable five thousand years ago with the development of the first civilization. The details of this first great change are probably beyond our recovery. However, we do know that it depended on two phenomena: the development of agriculture and the development of exploitation. Agriculture, that is the domestication of crops and livestock and the planting of crops in fields, gave man a secure surplus of food from the food producer. In a hunting and fishing economy it seems to take the food producer all his time to produce enough food for himself and his family. The moment we have agriculture, with its superior productivity of this form of employment of human resources, the food producer can produce more food than he and his family can eat. In some societies in these happy conditions, the food producer has simply relaxed and indulged himself with leisure. As soon, however, as we get politics, that is exploitation, we begin to get cities and civilization. Civilization, it is clear from the origin of the word, is what happens in cities, and the city is dependent (in its early stages, at any rate) on the existence of a food surplus from the food producer and some organization which can take it away from him. With this food surplus, the political organization feeds kings, priests, armies, architects, and builders, and the city comes into being. Political science in its earliest form is the knowledge of how to take the food surplus away from the food producer without giving him very much in return.

Now I argue that we are in the middle of the second great 2
change in the state of man, which is as drastic and as dramatic, and certainly as large as, if not larger than, the change from pre-civilized to civilized society. This I call the change from civilization to post-civilization. It is a strange irony that just at the moment when civilization has almost completed the conquest of pre-civilized societies, post-civilization has been treading heavily upon its heels. The student of civilization may soon find himself in the unfortunate position of the anthropologist who studies pre-civilized societies. Both are like the student of ice on a hot day—the subject matter melts away almost before he can study it.

These great changes can be thought of as a change of gear in 3
the evolutionary process, resulting in progressive acceleration of the rate of evolutionary change. Even before the appearance of man on the earth, we can detect earlier evolutionary gear-shiftings. The formation of life obviously represented one such transition, the movement from the water to the land another, the development of the vertebrates another, and so on. Man himself represents a very large acceleration of the evolutionary process. Whether he evolved from pre-existing forms or landed from a space ship and was not able to get back to where he came from, is immaterial. Once he had arrived on earth, the process of evolution could go on within the confines of the human nervous system at a greatly accelerated rate. The human mind is an enormous mutation-selection process. Instead of mutation-selection process being confined, as it were, to the flesh, it can take place within the image, and hence, very rapid changes are possible. Man seems to have been pretty slow to exploit this potentiality, but one suspects that even with primitive man, the rate of change in the biosphere was much larger than it had been before, because of the appearance of what Teilhard de Chardin calls the noosphere, or sphere of knowledge.

Civilization represents a further acceleration of the rate of 4
change, mainly because one of the main products of civilization is history. With the food surplus from agriculture it became possible to feed specialized scribes. With the development of writing, man did not have to depend on the uncertain memories of the aged for his records, and a great process of accumulation of social knowledge

KENNETH E. BOULDING

began. The past could now communicate, at least in one direction, with the present, and this enormously increased the range and possibility of enlargements of the contents of the human mind.

Out of civilization, however, comes science, which is a superior way of organizing the evolution of knowledge. We trace the first beginnings of science, of course, almost as far back as the beginning of civilization itself. Beginning about 1650, however, we begin to see the organization of science into a community of knowledge, and this leads again to an enormous acceleration of the rate of change. The world of 1650 is more remote to us than the world of ancient Egypt or Samaria would have been to the man of 1650. Already in the United States and Western Europe, in a smaller degree in Russia and in some other parts of the world, we see the beginnings of post-civilized society—a state of man as different from civilization as civilization is from savagery. What we really mean, therefore, by the anemic term "economic development" is the second great transition in the state of man. It is the movement from civilized to post-civilized society. It is nothing short of a major revolution in the human condition, and it does not represent a mere continuance and development of the old patterns of civilization. 5

As a dramatic illustration of the magnitude of the change, we can contemplate Indonesia. This is a country which has about the same extent, population and per capita income as the Roman Empire at its height. For all I know it is producing a literature and an art at least comparable to that of the Augustan age. It is, therefore, a very good example of a country of high civilization. Because of this fact, it is one of the poorest countries in the world. It is desperately anxious to break out of its present condition. Jakarta is a city about the size of ancient Rome, though perhaps a little less splendid. All this points up the fact that the Roman Empire was a desperately poor and underdeveloped society. The Roman cities seem to have been always about three weeks away from starvation, and even at its height it is doubtful whether the Roman Empire ever had less than seventy-five to eighty per cent of its population in agriculture. 6

Civilization, that is, is a state of society in which techniques are so poor that it takes about eighty per cent of the population to feed the hundred per cent. But we do have about twenty per cent of the people who can be spared from food-producing to build Parthenons and cathedrals, to write literature and poetry, and fight wars. By contrast, in the United States today we are rapidly getting to the point where we can produce all our food with only ten per cent of the population and still have large agricultural surpluses. But for the blessings of agricultural policy, we might soon be able to produce all our food with five per cent of the population. It may even be that agriculture is on its way out altogether and that within another 7

 AFTER CIVILIZATION, WHAT?

generation or so we will produce our food in a totally different way. Perhaps both fields and cows are merely relics of civilization, the vestiges of a vanishing age. This means, however, that even in our society, which is at a very early stage of post-civilization, we can now spare about ninety per cent of the people to produce bathtubs, automobiles, H-bombs and all the other conveniences of life. Western Europe and Japan are coming along behind the United States very fast. The Russians, likewise, are advancing toward post-civilization, although by a very different road. At the moment their ideology is a handicap to them in some places—especially in agriculture, which still occupies forty-five per cent of the people. And, if the Russians ever discover that super-peasants are a good deal more efficient than collective farms, they may cut away some of the ideology that hangs around their neck and move even more rapidly toward post-civilized society.

I'm not at all sure what post-civilization will look like but it will certainly be a world-wide society. Until very recently, each civilized society was a little island in a sea of barbarism which constantly threatened to overwhelm it. Civilization is haunted by the spectre of decline and fall, though it is noteworthy that in spite of the rise and fall of particular civilizations, civilization itself expanded steadily in geographical coverage, from its very beginnings. We must face the fact, however, that post-civilized society will be world-wide, if only because of its ease of communication and transportation. I flew last year from Idlewild to Brussels, and on glimpsing the new Brussels Airport out of the corner of my eye, I thought for a moment that we had come back and landed at Idlewild again. 8

The characteristic institutions of civilization are, as we have seen, first agriculture, then the city, then war, in the sense of clash of organized armed forces, and finally, inequality, the sharp contrast between the rich and the poor, between the city and the country, between the urbane and the rustic. The state is based very fundamentally on violence and exploitation, and the culture tends to be spiritually monolithic. 9

In post-civilization all these institutions suffer radical change. Agriculture, as we have seen, diminishes until it is a small proportion of the society; the city, likewise, in the classical sense, disintegrates. Los Angeles is perhaps the first example of the post-civilization, post-urban agglomeration—under no stretch of the imagination could it be called a city. War, likewise, is an institution in process of disintegration. National defense as a social system has quite fundamentally broken down on a world scale. The ICBM and the nuclear warhead have made the nation-state as militarily obsolete as the city-state, for in no country now can the armed forces preserve an 10

KENNETH E. BOULDING

area of internal peace by pushing violence to the outskirts. Poverty and inequality, likewise, are tending to disappear, at least on their traditional scale. In civilized societies the king or the emperor could live in a Versailles and the peasant in a hovel. In post-civilized society, it is almost impossible for the rich to consume on a scale which is more, let us say, than ten times that of the poor. There is no sense in having more than ten automobiles!

Another profound change in the passage from civilization to 11 post-civilization is the change in the expectation of life. In civilized society, birth and death rates tend to be about forty per thousand and the expectation of life at birth is twenty-five years. In post-civilized society, the expectation of life at birth rises at least to seventy and perhaps beyond. It may be that we are on the edge of a biological revolution, just as dramatic and far-reaching as the discovery of atomic energy and that we may crack the problem of aging and prolong human life much beyond its present span. Whether or not, however, we go forward to Methuselah, the mere increase of the average age of death to seventy is a startling and far-reaching change. It means, for instance, that in an equilibrium population, the birth and death rate cannot be more than about fourteen per thousand. This unquestionably implies some form of conscious control of births. It means also that a much larger proportion of the population will be in later years.

It is perfectly possible to paint an anti-utopia in which a 12 post-civilized society appears as universally vulgar or dull. On the whole, however, I welcome post-civilization and I have really very little affection for civilization. In most pre-civilized societies the fact that the life of man is for the most part nasty, brutish and short, does not prevent the poets and philosophers from sentimentalizing the noble savage. Similarly, we may expect the same kind of sentimentalizing of the noble Romans and civilized survivals like Winston Churchill. On the whole, though, I will not shed any tears over the grave of civilization any more than I will over pre-civilized society. The credit balance of post-civilization is large. It at least gives us a chance of a modest utopia, in which slavery, poverty, exploitation, gross inequality, war and disease—these prime costs of civilization— will fall to the vanishing point.

What we have at the moment is a chance to make a transition 13 to this modest utopia—a chance which is probably unique in the history of this planet. If we fail, the chance will probably not be repeated in this part of the universe. Whatever experiments may be going on elsewhere, the present moment indeed is unique in the whole four billion years of the history of the planet. In my more pessimistic moments, I think the chance is a slim one, and it may be

  AFTER CIVILIZATION, WHAT?   **643**

that man will be written off as an unsuccessful experiment. We must look at the traps which lie along the path of the transition, which might prevent us from making it altogether.

The most urgent trap is, of course, the trap of war. War, as I 14 have suggested, is an institution peculiarly characteristic of civilization. Pre-civilized societies have sporadic feuding and raiding, but they do not generally have permanent organized armed forces, and they do not generally develop conquest and empire; or if they do, they soon pass into a civilized form. An armed force is essentially a mobile city designed to throw things at another mobile or stationary city with presumably evil intent. As far as I know, not more than two or three civilizations have existed without war. The Mayans and the people of Mohenjodaro seem to have lived for fairly long periods without war, but this was an accident of their monopolistic situation and they unquestionably occupied themselves with other kinds of foolishness. If pre-civilized society, however, cannot afford war, post-civilized society can afford far too much of it, and hence will be forced to get rid of the institution because it is simply inappropriate to the technological age. The breakdown in the world social system of national defense really dates from about 1949, when the United States lost its monopoly of nuclear weapons. A system of national defense is only feasible if each nation is stronger at home than its enemies, so that it can preserve a relatively large area of peace within its critical boundaries. Such a system is only possible, however, if the range of the deadly missile is short and if the armed forces of each nation lose power rapidly as they move away from home. The technological developments of the twentieth century have destroyed these foundations of national defense, and have replaced it with another social system altogether, which is "deterrence."

"Deterrence" is a social system with properties very different 15 from that of national defense, which it replaced. Under national defense, for instance, it is possible to use the armed forces; under "deterrence" it is not—that is, if the deterring forces are ever used, the system will have broken down. We live in a society with a positive possibility of irretrievable disaster—a probability which grows every year. Herman Kahn recently said: "All we are doing is buying time, and we are doing nothing with the time that we buy." The armed forces of the world are caught in a technological process which not only destroys their own function, but threatens all of us. Even if a few of us do crawl out of the fallout shelters, it is by no means clear that we can put the world back together again. Even if the human race could survive one nuclear war, it is very doubtful that it could survive a second; and as the purpose of the first nuclear war would be to set up a political system which would produce the second, unless there is a radical change in attitude towards national defense, the prospects of

KENNETH E. BOULDING

the human race seem to be dim. Fortunately, "there is still time, brother" and evolution can still go on in the minds of men. The critical question is whether it can go on rapidly enough. The abolition of national defense, which is what we must face, is going to be a painful process, as we have come to rely on it to preserve many of the values which we hold dear. If the task can be perceived, however, by a sufficient number of people, there is at least a chance that we may avoid this trap before it is too late.

Even if we avoid the war trap, we may still fall into the 16 population trap. Population control is an unsolved problem even for the developed areas of the world, which have moved the furthest towards post-civilization. An equilibrium of population in a stable post-civilized society may represent a fairly radical interference with ancient human institutions and freedoms. In a stable post-civilized society, as I have suggested, the birth and death rates must be of the order of fourteen per thousand, and the average number of children per family cannot much exceed two. There are many social institutions which might accomplish this end. So far, however, the only really sure-fire method of controlling population is starvation and misery.

In many parts of the world—indeed, for most of the human 17 race for the moment—the impact of certain post-civilized techniques on civilized society has produced a crisis of growth, which may easily be fatal. In the tropics especially, with DDT and a few simple public-health measures, it is easy to reduce the death rate to nine or ten per thousand while the birth rate stays at forty per thousand. This means an annual increase of population of three per cent *per annum*, almost all of it concentrated in the lower age groups. We see dramatic examples of this phenomenon in places like the West Indies, Ceylon, and Formosa; but thanks to the activity of the World Health Organization, it is taking place rapidly all over the tropical world. Perhaps the most important key to the transition to post-civilization is heavy investment in human resources—that is, in education. The conquest of disease and infant mortality, however, before the corresponding adjustment to the birth rate, produces enormous numbers of children in societies which do not have the resources to educate them— especially as those in the middle-age groups, who after all must do all the work of a society, come from the much smaller population of the pre-DDT era.

Even in the developed countries, population control presents 18 a very serious problem. The United States, for instance, at the moment is increasing in population even more rapidly than India. The time when we thought that the mere increase in income would automatically solve the population problem has gone by. In the United States, and certain other societies, in the early stages of post-civilization, the child has become an object of conspicuous domestic consumption. The consumption patterns of the American spending unit seem to follow a certain *"gestalt"* in which household capital accumulates in a certain order, such as the first car, the first child, the washer and dryer, the second child, the deep freeze, the third child, the second car, the fourth child, and so on. The richer we get, the more children we can afford to have and the more children we do have. We now seem to be able to afford an average of something like four children per family, and as, in a post-civilized society, these four children all survive, the population doubles every generation. A hundred years of this and even the United States is going to find itself uncomfortably crowded. It can be argued, indeed, that from the point of view of the amenities of life we are already well beyond the optimum population.

The third trap on the road to post-civilization is the techno-   19
logical trap. Our present technology is fundamentally suicidal. It is based on the extraction of concentrated deposits of fossil fuels and ores, which in the nature of things are exhaustible. Even at present rates of consumption, they will be exhausted in a time span which is not very long measured against human history and which is infinitesimally small on the geological time scale. If the rest of the world advances to American standards of consumption, these resources will disappear almost overnight. On this view economic development is the process of bringing closer the evil day when everything will be gone—all the oil, the coal, the ores—and we will have to go back to primitive agriculture and scratching in the woods.

There are indications, however, that suicidal technology is   20
not absolutely necessary and that a permanent high-level technology is possible. Beginning in the early part of the twentieth century, it is possible to detect an anti-entropic movement in technology. This begins perhaps with the Haber process for the fixation of nitrogen from the air. A development of similar significance is the Dow process for the extraction of magnesium from the sea. Both these processes take the diffuse and concentrate it, instead of taking the concentrated and diffusing it, as do most processes of mining and economic production. These anti-entropic processes foreshadow a technology in which we shall draw all the materials we need from the virtually inexhaustible reservoirs of the sea and the air and draw our energy from controlled fusion—either artificially produced on the earth or from the sun.

This is why I so much resent spending half the world's   21
income on armaments—because the more we do this, the less chance we have of making the transition to a stable, high-level society. The human race is in a precarious position on its planet and it should act accordingly. It has a chance, never to be repeated, of making its great

KENNETH E. BOULDING

transition, and if it fails, at least one good experiment in intelligence will have gone to waste. I suppose there are similar experiments of this nature going on in other parts of the universe; but I must confess to a hopelessly anthropocentric prejudice in favor of planet earth. It's a nice planet, and I'm in favor of it and I have no desire to see its principal inhabitant blow it up or starve it out.

When we look at the nature of possible remedies for our immediate problems, it seems clear that we all are engulfed in a profound and appallingly dangerous misallocation of our intellectual resources. The misallocation lies in the fact that although all our major problems are in social systems, we persist in regarding them as if they were essentially problems in physical or biological systems. We persist in regarding agricultural problems, for instance, as one of crops, whereas it is clearly fundamentally a problem of farmers. We persist in regarding the flood-control problem as a problem of the river and we even turn it over to army engineers, who treat the river as an enemy. A flood, however, is no problem at all to a river. It is a perfectly normal part of its way of life. The flood, essentially, is a problem of people and of social institutions, of architecture and zoning. Professor Gilbert White, of the University of Chicago, suggests that after spending over four billion dollars on flood control in this country, we are more in danger of major disasters than we were before. What we really mean by flood control is the substitution of a major disaster every fifty or one hundred years for minor inconveniences every five or ten. 22

In national defense we have fallen into exactly the same trap. We regard this as a problem in physical systems and in hardware, whereas it is essentially a problem in social systems. Here again, we are building into our societies the eventual certainty of total disaster. In face of the fact that war and peace is the major problem of our age, we are putting practically nothing into peace research; even when we do put money into arms control and disarmament research we spend sixty million dollars for Project Vela, which deals wholly with physical systems, and one hundred and fifty thousand on Project Vulcan, which deals with social systems and with unanswerable questions at that. When we look at biological and medical research, and still more, research into population, the disparity is just as striking. We persist in regarding disease as a biological problem, whereas it is fundamentally a bio-social system. Yet the number of sociologists in our medical schools can be counted almost on the fingers of one hand. 23

Nevertheless, in spite of the dangers, it is a wonderful age to live in, and I would not wish to be born in any other time. The wonderful and precious thing about the present moment is that there is still time—the Bomb hasn't gone off, the population explosion may be caught, the technological problem can, perhaps, be solved. If the 24 human race is to survive, however, it will have to change more in its ways of thinking in the next twenty-five years than it has done in the last twenty-five thousand. There is hope, however, in the fact that we are very far from having exhausted the capacity of this extraordinary organism that we call man. I once calculated the capacity of the human nervous system in terms of the number of different states it might assume, which is a very rough measure. This comes to two to the ten billionth power, assuming that each of our ten billion neurons is capable of only two states. This is a very large number. It would take you ninety years to write it down at the rate of one digit a second. If you want a standard of comparison, the total number of neutrinos, which are the smallest known particles, which could be packed into the known astronomical universe (this is the largest physical number I could think of) could easily be written down in three minutes. I find it hard to believe, therefore, that the capacity of the human organism has been exhausted.

What we have to do now, however, is to develop almost a 25 new form of learning. We have to learn from rapidly changing systems. Ordinarily we learn from stable systems. It is because the world repeats itself that we catch on to the law of repetition. Learning from changing systems is perhaps another step in the acceleration of evolution that we have to take. I have been haunted by a remark which Norman Meier, the psychologist, made in a seminar a few months ago, when he said that a cat who jumps on a hot stove never jumps on a cold one. This seems precisely to describe the state we may be in today. We have jumped on a lot of hot stoves and now perhaps the cold stove is the only place on which to jump. In the rapidly changing system it is desperately easy to learn things which are no longer true. Perhaps the greatest task of applied social science at the moment is to study the conditions under which we learn from rapidly changing systems. If we can answer this question, there may still be hope for the human race.

QUESTIONS

1. According to Boulding, what distinguishes precivilization from civilization, and civilization from postcivilization?

2. Identify the main problems facing postcivilization.

3. What paradoxical language does the author employ in paragraph 2?

4. Would you label this essay as subjective or objective in writing style? Explain.

KENNETH E. BOULDING

5. Analyze the patterns of classification that serve to organize the essay. Explain the divisions involved in the classification schemes.

6. Examine the relevance of definition and of comparison and contrast to the development of the essay.

7. Discuss the reasoning process by which Boulding arrives at his conclusion in paragraph 25 that "We have to learn from rapidly changing systems."

8. What is the thesis of the essay? Where is it stated most clearly?

9. Comment on Boulding's statement: "If the human race is to survive . . . it will have to change more in its ways of thinking in the next twenty-five years than it has done in the last twenty-five thousand" (paragraph 24).

10. a. Explain your vision of postcivilization.
b. Write a classification essay on the possible types of civilizations that might emerge in the future.

Glossary of Terms

Abstract/concrete patterns of language reflect an author's word choice. Abstract words (for example, "wisdom," "power," "beauty") refer to general ideas, qualities, or conditions. Concrete words name material objects and items associated with the five senses—words like "rock," "pizza," and "basketball." Both abstract and concrete language are useful in communicating ideas. Generally you should not be too abstract in writing. It is best to employ concrete words, naming things that can be seen, touched, smelled, heard, or tasted in order to support generalizations, topic sentences, or more abstract ideas.

Acronym is a word formed from the first or first few letters of several words, as in OPEC (Organization of Petroleum Exporting Countries).

Action in narrative writing is the sequence of happenings or events. This movement of events may occupy just a few minutes or extend over a period of years or centuries.

Alliteration is the repetition of initial consonant sounds in words placed closely next to each other, as in "what a tale of terror now their turbulency tells." Prose that is highly rhythmical or "poetic" often makes use of this method.

Allusion is a literary, biographical, or historical reference, whether real or imaginary. It is a "figure of speech" (a fresh, useful comparison) employed to illuminate an idea. A writer's prose style can be made richer through this economical method of evoking an idea or emotion, as in E. M. Forster's biblical allusion in this sentence: "Property produces men of weight, and it was a man of weight who failed to get into the Kingdom of Heaven."

Analogy is a form of comparison that uses a clear illustration to explain a difficult idea or function. It is unlike a formal comparison in that its subjects of comparison are from different categories or areas. For example, an analogy likening "division of labor" to the activity of bees in a hive makes the first concept more concrete by showing it to the reader through the figurative comparison with the bees. Analogy in exposition can involve a few sentences, a paragraph or set of paragraphs, or an entire essay. Analogies can also be used in argumentation to heighten an appeal to emotion, but they cannot actually *prove* anything.

Analysis is a method of exposition in which a subject is broken up into its parts so as to explain their nature, function, proportion, or relationship. Analysis thus explores connections and processes within the context of a given subject. (See *Causal analysis* and *Process analysis*.)

Anecdote is a brief, engaging account of some happening, often historical, biographical, or personal. As a technique in writing, anecdote is especially effective in creating interesting essay introductions, and also in illuminating abstract concepts in the body of the essay.

Antecedent in grammar refers to the word, phrase, or clause to which a pronoun refers. In writing, antecedent also refers to any happening or thing that is prior to another, or to anything that logically precedes a subject.

Antithesis is the balancing of one idea or term against another for emphasis.

Antonym is a word whose meaning is opposite to that of another word.

Aphorism is a short, pointed statement expressing a general truism or idea in an original or imaginative way. Marshall McLuhan's statement that "the medium is the message" is a well-known contemporary aphorism.

Archaic language is vocabulary or usage that belongs to an early period and is old-fashioned today. A word like "thee" for "you" would be an archaism still in use in certain situations.

Archetypes are special images or symbols that, according to Carl Jung, appeal to the total racial or cultural understanding of a people. Such images or symbols as the mother archetype, the cowboy in American film, a sacred mountain, or spring as a time of renewal tend to trigger the "collective unconscious" of the human race.

Argumentation is a formal variety of writing that offers reasons for or against something. Its goal is to persuade or convince the reader through logical reasoning and carefully controlled emotional appeal. Argumentation as a formal mode of writing contains many properties that distinguish it from exposition. (See *Assumption, Deduction, Evidence, Induction, Logic, Persuasion, Proposition,* and *Refutation*.)

Assonance defined generally is likeness or rough similarity of sound. Its specific definition is a partial rhyme in which the stressed vowel sounds are alike but the consonant sounds are unlike, as in "late" and "make." Although more common to poetry, assonance can also be detected in highly rhythmic prose.

Assumption in argumentation is anything taken for granted or presumed to be accepted by the audience and therefore unstated. Assumptions in argumentative writing can be dangerous because the audience might not always accept the idea implicit in them. (See *Begging the question.*)

Audience is that readership toward which an author directs his or her essay. In composing essays, writers must acknowledge the nature of their expected readers—whether specialized or general, minimally educated or highly educated, sympathetic or unsympathetic toward the writer's opinions, and so forth. Failure to focus on the writer's true audience can lead to confusions in language and usage, presentation of inappropriate content, and failure to appeal to the expected reader.

Balance in sentence structure refers to the assignment of equal treatment in the arrangement of coordinate ideas. It is often used to heighten a contrast of ideas.

Begging the question is an error or fallacy in reasoning and argumentation in which the writer assumes as a truth something for which evidence or proof is actually needed.

Causal analysis is a form of writing that examines causes and effects of events or conditions as they relate to a specific subject. Writers can investigate the causes of a particular effect or the effects of a particular cause or combine both methods. Basically, however, causal analysis looks for connections between things and reasons behind them.

Characterization especially in narrative or descriptive writing, is the creation of people involved in the action. Authors use techniques of dialogue, description, reportage, and observation in attempting to present vivid and distinctive characters.

Chronology or chronological order is the arrangement of events in the order in which they happened. Chronological order can be used in such diverse narrative situations as history, biography, scientific process, and personal account. Essays that are ordered by chronology move from one step or point to the next in time.

Cinematic technique in narration, description, and occasionally exposition is the conscious application of film art to the development of the contemporary essay. Modern writers often are aware of such film techniques as montage (the process of cutting and arranging film so that short scenes are presented in rapid succession), zoom (intense enlargement of subject), and various forms of juxtaposition, using these methods to enhance the quality of their essays.

Classification is a form of exposition in which the writer divides a subject into categories and then groups elements in each of those categories according to their relationships to each other. Thus a writer using classification takes a topic, divides it into several major groups, and then often subdivides these groups, moving always from larger categories to smaller ones.

Cliche is an expression that once was fresh and original but has lost much of its vitality through overuse. Because terms like "as quick as a wink" and "blew her stack" are trite or common today, they should be avoided in writing.

Climactic ordering is the arrangement of a paragraph or essay so that the most important items are saved for last. The effect is to build slowly through a sequence of events or ideas to the most critical part of the composition.

Coherence is a quality in effective writing that results from the careful ordering of each sentence in a paragraph and each paragraph in the essay. If an essay is coherent, each part will grow naturally and logically from those parts that come before it. Following careful chronological, logical, spatial, or sequential order is the most natural way to achieve coherence in writing. The main devices used in achieving coherence are transitions, which help to connect one thought with another.

Colloquial language is conversational language used in certain types of informal and narrative writing, but rarely in essays, business writing, or research writing. Expressions like "cool," "pal," or "I can dig it" often have a place in conversational settings. However, they should be used sparingly in essay writing for special effects.

Comparison and contrast as an essay pattern treats similarities and differences between two subjects. Any useful comparison involves two items from the same class. Moreover, there must be a clear reason for the comparison or contrast. Finally, there must be a balanced treatment of the various comparative or contrasting points between the two subjects.

Conclusions are the endings of essays. Without a conclusion, an essay would be incomplete, leaving the reader with the feeling that something important has been left out. There are numerous strategies for conclusions available to writers: summarizing main points in the essay, restating the main idea, using an effective quotation to bring the essay to an end, offering the reader the climax to a series of events, returning to the beginning and echoing it, offering a solution to a problem, emphasizing the topic's significance, or setting a new frame of reference by generalizing from the main thesis. A conclusion should end the essay in a clear, convincing, or emphatic way.

Concrete (See *Abstract/concrete.*)

Conflict in narrative writing is the clash or opposition of events, characters, or ideas that makes the resolution of action necessary.

Connotation and denotation are terms specifying the way a word has meaning. Connotation refers to the "shades of meaning" that a word might have because of various emotional associations it calls up for writers and readers alike. Words like "patriotism," "pig," and "rose" have strong connotative overtones to them. Denotation refers to the "dictionary" definition of a word—its exact meaning. Good writers understand the connotative and denotative value of words, and must control the shades of meaning that many words possess.

Context is the situation surrounding a word, group of words, or sentence. Often the elements coming before or after a certain confusing or difficult construction will provide insight into the meaning or importance of that item.

Coordination in sentence structure refers to the grammatical arrangement of parts of the same order or equality in rank.

Declarative sentences make a statement or assertion.

Deduction is a form of logic that begins with a generally stated truth or principle and then offers details, examples, and reasoning to support the generalization. In other words, deduction is based on reasoning from a known principle to an unknown principle, from the general to the specific, or from a premise to a logical conclusion. (See *Syllogism.*)

Definition in exposition is the extension of a word's meaning through a paragraph or an entire essay. As an extended method of explaining a word, this type of definition relies on other rhetorical methods, including detail, illustration, comparison and contrast, and anecdote.

Denotation (See *Connotation.*)

Description in the prose essay is a variety of writing that uses details of sight, sound, color, smell, taste, and touch to create a word picture and to explain or illustrate an idea.

Development refers to the way a paragraph or essay elaborates or builds upon a topic or theme. Typical development proceeds either from general illustrations to specific ones or from one generalization to another. (See *Horizontal/vertical.*)

Dialogue is the reproduction of speech or conversation between two or more persons in writing. Dialogue can add concreteness and vividness to an essay, and can also help to reveal character. A writer who reproduces dialogue in an essay must use it for a purpose and not simply as a decorative device.

Diction is the manner of expression in words, choice of words, or wording. Writers must choose vocabulary carefully and precisely to communicate a message and also to address an intended audience effectively; this is good diction.

Digression is a temporary departure from the main subject in writing. Any digression in the essay must serve a purpose or be intended for a specific effect.

Discourse (Forms of) relates conventionally to the main categories of writing—narration, description, exposition, and argumentation. In practice, these forms of discourse often blend or overlap. Essayists seek the ideal fusion of forms of discourse in the treatment of their subject.

Division is that aspect of classification in which the writer divides some large subject into categories. Division helps writers to split large and potentially complicated subjects into parts for orderly presentation and discussion.

Dominant impression in description is the main impression or effect that writers attempt to create for their subject. It arises from an author's focus on a single subject and from the feelings the writer brings to that subject.

Editorialize is to express personal opinions about the subject of the essay. An editorial tone can have a useful effect in writing, but at other times an author might want to reduce editorializing in favor of a better balanced or more objective tone.

Effect is a term used in causal analysis to describe the outcome or expected result of a chain of happenings.

Emphasis indicates the placement of the most important ideas in key positions in the essay. As a major principle, emphasis relates to phrases, sentences, paragraphs—the construction of the entire essay. Emphasis can be achieved by repetition, subordination, careful positioning of thesis and topic sentences, climactic ordering, comparison and contrast, and a variety of other methods.

Episodic relates to that variety of narrative writing that develops through a series of incidents or events.

Essay is the name given to a short prose work on a limited topic. Essays take many forms, ranging from personal narratives to critical or argumentative treatments of a subject. Normally an essay will convey the writer's personal ideas about the subject.

Etymology is the origin and development of a word; tracing a word back as far as possible.

Evidence is material offered to support an argument or a proposition. Typical forms of evidence are facts, details, and expert testimony.

Example is a method of exposition in which the writer offers illustrations in order to explain a generalization or a whole thesis. (See *Illustration*.)

Exclamatory sentences in writing express surprise or strong emotion.

Expert testimony as employed in argumentative essays and in expository essays is the use of statements by authorities to support a writer's position or idea. This method often requires careful quotation and acknowledgment of sources.

Exposition is a major form of discourse that informs or explains. Exposition is the form of expression required in much college writing, for it provides facts and information, clarifies ideas, and establishes meaning. The primary methods of exposition are illustration, comparison and contrast, analogy, definition, classification, causal analysis, and process analysis (see entries).

Extended metaphor is a figurative comparison that is used to structure a significant part of the composition or the whole essay. (See *Figurative language* and *Metaphor*.)

Fable is a form of narrative containing a moral that normally appears clearly at the end.

Fallacy in argumentation is an error in logic or the reasoning process. Fallacies occur because of vague development of ideas, lack of awareness on the part of writers of the requirements of logical reasoning, or faulty assumptions about the proposition.

Figurative language, as opposed to literal language, is a special approach to writing that departs from what is typically a concrete, straightforward style. It is the use of vivid, imaginative statements to illuminate or illustrate an idea. Figurative language adds freshness, meaning, and originality to a writer's style. Major figures of speech include allusion, hyperbole, metaphor, personification, and simile (see entries).

Flashback is a narrative technique in which the writer begins at some point in the action and then moves into the past in order to provide crucial information about characters and events.

Foreshadowing is a technique that indicates beforehand what is to occur at a later point in the essay.

Frame in narration and description is the use of a key object or pattern—typically at the start and end of the essay—that serves as a border or structure to contain the substance of the composition.

Generalization is a broad idea or statement. All generalizations require particulars and illustrations to support them.

General/specific words are the basis of writing, although it is wise in college composition to keep vocabulary as specific as possible. General words refer to broad categories and groups, whereas specific words capture with force and clarity the nature of a term. General words refer to large classes, concepts, groups, and emotions; specific words are more particular in providing meanings. The distinction between general and specific language is always a matter of degree.

Genre is a type or form of literature—for example, short fiction, novel, poetry, drama.

Grammatical structure is a systematic description of language as it relates to the grammatical nature of a sentence.

Horizontal/vertical paragraph and essay development refers to the basic ways a writer moves from one generalization to another in a carefully related series of generalizations (horizontal), or conversely from a generalization to a series of specific supporting examples (vertical).

Hortatory style is a variety of writing designed to encourage, give advice, or urge to good deeds.

Hyperbole is a form of figurative language that uses exaggeration to overstate a position.

Hypothesis is an unproven theory or proposition that is tentatively accepted to explain certain facts. A working hypothesis provides the basis for further investigation or argumentation.

Hypothetical examples are illustrations in the form of assumptions that are based on the hypothesis. As such, they are conditional rather than absolute or certain facts.

Identification as a method of exposition refers to focusing on the main subject of the essay. It involves the clear location of the subject within the context or situation of the composition.

Idiomatic language is the language or dialect of a people, region, or class; the individual nature of a language.

Ignoring the question in argumentation is a fallacy that involves the avoidance of the main issue by developing an entirely different one.

Illustration is the use of one or more examples to support an idea. Illustration permits the writer to support a generalization through particulars or specifics.

Imagery is clear, vivid description that appeals to our sense of sight, smell, touch, sound, or taste. Much imagery exists for its own sake, adding descriptive flavor to an essay. However, imagery (especially when it involves a larger pattern) can also add meaning to an essay.

Induction is a method of logic consisting of the presentation of a series of facts, pieces of information, or instances in order to formulate or build a likely generalization. The key is to provide prior examples before reaching a logical conclusion. Consequently, as a pattern of organization in essay writing, the inductive method requires the careful presentation of relevant data and information before the conclusion is reached at the end of the paper.

Inference involves arriving at a decision or opinion by reasoning from known facts or evidence.

Interrogative sentences are sentences that ask or pose a question.

Introduction is the beginning or opening of an essay. The introduction should alert the reader to the subject by identifying it, set the limits of the essay, and indicate what the thesis (or main idea) will be. Moreover, it should arouse the reader's interest in the subject. Among the devices available in the creation of good introductions are making a simple statement of thesis; giving a clear, vivid description of an important setting; posing a question or series of questions; referring to a relevant historical event; telling an anecdote; using comparison and contrast to frame the subject; using several examples to reinforce the statement of the subject; and presenting a personal attitude about a controversial issue.

Irony is the use of language to suggest the opposite of what is stated. Writers use irony to reveal unpleasant or troublesome realities that exist in life, or to poke fun at human weaknesses and foolish attitudes. In an essay there may be verbal irony, in which the author says one thing but means another; or situational irony, in which the result of a sequence of ideas or events is the opposite of what normally would be expected. A key to the identification of irony in an essay is our ability to detect where the author is stating the opposite of what he or she actually believes.

Issue is the main question upon which an entire argument rests. It is the idea that the writer attempts to prove.

Jargon is the use of special words associated with a specific area of knowledge or a particular profession. Writers who employ jargon either assume that readers know specialized terms or take care to define terms for the benefit of the audience.

Juxtaposition as a technique in writing or essay organization is the placing of elements—either similar or contrasting—close together; positioning them side by side in order to illuminate the subject.

Levels of language refer to the kinds of language used in speaking and writing. Basically there are three main levels of language—formal, informal, and colloquial. Formal English, used in writing or speech, is the type of English employed to address special groups and professional people. Informal English is the sort of writing found in newspapers, magazines, books, and essays. It is popular English for an educated audience, but still more formal than conversational English. Finally, colloquial English is spoken (and occasionally written) English used in conversations with friends, employees, and peer group members; it is characterized by the use of slang, idioms, ordinary language, and loose sentence structure.

Linear order in paragraph development means the clear line of movement from one point to another.

Listing is a simple technique of illustration in which facts or examples are used in order to support a topic or generalization.

Logic as applied to essay writing is correct reasoning based on induction or deduction. The logical basis of an essay must offer reasonable criteria or principles of thought, present these principles in an orderly manner, avoid faults in reasoning, and result in a complete and satisfactory outcome in the reasoning process.

Metaphor is a type of figurative language in which an item from one category is compared briefly and imaginatively with an item from another area. Writers use such implied comparisons to assign meaning in a fresh, vivid, and concrete way.

Metonymy is a figure of language in which a thing is not designated by its own name but by another associated with or suggested by it, as in "The Supreme Court has decided" (meaning that the judges of the Supreme Court have decided).

Mood is the creation of atmosphere in descriptive writing.

Motif in an essay is any series of components that can be detected as a pattern. For example, a particular detail, idea, or image can be elaborated upon or designed so as to form a pattern or motif in the essay.

Myth in literature is a traditional story or series of events explaining some basic phenomenon of nature, the origin of humanity, or the customs, institutions, and religious rites of a people. Myth often relates to the exploits of gods, goddesses, and heroes.

Narration as a form of essay writing is the presentation of a story in order to illustrate an idea.

Non sequitur in argumentation is a conclusion or inference that does not follow from the premises or evidence on which it is based. The *non sequitur* thus is a type of logical fallacy.

Objective/subjective writing refers to the attitude that writers take toward their subject. When writers are objective, they try not to report their personal feelings about the subject; they attempt to be detached, impersonal, and unbiased. Conversely, subjective writing reveals an author's personal attitudes and emotions. For many varieties of college writing, such as business or laboratory reports, term papers, and literary analyses, it is best to be as objective as possible. But for many personal essays in composition courses, the subjective touch is fine. In the hands of skilled writers, the objective and subjective tones often blend.

Onomatopoeia is the formation of a word by imitating the natural sound associated with the object or action, as in "buzz" or "click."

Order is the arrangement of information or materials in an essay. The most common ordering techniques are *chronological order* (time in sequence); *spatial order* (the arrangement of descriptive details); *process order* (a step-by-step approach to an activity); *deductive order* (a thesis followed by information to support it); and *inductive order* (evidence and examples first, followed by the thesis in the form of a conclusion). Some rhetorical patterns such as comparison and contrast, classification, and argumentation require other ordering methods. Writers should select those ordering principles that permit them to present materials clearly.

Overstatement is an extravagant or exaggerated claim or statement.

Paradox is a statement that seems to be contradictory but actually contains an element of truth.

Paragraph is a unit in an essay that serves to present and examine one aspect of a topic. Composed normally of a group of sentences (one-sentence paragraphs can be used for emphasis or special effect), the paragraph elaborates an idea within the larger framework of the essay and the thesis unifying it.

Parallelism is a variety of sentence structure in which there is "balance" or coordination in the presentation of elements. "I came, I saw, I conquered" is a standard example of parallelism, presenting both pronouns and verbs in a coordinated manner. Parallelism can appear in a sentence, a group of sentences, or an entire paragraph.

Paraphrase as a literary method is the process of rewording the thought or meaning expressed in something that has been said or written before.

Parenthetical refers to giving qualifying information or explanation. This information normally is marked off or placed within parentheses.

Parody is ridiculing the language or style of another writer or composer. In parody, a serious subject tends to be treated in a nonsensical manner.

Periphrasis is the use of many words where one or a few would do; it is a roundabout way of speaking or writing.

Persona is the role or characterization that writers occasionally create for themselves in a personal narrative.

Personification is giving an object, thing, or idea lifelike or human characteristics, as in the common reference to a car as "she." Like all forms of figurative language, personification adds freshness to description, and makes ideas vivid by setting up striking comparisons.

Persuasion is a form of discourse, related to argumentation, that attempts basically to move a person to action or to influence an audience toward a particular belief.

Point of view is the angle from which a writer tells a story. Many personal and informal essays take the *first-person* (or "I") point of view, which is natural and fitting for essays in which the author wants to speak in a familiar way to the reader. On the other hand, the *third-person* point of view ("he," "she," "it," "they") distances the reader somewhat from the writer. The third-person point of view is useful in essays in which writers are not talking exclusively about themselves, but about other people, ideas, and events.

Post hoc, ergo, propter hoc in logic is the fallacy of thinking that a happening that follows another must be its result. It arises from a confusion about the logical causal relationship.

Process analysis is a pattern of writing that explains in a step-by-step way how something is done, how it is put together, how it works, or how it occurs. The subject can be a mechanical device, a product, an idea, a natural phenomenon, or a historical sequence. However, in all varieties of process analysis, the writer traces all important steps, from beginning to end.

Progression is the forward movement or succession of acts, events, or ideas presented in an essay.

Proportion refers to the relative emphasis and length given to an event, idea, item, or topic within the whole essay. Basically, in terms of proportion the writer gives more emphasis to a major element than to a minor one.

Proposition is the main point of an argumentative essay, the statement to be defended, proven, or upheld. It is like a *thesis* (see entry) except that it presents an idea that is debatable or can be disputed. The *major proposition* is the main argumentative point; *minor propositions* are the reasons given to support or prove the issue.

Purpose is what the writer wants to accomplish in an essay. Writers having a clear purpose will know the proper style, language, tone, and materials to utilize in designing an effective essay.

Refutation in argumentation is a method by which you recognize and deal effectively with the arguments of your opponents. Your own argument will be stronger if you refute—prove false or wrong—all opposing arguments.

Repetition is a simple method of achieving emphasis by repeating a word, phrase, or idea.

Rhetoric is the art of using words effectively in speaking or writing. It is also the art of literary composition, particularly in prose, including both figures of speech and such strategies as comparison and contrast, definition, and analysis.

Rhetorical question is a question asked only to emphasize a point, introduce a topic, or provoke thought, but not to elicit an answer.

Rhythm in prose writing is a regular recurrence of elements or features in sentences, creating a patterned emphasis, balance, or contrast.

Sarcasm is a sneering or taunting attitude in writing, designed to hurt by evaluating or criticizing. Basically, sarcasm is a heavy-handed form of irony (see entry). Writers should try to avoid sarcastic writing and to use more acceptable varieties of irony and satire to criticize their subject.

Satire is the humorous or critical treatment of a subject in order to expose the subject's vices, follies, stupidities, and so forth. The *intention* of much satire is to reform by exposing the subject to comedy or ridicule.

Sentimentality in prose writing is the excessive display of emotion, whether intended or unintended. Because sentimentality can distort the true nature of a situation or idea, writers should use it cautiously, or not at all.

Sensory language is language that appeals to any of the five senses—sight, sound, touch, taste, or feel.

Series as a technique in prose is the presentation of several items, often concrete details or similar parts of grammar like verbs or adjectives, in rapid sequence.

Setting in narrative and descriptive writing is the time, place, environment, background, or surroundings established by an author.

Simile is a figurative comparison using "like" or "as."

Slang is a kind of language that uses racy or colorful expressions associated more often with speech than with writing. It is colloquial English and should be used in essay writing only to reproduce dialogue or to create a special effect.

Spatial order in descriptive writing is the careful arrangement of details or materials in space—for example, from left to right, top to bottom, or near to far.

Specific words (See *General/specific words.*)

Statistics are facts or data of a numerical kind, assembled and tabulated to present significant information about a given subject. As a technique of illustration, statistics can be useful in analysis and argumentation.

Style is the specific or characteristic manner of expression, execution, construction, or design by an author. As a manner or mode of expression in language, it is the unique way each writer handles ideas. There are numerous stylistic categories—literary, formal, argumentative, satiric—but ultimately no two writers have the same style.

Subjective (See *Objective/subjective.*)

Subordination in sentence structure is the placing of a relatively less important idea in an inferior grammatical position to the main idea. It is the designation of a minor clause that is dependent upon a major clause.

Syllogism is an argument or form of reasoning in which two statements or premises are made and a logical conclusion drawn from them. As such, it is a form of deductive logic, reasoning from the general to the particular. The *major premise* presents a quality of class ("All writers are mortal."); the *minor premise* states that a particular subject is a member of that class ("Ernest Hemingway was a writer."); and the conclusion states that the qualities of the class and the member of the class are the same ("Hemingway was mortal.").

Symbol is something—normally a concrete image—that exists in itself but also stands for something else or has greater meaning. As a variety of figurative language, the symbol can be a strong feature in an essay, operating to add depth of meaning and even to unify the composition.

Synonym is a word that means roughly the same as another word. In practice, few words are exactly alike in meaning. Careful writers use synonyms to vary word choice, without ever moving too far from the shade of meaning intended.

Theme is the central idea in an essay; it is also termed the *thesis*. Everything in an essay should support the theme in one way or another.

Thesis is the main idea in an essay. The *thesis sentence,* appearing early in the essay (normally somewhere in the first paragraph) serves to convey the main idea to the reader in a clear and emphatic manner.

Tone is the writer's attitude toward his or her subject or material. An essay writer's tone may be objective, subjective, comic, ironic, nostalgic, critical, or a reflection of numerous other attitudes. Tone is the "voice" that writers give to an essay.

Topic sentence is the main idea that a paragraph develops. Not all paragraphs contain topic sentences; often the topic is implied.

Transition is the linking of ideas in sentences, paragraphs, and larger segments of an essay in order to achieve *coherence* (see entry). Among the most common techniques to achieve smooth transitions are: (1) repeating a key word or phrase; (2) using a pronoun to refer back to a key word or phrase; (3) relying on traditional connectives like "thus," "however," "moreover," "for example," "therefore," "finally," and "in conclusion"; (4) using parallel structure (see *Parallelism*); and (5) creating a sentence or paragraph that serves as a bridge from one part of an essay to another. Transition is best achieved when a writer presents ideas and details carefully and in logical order.

Understatement is a method of making a weaker statement than is warranted by truth, accuracy, or importance.

Unity is a feature in an essay whereby all material relates to a central concept and contributes to the meaning of the whole. To achieve a unified effect in an essay, the writer must design an effective introduction and conclusion, maintain consistent tone or point of view, develop middle paragraphs in a coherent manner, and above all stick to the subject, never permitting unimportant or irrelevant elements to enter.

Usage is the way in which a word, phrase, or sentence is used to express a particular idea; it is the customary manner of using a given language in speaking or writing.

Vertical (See *Horizontal/vertical.*)

Henry Adams, "The Dynamo and the Virgin," from *The Education of Henry Adams* by Henry Adams. Copyright 1918 by the Massachusetts Historical Society. Reprinted by permission.

Mortimer J. Adler, "How to Mark a Book," from *Saturday Review of Literature*, July 6, 1940. Copyright 1940 by Mortimer J. Adler; copyright renewed by Mortimer J. Adler. Reprinted by permission of author.

Woody Allen, "My Speech to the Graduates." Copyright © 1980 by Woody Allen. Reprinted from *Side Effects* by Woody Allen, by permission of Random House, Inc.

Maya Angelou, "The Deterioration of My Marriage," from *Singin' and Swingin' and Gettin' Merry Like Christmas* by Maya Angelou. Copyright © 1976 by Maya Angelou. Reprinted by permission of Random House, Inc.

Hannah Arendt, "The Human Condition," from *The Human Condition* by Hannah Arendt. Reprinted from *The Human Condition* by permission of The University of Chicago Press, © 1958.

Russell Baker, "Little Red Riding Hood Revisited," from *The New York Times*. Copyright © 1979 by The New York Times Company. Reprinted by permission.

James Baldwin, "Stranger in the Village," from *Notes of a Native Son* by James Baldwin. Copyright © by James Baldwin. Reprinted by permission of Beacon Press. "The Uses of the Blues," from *Playboy* 1963. Copyright © 1963 by James Baldwin. Reprinted by permission.

Amiri Baraka, "Expressive Language." Copyright © 1963 by LeRoi Jones, from *Home: Social Essays* (1966) by LeRoi Jones. By permission of William Morrow and Company. "Soul Food," copyright © 1962 by LeRoi Jones, from *Home: Social Essays* (1966) by LeRoi Jones. By permission of William Morrow and Company.

Mary Beard, "Women and Civilization," from *Understanding Women* by Mary Beard. Copyright 1931 by Longmans, Green, and Co. Reprinted by permission.

Ruth Benedict, "Are Families Passé?" from *Saturday Review*. Copyright 1948 by *Saturday Review*, December 25, 1948. All rights reserved. Reprinted by permission. "The Uses of Cannibalism," from *An Anthropologist at Work* by Margaret Mead. Copyright © 1959 by Margaret Mead. Reprinted by permission of Harper & Row, Publishers, Inc.

Franz Boas, "The Diffusion of Cultural Traits," from *Social Research*, September 1937. Copyright by *Social Research*. Reprinted by permission.

Kenneth Boulding, "After Civilization, What?" from *The Bulletin of the Atomic Scientists*, October 1962. Reprinted by permission of *The Bulletin of the Atomic Scientists*, a magazine of science and public affairs. Copyright © 1962 by the Educational Foundation for Nuclear Science, Chicago, Ill.

Elizabeth Bowen, "The Big House," from *Collected Impressions* by Elizabeth Bowen. Published in 1950 and copyright by Alfred A. Knopf, Inc. Reprinted by permission, and also by permission of Longmans, Green and Co.

Art Buchwald, "To Clone or Not to Clone," from *The Buchwald Stops Here*.

Acknowledgments

Reprinted by permission of G. P. Putnam's Sons. Copyright © 1976, 1977, 1978 by Art Buchwald.

Albert Camus, "The Myth of Sisyphus," from *The Myth of Sisyphus and Other Essays*, by Albert Camus, translated by Justin O'Brien. Copyright © 1955 by Alfred A. Knopf, Inc. Reprinted by permission of Alfred A. Knopf, Inc.

Rachel Carson, "The Changing Year," from *The Sea around Us* by Rachel Carson. Copyright 1950, 1951, 1961 by Rachel L. Carson; renewed 1978 by Roger Christie. Reprinted by permission of Oxford University Press, Inc.

Kenneth B. Clark, "The Science of Human Morality," from *Paths of Power* by Kenneth B. Clark. Copyright © 1974 by Kenneth B. Clark. Reprinted by permission of Harper & Row, Publishers, Inc.

Arthur C. Clarke, "The Planets Are Not Enough." Reprinted by permission of the author and the author's agents, Scott Meredith Literary Agency, Inc., 845 Third Avenue, New York, New York 10022.

Robert Coles, "I Listen to My Parents and I Wonder What They Believe," from *Redbook*, February 1980. Reprinted by permission of Dr. Robert Coles.

Harry Crews, "Why I Live Where I Live," from *Esquire*, September 1980. Copyright © 1980 by Harry Crews. Reprinted by permission of Paul R. Reynolds, Inc., 12 East 41st Street, New York, N.Y. 10017.

Joan Didion, "In Bed," from *The White Album* by Joan Didion. Copyright © 1979 by Joan Didion. Reprinted by permission of Simon and Shuster, a Division of Gulf and Western Corporation. "On Keeping a Notebook," from *Slouching towards Bethlehem* by Joan Didion. Copyright © 1966, 1968 by Joan Didion. Reprinted by permission of Farrar, Straus, and Giroux, Inc.

W. E. B. Du Bois, "On the Meaning of Progress," from *The Souls of Black Folk*. Contained in *Three Negro Classics*, Avon Books. Reprinted by arrangement.

Albert Einstein, "The Common Language of Science," from *Out of My Later Years* by Albert Einstein. Reprinted by permission of the Estate of Albert Einstein.

Loren Eiseley, "How Natural Is Natural? from *The Firmament of Time* by Loren Eiseley. Copyright © 1960 by Loren Eiseley; copyright © 1960 by The Trustees of the University of Pennsylvania. (New York: Atheneum, 1960.) Reprinted with permission of Atheneum Publishers.

F. M. Esfandiary, "The Mystical West Puzzles the Practical East," *The New York Times Magazine*, February 5, 1967. Copyright © 1967 by The New York Times Company. Reprinted by permission.

William Faulkner, "Address upon Receiving the Nobel Prize for Literature," *Essays, Speeches & Public Letters by William Faulkner*, edited by James B. Meriwether. Reprinted by arrangement with Random House, Inc.

Frances Fitzgerald, "America Revised: History Schoolbooks in the Twentieth Century," from *America Revised*. Copyright © 1979 by Frances Fitzgerald. By permission of Little, Brown and Company in association with Atlantic Monthly Press.

E. M. Forster, "My Wood," from *Abinger Harvest* by E. M. Forster. Copyright 1936, 1964 by E. M. Forster. Reprinted by permission of Harcourt Brace Jovanovich, Inc., and Edward Arnold (Publishers) Ltd.

Sigmund Freud, "Libidinal Types," *International Journal of Psychoanalysis*, vol. 13, 1932. Reprinted by permission.

Ellen Goodman, "Bamama Goes to College." Copyright © 1980, The Boston Globe Newspaper Company/ Washington Post Writers Group. Reprinted with permission.

J. B. S. Haldane, "On Being the Right Size," from *Possible Worlds* by J. B. S. Haldane. Copyright 1928 by Harper

& Row, Publishers, Inc.; renewed 1965 by J. B. S. Haldane. Reprinted by permission of Harper & Row, Publishers, Inc., the Author's Literary Estate, and Chatto and Windus Ltd.

Edith Hamilton, "Roots of Freedom," from *The Ever-Present Past* by Edith Hamilton. Reprinted with the permission of W. W. Norton and Company, Inc. Copyright © 1964 by W. W. Norton and Company, Inc. "The Lessons of the Past." Reprinted by permission of John D. Gray, Executor of the Estate of Doris Fielding Reid.

S. I. Hayakawa, "Sex Is Not a Spectator Sport," from *Through the Communication Barrier* by S. I. Hayakawa. Copyright © 1979 by S. I. Hayakawa. Reprinted by permission. "Words and Children," from *Through the Communication Barrier* by S. I. Hayakawa. Copyright © 1979 by S. I. Hayakawa. Reprinted by permission.

Karen Horney, "The Oedipus Complex." Reprinted from *New Ways in Psychoanalysis* by Karen Horney, M.D.; with permission of W. W. Norton and Company, Inc. Copyright 1939 by W. W. Norton and Company. Copyright renewed by Marianne von Eckardt, Renate Mintz, and Brigitte Swarzenski.

Langston Hughes, "Salvation," from *The Big Sea* by Langston Hughes. Copyright 1940 by Langston Hughes. Reprinted by permission of Farrar, Straus and Giroux, Inc.

Aldous Huxley, "Time and the Machine," from *The Olive Tree* by Aldous Huxley. Copyright 1937 by Aldous Huxley; renewed 1965 by Laura A. Huxley. Reprinted by permission of Harper & Row, Publishers, Inc., Mrs. Laura Huxley, and Chatto and Windus Ltd.

Jane Jacobs, "Conserving Old Work by Adding New," from *The Economy of Cities*, by Jane Jacobs. Copyright © 1969 by Jane Jacobs. Reprinted by permission of Random House, Inc.

Carl Gustav Jung, "The Mother Archetype," from "Archetypes and the Collective Unconscious," in *The Collected Works of C. G. Jung*, trans. R. F. C. Hull, Bollingen Series XX, vol. 9, I. Reprinted by permission of Princeton University Press.

Pauline Kael, "Movies on Television," from *Kiss Kiss Bang Bang* by Pauline Kael. Copyright © 1967 by Pauline Kael. First appeared in *The New Yorker*.

Immanuel Kant, "The Ethical Systems of the Ancients," from *Lectures on Ethics*. Hackett Publishing Co., Inc., Indianapolis, Indiana. Copyright © 1980. Reprinted by permission.

Maxine Hong Kingston, "The American Father," from *China Men*, by Maxine Hong Kingston. Copyright © 1977, 1978, 1979, 1980 by Maxine Hong Kingston. Reprinted by permission of Alfred A. Knopf, Inc.

Joseph Wood Krutch, "The New Immorality." Copyright © 1980 by *The Saturday Review*. All rights reserved. Reprinted by permission.

Katherine Kuh, "Breakup: The Core of Modern Art," from *Breakup: The Core of Modern Art* by Katherine Kuh. Copyright © 1965 by Cory, Adams, and MacKay Ltd., London, England. By permission of Little, Brown and Company in conjunction with the New York Graphic Society.

D. H. Lawrence, "Do Women Change?" from *Phoenix II: Uncollected Papers* by D. H. Lawrence. Copyright © 1959, 1963, 1968 by the Estate of Frieda Lawrence Ravagli. Reprinted by permission of Viking Penguin, Inc. "Why the Novel Matters," from *Phoenix: The Posthumous Papers of D. H. Lawrence*. Copyright 1936 by Frieda Lawrence, renewed 1964 by the Estate of Frieda Lawrence Ravagli. Reprinted by permission of Viking Penguin, Inc.

Ursula K. LeGuin, "American Science Fiction and the Other." Reprinted with permission from Berkley Publishing Corporation. Ursula K. LeGuin copyright © 1979.

Carson McCullers, "Home for Christmas," from *The Mortgaged Heart* by Carson McCullers. Copyright © 1971 by Floria V. Lasky. Reprinted by permission of the publisher, Houghton Mifflin Company.

Phyllis McGinley, "Suburbia: Of Thee I Sing," from *The Province of the Heart* by Phyllis McGinley. Copyright 1949 by Phyllis McGinley, renewed 1977 by Julie Elizabeth Hayden and Phyllis H. Blake. Reprinted by permission of Viking Penguin.

Marshall McLuhan, "Sight, Sound, and the Fury," from *Commonweal* magazine, April 9, 1954. Reprinted by permission of Commonweal Publishing Company, Inc.

Marya Mannes, "How Do You Know It's Good?" *Glamour* magazine, November 1962, copyright © 1962 by Marya Mannes. Reprinted by permission of Harold Ober Associates Incorporated. "The New Therapy," in *Last Rights: A Case for the Good Death* by Marya Mannes. Copyright © 1973 by Marya Mannes. By permission of William Morrow and Company. "Wasteland," from *More in Anger*. J. B. Lippincott Co., 1958, © 1958 by Marya Mannes. Reprinted by permission of Harold Ober Associates Incorporated.

Rollo May, "Powerlessness Corrupts," reprinted from *Power and Innocence* by Rollo May, with the permission of W. W. Norton and Company, Inc. Copyright © 1972 by Rollo May.

Margaret Mead, "A Day in Samoa," from *Coming of Age in Samoa* by Margaret Mead. Copyright 1928, renewed 1955 by Margaret Mead. By permission of William Morrow and Company. "One Vote for This Age of Anxiety." *New York Times*, May 20, 1965. Copyright © 1965 by The New York Times Company. Reprinted by permission.

A. J. Mojtabai, "Polygamy," from "Hers" essay, *New York Times*, June 5, 1980. Copyright © 1980 by The New York Times Company. Reprinted by permission.

N. Scott Momaday, "The Way to Rainy Mountain." Reprinted by permission from *The Way to Rainy Mountain*, by N. Scott Momaday, © 1969 by The University of New Mexico Press. First published in *The Reporter*, January 26, 1967.

Louis Mumford, "The Social Concept of the City," from *The Culture of Cities* by Lewis Mumford, copyright 1938 by Harcourt Brace Jovanovich, Inc.; copyright © 1966 by Louis Mumford. Reprinted by permission of the publisher.

Anaïs Nin, "Morocco," from *The Diary of Anaïs Nin*, volume II, copyright © 1967 by Anaïs Nin. Reprinted by permission of Harcourt Brace Jovanovich, Inc. "Notes on Feminism." Reprinted from *The Massachusetts Review*. © 1972 The Massachusetts Review, Inc.

Michael Novak, "Sports: A Sense of Evil," from *The Joy of Sports*, copyright © 1976 by Basic Books. Reprinted by permission.

George Orwell, "Marrakech," from *Such, Such Were the Joys* by George Orwell, copyright 1945, 1952, 1953, 1980 by Sonia Brownell Orwell; copyright © 1973 by Sonia Pitt-Rivers. Reprinted by permission of Harcourt Brace Jovanovich, Inc., the Estate of the late George Orwell, and Martin Secker and Warburg. "Politics and the English Language," from *Shooting an Elephant and Other Essays* by George Orwell, copyright 1950 by Sonia Brownell Orwell; copyright © 1978 by Sonia Pitt Rivers. Reprinted by permission of Harcourt Brace Jovanovich, Inc., the Estate of the late George Orwell, and Martin Secker and Warburg. "Shooting an Elephant," from *Shooting an Elephant and Other Essays* by George Orwell, copyright 1950 by Sonia Brownell Orwell; copyright © 1978 by Sonia Pitt Rivers. Reprinted by permission of Harcourt Brace Jovanovich, Inc., the Estate of the late George Orwell, and Martin Secker and Warburg.

Sylvia Plath, "A Comparison," from *Johnny Panic and the Bible of Dreams* by Sylvia Plath. Copyright © 1962 by Sylvia Plath. Reprinted by permission of Harper & Row, Publishers, Inc.

J. B. Priestley, "Wrong Ism," from *Essays of Five Decades* by J. B. Priestley. Copyright © 1966 by J. B. Priestley. By permission of Little, Brown and Company in association with the Atlantic Monthly Press.

Santha Rama Rau, "By Any Other Name," from *Gifts of Passage* by Santha Rama Rau. Copyright 1951 by Visanthi Rama Rau Bowers. Originally appeared in *The New Yorker*. Reprinted by permission of Harper & Row, Publishers, Inc.

Bertrand Russell, "Can Religion Cure Our Troubles?" from *Why I Am Not a Christian* by Bertrand Russell. Copyright © 1957 by Allen and Unwin. Reprinted by permission of Simon and Shuster, a Division of Gulf and Western Corporation. "The Study of Mathematics," from *Mysticism and Logic* by Bertrand Russell. Copyright 1929 by Allen and Unwin, Ltd. Reprinted by permission.

Saint Augustine, "Adult Cruelty and Folly," from *The Confessions of St. Augustine*, translated by John Ryan. Copyright © 1960 by Doubleday and Company, Inc. Reprinted by permission of the publisher.

Jean-Paul Sartre, "American Cities," from *Literary and Philosophical Essays* by Jean-Paul Sartre. Copyright © 1955 by S. G. Phillips Inc. Reprinted by permission.

Budd Schulberg, "The Wonderful Lousy Poem," from *Family Weekly*, October 11, 1964. Copyright © 1964 by Budd Schulberg. Reprinted by permission.

John Simon, "The Corruption of English," reprinted from *Paradigms Lost: Reflections on Literacy and its Decline* by John Simon. Originally entitled "Pressure from Above" and "Pressure from Below" which appears in *The State of the Language* published by Berkeley, University of California Press, copyright © 1976, 1977, 1978, 1979, 1980 by John Simon. By permission of Clarkson N. Potter, Inc.

Geneva Smitherman, "White English in Blackface, or Who Do I Be?" from *The Black Scholar*, May–June, 1973. Copyright © 1973 by The Black Scholar. Reprinted by permission.

John Steinbeck, "Americans and the Land," from *America and Americans* by John Steinbeck. Copyright © 1966 by John Steinbeck. Reprinted by permission of Viking Penguin Inc.

Dylan Thomas, "A Visit to Grandpa's," from *Portrait of the Artist as a Young Dog* by Dylan Thomas. Copyright 1940 by New Directions Publishing Corporation. Reprinted by permission of New Directions Publishing Corporation and David Higham Associates Limited.

Lewis Thomas, "On Societies as Organisms," from *The Lives of a Cell* by Lewis Thomas. Copyright © 1971 by the Massachusetts Medical Society. Originally appeared in the *New England Journal of Medicine*. Reprinted by permission of Viking Penguin Inc.

Virgil Thomson, "Taste in Music," originally published in the New York *Herald Tribune*, July 16, 1944. Copyright 1944 and 1971 by Virgil Thomson. Reprinted with the permission of the copyright owner.

James Thurber, "The Night the Bed Fell." Copyright 1933, 1961 by James Thurber. From *My Life and Hard Times* published by Harper & Row. Reprinted by permission of Mrs. James Thurber.

Alexis de Tocqueville, "Some Reflections on American Manners," from *Democracy in America* by Alexis de Tocqueville, translated by George Lawrence; J. P. Mayer and Max Lerner, eds. Translation copyright © 1966 by Harper & Row, Publishers, Inc. Reprinted by permission of Harper & Row, Publishers, Inc.

Arnold Toynbee, "Why I Dislike Western Civilization" from *The New York Times*, 1964. Copyright © 1964 by The New York Times Company. Reprinted by permission.

Barbara W. Tuchman, "An Inquiry into

the Persistence of Unwisdom in Government," from *Esquire* magazine, May 1980. Reprinted by permission of Russell and Volkening, Inc., as agents for the author. Copyright © 1980 by Barbara W. Tuchman.

Mark Twain, "The Mesmerist," from *Mark Twain in Eruption* by Mark Twain, edited by Bernard DeVoto. Copyright 1922 by Harper & Row, Publishers, Inc.; renewed 1940 by The Mark Twain Company. Reprinted by permission of Harper & Row, Publishers, Inc.

Judith Viorst, "How Books Helped Shape My Life," from *Redbook*, July 1980. Copyright © 1980 by Judith Viorst. Reprinted by permission.

Robert Warshow, "The Gangster as Tragic Hero," from *The Immediate Experience* by Robert Warshow. Reprinted by permission of Paul Warshow.

E. B. White, "Calculating Machine," from *The Second Tree from the Corner* by E. B. White. Copyright 1951 by E. B. White. Originally appeared in *The New Yorker*. Reprinted by permission of Harper & Row, Publishers, Inc. "Once More to the Lake," from *Essays of E. B. White*. Copyright 1941 by E. B. White. Reprinted by permission of Harper & Row, Publishers, Inc.

John Williams, "The Figure Eight." Copyright © John A. Williams. Reprinted by permission of the author.

Richard Wright, "The Psychological Reactions of Oppressed People," from *White Man, Listen!* by Richard Wright. Copyright © 1957 by Richard Wright. Reprinted by permission of Doubleday and Company, Inc.

Index

ADAMS, HENRY, 629
ADDISON, JOSEPH, 89, 163
Address upon Receiving the Nobel
   Prize for Literature, 578
ADLER, MORTIMER, 326
Adult Cruelty and Folly, 141
Aes Triplex, 504
After Civilization, What?, 639
Allegory of the Cave, The, 467
ALLEN, WOODY, 592
America Revised, 253
American Cities, 113
American Father, The, 38
American SF and the Other, 397
Americans and the Land, 572
ANGELOU, MAYA, 44
Are Families Passé?, 285
ARENDT, HANNAH, 488
Art of Political Lying, The, 360
Art of Procuring Pleasant Dreams,
   The, 145
AUGUSTINE, ST., 141

Bachelor's Complaint, A, 157
BACON, FRANCIS, 172
BAKER, RUSSELL, 323
BALDWIN, JAMES, 438, 580
Bamama Goes to College, 150
BARAKA, AMIRI, 143, 334
BEARD, MARY, 622
BENEDICT, RUTH, 184, 285
Big House, The, 84
BOAS, FRANZ, 194
BOSWELL, JAMES, 58
BOULDING, KENNETH E., 639
BOWEN, ELIZABETH, 84
Break-Up: The Core of Modern Art,
   410
BUCHWALD, ART, 548
By Any Other Name, 22

Calculating Machine, 326
CAMUS, ALBERT, 484
Can Religion Cure Our Troubles?, 495
CARSON, RACHEL, 532

Changing Year, The, 532
Circle of Governments, The, 274
CLARK, KENNETH B., 561
CLARKE, ARTHUR C., 553
COLES, ROBERT, 453
Common Language of Science, The,
   519
Comparison, A, 389
Conserving Old Work by Adding
   New, 239
Corruption of English, The, 364
CREWS, HARRY, 63

Day in Samoa, A, 69
Death of the Moth, The, 177
DE QUINCEY, THOMAS, 401
Deterioration of My Marriage, The, 44
DIDION, JOAN, 202, 311
Diffusion of Cultural Traits, The, 194
DONNE, JOHN, 493
Do Women Change?, 152
DU BOIS, W. E. B., 265
Dynamo and the Virgin, The, 629

Economy, 79
EINSTEIN, ALBERT, 519
EISELEY, LOREN, 529
Election, An, 242
EPICURUS, 459
ESFANDIARY, F. M., 611
Ethical Systems of the Ancients, The,
   471
Expressive Language, 334

FAULKNER, WILLIAM, 578
Figure Eight, The, 18
FITZGERALD, FRANCES, 253
FORSTER, E. M., 235
FRANKLIN, BENJAMIN, 145, 189
   526
FREUD, SIGMUND, 220

Gangster as Tragic Hero, The, 422
GOLDSMITH, OLIVER, 242, 568
GOODMAN, ELLEN, 150

HALDANE, J. B. S., 542
HAMILTON, EDITH, 464, 602
HAYAKAWA, S. I., 134, 318
HAZLITT, WILLIAM, 407
Home for Christmas, 9
HORNEY, KAREN, 229
How Books Helped Shape My Life, 383
How Do You Know It's Good?, 415
How Natural Is Natural?, 529
How to Mark a Book, 326
HUGHES, LANGSTON, 1
Human Condition, The, 488
HUXLEY, ALDOUS, 550
HUXLEY, T. H., 512

I Listen to My Parents and I Wonder What They Believe, 453
In Bed, 202
Inquiry into the Persistence of Unwisdom in Government, An, 295
IRVING, WASHINGTON, 67

JACOBS, JANE, 239
JUNG, CARL GUSTAV, 216

KAEL, PAULINE, 427
KANT, IMMANUEL, 471
KINGSTON, MAXINE HONG, 38
KRUTCH, JOSEPH WOOD, 477
KUH, KATHERINE, 410

LAMB, CHARLES, 157
LAWRENCE, D. H., 152, 391
Lead Poisoning, 526
LEGUIN, URSULA K., 397
Lessons of the Past, The, 602
Libidinal Types, 220
Little Red Riding Hood Revisited, 323

McCULLERS, CARSON, 9
McGINLEY, PHYLLIS, 105
MACHIAVELLI, NICCOLO, 274
McLUHAN, MARSHALL, 339
MANNES, MARYA, 132, 211, 415
Marrakech, 99
MAY, ROLLO, 180
MEAD, MARGARET, 69, 617
Mesmerizer, The, 4
Modest Proposal, A, 277
MOJTABAI, A. G., 137
MOMADAY, N. SCOTT, 73
Morocco, 123

Mother Archetype, The, 216
Movies on Television, 427
MUMFORD, LEWIS, 259
My Speech to the Graduates, 592
Mystical West Puzzles the Practical East, The, 611
Myth of Sisyphus, The, 484
My Wood, 235

National Prejudices, 568
New Immorality, The, 477
New Therapy, The, 211
Night the Bed Fell, The, 28
NIN, ANAÏS, 23, 206
No Man Is an Island, 493
Notes on Feminism, 206
NOVAK, MICHAEL, 480

Oedipus Complex, The, 229
Of Envy, 172
Of the Meaning of Progress, 265
On Being the Right Size, 542
Once More to the Lake, 93
One Vote for This Age of Anxiety, 617
On Gusto, 407
On Keeping a Notebook, 311
On Keeping a Private Journal, 309
On Societies as Organisms, 522
On the Knocking at the Gate in Macbeth, 401
ORWELL, GEORGE, 51, 99, 348

Planets Are Not Enough, The, 553
PLATH, SYLVIA, 389
PLATO, 467
Politics and the English Language, 348
Polygamy, 137
Powerlessness Corrupts, 180
PRIESTLEY, J. B., 245
Psychological Reactions of Oppressed People, The, 224

RAU, SANTHA RAMA, 22
Remarks Concerning the Savages of North America, 189
Roots of Freedom, 464
Royal Exchange, The, 89
RUSSELL, BERTRAND, 495, 540

Salvation, 1
SARTRE, JEAN-PAUL, 113
SCHULBERG, BUDD, 14
Science of Human Morality, The, 561

Sex Is Not a Spectator Sport, 134
Shooting an Elephant, 51
Sight, Sound, and the Fury, 339
SIMON, JOHN, 364
SMITHERMAN, GENEVA, 372
Social Concept of the City, The, 259
Some Reflections on American
    Manners, 249
Soul Food, 143
Sports: A Sense of Evil, 480
STEINBECK, JOHN, 572
STEVENSON, ROBERT LOUIS, 504
Stranger in the Village, 580
Study of Mathematics, The, 540
Suburbia: Of Thee I Sing, 105
Sunday in London, A, 67
Superstitious Household, A, 163
SWIFT, JONATHAN, 167, 277, 366

Taste in Music, 448
THOMAS, DYLAN, 32
THOMAS, LEWIS, 522
THOMSON, VIRGIL, 448
THOREAU, HENRY DAVID, 79, 309
THURBER, JAMES, 28
Time and the Machine, 550
To Clone or Not to Clone, 548
TOCQUEVILLE, ALEXIS DE, 249
TOYNBEE, ARNOLD, 595
Treatise on Good Manners and Good
    Breeding, A, 167

TUCHMAN, BARBARA W., 295
TWAIN, MARK, 4

Uses of Cannibalism, The, 184
Uses of the Blues, The, 438

VIORST, JUDITH, 383
Visit to Grandpa's, A, 32

WARSHOW, ROBERT, 422
Wasteland, 132
Way to Rainy Mountain, The, 73
We Are All Scientists, 512
Wednesday, 12 January 1763; A Man
    of Pleasure, 58
We Should Seek Our Own Pleasure,
    459
WHITE, E. B., 93, 326
White English in Blackface; or Who Do
    I Be?, 372
Why I Dislike Western Civilization, 595
Why I Live Where I Live, 63
Why the Novel Matters, 391
WILLIAMS, JOHN, 18
Women and Civilization, 622
Wonderful Lousy Poem, The, 14
WOOLF, VIRGINIA, 177
Words and Children, 318
WRIGHT, RICHARD, 224
Wrong Ism, 245